Y0-CCH-972

THE
HISTORIA REGUM BRITANNIE
OF GEOFFREY OF MONMOUTH
III

A Summary Catalogue of the Manuscripts

THE
HISTORIA REGUM BRITANNIE
OF GEOFFREY OF MONMOUTH

ISSN 0267–2529

I

Bern, Burgerbibliothek, MS. 568
Edited by Neil Wright

II

The First Variant Version: a critical edition
Edited by Neil Wright

THE
HISTORIA REGUM BRITANNIE
OF GEOFFREY OF MONMOUTH

III

A Summary Catalogue of
the Manuscripts

Julia C. Crick

D. S. BREWER

First published 1989 by D. S. Brewer, Cambridge

D. S. Brewer is an imprint of Boydell & Brewer Ltd
PO Box 9, Woodbridge, Suffolk IP12 3DF
and of Boydell & Brewer Inc.
Wolfeboro, New Hampshire 03894–2069, USA

ISBN 0 85991 213 2

British Library Cataloguing in Publication Data
Geoffrey, *of Monmouth, 110?–1154*
    The historia regum Britannie of Geoffrey of Monmouth.
    3 : A summary catalogue of the manuscripts.
    1. England. Kings, ancient period
    I. Title
    936.2'009'92
    ISBN 0–85991–213–2

Library of Congress Catalog Card No. 84–24170

The paper used in this publication meets the minimum requirements of American National Standard for Information Sciences – Permanence of Paper for Printed Library Materials, ANSI Z39.48–1984.

Printed in Great Britain by Woolnough Bookbinding Ltd, Irthlingborough, Northants

CONTENTS

M.F.W. & G.M.C. *in memoriam*

PREFACE

This catalogue is a by-product of the first two years of my doctoral research into the readership and circulation of Geoffrey of Monmouth's *Historia regum Britannie*. The *Historia* has achieved notoriety perhaps for the combination of its largely pseudo-historical contents and widespread influence and acceptance into the mediaeval canon of historical texts. Geoffrey wrote in the 1130s, a time of political and intellectual ferment which he, a secular canon of St George's, Oxford, with high connections, was well placed to observe. In this climate, he constructed a narrative tracing the monarchy in Britain from its glorious roots in the pseudo-historical past: the Trojan remnant represented by Brutus, the eponymous founder of the British people. Scholars have naturally been curious about the impact of this sudden revelation of previously unknown centuries of the island's history. Literary reaction has received some degree of attention. The material evidence of the popularity of the *Historia* – the enormous number of surviving manuscripts – is, on the other hand, almost untouched. My study, based on a survey of extant witnesses, seeks, using the evidence of text-history and manuscript ownership, to investigate this second area. It is hoped that my findings will be published in a sequel to the present volume.

My original aim was perhaps more ambitious than I realised. Thanks to the considerable efforts of Dr David Dumville and others, the list of 187 manuscripts of the *Historia* published by Acton Griscom in 1929 had grown by 1985 to 215 (a total which still stands despite additions and deletions). By that time a substantial stock of microfilms of these manuscripts had been acquired, with the help of a grant from the Vinaver Fund under the supervision of Dr Richard Barber of Boydell & Brewer Ltd. As the published material about these manuscripts was often inaccurate or incomplete, amounting, in some cases, only to a statement of title and, perhaps, date, it was clear that it would be necessary to compile a collection of formal manuscript-descriptions for my own use to accompany my notes on text-history. I owe to Richard Barber the suggestion to publish what resulted.

The catalogue would not have appeared in its present form without considerable assistance from various quarters. I could not have completed the survey on which it is based without access to the microfilm collection just mentioned, whose extensiveness is due to the ingenuity, efficiency, and perseverance of Richard Barber and his former assistant, Amanda Hummel. Their work has made it possible to include many manuscripts unknown to previous editors, especially those only recently added to our constantly growing list. I am indebted to Richard Barber, David Dumville, Sue Edgington, and Anne Sutton for contributing references to further manuscripts in the course of the survey. Thanks are due to Richard Barber again: for his unfailing patience and good humour in managing the publication of this enterprise.

David Dumville, who supervised my doctoral work, has been an essential agent in the development of the catalogue. The foundations for the work were laid by his revision of Griscom's list of manuscripts (see 'The manuscripts') and the project has continued to profit from his involvement. Despite his own heavy workload, he has overseen the preliminary and subsequent stages of the production of this book, and has latterly carried out the unenviable task of imposing some professional order on a mass of material accumulated over an extended period. In the process he has eliminated numerous errors besides contributing a great deal from his encyclopaedic knowledge of the literature. He is also largely responsible for the list of *Prophetie*-manuscripts found in Appendix VII.

I am also pleased to acknowledge the contribution of Neil Wright, editor-in-chief of the Geoffrey of Monmouth Research Project. His edition of Bern, Burgerbibliothek, MS. 568 has been fundamental to the survey. I am especially indebted to him for my knowledge of Hammer's unpublished work on the Second Variant, and for making available parts of his own work on the First Variant prior to publication. He has also drawn my attention to items of importance at various stages. The catalogue has greatly benefited from his comments on and corrections of draft versions and I owe to him the identification of a number of texts and especially of Classical allusions.

Eighty-one of the 215 manuscripts included here are known to me only from microfilm or photograph. Undertaking the description of manuscripts at such remove may seem a hopelessly error-prone business; there is, however, at least one large-scale project which, like the present one, would have been impracticable without such a method. This is the scheme begun in 1962 at the University of Notre Dame, Indiana, where microfilms of the entire holdings of the Biblioteca Ambrosiana in Milan (amounting to about ten thousand volumes) were deposited and, between 1978 and 1982, catalogued.

The convenience of reference offered by microfilm is, of course, offset by serious disadvantages. Apart from obvious difficulties such as sheer illegibility (due to a faded or out-of-focus film), basic information about the manuscript, for example about the constituent parts of the volume, must often be sacrificed.

Unless stitching or quire-signatures are clearly visible, information about the construction of the book must often be supplied from published descriptions. The problem is compounded by photographers who, for reasons of economy, have excluded flyleaves or blank leaves in the middle of a text. This is to say nothing of the problems caused by the accidental omission of a frame on a microfilm. Another handicap which the use of microfilm creates for the would-be cataloguer is the loss of a sense of the book's size. This is important not only in gauging the scale of the volume but in assessing its script, whose appearance may be distorted when artificially shrunk or blown up.

Some of these problems have, however, been alleviated by the expert contributions of a number of people. Like all those who have assisted in the production of the catalogue, they cannot of course be held responsible for any distortions which their information has suffered at my hands. Large parts of the entries for the Aberystwyth manuscripts, particularly the DESCRIPTION and HISTORY sections, are derived from manuscript-descriptions generously made available by Daniel Huws of the National Library of Wales, who in addition provided me with dimensions and collations of two further manuscripts. William O'Sullivan deciphered an inscription in Dublin, Trinity College, MS. 496 (which I could not make out on the microfilm) and supplied other valuable information about it. Much of the physical descriptions of the Bruxelles manuscripts is derived from notes made by David Dumville and Michael Lapidge at the Bibliothèque Royale in September 1986. I am also indebted to Dr Lapidge for first-hand information about Arras, BM, 598 and Paris, BN, lat. 5697.

There is only one manuscript included here of which I have not myself seen substantial parts (whether on microfilm or photograph, or in the flesh). This is Notre Dame, University Library, MS. 40. The corresponding entry in the catalogue, therefore, is solely dependent on information very generously supplied by Dr Maureen Boulton and Kent Emery Jr. Thanks are due to Richard Barber and David Dumville for securing the assistance of these Notre Dame scholars.

The Leningrad manuscript, once in the possession of King Richard III, was the last to be added to our list. We owe its inclusion entirely to Anne Sutton and Livia Visser-Fuchs, who encountered it in the course of their detailed study of the library of that king and notified us of its existence. I am further indebted to them for the loan of their microfilm and for generously making available before publication drafts of their article on the manuscript.

Further invaluable information and assistance has kindly been provided by others including Cecily Clark, Professor Christopher Brooke, Dr James Carley, Dr Simon Keynes, Dr Nigel Morgan, Max Niedermeyer, Oliver Padel, Jayne Ringrose, and variously by fellow research students at Cambridge; I have several of them to thank for moral support as well. My primary debt here, however, is to David Dumville, Neil Wright, and especially Dr Andrew Gilbert.

I am also indebted to librarians and library staff for their cooperation and assistance: in Cambridge, the University Library, the libraries of Corpus Christi, Gonville and Caius, St John's, Sidney Sussex, and Trinity Colleges and of the Fitzwilliam Museum; in London, the British Library, and the libraries of Lambeth Palace and the College of Arms; in Oxford, the Bodleian, and the libraries of All Souls' College, Christ Church, and Magdalen College; in Paris, the Bibliothèque Nationale. Among these, particular mention must be made of Cambridge University Library. The extensiveness of its collections and the convenience of open-shelf access have enabled me to track down and consult with relative speed many of the obscurer items included in the bibliography. This has greatly eased the difficulties associated with certain aspects of this catalogue's production. Some of the library's staff deserve particular thanks. Apart from the assistance of Jayne Ringrose, noted above, I must also acknowledge the patience of Godfrey Waller and the staff of the Manuscripts Reading Room, who, since 1985, have uncomplainingly housed for me the microfilm collection.

I also owe a special debt to the Hon. Mrs John Southwell, whose interest and kind hospitality made it a pleasure to include the only *Historia*-manuscript in private hands known to us.

I am uncomfortably aware that errors and deficiencies must still lurk within the catalogue despite strenuous efforts to seek them out and correct them. Many defects will not of course emerge until the catalogue is used. I should be very grateful, therefore, to hear of readers' corrections and additions. These may be sent to me via the offices of Richard Barber at Boydell & Brewer Ltd., P.O. Box 9, Woodbridge, Suffolk.

The list of *Historia*-manuscripts has continued to grow during the progress of this work; there is no reason to think that it will now cease to do so. The members of the Geoffrey of Monmouth Research Project will be very grateful to be informed of any further additions. Such references may also be sent to Dr Barber at the above address.

J. C. Crick
Gonville & Caius College, Cambridge
January 1989

NOTES FOR THE USER

The manuscripts are arranged by library in strict alphabetical order and are generally described in their entirety including, where necessary, *membra disiecta* now housed separately. Units within a manuscript are omitted from descriptions only if it is beyond doubt that their association with the *Historia*-manuscript in question was post-mediaeval. Certain of the Cottonian manuscripts in the British Library, for example, are constructed of rematched parts of mediaeval volumes, the remainder of the originals being shelved elsewhere in the same library.

Each entry has been arranged in six sections: a heading followed by notes on the *Historia* itself, the other contents of the manuscript, a physical description, indications of history, and a brief bibliography.

(i) **SHELFMARK** (asterisked if manuscripts have been examined at first hand – the remainder have been described from microfilm only)
Date
Mediaeval provenance, if known (with order of religious house where appropriate)
Number of folios or pages (flyleaves given in lower-case Roman numerals)
Second-folio reference

(ii) **HRB**
Second-folio reference (if HRB located in a different unit from that beginning the volume).

Number of chapters present. The sequence given by Faral (*La Légende*, III) is used. §§1–5 bear the dedications, §§109–110 form the introduction and dedication to the Prophecies of Merlin which follow in §§111–117; the narrative constitutes the remainder – §§6–108, 118–208.

Nature of the dedication, if present. (Arguments attaching to these have been conveniently summarised by Wright, *The Historia Regum Britannie of Geoffrey of Monmouth, I*, pp. xii–xvi.)
The most commonly found dedication is that to Robert, earl of Gloucester.

This occupies §3; §4 is then absent. There are in addition two forms of double dedication (contained in §§3 and 4): to Robert and Waleran, earl of Meulan; and to King Stephen and Robert. There is also the so-called 'nameless dedication', identified by Jacob Hammer, a reworked form of the single dedication, from which the name of the dedicatee has been omitted.[1]

Rubrics (concentrating especially on those at opening, end, and *Prophetie Merlini*)

Book-divisions (numbered in upper-case Roman numerals unless a different form of numbering is found in the manuscript)

Peculiarities – details of lacunae, interpolations, abbreviations, variants
There are two recognised variant versions of the text. The first, edited by Hammer in 1951[2] and now by Neil Wright,[3] represents a substantial reworking of the text which, it is thought, was not carried out by Geoffrey himself though completed within his lifetime. The Second Variant is more of an abbreviation; material extraneous to the narrative – speeches, for example – has been omitted. This has not been printed, although Hammer was working on an edition at the time of his death. The only published account of Hammer's work was provided by Hywel Emanuel.[4]

Other items – published
i. *Merlinus iste*. A note about Merlin beginning thus is found before the beginning of the Prophecies or, more usually, after the end, in certain manuscripts. It was printed by Jacob Hammer from Lincoln Cathedral MS. 98 ('Some additional manuscripts', p. 239).
ii. *Pudibundus Brito*. A reworked form of §§109–110 in which the usual dedication to Alexander, bishop of Lincoln, is replaced by a more florid and poetic passage. Printed by Faral from Paris, BN, MS. lat. 6233 ('Geoffroy', pp. 31–32).

Other items – unpublished
These include a letter purportedly sent by the dying Arthur to Hugh, *capellanus*. Notification should also be given here of a particular form of §118 and the beginning of §119. The opening phrase of §118 'Cum igitur . . . prophetasset Merlinus' is replaced by 'Merlinus uero incipiens coram rege Uortigerno prophetare', after which the text proceeds as normal to the end of the first sentence of §119 '. . . Aurelius Ambrosius'. This block of text is displaced in

---

[1] Printed by Hammer (from Sankt Gallen, Stiftsbibliothek, MS. 633), 'Some additional manuscripts', p. 237; see also Hammer, 'Remarks', pp. 528–30.
[2] *Geoffrey.*
[3] *The Historia Regum Britannie of Geoffrey of Monmouth, II.*
[4] 'Geoffrey of Monmouth's *Historia*'.

two of the manuscripts in which it is found, occurring immediately before instead of after the Prophecies (§§111–117). The closing phrase of the passage is continued in the same two manuscripts: 'Cum germano suo decem milibus militum comitatus'.

(iii) CONTENTS
folio/page-reference; opening rubric, extract from final rubric or other indication of title; incipit . . . explicit; edition/source of further information

Incorrect foliation has been dealt with in two ways. Where a folio has been skipped and this omission has not been remedied in the manuscript, the unnumbered leaf will be designated by the number of the folio which it follows plus an asterisk. Where the sequence of numbers is itself faulty, the existing foliation is given in quotation marks and the actual number indicated in brackets.

Where appropriate a bracketed general title will precede more detailed descriptions of a series of items.

A short line indicates division between physically separable units.

(iv) DESCRIPTION
SIZE in centimetres

QUIRING with any quire-signatures, catchwords, etc. (divisions between units of text are indicated by a separating semi-colon). Unless quire-markings in the manuscript specify otherwise, quires of flyleaves are usually indicated by lower-case letters and quires in the main part of the manuscript by upper-case Roman numerals. Leaves within the quire are referred to by Arabic numerals; where necessary, folio- or page-references are included in the information describing individual quires. Units within the volume are usually referred to by upper-case letters, unless these would duplicate the system of quire-signatures used within the manuscript (in which case units are marked (i), (ii), etc.).

PRICKING whether in both margins (indicating that the leaves were folded before pricking) or in one only.

RULING number of written lines, whether beginning below or above top ruled line (compare the observations of Ker, 'From ''above top line'' '), number of columns, nature of boundary-lines.

SCRIPT type of script, noting particular letter-forms and usages of value for dating[5] or illustrating characteristics or idiosyncrasies of the hand in question.

DECORATION

---

[5] See, for example, Ker, *English Manuscripts in the Century after the Norman Conquest*; Parkes, *English Cursive Book Hands*; Lieftinck, 'Pour une nomenclature'.

(v) HISTORY
Ex-libris, inscriptions of ownership (concentrating on earlier evidence)

(vi) BIBLIOGRAPHY
Short titles only (full bibliography may be found at the end of the book)

There are also appendices: manuscripts in private hands, extracts of the *Historia*, manuscripts located but which it has not been possible to include in the survey for practical reasons, manuscripts whose present location is unknown, lost manuscripts, witnesses excluded from the catalogue on the grounds of being abridgments, and manuscripts of Geoffrey's other known works, the *Prophetie Merlini* and *Uita Merlini*. The volume has been indexed by contents of the manuscripts, first lines of Latin verse, and origin/provenance.

To avoid the introduction of further inaccuracies, capitalisation in transcriptions has been normalised and abbreviations usually expanded silently. Where intervention is unavoidable, the following conventions are used: [ ] signify editorial supply, for example in transcribing a nearly illegible passage or an ambiguous abbreviation, < > indicate emendation.

LIST OF MANUSCRIPTS OF THE *HISTORIA*

CATALOGUE

1 ABERYSTWYTH, NATIONAL LIBRARY OF WALES, MS. 2005
(PANTON 37), fos 63r–72v

Saec. xviii

96 fos (paper) in whole volume, of which only 10 fos considered here. Entire volume prefaced by a note 'Mr. John Jones of Gelli Lyfdy's notes on an ancient British History transcribed by me Evan Evans 1774 at Wrexham.

'With an account of a Curious Copy of the British history translated by Galfridus of Monmouth, and some extracts from the same to be compared with the Latin and British copies of that history in print and manuscript'.

On 63r 'An account of a Curious Manuscript which now belongs to Doctor Treadway Nash near Be[ ]ere Worcester 1773 bought out of the library of the late Mr. Lewis Morris of Penbryn in Cardiganshire. This seems to be the first edition of Galfrid's history ... This manuscript was bought by me Lewis Morris of Galltvadog in Cardiganshire of Thomas Osborn bookseller of Grays Inn July 1753'. Doctor Tread-way Nash may be identified as the historian of Worcestershire (whose *Collections* were published in 1781/82). The flyleaf of his manuscript, according to the transcription in NLW, MS. 2005 (64v), bore the inscriptions 'Liber communitatis domus alme uirginis Marie iuxta Dublinam' and 'Sum Patricii Dowdal x Iulii accomodat. Wilielmo Ryano'.

HRB 65r–72v

§§5, 6–8 (*med.*), 54–55, 206–208.

Rubrics at §5 'Incipit historia Britonum a Galfrido Arturo Monemutensi de britannica lingua in Latinum translata'; after §208 'Explicit historia Britonum a magistro Galfrido Monemutensi in Latinum translata'.

Copy of First Variant witness: Wright siglum P, *The Historia Regum Britannie of Geoffrey of Monmouth, II*, pp. lxxxvii–lxxxviii.

CONTENTS (listed on 63r–64r)

'Of the nature and property of animals from Aristotle', Dares Phrygius, HRB (divided into twelve books 'but not always distinguished nor in chapters'), Commentary on Prophecies of Merlin, Latin verses on Ireland and Scotland ('Regnum Scotorum ...'), 'The articles of Munster A. D. 1310', Sibylline prophecies, Giraldus Cambrensis's *Topographia Hiberniae* and *Expugnatio Hibernica*.

BIBLIOGRAPHY

Evans, *Report on Manuscripts in the Welsh Language*, II.843–45.

Hammer, *Geoffrey*, p. 8.

Parry, 'A Variant Version'.

Wright, *The Historia Regum Britannie of Geoffrey of Monmouth, II*, pp. lxxxvii–lxxxix.

3

2 ABERYSTWYTH, NATIONAL LIBRARY OF WALES, MS. 11611

(*OLIM* CLUMBER 46)

Saec. xii *med./2*   Mediaeval provenance: ?
105 fos   2nd fo: *progessus inde Nectanabus*

HRB 34v–105r.

§§1–3, 5–93 (*ex.*), 104 (*med.*) –150 (*med.*), 171 (*med.*) –174 (*ex.*), 190 (*med.*) –194 (*in.*), 207 (*ex.*) –208. Nameless dedication.

Rubrics at §1 (34v) 'Incipit hystoria Britannorum', after §208 (105r) 'Explicit'.
No book-divisions.

Text lost between 75v (ends 'Aurelius Ambrosius, Utherpendragon' §93) and 76r (opens 'Suos et adstantes principes inuaserunt' §104); 100v (ends 'in modum uo-raginis, sorbendoque' §150, at end of quire) and 101r (opens 'regi Medorum obuiaret' §171); 102v (ends 'ad perstandum hortabatur' §174) and 103r (opens 'nullatenus impetrari potuisset' §190); 104v (ends 'in Kidalentam urbem applicant. Deinde' §194) and 105r (opens 'a Britannica Gualenses' §207).

CONTENTS

1r–9v: 'Incipiunt gesta Alexandri magni'. 'Aegypti sapientes satis genere diuino . . . lituo intonat atque ad bel-.' Ed. Kuebler, *Iuli Valeri Alexandri Polemi res gestae*, pp. 1–168.

9v–17v: 'Epistola Alexandri regis magni Macedonum missa ab India ad Aritotilem (*sic*) preceptorem suum' (from rubric on 17v). Begins imperfectly. 'Diuiciis regia gaza repleti sumus . . . et animi et industrie optime Aristotilis ponderaris.' Ed. Walther Boer, *Epistola Alexandri*.

17v–25r: 'Disputacio inter Alexandrum inperatorem (*sic*) et Dindimum regem Brag-manorum'. 'Alexander imperator cum ei non sufficeret . . . per nos fieri et esse meliorem.'

25r: 'Responsio Alexandri'. 'Sepius ad aures . . . ut prebeas responsa quesitis.'

25r–30v: 'Desiderantem te Alexander . . . qui se non agnoscunt esse mortales'.
30v–32r: 'Responsio Alexandri'. 'Tu nunc ideo beatum . . . aut inuidie quod a meliore prestantur.' Fos 25r–32r, correspondence of Alexander and Dindymus, ed. Kuebler, *Iuli Valeri Alexandri Polemi res gestae*, pp. 169–89.

32r–34v: 'Incipit prologus [ ] uita Bragmanorum'. 'Mens tua que et discere . . . qui Petrum et Paulum sanctos apostolos interemit.' *Commonitorium Palladii*, ed. Pfister, *Kleine Texte zum Alexanderroman*, pp. 1–5.

DESCRIPTION

SIZE 23 x 17 cm.

QUIRING Some original signatures (from .i. on 8v to .iiii. on 26v). Also Early Modern letters on first recto of each quire. I⁸, II⁸ (lacks 2–7: fos 9–10), III–X⁸, XI⁸ (lacks 2–7: 75–76), XII–XIV⁸, fos 101–105 uncollatable. Loss of text indicates that two quires may be lacking after 100, and perhaps six leaves after 102 and again after 104.

PRICKING Visible in outer margins.

RULING Single column with double vertical boundary lines. Top line written. 27–29 lines.

SCRIPT Four-line Protogothic in several hands. Minims and descenders are ticked. Straight and round **d** are found, final round **s** is frequent in one hand. e-caudata occurs occasionally. *Et*-nota is standard but occasionally ampersand is found or *et* is unabbreviated. The horizontal of **t** is often just pierced but **a** has the Caroline form.
DECORATION Capitals have shaded ornament, split shafts (etc.) in red, blue, green, and buff.

HISTORY
On fo 1 'Est Petri Moesan Doc. Theo.', in sixteenth-century hand. Also on fo 1 'Capucinorum Usui' (eighteenth-century) and in another hand 'Salinensium'.

BIBLIOGRAPHY
Davies *et al.*, *Handlist*, IV.44.
Hammer, 'Some additional manuscripts', pp. 240–41.

3 ABERYSTWYTH, NATIONAL LIBRARY OF WALES, MS. 13052
(*OLIM* PHILLIPPS 32)

Saec. xiii$^{1/in.}$ Mediaeval provenance: ?France
ii + 60 + ii fos 2nd fo: *resisteret. Arguebat enim*

HRB 1r–60v.
§§1–3, 5–208. Nameless dedication.
Rubrics at §1 (1ra) 'Incipit in historiam Britannorum prefatio Gaufridi Monomutensis', §5 (1rb) 'Explicit prefatio. Incipit historia', §118 (33rb) 'Explicit prophetia Merlini', after §208 (60vb) 'Explicit histori (*sic*) Britannorum'.
No book-divisions.
No other contents.

DESCRIPTION
SIZE 26 x 17 cm.
QUIRING I–VII^8, VIII^4.
PRICKING Visible at outer edges only.
RULING Two columns of 40 lines. Written above top ruled line. Central vertical margin divided.
SCRIPT Gothic bookhand with some lozenged minims. It lacks a regimented aspect; some roundness is retained. Juncture of **e** and **o** after **d**, **h**, and **p** and sometimes after **b**. **a** has the Caroline form, final **s** is tall or round, straight-backed **d** occurs, but rarely. *Et*-nota is crossed. The horizontal of **t** is just pierced. **u** and round **d** when starting a line have trailing approach-strokes. The tops of the ascenders of **b**, round **d**, and **h** have diagonal hairlines.
DECORATION Capitals have a simple outline or foliate decoration. There is no filigree.

BIBLIOGRAPHY
Davies *et al.*, *Handlist*, IV.351.

4 ABERYSTWYTH, NATIONAL LIBRARY OF WALES, MS. 13210
(*OLIM* PHILLIPPS 26233)

Saec. xiii² Mediaeval provenance: Robertsbridge, Sussex (Cistercian)
i + 64 + i fos 2nd fo: *raptam. grauiter tulit*

HRB 11ra–64rb

§§5–108, 111–187 (*in.*), 203–208. Dedicatory chapters absent.

§§1–3 (dedicated to Robert of Gloucester) written in margin of 10v, Early Modern hand.

Rubrics at §5 (10vb) '[I]Nncipit (*sic*) hystoria Brittonum tracta ab antiquis libris Brittonum', §6 (11ra) 'Incipit narratio', §111 (23ra) '. . . Incipit liber .vii. de propheciis Merlini', after §208 (64rb) 'Explicit hystoria Brittonum correcta et abbreuiata'.

Book-divisions: II §23 (15va), III §35 (18vb), IV §54 (23ra), V §73 (28ra), VI §90 (32va), VII §111 (38rb), VIII §118 (42ra), IX §143 (49rb), X §163 (56ra), XI §177 (61rb).

Four folios lost after 62. 62v ends 'cum feris' §§186/187; 63r begins 'edentes et bibentes' §203.

Conflation of First with Second Variant. Wright, siglum a: *The Historia Regum Britannie of Geoffrey of Monmouth, II*, pp. lxxviii–lxxix.

CONTENTS

i: flyleaf. Blank except for Phillipps crest and modern note of contents.

1r–10vb: 'Epistola Cornelii ad Crispum Salustium in Troianorum hystoria que in Greco a Darete hystoriographo facta est. Cornel[ius] Gaio Crispo salutem'. 'Cum multa Athenis studiosissime agerem . . . Neoptolemus. Penthesileam.' Ed. Meister, *Daretis Phrygii De Excidio Troiae Historia.*

11ra–64rb: HRB.

64rb/va: note on place-names in HRB (in grade of script of rubrics in HRB). 'Armorica siue Latauia id est minor Britannia . . . qui fluuiis Loegriam secernit a Deira et Albania.' Ed. Dumville, 'Anecdota'.

Found also in London, BL, Cotton Titus A.xxvii and Lambeth Palace 401, Heidelberg, Universitätsbibliothek, MS. 9.31, Oxford, Bodleian, MS. Digby 196.

64v: in Early Modern hand, dedicatory letter of William of Malmesbury to Robert of Gloucester. 'Domino uenerabili et famoso comiti . . . quamuis a maiore parte uocauerim gesta regum Anglorum.' Ed. Stubbs, *Willelmi Malmesbiriensis monachi de gestis regum*, II.355–56.

DESCRIPTION

SIZE 25 x 17 cm.

QUIRING a (singleton: i), I–V¹², now VI⁴ (?originally VI⁸, now lacking 5–8).

RULING Two columns, single vertical boundary-lines, 35 written lines, written below top line. Double line drawn in margins at foot and outer edge.

SCRIPT Orderly, fairly formal Gothic bookhand. Minims not broken. Small flat tops to b, h, l, and straight-backed d. Juncture of e and o after b, d, h, p. Final s round. Crossed *et*-nota. Pierced t. Top of two-compartment a closed by hairline. Straight-backed **d** fairly frequent. Rubrics and 'Armorica siue Latauia' in similar script with tall, thick ascenders with split and looped tops (chancery influence).

DECORATION Unfiligreed capitals. In two colours at major divisions in HRB.

HISTORY

In script of rubrics, at foot of 64v, 'Hanc hystoriam Brittonum scripsit frater Willelmus de Wodecherche laicus quondam conuersus Pontis Roberti cuius anima requiescat in pace. Amen'. Cistercian house of Robertsbridge, Sussex. William Woodchurch is known to be the scribe of another manuscript, Oxford, Bodleian Library, MS. Bodley 132 (*S.C.* 1893): Ker, *Medieval Libraries*, p. 296.

At the foot of 1r in ?sixteenth-century hand, 'Gabriel Pulteney'. This manuscript was in the possession of Archbishop Parker in the sixteenthcentury, at which stage it was bound with Phillipps MS. 26641 (a version of William of Malmesbury's *Gesta Regum Anglorum*) and MS. 26642 (Giraldus Cambrensis, *Topographia Hiberniae*): *Bibliotheca Phillippica*, pp. 42–45; Strongman, 'John Parker's manuscripts', pp. 22–23.

Notes in sixteenth-century hand concerning text of HRB on 11r and 64r, possibly in Parker's hand. See Wright, *The Historia Regum Britannie of Geoffrey of Monmouth, II*, pp. lxxviii–lxxix; Huws & Roberts, 'Another manuscript'.

BIBLIOGRAPHY

Davies *et al.*, *Handlist*, IV.503–4.

Dumville, 'The manuscripts', p. 121.

Huws & Roberts, 'Another manuscript'.

Wright, *The Historia Regum Britannie of Geoffrey of Monmouth, II*, pp. lxxviii–lxxix.

5 ABERYSTWYTH, NATIONAL LIBRARY OF WALES, MS. 21552

Saec. xiii   Mediaeval provenance: ?English
i + 84 + ii fos   2nd fo: *anni emensi*

HRB 1r–83vb.

§§1–3, 5–208 [with *Merlinus iste* passage in the lower margin after §117]. Dedicated to Robert of Gloucester.

Rubrics at §1 (1ra) 'Galfridi Arturi Monemutensis de gestis Britonum prologus incipit', §5 (1rb) 'Explicet (*sic*) prologus. Britanie (*sic*) insule descripcio incipit', §6 (1va) 'Explicit prologus de descripcione et commendacione Britannie. Hic incipit liber primus Bruti', §109 (41rb) 'Incipit prologus in prophecias Merlini', §118 (46va) 'Expliciunt prophecie Merlini. Sequitur liber .viii. unde supra', after §208 (83vb) 'Deo gracias. Explicit iste liber Deo gloria qui incepit et compleuit. Amen'.

Book-divisions: I §6 (1va), II §23 (8rb), III §35 (13va), IV §54 (19rb), V §73 (25vb), VI §89 (32ra), VII §118 (46va). No capitals or rubrication completed after 48r.

Merlinus iste passage added in hand of text in lower margin of 46v. *Signes de renvoi* at end of §117 and also before the marginal addition. No other contents. Folio 84 ruled but not written.

DESCRIPTION
SIZE 20.2 x 15.5 cm.
QUIRING Indicated by catchwords. I–VII¹².
PRICKING Visible in outer margin only.
RULING Two columns of 34 written lines, beginning below top ruled line. Double vertical boundary lines at outer edges.
SCRIPT Heavy Gothic bookhand approaching two-line proportions. Juncture of **a** and **e** after **b, d, p**. Also fusion of **oc, ba**, etc. Ascenders are tagged, double **l** has a flat top. **a** is two-compartment, **t** is pierced, tall **s** is found finally. Brown ink.
DECORATION Only completed as far as 48r. Blue and red initials with contrasting filigree sometimes running the length of the margin. Major initials are more elaborately filigreed.

HISTORY
Marginal notes in several hands, including sixteenth-century annotations showing interest in Oxford, Cornwall, and Brittany. Inside front cover is the bookplate of Alexander Murray of Broughton, Wigtown (Scotland), a Member of Parliament (*ob.* 1750). It covers the remains of an earlier bookplate.

BIBLIOGRAPHY
Dumville, 'The manuscripts', p. 125.

6 ABERYSTWYTH, NATIONAL LIBRARY OF WALES, MS. LLANSTEPHAN 176
(*OLIM* PHILLIPPS 9162)

Saec. xiii² [?1260x1270]

ii + 208 + ii fos

Origin: England, ?Hyde Abbey, Winchester (Benedictine)
2nd fo: [*re*]-*digere decreui*

HRB 110va–199rb
§§1–3, 5–208. Dedicated to Robert of Gloucester.
Only rubric after §208 (199rb) 'Explicit hystoria Britonum'.
Book-divisions: II §23 (119v), III §35 (125r), IV §54 (132r), V §73 (140r).

CONTENTS
1r–64v: 'Incipit tractatus de legibus et consuetudinibus regni Anglie tempore regis .H. secundi compositus iusticie gubernacula tenente illustri uiro Ranulfo de Glaneuilla . . .'. 'Regnoque insurgentes oportet esse decoratam . . . curiam tractari non decuit.' Ed. Woodbine, *Glanvill.*
64v–81v: 'Bref de dreit'. *Capitula*-list followed by text (65rb) with rubric 'Cest le primer bref de dreit'. 'Henri par la grace Deu rey de Engleterre . . . per bons sumons.' Truncated. Ed. Turner, *Brevia placitata*, pp. 1–38.
82–85: added leaves written in informal fourteenth-century hand.
82r: on alchemy. 'Pur turner plum en color dor . . . de ore ke uos uoiles.'

82v–83r: 'Ici comence le liuer de xii ewes'. 'La primer est ewe rouge . . . en ceste liuerette. Deo gracias.' Cf. Thorndike & Kibre, *Incipits*, col. 1432; Singer, *Catalogue*, II.710 (no. 1063.xxi).

83r: 'Pur suz aurer checun maner de metal . . . seit fondu'.

83v–84v: various tracts on colour and alchemy. 'Pur fer colur dor a peintur. e a escriuer . . . une feiz sullimez.'

84v–85r: '.7. sunt corpora etc (*sic*) oportet ergo . . . omnia alia uaria sunt'.

85v: blank.

86r–90v: 'En quanz poinz passe le bref de mort de ancestr. le bref de nouele desseysine . . . la es soigne ni gist pas'.

91r–110ra: 'Hic incipiunt breuia de recto et alia que in curia regis perpetrantur'. 'Rex tali salutem . . . per quos inquisitio illa facta fuerit.'

110v–199r: HRB.

199v–200r: blank.

200v: 'Ordo eligendi prelatum'. 'Primo uocandi sunt omnes qui debent et presunt commode interesse . . . hoc modo utilis.' In Anglicana script.

201r–204r: blank.

204v–205v: 'Iohanni pariter Petro Laurencio . . . Quam beneficiens uxoris equitas'. Walther, *Initia*, I.960, no. 18302. First line trimmed away. Order of lines different from that printed (under the title *Golias de coniuge non ducenda*) by Wright, *The Latin Poems*, pp. 77–85.

206r: blank.

206v: top of text trimmed away. '. . . Sciant quod hanc conuencionem fecit Willelmus Wynton. episcopus cum Galfrido abbate sancti Petri noui monasterii coram me et baronibus meis. Reddidit ipse episcopus in manu mea Hydam.'

207r: blank.

207–208r: medical recipes (Latin) and (207v) diagram of four concentric circles with series of letters between outer two rings.

DESCRIPTION

SIZE 18.5 x 14 cm.

QUIRING a^2, I–II^8, III^{12}, IV^{10}, V–VII^{12}, VIII^{12} (8 lacking: fos 75–85), IX^{10}, X^{12}, XI^{10}, XII^{16} (118–133), XIII–XVII^{12}, XVIII^{10} (lacks 9: fos 194–202), 203 uncertain attachment, XIX^4 (207v pasted to stub conjoint with 204; 208 former pastedown).

RULING Two columns, central margin divided vertically. Writing below top line; 31 written lines.

SCRIPT Gothic minuscule, not of most formal grade. Juncture of **de** and sometimes **po**. Two-compartment **a** usual, pierced **t** and **p**. Tall final **s**, *et*-nota crossed. Flat top on double **l**, **b** tagged to left.

DECORATION Blue or red filigreed capitals.

HISTORY

Text on 206v (written in Anglicana script of *ca* 1300, but mentioning abbot of New Minster (Hyde) 1106–24) and nature of register of writs suggest English origin, Hyde Abbey, Winchester (*ex inf.* Daniel Huws); now Watson, *Medieval Libraries*, p. 39. Nineteenth-century *ex-libris* on ii r: 'De la Bibliothèque de la Chevalière D'Eon'.

BIBLIOGRAPHY
Dumville, 'The manuscripts', p. 121.
Evans, *Report on Manuscripts in the Welsh Language*, II.768.

7 ABERYSTWYTH, NATIONAL LIBRARY OF WALES, MS. LLANSTEPHAN 196

Saec. xv or later   Mediaeval provenance: ?
180 pages   2nd fo: *Eneas post Troianum*

HRB pp. 1b–145b.
§§1–3, 5–208 [prefaced by Arthur's letter]. Dedicated to Robert of Gloucester.
Rubrics at top 1a 'Incipit tractacio historie Bruti', at §5 (2a) 'De insula Britannie', §6 (3a) 'De fuga Enee post bellum Troie', §110 (p. 73b) 'Prologus de prophetia Merlini', §118 (p. 82a) 'Hic finitur prophetia Merlini', after §208 (145rb) 'Explicit tractacio historie Bruti cum prophetia Merlini'. Other rubrics passim at chapter-divisions.
Book-divisions: II §23 (p. 17), III §35 (p. 24), IV §54 (p. 35), V §73 (p. 47), VI §89 (p. 58), ?VII §143 (p. 98; 'Liber s.').
Arthur's letter (see below) is also found in Oxford, Bodleian, MSS. Bodley 233 and Rawlinson B.189, and in Würzburg, Universitätsbibliothek, MS. M.ch.f.140.
It prefaces the *Historia* in Llanstephan 196 only: otherwise it follows §178.

CONTENTS
p. 1a/b: introduction to HRB. 'Littere quas misit Arturus inuictus rex Britannie Hugoni cappelano de Branno super secanam cum palefrido.' 'Arturus Dei gracia . . . pro dignitate tue promocionis famulabitur.'
pp. 1b–145b: HRB.
pp. 145b–147b: 'Prophetia Merlini' (rubric in margin of p. 147) 'Sicut rubeum draconem albus expelleret . . . impacietur illi irrogare iniuriam.' Ed. Schulz, *Gottfried*, pp. 464–65. Ends imperfectly: most of outer column of pp. 147–148 cut away.
p. 148: blank except for notes entitled 'Prophetia Ezechiellis'.
pp. 149–172: 'Incipit tractacio prophetie de Brydlington . . . sequitur primum capitulum'. 'Febribus infectus requies fuerat michi lectus . . . ad mortem tendo morti mea carmina pendo.' Cf. Wright, *Political Poems*, I.128–211. Walther, *Initia*, I.316, no. 6296.
pp. 172–173: 'Sequitur prophetia Sancti Thome Cantuar[ ] archiepiscopi'. 'Quando ego Thomas Cantuariensis archiepiscopus exul . . . inclusa in quodam uase plumbeo.'
p. 173: 'Sompnium ducis Gloucestrie'. 'In Domino confido morte dura nunc pereo . . . Deum uenerari memento.'
pp. 173–174: 'Prophetia fratris Roberti de Seyo'. 'Post hec factum est uerbum . . . flos et columba ingemiscet.'
p. 174: short note. 'Anglia transmittet leopardum lilia Galli . . . quo dabit hic herimita.' Walther, *Initia*, I.52, no. 1026.
pp. 174–175: 'Pronosticon (*sic*) Armenie de sexto Hibernie contenta in litteris quas

quidam frater Conradus tunc in partibus Ierusalem misit domino Galfrido de Langley'.
'Cum propter quoddam enorme ... diuisi sumus propter fatuitatem nostram ab
inuicem.'
pp. 175–176: 'Regnum Scotorum fuit inter cetera regna ... Christe Iesu uadunt anglica
templa cadunt'. Walther, *Initia*, I.864, no. 16547.
pp. 177–180: ?blank.

DESCRIPTION
SIZE   26 x 19.5 cm.
QUIRING   Some catchwords. I–IX^8, X^4 (pp. 145–152), pp. 153–180 uncollatable.
RULING   pp. 1–147 – single column, 34–36 lines, single boundary lines, ruling above
top written line. pp. 149–176 – two columns, 29–32 lines or more.
SCRIPT   Four-line, Secretary-influenced hand with heavy shading and formal aspect.
Tops of ascenders turned under and almost angled. Looped **d** angular, flat top of g
pierces the upright strokes, a is two-compartment with a pinched top. Descenders taper
and slant.
DECORATION   Plain red initials.

HISTORY
In 1555 in possession of William Bowyer, his no. 64 (note on fo 1).

BIBLIOGRAPHY
Evans, *Report on Manuscripts in the Welsh Language*, II.781.

8   ABERYSTWYTH, NATIONAL LIBRARY OF WALES, MS. PENIARTH 42

Saec. xii/xiii   Mediaeval provenance: ?England
vi + 77 + xi fos   2nd fo: *Pirrus etenim filius*

HRB 1r–77r
§§1–3, 5–109, 111–208. Dedicated to Robert of Gloucester.
No rubrics.
No book-divisions.

CONTENTS
1r–77r: HRB.
77v: list of kings to Henry III in cursive hand of fourteenth century. 'Aldredus rex
primus ... Henericus (*sic*) filius eius rex [ ] post eum regit .lvi. annos.'

DESCRIPTION
SIZE   17.3 x 13 cm.
QUIRING   I–IX^8, X^4 (+ 1 after 4).
RULING   Single column of 28 lines; double vertical boundary-lines.
SCRIPT   Slightly angular four-line minuscule; varying practices. Sometimes compact
minim-space, juncture of **d** with **e** and **o**, crossed and uncrossed *et*-nota. Elsewhere

11

no juncture and persistance of tall s in final position but occasional appearance of crossed *et*-nota as well as the uncrossed form and ampersand. Tops of some ascenders tending to split.

DECORATION Red and blue flourished capitals.

HISTORY
Belonged to Sir John Prise (*ob.* 1555): see Ker, *Books, Collectors and Libraries*, p. 486.

BIBLIOGRAPHY
Evans, *Report on Manuscripts in the Welsh Language*, I.377.

9 ABERYSTWYTH, NATIONAL LIBRARY OF WALES, MS. PENIARTH 43

Saec. xiv^1 ?   Mediaeval provenance: ?English
i + 177 + iii fos   2nd fo: *Hic furtiue ueneri* (11r)

HRB 10r–177r.
§§5–108, [109–110 *pudibundus Brito*], *Merlinus uero incipiens* passage, 111–117 'in fletum prorumpent pliades', 119 'Rumore itaque'–208. Dedicatory section absent.
Note above §1 (10r) in hand of text 'In nomine trino hoc opus incipio', and rubrics under §6 (10v) '.i. liber historie gentis Britonum', under §111 (92v) 'Incipiunt prophetie Merlini', after §208 (177r) 'Explicit historia gentis Britonum'.
Book-divisions: I §6 (10v), II §23 (24v), III §35 (35r), IV §54 (47r), V §72 (59v), VI §89 (73v), §143 'ultimus' (121v).
Interpolation (91v–92r) after §110 'Merlinus uero incipiens coram rege . . . .x. milibus militum comitatus'.

CONTENTS
1r–5v: blank except for inscription on 2v; see below, HISTORY.
6r–8r: 'De gigantibus' (according to final rubric). 'Anglia olim Albion dicebatur . . . de primis habitatoribus huius terre.' Written in Anglicana hand.
8v–9v: blank.

10r–177r: HRB.

DESCRIPTION
SIZE 14 x 9.5 cm.
QUIRING Catchwords beginning with first quire of HRB indicate arrangement in twelves. a^{12} (lacking 1, 4–5: fos 1–9, ?originally only fos 1–3, 6–8); I–XIV^{12}.
RULING One column of 23 lines.
SCRIPT Small, rounded, two-line bookhand. Simple strokes because of size. Ascenders have flat hairline-tops, *et*-nota is crossed, t is pierced. Round s is standard finally but tall form is used elsewhere. Juncture of e and o after d and p.
DECORATION Blue capitals with red filigree at book-divisions.

HISTORY
Fifteenth-century marginal notes showing historical interest, especially in London. In Secretary-hand on 2v: 'Johan Bates [*bis*]. [ ] uniuersi per presentes me Joh*an* Bates in com[ ] Oxon[ ]'.

BIBLIOGRAPHY
Evans, *Report on Manuscripts in the Welsh Language*, I.377–78.

10 ABERYSTWYTH, NATIONAL LIBRARY OF WALES, MS. PORKINGTON 17
(*OLIM* ORMSBY-GORE COLLECTION, MS. 17)

Saec. xiii²?   Mediaeval provenance: ?England
v + 90 + iii fos   2nd fo: *pluresque alios secum*

HRB 1r–86r.
§§1–3, 5–208. Dedicated to Robert of Gloucester.
Rubrics at foot 1r 'Incipit liber Bruti', at §5 (1rb) 'De Brittania', §109 (39vb) 'Item de Merlino', §110 (39vb) 'De Alexandro Lincolinensi episcopo', §111 (40ra) 'De prophecia Merlini que dicit', after §208 (86r) 'Explicit liber Bruti'. Other rubrics at every chapter.
No book-divisions.

CONTENTS
i–v: paper flyleaves with notes on contents in Early Modern and later hands on i–ii.
1r–86r: HRB.
86v: 'Co est la chartre au diable fet al ci[ ]'. 'Beau mester le me diez . . . assez autres sans cuntredit' (58 lines).
87r–88r: 'Mester enseingne mauez tres bien . . . uers son prome e uers nostre seingnur'.
88r–89r: ?blank
89v–90r: 'Beati qui esuriunt . . . tunc demum liberantur'. Walther, *Initia*, I.106, no. 2098. Ed. Wright, *The Political Songs*, pp. 224–30.

DESCRIPTION
SIZE 13.5 x 8.5–9.5 cm.
QUIRING i–v, I–II¹⁰, III–IV¹², V¹⁴, VI–VII ¹², VIII ⁸, iii. No signatures or catchwords.
RULING Two columns of 30 written lines, written below top line. Frame of two parallel lines drawn in outer and lower margins. No ruling after HRB. 86v–88r in two columns of 26–32 lines. 89v–90r in a single column of about 20 lines.
SCRIPT HRB in a peculiar form of Gothic. Stiff aspect with frequent use of straight-backed **d** although round form is found, especially joined to **e**. No other juncture. Tall final **s** occurs most frequently but round **s** is found and also a 3-shaped form. **t** is uncrossed but **a** has the two-compartment form. *Et*-nota is crossed and **x** has a horizontal bar. Ascenders have heavy flat tops.

Additions in two forms of Anglicana, both to be dated before the mid-fourteenth century. (i) Split ascenders, long **r**, Caroline type of **a** which, like **s**, is larger than neighbouring minims. **e** is simple and **d** looped. (ii) Tapering and heavy strokes on **b**, **r**, long **s**, the ascender of **d**. Ascenders have split tops. **a** has two-compartment form. DECORATION Capitals are prominent with showy, rather crude filigree or feathered ornament (in red and blue with green and red scrollwork: Griscom & Jones, *The Historia*, p. 35).

BIBLIOGRAPHY
Dumville, 'The manuscripts', p. 121.
Griscom & Jones, *The Historia*, pp. 34–37, 563, & pl. IV.
Hammer, 'Some additional manuscripts', p. 240, n. 27.

11   ABERYSTWYTH, NATIONAL LIBRARY OF WALES, MS. WYNNSTAY 14

Saec. xv   Mediaeval provenance: Britain
20 fos   2nd fo: *ueterum prosapia*

HRB 1r–20v.
§§1–3, 5–60 'ut predictum est insurrexisset'. Dedicated to Robert of Gloucester.
No rubrics or book-divisions extant.
No other contents.

DESCRIPTION
SIZE   19.5 x 14 cm.
QUIRING   I^{20} (paper).
RULING   Frame-ruled. 36 lines written.
SCRIPT   Cursive minuscule with long descenders. No obvious pointing of descenders but script slightly splayed. The loop of ascenders is approaching angularity. **r** often has the long form, **d** has a looped ascender and its lobe is sometimes pinched, **e** has the looped or the simple form, *et* is not abbreviated. The upright of **t** rises well above the cross-stroke.
DECORATION   Capitals not completed.

HISTORY
At top of 1r in hand similar to that of the text, 'Et est iste liber Reginaldi de Wolston. canon. Hereford.': not listed by Ker, *Medieval Libraries*, pp. 268–69 or p. 423, as a donor of books. One Reginald Wolstone recorded as prebendary of Hinton 1396–1411: John Le Neve, *Fasti Ecclesiae Anglicanae, 1300–1541*, II.27. As Daniel Huws has pointed out (unpublished manuscript-notes), this date-range probably indicates that the inscription belonged to some ancestor of this volume, and not to Wynnstay 14 itself.

BIBLIOGRAPHY
Dumville, 'The manuscripts', p. 125.

12 ALENÇON, BIBLIOTHEQUE MUNICIPALE, MS. 12

Saecc. x + xii^{1/med.} + xii²

187 fos

Mediaeval provenance: Saint-Evroul,
Normandy (Benedictine)
2nd fo: *et particulas quas*
2nd fo of twelfth-century volume
(62r): *dixit quia non est*

HRB 169r–187v

Merlinus iste passage ('Merlinus iste inter Britones sapientissimus . . . malus spiritus futura propalare consueuit') + §§118–208. No rubrics or book-divisions but larger capitals at §§143, 163, 177 (where book-divisions often made).

CONTENTS

i–ii: twelfth-century flyleaves (early). 'Non est idem ordo duodecim prophetarum apud Hebreos . . . Quia ipsi asee[ ].'

1r–57v: *Anicii Manlii Seuerini Boetii ex cons. ordi. patr. philosophias consolationis* (from rubric on 7r). 'Carmina qui quondam studio florente peregi . . . cum ante oculos agitis iudiciis cuncta cernentis.' Boethius's *De Consolatione Philosophiae*. Ed. Buchner, *Anicius Manilius Severinus Boethius*.

57v: four lines of verse 'Ut gaudere solet fessus iam nauta labore . . . Exultat uiso lassus et ipse quidem'. Schaller & Könsgen, *Initia*, p. 746, no. 16856.

57v: diagram of names of disciplines – Theorica, eloquentia, sapientia, etc. – arranged as a diamond.

58r: 'Uersus Platonis de Deo' (script as before), 31 lines. 'Omnipotens annosa poli quem suscipit aetas . . . Quicquid id est uegetum quod per cita corpora [ ].' Schaller & Könsgen, *Initia*, p. 504, no. 11308. Tiberianus, *Carmen* 4. Ed. Baehrens, *Poetae*, III.267–68.

58v: diagram of the winds.

59r: contents-list.

59v: diagram of liberal arts, as 57v.

60: twelfth-century flyleaf (taken from two-column, ?liturgical, book).

61r–69v: 'Incipit uita sancti Seueri archipresulis et confessoris'. 'Quotienscunque uirorum gesta fortium eorumque laudabiles . . . Iohannis extitit consummator.' *BHL* 7683.

69v–74v: 'Incipit prologus passionis sanctorum martyrum Crisanti et Darie uirginis que recolitur kalendas Decembris'. 'Historiam priorum sanctorum ad edificationem nostram Deus uoluit peruenire . . . cui est honor gloria et potestas in secula seculorum. Amen.'

74v–76r: 'Incipit quoddam scriptum de sancto Brictio quomodo exagitatus sit a diabolo'. 'Quodam tempore dum beatus Martinus . . . atque ad locum quo tendebat die tandem certio peruenerunt.' Sulpicius Seuerus, *Dialogi*, III.51. Ed. Halm, *Sulpicii Severi libri*, pp. 213–14.

76r/v: 'Incipit passio sancte Eufemie uirginis'. 'Sancta Eufemia filia Philfronis senatoris . . . templum magnificum.'

77r–83v: 'Incipit prologus passionis sancte Anastasie martirii'. 'Omnia que a sanctis gesta sunt . . . ad laudem nominis sui usque in finem seculi. Amen.'

83v–94v: 'Incipit uita sancti Remigii Remensis archiepiscopi et confessoris'. 'Post uindictam scelerum que facta est . . . sed obstat nisui eius sacerdotis iniuria.' *BHL* 7155.

94v–101v: 'Incipiunt gesta sancte Marie Magdalene', Odo of Cluny. 'Quanquam (*sic*) per quattuor mundi climata . . . ad huc inter iacente consecutus est.' *BHL* 5439.

101v–106r: 'Incipit prologus in passionem sancti Pontii martyris'. 'Quis poterit credere nisi Deo tribuente . . . cui est h (*sic*) honor gloria imperium et potestas in secula seculorum. Amen.' *BHL* 6896.

106r–114r: 'Incipit prologus in uitam sancti Ansberti episcopi et confessoris'. 'Uenerando et omni honore amplectendo eximio sacerdoti Christi Hildeberto . . . cui est honor et potestas decus et imperium per infinita seculorum secula. Amen.'

114r–119r: 'Incipit prologus in uitam sancte Austreberte uirginis'. 'Si ruens mundus et uelut arbor incisa securibus . . . Deus per interminata secula seculorum. Amen.' *BHL* 831.

119r–123v: 'Incipit prologus in uitam sancti Amandi episcopi et confessoris'. 'Scripturus uitam sancti Amandi habitatorem eius inuoco spiritum sanctum . . . cui est honor et gloria laus et imperium per infinita secula seculorum. Amen.' *BHL* 332.

123v–125r: 'Incipit uita sancti Hylarii Pictauensis episcopi'. 'Igitur beatus Hylarius Pictauorum urbis episcopus . . . qui sine fine uiuit et regnat in secula seculorum. Amen.'

125r–127r: 'Incipit passio sanctorum Marcellini et Petri'. 'Benignitas saluatoris nostri martirum perseuerantia comprobata . . . cui est honor et gloria et potestas per infinita secula seculorum. Amen.' *BHL* 5230.

127r–130r: 'Incipit passio sanctorum Alexsandri (*sic*) pape Hermetis Euentii et Teodoli martirum'. 'Quinto loco a beato Petro apostolo . . . Benedictus Deus in secula seculorum. Amen.' *BHL* 266.

130r–132v: 'Incipit prologus in gesta sanctorum apostolorum Petri et Pauli'. 'Licet plurima de sanctis apostolorum signis Petri et Pauli . . . et sanctificatione spiritus sancti cui est honor et gloria in secula seculorum. Amen.' *BHL* 6663.

132v–135v: 'Incipit prologus in uitam sancti Cucufatis martiris'. 'Gloriosos sanctorum triumphos preconiis deuotis attollere . . . cenobium debito cum honore est reconditum.' *BHL* 1998.

135v–139r: 'Incipit passio sancti Uincentii leuite et martyris'. 'Probabile satis est ad gloriam Uincentii martiris . . . qui uiuit et regnat Deus per infinita secula seculorum. Amen.' *BHL* 8628.

139r–140r: 'Incipit sermo sancti Augustini de eodem sancto Uincentio leuita et martyre'. 'In passione que nobis recitata est . . . cum patre et spiritu sancto in secula seculorum. Amen.' Ed. Migne, *Patrologia Latina*, XXXVIII.1255.

140r–141r: 'Incipit alius sermo eiusdem doctoris de sancto Uincentii'. 'Cunctorum licet dilectissimi gloriosas martirum passiones . . . uiuit et regnat Deus per omnia secula seculorum. Amen.' Ed. Migne, *Patrologia Latina*, XXXIX.2095–98.

141r–153v: 'Incipiunt miracula de sancto Benedicto'. 'Foca imperatore post octo annorum curricula . . . Hoc quomodo incolumitatem adeptus propria reuisit.'

16

153v–161r: 'Incipit passio sanctorum Machabeorum'. 'Principium meum philosofico quidem sermone . . . in uirtute patris et filii et spiritus sancti. Amen.' *BHL* 5111.

161r–164r: 'Incipit passio sancte Marie uirginis'. 'Adrianus et Antonius imperatores per omnes populos quos regebant legem miserunt . . . per omnia secula seculorum. Amen.'

164r–169r: 'Incipit prologus in uitam sancti Serenici confessoris'. 'Postquam diuine celsitudo maiestatis . . . atque ut imperatum est que scripta comperimus legentium memorie fideli narratione protulisse.' *BHL* 7591.

169r–187v: HRB (begun in two columns under previous single-column text).

DESCRIPTION

SIZE   31 x 25.5 cm.

QUIRING   No indication of quiring in early volume (fos 1–59). Some signatures in B (.iiii. 92v, .v. 100v, .vi. 108v, .vii. 116v, .viii. 124v, .viiii. 132v, .x. 140v, .xii. 149r, .xiii. 164v) suggesting I–XIII[8] (beginning at 60). 165–187 – collation not reconstructable from microfilm.

PRICKING   Outer margin only throughout.

RULING   Double vertical boundary-lines; writing below top ruled line in both parts. Boethius in single column of 24 written lines with marginal and interlinear glosses. fos 61–163 – single column of 36 lines; fos 164r–169r – single column of 29–35 lines; HRB – double column of 39–47 lines.

SCRIPT   Boethius in spacious Caroline minuscule, forward-leaning, generally canonical forms but f trails below the line and e-caudata is occasionally found. *Uitae* in several collaborating Protogothic hands with varying usage but generally small-headed a and sometimes straight-backed g. Ampersand only. Some use round d but e-caudata, others only straight-backed d but no e-caudata. Final round s found in one hand with no e-caudata, standard round d. HRB in similar but smaller and less ordered script, several hands. No e-caudata. Final round s and standard round d in some hands. No signs of juncture. Ticks on minims and some descenders.

DECORATION   Romanesque with fine, delicate single-line scrolling, sometimes outlines of foliate interlace. A few capitals in A. Simple interlace, some biting animals.

HISTORY

Boethius listed among books of Saint-Evroul in twelfth century: Nortier, *Les Bibliothèques*, p. 120.

BIBLIOGRAPHY

Crick, 'Manuscripts', pp. 159–60.

Omont, *Catalogue général*, II.485–87.

13 ARRAS, BIBLIOTHEQUE MUNICIPALE, MS. 583 (871)

Saec. xiii   Provenance: Saint-Vaast, Arras (A.D. 1698)
75 fos   2nd fo: *ut ipsos inermes*

HRB 1r–39rv

§§1–3, 5–18 (*in.*), 21–33 (*ex.*), 39 (*in.*) –50 (*ex.*), 55 (*ex.*) –88 (*ex.*), 95 (*ex.*) –108,
111–118 (*med.*), 124 (*med.*) –162 (*in.*), 165 (*ex.*) –208. Dedicated to Robert of
Gloucester.

1r: 'Prologus sequentis operis'. No closing rubric.

Some book-divisions: §5 (1r), §25 (4r), §73 (12v) 'Liber Quintus'.

Text lost between 3v (§18 'ex illis imbertus nomine') and 4r (§21 'Coriniensem
exemplum ducis'); 6v (§33 'quo ille sopitus fuerat') and 7r (§39 'Ex cemento et
lapidibus'; 8v (§50 'nemore uenans obuiauit') and 9r (§55 'ut comminatus es infra'),
15v (§88 'fauerent inquietarent. Per mariti-') and 16r (§95 '-girno magis ac magis').
On 18rb text ends mid-column 'Quid contra nefandam gentem ageret. (U)ocatis', end
of §105, first word of §106. Rest of 18r, 18v, and 19r/v blank. Text resumes on 20r
with large capital 'Postquam igitur [ ] Britones nefandum' (in Wright reads 'Ut igitur
inceptum nefandum'), last sixteen lines of §105. §§109–110 omitted – no physical
loss here. Text lost between 22v (§118 'tibi in presidium sed') and 23r (§124 '-toria
lucisitis enim'); 30v (§162 'Erant dixerunt promiserunt' and 31r (§165 'mandauerat
Arturo ut').

CONTENTS
1r–39r: HRB.

39v–75v: 'Incipit hystoria Hebreorum'. 'Status imperii iudaici breuiter . . . deflebant
singuli tamquam proprias orbitates.' See Hammer & Friedmann, 'Status imperii
iudaici'.

Rest of 75v blank.

DESCRIPTION
SIZE 22 x 30.2 cm.

QUIRING No signatures but catchwords on 9v, 30v, 64v and 74v. Loss of text suggests
leaves missing after fos 3, 6, 8, 15, 22, 30.

PRICKING In both margins.

RULING Two columns throughout, of 46 lines.

SCRIPT Small, black, compact minuscule. Many hairlines. Juncture of **de**, **po** and
sometimes **do**. Crossed *et*-nota used. **g** has 8-form, **d** is round-backed. Absence of
two-compartment **a** and pierced **c** suggest date not after mid-thirteenth century.

DECORATION Usual filigreed initials.

HISTORY
On 1r above text, in round, flourished hand, 'Bibliothecae mo*naste*rii Vadasti (*sic*)
Atrebaten. 1698', with shelfmark G.18 which is repeated at foot of page.

BIBLIOGRAPHY
Quicherat, *Catalogue général*, IV.233–34.

Saec. xii² + **xii/xiii**   Mediaeval provenance: Vauluisant (Cistercian)
i + 177 + i fos   2nd fo: [*nu*]-*mero annorum ab Adam*
                                        2nd fo: [*celsitudi*]-*nem tue potentie*

HRB 133ra–176va
§§1–3, 5–208. Nameless dedication.
Rubrics at §1 (132r) 'Incipit in historiam Britannorum. Prefacio Gaufridi Monomutensis', after §110 (156ra) 'Incipit prophetia Merlini', after §117 'Explicit', after §208 (176v) 'Explicit historia Britanorum'.
No book-divisions.

CONTENTS
Flyleaf with Early Modern contents-list on verso.
1r–104r: 'Incipit epistola Freculfi episcopi ad Elis\ich/arum magistrum suum in opere subsequenti'. 'Domino preceptoris desiderantissimo Elisacharo . . . librorum fecimus finem.' Freculf of Lisieux, *Chronicon*, divided here into seven books, but omitting second of the two books printed by Migne. Ed. Migne, *Patrologia Latina*, CVI.917–1116.
104ra/vb: collection of extracts from chronicles as found in Auxerre, BM, MS. 70. Cites Eusebius, Isidore, Bede, Jerome, Prosper, Orosius. 'Ex libro Iulii Africani qui primus Latinorum post Christi aduentum scripsit de temporibus atque etatibus seculi'. 'Ab Adam usque ad diluuium anni .ii(m).cc.xlii . . . ad presentem annum fiunt .vi.viiii..' Cf. Paris, BN, lat. 8501A, fos 37v–39v.
104vb–106va: 'De discretione temporum'. 'Prima etas in exordio . . . qui est aera dclxvi .v(-).dccc.lvii.'
(106va–107vb: poems of Ausonius, *De xii Caesaribus per Suetonium Tranquillum scriptis*)
106va/b: 'Incipit epistola ad Hesperium filium'. 'Cesareos proceres in quorum regna secundis . . . nomina res gestas uitamque obitumque peregit.' Schaller & Könsgen, *Initia*, p. 87, no. 1826.
106vb: 'Incipiunt monostica de ordine imperaorum (*sic*)'. 'Primus regalem patefecit Iulius aulam . . . Erant quem caluum dixit sua Roma Neronem.' Schaller & Könsgen, *Initia*, p. 560, no. 12558.
106vb: 'Item monostica de etate imperii eorum'. 'Iulius ut perhibent diuus triedenda (*sic*) regnat . . . Quindecies seuis potitur dum frater habenis.' Schaller & Könsgen, *Initia*, p. 381, no. 8522.
106vb–107ra: 'Item monostica de obitu singulorum'. 'Addidit Augustum diuis matura senectus . . . Sera grauem perimunt sed iusta piacula fratrem.' Schaller & Könsgen, *Initia*, p. 381, no. 8521 (lacking line 1).
107ra/vb: 'Incipiunt tetrastica'. 'Nunc et predictos et regni sorte sequentes . . . antoninorum nomina falsa gerens.' Schaller & Könsgen, *Initia*, p. 475, no. 10735.
(107vb–108rb: poems of Ausonius from *Liber eclogarum*)
107vb–108ra: 'Incipiunt monostica de erumpnis Herculis'. 'Prima Cleonei tolerata

erumpna leonis . . . Cerberus extremi supprema est meta laboris.' Schaller & Könsgen, *Initia*, p. 556, no. 12481.

108ra: 'Incipiunt (*sic*) de institucione uiri boni'. 'Uir bonus et sapiens qualem uix repperit unum . . . Offensus paruis det palmam et premia cunctis.' Schaller & Könsgen, *Initia*, p. 765, no. 17263.

108ra/b: 'Incipit de Pitagoricis diffinicionibus'. 'Est et non cunctis monosillaba nota frequenter . . . Qualis uita hominum duo quam monosillaba uersant.' Schaller & Könsgen, *Initia*, p. 210, no. 4582. Also in Paris, BN, lat. 8501A, 32va.

108rb: 'Incipit de etatibus animancium'. 'Ter binos deciemque nouem super exit in annos . . . Cetera secreta nouit Deus arbiter eui.' Schaller & Könsgen, *Initia*, p. 720, no. 16238. Paris, BN, lat. 8501A, 32va. Last of items found also in Auxerre, BM, MS. 70. See below, HISTORY.

108v–109v: *Diffiniciones Ciceronis*. 'Nulle sunt occultiores insidie quam . . . Nichil enim tam mortiferum ingeniis quam luxuria est.' Cf. Paris, BN, lat. 8501A, fos 32v–33r.

109v–116vb: Letter of Alexander to Aristotle (rubric no longer visible). 'Semper memoram tui . . . et animo et industria obtime Aristoteles ponderatis.' Ed. Walther Boer, *Epistola Alexandri*.

116vb–127rb: 'Incipit epistola Daretis Frigii de excidio Troianorum' (rubric on 117ra), preceded by usual prefatory letter. 'Cornelius nepos Salustio Crispo . . . Palomonem. Epistrophium. Scidium.' Ed. Meister, *Daretis Phrygii De Excidio Troiae Historia*.

127va–128vb: moral poem. 'Tot tibi mala meis manibus lectissima carpsi . . . Qui fratri ignoscit ignoscit Christi et illi.' Also found in Paris, BN, lat. 4887. Walther, *Initia*, I.1013, no. 19325.

128vb–129va: 'Incipiunt uersus Fortunati episcopi in consolacione defunctorum'. 'Aspera conditio et sors inreuocabilis hore . . . candida seu rubeis lilia mixta rosis.' Schaller & Könsgen, *Initia*, p. 53, no. 1112.

129va–130va: 'Incipiunt uersus Bede presbiteri de aduentu iudicii'. 'Inter florigeras fecundi cespitis herbas . . . ac domini benedicere secla (*sic*) per omnia Christum.' Ed. Fraipont, *Bedae venerabilis opera. Pars III Opera homiletica. Pars IV Opera rhythmica*, pp. 439–44. Walther, *Initia*, I.479, no. 9456.

130va–132v: poem ?by Ansellus of Fleury. 'In Salomonis ferculo quod construxit . . . de libano faciat esse congruum.' Schaller & Könsgen, *Initia*, p. 354, no. 7917.

133r–176va: HRB

176vb: opening of *De remediis fortuitorum*, pseudo-Seneca. 'Ad Callionem quondam . . . esse mortiferum.' Truncated before end.

Final flyleaf with notes about contents as before fo 1.

DESCRIPTION

SIZE 34.6 x 23.3 cm.

QUIRING No signatures in HRB but in A on 8v (I), 16v (II), 24v (III), 32v (IIII), 48v (VI), 56v (VII), 64v (VIII), 104v (XIII), 112v (XIIII), 120v (XV), 128v (XVI), indicating I–VIII [8], ?IX–XII [8], XIII–XVI [8]. HRB apparently added to slightly earlier unit.

PRICKING In both margins.

RULING In two columns throughout. Fos 1–132 – 34 lines per page. HRB – 40/41 lines.

SCRIPT HRB in script not unlike rest of manuscript, but later hand. Pointed tops to some minims, thickened feet, juncture of po, de, do but straight-backed d occurs (round d predominates). *Et*-nota standard (occasionally crossed), both straight and round s finally. Tall s and f broken in middle. Horizontal of t occasionally pierced.

DECORATION Romanesque initials with simple scrolled ornament.

HISTORY

Contents of 1r–108rb as in Auxerre, BM, MS. 70 (67) (dated *ca* 1200), which bears thirteenth-century *ex-libris* of Cistercian abbey of Pontigny. C. H. Talbot identified the manuscript with number 176 in the Pontigny collection but this has been rejected by M. Peyrafort-Bonnet: 'Les manuscrits 49 et 91 [at Auxerre] ne provient pas de Pontigny, mais d'une autre abbaye cistercienne: Vauluisant, dont les deux volumes portent des cotes anciennes' (for references to both identifications, see below). Vauluisant was in the diocese of Sens and in the line of Cîteaux.

N.B. Contents also related to those of Paris, BN, MS. lat. 4887 which contains Freculfus, a chronicle-collection, and some poems of Ausonius, the moral poem, Fortunatus's *De consolatione defunctorum* and Bede's *De die iudicii*.

BIBLIOGRAPHY

Molinier, *Catalogue général*, VI.38–39.

Peyrafort-Bonnet, 'La dispersion', p. 106.

Talbot, 'Notes', especially p. 168.

15   BERN, BURGERBIBLIOTHEK, MS. 568

Saec. xii *ex.* [*post* 1175]   Origin: ?Fécamp
198 + 2 fos   2nd fo: *ostium sed aliunde*

HRB 18r–79v

§§1–208. Dedicated to King Stephen and Robert of Gloucester.

No original rubrics but above §111 (47v) in cursive hand of ? *ca* 1300 'Incipiunt prophetie Mellini'.

No book-divisions.

CONTENTS

i: flyleaf.

1r–2r: letter of Emperor Frederick Barbarossa to Hillin, archbishop of Trier. 'F. Romanus imperator et semper augustus dilecto suo H. uenerabili Treuerensi archiepiscopo . . . prout dominus dederit resistant.' Ed. Pertz, 'Mittheilungen', pp. 418–26.

2r/v: Hillin to Pope Hadrian IV (1154–59). 'Domino et patri A. summo et uniuersali pontifici H. sancte Treuerensis ecclesie humilis minister . . . in uitam eternam temporibus suis.' Ed. Pertz, 'Mittheilungen', pp. 426–28.

2v–4r: Hadrian IV to bishops of Trier, Mainz, and Köln (1158). 'A. seruus seruorum Dei dilectis in Christo fratribus H. [ ]reuensi A. Maguneiensi F. Coloniensi . . . quia non expedit fraternitati uestre scisma regni et ecclesie.' Ed. Pertz, 'Mittheilungen', pp. 428–34.

4r/v: Alexander III to Roger, archbishop of York, and the English episcopate (1166). 'A. episcopus seruus seruorum Dei archiepiscopo Eboracensi et uniuersis Anglie episcopis salutem . . . Datum Lateranis nono Aprilis.' Ed. Migne, *Patrologia Latina*, CC.406–7.

4v: Henry II of England to his son Henry (1170). 'H. rex Anglie et dux Normannie . . . Test. Rot. archiepiscopo Rothomag. apud Chinum.' Edd. Robertson & Sheppard, *Materials*, VII.346–47.

4v–5v: Pope Alexander III to Roger, archbishop of York, and Hugh, bishop of Durham (1170). 'A. episcopus seruus seruorum Dei Rog. archiepiscopo Eboracensi et H. Dunelmi episcopo salutem . . . conueniat. Datum Ferenti .xvi. kl. Octobris.' Ed. Migne, *Patrologia Latina*, CC.703–5.

5v–6v: letter of Alexander III to bishops of London, Salisbury, Exeter, Chester, Rochester, St Asaph, and Llandaf. 'A. episcopus seruus seruorum Dei uenerabilibus fratribus Londoniensi Salesberiensi (etc.) . . . euitari. Datum Ferenti .xvi. kal. Octobris.' Ed. Migne, *Patrologia Latina*, CC.700–2.

7r/v: 'Qu[ero Deum] testem circundederam mihi uestem . . . Qui nec erant nec erunt mihi fratres deseruerunt'. Walther, *Initia*, I.783, no. 15088.

8r: 'Post dubiam post nugatorium fortune gloriam . . . quam referens honoris'. Walther, *Initia*, I.741, no. 14313.

8r/v: 'Nec mare flumini nec lumini sol supplicat . . . homo sed plus homine'. Walther, *Initia*, I.599, no. 11689.

9r–15v: Peter Alphonsus, *Disciplina clericalis*, acephalous. 'Leuius poterit requirere dampnum tuum . . . misericordiam consecutus fuisset.' Edd. Hilka & Söderhjelm, *Die Disciplina clericalis*.

15v–17v: added in near contemporary hand 'Baucis. Glicerium. Traso. Dauus. Birria'. 'Baucis amica sibi spe lucri sedula nutrix . . . Glicerio fruitur atque potitus abit.' Ed. Orlandi, 'Baucis et Traso'.

17v: five lines of verse. 'Cuius totus eram cuius me cura regebat . . . qui sic diligeret nec sic nec talis abiret.' Walther, *Initia*, I.176, no. 3526.

17v: in informal fourteenth-century hand. List of British kings from Brutus to Arthur. 18r–79v: HRB.

80r–83r: Bede, *Historia ecclesiastica gentis Anglorum*, I.15, 23, 25, 26, 34; II.1–3, 5. 'Anno ab incarnatione Domini quadrigentesimo nono Mauritianus cum Ualentiniano . . . qui cum filio suo Oisc inuitatus a Wrtigerno Britanniam primus intrauit ut supra retulimus.' Edd. Colgrave & Mynors, *Bede's Ecclesiastical History*.

83v–120r: 'Incipit prologus in uitam sancti regis Edwardi ad gloriosum regem iuniorem Henricum', by Aelred of Rievaulx. 'Multis ueterum studio fuisse didicimus . . . omnium corda commouit.' Ed. Migne, *Patrologia Latina*, CXCV.737–90. *BHL* 2423.

120v: blank except for notes in late mediaeval hand.

121r–137v: 'Incipiunt epistole Arn. Lex. episcopi edite ad Egidium arch. Rot.'. 'Epistolas que aliquando diuersis a me fere destinare personis . . . uel mandatis audeat obuiare.' Ed. Barlow, *The Letters*, nos 1, 4, 11, 30, 5, 16, 8, 7, 17, 22, 15, 18–21, 9, 13, 26, 24.

137v–140r: 'Alex. papa Arnulf. Luxou. episcopo'. Pope Alexander III to Arnulf, 1160. 'Alexander episcopus seruus seruorum Dei . . . ac sollenniter excommunicasse cognoscas. Data Amagn. kl. Aprilis.' Ed. Giles, *Arnulfi Lexoviensis episcopi episto-lae*, pp. 112–16.

140r–163v: further letters of Arnulf beginning 'Ad archiepiscopos et episcopos A. de s. c. d. papa Alex.'. 'Quanta tempestate laborat ecclesia . . . et mihi gratiam diuine propitiationis augeret.' Ed. Barlow, *The Letters*, nos 28, 23, 29, 33–35, 38, 40, 43, 39, 45, 46, 27, 32, 14, 25, 31, 12.

(163v–176v: sermons of Arnulf of Lisieux)

163v–164r: 'Ad Egidium Rothomagensem archidiaconum'. 'Sermonem habitum in concilio Turonensi . . . equitate cognoscas.' Ed. Migne, *Patrologia Latina*, CCI.151–52.

164r–165r: 'Sermo habitus in concilio Turonensi tempore scismatis sub Alexandro papa'. 'Hodiernum sermonem domini et patres mei mihi domini nostri qui presidet . . . sermone adimpleat oportuno.' Ed. Migne, *Patrologia Latina*, CCI.153–54A.

165r–171v: 'In omni itaque sermone Domini et patres mei karissimi . . . eterne retributionis inferre'. Ed. Migne, *Patrologia Latina*, CCI.154A-161.

171v–176v: 'Quis putas fidelis seruus et prudens quem constituit dominus . . . cui est honor et gratia in secula seculorum. Amen'. Ed. Migne, *Patrologia Latina*, CCI.161–67.

176v–184r: letters of Arnulf. 'Sustulit uirum gloriose memorie Innocentium papam . . . non nisi fortuitos experietur euentus.' Ed. Barlow, *The Letters*, nos 2–3, 37, 53, 47, 52, 51.

(184r–188v: verse attributed to Arnulf, ed. Migne, *Patrologia Latina*, CCI.195–200)

184r/v: 'De natiuitate Domini'. 'Semper ab eterno nascens ex tempore nasci . . . Exit et erecto porta negata patet.' Walther, *Initia*, I.916, no. 17484.

184v–185r: 'Ad Henricum Wintoniensem episcopum'. 'Quod per multiplices dispensat gratia formas . . . Nescio plus placeas proficiasue magis.' Walther, *Initia*, I.850, no. 16292.

185r/v: 'De induatione uernali'. 'Quicquid hiemps tanquam ueteri deforme senecta . . . Perpetuaque fluant tempora temperie.' Walther, *Initia*, I.832, no. 15987.

185v–186r: 'De alterna temporum successione'. 'Tempora circuitu ueteri reuoluta uicissim . . . Et uariata mouens inuariata manet.' Walther, *Initia*, I.1002, no. 19112.

186r/v: 'Item idem ad poetam mendicium laudem et munus uersibus postulantem'. 'Versus mendicos et muse pauperis ausum . . . Laudibus impleri muneribusque manum.' Walther, *Initia*, I.1062, no. 20250.

186v: 'Versus eiusdem ad sceuam de anu non reformanda'. 'Sceua senescentis domine marcere decorem . . . Multiplicatque cutem multiplicata dies.' Walther, *Initia*, I.907, no. 17310.

186v–187r: 'Item ad iuuenem et puellam affectuosius se inuicem intuentes'. 'Occurrunt blando sibi lumina uestra fauore . . . Et letos parient anxia uota dies.' Walther, *Initia*, I.673, no. 13120.

187r/v: 'Item ad lasciuos sodales'. 'Mens \mea/ uirtutum studiis a tempore primo . . . Nec luci tenebras contrabit ipsa sue.' Walther, *Initia*, I.557, no. 10916.

187v: 'Epitaphium regis Henrici primi'. 'Henrici cuius celebrat uox publica nomen . . . soluisset. Secuit prima decembris eum.' Walther, *Initia*, I.388, no. 7697.

187v–188r: 'Quomodo pauperi uel diuiti sit donandum'. 'Res simplex triplici uicio dampnata datoris . . . Ne parcam prodant dona recisa manum.' Walther, *Initia*, I.870, no. 16648.

188r: 'Epitaphium Matildis imperatricis'. 'Regia progenies stirps regia Cesaris uxor . . . Creditur eternum continuasse diem.' Walther, *Initia*, I.862, no. 16504.

188r/v: 'Regis mater erat et regibus orta Matildis . . . De nostram ad uerum nocte reuecta diem'. Walther, *Initia*, I.863, no. 16528.

188v: 'Sic cruce tollo crucem moriens de morte triumpho . . . Res signo morti uita corona iugo'. Walther, *Initia*, I.950, no. 18107.

188v: 'Uersus Landrici de Anschitillo'. 'Porrum portaui monacho quem semper amaui . . . Te colo digne coli nam sine labe doli.' Walther, *Initia*, I.738, no. 14272. Ed. Laporte, 'Epistulae Fiscannenses', p. 18.

(188v–197v: material relating to abbey of Fécamp)

188v–190r: 'Uenerabili fratri et amico interiori Anch. (*sic*) Herueus puer eius sanctitatis . . . Uale iterum et dominus tecum sit'. Ed. Laporte, 'Epistulae Fiscannenses', pp. 18–20.

190r–191v: Pope Alexander III to Henry II of England (1168). 'Dominus papa domino regi. Excellentie tue nuntios dilectos scilicet filios nostros . . . ac circumueniri possimus.' Ed. Migne, *Patrologia Latina*, CC.464–66.

191v–192r: Alexander III to English bishops (1169). 'Uniuersis episcopis Anglie. Super discretione uestra satis compellimur admirari . . . nullatenus teneamini. D. beneuale .vii. kal. maii.' Ed. Migne, *Patrologia Latina*, CC.579–80.

192r–193r: 'Uenerabili et dilecto fratri .A. .H. omnium seruorum Dei minimus . . . necesse est. Uale amplius quam dicere possum'. Ed. Laporte, 'Epistulae Fiscannenses', pp. 20–22.

193r/v: 'A. uenerabili fratri suo et amico Herueus totus eius salutem . . . michi factum reputabo. Ualete'. Ed. Laporte, 'Epistulae Fiscannenses', pp. 22–23.

193v–194r: 'Desiderato et amico interiori Ansch. uenerande bonitatis . . . quomodo id fieri debeat'. Ed. Laporte, 'Epistulae Fiscannenses', pp. 23–24.

194r/v: 'Uenerabili fratri et desiderato Ansch. Herueus ab etate puerili socius . . . Uiue memor nostri sum memor ecce tui.' Ed. Laporte, 'Epistulae Fiscannenses', pp. 24–25.

194v–195v: 'Uenerando fratri et amico speciali Roberto Gaufridus . . . uel indignantis amici scripta accepero'. Ed. Laporte, 'Epistulae Fiscannenses', pp. 25–26.

195v–196v: 'Omnibus sancte matris ecclesie fidelibus et filiis frater .H. . . . obtineat beatitudinem. Ualete'. Ed. Laporte, 'Epistulae Fiscannenses', pp. 26–27.

196v–197r: 'Reuerentissimo domino et patri .H. Dei gratia abbati .R. humilis prior Norwicensis eiusdemque loci conuentus salutem . . . ualeat sanctitas uestra'. Ed. Laporte, 'Epistulae Fiscannenses', pp. 27–28.

197r/v: 'Adrianus episcopus seruus seruorum Dei uenerabili fratri Hug. Rothom. archiepiscopo salutem ... studebimus confirmare. Datum Lat. .ii. kl. Ian.'. Ed. Laporte, 'Epistulae Fiscannenses', pp. 28–29.

197v–198v: 'Nullum inter onera grauius onus ... Ualete. Iterum <dico si locum>'. Truncated at foot of page. Ed. Laporte, 'Epistulae Fiscannenses', pp. 29–31.

199–200: flyleaves cut from document of 1481–84, relating to area south of Beauvais.

DESCRIPTION

SIZE 20 x 14 cm.

QUIRING A^2 (fos 1–2), B^{12} (lacks 7–12: fos 3–8), lacuna, C^8, D^2 (fos 17–18), E-H^8, J-M^8; I–IV^8, V^6 (fos 115–120); I^{10} (3, 9 cancelled: fos 121–128), II–VIIII^8, X^6 (193–198); a^2 (199–200).

PRICKING Visible in both margins in places.

RULING Single column of 34–35 lines in HRB. More variable elsewhere. Two columns on 7r/v and also for additions 15v–17v.

SCRIPT Four-line Protogothic. Final s tall (occasionally round), round d usual but straight-backed form occasionally found, uncrossed et-nota, ct-ligature. No juncture. Occasional e-caudata (rare). Several hands with varying degrees of lateral compression.

DECORATION Romanesque, some with split shafts or bosses, some with scrolled ornament. Green, red, blue.

HISTORY

The presence of the Fécamp letter-collection (fos 188–197) suggests early association with that house. In north-west France in Early Modern period. See Wright, *The Historia Regum Britannie of Geoffrey of Monmouth, I*, pp. xxxv–xliii.

BIBLIOGRAPHY

Hagen, *Catalogus codicum Bernensium*, pp. 458–60.

Laporte, 'Epistulae Fiscannenses'.

Pellegrin, 'Essai d'identification', especially p. 25.

Wright, *The Historia Regum Britannie of Geoffrey of Monmouth, I*, especially pp. xx–xlvi.

16 BOULOGNE-SUR-MER, BIBLIOTHEQUE MUNICIPALE, MSS. 180 + 139 + 145

Saec. xiii ?$^{med./2}$ Provenance: Mont-Saint-Eloi, Arras (Augustinian)

74 + 61 + 69 fos   2nd fo: [*pro*]-*geniem Heleni filii Priami*

HRB 2ra–72va.

§§1–3, 5–208. Dedicated to Robert of Gloucester.

No opening or closing rubrics. At §110 (37va) 'Incipit prologus in prophetia Mellini', §111 (37vb) 'Explicit prologus'.

Book-divisions at §23 (8v) II, §35 (13r) III, §54(18v) IV, §73 (24v) V, §89 (30r) VI, §143 (50r) VII, §177 (64r) XI. No indication of beginnings of books VIII–X. Some omissions from text, for example in §62 and §151.

CONTENTS
MS. 180
1: blank
2ra–72va: HRB.
72va–74v: *Prophetie Merlini* with gloss. 'Sedente itaque rege . . . ex quibus uulpis et lupus' (truncated). HRB §§111–116.41. Not listed by Eckhardt, 'The *Prophetia Merlini*'.
MS. 139
1: blank.
2ra: erased passage at top of column.
2ra–69vb: 'Status iudaici imperii breuiter in hec libello annotatus est . . . et deflebant singuli tanquam proprias orbitates'. See Hammer and Friedmann, 'Status imperii iudaici'.
MS. 145
1: blank.
2ra–61vb: 'Incipit liber primus de gestis et successione regum Francorum qui Merouingii dicti sunt' (rubric on 2vb), preceded by *capitula*-list. Truncated at end. 'Domino patri et sanctissimo .P. uenerabili Atrebatensi ecclesie episcopo . . . occupandi cuius pars maxima per.' Chronicle of Andreas Sylvius with continuation of William, abbot of Andres (near Boulogne). Andrew of Marchiennes. See Werner, 'Andreas'.

DESCRIPTION
QUIRING Catchwords indicate arrangement mainly in twelves, regularly so in HRB. Apparently MS. 139 originally followed MS. 180 (HRB) as the words '[ ]cules eius et faciem' may be discerned in the erasure on 2r of MS. 139. These come from the section of *Prophetie Merlini* immediately following that with which MS. 180 ends.
PRICKING Visible in outer margin.
RULING Two columns of 26 written lines, written below top ruled line.
SCRIPT Small, thick, practised Gothic bookhand. Nearly two-line proportions -- semi-quadrata. Juncture of e and o with d, h, p, and more general fusion of opposing curves. Final round s standard, *et*-nota is crossed, two-compartment a and pierced t occur in places.
DECORATION Red and blue capitals alternately with elaborate and handsome filigree in contrasting colour. Main initials (two-colour) in a square of intricate filigree.

HISTORY
On 2r, MS. 180 (Early Modern hand): 'Bibliothece quon[ ] Montis Sancti Eligii'.

BIBLIOGRAPHY
Quicherat, *Catalogue général*, IV.659, 662–23, 683.

17 BRUGES, BIBLIOTHEQUE DE LA VILLE, MS. 428

Saec. xiii/xiv   Provenance (1641): Les Dunes (Cistercian), diocese of Thérouanne
76 fos   2nd fo (the original lost): *presidium illius expectabat*

HRB 1r–48v
Acephalous. §§5 ('plage freto ad Gallias nauigatur') –109, 118–208. Dedicatory section (§3) lost.
No closing rubric.
Book-divisions: I §6 (1r), III §35 (10r).
Second Variant Version. Hammer's siglum F: Emanuel, 'Geoffrey of Monmouth's *Historia*', p. 104.

CONTENTS
1r–48v: HRB.
48vb–51rb: 'Editio Gaufridi Monemutensis de edictis Merlini Ambrosii'. HRB §§110–116.54 'et ueneratus interibit'. Rubric at §111 (49ra) 'Incipit liber Ambrosii Merlini'.
51rb–54rb: 'Liber Methodii episcopi ecclesie et martyris Christi de Hebreo transtulit in Latinum quem beatus Ieronimus in opusculis suis collaudauit'. 'Sciendum nobis est . . . et iudicium Dei appropinquabit.' Cf. Sackur, *Sibyllinische Texte*, pp. 59–96.
54v: blank.
55ra–59rb: 'Incipit liber tercius de ira ad Nouatum'. 'Quod maxime desiderasti Nouate . . . immortalitas aderit.' Seneca, *Dialogi* IV. Ed. Reynolds, *L. Annaei Senecae Dialogorum libri duodecim*, pp. 93–128.
59rb–63va: 'Liber de uita beata ad Gallionem'. 'Uiuere Gallio frater omnes beate uolunt . . . nauem soluere quam laudet nauigationem.' Seneca, *Dialogi* VII. Ed. Reynolds, *ibid.*, pp. 167–206.
62va–69rb: *Liber de breuitate uite* and *Consolatio ad Polybium*. 'Maior pars mortalium Pauline . . . grauis fremitus circumsonat.' Seneca, *Dialogi* X. Ed. Reynolds, *L. Annaei Senecae Dialogorum libri duodecim*, pp. 279–339.
69rb–73rb: *Liber ad Marciam de morte filii*. 'Nisi te Marcia scirem . . . ista iam nouit.' Seneca, *Dialogi* VII. Ed. Reynolds, *L. Annaei Senecae Dialogorum libri duodecim*, pp. 129–66.
73rb–76va: *Liber ad Helbiam matrem de consolatione filii*. 'Sepe iam mater optima . . . uadit omnibus seculis.' Seneca, *Dialogi* XII. Ed. Reynolds, *L. Annaei Senecae Dialogorum libri duodecim*, pp. 291–317.
76va: 'Epitaphium Senece'. 'Cura labor meritum sumpti pro munere . . . ossa tibi.' Ed. Riese, *Anthologia*, II.126, no. 667.

DESCRIPTION
SIZE 32.4 x 24.7 cm.
QUIRING Originally two volumes: 1–54; 55–76. Catchwords in first unit. Folio 6 is merely as slip between fos 5 and 7. Catchwords on 17v, 22v, 29v. I⁴, II¹² (+ slip after 1: 5–17), III (5 fos), IV (7 fos); the remainder uncollatable from microfilm.
PRICKING In both margins.

27

RULING Two columns of 42 lines. Ruling above top written line. Single vertical boundary-lines. Two extra lines ruled along margins at head and foot.
SCRIPT Formal bookhand. Minims with pointed ends, short ascenders and descenders, and heavy pen-strokes. Juncture of e and o with d, h, and p. Fusion of other curves (for example, co). a usually in two-compartment form, horizontal of t is pierced, final s is round but initial d is often straight-backed. At edge of text, ascenders and cross-strokes sometimes trail into the margin. Et-nota is crossed.
DECORATION Capitals are infrequent and only filigreed at the beginning of the book, which suggests that the decoration is incomplete.

HISTORY
Related to Bruges MS. 424 in which are found the works on fos 55–69 of this manuscript. On 65rb of our manuscript are found marginal notes in the hand of the annotator of MS. 424. A title on the flyleaves of the first part of MS. 428 indicates that the HRB was originally preceded by the history of Dares Phrygius. Identified as the copy listed by Sanderus in 1641 at the Cistercian abbey of Les Dunes: Isaac, *Les Livres*, p. 285.

BIBLIOGRAPHY
A. de Poorter, *Catalogue*, pp. 483–85.

18   BRUXELLES, BIBLIOTHEQUE ROYALE DE BELGIQUE, MS. 8495–8505 (3472)

Saecc. xvi + xii/xiii + xvii   Mediaeval provenance: ?
20 + 16 + 168 fos   2nd fo (22r): *si quid absque certo auctore*

HRB 21r/v
§204 ('digne susceptus est') –§208.
Final rubric 21v, 'Explicit edicio Gaufridi Arturi Monumetensis de gestis Britonum'.

CONTENTS
1r: contents-list.
3r–11v: Bollandists's collections, kalendar (3v blank).
12r/v: blank.
13r–19r: (different hand) 'Quae sequuntur excerpta sunt ex missali elegantissimo ad usum Anglicanae ecclesiae data coenobio Gemmeticensi a Roberto qui eius quondam abbas fuerat tuncque episcopus Londoniensis . . .'.
All versos left blank.
19v–20v: blank.

21r/v: HRB.
21v–33r: Henry of Huntingdon, notes on English saints. '[D]e uiris illustribus Anglorum et que per eos deitatis omnipotencia . . . Et iam hic de gloriosis operibus Dei liber

explicit.' *Historia Anglorum*, Bk. IX (sometimes X). Not included by Greenway, 'Henry of Huntingdon and the manuscripts'.
33v: blank, unruled.
34r–35v: displaced section of previous text. 'regum Sebbi et Sigehere . . . et anime et corpore sempiternam.' Should be arranged fos 21–25, 34–35, 26–33, 36.
36r/v: blank parchment.

37r–204: seventeenth-century Bollandist collections (on paper). Letters and notes on saints and saints' days. Mainly Latin, some French.

DESCRIPTION
SIZE 22.2 x 15.5 cm; 17.5 x 11.3 cm.
QUIRING Two mediaeval parchment quires I⁴ (21–24), II¹² (25–36). II should be subdivided as follows: a⁴ (25, 34–35, 26), b⁸ (27–33, 36). Rest of volume paper.
PRICKING Mostly trimmed away but occasionally visible at outer edge.
RULING Single column, 32 lines then 27–28 lines. Ruling above top written line.
SCRIPT Several hands, Protogothic minuscule. First has short ascenders, minims thickened at each end but not broken. Tall final s (round in abbreviation), Caroline a, juncture of de and do only. Crossed *et*-nota. Other collaborating hands. One four-line, antiquated-looking with peculiar shading, straight hairline feet, ct-ligature, straight-backed d as well as round form, no juncture. Frequent final round s. Third hand large and bold with ampersand and straight-backed d only, no juncture but occasional final s. Pinched h. Bollandist material in many Early Modern hands.
DECORATION Romanesque capitals.

BIBLIOGRAPHY
Van den Gheyn, *Catalogue*, V.474–76.

19 BRUXELLES, BIBLIOTHEQUE ROYALE DE BELGIQUE, MS. 8536–8543 (1489)

Saec. **xii**^*med./2* + xiii   Mediaeval provenance: Saint-Bernard opt Scheldt, Belgium (Cistercian)
i + 140 fos   2nd fo: *Italia indignantibus parentibus*

HRB 1r–72r.
§§1–3, 5–208. Nameless dedication (§3).
Later rubrics. At §1 (1r) 'Incipit prefatio in hystoria Britonum', §5 (1r) 'De longitudine et latitudine [ ] et situ [ ]', and also in margin 'Explicit prefatio. Incipit prologus'. Few rubrics after §15 but in margin beside §110 (38r) 'Incipit prologus de prophetia Merlini'.
Book-divisions apparently contemporary with rubrics: I §6 (1v), II §23 (8v), III §35 (13v), IIII §54 (19r), V §73 (25r), VI §89 (30v), Prophecies of Merlin §110, VIII §118 (42r), IX §143 (50r), X §163 (57r), XI §177 (63v).

CONTENTS
i: blank except for titles (?sixteenth-century and later) on recto.
1r–72r: HRB.
72v: blank except for inscription (see below, HISTORY).

73r–98r: 'Incipit prologus magistri Hugonis prioris sancti Laurencii de naturis auium'.
'Desiderii tui karissime peticionibus satisfacere cupiens . . . per bonas operacionem
conformem reddit.' By Hugh of Saint-Victor. Ed. Migne, *Patrologia Latina*,
CLXXVII.13–164.
116r–126v: 'Incipit prologus magistri Hugonis prioris sancti Laurencii de medicina
anime'. 'Cogis me frater karissime ut ea que de medicina anime . . . ut emplaustrudo
uerecundie fronti superponat.' By Hugh of Saint-Victor. Ed. Migne, *Patrologia
Latina*, CLXXVI.1183–1202.

127r/v: '[ ]iunt namque doctores quod Moyses qui ut de eo scriptura testatur . . . que
omnia propter fastidium declinamus'.
128r–134r: 'Incipit passio sancte Theodosie uirginis'. 'In illis temporibus Diocletiano
quater imperante . . . et partem cum ipsa obtinebunt in secula seculorum.' *BHL* 8090.
134r–135v: *Passio beate Barbare uirginis*. 'Temporibus Maximiani imperatoris erat
quidam satrapa Diosorus nomine . . . Est ibi tunc ubi nunc sibi soli sufficit ipse.' *BHL*
913.

136r–140v: 'Sermo domini Odonis Cantuarie monachi in honore sancte crucis in die
nostre redemptionis'. 'Ita uos hodie fratres erga crucem Christi . . . in mortem
resolutus emitteret.' Ed. de Clercq, *The Latin Sermons*, pp. 43–84, l. 14. MS. B2 (*ibid.*,
p. 9).

DESCRIPTION
SIZE 24 x 16.5 cm.
QUIRING Four volumes, of which the first is the earliest. A I–IX⁸, with signatures; B
(73–126) X–XIV⁸, XV⁸ (lacks 7–8: fos 121–126); C (127–135); D (136–140); both
uncollatable.
PRICKING Visible in outer margin in A, C, and D.
RULING A – single column, 36 lines, top line written; B – single column, 30 lines; C
– single column, 34 lines; D – double column, 40 lines.
SCRIPT HRB – Protogothic minuscule with ampersand and frequent use of e-caudata.
g has straight back, round d standard, ct-ligature. Very dark brown ink. B – small,
thirteenth-century Protogothic minuscule. Crossed *et*-nota with extended top. Juncture
of e and o after d and p. Tall ascenders with split or tagged tops. Final tall s. C – strange
untidy script, closely written. *Et*-nota, occasional round s but straight-backed d still
occurs. i distinguished from other minims by tag at foot. D – small hand with crossed
et-nota or ampersand and juncture of de and do. Straight-backed d also found. h
pinched.
DECORATION Most capitals in HRB of type found in northern France and Low
Countries: split shafts with cross-hatched scroll-decoration, animal heads, etc. First

two capitals in green and orange with filigree, ?not original but added at same time as rubrics. B – filigreed capitals, historiated opening initial and spaces left in text, presumably for illustrations. C – filigreed. D – plain.

HISTORY
Inscription on 72v in formal hand ?of later thirteenth-century, 'Hunc librum dedit magister Martinus de Lyra domui loci sancti Bernardi. Retribuat illi Deus uitam eternam. Amen. Quicumque eum abstulerit uel aliquid ab eo defraudauerit nouerit se esse excommunicatum. Nec remittetur peccatum donec restituatur ablatum. Anima magistri Martini supradicti de Lira datoris huius pulcherrime hystorie per misericordiam Dei requiescat in pace. Amen.' *Locus sancti Bernardi* may be identified as Lieu-Saint-Bernard, the Cistercian abbey of Saint-Bernard opt Scheldt, near Antwerp (founded at Viemdes in 1233 or 1237, moved site in 1246).

BIBLIOGRAPHY
Van den Gheyn, *Catalogue*, II.385–86.

20 BRUXELLES, BIBLIOTHEQUE ROYALE DE BELGIQUE, MS. 9871–9874

Saec. ?xii/xiii   Mediaeval provenance: ?
i + 155 fos   2nd fo: *uita. Non est michi*

HRB 86r–155v.   2nd fo: *culmen honoris perueniret*
§§1–3, 5–108, 111–112, 117–180 'que lingua Anglorum stragen uocatur'. Deliberately truncated. Nameless dedication.
Rubrics at §1 (86ra) 'Incipit prologus Gaufridi Monemutensis in hystoriis regum Britannie', §5 (86rb) 'Explicit prologus. Incipit hystoria', interpolation 'Ego Merlinus rogatus' (see below) after §143, 'diademate insignuit' (*sic*), (140r) 'Prophetia Merlini de Arturo', after §180 (155vb) 'Explicit historia regum Britannie'.
Compressions §§83–84, 173–174 as in Montpellier, BM, MS. 92. Interpolated section 140rb/va after 'regni diademate insign<i>uit' (§143) 'Ego Merlinus rogatus ab Arturo ... tanto minus sapiens sibi uidebitur'. Unique to this manuscript.

CONTENTS
1r–49ra: 'Incipit actus Sancti Iohannis theologi et Prochori eius discipuli'. 'Actum est post assumptionem Domini nostri ... glorificantes Patrem et Filium et Spiritum Sanctum in secula seculorum. Amen.' *BHL* 4323.
49ra–57va: 'Incipit sermo de Sancto Iohanne'. 'Hodie dilectissimi sancte nobis leticie gaudia geminantur ... per omnia secula seculorum. Amen.' Ed. Migne, *Patrologia Latina*, CXLIV.857–66.
57va–65vb: 'Sermo de eodem', by Peter Damian. 'Gaudemus fratres karissimi copiosum uestre fraternitatis adesse conuentum ... uiuit et regnat in secula seculorum. Amen.' Ed. Migne, *Patrologia Latina*, CXLIV.866–75.
65va–85ra: 'Incipit argumentum Sancti Bernardi abbatis in euangelio missus est'.

'Scribere me aliquid et deuotio iubet . . . una in deitate substantia et in qua unus cum eis spiritus sanctus uiuit et regnat Deus per omnia secula seculorum. Amen.' Schneyer, *Repertorium*, I.442, nos 8–11.

85v: prayers and notes in various hands (twelfth- to fourteenth-century).

86r–155v: HRB.

DESCRIPTION

SIZE 28 x 18.5 cm.

QUIRING Elaborate quire-signatures indicate a sequence of eights beginning at 86r (HRB) and therefore two separate volumes.

A – I–X⁸, [XI]⁶ (lacks 6: fos 81–85; erasure on 85r/v). B – I–VIII⁸, [IX]⁸ (lacks 7–8: fos 150–155).

PRICKING Visible at outer edge only.

RULING Two columns of 31 lines. Ruling above top written line in both volumes.

SCRIPT Rigid minuscule with Romanesque proportions but lateral compression. Some juncture of e and o with b, p, h. Round s frequent finally. Straight-backed d and occasionally the round form. Upper section of a is open, *et*-nota is uncrossed but t is pierced. Stiffness and combination of features are reminiscent of German script. Dark brown ink. First part of book slightly later-looking. Round d standard and used in juncture.

DECORATION Red and orange-red initials with green elaboration. Fairly florid.

BIBLIOGRAPHY

Not catalogued by Van den Gheyn.

21 BRUXELLES, BIBLIOTHEQUE ROYALE DE BELGIQUE, MS. II.1020 (3791) (*OLIM* PHILLIPPS 11603)

Saec. xiii¹ᐟᵐᵉᵈ·   Mediaeval provenance: Saint-Martin, Tournai
139 fos   2nd fo: *esse rectissimam. Rursus uero*

HRB 90r–137v.

§§1–3, 5–208. Dedicated to Robert of Gloucester.

Rubrics at §1 (89vb) 'Prologus in hystoria Brittannica', §110 (114ra) 'Prologus in prophetia Merlini', §111 (114rb) 'Incipit prophetia Merlini. Liber vii'. After §208 (137v), in ?fourteenth-century hand: 'Ego Galfridus Monemutensis'. Book-divisions at §5 (90r) I, §23 (94v) II; §35 (97v) III, §54 (101r) IIII, §73 (105r) V, §89 (109r) VI, §111 (114r) VII, §122 (117v) VIII, §143 (122v) IX. Large capital and space for rubric at §177 (132r).

CONTENTS

1r–38r: 'Incipit liber domni Herimanni abbatis de restauratione ecclesie sancti Martini Tornacensis' (rubric on 1rb). 'Dilectissimis dominis patribus fratribus et filiis ʻ. . .

indictione .viii. concurrentur .v. epacta .xi..' Then continued in informal hand to 1331 (Iuo to Egidius).

38va–89vb: 'Status imperii iudaici breuiter in hoc libello . . . et deflebant singuli tanquam proprias orbitates'. In two books, each preceded by *capitula*-list. See Hammer and Friedmann, 'Status iudaici imperii'.

90r–137v: HRB.

138: recto blank. On verso in late mediaeval hand 'Catalogus regum Britannie' ('Brutus . . . Cadualadrus').

DESCRIPTION

SIZE 33.5 x 24.5 cm.

QUIRING Some catchwords. I–III^8, IV^8 (lacks 7; fos 25–31); fo 32 singleton glued to fo 33; V–VIII^8, IX^6, X^{10} (fos 71–80; 74 mutilated), XI–XVI ^{8}, XVII^2 (fos 137–138).

PRICKING In both margins.

RULING Two columns of 39 lines.

SCRIPT Of one type throughout – a regular and stylish Gothic book-hand. No strict lateral compression or compactness of the minim-space but juncture of e and o with b, d and p is frequent. a has the Caroline not the two-compartment form, the horizontal of t is pierced, *et*-nota is crossed. Ascender of d when initial often trails into the margin.

DECORATION Filigreed initials in blue and red.

HISTORY

On 137v in informal hand of ?thirteenth century: 'Liber sancti Martini Torn. seruanti benedicto. Auferenti maledicto amen, amen fiat fiat' (Benedictine house of Saint-Martin, Tournai). Listed in the seventeenth century among books of that house: Sanderus, *Bibliotheca belgica manuscripta*, I.128.

BIBLIOGRAPHY

Van den Gheyn, *Catalogue*, VI.131.

22   CAMBRIDGE, CLARE COLLEGE, FELLOWS' LIBRARY, MS. 27 (N'.1.5)

Saec. xiii^2 (?*ante* 1272)   Mediaeval provenance: ?St Albans (Benedictine)

i + 75 + i fos   2nd fo: *gentem paganorum perfidam*

HRB 24ra–75vb

§§1–3, 5–116 'mente opprimetur', 156 'Badonie. Ionathan Dorescestrensis'-208. Dedicated to Robert of Gloucester.

No rubrics or book-divisions.

Second Variant. Hammer's MS. P: Emanuel, 'Geoffrey of Monmouth's *Historia*', p. 104.

CONTENTS

Flyleaf: Latin document written in cursive hand of ?late fourteenth century, 'Tempore regis R.'.

1ra–19va: 'Incipit hystoria Turpini Remensis ecclesie archiepiscopi de famosissimo rege Karolo magno quomodo terram Hyspanicam et Galecianam a potestate Sarracenorum liberauit' (rubric on 1ra after preface). Preceded by prefatory letter to Leoprand and *capitula*-list. Text begins 1va 'Gloriosissimus namque Christi apostolus Iacobus . . . sua predicacione ad Dominum conuertit'. Ed. Meredith-Jones, *Historia Karoli*. Listed as of undetermined filiation by de Mandach, *La Geste de Charlemagne*, p. 398.

19va/b: 'Ex genere Priami fuit Meroueus qui genuit Childericum . . . Ludouicus genuit Philippum qui nunc regnat'. Also in Cambridge, Corpus Christi College, MS. 292, Cambridge, St John's College, MS. G.16, and London, BL, Harley 6358.

19vb–20ra: 'Anno ab incarnacione Domini .dccc.lxxvi. Rollo cum suis Normanniam penetrauit . . . Mortuo Iohanne successit ei Henricus filius eius.'

20ra–22ra: Herman de Valenciennes, On the Assumption of Our Lady. 'Seignurs ore escutez ke deu uous beneie . . . Put hum ceu chose aprendre dunt un purra ioir.' Cf. Meyer, 'Les manuscrits français de Cambridge: ii', pp. 368–69.

24ra–75vb: HRB.

75vb: regnal list of English kings from Alfred to Henry III. 'Aluredus rex qui primus totum regnum Anglie possedit regnauit .xxxi. annos . . . [ ]enricus filius eius regnauit.'

DESCRIPTION

SIZE 35 x 21.5 cm.

QUIRING Flyleaf. I^{12}, II^{12} (11 lacking: 13–23), III–VI^{12}, VII^4 (72–75), flyleaf. Some catchwords. HRB begun on fresh quire.

PRICKING Visible in outer margins only.

RULING Two columns of 38–39 lines. Single vertical boundary-lines but divided central margin (between columns).

SCRIPT Round and nearly two-line. Juncture of b, d, p, with e; and d, h, p, with o. Also *Verschrenkung*: oc, od, pa, etc. t usually pierced. a has both two-compartment and Caroline form. Crossed *et*-nota, round d standard. Final s usually round but tall form also occurs. Ascenders very short with indented or tagged tops. Script concords with date suggested by regnal lists on 19v–20r and 75v which stop at reign of Henry III (*ob.* 1272).

DECORATION Gothic capitals with elaborate filigree. Historiated initial on 24r. Full-colour picture 20ra (described by James, *A Descriptive Catalogue of the Western Manuscripts in the Library of Clare College*, p. 45). Marginal line-drawing on 36r (see below, HISTORY).

HISTORY

St Albans provenance suggested by M. R. James as flyleaf (before text) mentions Wymondham and Tittenhanger, two possessions of the abbey. This suggestion has been corroborated by the identification of a marginal drawing on fo 36 as the work of an artist connected with the school of Matthew Paris (at St Albans): Morgan, 'Matthew Paris', p. 90, n. 22 & p. 92.

BIBLIOGRAPHY
James, *A Descriptive Catalogue of the Western Manuscripts in the Library of Clare College*, pp. 43–45.

23   *CAMBRIDGE, CORPUS CHRISTI COLLEGE, MS. 281

Saec. xii*med./2*   Mediaeval provenance of A: ?
                                          Origin of B: ?St Andrew's, Northampton;
                                          Mediaeval provenance of B: Burton
iii + 79 + 54 + 22 fos   2nd fo: *Pluribus quoque*

HRB 1r–77r.

§§1–3, 5–208. Dedicated to Robert of Gloucester.

Original rubrics at §1 'Incipit prefatio in libro Brittonum', §5 (1r) 'Explicit prefatio. Incipit liber', other marginal rubrics as at §27 (9v) 'In hoc tempore renabat (*sic*) David rex in Iudea'. Added rubrics in ?Early Modern hand §1 (1r) (in red, formal Gothic) 'Gaufredus Monumetensis', §109 (29r) 'De prophetiis Merlini', after §208 (77r) 'Finis'.

Book-divisions added in same late hand as second set of rubrics: II §72 (19v), III §98 (26r), IV §109 (29r), V §119 (35r), VI §133 'Apparente' (41r), VII §143 (45v), VIII §179 (67r), IX §190 (70r).

Sections of the text written in capitals: §64 'In diebus illis natus est Dominus noster ... obligabatur', §77 'Inter ceteros utriusque ... conualauerunt' (*sic*) (this last passage is also found in capitals in London, BL, Cotton Titus C.xvii).

CONTENTS

i–ii: Early Modern document (in Latin) with blank verso of document now forming inside of bifolium.

i v: note in sixteenth-century hand, 'In the masters Lodginge Gaufridus monumetensis Annales Burtonenses Historiola de terra sancta'.

ii r: unimportant note on Geoffrey of Monmouth (as bishop of St Asaph) in different sixteenth-century hand.

iii: paper leaf. Blank recto but poem by Madog of Edeirnion on verso written in Humanist Cursive. 'Strenua cunctorum delectatum gesta proborum ... ex libris densis collegit nos refouens his.' Poem by Madog of Edeirnion. Walther, *Initia*, I.977, no. 18633. Ed. Hammer, *Geoffrey*, p. 18, from Cardiff MS. 2.611.

1r–77r: HRB.

77v–78r: Richard of Poitou, verses in praise of England (32 lines). 'Uenimus ad naues conscendere me prohibebat ... Quamque uidebatur mors prope terra procul ... ac monstrare potest officiosa manus.' Ed. Wattenbach, 'Verse aus England', pp. 600–1. Walther, *Initia*, I.1054, no. 20097.

78v–79r: further verses as above (42 lines). 'Anglia terra ferax et fertilis angulus orbis ... Terminat hora diem terminat a\u/ctor opus.' Ed. Wattenbach, *Verse aus England*, pp. 601–2. Walther, *Initia*, I.52, no. 1021.

79r: two notes in a Humanist Cursive hand. 'Epitaphium Lewelini magni'. 'Hic iacet Anglorum tortor tutor Wenedorum . . . forma futurorum dux lux laus lex populorum.' 'De Sancto Patricio.' 'Hic iacent in duno (*sic*) tumulo . . . atque Columba pius.'
79v: unruled and blank except for notes in a different (post-Dissolution) sixteenth-century hand. 'Anni ab origine mundi ad Christum ad Iesum duo cent. minus uno milia quinque.'

1r–34v: Annals of Northampton to 1294 (entries made at various times). For identification see Anderson & Anderson, *The Chronicle of Melrose*, p. xxxi. 'Anni ab incarnatione Domi[ ].' 'Primus annus Domini .iiii. annus fuit prime ordinis indictione . . . que non insurrexerunt in regem ex[ ]tis Melenith et Tempseth.'
35r–37v: document expressing claim of Edward I to Scotland. '[ ]dward par la grace Deu rey de Engletere, seygnur de Irelande . . . le rey Edward ke ore est ke Deu gard.'
38r–48r: Annals of Northampton continue, 1259–1339 (resuming in hand found on 34v). '1295. Hoc anno postquam sedes Romana uacauerat per tres annos . . . et in mense Marcio regressus est rex in Angliam.'
48v–49r: in sixteenth-century hand. 'Thomas de la Moore in libro suo de morte et uita Edwardi secundi.' 'Mittuntur littere increpatorie custodibus . . . minis terribilibus in fugam coactiuis affligere non cessauit.'
49v–54v: ruled but blank.

1r–22v: 'Expedicio contra Turcos circa anno Domini 1094' (rubric in sixteenth-century hand), by Peter Tudebode. 'Cum iam appropinquasset ille terminus . . . et per infinita seculorum secula dicat omnis spiritus. Amen.' Edd. Hill & Hill, *Petrus Tudebodus*.

DESCRIPTION
SIZE 25.5 x 13 cm.
QUIRING Three volumes, separately foliated but bound as one. I–III⁸, IV⁸ (lacks 6–8: 25–29), V–IX⁸, X⁶, XI⁴; a¹², b⁸ (lacks 8: 13–19), c⁸ (lacks 8), d⁸, e¹², f⁸; A–B⁸, C⁸ (lacks 7–8).
PRICKING Mostly in outer margins only, but in inner also in some places in HRB.
RULING One column throughout. HRB in 29–36 lines (depending on hand), sometimes with double vertical boundary-lines (otherwise single). Written above top line. Early part of second volume ruled in 30 lines, later very variable. Volume 3 also in 29 lines.
SCRIPT HRB in at least two collaborating hands. Well written four-line Protogothic. Ampersand and *et*-nota occur with equal frequency, e-caudata is fairly common. One hand is upright with separated letters with pointed tops. Another is rounder, written with a broader nib. No round s. Volume 2 in numerous hands, of which the first runs to the annal dated 1140 (19v). Volume 3 similar to 1 but slightly later, with more frequent use of *et*-nota.
DECORATION Handsome capitals in volume 1. Red or green, occasionally pale brown. Sometimes using two colours, and elaborate in places. Volume 3 similar decoration but blue also used.

HISTORY

In formal, very late Gothic, on strip pasted to foot of first recto of second volume, 'Iste liber est de communitate Burtonie etc.'. Connection with St Andrew's, Northampton, suggested by James (*A Descriptive Catalogue of the Manuscripts in the Library of Corpus Christi College*, II.46) on the grounds of a list of houses of the Cluniac order, to which St Andrew's belonged, and references in the Annals to the foundation of that house in 1083 and, at the entry for 1237, of a miracle which happened 'In hoc monasterio beati Andreae'. A. O. and M. O. Anderson noted a weak connection between the annals in this manuscript and section C of the Chronicle of Melrose, and also that certain items in the Annals of Lewes are 'closely cognate' with the annals of Northampton: *The Chronicle of Melrose*, p. xxxi.

BIBLIOGRAPHY

James, *A Descriptive Catalogue of the Manuscripts in the Library of Corpus Christi College*, II.45–48.

Ker, *Medieval Libraries*, p. 15.

24   *CAMBRIDGE, CORPUS CHRISTI COLLEGE, MS. 292

Saecc. xvi + xiii ?[1] + xiv   Mediaeval provenance: ?? Peterborough
                                                                                    (Benedictine)
i + 123 fos   2nd fo (fo 2): *Eneas post*

HRB 1r–12v, 13r–78v.

§§1–3, 5–31 'maritem. Illud' supplied in sixteenth-century hands (resembling printed textura).

§§31 '[ ] autem affirmo quod numquam te eo honore' –208. 2nd fo: *indicaret ipsum* (fo 14)

No rubrics or book-divisions in original part of manuscript. Rubrics in sixteenth-century section between chapter-divisions, as at §1 (1r): 'Inclitissmo (*sic*) principi domino Roberto Claudiocestriae duci inuictissimo Galfridus Monemutensis cum omni ueneratione salutem'. This rubric found in Cavellatus's edition of 1508: *Britannie utriusque regum et principum origo*.

Fo 38 should precede fo 37 (no loss of text). 36v ends 'indutum Londonias atque uix' (§94) which is continued on 38r 'annuente populo in regem erexit'. 38v ends 'a tali crimine' (§96), continuing on 37r 'purgabant. Re tandem'.

CONTENTS

i: blank flyleaf of the same type of membrane as following quire.

1r–12v, 13r–78v: HRB.

79r–99v: 'Incipit historia Turpini Remensis ecclesie de famo<sissimo> rege Karolo magno quomodo terram Hispanicam et Galetianum a potestate Sarracenorum liberauit' (rubric on 79r following dedicatory letter) with dedicatory letter and *capitula*-list. 'Turpinus Dei gratia archiepiscopus Remensis . . . et Christo subiugare uolebat relinquire.' Imperfect at end.

100r–101v: completed in same sixteenth-century hand as is found in quire II: 'et auunculum liberare aut illum dimittere . . . beatus Mattheus apostolus et euangelista sua predicatione ad Dominum conuertit'. Ed. Meredith-Jones, *Historia Karoli*. de Mandach's MS. C 19: *La Geste de Charlemagne*, p. 387.

101v: in same hand as preceding, two notes (as found in Cambridge, Clare College, MS. N′.1.5 and St John's College, MS. G.16). 'Ex genere Priami fuit Moroueus qui genuit Childericum . . . Ludouicus genuit Philippum.' 'Anno ab incarnacione Domini .d.ccc. .lxxvi. Rollo cum suis Normanniam penetrauit . . . mortuo Henrico regnauit Edwardus filius eius.'

102r: blank.

102v–107v: in informal sixteenth-century (post-Dissolution) hand. 'Hec est conuentio et finis quam Willmus (*sic*) rex Scotie cum domino suo Henrico Anglie filio Matildis imperatricis . . . et episcopatum suum in pace habere permittat.' Discussed by Stones & Simpson, *Edward I and the Throne of Scotland*, I.160.

108r–122v: 'Statuta edita tempore .E. secundo anno Christo apud Ebor. in quibus locum habunt regia prohibicio'. Series of documents concerning Scotland in fourteenth-century hand with title added in slightly later hand.

108r–110v: 'Magna carta concessa eidem clero per eundem in hec uerba'. 'Rex omnibus ad quos presentes littere peruenerint salutem . . . et per ipsum regem et consilium.'

110v–112v: 'Bulla quam papa misit regi Anglie pro Scotis etc.' (Pope Boniface VIII to Edward I). 'Bonifacius episcopus seruus seruorum Dei karissimo in Christi filio Edwardo regi Anglie . . . Scimus fili et longi iam temporis spacio . . . Datum Anagn. .v. kal. Iulii pontificatus nostri anno quinto.' Ed. Stones, *Anglo-Scottish Relations*, pp. 162–74.

112v–116v: 'Responsio .R. Anglie propter negocio (*sic*) Scotie Domino papa missa etc.'. 'Sanctissimo in Christo patri domino infrascripta non in forma nec in figura iudicii . . . Datum apud Kemesoye .vii. die Maii anno Domini millesimo trescentesimo primo et regni nostri uicesimo nono.' Ed. Stones, *Anglo-Scottish Relations*, pp. 192–218.

116v–118v: 'Littera quam comites et barones Anglie miserunt domino pape super negocio (*sic*) Scotie'. 'Sanctissimo in Christo patri domino .H. diuina prouidencia sancte romane a uniuersalis ecclesie summo pontifici . . . sancta romana ecclesia mater per cuius ministerium fides catholica gubernatur . . . Datum apud Licoln. duodecimo die Febr. anno Domini .m.ccc..'

118v–119r: 'Papa mandat archiepiscopo Cant. quod presentes .R. Angl. litteras quas sibi mittit pro Scotis'. 'Bonifacius episcopus seruus seruorum Dei . . . Frequens et inculcata fide dignorum . . . Amagni. .iiii. kl. Iulii pontificatus nostri anno quinto.'

119r–120v: 'Certificacio archiepiscopo domino papa missa super negocia Scotie'. 'Sanctissimo patri in Christo et domino suo reuerendo si placet domino Bonifacio diuina prouidencia . . . .' 'Cum promptitudine iuxta posse parendi mandatis papalibus ac preceptis . . . Datum apud idus Otteford. .viii. Octobr. anno Domini .m. trecentesimo.'

120v–121v: 'Carta regis .E. filii regis .E. de protectione bonorum ecclesie'. '.E. Dei gratia . . . Sciatis quod cum celebris memorie Dominus .E. . . . per ipsum regem et concilium.'

121v–122v: '[ ] super statuto et carta rex uic. Kanc. salutem. Cum celebris memorie dominus .E. . . . test. meipso apud Ebor. .xxiiii. die Nouembr. anno regni nostris .x.'. 123r/v: in sixteenth-century (post-Dissolution) hand. 'Haec charta refertur in Schoti-chronicon (*sic*) libro decimo tercio cap. 13 sed quis pinxit leonem ipsi considera circa annum Domini 1328.' 'Uniuersis presentes litteras inspecturis Edwardus Dei gratia rex Anglie . . . in cuius rei etc.' Ed. Stones, *Anglo-Scottish Relations*, pp. 322–24.

DESCRIPTION

SIZE 24.5 x 17.5 cm.

QUIRING I[8] (+ 1 – fo i – before 1), II[4]; III ?[8] (?wants 1–3: fos 13–17), IV–XIII[8], XIV[2] (98–99); XV[2] (100–101), XVI[6] (102–107); XVII[16] (108–123). Catchwords visible on most quires between III and XIII (in thirteenth-century part of book).

PRICKING In outer margin only.

RULING Single column. Thirteenth-century part of the book (13r–99v) in 33–34 lines with double vertical boundary-lines. Q. I 30–31 lines; Q. II 33 lines. 108r–123v – approximately 29 lines.

SCRIPT Thirteenth-century part of book homogeneous but seemingly in more than one hand. Heavy bookhand with flat tops to ascenders and short ascenders and descenders. Dark brown ink. *Et*-nota crossed, **a** has Caroline form, horizontal of **t** is sometimes pierced, **s** is usually tall. Occasional juncture of round **d** with **e** and **o**, also following **h** and **p**.

Opening quires in separate sixteenth-century hands. Fourteenth-century documents in Anglicana hand with fairly compact letter-bodies and long descenders, simple unlooped **e** and two-compartment **a** formed by a looped stroke. Ascenders are occasionally split but they usually turn over to right only (suggesting date after first quarter of the century).

DECORATION Red or blue capitals, mostly plain but simple filigree on larger capitals at textual divisions.

HISTORY

This manuscript matches the entry in the fourteenth-century catalogue of Peterborough Abbey, 'Historia Britonum, Gesta Karoli Magni in hispanica quomodo liberauit uiam Iacobitanam a potestate paganorum': James, 'List of manuscripts', p. 77. The *Historia Turpini* is associated with Geoffrey's History in ten extant manuscripts but only three of them bear a rubric comparable with the description given in the book-list. These are this manuscript, Cambridge, Clare College 27 and Paris, BN lat. 5697. Corpus Christi 292 is the only one of these which seems originally to have contained only these texts and in this order.

Although this is the best candidate for identification with the reference from Peterborough, the identification must remain tentative considering how frequently the two histories are associated and that the equivalence between the entry in the list and the rubric in the manuscript is not exact.

BIBLIOGRAPHY

James, *A Descriptive Catalogue of the Manuscripts in the Library of Corpus Christi College*, II.67–69.

25 *CAMBRIDGE, CORPUS CHRISTI COLLEGE, MS. 414

Saec. xiv   Mediaeval provenance: ?
iii fos + 560 pp.   2nd fo (p. 5): *uincit edo[ ]ut*

HRB pp. 421–562
§§1–3, 5–208. Dedicated to Robert of Gloucester.
Only original rubric is before §110 (p. 495) 'Prefacio'. Title in sixteenth-century hand above §1 (p. 421) 'Gaulfridus Monumetensis (*sic*)' and also in same hand on p. 496 'Hic incipit prophetia Merlini' and on p. 504 'Finis prophetie Merlini'.
Original book-divisions, entered informally in margins: 2 §23 (p. 433), 3 §35 (p. 445), 4 §54 (p. 456), 5 §73 (p. 468).

CONTENTS
i–ii: flyleaves taken from document with outer (written) side of bifolium mounted on paper.
i v: contents-list in Humanist Cursive.
p. 1: note in same hand on Gervase of Tilbury.
p. 2: in ?same hand again. 'In gratiam eorum qui huiusmodi abbreuiationibus antiquorum non sunt exercitati.' Note in another, more cursive, sixteenth-century hand. 'Duo sunt imperator<es> Auguste . . . in sortem Domini uocati nuncupantes.'

---

pp. 3–242: 'Ocia imperialia', Gervase of Tilbury. 'Serenissimo domino suo Ottoni quarto romano imperatori semper augusto Geruasius Tilberiensis . . . aput deuotum dominum imperatorem.'
pp. 242–248: 'In epistola Alexandri ad Aristotilem prope principium' (marginal rubric). 'In libro de situ Indie et generibus hominum et ferarum ita legitur . . . eo tempore et Theodotus.' Imperfect at end.
pp. 249–275: 'Incipiunt gesta Alexandri magni et eius genere atque uita'. 'Egipti sapientes sati genere diuino . . . uino et ueneno superatus atque extinctus occubuit.' Ed. Kuebler, *Iuli Valeri Alexandri Polemi res gestae*, pp. 1–168.
pp. 275–316: 'Hystoria belli Roscidiuallis' (according to final rubric). History of Pseudo-Turpinus with prefatory letter and *capitula*-list. 'Turpinus Dei gratia archiepiscopus Remensis . . . sua predicacione conuertit ad Dominum.' Ed. Meredith-Jones, *Historia Karoli*. This manuscript discussed by de Mandach, *La Geste de Charlemagne*, p. 375.
pp. 317–320: blank and unruled except for p. 320.
pp. 321–343: 'De bello troiano' (added title). 'Cornelius Nepos Salustio Crispo suo salutem . . . Palamonem. Ephistrephum (*sic*). Scidium.' Ed. Meister, *Daretis Phrygii De Excidio Troiae Historia*.

pp. 343–349: *Epistola Ualerii ad Ruffinum de non ducenda uxore* (from final rubric). 'Loqui prohibeor et tacere non possum . . . uel scripsisse uidear uale. Amen.' Edd. & transl. James *et al.*, *Walter Map: De nugis curialium*, pp. 288–83 (Dist. IV.3–5).

pp. 349–366: 'Incipit exposicio eius' (commentary on preceding text). 'Loqui prohibeor et tacere non possum etc. Hec epistola continet principatus tria . . . autem amara est rugose frontis tristis offenditque correptos.'

pp. 367–397: 'Incipit tractatus de ortu deorum et integumentis breuibus et utilibus'. 'Dii quos pagani finxerunt et adhuc colendo uenerantur homines olim fuisse producuntur . . . constat esse uelocissimum.'

397–419: 'Incipit hystoria de itinere et aduentu Enee in Ytaliam'. 'Superius autem excidio Troie secundum Daretem . . . et cepit Albanum ciuitas Rome subiecta est, etc.' Also found in Cambridge, St John's College, MS. G.16.

pp. 419–421: Story of Albina. 'Anglia modo dicta olim Albion dicebatur . . . et sic ueritas clarescit historie de primis habitatoribus huius terre, etc.'

pp. 421–562: HRB.

DESCRIPTION

SIZE 20 x 14.5 cm.

QUIRING i–ii, pp. 1–2 flyleaves; I^{10} (pp. 3–22), II–III^{10}, IV^{10} (?10 lacking); V^{10}, VI^{12}, VII–VIII^{10}, IX^{10} (lacks 1: pp. 165–182), X–XI^{12}, XII^{6}, XIII^{4} (lacks ?4), XIV^{12}, XV^{8}, XVI^{2} (pp. 389–392), XVII^{10}, XVIII^{4} (pp. 313–320), XIX^{10} (pp. 321–340), XX–XXI^{8}, XXII–XXIX^{12}. Some catchwords.

PRICKING In outer margin only (the pricks are often large holes).

RULING Single column throughout. 36–38 or 42 lines for HRB, varying according to scribal portions.

SCRIPT Several different hands, but volume is apparently single production. Opening hand of volume recurs: nearly two-line, informal script with many letters highlighted in red; looped round **d** and two-compartment **a**, long **r**, **s** falls slightly below the line, little compression or signs of juncture. Also small English hand with looped **d** and two-compartment **a**, simple form of **e**, long **r** and crossed *et*-nota. No split ascenders. Formal bookhand (not found in HRB) with artificiality of late Gothic, broken strokes, pointed tops to letter-bodies, indented tops to ascenders and some hairlines. Apparently written in collaboration with other hands.

DECORATION Rather crude red capitals.

HISTORY

On Parkerian flyleaf (pp. 1–2), see McKisack, *Medieval History*, p. 36.

BIBLIOGRAPHY

James, *A Descriptive Catalogue of the Manuscripts in the Library of Corpus Christi College*, II.300–3.

26   *CAMBRIDGE, FITZWILLIAM MUSEUM, MS. 302
(*OLIM* PHILLIPPS 203)

Saec. xiii   Mediaeval provenance: ?England
ii + 100 + ii fos   2nd fo: [*genu*]-*itque filium cui nomen erat*

HRB

§§1–3, 5–107 'in presenciam ipsius adducti', §110 '-tis tue dilectio' –208.
Dedicated to Robert of Gloucester.
Rubrics at §1 (1r) 'Hic incipit prologus Galfridi Arturi Monemutensis de gestis regum
Brittannie insule', §5 (1r) 'Explicit prologus. Hic incipit descriptio Britannie insule',
after §208 (90v) 'Explicit liber de historiis regum Brittannie insule'.
Book-divisions: I §6 (1v), III (*sic*) §23 (9v), III §35 (15v), IIII §54 (22v), V §73 (30r),
VI §89 (37v), VII §111 (47r), VIII §118 (52v), IX §143 (63r), X §163 (72r), XI §177
(80v).
Hiatus in text caused by loss of folio between fos 46 and 47.

CONTENTS

Flyleaf: blank except for recto which bears Phillipps shelfmark and crest and a note
at top in Early Modern hand.
1r–90v: HRB.
90v–99r: 'Hic incipiunt uaticinia [ ]'. 'En lestorie de Bretaigne maior dunt li breton
primes furent seignor Tronum escrit quil la perdirent . . . kien romanz translata le
Merlin.' Translation of *Prophetie Merlini* attributed to Helys of Winchester. Other
copies: Oxford, Bodleian Library, MS. Hatton 67 (*S.C.* 4075); Durham, Cathedral
Library, MS. C.IV.27 (see Wormald & Giles, *A Descriptive Catalogue*, I.291).
99v–100r: 'Non me permittas Domine famulum tuum a te separari . . . saluator mundi
qui cum patre et spiritu sancto uiuis et regnas Deus per omnia secula seculorum amen'.
100v: part of *Folie Tristan*, different hand. 'Et quant Tristan uint dewant li rei . . . de
d[ ]ire.' See Dean & Kennedy, 'Un fragment'.

DESCRIPTION

SIZE 17 x 11.5 cm.
QUIRING a², I–IV¹⁰, V¹⁰ (lacks 7: 41–49), VI–IX¹⁰, X¹² (lacks 12: 90–100), b⁴ (lacks
1, 3). First four quires marked by signatures.
PRICKING Outer margin only, where extant.
RULING Single column of 33 written lines. Written below top ruled line. Single
vertical boundary-lines.
SCRIPT Heavy four-line script written with broad nib. Round **d** standard (nearly
two-line), crossed *et*-nota, **t** just pierced. **e** and **o** following **d** and **p** approach juncture.
At foot of page, very long descenders decorated with groups of diagonal hairlines;
some ascenders at top of page decorated similarly. Script same throughout book except
for 100v which is written in informal hand, with thick uprights, double-split ascenders
(?*ca* 1300).
DECORATION Plain capitals except for those on fo 1 which have crude filigree. Red
and green.

HISTORY

Inscription of ownership (top 1r) of Franciscus Bordeman, 1586. Flyleaf bears Phillipps shelfmark and note of sale in 1897 and acquisition by the Museum in 1919. Correspondence (undated) at front of volume from Seymour de Ricci mentions that it was bought by Quaritch in the Phillipps sale, but then sold to W. Percy Sladen of London, who died in 1900. Unimportant note (top of flyleaf before text) in Early Modern hand in English.

BIBLIOGRAPHY

Dean & Kennedy, 'Un fragment'.
Wormald & Giles, *A Descriptive Catalogue*, I.290–92.

27   *CAMBRIDGE, FITZWILLIAM MUSEUM, MS. 346

Saec. xv   Mediaeval provenance: ?English
i + 26 + i fos   2nd fo: [*Brito*]-*nes olim ante ceteros*

HRB 1r–26v
§§1–3, 5–52 'cui Samuel. Penyses cui'. Dedicated to Robert of Gloucester.
No original rubric or book-divisions but spaces left for large capital and rubrics at §§1, 5, 23, 35. Note in modern hand at top fo 1, 'Galfrid[i] Monemutensis cronica'.
Chapter-divisions, added in pseudo-Gothic hand, correspond with divisions in translation by Aaron Thompson (1719): Wormald & Giles, *A Descriptive Catalogue*, I.339.
No other contents but notes on outer wrapper (see below, HISTORY).

DESCRIPTION

SIZE 21.5 x 14 cm.
QUIRING I–III^8 (marked by signatures), IV (2 singletons). Numerous modern paper flyleaves at either end and the whole enclosed in a thick parchment wrapper.
PRICKING Outer edge only.
RULING Single column of 27 written lines. Written below top ruled line line. Single vertical boundary-lines.
SCRIPT Dark brown ink. Four-line ?Bastard script. Very upright minims in round **d**, **p**, **h**, etc. but descenders of **f** and **s** fall below the line, although they do not taper. Juncture of **e** and **o** after **d** and occasionally **p**. Diagonal hairlines trail from **x** (which is barred), 2-shaped **r** and the *con-* compendium. Final **s** is round; **a** has two-compartment form. Ascenders curl over at top but are not angled.
No decoration.

HISTORY

Various notes inside front cover of outer wrapper. Signature 'Tho. Martin', Thomas Martin of Palgrave (1687–1771). Underneath in Early Modern hand: 'I have this Brittish History by Jeffrey of Mounmouth Translated into English by Aaron Thompson late of Queens College Oxon: with a large preface wherein he endeavours to prove the author to be a more faithfull Historian, than he is generally esteemd. to be etc.'. Thompson's translation was published in 1719, and reprinted by J. A. Giles in 1842. Also bookplate of John Brand (1744–1806) and record of the manuscript's sale in 1807 for L 1.13s.0d. Note by J. A. Giles stating that he collated the manuscript in February 1842. It is his manuscript 3: Giles, *Galfredi Monumetensis Historia Britonum*, p. 240. Signature 'R. Farmer' (he sold the volume in 1798). Giles noted that it had formerly been in Farmer's collection and was 'now' owned by James Bohn. See Griscom & Jones, *The Historia*, p. 16.

BIBLIOGRAPHY
Dumville, 'The manuscripts', p. 122.
Wormald & Giles, *A Descriptive Catalogue*, I.338–39.

28 *CAMBRIDGE, GONVILLE & CAIUS COLLEGE, MS. 103/55

Saec. xii *ex.*   Mediaeval provenance: ? England
ii + 78 fos   2nd fo: *precepit magis suis explorare*

HRB 1r–78v
§§1–3, 5–205 'fatale tempus superueniret'. Dedicated to Robert of Gloucester.
Rubrics at §1 (1r) 'Domino Rodberto comiti', §18 (6r) 'Qualiter Brutus cum Pictuensibus pugnauit', and similarly elsewhere but not at Prophecies or after end of text.
No original book-divisions but some indicated in modern coloured pencil.
Gloss on Prophecies §§111–115 (*med.*), fos 42v–43v.
Some sentences out of sequence in §5 but no loss of text.

CONTENTS
ir–iir: 'H[ ] tres paginae sunt manuscriptum principium Henrici Huntingdonensis' (note in Humanist Cursive at top of ii r). 'Britannia igitur beatissima est insularum . . . de lingua tamen quamque unam inter ceteras Deus ab exordio linguarum instituit mirandum uidetur.' Henry of Huntingdon, *Historia Anglorum*, I.1–8. Ed. Arnold, *Henrici archidiaconi Huntendunensis Historia Anglorum*, pp. 5–136.
1r–78v: HRB. Ends imperfectly.

DESCRIPTION
SIZE 26 x 18 cm.
QUIRING No catchwords. a (2 singletons), I–IX⁸, X⁸ (6, 8 lacking: 73–78).
PRICKING At outer edges only.
RULING HRB in 34 written lines, written above top ruled line; double vertical boundary-lines. Flyleaves with 39 lines, layout as for HRB.
SCRIPT HRB in deliberate and rather awkward Protogothic. Crossed *et*-nota indicates later date than aspect suggests. Ampersand usual. Short ascenders and descenders but four-line script. Flattish tops to ascenders. Round s usual in abbreviations and in final position, straight-backed **d** is more common than round. Flyleaves in slightly later-looking glossing script. Small and compact with two-line round **d**, crossed *et*-nota. g not cranktailed, a Caroline, no round s.

DECORATION Quite ornate initials (also suggesting later date) in red, green, or blue with filigree (face sometimes drawn inside letter).

HISTORY
Note on verso of ii, 'Stephanus Valengerius. Socius Collegii Goneuilli et Caii dono dedit collegio predicto anno Domini .1567.'. Verse (by John Bever) on 2v in margin by §8: 'Uersus Bruti. Sit mihi libertas pocius maciesque famesque quam sim seruili condicione satus'. On Bever's verses see Hammer, 'A Note', p. 231.

BIBLIOGRAPHY
James, *A Descriptive Catalogue of the Manuscripts in the Library of Gonville and Caius College*, I.103.

29   *CAMBRIDGE, GONVILLE & CAIUS COLLEGE, MS. 249/277

Saec. xv (?1464)   Mediaeval provenance: ? Cambridge
iii + 250 fos (+ 141*; no fo 215)   2nd fo: *quod corpus eius*

HRB 151r–177va
§§1–3, 5–208. Dedicated to Robert of Gloucester.
Rubrics before §1 (151r) 'Brutus sed est Galfridus Monemutensis de gestis Anglorum' (?later), and 'Primus liber Bruti', §110 (164vb) 'Incipit prologus de prophetia Merlini'. After §208 (177va), 'Amen'.
Book-divisions: II §23 (153va), III §35 (155va), IV §54 (157vb), V §73 (160rb), VI §89 (162rb), VIII §118 (166rb), IX [ ], X §163 (172ra), XI §177 (174va).

CONTENTS
i–iii: flyleaves from thirteenth-century civil law book, with gloss. Notes in mediaeval and Secretary hands.
1r: half-leaf. Verses in fifteenth-century hand. 'Militis uxorem clamidis mercede subegit ...' Walther, *Initia*, I.563, no. 11032. Printed by James, *A Descriptive Catalogue of the Manuscripts in the Library of Gonville & Caius College*, I.301.
1v: blank.
2r: fifteenth-century contents-list.
2v: blank.
3r–9v: 'Tabula libri policronicon'. 'Abel et de morte eius ... de Zorobabel.' Alphabetically arranged with book- and *capitulum*-references.
10ra–127rb: 'Primus liber policronicon' (running title), Ranulph Hidgen. 'Post preclaros arcium scriptores quibus circa rerum noticiam ... et palam in eorum sermonibus predicantes.' In seven books. Edd. Babington & Lumby, *Polychronicon*.
127rb/vb: 'How longe every kynge reygned fro Willyam Conquerer unto kynge Henry the Vth inclusiue' (added rubric). 'Thys myghty William duke off Normandye ... Lyth att Westmenstre not ferre from saynt Edward.' John Lydgate's *Kings of England*.
128r–133v: inserted quire with table of dates and events in Latin compiled by John

Herryson. 'Ricardus secundus fuit coronatus apud Westmon. septimo kl. Augusti . . . .' From 1377 to 1469. Ed. Smith, *Abbreuiata cronica*, pp. 3–14.

134ra–150vb: 'Incipit liber primus Tulli in sua noua rethorica'. 'Etsi in negociis secularibus impediti . . . si rationes precepcionis diligencia consequemur exercitacionis.' Six books. *Ad Herrenium*, attributed to Cicero. Ed. Marx, *M. Tulli Ciceronis quae manserunt omnia. Fasc.*1.

151ra–177va: HRB.

177va: several verses (see James, *A Descriptive Catalogue of the Manuscripts in the Library of Gonville and Caius College*, I.302).

177vb–180vb: *Carmen Brydlington* (from final rubric), prophecy of John of Bridlington. 'Febribus infectus requies fuerat mihi lectus . . . ad mortem tendo morti mea carmina pendo.' Walther, *Initia*, I.316, no. 6296. Cf. Wright, *Political Poems*, I.128–211.

181ra/vb: 'Uaticinium cuiusdam spiritus tempore regis Iohannis'. 'Extincto herede regnans . . . ad amissam pascuam reuocando.'

181vb–182ra: 'Uersus ad cognoscendum [ ]'. 'Tolle capud mercis bis cancri luna suum dat . . . hostibus expulsis iudicis usque diem.' Cf. Ward, *Catalogue of Romances*, I.307 & 311.

182ra/b: 'Uaticinium Scocie [ ] gentis s.'. 'Regnum Scotorum fuit inter cetera regna . . . sanguine saxonico inuncta redibit humus.' Walther, *Initia*, I.864, no. 16547.

182rb: 'Gildas'. 'Ter tria lustra tenent cum semi tempora sexti . . . in studii muros leopardi ui [ ]turos.'

182rb/va: 'Uersus Gilde'. 'Cambria Carnerwan Anglie natum dabit agnum . . . p[ ]a cunctorum tibi formam dat futurorum.' Cf. Dublin, Trinity College, MS. 172.

182va: 'De aduentu Normannorum'. 'Gens Normannorum consensu fulta priorum . . . Ultra petent et fers uile iugatus eis.'

182va: 'Uaticinium Anglie'. 'Anglorum regnum Bastard[ ] bello superabit . . . Qui plura Dei satis exprimitur tua peticio.'

182vb: 'Uersus H.meg.'. 'Quando sambucus fert seresa fructificando . . . Qui non errant fiant Franci sibi certi.'

182vb: 'Gallorum leuitas Germanos iustificabit . . . Gens periet subito petro testante perito.' Walther, *Initia*, I.353, no. 7015. Holder-Egger, 'Italienische Prophetieen', pp. 125–26.

182vb: 'Uaticinium unius sibillarum Ytalie'. 'Ueniet aquila ardens ?coniungemur leopard[um] cum leone genus . . . et archana illius denudabit.'

182vb–183ra: 'Uaticinium regine austri sibille'. 'Regina austri que uenit ad Salamonem . . . coacti quia preliis superacti.'

183ra. 'Uaticinium si Wallie de eodem s.'. 'Catulus linxeus in lupum rapidum conuertetur . . . et ad sidera conuolabit.' Also found in London, BL, MSS. Cotton Faustina A.viii and Royal 12.C.xii.

183ra/b: 'Uaticinium Tholeti'. 'Quoniam superbus pestis . . . senio confectus moretur aquis.'

183rb: 'Merlinus'. 'In ceterisque Merlinus dixit Arturo . . . plus dabit hic orbi quam dabit orb. ei.'

183rb/va: 'Uaticinium paganorum'. 'Pagani ?habentes uaticinia quam plura . . . et hoc est quo Dei suspensus a magistre (*sic*) cade[ ].'

183va: 'Uaticinium armo. de eodem [ ]'. 'Ueniet ab occidente Francorum quidam rex Britannie . . . triumphator recedet.'

183va/b: 'Sibylla'. 'A longe petra ueniet sed non erit ecclesia . . . gaudebit se uictorem succumbus humilior.'

183vb: 'Merlinus Syluestris'. 'Misterium hominis cuius n. id est moratur in tribus montibus . . . et omnia regna Francorum bestias adorabunt.'

183vb: 'Prophetia magistri Roberti de Sey'. 'Post hoc factum est uerbum Domini . . . columba ingemiscet.'

183vb (foot): note in hand of text. 'Gallus rex Francie. Caus rex Cicilie. leo rex Grecie . . ..'

184ra–190ra: *Tullius in sua ueteri rethorica* (from final rubric). Cicero, *De inuentione*. ?Incomplete. 'Sepe enim et multum boni ne an mali . . . cum approbacione alter utra tum utraque.' Ed. Friedrich, *M. Tulli Ciceronis opera rhetorica*, I.117–?

190v: blank, unruled.

191ra–193rb: 'Cronica fundacionis destruccionis et renouacionis uniuersitatis et ciuitatis Cantabrigg. nostre matris immaculate', Nicholas Cantelupe. 'Anno a mundi creacione 4321 inclitus Bartruth rex Britonum . . . alias Adelstanus alias Ethelstanus.' Cf. fos 247r–249v. Ed. Hearne, *Thomae Sprotti Chronica*, pp. 262–80.

193rb/va: various continuations (see James, *A Descriptive Catalogue of the Manuscripts in the Library of Gonville and Caius College*, I.303). 'Anno a mundi creacione 4824 . . . cui uniuersitati honor et gloria. Amen.'

194ra–216rb: *Libri Tullii de officiis* (from final rubric). 'Quamquam te Marce . . . si talibus monumentis preceptisque letabere.'

216va–217ra: *Abstractum prophicie* (*sic*) *Iohannis de Rupecissa* (from final rubric). 'Ix modellis (*sic*) ewangelice sanctitatis predilectissimo patri . . . et quomodo mundum seducet, etc. Terminabitur opus Iohannis de Rupecissa, Deo gracias.' Extract from *Uade mecum in tribulatione*, Iohannes de Rupescissa. See Bignami-Odier, *Etudes*, p. 249.

217rb/va: 'Hic incipit narracio de quadam uisione sancti Thome Cant. archiepiscopi de unccione regum Anglie'. 'Quando ego Thomas . . . et omnes reges paganorum ab illorum populorum facie formidabunt.'

217vb–218ra: 'Hec prophetia Merlenis (*sic*) Siluestris Anglorum regi Edwardi sancto huius nominis tercio reuelata fuit per spiritum sanctum . . .'. 'Arbor fertilis decisa est a trunco proprio . . . H. retulit paruo carmine plura notans.'

218ra/b: 'Prophicia Hemerici determinando teros regionum pape ac regum'. 'Lilium regnans in nobili parte mundi . . . quia omnia in prima causa promissa permanebunt.' 'Lilium rex Francie . . . signum mirabile signum crucis.'

218va: 'Concluccio hec deducta .xxi. die mensis Marcii anno Christi 1467 . . .'. Prognostic for 1468. 'Et per peritos astrologos calculatum erat . . . modo in condicionibus humanorum.'

219ra–227ra: Cicero, extract from *De Oratore*. 'Cogitanti mihi sepe numero et memoria uetera repetenti . . . ueritate ut tu putas.' Ed. Kumaniecki, *M. Tulli Ciceronis scripta quae manserunt omnia. Fasc. 3.*

227v–228r: prophecy. 'When ye cokke in ye north has bylde hys neste . . . and in ye uale off Iosaphath berede schall he be.' Ed. Brandl, 'The Cock in the North', pp. 1166–74, & p. 1163.

228v: 'Quomodo ille rex habet diuersa imposita nomina qui inueniret sanctam crucem'. 'Sanctus Thomas uocat eum regem uirginum . . . Machametus uocat eum rosam Britannie nomine Edwardi 4ti.'

229r–234vb: 'Incipit liber prouincialis ubi sunt omnes ciuitates mundi'. 'In ciuitate Romana sunt quinque ecclesie que patriarchales dicuntur . . . et de edificacione urbis ad natiuitatem Christi .dcc.lii. annos.' Cf. Miraeus, *Notitia episcopatuum*, pp. 65–91 etc.

234vb–235r: addition, probably in hand of one of Caius's secretaries (Professor C.N.L. Brooke informs me that this is not – as James had stated – Caius' own hand but that of one of his secretaries). 'Insurrexio crudelitas et spolia oppidanorum in academicos'. 'Memorandum quod die sabati proximo post festum Corporis Christi . . . quidam uariis penarum generibus sunt cruciati.' Cf. 250r. Ed. Hearne, *Thomae Sprotti Chronica*, pp. 258–61.

235v–236r: genealogical tree of English kings from Henry III to Edward IV.

236v–243r: summary in diagrammatic form of biblical history from Creation to disciples of Christ. Begins with summary of the seven days of creation: 'Lux firmamentum mare terraque lumina pisces et uolucres pecudes fera reptile cum prothoplasto'.

243v: blank.

244r: blank except for note at top on capture of a Scottish warship in third year of Henry VIII (1511–12).

244v–245r: notes on observation of celestial phenomena.

245v: blank except for a few notes.

246r/v: more notes in Herryson's hand on celestial phenomena etc., dated 1469/70.

247r–247v: in formal late Gothic, false statutes of the University of Cambridge. 'Honorius episcopus seruus seruorum Dei dilectis filiis doctoribus et scolaribus uniuersitatis Cantebrigie studentibus salutem . . . Idus Iulii pontifici nostri anno secundo.' Printed by Hearne, *ibid.*, pp. 253–58.

247v–249v: 'Omnia suprascripta de origine multiplici destruccione et reedificaione huius [ ] uniuersitatis in policronicon et aliis ?<cronicis> auctoritate plenis satis clare habuntur' (final rubric). 'Anno a mundi creacione 4321 inclitus rex Britonum Gurguint . . . alii. uocatur Aethelstanus alii. Adelstanus alii. Ethelstanus.' Ed. Hearne, *ibid.*, pp. 262–80.

250r: copy of *Insurrexio* (cf. 234v). 'Memorandum quod die sabati . . . quidam uariis penarum generibus sunt cruciati.'

250v: blank.

DESCRIPTION

SIZE 39.5 x 27.5 cm.

QUIRING a⁶ (3–5 cut down: fos i–iii), b² (1 mutil.: fos 1–2); I⁸ (8 lacking: 3–9), II–XV⁸, XVI⁸ (adds six after 6: fos 122–135), XVII⁸ (136–141, 141*, 142), XVIII–

XXIII⁸, XXIV⁶ (lacks 1, 4, 6: 191–193), XXV–XXVI⁸, XXVII⁸ (210–214, 216–218), XXVIII⁸, XXIX ?² (fos 227–228), XXX⁸, XXXI¹⁰ (lacks 8, adds one after 9: 237–246); XXXIII⁴ (fos 247–250).

PRICKING For boundary-lines only.

RULING Frame-ruled. Two columns of 55–56 lines written (variable number).

SCRIPT HRB in small hand, brown-grey ink. Rapid, heavily abbreviated script. Long **r**, simple round **a**, looped **e** and **d**, crossed *et*-nota. Looped tops, no angularity. Several other hands in volume. That of Herryson is coarse, large, and more angular with fewer looped letters. Script of second volume is formalised Gothic with broken strokes and lozenged feet. Ascenders have indented tops. Not many hairlines. **x** has horizontal bar.

DECORATION Mostly red or blue capitals with crude filigree. Opening page of *Policronicon* has coarsely drawn border of flowers and coat of arms. In second volume, initials have a blue outline and red decoration and are enclosed in squares of elaborate red filigree.

HISTORY

On the chronicle (expressing Yorkist sympathies) of Herryson (or Harryson) see Gransden, *Historical Writing in England: ii*, p. 250. Herryson became an M.A. of the University of Cambridge before about 1448–50, and spent most of his career in that town as priest and chaplain. He died *ca* 1473: Emden, *A Biographical Register in the University of Cambridge*, p. 290. The manuscript was certainly at Gonville & Caius College in the early eighteenth century and had probably been there since its production: Hearne quotes a letter 'ab amico doctissimo Cantabrigiensi' of 1719 which mentions three copies of Cantalupe's *Historiola* including one 'at Caius College copied out *an.* 1464. by John Herryson Doctor in Sacris Medicinis' (Hearne, *Thomae Sprotti Chronica*, p. 246).

BIBLIOGRAPHY

James, *A Descriptive Catalogue of the Manuscripts in the Library of Gonville and Caius College*, I.300–5.

30 *CAMBRIDGE, GONVILLE & CAIUS COLLEGE, MS. 406/627

Saec. xii/xiii Mediaeval provenance: Bridlington (Augustinian)
ii + 58 + ii fos 2nd fo: *Grecorum liberarentur*

HRB 1r–58r

§§1–3, 5–208. Dedicated to Robert of Gloucester.

No opening or closing rubrics but note after §208 (58r), 'Causam mortis deplorabant uite uiam quid ignorant ad salutis portum uolant cum sit iudex dominus c[ ] iustus deprauatur committat reus datur legis lator condemnatur astat iudex comminus'. Occasional marginal notes in red or ink in hand of text, as beside §21 (foot of 6r) 'Albion est insula gigantum'.

Only marked book-division: III §35 (11r). Large initials also at §§23, 89, etc. (where divisions were often made).

No other contents. Flyleaves have some notes in mediaeval and Secretary hands.

DESCRIPTION
SIZE 18 x 14.5 cm.
QUIRING One signature (*vii*) at foot of 58v. a^2, I–VI^8, VII^{10} (49–58).
PRICKING At outer edge only.
RULING Single column of 34–35 lines. Writing above top line.
SCRIPT At least two hands, both very small, of glossing type, dark brown or black ink. Main hand has four-line proportions, not very compressed. Round **d** standard (sometimes cursive *de* digraph) but tall or cedilla-like s in final position. Ligatures of N with S and T. e-caudata occurs, *et*-nota predominant, but also ampersand. Subsidiary hand is later-looking with crossed *et*-nota and more angularity. Some descenders beginning to split. No round s. Straight-backed **d** occurs but rarely. Crank-tailed g.
DECORATION Opening capital formed of heavy foliate interlace drawn in ink and filled with red, green, and blue. Those at §5 and §35 historiated (heads of kings, etc.) but not fully coloured. Other major capitals, such as that at §1. Minor initials in red, green or blue (red is lobster-coloured and rubs off on offset; cf. the Sawley manuscripts Cambridge, Corpus Christi, MS. 139 and University Library, MS. Ff.1.27), occasionally with scrolling or filigree.

HISTORY
Inscription in Anglicana hand of ?early fourteenth century (top of 1r): 'Liber sancte Mar. de Bridelington. Qui hunc alienauerit, anathema sit'. Augustinian priory of St Mary founded in early twelfth century: Knowles & Hadcock, *Medieval Religious Houses: England and Wales*, p. 149.

BIBLIOGRAPHY
James, *A Descriptive Catalogue of the Manuscripts in the Library of Gonville and Caius College*, II.472.

31   *CAMBRIDGE, GONVILLE & CAIUS COLLEGE, MS. 450/391

Saec. xvii   Origin: ?England
66 fos numbered 9–74   2nd fo: *quod fere quemque nobilissimi*

HRB 9r–74v
§24 'Socios largitur nihil' –§193 'Hiberniam insulam adiuit' [§§109–110 in *pudibundus Brito* form]. Opening dedication lost.
Extant rubrics at §109 (41r) 'Prologus Galfridi in uaticinationes Merlini', §111 (41r) 'Incipiunt uaticinia Merlini Ambrosii'. Brief summary of chapter at each division.
No book-divisions.
No other contents.

DESCRIPTION
SIZE 30.5 x 20 cm.

QUIRING Paper. First quire gone (1^8). No catchwords, tightly bound. II–VIII^8, IX^8? (lacks 3–8: 73–74).
RULING None visible. Single column of 40–44 lines (variable) written.
SCRIPT Rapid with long slanting ascenders and descenders and compact letter-bodies. Leans to right, is not splayed. Current letter-forms – **p**, **e**, and **h** often written in single stroke (**e** often looped). **a** has the simple round form. **d** is not looped except in ligature. Dark grey ink. James suggested possible link with Caius MS. 445/741, a transcription made by William Yonger, librarian of the college, in 1631. Comparison of the hands leads me to doubt this identification.
DECORATION No capitals but opening few words of each chapter written in formal, angular, double-size script. Heavily shaded.

BIBLIOGRAPHY
James, *A Descriptive Catalogue of the Manuscripts in the Library of Gonville and Caius College*, II.523.

32 *CAMBRIDGE, ST JOHN'S COLLEGE, MS. G.16 (184)

Saec. xiv$^{2/ex.}$ Mediaeval provenance (*ca* 1500): Exeter Cathedral
iii + 322 + ii fos   2nd fo: *ipsum facie ad faciem*
2nd fo of this volume (fo 45): *curia Arthuri*

HRB 44rb–103rb
§§1–3, 5–208. Dedicated to Robert of Gloucester.
Rubrics at §1 (44r) 'Incipit prologus', §5 (44va) 'Incipit primus liber de situ et regibus Britannie et qui prius eam inhabitauerunt', §108 (74ra) 'De uerbis Merlini', §109 (74rb) 'Uerba auctoris', §111 (74va) 'Incipiunt uaticinia Merlini coram Uortegirno edita', after §208 (103rb) 'Explicit'.
Book-divisions (not all rubricated but indicated by restarting of the sequences of *capitula*-numbers): I §5 (44va), II §35 (54ra), III ?§111 (74va), IV ?§119 'Rumore' (78ra), VI §143 (84va), VII §187 (98rb).
Interpolation after §5 of passage 'Anno ante incarnacionem . . . annis peractis' as in Glasgow, UL 331, London, BL, Cotton Vespasian E.x, and Oxford, Bodleian, Rawlinson B.148.
Text followed by verses: 'Librum scribendo compleui sine iocundo / scribere non posco requiescere fessus hanelo / hec Rogere tibi proposse polita peregi / mente manu lingua tandemque labore peracta / me precor indignum reputes ne semper amicum / promissis precio sum dignus iure peracto. Explicit.' *Colophons*, V.259, no. 16787. Same found in [Paris, BN, MS. lat. 4999A +] Manchester, John Rylands Library, MS. lat. 216.

CONTENTS
i: blank except for contents-list in late mediaeval informal hand on verso and a few notes.
ii r: blank except for invocation.

ii v–iii r: poem written in orderly and upright English Cursive hand. 'Pergama flere uolo fato Danais data solo . . . femina fatalis femina feta malis.' Printed by Hammer, 'Some Leonine summaries', pp. 121–22. Walther, *Initia*, I.723, no. 13985.

iii rb/v: blank except for six-line verse on iii rb. 'In nucem dentes dux uane Karolus armat . . .'. Printed by James, *A Descriptive Catalogue of Manuscripts in the Library of St John's College*, p. 218. Not listed by Walther or Schaller & Könsgen.

1r–38va: 'Liber Alexandri uictoris tocius orbis in .xii. annis' (according to final rubric). 'Quippe Egipti scientes mensuram terre . . . duodecima Alexandria est que dicitur Egiptus'. *Historia de preliis*, recension J.3. See Pfister, 'Die Historia de Preliis'.

38va–41vb: 'Quomodo Alexander iuit ad Paradisum'. 'Cum igitur Alexander nobili et multiformi preda onustus . . . uino et ueneno superatus atque extinctus occubuit.'

41vb: *Epitaphium Alexandri*. 'Primus Alexander pillea natus in orbe . . . bissenis postquam populos dimicauerat annis.' Walther, *Initia*, I.759, no. 14648.

Underneath, in different hand but similar script, 'Gesta Alexandri magni regis Macedonum'. '[Q]uicquid in humanis constat uirtutibus altis . . . succubuit leto sumpto cum melle ueneno.' See Hill, '*Epitaphia Alexandri*', p. 98. Walther, *Initia*, I.833, no. 15990.

42r/v: blank, unruled.

43ra–44rb: list of *capitula* to HRB. 'Incipit primus liber de situ et regibus Britannie et qui prius eam inhabitauerunt . . . De Iuor et Ini.'

44rb: prophecy. 'Gallorum leuitas Germanos iustificabit . . . sub quo tunc uana cessabit gloria cleri.' Ed. Wattenbach, 'Italienische Prophetieen', pp. 125–26. Walther, *Initia*, I.353, no. 7015.

44rb–103(112)rb: HRB.

103va–104(113)rb: 'Incipit prophetia aquile Scheftonie'. 'Arbor fertilis a primo trunco . . . qui pacifico regno accedit.' Ed. Schulz, *Gottfried*, pp. 463–65.

104rb–107(116)ra: 'Incipit distinctio aquile Scheftonie'. 'Arbor fertilis . . . pars uero tertia in patria permanens uilis et uacua reperietur.' Commentary on preceding work. Found also in Leningrad, Saltykov – Shchedrin State Public Library, MS. lat. F.IV.76.

107ra–109(118)va: *Gesta Saluatoris*. 'In diebus Tyberii Cesaris anno imperii eius .xv. . . . cauentes usque in hodiernum diem.' ?Cf. Tischendorf, *Evangelia Apocrypha*, pp. 471–86.

109va–110(119)v: ruled but blank.

111(113 (*sic*))r–251(270)vb: 'Incipit prologus historie Anglorum contexte ab Henrico archidiacono ad Alexandrum Lincolniensem episcopum anno ab incarnacione Domini nostri milleno centesimo .xl. quinto'. 'Cum omni fere literarum studio dulce laboris . . . me rapuit me detinuit blandita libido.' Edition of 1148: Greenway, 'Henry of Huntingdon and the manuscripts', p. 117.

251(270)vb–254(273)va: 'De omnibus sibillis et de nominibus earum et de origine et patria et actibus earum a diebus Alexandri magni'. 'Sibille generaliter omnes femine dicuntur prophetantes . . . et regnauit Dominus cum sanctis in secula seculorum. Amen.' Ed. Sackur, *Sibyllinische Texte*, pp. 177–87.

254(273)va–256(275)vb: 'Principium hystorie magni Alexandri filii Philippi Mace-donis'. 'Mortuo Philippo rege Grecorum anno ab Adam .v.dcccc.l.xxxviii. . . . nam si non peteret rex tamen ista forent.'

256(275)vb–262(281)rb: 'Epistola Alexandri magni Macedonis ad Aristotilem magistrum suum de omnibus mirabilibus que ipse fecit et uidit'. 'Semper memor tui . . . et industrie nostre argumentum optime Aristotiles in perpetuum iudicium nostrum.' Ed. Walther Boer, *Epistola Alexandri*.

(262(281)rb–270(289)ra: extracts from Godrey of Viterbo, *Pantheon*)

262(281)rb/va: 'De Gog et Magog quos Alexander similiter inter montes conclusit'. 'Finibus Indorum species fuit una uirorum . . . alpeque multiplici gens ea clausa fuit.' Ed. [Herold], *Pantheon*, cols 266–67.

262(281)va/b: 'Ex scriptis Ysidori'. 'Nota quod Alexander clausit illos ereis portis . . . et reliqui libri dent pociora tibi.' *Ibid.*, col. 267.

263(282)ra–264(283)ra: 'De disputacione inter Alexandrum et regem Bragmanorum Dindimum nomine'. 'Bragmanides uidit nec eos seruire coegit . . . gesta sub Antiocho promere musa ueni.' *Ibid.*, cols 267–70.

264(283)ra–265(284)ra: 'Hystoria romana mortuo Alexandro'. 'Post mortem Alex-andri in diuersis mundi partibus Romani triumphare ceperunt . . . utraque romano consule facta suo.' *Ibid.*, cols 270–73. On fos (282)-(284) see Hahn, 'Notes', p. 276.

265(284)ra–270(289)ra: 'Hystoria Anglorum et Saxonum secundum magistrum Gotifridum Uiterbiensium'. 'Cronica que perhibent regnasse Dioclicianum . . . uiribus et gladiis prefuit esse uiris.' *Ibid.*, cols 606–17.

270(289)ra/b: 'Hystoria de lege et natura Saracenorum et de uita et origine et lege Machometi prophetie earum qui fuit et cepit (*sic*) temporibus Heraclii impertoris (*sic*) Romanorum'. 'Saraceni peruerse se putant esse ex Sara . . . Abderrahaman igitur Mahomath qui regnauit in Corduba.'

270(289)rb–272(291)rb: 'Item de eodem Machometh quem Saraceni colunt et uener-antur'. 'Homo ille qui dictus et Mahomath hysmaelita . . . secundum tradicionem Mahomet describemus.'

272(291)rb–273(292)ra: 'Item de fide et credulitate Saracenorum'. 'Credunt igitur Sarraceni unum esse Deum . . . et si tunc non peniteat occidatur.' Also in Cambridge, University Library, MS. Dd.1.17.

273(292)ra–280(299)rb: 'Cronica de doctrina Grecorum tripartita ab Adam usque ad imperatorem Fridericum primum secundum magistrum Gotifridum Uiterbiensem'. 'Adam cum esset annorum ducentorum .xxx. genuit Seth . . . et insuper .xlii. quibus ipse Fridericus regnauit.'

280(299)rb–285(304)rb: 'Incipit tractatus cronicorum de omnibus regibus Israel qui regnauerunt super .x. tribubus in Samaria usque ad captiuitatem eorum sub Salmaua-sar rege Assiriorum'. 'Reges quotquot regnauerunt in .x. tribubus Israel . . . in antea fuerunt imperatores et pontifices sicut superius in ordine continetur.' Lists of Old Testament kings and high priests, of the early patriarchs of Jerusalem, Alexandria, and Antioch, and of bishops of Byzantium, followed by notes on liturgical matters.

285(304)rb–286(305)vb: 'Incipit liber Methodii episcopi de principio seculi'. 'In nomine Christi incipit liber Methodii . . . .' 'Sciendum namque est nobis fratres karissimi . . . qui cum Deo patre et Spiritu Sancto uiuit et regnat Deus per infinita secula seculorum. Amen.' Compare ed. Sackur, *Sibyllinische Texte*, pp. 56–96.

286(305)vb–288(307)vb: 'De Antichristo incipit'. 'De Antichristo scire uolentes primo notabitis quare sic uocatus sit . . . modo habemus pacem et securitatem et cum talia dixerint subito ueniet subitan<e>us eis interitus.' Version by Albuinus. Ed. Verhelst, *Adso Dervensis*, pp. 68–74 & 65.

289(308)ra–306(325)ra: 'Turpinus episcopus de bello Roscidiuallis'. 'Turpinus Dei gratia archiepiscopus Remensis . . . beatus Matheus apostolus et ewangelista sua predicacione ad Dominum conuertit.' Ed. Meredith-Jones, *Historia Karoli*.

306(325)rb: genealogical note on Frankish kings. 'Ex genere Priami fuit Meroueus qui genuit Childericum . . . Ludowycus genus Philippum qui modo regnat.'

306(325)rb/va: 'Anno ab incarnacione Domini .dccc.lxxvi. Rollo cum suis Normannia penetrauit . . . mortuo patre successit Edwardus filius qui modo feliciter regnat.' Both this and the previous item are found in Cambridge, Clare College, MS. N'.1.5.

306(325)va–315(334)va: 'Incipit hystoria Daretis Troianorum Frigii de Greco in Latinum translata a Cornelio Nepote' (rubric on 325vb) with usual prologue. 'Cornelius Salustio Crispo suo salutem . . . Memnonem Neoptolemus Pentesileam.' Ed. Meister, *Daretis Phrygii De Excidio Troiae Historia*.

315(334)va: 'Epitaphium Hectoris'. 'Defensor patrie iuuenum . . . et merens hac tumulauit humo.'

315(334)va: 'Epitaphium Achillis'. 'Pelides ego sum Tetidis notissima proles . . . fraude peremptus humum.'

315(334)va–326(345)rb: 'De itinere et aduent<u> Enee in Italiam'. 'Superius autem excidio Troie secundum Daretem . . . et ad Romanos translatum est et cepit Albanum ciuitas Rome subiecta esse.' Also found in Cambridge, Corpus Christi College, MS. 414.

326(345)va–328(347)rb: 'Narracio ex libro qui Grece uocatur Suda quem tempore Theodosii iuuenis composuerunt uiri sapientes isti Hendemus. Rector. Erigenius . . . Zopirion et Polion'. 'Temporibus piissimi imparatoris (*sic*) Iustiniani fuit quidam princeps Iudeorum. Theodosius . . . ut familiari amico Philippo apud Iudeos absconditum secretum propalauit.' From Robert Grosseteste's translation of the lexicon of Suidas, entry on *Iesus*: Harrison Thompson, *The Writings*, pp. 64–65.

328(347)rb–346(365)vb: 'Testamenta .xii. patriarcharum filiorum Iacob'. 'Transcriptum testamenti Ruben . . . et habitauerunt in Egipto usque ad diem exitus eorum de terra Egypti'. *Incipit* written as continuation of the rubric.

347(366)r: in a later, Secretary hand. 'Igitur cum Thobias putaret orationem suam . . . omnia quecumque precepisti michi pater faciam.' Tobit IV and V.1.

366v–367r: erased inscriptions, see HISTORY.

367v, iv–v: blank.

DESCRIPTION
SIZE 22 x 16 cm.

QUIRING Homogeneous appearance but sequences of catchwords, then signatures, indicate three separate volumes. Signatures run from .II. (58v) to .VIII. (106v) then .I. ('127'v) to .XVI. ('297'v) after which the signatures and some of the catchwords are trimmed away. a⁴ (4 lacking: i–iii), I–V⁸, VI ?² (fos 41–42); VII–XIV⁸, XV⁴; XVI–XIX⁸, XX–XXII¹², XXIII–XL⁸, b². Early pagination with some errors: leaps from ?80 to 90; after 170 next fos are numbered 180, 190, 200 then 201 . . .

PRICKING Holes at outer edge and in lower margin (for boundary-lines).

RULING In HRB, two columns of 40–44 lines. Written below top ruled line. Same throughout volume.

SCRIPT HRB in small, regular, Gothic bookhand. Fairly formal. Short ascenders and descenders with cleft ends. Juncture of **e** after **b** and **d** and of **o** after **d**. **ba** also fused. No juncture after **h**. Hairline on *et*-nota (always crossed) and tag on 2-shaped **r** but not on **h**. **a** is constructed of two uprights joined by hairlines. Fos 1–41 in a similar script but a larger and less delicate hand. Hand of HRB is also found in final unit of the codex.

DECORATION Blue capitals with red filigree. Occasionally more elaborate decoration but not within HRB. Initial in gold blocked out in blue and pink with white highlights at opening of Dares Phrygius. Historiated initial, also with gold letter, at opening of *Historia Anglorum* (111r).

HISTORY

Notes in one hand at top 1r: 'Joh(ann)es Parker miles' and 'W. Crashawe 1610': see Strongman, 'John Parker's manuscripts', p. 11 and references.

On 336v, erased inscription deciphered by R. A. B. Mynors (letter to the College Librarian, 10.12.1950) recording transfer of this book on 3rd April 1493 from one Patrick to Thomas Austell for it to be passed on to other members of the cathedral clergy. Thomas Austell has been identified as the treasurer of Exeter Cathedral between 1492 and 1515: see John Le Neve, *Fasti Ecclesiae Anglicanae, 1300–1541*, IX.12.

BIBLIOGRAPHY

James, *A Descriptive Catalogue of Manuscripts in the Library of St John's College*, pp. 217–22.

33   *CAMBRIDGE, ST JOHN'S COLLEGE, MS. S.6 (254)

Saec. xv¹?   Mediaeval provenance: ?John Mablethorpe
143 fos   2nd fo: *modum doluit. Reuocauitque*

HRB 1r–53v

§§1–3, 6–208. Dedicated to Robert of Gloucester.

Rubrics above §1 (1r) 'Prologus', at §6 (1r) 'Incipit liber de gestis Britonum primus. Capitulum primum', §109 (27r) 'Incipit prologus Gaufridi Monemutensis in prophetias Merlini', §118 (30r) 'Expliciunt prophetie Merlini. Sequitur capitulum .ii.', after §208 (53v) 'Explicit cronica de gestis Britonum'.

Book-divisions: I §6 (1r), II §27 (6v), III §43 (10v), IV §64 'In diebus illis natus est' (15v), V §98 (24r), VI §111 (27r), VII §127 (32r), VIII §143 (36v), IX §175 'Disgregati' (47r).

No physical break between §3 and §6.

CONTENTS
1r–53v: HRB.
54r–57v: 'Sermo beati Augustini. De oracione Dominica'. 'Beatus apostolus tempora ista quando futurum erat . . . cui est honor et gloria in secula seculorum. Amen.'
58r–60v: ruled but blank.
61r–143r: 'Incipit prologus uenerabilis Bede presbiteri in librum ecclesiastice historie de gestis Anglorum'. 'Gloriosissimo regi Ceolwlfo Beda famulus Christi et presbiter . . . fructum pie intencionis inueniam.' In five books. Edd. Colgrave & Mynors, *Bede's Ecclesiastical History*.
143r: short note. 'Lindisfarne dicitur insula que a wlgo Halig elond appellatur . . . sedes episcopalis in Dunhelmum translata est.'
Same text found in eleventh-century copy of Bede's *Historia* (Cambridge, Trinity College, MS. R.7.5 [43]): see Colgrave & Mynors, *ibid.*, pp. xlvii–xlviii.
143r/v: start of an alphabetical table to the *Historia*. 'Abbas quidam pererat (*sic*) et monasteriis et episcopis illius insule . . . Arturi nomen magnificatum est in procul multos terrens et elatum est cor eius.'

DESCRIPTION
SIZE 30 x 20 cm.
QUIRING Indicated by catchwords. I–VI^{12}, VII^{12} (lacks 12: fos 73–83), VIII–XII^{12}.
PRICKING Visible at outer edges only.
RULING Single column of 43 lines. Single vertical boundary-lines, ruling above top written line.
SCRIPT Four-line formal cursive with upright descenders and minims. Some angularity in the bows of **g** and **d** but basic roundness retained. **a** has the looped two-compartment form, **d** is round and sometimes looped, **e** has the simple form. **t** is pierced, *et*-nota is uncrossed. 8-shaped final **s** standard. This script is found in double size in a motto following HRB and in the other texts. Slightly weak black ink. Single hand.
DECORATION Blue capitals with coarse red filigree. Running title at top of each page.

HISTORY
On 53v and 143r: 'Laus tibi Iesu dulcedo unus semper. M. J. M.'. Perhaps John Mablethorpe, fellow of Lincoln College, Oxford: Ker, *Books, Collectors and Libraries*, p. 316, n. 75. Mablethorpe, who owned a number of manuscripts, was at Lincoln College in the 1430s and 1440s, before moving to Eton: Emden, *A Biographical Register of Oxford to A.D. 1500*, II.1198–99.

BIBLIOGRAPHY
James, *A Descriptive Catalogue of Manuscripts in the Library of St John's College*, p. 290.

Saec. xii/xiii   Mediaeval provenance: Wells Cathedral, Somerset
i + 178 fos   2nd fo: [*se*]-*se aeri insere ac miscere*

HRB 113va–177va
§§1–3, 5–208. Dedicated to Robert of Gloucester.
Rubrics at §1 (113va) 'Prologus Galfridi in hystoria Britonum', no closing rubric.
Book-divisions (indicated in margin): II §23 (119v), III §35 (123v), IIII §89 (138v),
?V §111 (145v), VI §118 (149r), VII §163 (156v).

CONTENTS
i: flyleaf. Recto mostly obscured by parchment leaf pasted on to it but note in English,
?of the fifteenth-century, still visible ('Now I am as I was euen as I s<chol>de be/ He
that makyth me nogt [ ] euyl mote he the'). New leaf carries ?seventeenth-century
note of ownership (see below, HISTORY).
i v bears contents-list in formal Protogothic hand.
1ra–39rb: 'In prologus in libro ermeneumatum' (of Old and New Testaments).
'Quoniam sunt non nulli in conuentu fratrum minorum eruditi . . . uel principium et
finis. Amen id est uerum est.'
39rb–41ra: 'Incipit liber Fulgentii episcopi ad Calcidium de quibusdam nominibus .i.
lxii.'. 'De tuorum preceptorum Domine serie nostra quicquam . . . Nescio quorsum
mihi tua uerba delenifice ueniant.'
41ra–45ra: 'Incipiunt interpretationes Echirii episcopi de nominibus hebraicis ac
uariis uocabulis atque expositione rerum diuersarum de nominibus heb\r/aicis'. 'Ado-
nay in Latinum significat Dominus Sabaoth exercituum siue uirtutum . . . Tropologia
moralis intellectus. parabola similitudo.'
45ra/b: list of animal cries arranged alphabetically in four columns. 'Accipiter pipat.
Anas trinnit . . . Ursus seuit.' Fourth column: 'Cella pinaria non penuria dicendum . . .
Calue uero ossaque sunt et singulariter calua'. Continues in same hand as Dares (on
fos 104r–113v).
45va–55va: 'Incipiunt differentie similium partium orationis a Cicerone et ab aliis
sapientibus uiris in sensu et litteratura per alphabetum. Disposite .iii. Incipit de .A..'
'Inter absconsum et absconditum. Absconsum consuetudinis. Absconditum rationis
est . . . ubi temperis finit.'
55va–58rb: 'Incipit de diuersis partibus in eadem significione positis'. 'Uecurio suo
. . . redintegrare.'
58rb: List of virtues and vices.
59ra–71rb: 'Incipit liber primus domini Bede presbiteri de ortographia'. 'Aeternus
aetas . . . et non numquam prandeo et necnon est libera a res michi.' Ed. Jones, *Bedae
Venerabilis opera. Opera didascalica*, I.7–57.
71rb–73rb: 'Incipit de numero iuxta latinos', on Roman and Greek numbers, then on
computation of digits. 'Per .i. litteram repsentatur (*sic*) unitas per .v. quinque . . . in
uicem digitis super caput implicabis.'
73va: '[ ]d extrahendam radicem alicuius numeri primo consideradum (*sic*) est . . . uel
quantum poterit ex eo et sic deinceps.'

73va–76vb: 'Littera est nota elementi. Que cum scribitur et in uoce minime resonat . . . ut pape euax'.

76vb–77ra: 'Grama grece littera interpr. latine . . . et clanculo ferale quoddam eructat aconitum'.

77ra–81va: 'Incipit epilogus. Omnium uerborum perfectam et equalem declinationem habentium in .o. uel in .or. desinentium tam necessarium minus eruditis et in arte gramatica parum exercitatis quam introductorium'. 'Omnia uerba perfectam et equalem habentia declinationem . . . enim tempus proximum presenti tempori.'

81va–89vb: 'Incipiunt partes secundum ordinem litterarum alphabeti excerpte et collecte de libro ethimologiarum beati Ysidori episcopi'. 'Anapestus repercussus. Analogia similium comperatio . . . Dum eum Maria et parentes ad templum detulerunt.' Unidentified extract from Ysidore, *Etymologiae* (the whole ed. by Migne, *Patrologia Latina*, LXXXII.73–728).

90ra–95ra: 'Incipiunt partes per dispositionem litterarum alfabeti excerpte de Prisciano iuxta magistri Petri expositionem cognomento Helie.' 'Apostropha componitur ab *apo* quod est retro et *strophos* quod est conuersio . . . Quis primus loco et tempore et ordine dignitatis similiter et ultimus.'

95ra/b: 'Q[uesti]o de constructione'. 'Cum dicitur ego et tu legimus . . . quod construatur cum tu.'

95rb–96rb: 'Q[uesti]o de nomine et gerundiuo'. 'Quem legendus . . . ut luctor respectu communis ut osculor.'

96va–97va: 'Nomen est pars orationis que unicuique subiectorum . . . de quibus singulis hinc tractabimus.'

97va–103rb: 'De patronomico'. 'Patronomicum est quia a propriis tantummodo deriuatur . . . Ego nam apicularum opera congestum non feram.'

103va/b: (in same hand as end of Dares) 'Hoc differt inter uesper uesperis masculini generis . . . et pretereundo alienus'.

104ra–113va: 'Prologus Salustionis (*sic*) in hystoria Daretis de bello Troiano'. 'Salustio Crispo suo salutem . . . Andromacam et Helenum .i. .cc. hucusque hystoria Daretis scripta est.' Ed. Meister, *Daretis Phrygii De Troiae Excidio Historia*.
113va–177va: HRB.
177va/b: on division of world. 'Post diluuium tribus filiis Noe orbem terrarum . . . clamoribus suis prodigia uentura presagientibus.'
177vb–178ra: *Mirabilia Britannie*. 'Est et aliud stagnum in regione Huic . . . uel magnum uel paruum inuenitur.' On this and previous item, see Dumville, 'Anecdota'.

DESCRIPTION
SIZE 26 x 18 cm.
QUIRING Two sets of signatures: i–xiii in grammatical material (6v–96v), .i.- .ix. in Dares and HRB (112v–176v). ?I^6 (+ one before 1: fos i, 1–6), II–III^8, IIII ?^{6} (23–28), V–XII^8, XIII^4 (93–96), XIV^8 (8 lacking); XV ?^{8} (4 canc., + bifolium after 3: 104–112), XVI–XXIII^8, XXIV^4 (lacks 3, 4: 177–178). The two units joined at an early stage as hand of second appears on 45r and 103v.
PRICKING Outer edges only.

RULING Two columns throughout with single vertical boundary-lines and divided central margin; top line written. A 35–38 lines, B 36 lines.

SCRIPT B in informal four-line minuscule. Tops of ascenders of **b**, **h**, **l** slightly forked. Ampersand standard (but *et*-nota in corrections), no round s, round **d** frequent but straight-backed form also found. **d** approaching juncture with **e** and **o**. ct-ligature. **a** has small head, **h** is pinched. Brown ink. A in compact and upright, not broken, black minuscule. Round **d** very frequent, final s standard, uncrossed *et*-nota. Juncture of **de**. **a** not two-compartment. Flat hairline tops to **b**, **d**, **h**, **l**. Ascender of round **d** trails into margin when starting a line. Seems later in date than script of B but appearance of hand of B on some folios (see above) shows this to be impossible.

DECORATION Unfiligreed Romanesque capitals in red or faded brown-red. In A green also used (in rubrics and initials).

HISTORY
Note on leaf attached to i r, in seventeenth-century hand, 'To the worshipfull my good frynde Mr. Doctor Warde mr. of Sidney Colledge in Cambridge'. Samuel Ward (ob. 1643), master of Sidney Sussex College: Lee, *Dictionary of National Biography*, LIX.335–36. Contents suggest it belonged to Wells Cathedral, Somerset: Ker & Watson, *Medieval Libraries*, p. 67.

BIBLIOGRAPHY
James, *A Descriptive Catalogue of the Manuscripts in the Library of Sidney Sussex College*, pp. 53–55.

35 *CAMBRIDGE, TRINITY COLLEGE, MS. R.5.34 (725)

Saec. **xv** + xvi   Mediaeval provenance: ?
ii + 267 fos   2nd fo (12r): *belle ad pristinam dignitatem*

HRB 11r–32r, 32r–34v.
§§1–3, 5–101 'uincebat namque nuncias suos per'. Fo 32 cut horizontally under text and pasted to new leaf where continuation of text to end of §108 begins in later hand (fos 32r–34v). Dedicated to Robert of Gloucester.
Only original rubric at top 11r 'Historia Galfridi Monumetensis', after added section (34v) 'Hic explicit tercius liber Galfridi Monumetensis et desunt libri de historia [quinque cancelled] sex'.
Second Variant Version (not recorded by Hammer): Crick, 'Manuscripts', p. 162.

CONTENTS
i–ii: parchment flyleaves cut from a Latin document written in a ?sixteenth-century hand. Centre of bifolium blank except for Early Modern contents-list on recto of i.
1: paper. Blank except for College bookplate on verso.
2r–5v: list of contents of William of Malmesbury's *Historia Pontificum Anglorum*, in sixteenth-century hand. 'Capit. Phrohemium (*sic*) primum Prohemium secundum De Constantino Seuero . . . 54 De ?literare amore.'
6r–10v: blank.

11r–34v: HRB.

35r–58v: blank.

59r–61r: account by Sir Robert Wingfield of his discovery and transcription of documents about the attempt of the English to gain separate representation at the Council of Constance and the opposition of the French to that attempt. In Humanist minuscule. 'Agenti mihi nuper serenissimi ac potentissimi regis Anglie . . . transfundatur uale excellentissime eques et me ut facis [ ].'

61r–67v: French *protestacio* against the English (3.3.1417). 'Ad inuincibilem ueritatem et iustitiam . . . peto mihi fieri instrumentum publicum uel publica ad futuram rei memoriam.' Ed. Mansi, *Sacrorum Conciliorum noua et amplissima Collectio,* XXVII.1022–31.

68r–70v: blank.

71r–72r: 'Placeat ex isto auisari (*sic*) contra illos qui laborant ad sumptorum quinte nacionis in hoc sacro concilio, etc.'. Proposal that *nationes* in the council should be replaced by a division of Latin Christendom into four. 'In tota christianitas debet utique diuide in quattuor naciones . . . ita diuiditur nacionem.'

72r–81v: English *protestatio* (31.3.1417). 'Ut consuperabilis ueritas et iusticia eo ualidius . . . in omnibus et singulis premissorum prout opus fuerit locis et temporibus opportunis.' Ed. Mansi, *ibid.,* XXVII.1058–70.

82r: blank.

82v: endorsement addressing documents to Thomas Rodebourne.

83r: blank.

83v: prologue to following work supplied in hand which completed HRB. 'Incipit . . . Malmesber. in gesta Anglorum' (partly trimmed away). 'Domino uenerabili et famoso comiti . . . a maiori parte uocandum gesta regum Anglorum.'

84r–145v: 'Incipit prologus domni Willelmi monachi Malmesburiensi in primo libro de gestis regum Anglorum'. 'Res Anglorum gestas Beda uir maxime doctus . . . transcensis alpibus uenit Gallias aduentus circa ferebatur.' Ed. Stubbs, *Willelmi Malmesbiriensis monachi. De gestis regum Anglorum.* MS. Ar: *ibid.,* I.lxxii–lxxiii. In late Gothic bookhand.

89v blank but ruled. Apparently no textual hiatus.

146r–182v: continued in Secretary hand. 'Aduentus circa ferebatur perspicua quod uiolencia Guillelmi Roma extrusus . . . qui non erraui eligendi iudicio. Laus Deo.'

183r/v: blank.

184r–206r: 'Incipit prologus Anglorum ad Robertum comitem Glocestren.' in hand of continuator of HRB. 'Domino amantissimo Roberto filio regis Henrici . . . ab his qui interfuere ueritatem accepero.' Ed. Potter, *Historia Novella.*

206v–208v: blank.

209r–256v: in different but similar hand to preceding. 'Prologus librum .v. Wilelmi Malmesb. de pontificibus.' 'Totius Anglie quaquauersum porrigitur episcopatibus . . . estiuis etiam mensibus pluuiis et luteus.' Ed. Hamilton, *Willelmi Malmesbiriensis monachi. De gestis pontificum.*

257r–265vb: '[ ]heodosius de uita Alexandri'. In fifteenth-century hand, two columns.

'Rex Cecilie Alexandrum ad conuiuuium inuitauit . . . id est potestate sue diu di [ ]tatis, etc.'

266ra–267va: 'Repleta fructu iusticie ad phil[ ]p°. Ut uas supereffluat . . . omne al. benedictione. Amen. Amen. Amen'.

DESCRIPTION

SIZE 27 x 21 cm.

QUIRING Mostly paper, but outer bifolium of some quires parchment. Three distinct fifteenth-century units (HRB fos 11r–32r; *Gesta Regum* fos 84r–145v; *Uita Alexandri* fos 257r–265v) joined by material in sixteenth-century hands. a², I ?¹² (?1–2 cancelled), II¹⁴ (fos 11–24), III⁸ (+3 after 8, 8 split and glued on to following folio: 25–34), fos 35–158 uncollatable, I¹², II¹⁴ (lacking one leaf: fos 171–183); fos 183–256 uncollatable; I ?¹² (257–259, 259*, 260–267).

PRICKING None visible.

RULING 1–83 – frameruled. Single column, up to 47 lines written. 84–145 – ruled in grey ink, single column, 45 written lines, written below top line. 257–265 – double column of 53 lines.

SCRIPT Miscellaneous.

HRB – four-line cursive with looped e, pierced t, simple round a. g and looped round d not yet angular. Ascenders turn under at top, not angled. Short r. Script of continuation later with v-like r, horned a, pierced g.

DECORATION In HRB – blue capitals with crude red filigree at §§1 and 5; not completed elsewhere.

HISTORY

HRB, *Gesta regum*, and fos 257–267 in various fifteenth-century hands. Remainder dates from sixteenth-century.

Listed by John Parker among the books at the house of his father, Matthew, at Bekesbourne: Strongman, 'John Parker's manuscripts', p. 15.

BIBLIOGRAPHY

James, *The Western Manuscripts in the Library of Trinity College*, II.203–4.

36   *CAMBRIDGE, TRINITY COLLEGE, MS. R.7.6 (744)

Saec. xiii¹?   Mediaeval provenance: ?

ii + 56 + ii fos   2nd fo: *arguebat enim*

HRB 1r–56r.

§§1–3, 5–195 (*med.*), 200 (*med.*) –208. Nameless dedication.

Rubrics at §1 (1r) 'Incipit prologus hystorie Brithonum et Anglorum', §5 (1r) 'Descripcio Britannie', §6 (1v) 'Incipit hystoria', §111 (31v) 'Prophecie Merlini', after §208 (56r) 'Explicit Brutus de uita regum Anglie'. No book-divisions.

Hiatus in text due to loss of a leaf after fo 54. 54v ends 'audita est. Ut Gildas' (§195) and 55r begins 'aufferent. At Pianda timens' (§200).

No other contents. Flyleaves are blank paper except for Early Modern title on the recto of the first: 'Monumetensis Historia Britonum'. Ends of a parchment binding strip visible outside flyleaves (written in bookhand of late thirteenth or early fourteenth century with some glosses, two columns, brown ink).

DESCRIPTION
SIZE 24 x 15 cm.
QUIRING I^8, II^{14}, III–IV^{12}, V^{10} (9 lacking; + 1 after 10).
PRICKING In outer margin only.
RULING Single column of 37–38 written lines. Single vertical boundary-lines. Writing below top ruled line.
SCRIPT Small and rather disorderly with upright strokes. Ascenders have slanting tops. a has the Caroline form; t is not pierced. Final s is round or tall. *Et*-nota is crossed. Sometimes juncture of e and o after d and p.
DECORATION Unornamented capitals at most chapters in blue, red, and blue-green. §§1 and 111 have larger capitals in two colours with asterisk or star design inside letter.

BIBLIOGRAPHY
James, *The Western Manuscripts in the Library of Trinity College*, II.222–23.

37 *CAMBRIDGE, TRINITY COLLEGE, MS. R.7.28 (770)

Saec. xiii^1 (+ xii + xiv–xv)   Mediaeval provenance, parts II and III:?
                                     ? (Origin & mediaeval provenance, part I:
                                     Bury St Edmunds, St Neots)
74 + 120 + 18 pp.   2nd fo: [*ori*]-*entalibus suis partibus*

HRB pp. 75–194   2nd fo: *ferino ritu*
§§1–3, 5–208. Dedicated to Robert of Gloucester.
Rubrics at §1 (p. 75) 'Incipit prologus Gaufridi in his[toria] Britonum', after §208 (p. 194) 'Finit historia Britonum'.
No book-divisions.
Prophetie §§111–113 have marginal gloss.
§25 is truncated (p. 86). It ends 'cum [p]ace et diligencia .xl. annis' and §26 begins 'Quo defuncto discordia erat'.
Lower part of p. 87 (under §31) is taken up with notes in elegaic couplets on the names of Old Testament figures, with the rubric 'Nomina patriarcarum et uersibus ita'. 'Pro nobis Christum sanctorum nomina patrum signant de quorum carne fit ipse caro . . . constristans rebrobos (*sic*).' p. 88 is blank. Text of §31 resumes without loss on p. 89: 'Nempe ego dilexi te'.

CONTENTS
Unconnected with HRB.
pp. 1–74: Annals of St Neots. 'Igitur Brittannia Romanis usque ad Gaium Iulium

Cesarem . . . et Rollonem ducem Northmannorum.' Edd. Dumville & Lapidge, *The Annals*, pp. 1–107. See also Dobbie, *The Manuscripts of Caedmon's Hymn*, p. 90.

---

pp. 75–194: HRB.

---

pp. 195–198: flyleaves taken from account (worn) written in Secretary-hand in English.

pp. 195 and 198 are blank.

pp. 199–202: 'Feodum comitum Gloucestrie et heredum suorum intronizacionem archiepiscopi uel electi in archiepiscopatum Cant.'. 'Comes predictus summoniri debet per quindenam . . . pro feodum camerarum intronizantis.' In fourteenth-century Gothic bookhand.

pp. 203–207: 'Quantum archiepiscopi in archiepiscopatum uixerunt et in quo gradu et dignitate prius erant'. '[A]ugustinus primus archiepiscopus Cant. . . . Hic erat prius archidiaconatus Essexie.' Ends at 1313 with Robert Wynchelsey.

pp. 208–210: continued in a more cursive hand to 1381 (William Courtney).

p. 210: further continuation from Thomas Arundel to Matthew Parker in a Parkerian hand.

p. 211: flyleaf as pp. 195–198.

DESCRIPTION

SIZE 16 x 11.5 cm.

QUIRING Three separate volumes with catchwords in HRB section only. I^{10} (10 lacking: pp. 1–18), $II–III^8$, IV^{10} (lacks 3 and 7: pp. 51–66), V^6 (lacks 3, 5); VI^6 (+ singleton after 3: pp. 75–88), VII^6 (pp. 89–100), $VIII–XII^8$, XIII^8 (8 lacking: pp. 181–194); XIV^{10} (lacks 2: pp. 195–210).

PRICKING Trimmed away in HRB.

RULING HRB in single column of 37–42 lines. Written below top line (ruled at about height of two lines); double vertical boundary-lines.

SCRIPT HRB written in a very small, four-line, script resembling glossing hand. Dark brown ink. No real juncture, probably because of size, but de written closely. *Et*-nota is standard and is uncrossed. It is found finally in words. d is round, t is not pierced, a has the Caroline form, sometimes with a tall upright. Final s is tall and extends below the line. The Insular compendia for *est* and *enim* are found.

DECORATION Simple unfiligreed initials in orange or green.

HISTORY

A was written at the Benedictine abbey of Bury St Edmunds in the 1120s or 1130s: Dumville & Lapidge, *The Annals*, p. xix; Ker & Watson, *Medieval Libraries*, p. 6.

BIBLIOGRAPHY

Dumville & Lapidge, *The Annals*, pp. xv–xxi.

James, *The Western Manuscripts in the Library of Trinity College*, II.239–40.

Ker & Watson, *Medieval Libraries*, p. 6.

38 *CAMBRIDGE, TRINITY COLLEGE, MS. O.1.17 (1041)

Saec. xiv[1]   Mediaeval provenance: Whalley Abbey (Cistercian)
ii + 274 fos (7–60, 70–288; + 217a)   2nd fo: *similia nescio unde indesinenter*

HRB 110r–181r
§§1–3, 5–108, 118 (*in.*) –208, 111–117. Dedicated to Robert of Gloucester.
Rubrics at §1 (110r) 'Incipit prologus Galfridi Monemut(ensis) in historiam Brito-
num', §6 (110v) 'Incipit historia', after §108 (177r) 'Explicit', before §111 (177r)
'Incipit prophetia Merlini', after §117 (181r) 'Explicit'.
No book-divisions.
Text jumps from end of §108 to §118 'Wortigirnus uero pre ceteris' (149r). No
physical loss. There is a marginal note, 'inserenda prophetia'.

CONTENTS
1r/v: flyleaf, blank except for bookplate and a few notes on verso.
2r/v: fragment from *Uisio de spiritu Guydonis*. 'Audiebant unam tenuem uocem . . .
disponitur ad [ ].'
3–6: lacking.
7r–105r: 'Incipit prologus in librum quem moderni Itinerarium beati Petri uocant'.
Pseudo-Clementine *Recognitiones* in ten books. 'Tibi quidem papa Gaudenti nostrorum insigne decus doctorum . . . et non minorem ei graciam quam apostolo exhiberet.'
Ed. Rehm, *Die Pseudoklementinen: ii*, pp. 3–371 (see p. LXXIX on this manuscript).
(105r–109r: lists and notes with rubric on 109r, 'Explicit secundum Rogerum')
105r: list of some European rulers. 'Imperator Romanorum . . . rex Commacie (*sic*).'
105r–109r: account of churches of Christendom with lists of cardinals and archbishops. 'In ciuitate romana sunt quinque ecclesie principales . . . archiepiscopus
Colocensis qui dicitur Rodo nullum habet suffraganum.' Cf. ed. Miraeus, *Notitia
episcopatuum*, pp. 65–91.
109v: blank.
110r–181r: HRB followed by Prophecies of Merlin.
181v: blank.
182r–193v: *Meditationes* attributed to Bernard of Clairvaux. 'Multi multa sciunt et
. . . qui uiuit et regnat in secula seculorum. Amen.' Ed. Migne, *Patrologia Latina*,
CLXXXIV.485–508.
193v–199v: 'Domine Deus meus da cordi meo te desiderare . . . in tui unitate uiuit et
regnat per infinita secula seculorum. Amen'.
199v–200r: note on faith. 'Fides est substantia rerum . . .'
200r: (addition) 'Uita Sancti Brandani'. 'Uana uanis garriat pagina pagana . . . Dulcis
sitis pia sunt uiam hanc experto.' BHL 1445. See Kenney, *The Sources*, p. 416, no.
203.
200v–212v: 'De Nectanabo mago quomodo magnum genuerit Alexandrum'. 'Egypti
sapientes sati genere diuino primi feruntur . . . uino et ueneno superatus atque extinctus
occubuit.' Iulius Ualerius's Epitome of *Gesta Alexandri*, ed. Kuebler, *Iuli Valeri
Alexandri Polemi res gestae*, pp. 1–168.
212v–244r: *Gesta Normannorum Ducum*, D-redaction. 'Pio uictorioso atque ortho-

doxo summi regi [ ] Anglorum . . . ob Aluredi fratris regis mortem ab eis iniuste perpetratam.' Ed. Marx, *Guillaume de Jumièges.*

244r–250v: 'Sequitur genealogia Edwardi regi'. 'Anno Domini .m.lxxiiii. tres de prouincia Merciorum . . . cui successit Edwardus filius eius et regn. annis .l. et pl.' Genealogy of English kings, Henry I to Edward III.

251–264v: 'De infancia Christi'. 'De commoracione beate Marie in Israel . . . omnes qui uidebant eum glorificabant Deum omnipotentem qui est benedictus in secula seculorum.'

264v: deed. Underneath, in hand of similar type, 'Paceat uniuersis presentes quod ego frater R. de Warwych. ordinis Cistri. quondam abbas monasterii de C. Recepi de religione . . . in yyeme. Anno r. r. Edwardi tercii post conquestum.'

265r/v: Urbain le Courtois, on conduct and manners. 'Un sages homme de grant valur . . . Chier filz a deux uous comant.' Ed. Meyer, 'Les manuscrits français de Cambridge: iii', pp. 71–73.

266r–273v: Dialogue between love and a knight. 'Uolez escuter un deduit . . . De me soiez en compaynie.' Ed. Meyer, *ibid.*, pp. 73–74. ?By Nicholas Bozun: Vising, *Anglo-Norman Language and Literature*, p. 72.

Legend of the wood of the Holy Cross. 'Ki uoudra sauer et oyr de la verraie croiz dnt. . . . tut temps et empire sanz fyn. Amen.' See Meyer, *ibid.*, p. 74.

277r–287v: 'Incipit speculum sancti Edmundi archiepiscopi de tempore mundi'. 'En le honour e. el noun nostr. douz seignur Iesu . . . deuez penser coment il a cele hure de la mie [ ].' Prose translation of *Speculum* of Edmond de Pontigny: Vising, *Anglo-Norman Language and Literature*, p. 57.

287v–288v: various scribbles (fourteenth- to sixteenth-century) including verse concerning date of Easter, 'A festo stelle numerando perfice lune . . .'. Walther, *Initia*, I.2, no. 35.
Stub after 288.

DESCRIPTION
SIZE 20 x 14 cm.
QUIRING Foliation incorrect. a² (fos 1–2), fos 3–6 lacking, I–V¹⁰, XV¹⁰ (57–60, 70–75), VII–IX¹⁰, X⁴ (106–109), XI¹⁰, XII 16, XIII–XV⁸, XVI¹², XVII⁴ (fos 172–175), XVIII⁶, XIX⁸, XX¹², XXI–XXII⁸, XXIII¹⁰ (217a–226), XXIV–XXVI⁸, XXVII¹², XXVIII² (fos 263–264), XXIX¹², XXX fos 277–288.
PRICKING Both margins.
RULING Single column of 33–40 written lines. Written below top ruled line. Usually single vertical boundary-lines.
SCRIPT HRB in a formal sort of Anglicana. Brown ink. Some split ascenders but more usually turned over at top, split long r, simple not curled e, two-compartment looped a of minim height. d is round and looped with heavy stroke but script in general not highly shaded. Final round s.
DECORATION Capitals are blue or red with red or purple filigree. Numerous coloured paragraph marks.

HISTORY
On verso of stub after 288 in sixteenth-century hand (see James, *The Western*

Manuscripts in the Library of Trinity College, III.19) 'Iste liber procuratus? fuit per Rogerum de Lind[eley?] Wadedulphus [ ]'.
On 267r, in angular cursive hand of perhaps the late fifteenth century, 'Liber mon. de Whalley, Whalley'. Cistercian abbey of Whalley, Lancashire.

BIBLIOGRAPHY
James, *The Western Manuscripts in the Library of Trinity College*, III.16–19.
Ker, *Medieval Libraries*, p. 197.
Meyer, 'Les manuscripts français de Cambridge: iii', p. 68.
Van Houts, *Gesta Normannorum Ducum: een studie*, pp. 211–12.

39   *CAMBRIDGE, TRINITY COLLEGE, MS. O.2.21 (1125)

Saec. xiii/xiv   Mediaeval provenance: ?
140 fos   2nd fo: *duos colores*

HRB 5r–117v.
§§1–208. Dedicated to Robert of Gloucester and Waleran of Meulan.
Rubrics at §1 (5r) 'Incipit prologus super librum hystoriarum regum Britannie', §5 (5v) 'Descripcio insule', after §208 (117v) 'Ualete'. Many marginal rubrics but none at §§109–111.
No book-divisions.

CONTENTS
1r: Early Modern contents-list, shelfmarks, and note 'Le: Fludd' (cf. Cologny-Genève, Bibliothèque Martin Bodmer, MS. Bodmer 70).
1va/b: 'Cur mundus militat sub uana gloria . . . felix qui poterit mundum contempnere'. Walther, *Initia*, I.197, no. 3934.
2r–4r: 'Tractatus de signis et moribus natalibus hominum ad regem magnificum Alexandrum qui dominatus fuit toti orbi dictus monarcha in septentrione' (from final rubric). 'Et inter ceteras res illa est . . . ad meliorem et probabiliorem partem.' From the *Secreta Secretorum*: ed. Steele, *Opera hactenus inedita Rogeri Baconi*, V.25–172.
4v: blank.
5r–117v: HRB.
117v–119r: 'Uisio beati Pauli: De penis inferni'. 'Dies dominicus electus in quo gaudebunt angeli et archangeli . . . amictus lumine sicut uestimento, etc.' This manuscript not mentioned by Silverstein, *Visio Sancti Pauli*, pp. 220–22.
119v: blank.
120r–133v: 'Chere soer puis ceo ke uus me priastes'. French verse with marginal English gloss. 'Femme ke aproche soun tens . . . Blaunche poudre ho la grose dragee.' Treatise on the French language attributed to Walter de Bibelesworth: Vising, *Anglo-Norman Language and Literature*, pp. 75–76 and p. 95.
134r–138r: 'Epistola Ar[istotilis] ad Alexandrum' (from final rubric). 'Nunc uero prius tradere uolo doctrinam medicinalem . . . a cuius medio usque ad medium marcii

hyemps fundatur.' Not the usual text known by this name. There is a note above the text on 134r in Humanist Cursive: 'Alterius pars est'.

138v–139r: *Secreta Ypocratis* (from final rubric). 'Peruenit ad nos quod cum Ypocras morti apropinquasset precepit . . . quod desiderauit dulcia in principio egritudinis.'
139–140v: medical recipe (English) and notes on the More family, in various hands. Printed (with photographs) by Chambers, *The Place of St. Thomas*, pp. 123–24, 119–120.

DESCRIPTION
SIZE 21.5 x 14.5 cm.
QUIRING Marked by catchwords from quires II to X. I⁴, II–VIII¹², IX–X¹⁰ XI¹² (lacks 12: 109–119), XII¹², XIII¹² (lacks 9–11: 132–140). Several items are codicologically distinct but the script suggests that the book was a unit from an early stage.
PRICKING At outer edges only.
RULING HRB in single column of 30 lines as is following work (viz 5r–119v). 1v in two columns of 32 lines, 120–133 31 lines, 134–138 36–37 lines, 138v 43 lines.
SCRIPT HRB in bookhands with cursive features by more than one scribe. Dark brown ink. Crossed *et*-nota, a constructed of two verticals joined by hairlines. Juncture only of e and o after b, d, and p in one hand but elsewhere juncture after h. In the conservative hand t is not pierced, tall s is found, and double l lacks a flat top, unlike the other scribal portion (s). The nature of other hands in the volume suggest that the codex was an early unit: the hand of the *Uisio* is close to that of fos 148v–149r; fos 2r–4r resemble fos 134r–138r and also the preceding French verses. Varies from thin and broken script to broad. The script of *Secreta Ypocratis* resembles that of HRB; the hands of HRB are not apparently found in the rest of the volume, however.
DECORATION Blue or red capitals without filigree throughout volume, except for opening capital in HRB which has purple ink filigree.

BIBLIOGRAPHY
Griscom & Jones, *The Historia*, p. 32 & pl. III.
James, *The Western Manuscripts in the Library of Trinity College*, III.113–15.

40 *CAMBRIDGE, UNIVERSITY LIBRARY, MS. Dd.1.17 (17)

Saec. xiv *ex.* (*post* 1381) Mediaeval provenance: ?Glastonbury Abbey (Benedictine), Somerset
i + 245; 90; 86 + i fos 2nd fo (now fo 1): *que uulgares cronice*

HRB 111r–121ra.
§§117 'sole litigabat. Ascendet uirgo sagittarii' –145 'flumina supra montem', §§160 'exigamus quod a uobis' –208. Dedication lost.
Rubrics after §117 (111r) 'Explicit prophecia', after §208 (121ra) 'Explicit hystoria de gestis Britonum'. No book-divisions extant.
Text of §179 compressed.

CONTENTS

2r–97vb: *Polychronicon* of Ranulph Higden, imperfect at both ends. 'Que uulgares cronice que Dionysium predicium sequuntur . . . ad Angliam recesserunt uel mali . . .' Edd. Babington & Lumby, *Polychronicon.*

98–110: lost according to modern note in the manuscript.

111r–121ra: HRB.

121ra–122vb: Henry of Huntingdon's letter to King Henry I. '.H. minister seruorum Dei .H. illustri regi Anglorum salutes et orationes.' 'Cum mecum propter ea que responsione tua accepi tractarem . . . de tua generacione siue progenie sanctissima. Ualete.' Greenway, 'Henry of Huntingdon and the manuscripts', p. 120.

122vb–129ra: 'De gestis Karoli regis Gallorum'. 'Gloriosissimus Christi apostolis (*sic*) Iacobus . . . magis enim deficeret manus [?etc.] et calamus quam historia. Explicit hystoria de gestis Karoli.' Ed. Smyser, *The Pseudo-Turpin.* On the equivalence of Dd.1.17 with Smyser's MS. R see de Mandach, *La Geste de Charlemagne*, p. 368.

129ra–159ra: 'Incipit cronica fratris Martini de ordine fratrum predicatorum et domini[ ]'. 'Quoniam scire tempora summorum pontificum Romanorum . . . et animauit suscepta negocia sollicite prosequenda.' The Chronicle of Martinus Polonus with continuation (beginning at 156ra 'animos Romanorum reuocauit') as printed in MGH, SS, XXII and XXX.1, pp. 713–14. Von den Brincken, 'Studien', p. 528 (class IIIb).

159rb–160va: 'Diuisio regni Anglie in regna et postea de monarchis et de conquestu per Willelmum' (according to later contents-list on 1v). 'Primis (*sic*) habuit Kanciam . . . tanquam stipendarius regis Francie'. Ends with reference to Richard II's marriage to Anne of Bohemia in 1381: Hardwick *et al.*, *Catalogue*, I.18.

160va–203va: Guido delle Colonne. 'Licet cotidie uetera recentibus obseruant . . . Anno dominice incarnacionis .m.cc. octuagesimo septimo eiusdem primo indiccionis febr.. Amen.' Ed. Griffin, *Historia Destructionis Troiae.*

203vb–204rb: 'Prophecia Iohannis de Lignunbio sollempnissimi doctoris dec[retorum] uniuersitatis Bononie'. 'Regnum Spiritus sancti distinguuntur in Iacob filii Isaac . . . et ibi clarius uidebitis.' Written after 1378.

204rb–230vb: 'Incipit historia Ierosolimitana capitulum .i. cur Dominus terram sanctam uariis flagellis et sub alterius casibus exposuit. Incipit hystoria Ierosolimitana secundum magistrum Iacobum de Uitri' (from rubric on 204vb) preceded by *capitula.* Text begins 204vb 'Terra sancta promissionis Deo amabilis . . . et a sancta romana ecclesia de die in diem expectantes'. Ed. Bongars, *Gesta Dei per Francos*, I.ii, pp. 1049–1124.

231ra–261v: 'Liber uocatus beliallis et [ ]' (later title). 'Uniuersis Christi fidelibus atque orthodoxe sancte matris ecclesie fidei cultoribus . . . cum legeritis dicatis Deo multiplicasti magni-'. Jacobus Theramicus Belial, *Consolatio Peccatorum.* Imperfect at end.

262: lacking.

1r–6ra: 'Incipit testamentum patriarcharum'. 'Trascriptum (*sic*) testamenti Ruben . . . usque ad diem exitus eorum de terra Egypti.'

6ra: prayer. 'Audi pater omnipotens audi miserum . . . tibi pia plorans compatitur uirgo Maria, etc.'

6ra–38va: 'Cronica Martiani Scoti de gestis regni Anglorum usque ad obitum Stephani et initium regni Henrici secundi qui fuit filius imparatritis (*sic*) et Galfridi Plantegen. comitis Andegauie' (from final rubric). 'Cum in omni fere litterarum studio . . . spiritus es caro sum. Te nunc intrante reuixi.'
The beginning and end of this compilation are taken from Henry of Huntingdon's history and the middle from the Durham *Historia post Bedam*. See Greenway, 'Henry of Huntingdon and the manuscripts', p. 120. For other copies see Arnold, *Henrici archidiaconi Huntendunensis Historia Anglorum*, p. xliv.

38va–56rb: 'Liber domini Marti Pauli de Uenet. de condicionibus et consuetudinibus orientalium regionum' (from final rubric). 'Librum prudentis honorabilis ac fidelissimi domni . . . ad diuersas prouincias et regiones deferuntur.' Cf. Iwamura, *Manuscripts*.

56rb–70vb: 'Iste liber intitulatur flos ystoriarum terre orientis quem compilauit frater Haytonus dominus Chursi consanguineus regis Armenie . . .' 'Diuiditur autem liber iste in quatuor partes . . . qui potens est Deus in secula seculorum. Amen.' Ed. *Recueil des Historiens des Croisades, Documents arméniens*, I.255–363.

71ra/b: *Fides Saracenorum* (according to final rubric). 'Credunt Saraceni unum Deum creatorem esse . . . de paradiso et inferno.'

71rb–74va: 'Tractatus de ortu processu et actibus Machometi' (according to final rubric). 'Ad ostendendum quod Machometus . . . sicut patet in omnibus supradictis.' Also in Cambridge, Gonville & Caius College, MS. 162/83 (fos 1r–11v).

74vb–79rb: 'Tractatus de statu Saracenorum de Machometo pseudo prophetia eorundum ipsa gente et eorum fide qua utuntur et hec est rubrica' (from final rubric), by William of Tripoli. 'Uenerabili patri ac domino Theobaldo . . . laus sit Deo in secula seculorum. Amen. Opusculi consummacio hec est.' Cf. Cambridge, Gonville and Caius College, MS. 162/83 (fos 12r–25v). Ed. Prutz, *Kulturgeschichte der Kreuzzüge*, pp. 575–98.

79rb–79vb: 'Tempore Bonifacie pape IIII Romani pontificis . . . cibus ciborum uestentur generibus'. Truncated at end.

80–82: excised. According to contents-list (1v) contained 'Somnium beati Thome martiris post decessum ab Anglia' and 'Processus fratris Nicholai Wysebeche de unccione regis Anglie'.

83r–93va: 'Liber sancti Gilde abbatis et historiographi Anglorum et cetera' (according to final rubric). 'Aque torrentem uiue ex undantibus irrigua . . . cui sit honor et gloria in secula seculorum. Amen.' Gildas, *De Excidio Britannie*, acephalous. Ed. Mommsen, *Chronica Minora*, III.1–85, at pp. 25–85 (on this manuscript, see p. 14). Marked up for printing: see Bromwich, 'The first book', pp. 273–75.

1r–31ra: 'Dialagus petii Plowman' (from final rubric). 'Yn a somer seson whan softe was the sonne . . . and sith he gradde after grace til I gane awake.' B-text, ed. Kane & Donaldson, *Will's Vision* (see pp. 2–3 for this manuscript).

31rb–32rb: 'How men that ben in hele sholde uisite sike folk'. 'My dere sone or doughter . . . for in thy merciful handes I put it. Amen. Amen.' *Uisitatio infirmorum* attributed to Richard Rolle. Ed. Horstman, *Richard Rolle*, II.449, 450.

32va–53vb: Sir John Mandeville's Travels. 'For as muche as the land over the see . . .

and holy gost that lyuees and regnees god with outen ende. Amen. Amen. Per charite.'
Cf. Vogels, *Handschriftliche Untersuchungen*, p. 12. Fo 37 lacking.

54r–63rb: 'In Rome was an emperour . . . that never in erth 3ed schodde. Amen. Amen for charite'. Printed from this manuscript by Wright, *The Seven Sages*, pp. 1–116.

63va–87vb: 'Incipit concordia quatuor euugelistarum (*sic*) historie ordo euangelice et euangeliorum manuale breuiarium' (rubric on 65ra). 'Clemens Lantoniensis ecclesie presbiter . . . ad turbas ordinis rem patet.' Imperfect at end. Latin concordance of the Gospels. See Lapidge & Sharpe, *A Bibliography of Celtic-Latin*, p. 21, no 45.

88–92: excised.

DESCRIPTION

SIZE 44 x 31 cm. Foliated as for three volumes.

QUIRING Mostly indicated by catchwords. Generally even absent leaves foliated. i Singleton, I^{12} (1 lacking: fos 2–12), II–V^{12}, VI^{12} (7 lacking: fos 61–66, 68–72), VII–VIII^{12}, IX^{12} (?lacks 2–12: fo 97), fos 98–110 lacking, X^{12} (6 and 7 mutilated, 1–2 lacking: fos 111–120), XI^{12}, XII^{12} (lacks 6 and 7: fos 133–144), XIII–XXI^{12}, XXII^{10} (lacks 10: fos 253–261), singleton (flyleaf). ii I–VI^{12}, VII^{12} (8–10 lacking: 73–84), VIII^{12} (10–12 excised [unnumbered]: fos 85–93). iii I–III^{12}, IV^{12} (1 lacking [i.e. 37]: fos 38–48), V–VII^{12}, VIII^{8} (lacks 4, 5–8 excised: 85–87), singleton (flyleaf).

PRICKING At outer edges only. Frame of double lines ruled in the margin.

RULING Two columns of 52 lines, single vertical boundary-lines.

SCRIPT Formal type of Gothic bookhand. a has looped two-compartment form, t is well pierced. Only remaining juncture is d with e. Final round s is standard and occurs in other positions. 2-shaped r is frequent. Thick upright strokes, hair-lines on *et*-nota (which is crossed) but not elsewhere. Titles in *textura* double the height of the main script. In iii the Middle English texts are written in a more cursive script: long r, looped tops to ascenders, etc.

DECORATION Main capitals are blue with red filigree decoration (patterns left in reserve inside the letter, squared off). Red or blue paragraph-marks at minor divisions.

HISTORY

A connection with Glastonbury has been made on the basis of the presence of the text of Gildas, an extremely rare work. M. R. James (unpublished Cambridge University Library manuscript-notes) quoted the preface to Josselin's edition of Gildas of 1568, in which the locations of only two manuscripts of the work are mentioned: one at Canterbury (now BL Cotton Vitellius A.vi) and one at Glastonbury. The Glastonbury attribution of this manuscript is recorded, but queried, by Ker & Watson, *Medieval Libraries*, p. 38.

There is considerable similarity between the contents and appearance of this volume and that of a similar date from the church of St Peter's, Cornhill, in London: London, BL, MS. Royal 13.D.i.

A sixteenth-century *ex-libris* is found on C, fo 34r: 'This is Robert Hertmorye[ ] bok[ ]'. The volume was listed by Bernard in 1697 among the books of John Moore, bishop of Norwich (1646–1714): Bernard, *Catalogi*, II.i, p. 368, no. 9475.

BIBLIOGRAPHY
Bromwich, 'The first book', pp. 273–75, with plate.
Hardwick *et al.*, *A Catalogue*, I.15–26.
Kane & Donaldson, *Will's Vision*, pp. 2–3.
Seymour, 'The English manuscripts of Mandeville's Travels'.

41 *CAMBRIDGE, UNIVERSITY LIBRARY, MS. Dd.4.34 (209)

Saec. xiv   Mediaeval provenance: ?England
i + 68   2nd fo: *erant ceteri*

HRB 1r–68rb
§§6–208 [109–110 *Pudibundus Brito* form]. Dedicatory section (§3) absent.
No opening rubric. After §208 (68rb) 'Explicit liber hystorie gentis Britonum'.
No book-divisions.

CONTENTS
i: blank except for note of title on recto (Early Modern) and erased Latin *ex-libris* inscription (not recoverable under ultra-violet) and library bookplate on verso.
1r–68rb: HRB.
68rb: poem beginning under final rubric of HRB, 'Dic Cayphe mercede capud dampnatur alumpni . . . Et babel Archadie perfusa cruore rudebit'. Walther, *Initia*, I.218, no. 4348. Also found in Wien, ?Österreichische Nationalbibliothek, MS. 609, fos 23v–24r, and elsewhere. Ed. Roth, 'Lateinische Gedichte', pp. 9–10.
68v: diagram of three concentric circles with various notes (in hand of HRB) beginning 'Sceptriger Arturus in bello stans quasi murus'.
69–72: lacking.

DESCRIPTION
SIZE 23 x 15.5 cm.
QUIRING I^{12} (?+ i before 1 – parchment flyleaf: fos i + 1–12), II–V^{12}, VI^{12} (9–12 lacking: 61–68). Followed by blank paper flyleaves ii–iii.
PRICKING At outer edge.
RULING Two columns of 39 lines with double vertical boundary-lines and divided central margin. Ruling above top written line.
SCRIPT Fairly formal Gothic. Short ascenders and descenders, round final s, **a** constructed of two vertical strokes joined by hairlines. Minims not lozenged but sometimes tagged at the top, as are ascenders. Fusion of **a, e, o** with curves of **b, d, h, p**.
DECORATION Red, light and dark blue filigreed capitals. Opening initial in two colours with pattern left in reserve and alternate red and blue scrolls along left and upper edge of text. Capitals in text picked out in red.

71

HISTORY
Erased note in ?Secretary hand on 1v. Mentions 'Full[ ]ton'.

BIBLIOGRAPHY
Hardwick *et al.*, *A Catalogue*, I.234.

42   *CAMBRIDGE, UNIVERSITY LIBRARY, MS. Dd.6.7 (324) + OXFORD, BODLEIAN LIBRARY, MS. BODLEY 585 (*S.C.* 2357), FOS 1–47*

*CAMBRIDGE, UNIVERSITY LIBRARY, MS. Dd.6.7

Saec. xv (1440–48)   Mediaeval provenance: St Albans (Benedictine)
ix + 154 + i   2nd fo: *auditis ille confestim*

HRB 6v–152v.
§§1–3, 5–208. §110 followed by end of *pudibundus Brito* version. Dedicated to Robert of Gloucester.
Rubrics at §1 (6v) 'Incipit prologus Gaufridi Monemutensis ad Robertum comitem Glaudiocestrie in historia Britonum', §5 (7r) 'Commendacio insule', after §108 (85v) 'Incipit prologus in prophecias Merlini', at §111 (86v) 'Incipit prophetia Merlini', after §208 (152v) 'Explicit historia Britonum a Galfrido Monemutensi de Britanico in Latinum translata' (opening and closing rubrics in red).
Divided into twelve parts marked at §23 (28v) II, §54 (48v) III, §73 (60v) IV, §89 (71v) V, §98 (77v) VI, §118 (94r) VIII, §143 (110v) IX, §163 (124v) X, §177 (136v) XI, §188 (141r) XII. *Prophetie Merlini* presumably forms seventh part. *Capitula* numbered serially in each part (arabic numerals). Table of *capitula* between §§3 and 5 occupying 8r–16r (top).

CONTENTS
i–ix: mostly blank but on i r 'Stapulforde Taney' (? hand of text), on ii r 'Suerder' (?sixteenth-century), and iii r Early Modern copy of *ex-libris* on 1r.
1r–6v: 'Hic incipit qualiter primo ista terra fuerat inhabitata'. 'Euolutis a mundi constitucione . . . nomen prius impositum huic terre. Explicit.' Also found in Oxford, Bodleian Library, MS. Rawlinson B.189.
6v–152v: HRB.
152v: two-line poem beginning 'Urbs Uerolamia tua . . .'. Walther, *Initia*, I.1035, no. 19738.
152v–154v: 'Offa rex Merceorum potentissimus . . . semper in speculum summe religionis euasit'. Text mainly concerning St Alban and the monastery.
154 a slip only.
Final flyleaf: deed of 33 Elizabeth concerning property in East Malling, Kent.

*OXFORD, BODLEIAN LIBRARY, MS. BODLEY 585

CONTENTS

1r–17v: 'Tractatus de uita et nobilitate et martirio sanctorum Albani et Amphibali de quodam libro Gallico excertus et in Latinum translatus'. 'Iulius Cesar primus Romanorum imparatorum (*sic*) . . . urbs Uerolamia sua quam imperia in [ ].' *BHL* 214.

17v–18r: opening of HRB, very faint (?erased). §§1–3, 5 (*in.*) –5 'pignus suauis soporis in'.

18v–47r: 'De granario magistri Iohannis Wethamstede' (extracts only). 'Anglia que secundum Solinum de mirabilibus mundi . . . sanguine sitisti sanguinem bibe.'

47*: blank.

DESCRIPTION

SIZE 19 x 14.5 cm (CUL Dd.6.7); 21 x 14.5 cm (Bodley 585).

QUIRING a^{10} (lacks 10: fos i–ix), I^8, II^8 (slip before 3: 9–17), III–XVIII^8, XIX^8 (slip after 8), b^2 (2 cut down). Bodley 585 I–V^8, VI^8 (fos 41–47*).

PRICKING At outer edges.

RULING One column of 23 lines, written below top ruled line; single vertical boundary-lines.

SCRIPT Thick strokes, rather crude, apparently in a single hand. Simple forms of **a** (not two-compartment), round **d**, **e** and **g**. Few descenders – **s** usually tall with round or high form in final position. Ascenders often have tagged or flat tops. *Et*-nota is sometimes double-barred. Occasional fusion of **d** with **e** or **o**. **x** has horizontal cross-stroke and 2-shaped **r** curls below the line.

DECORATION Red initials with no ornament.

HISTORY

CUL Dd.6.7

At top of 1r, in late mediaeval hand: 'Liber monasterii S. Albani'. Probably in same hand at foot of 152v: 'Liber domini Edmundi Shenley'. This monk of the abbey (who may have been the scribe of this book) moved to Wymondham before December 1448. The presence of Abbot John Whethamstede's *Granarium* in the collection provides the other terminus of 1440: Watson, *Catalogue of Dated and Datable Manuscripts c. 435–1600 in Oxford Libraries*, I.19 (no. 204). (On Whethamstede's sceptical treatment of Geoffrey's *Historia*, see Keeler, *Geoffrey of Monmouth*, pp. 80–85.)

BIBLIOGRAPHY

Dumville, 'The manuscripts', p. 118.

East, 'Manuscripts', p. 484.

Hardwick *et al.*, *A Catalogue*, I.292–93.

Howlett, 'A St Albans historical miscellany' (with 2 plates).

Ker & Watson, *Medieval Libraries*, p. 60.

Watson, *Catalogue of Dated and Datable Manuscripts c. 435–1600 in Oxford Libraries*, I.19 (no. 204); II, pl. 396.

43 *CAMBRIDGE, UNIVERSITY LIBRARY, MS. Dd.6.12 (329)

Saec. xii*med/2* + xv *ex.*
iii + 125 fos (but 2–8 lacking) + i

Mediaeval provenance: ?
2nd fo: (lacking;
9r now follows fo 1) *minimum cum his uerbis*

HRB 1r–v, 9r–116r.

§§1–3, 5–5 'Postremo quinque inhabitatur populis', 18 'minimum cum his uerbis' – 208. Dedicated to Robert of Gloucester.

Rubrics at §1 (1r) now nearly illegible 'Incipit editio [Galfridi Arturi Monemutensis] de gestis Britonum', §5 (1v) ?'Descriptio insule', no original final rubric.

Book-divisions at §23 (12r) II, §35 (19r) III, §54 (28r) IIII, §73 (37v) V. Large capitals without rubrics at §89 (46v), 109 (59v), 118 (69v), 143 (82v). Lacuna in text before §18 caused by loss of fos 2–8 (indicated in foliation: text resumes on 9r).

CONTENTS

i–iii: fragments of ?service-book (text in formal Gothic with extracts of music overwritten with account dating from *ca* 1300, see below).

1r/v, 9r–116r: HRB. 2–8 lacking.

116r–118v: brief chronology of British kings (fifteenth-century). 'Anno Domini millesimo ducentissimo quadragesimo quinto . . . in comitatu Lyncolnie et obtinuit uictoriam.' From 1245 to the Battle of Stoke, 1487.

119r–124r: blank.

124v–125, flyleaves i–iii: fragments of ?service-book (text in formal Gothic with extracts of music) overwritten with account dating from *ca* 1300 (see below).

DESCRIPTION

SIZE 20 x 13.5 cm.

QUIRING a⁴ (2 cancelled: fos i–iii), I⁸ (lacks 2–8: fo 1), II–IV⁸, V¹² (lacks 2–3: 33–42), VI–VII⁸, VIII¹² (60 cut down, 10–12 lacking: fos 59–67), IX–X⁸, XI⁶ (fos 84–89), XII¹⁰, XIII–XIV⁸, XV uncollatable: fos 116–125. No loss of text except in quire I. Paper flyleaves before a⁴ and after XV.

PRICKING Most outer prickings trimmed away. Inner prickings only on fos 61–67, coinciding with the output of one old-fashioned hand.

RULING Single column of 25–28 lines, single vertical boundary-lines.

SCRIPT Protogothic minuscule in several collaborating hands of varying degrees of formality. Most are in a four-line script with short ascenders and an English roundness. Majuscule forms occur occasionally mid-word and in ligatures. The head of a often rises above neighbouring letters. Usages range from the most conservative hand in which straight d, tall s and ampersand only are found with frequent e-caudata, to the final hand in which round d and s and the *et*-nota are standard and e-caudata rare. Less conservative hand begins 68r after break in *Prophetie*, at start of Q. IX.

DECORATION Major initials in several colours (red, green, blue) with stylised foliate filling. Other capitals have split shafts and decorative bosses but towards the end of the manuscript there are plain red capitals only.

HISTORY
No inscriptions of ownership but first flyleaves cut from account (?*ca* 1300) in which personal names are followed by West-Country and Wiltshire place-names, as 'Ricardus de Malemesburiensi' (*sic*). No. 908 among books of John Moore, bishop of Norwich (1646–1714).

BIBLIOGRAPHY
Hardwick *et al.*, *A Catalogue*, I.295.

44   *CAMBRIDGE, UNIVERSITY LIBRARY, MS. Dd.10.31 (590)

Saec. xiii (*post* 1264)   Origin: ?England
fos 9–80, 105–112, 137–194   2nd fo: *multis postmodum*

HRB 9r–80v.
Truncated at both ends. §20 'Hostes celeriter inuasit' –§175 'et isti tunc libertatem quem illi eisdem demere' [§§109–110 in *pudibundus Brito* form]. Dedication (§3) lost.
No rubrics extant. No book-divisions.

CONTENTS
1–8: lost.
9r–80v: HRB.
81–104: lost.
105r–110va: chronicle of eleventh- and twelfth-century Anglo-Norman history. Acephalous. '-ana lege sibi sociata . . . a duce Normannorum Willelmo superatus est'.
110vb–146v: annals organised by regnal years to the battle of Lewes in 1264. Middle lost. 'In diebus sanctissimi regis Edwardi . . . anno isto obiit regina Matil-' (110vb–112v); 113–36 lost; 'feria .vi. ante festum . . . et suis emolumentum et regis nomen reseruans. Explicit' (137r–146v). Also found in Oxford, Magdalen College, MS. lat. 199 (fourteenth-century, no other contents; text ends differently from here). According to Coxe, text compiled in 1254 from the Annals of Waverley with reference to the works of William of Malmesbury, Henry of Huntingdon, John of Worcester, Aelred of Rievaulx, and Ralph Diceto: Coxe, *Catalogus codicum manuscriptorum qui in collegiis aulisque Oxoniensibus hodie adservantur*, II.i, 90.
147r–156va: 'Incipit catalogus siue cronica omnium pontificum et imperatorum Romanorum . . .'. 'Dominus noster Iesus Christus primus et summus pontifex . . . Sed Saraceni eam postea recuperauerunt.'
157r–170va: 'Epistola Cornelii ad Crispum Salustium in Troianam historiam que in Greco de Darete historiograffo facta est'. 'Cornelius Gayo Crispo salutem . . . Mennonem. Neoptholemus. Pentessileam.' Ed. Meister, *Daretis Phrygii De Excidio Troiae Historia*.
170va: notes in faint Secretary hand. 'Commendacio historia(?)'; 'Plus ferus ille fero plus pando plusque leone . . .'.

171r–194vb: poems in French, beginning 'Le russinole uoleit a mer', as printed (from this manuscript) by Meyer, 'Les manuscrits français de Cambridge: ii', pp. 241–62.

DESCRIPTION

SIZE 25 x 17 cm. Many paper flyleaves before and after text.

QUIRING Catchwords at end of each quire. Foliation includes absent leaves. Quire of 8 lacking; I–IX^8; 3 quires lacking (81–104); X^8 (fos 105–112); 3 quires lacking (113–136); XI–XII^8, XIII^4 (fos 153–156), XIV^8, XV^6, XVII–XVIII^8; at least one quire lacking (catchword at end of XVIII).

PRICKING Mostly trimmed away. At outer margin only.

RULING Two columns of 30 lines mostly, but 29–35 written lines fos 171–194 (poems). Writing below top ruled line.

SCRIPT Similar type throughout volume – angular, heavily-shaded minuscule written with wide nib. Short ascenders and descenders, some ascenders indented at top, some minims lozenged. Usually a has the two-compartment form and t is pierced. Unlooped round d is standard as is crossed et-nota and final round s. Juncture of d and p with e and o. Dark brown ink.

DECORATION Blue or red capitals with contrasting filigree (sometimes in dark green). Coloured paragraph-marks in text.

HISTORY

No. 824 among books of John Moore, bishop of Norwich (1646–1714).

BIBLIOGRAPHY

Hardwick et al., A Catalogue, I.427–28.

Meyer, 'Les manuscrits français de Cambridge: ii', p. 241.

45   *CAMBRIDGE, UNIVERSITY LIBRARY, MS. Dd.10.32 (591)

Saec. xiv ^{2} Mediaeval provenance: ?

82 fos   2nd fo: [inquie]-tudini Grecorum resistere

HRB 1r–63r.

§1–3, 5–208. Dedicated to Robert of Gloucester.

Rubrics at §1 (1r) 'Hic incipit liber Britonum qui uocatur Brrutus (sic) de gestis Ang[ ]', §21 (6r) 'Hic applicuit Brutus in terram Britannie uocatam modo Angliam'; there are various other similar rubrics commenting on content but no final rubric. Book-division indicated at §23 (7r) only: 'Liber secundus'.

CONTENTS

1–63r: HRB.

63r–82r: continuation in French to Edward I in different hand. 'Epar long tenps apres il aueit en Engletere un rey . . . de qi alme dieux eit mercy. Amen.'

82v: blank.

DESCRIPTION
SIZE 24.5 x 15.5 cm.
QUIRING Some catchwords. I–VI^{12}, VII^{12} (lacks 11, 12).
PRICKING At outer edge.
RULING One column of about 35 lines with single boundary-lines. Writing below top ruled line.
SCRIPT HRB in single hand apparently. Upright Anglicana Formata. Two-compartment a often rises above minim-height. d is looped; cursive long r is found but the 2-shaped form is usual.
French continuation in another, similar hand.
DECORATION Blue initials, occasionally with red filigree. Both crude.

HISTORY
At foot of 1r 'Sub de R: le Fe: J:h' ?

BIBLIOGRAPHY
Hardwick *et al.*, *A Catalogue*, I.478–79.

46   *CAMBRIDGE, UNIVERSITY LIBRARY, MS. Ee.1.24 (913)

Saec. xv   Mediaeval provenance: ?
i + 53 fos   2nd fo: *nationes ipsius fama*

HRB 1r–53v.
§§1–3, 5–208. Dedicated to Robert of Gloucester.
Title (contemporary) above §1 'Historia Britonum' (and above that in same hand 'Iesus Maria'). After §208 (53v) 'Deo gratias. Explicit liber de gestis Britonum', with additional note in same hand, 'Durauit autem regnum Britonum a Bruto primo conquisitore usque ad Cadwaladrum qui fuit ultimus de illa gente duobus milibus et 76 annis sub C et duobus regibus preter Wallenses et Cornubienses. Angli autem qui et Saxones dicti sunt CCC 77 annis ante aduentum Normannorum'.
No book-divisions.
No other contents but numerous paper flyleaves, the last of which (facing 1r) has nineteenth-century title and shelfmark and traces of a bookplate.
No other contents.

DESCRIPTION
SIZE 20.5 x 14 cm.
QUIRING Indicated by signatures. Paper. I–IV^{12}, V^6 (lacks 6).
RULING Frame-ruling, 39–45 lines written.
SCRIPT Small, rapid, ugly cursive with long descenders of f and s. Simple round forms of a, d and e. Looped ascenders. Minim-letters hard to distinguish. t pierced. Dark grey ink.
DECORATION Undecorated initials in red, often faded to purple-grey.

BIBLIOGRAPHY
Hardwick *et al.*, *A Catalogue*, II.20.

47 *CAMBRIDGE, UNIVERSITY LIBRARY, MS. Ff.1.25 (1158), part 5

Saec. xiv ?[1]   Mediaeval provenance: ?
i + 35 + 4 + ii fos   2nd fo: *Romanorum instinctu*

HRB 12r–48v + 45* – 48*v.

§§1–3, 5–184, 186–191 'in Britanniam sunt reuersi' (foot of 44v). Continued in hand of one of Matthew Parker's secretaries: no loss of text §191 'subceptoque regni' –208. Dedicated to Robert of Gloucester.

Rubrics at §1 (12r) 'Incipit prologus Gauffridi Monemutensis in sequentem historiam', §5 (12r) 'Descripcio britannice insule', §109 (31v) 'Prefacio hystoria et epistola de interpretacione propheciarum Merlini', §111 (31v) 'Incipiunt prophecie Merlini ex mistica pugna draconum', after §208 (48*v) 'Explicit historia Britonum' (sixteenth-century). Also rubrics at each main textual division summarising contents.

Book-divisions at §54 (21r) II, §98 (29r) III, §143 (37v) IV. Each book subdivided into *capitula*.

Second Variant Version. Hammer's siglum X: Emanuel, 'Geoffrey of Monmouth's *Historia*', p. 104.

CONTENTS
1–9: lacking.
9*v: Parkerian introductory note about Ponticus Virunnius's epitome, the *Historia* and its author.
10r–12r: 'Incipiunt capitula primi lib\ri cronici ueł historie Britannie', (section marked ∨ rewritten in ?sixteenth-century hand). 'Descripcio quantitatis et multimode opulencie . . . et anglice ystorie tractanda distribuit.'
12r–48v: HRB.
49–50: flyleaves – sixteenth-century document, Latin and English.
N.B. Ff.1.25 is a Parkerian compilation of historical texts. Volumes 1 and 4 are thirteenth-century and apparently unconnected before Parker's time. Volumes 2 and 3 are Parkerian supplements, texts appropriate to the collection.

DESCRIPTION
SIZE 26.5 x 18 cm.
QUIRING 1–9 gone, Parkerian singleton before text (9*), I¹² (lacks 1–9: fos 10–12), II–III¹², IV¹⁰ (lacks 9–10: 37–44), with additional Parkerian quire V⁴ (fos 45–48), b² singletons.
PRICKING At outer edge.
RULING Single column of 53–59 lines; single vertical boundary-lines.
SCRIPT Several round, informal English hands. Brown ink. Nearly two-line Anglicana script with looped a and d (backwards), long cursive r. Little angularity. Crossed *et*-nota. Tops of ascenders are looped and sometimes split, curling to the left as well. Parkerian additions in elaborate Secretary script with one-compartment a but looped e. Bow of initial a often extended upwards into a diagonal. Dark grey ink.
DECORATION Spaces originally left for initials. Filled by later plain ink capitals.

HISTORY

Bears marks of Matthew Parker's secretaries: McKisack, *Medieval History in the Tudor Age*, p. 65, n. 1. Given by Parker, the codex was originally bound in two volumes. That containing the *Historia* was reported lost in 1732 and again in 1760: see McKitterick, *Cambridge University Library*, pp. 213 & 217.

BIBLIOGRAPHY

Hardwick *et al.*, *A Catalogue*, II.315–18.

48   *CAMBRIDGE, UNIVERSITY LIBRARY, MS. Ii.1.14 (1706)

Saec. xii²/ᵉˣ·   Mediaeval provenance: possibly Wales

ii + 129 + ii   2nd fo: [*fera*]-*rum generibus repleta*

HRB 1r–128v.

§§1–207 'sub duce Adelstano qui primus inter eos diadema portauit'. Dedicated to Robert of Gloucester and Waleran of Meulan (§§3–4).

No surviving opening rubric. After text finishes mid-page (128v), in same hand: 'Explicit'. No other rubrics or book-divisions.

Similar ending found in New Haven, Yale University Library, MS. 590.

No other contents but notes on 129v in the hand of Mark Broughton (sixteenth-century) who also made annotations in the manuscript. Paper flyleaves blank except for note in Welsh at top of first recto 'Isa fen asw' (?seventeenth-century) and on paste-down at end 'Yr isa dan y fen asw' (also found in MSS. Ii.4.4 and Kk.3.21).

DESCRIPTION

SIZE 21.5 x 16 cm.

QUIRING Some signatures extant, on 8v (I), 24v (III), 36v (IIII). I–III⁸, IIII¹², V–XV⁸, XVI⁶ (lacks 6: 125–129).

PRICKING In outer margin only.

RULING Single column of 22–24 lines, writing above top line, double vertical boundary-lines.

SCRIPT More than one hand. Initially a stiff, upright minuscule. Minim-letters have small feet and regularly pointed tops. Generally short ascenders, some lateral compression. Both ends of minims and uprights finished with small flat stroke. Ampersand and *et*-nota, round and straight-backed d used (round form less frequent). Final round s frequent but tall form also found. **a** large- or trailing-headed, **g** has 8-form. Some e-caudata. q-caudata used for *que*, etc. Occasional ligatures using majuscules: **N + S** or **T**, **a** + crossed **R** for -*arum*.

DECORATION Opening initial in green with stylised foliate filling in green, beige, and red. Minor capitals sometimes filled or with single-line feathering, bosses, split shafts, etc. In one to three colours (green, brown, red), usually two.

HISTORY

On 129v 'Pertinet ad Marcum Broughton' (sixteenth-century).

M. R. James conjectured a Welsh mediaeval provenance: 'I incline to suggest Margam Abbey as the home of the book. Robert of Gloucester was its founder. Note that Ii.4.4, which also has the double dedication of Geoffrey's work, has like this a Welsh scribble in it' (Cambridge University Library manuscript-notes, unpublished).

BIBLIOGRAPHY

Griscom, 'The date of composition'.
Griscom & Jones, *The Historia*, pp. 30–33, plates I & VII.
Hardwick *et al.*, *A Catalogue*, III.327–28.

49   *CAMBRIDGE, UNIVERSITY LIBRARY, MS. Ii.4.4 (1801)

Saec. xii *ex.*   Mediaeval provenance: ?Britain
ii + 134 + i fos (but foliated to 135)   2nd fo (2r): *tam crebris et magnificis*

HRB 58r–133v.   2nd fo (59r): *Eneas post Troianum*
§§1–208. Dedicated to Robert of Gloucester and Waleran of Meulan.
Rubrics at §5 (58vb) 'Explicit prologus. Incipit historia Britonum' (rest of column blank), before §111 (97v) 'Incipit prophecia Merlini'. No opening or closing rubrics. No book-divisions.

CONTENTS

i–ii: parchment flyleaves. Blank except for modern note of contents + bookplate on i v and on i r, in fourteenth-century Anglicana (written upsidedown), 'Adam primus homo damnauit secula pomo'.
1r–57rb: 'Incipit prologus Fulcheri presbiteri de captione Ierusalem' (rubric on 1v) preceded by *capitula*-list and followed by text. 'Placet equidem uiuis prodest etiam mortuis . . . ad superos uehitur angelicis manibus' (from beginning of prologue to epitaph of Giraldus which concludes the work; no loss of text between fos 56 and 57). Ed. Hagenmeyer, *Fulcherii Carnotensis Historia*.
57v: blank.
58–133v: HRB.
134 excised.
135: blank, unruled.
iii: as i–ii.

DESCRIPTION

SIZE 27 x 17.5 cm.
QUIRING Two volumes as indicated by signatures on the second unit. a² (i–ii), I–VII⁸; I⁸ (+ 1 before 1 [= last leaf of previous work], stub after 8: 57–65), II–V⁸, VI¹⁰ (98–107), VII–IX⁸, X ?4 (3 lacking: fos 132–135), b² (2 lacking: fo iii). Signatures I–VI, VIII–IX extant in this second section.

PRICKING Outer prickings mostly trimmed away. Some inner prickings extant in both halves of the book.

RULING Similar throughout book. Two columns with single boundary-lines; writing above top ruled line. 30 lines mostly but occasionally 29 in Fulcher's *Historia*.

SCRIPT Different hands in A and B but comparable script. Tall and massive Proto-gothic in several hands. Straight **d** and ampersand are standard, probably indicative of the level of formality rather than an accurate dating criterion. Final round s occurs. Horizontal compression and some angularity. e-caudata is found occasionally.

DECORATION Similar in parts A and B – elaborate and fine. Large capitals in red, green, light brown, and cobalt blue. Main part of letter in one colour with delicate foliate or feathered decoration in other colours. In A, minor capitals often in two colours. In B, they are smaller, plainer, and mostly red or green.

HISTORY
On i v, in (Early) Modern hand, the Welsh note 'Yr isa dan y Fen asw' (cf. MS. Ii.1.14).

BIBLIOGRAPHY
Hardwick *et al.*, *A Catalogue*, III.440.

50   *CAMBRIDGE, UNIVERSITY LIBRARY, MS. Ii.4.12 (1809)

Saec. xiv *in.*   Mediaeval provenance: Norwich (Benedictine Cathedral Priory)
ii + 179 + ii fos (fo 95 lost)   2nd fo: *maxime quod a Deo*

HRB 97r–180r.
§§1–3, 5–208 [with *Merlinus iste* chapter before §118 (144v)]. Dedicated to Robert of Gloucester.

No opening or closing rubrics. Occasional marginal rubrics as at §6 (98r): 'Natus est Brutus'.

No book-divisions.

Second Variant Version (not known to Hammer or Emanuel): Crick, 'Manuscripts', p. 162.

CONTENTS
i–ii, iii–iv (before and after text): fragments from a service-book.
1r–89vb: 'Summa magistri Richardi'. 'Qui bene presunt presbiteri duplici honore digni habeantur ... Hic ergo erat consummatus.' *Summa* of Richard Wetherset, chancellor of the University of Cambridge (*fl.* 1250).
90ra–91ra: 'Incipiunt capitula super summa Ricardi'. 'Quales debent esse presbiteri ... et de hiis quibus Christus infirmatur.'
91rb–96: blank. 95 excised.
97r–180r: HRB.
180v: prayers and devotional quotations in various types of hand.

DESCRIPTION

SIZE 24.5 x 17.5 cm.

QUIRING Paper flyleaves followed by a^2, I–VII^{12}, VIII^{12} (lacks 11: 85–96), IX–XV^{12} and b^2, before more paper flyleaves. Absent leaves foliated.

PRICKING Visible only at inner edge.

RULING HRB in a single column of 31 lines. Flyleaves and *Summa* in two columns of 32 and 31 lines respectively.

SCRIPT Gothic bookhand but not of highest grade. Minims lozenged at top only. **a** constructed of two verticals joined by hairlines. *Et* unabbreviated; final s is usually tall. Juncture of **b, d, h, p** with **e** and **o**, even **a**. Brown ink.

DECORATION Mainly blue or red with contrasting filigree. Trefoil shapes left in reserve in centre of letter. Opening capital of each work blue and red with bird or animal left in reserve. Capitals in text picked out in red.

HISTORY

On top of 1v in hand apparently not far in date from that of the text: 'Rogeri de Bliclingge monachi'. Norwich pressmark (antedating the second quarter of the fourteenth century): see Ker, *Books, Collectors and Libraries*, p. 257. Flyleaves at end taken from the Advent Office of the Benedictine Cathedral Priory of Holy Trinity, Norwich.

BIBLIOGRAPHY

Hardwick *et al.*, *A Catalogue*, III.451–52.

Ker, *Medieval Libraries*, p. 137.

51   *CAMBRIDGE, UNIVERSITY LIBRARY, MS. Ii.4.17 (1814)

Saec. xv   Mediaeval provenance: ?

2 paper + iii + 91 + 2 paper   2nd fo: *mulier puerum*

HRB 1r–91r.

§§1–3, 5–208. Dedicated to Robert of Gloucester.

Rubrics at §1 (1r) 'Hic incipit prologus Galfridi Arthuri Monemuth. de gestis Britonum in Angl.', §5 (1r) 'Explicit prologus. Hic incipit descripcio Britannie insule que nunc Anglia uocatur', §6 (1v) 'Hic incipit primus liber de gestis Britonum in Anglia dudum uocata Magna Britannia', §110 (49r) 'Incipit prologus de prophetia Merlini', §158 ('Lucius rei publice procurator') (72r) 'Littera missa ab imperatore Lucio ad Arthurum regem', after §208 (91r) 'Explicit liber de historiis regum Britannie'.

Book-divisions at §23 (10r) II, §35 (16r) III, §54 (23v) IV, §73 (32r) V, 89 (39r) VI, §111 (49r) VII, §118 (54v) VIII, §143 (65r) IX, §177 (81v) X.

CONTENTS

1r–91r: HRB.

91v: note on weights and measures. 'Tria grana ordei faciunt pollicem . . . grana ad quart. .xi.' *Assisa de ponderibus et mensuris.*

Flyleaves [2 paper + i–iii; 2 paper after text]: index of proper names, etc., from the *Historia* in the hand of Abraham Wheloc (*ob.* 1653). Parchment flyleaves (i–iii) original: on verso of i there are recipes in a hand close to that of the text.

DESCRIPTION
SIZE 22.5 x 17cm.
QUIRING a (paper bifolium), b^4 (lacks 1), I–XI^8, XII^6 (lacks 4–6), c^2 (paper bifolium). Catchwords on last verso of each quire.
PRICKING For frame-ruling.
RULING In frame, about 25–29 lines usually.
SCRIPT Four-line Secretary script. Angular bow of **d, g**, etc. Descenders taper but are not slanting, ascenders loop over angularly at top. **a** has two-compartment looped form. **e** in ligature has the single-stroke, curled form. **t** is well pierced. Long cursive **r** is used.
DECORATION Blue and red filigreed capitals. Patterns square off the letter, decorative spaces left within it. Opening initial is in gold with solid coloured ground of blue and brown with white highlighting.

HISTORY
No *ex-libris* inscription but at top of ii r in ?seventeenth-century hand is a memorandum mentioning Sir William Skeryngton and Elizabeth, abbess of Syon, as well as the County of Middlesex. Erasure under text on 91r.

BIBLIOGRAPHY
Hardwick *et al., A Catalogue*, III.454.

52   *CAMBRIDGE, UNIVERSITY LIBRARY, MS. Kk.6.16 (2096)

Saec. xiv^1 [1327]   Origin: Worcester
ii + 163 + ii fos   2nd fo: *uix mille ho\<minu\>m*

HRB 12r–146r
§20 'Contra quos Brutus etiam'–§33 'ultra modum commota in odium' (23v); §62 'Enniauni correctus' (24r)–208. Dedicatory section lost.
Rubrics after §117 (76r) 'Explicit prophecia Merlini', after §208 (146r) 'Explicit historia Bruti. Script. Wigorn. anno Domini .m.ccc. uicesimo septimo. Amen'.
No book-divisions.

CONTENTS
1r: blank except for title 'Historia B[ ]'.
1v–7r: extracts from Orosius and Hegesippus. 'Orosius de ormesta mundi contra paganos scripsit beato Augustino . . . hec ab Egesippo colliguntur.'
(7r–10v: various notes in sixteenth-century hands)
7r–8r: on the foundations of York, Winchester, Bath, Leicester, Babylon, with notes on Troy, Rome, and Belinus and Brennius. 'Nota cronicas notabiles sequentes . . . ultra Sabrinam in Wallias.'

8v–10r: verse. 'O myghty mars that marrith many a wight . . . by the sonne and the mone euery dele.'

10r/v: note. 'Anno .xii. Henrici VII memorandum that John Wright, prophesur examined before my lord Cardinal, my lord Treasurer, my Lords of Bathe . . .' Possibly written in about 1496/7, the date of the document. Continued on 11v.

11r: (in original hand) extract from Josephus. 'Secundum Iosephum libro .vii. antiquitatum . . . anni .mmm.d.xiii. menses .vi. dies .x. hec Iosephus.'

Note beneath in ?sixteenth-century (post-Reformation) hand on early Britons.

11v: continuation of note on 10r/v.

12r–146r: HRB.

146r–153v: prophecy of John of Bridlington. '[F]ebris infectus requies fuerat mihi lectus . . . Ad [mort]em tendo [ ]a pendo.' Walther, *Initia*, I.316, no. 6296. In different hand from HRB, later. Remainder of 153v illegible.

154r/v: Vision of St Thomas of Canterbury. 'Quando ego Thomas Cantuariensis archyepiscopus . . . inclusa cum hac cedula in uase plumbeo.'

155r: 'De Henrico 6'. 'Flamine romano crescit britannicus honor . . . ac unitur omne.' Walther, *Initia*, I.330, no. 6576. Later hand. Another prophecy beneath, in same hand. 'Ter tria lustra tenet . . . clerumque reducet.'

155v–156r: 'Hic incipit prophecia quam composuit Holpes ph[ilosoph]us'. 'Gallorum nouitas Germanos iustificabit . . . rex erit Anglorum regum de stirpe priorum.' Walther, *Initia*, I.353, no. 7015.

156v: 'Prophecia sancti Thome martyris' (according to final rubric). 'Cesaris imperium per tempora longa latebit . . . in studii muros leopardi ui ructuros.' Walther, *Initia*, I.116, no. 2307.

156r–157r: 'Prophecia quam Gyldas abbas de Glastynberi composuit' (according to final rubric). 'Regnum Scotorum fiet inter cetera regna . . . h[ ] retulit paruo carmine plura uocans.' Walther, *Initia*, I.864, no. 16547.

157v–158r: notes in various sixteenth-century (post-Reformation) hands.

158v: not legible.

159r: 'Anno cephas mille canis catulus cocodrille . . . debeat ad regnum dat Aprilis nobile signum'.

159v: 'Incipit prophecia Willelmi de Stapulton quondam forestarii [ ] foresta de Ingelwode anno Domini millesimo .ccc.lxxix'. 'Anno cephas mille canis catulas cocadrille . . . Quos creasti Domine peccatoribus misere.' Walther, *Initia*, I.58, no. 1128.

160r–161r: 'Hermenis dominus sapientum dixit post annum a criacione (*sic*) mundi 6376 . . . Si fiat metrum falsum tibi discute tetrum.'

161r/v: 'Hii uersus sequentes inueniebantur in tarde scripti . . .', description of discovery of verses in church in Anjou. 'Dum nubilum (*sic*) scisma dum cancer ui roborabit . . . et aliis animalibus hys complet. rex noster, etc.' Dated 1417. Walther, *Initia*, I.247, no. 4909.

162r: 'Duo sunt genera principatuum . . . Hec nota secundum intent. Ar[ ]'.

162v: 'Prophesia (*sic*) abbatis Joachim'. 'Carolus Philippi filius . . . imperator post Fredericum tercium.'

163: blank except for notes and inscriptions of ownership (see below, HISTORY).

DESCRIPTION

SIZE 14.5 x 9.5 cm.

QUIRING a^2, I^{10}, II^{14}, III^{10}, IV^{14}, V^{10}, VI^{14}, VII^{10}, VIII^{14}, IX^{10}, X^{14}, XI^{10}, XII^{14}, XIII^{10}, $XIV?^{10}$ (lacks 10: 155–163), b^2.

PRICKING For frame-ruling.

RULING 28 lines ruled inside frame. Single column. 49 lines in *Prophetie Merlini*.

SCRIPT HRB written in small, nearly two-line, Anglicana. Brown ink. Some forked ascenders. Looped round **d**, pierced **t**, 2-shaped **r** and two-compartment **a** (constructed of verticals joined by hairlines); final looped **s** tends to be larger than minim-size. Crossed *et*-nota standard.

Various other hands, that of fos 1v–7r similar to HRB. Fos 164r–157r written mostly in small, fairly cursive hand, grey ink, perhaps slightly later in date than main hand: long **r**, looped ascenders, large final **s**.

DECORATION Red or blue capitals, occasionally filigreed with the other colour.

HISTORY

Date and place of origin indicated in closing rubric of HRB (146r), see above. On 158r in sixteenth- (or late fifteenth-) century hand. 'Iste liber est Thome Pooche questoris quem accomodauit fratri magistro Lynwode qui magister quam plurima hic intitulauit quem quia non in uendicione concordauer[unt] reddidit in presentia Partrich. quondam magistri dicti Thome'. Also in sixteenth-century hand, 163r, 'Lyndwode'. In seventeenth-century hand on 163v: 'Nicholas Ferrar ex dono magistri Danielis Birkett'. H. L. Pink identified Ferrar with the member of Clare Hall (viz. Clare College) of that name who died in 1637 (Cambridge University Library manuscript-notes, unpublished).

Also on 163v in ?sixteenth-century hand, 'W. Staunton'. Also 'Mary'.

BIBLIOGRAPHY

Hardwick *et al.*, *A Catalogue*, II.714–15.

Robinson, *Catalogue*, I.37, no. 71.

53 *CAMBRIDGE, UNIVERSITY LIBRARY, MS. Mm.1.34 (2295)

Saec. xii/xiii	Mediaeval provenance: ?
57 fos	2nd fo: *regem ceterosque grecos*

HRB 3r–57v.

§§1–3, 5–208. Nameless dedication.

Rubrics at §1 (3r) 'Incipit [prologus] historie Britonum', after §5 (3v) 'Explicit prologus. Incipit historia', after §8 (4r) 'Historia Britonum', §111 (32r, in margin) 'Uaticinium Merlini', after §208 (57v) 'Explicit historia regum Britannie'. Occasional other rubrics.

No book-divisions.

No other contents but flyleaves (1r–2v) are fragments of a fourteenth-century breviary with part of the Common of Virgins.

DESCRIPTION
SIZE 19 x 13.5 cm.
QUIRING Text divided into eights marked on last verso of quire by signatures and on first recto by letters. a² (fos 1–2), I–VI⁸, VII⁸ (lacks 8: fos 51–57).
PRICKING In outer margin only.
RULING Single column of 37 lines. ?Writing above top ruled line.
SCRIPT Small, closely-written Protogothic with cursive features. No juncture, *et*-nota uncrossed, no round s. Straight d and ampersand still occurring in places. No e-caudata. Split ascenders of b, h, l, d. a small-headed, g straight-backed, t slightly pierced. Lack of juncture perhaps results from smallness of script.
DECORATION Red capitals with some double strokes, bosses, etc., but no ornament external to the letter-form.

BIBLIOGRAPHY
Hardwick *et al.*, *A Catalogue*, IV.124.

54   *CAMBRIDGE, UNIVERSITY LIBRARY, MS. Mm.5.29 (2434)

Saec. xii *med.*   Mediaeval provenance: England (?Midlands, E. Anglia)
179 fos   2nd fo (3r): [*mi*]-*sit qui erant polliciti*

HRB 21r–107r.
§§1–3, 5–208 [*Merlinus iste* chapter after §117 (71v)]. Dedicated to Robert of Gloucester.
Rubrics before §1 (20v) 'Incipit prologus Gaufridi Monemutensis in sequentem hystoriam', before §5 (21v) 'Descriptio Britannice insule', after §5 (22r) 'Explicit descriptio Britannie insule. Incipit hystoria Britonum', after §208 (107r) 'Explicit hystoria Britonum'. No rubrics for Prophecies.
No book-divisions.
Second Variant Version. Hammer siglum E: Emanuel, 'Geoffrey of Monmouth's *Historia*', p. 104. Exemplar of Lincoln 98.

CONTENTS
1: lost.
2r–16r: 'Incipit hystoria Daretis Troianorum Frigii de Greco translata in Latinum a Cornelio nepote' (rubric on 2v) preceded by letter of Cornelius. 'Cornelius Salustio Crispo suo salutem . . . Palamonem. Epistrophum. Scidium.' Ed. Meister, *Daretis Phrygii De Excidio Troiae Historia*.
16r–20v: 'Incipit prophetia Sibylle'. 'Sibylle generaliter omnes femine dicuntur prophetantes . . . regnabunt cum illo in secula seculorum. Amen.' Ed. Sackur, *Sibyllinische Texte*, pp. 177–87.
21r–107r: HRB.
107v–118v: 'Incipit gesta Britonum a Gilda sapiente composita'. 'A principio mundi

usque ad diluuium . . . solus in extremis finibus cosmi est.' *Historia Brittonum*, ed. Faral, *La Légende*, III.5–61.

118v–119v: 'Bedan' chronology. 'Quinquagesimo ergo quarto anno hoc est sexto decimo anno . . . qui sunt ab exordio mundi usque in presens.' Found in Cambridge, University Library, MS. Ff.1.27 (1160) and elsewhere.

119v–122v: 'Incipit libellus Bemetoli quem beatus Ieronimus de Greco in Latinum transtulit uel composuit'. 'Anno .dcccc. tricesimo mortuus est Adam . . . honor perhennis in secula seculorum. Amen.' Compare edition of pseudo-Methodius by Sackur, *Sibyllinische Texte*, pp. 59–96.

122v–123r: genealogy of the counts of Flanders. 'Hildricus Harlebecensis comes genuit Ingelramnum . . . et ex ea duos filios suscepit. Baldeuuinum et Willemmum.'

123r: 'Hec sun (*sic*) nomina Francorum regum'. 'Clodoueus . . . Lodouicus' (son of Philip Augustus).

123v–128r: Henry of Huntingdon, *Historia Anglorum*, Book I.1–13 *med.*. 'Britannia igitur beatissima est insularum . . . Illa inquam uirtus que semper in asperrimis.' Ed. Arnold, *Henrici archidiaconi Huntendunensis Historia Anglorum*, pp. 5–17.

128v–129v: blank (end of quire).

130r/v: 'Anglia habet in longitudine .dccc. miliaria a Penuithflete . . . Staffordesire .d. hide'.

130v–144rb: 'Incipiunt gesta Alexandri regis magni Macedonum' (rubric on 131v), preceded by *capitula*. 'Egypti sapientes . . . superatus atque extinctus occubuit.' Ed. Kuebler, *Iuli Ualeri Alexandri Polemi res gestae*, pp. 1–168.

144rb: 'Epitaphium'. 'Primus Alexander pillea natus in urbe . . . ferroque regna lesit.' Walther, *Initia*, I.759, no. 14648.

144v: 'Quiquid in humanis constat uirtutibus altis . . . succubuit leto sumpto cum melle ueneno'. Reproduced by Hill, '*Epitaphia Alexandri*', p. 98. Walther, *Initia*, I.833, no. 15990.

144v–150v: 'Incipit epistola Alexandri regis magni Macedonum ad magistrum suum Aristotilem'. 'Semper memor tui etiam . . . nominis mei fama habeatur in gloria.' *Gesta Alexandri*, printed from this manuscript by DiMarco & Perelman, 'The Middle English Letter'.

151r–155r: 'Alexandri magni regis Macedonum et Dindimi regis Bragmannorum de philosophia per litteras facta collatio' (rubric on 150v). 'Sepius ad aures . . . aut inuidie quod a meliori prestantur.' Ed. Kuebler, *Iuli Valerii Alexandri Polemi res gestae*, pp. 169–89.

155r–156v: 'Praua (corr. to parua) recapitulacio de eodem Alexandro et de suis'. 'Tempore quo hic Alexander natus legitur . . . et egregie uicisse narratur.' Ed. Ross, '*Parva Recapitulacio*', pp. 199–203.

156v–157r: two notes. 'Notum sit omnibus fidelibus statutum . . . idus Iulii ciuitas Ierusalem capta fuit.' 'Hec sunt reliquie que apud Constantinopolim in capella imperatoris monstrantur . . . caput Sancti Pantaleonis martiris.' First is preceded by petition: 'Exora Cristum qui librum legeris istum / [U]t det scriptori (glossed 'Ernulfo') quicquid debetur honori'.

157v–160v: 'Incipit sermo quomodo primitus sancta arbor creuit in qua salus mundi

pependit'. 'Zancta (*sic*) et diuina eloquia fratres . . . ipseque Dominus Iesus Christus.'
Ends imperfectly but reconstructable from Lincoln 98.

Ed. from this manuscript (and Hereford, Cathedral Library, MS. P.2.iv) by Mozley,
'A new text', pp. 117–27.

DESCRIPTION

SIZE 27 x 17.5 cm.

QUIRING Indicated by signatures. I[8] (1 lacking: fos 2–8), II–XIII[8], XIIII[10] (lacks 7:
fos 105–113), XV–XIX[8], XX[8] (6 lacking: fos 154–160). Signatures present except for
quires V and VI.

PRICKING Visible in outer margins only.

RULING Single column of 32–40 lines. Top line written. Single boundings.

SCRIPT Mostly written in one type of hand, a solidly proportioned form of Anglo-
Norman Protogothic minuscule. Short ascenders and descenders, little compression.
Ampersand, tall **s** and straight **d** are standard in some areas of the book but medial
round **d** and final round **s** occur. e-caudata is common. **a** often has an overhanging
head. The tops of minims and **f**, **p**, and tall **s** are thickened. 156v–157r (the two notes)
– written in a more cursive documentary type of hand with extended ascenders and
descenders, round **d** (when avoiding descenders), and *et*-nota as well as ampersand.
Some letter forms are also found in the rest of book. Its position within the work of
the more formal hand(s) suggests contemporaneous production (even the possibility
that this is a lower grade of script available to a practitioner of bookhand).

DECORATION Striking. Opening rubrics usually in large, fleshy, foliate-type square
capitals with alternate syllables or words (etc.) in green and pink or green and red.
Often accompanied by decorated initial.

HISTORY

Verse on 157v names scribe as Ernulf (unidentified). Ker notes this name occurring
twice in twelfth-century book inscriptions – the twelfth-century bishop of Rochester
of that name and another Ernulf who donated books of Gloucester – neither of whom
may be associated with our scribe: Ker, *Medieval Libraries*, pp. 265, 297.

Little is known of the book's early history. M. R. James presumed that the absent first
leaf had carried any marks of ownership. The volume is related to a Peterborough
book, Oxford, Bodleian Library MS. Bodley 163 (*S.C.* 2016), from which a block of
texts was derived: the *Historia Brittonum*, *Libellus Bemetoli*, the genealogy of the
counts of Flanders, and the notes on French kings. Our manuscript in its entirety was
the exemplar for Lincoln Cathedral MS. 98. James suggested a place of origin for
Mm.5.29: 'I have an impression that this fine book is from a Northern house: it is not
in the Durham catalogue' (Cambridge University Library manuscript-notes, unpublished). On 128v (otherwise blank) in ?seventeenth-century hand 'Liber Gulihelmus
Saunderus', repeated with varying spelling on the same leaf. (*Dictionary of National
Biography* does not supply a suitable candidate.)

Listed among books of John Moore, bishop of Norwich, in 1697 by Bernard, *Catalogi*,
II.1, pp. 363–64, no. 9277.

BIBLIOGRAPHY
Hardwick *et al.*, *A Catalogue*, IV.336–59*.
Hill, '*Epitaphia Alexandri*'.
Hill, 'The Middle English and Latin versions'.

55   CARDIFF, SOUTH GLAMORGAN CENTRAL LIBRARY, MS. 2.611

Saec. xiii/xiv   Mediaeval provenance: ?Wales
132 fos   2nd fo: *Priamus respondit* (acephalous text)

HRB 10r–130v
§§1–3, 5–137 (*in.*), 138 (*med.*) –208. Dedicated to Robert of Gloucester. Rubrics at
§1 (10r) 'Hystoria Britonum', §110 (in margin, 69v) 'Epistola .G. Monumutensis
episcopo Lincoll. directa', after §208 (130v) 'Explicit tractatus'.
No book-divisions.
Lacuna in text caused by loss of folio after 87. 87v ends 'Denique pacificatis
acquilonaribus' (§137) and 88r begins 'nam et ipse ad obsidionem' §138.
Mixed vulgate and First Variant text (Variant partly §§5–108, then sparingly §§178–
208). Wright siglum c: *The Historia Regum Britannie of Geoffrey of Monmouth, II*,
pp. lxxix–lxxx.

CONTENTS
1r–9r: Dares Phrygius, acephalous. 'cessat de imperio Agamemnonis conqueri . . .
Protenorem et alios quinque. Hactenus id Dares Frigius mandauit litteris.' Ed. Meister,
Daretis Phrygii De Excidio Troiae Historia.
9r/v: genealogy of the Trojans. 'Notandum quod Ciprius quidam filius Yewan . . . a
quibus tres partes Britannie nomina sortita sunt.' Also in Exeter Cathedral, MS. 3514.
9v–10r: poem prefacing HRB by Madog of Edeirnion. 'Strenua cunctorum delectant
gesta proborum . . . Ex libris densis collegit uos refouens his.' Printed by Hammer,
Geoffrey of Monmouth, p. 18. Also in Cambridge, Corpus Christi College, MS. 281.
Walther, *Initia*, I.977, no. 18633.
10r–130v: HRB.
130v–132v: 'Prophetia Merlini siluestris'. 'Arbor sterilis a primo trunco decisa . . .
qui pacificato regno occidet.' Ed. Schulz, *Gottfried*, pp. 463–65.
132v: 'Epithaphium (*sic*) Arturi (four lines)'. 'Quem morum probitas commendat
laude perhenni . . . Arturi iacet hic coniunx tumulata secunda.' Known to Adam of
Domerham: Nitze, 'The exhumation of King Arthur', p. 361.

DESCRIPTION
SIZE ?
QUIRING I–VII^{12}, VIII^{12} (4 lacking: 85–95), IX–XI^{12}, ?singleton (132). At least one
quire lost before I.
RULING Single column of 24 lines.
PRICKING Not visible.
SCRIPT Informal bookhand of a rather disorderly aspect. Final s cedilla-shaped or

tall. **a** has small head but two-compartment form sometimes found. **t** slightly pierced. Round **d** has fairly long ascender. Juncture of **e** and **o** after **b**, **d** and **p**. Crossed *et*-nota. Small approach-strokes to tops of ascenders. Some ascenders extended at top of page. DECORATION Simple unfiligreed capitals. Catchwords and some opening letters ornamented with sketches of heads etc.

HISTORY
Perhaps written on the French/German border, possibly near Metz (see Hammer, *Geoffrey*, p. 8, n. 10). Marginalia in this manuscript also found in Ushaw College, MS. 6, the ultimate source of central section of this manuscript: Dumville, 'The origin of the C-text', p. 318.

BIBLIOGRAPHY
Dumville, 'The origin of the C-text'.
Hammer, *Geoffrey*, pp. 18–19.
Wright, *The Historia Regum Britannie of Geoffrey of Monmouth, II*, pp. lxxix–lxxx.

56 COLMAR, BIBLIOTHEQUE MUNICIPALE, MS. 448 (14)

Saec. xii[2]   Mediaeval provenance (fifteenth-century):
                                Marbach, dioc. Basel (Augustinian)
(?ii +) 74 + i fos (73 foliated)   2nd fo: [*Cassibel*]-*lanus tamen pietati*

HRB 1r–73v
§§51 (*med.*) –115.28, 116.41–181 (*in.*), 189 (*med.*) –200 (*in.*), 201 (*ex.*) –208. Dedicatory section lost.
Rubrics at chapter-divisions. §109 (26r) 'Relatio historiagrafi de Merlino', §110 (26v) 'Prefatio', §111 (26v) 'Incipiunt prophetie Merlini', after §208 (73v) 'Explicit liber'. No extant book-divisions.
§51 begins '-untur. Potiti uero uictoria'. Lacunae caused by loss of first three quires, then of folios between 28v (ends 'foliorum adnichilabit. Dein-' §115) and 29r (begins 'procreabuntur in nido' §116), 66v (ends 'totius insule tenens' §181) and 67r (begins 'Adedelfridus (*sic*) ciuitate capta' §189), 71v (ends 'et argenti Cadual-' §200) and 72r (begins 'diuina celebrantur' §201).
No other contents. Rear flyleaf from twelfth-century kalendar (November and December). According to Schmitt (*Catalogue général*, LVI.166) similar leaf before text, preceded by fragments of treatise on the Devil (fifteenth-century).

DESCRIPTION
SIZE 20.5 x 14 cm.
QUIRING Some signatures on first recto or last verso of quire, beginning .iiii. on 1r (.v. 15v, .vi. 16r, .vii. 31v, .viiii. 47v, .x. 48r, .xii. 64r, .xiii. 70r. a ?2 singletons, IV[8], V[8] (9–10, 10*, 11–15), VI[8] (+1 after 8: fos 16–24), VII[8] (lacks 5), VIII–XI[8], XII[8] (4–5 lacking: 64–69), XIII ?[8] (?3–6 lost, + singleton after 8: fos 70–73, flyleaf). Numbering duplicated at fo 10.

PRICKING Outer margin only.

RULING Single column of 27–28 lines.

SCRIPT Four-line Protogothic with upright and rather stiff strokes, compact minims. *Et*-nota standard, no round s. Round d found in one hand but elsewhere straight-backed form only. Caroline form of **a**. Top of **p** slightly pierced. **g** has dropped waist. Continental origin.

DECORATION Romanesque capitals (vermilion) with some simple single-line scrolling.

HISTORY

On 24v under §105 'Liber domus sancti Augustini et omnium sanctorum in Marpach (*sic*) ordinis canonicorum regularium dyoc. Basilien. prope Columbariam' (fifteenth-century). Marbach in diocese of Basel, near Colmar.

Text on first flyleaf mentions Brother Caspar of Marbach, and is dated 1472 (Schmitt, *Catalogue général*, LVI.166–67).

BIBLIOGRAPHY

Crick, 'The manuscripts', p. 158.
Schmitt, *Catalogue général*, LVI.166–67.

57 COLOGNY-GENEVE, BIBLIOTHEQUE MARTIN BODMER, MS. BODMER 70

Saec. xv ?[1]   Provenance: ?English
114 fos   2nd fo: [*superueni*]-*ente Ascanius regia potestate*

HRB 1r–109v

§§1–3, 5–189 (*ex.*), 191 (*ex.*) –208. Dedicated to Robert of Gloucester. No opening rubric. After §208 'Explicit hystoria Britonum'.

No book-divisions.

Tally of kings to 'c<entesimu>s Kawaladrus'.

Lacuna caused by loss of folio between 103 (ends 'dux Cornubie et Margadud' §189) and 104 (begins 'Prodiderunt. Postremo Karenticum regem' §191).

CONTENTS

1r–109v: HRB.

109v: on the Heptarchy, truncated. 'Quando Saxones Angliam sibi subiugarunt . . . in quo est Lincolnia. Leycestria. Northamton. Huntendon. Hertford.'

110r: note on Edward I and his coronation, acephalous. 'qui in adolescencia obierunt . . . qui tempore suo moribus et sciencia precipue in uniuersali ecclesia claruit excellenter.'

110v: note on defeat at Bannockburn of Edward II by Robert Bruce (1314). 'Memorandum quod anno Domini .m.ccc.xiiii. Inito conflictu . . . et incarcerati et postea redempti.'

111–114: blank except for note on 113v (see HISTORY, below) and note on 114v on peasant revolt in Norfolk (1549).

DESCRIPTION
SIZE 19.5 x 13 cm.
QUIRING Indicated by catchwords. I–VIII^8, IX^8 (lacks 5, no text lost: 65–71), X–XIII^8, XIV^8 (lacks 1, 8: fos 104–109), XV^8 (lacks 1, 7–8: fos 110–114).
RULING Frame-ruling only. 26–27 lines written.
SCRIPT More than one hand. Cursive with some angularity. No slope. Long descenders, ascenders angled at top and curled under. Final round s, occasional sigma-form, but usually long. Two-compartment a initially, otherwise pinched round form. Long r with little shoulder, also 2-form. t has ascender. Some angularity in round d but not g. e usually has simple form, occasionally curled.
DECORATION Plain capitals.

HISTORY
On 113v in angular secretary hand 'Liber Roberti llooyde alias ffloode', perhaps Robert Fludd 1573–1637 (see Pellegrin, *Manuscrits latins de la Bodmeriana*, p. 119). N.B. 'Le: Fludd' also found in Cambridge, Trinity College, MS. O.2.21. Other names as described by Pellegrin, *ibid.*: 1r 'John Blesocv' (?fifteenth-century), 114v 'John Baunt' (?sixteenth-century).

BIBLIOGRAPHY
Crick, 'Manuscripts', p. 160.
Pellegrin, *Manuscrits latins de la Bodmeriana*, pp. 119–22.

58 DÔLE, BIBLIOTHEQUE MUNICIPALE, MSS. 348+349

Saecc. xvi + xiii   Mediaeval provenance: ?
59 + 68 fos   2nd fo A: *Ei quoniam ex quo*

HRB B 1r–68v   2nd fo B: *me eamque fecit pregnantem*
§§1–3, 5–159 'qui discidio ueterum nostrorum inuitati'. Nameless dedication.
Rubrics at §1 (1r) 'Incipit hystori[ ] de origine Brittonum translata a Gaufrido Monumetensi de brittannica lingua in Latinum', §5 (1r) 'Explicit praefa[ ]', §6 (1v) 'Textus hystorie incipit', §109 (46r) 'Reuelatio hystoriografi de Merlino', §110 (46r) 'Reuelatio hystoriografi de eodem', §111 (46r) 'Incipiunt prophetie Merlini'. Other rubrics summarising action.
No book-divisions.

CONTENTS
Notes on contents of manuscript, signed by (the elder) Pallu.
A 1r–9v: 'De gestis Francorum libri tres', opening supplied in hand of P. Pierre-François Chifflet (1592–1682, member of Jesuit order). 'Cum animaduerterem quam plurimos . . . delatum ibi [ ] tumulatum.'
10r–57v: original manuscript, same text continues 'iurauerat se nullatenus nociturum

Neustriam . . . connumerantur ibi sit timor unde tibi'. Partially ed. by de Wailly, 'Examen', pp. 403–5.

58r–59v: notes of dates of Easter, etc. 'Inni (*sic*) Domini .m.cc.v. inditio viii epacta .xxviii. . . . inni (*sic*) Domini .m.cc.xxxiii. . . . nonum aprilis luna .xix..' Final entry, for 1234, made in more informal hand.

B 1–68v: HRB, truncated at end.

DESCRIPTION
SIZE 26.1 x 18 cm.

QUIRING A – no indications of arrangement. B – catchwords indicate quires of twelve after I^8 ($II–VI^{12}$).

PRICKING At outer edge only.

RULING Single column of 36 written lines, writing below top ruled line.

SCRIPT Similar in A and B. Fluent, almost two-line Gothic minuscule. Minims ticked but not lozenged. Juncture of **e** and **o** with **d** and **p**. Pierced **t** but both single- and double-compartment forms of **a** found. Crossed *et*-nota.

BIBLIOGRAPHY
Gauthier, *Catalogue général*, XIII.446.

59   DOUAI, BIBLIOTHEQUE MUNICIPALE, MS. 880 (835)

Saec. xii$^{2/ex.}$ Mediaeval provenance: Anchin (Benedictine)
114 fos   2nd fo (15r): [*mi*]-*nistrat. Omni etenim*

HRB 14va–88va

§1–3, 5–208. Dedicated to Robert of Gloucester.

No opening or closing rubrics. Before §5 'Explicit prologus. Incipit historia Britannorum'. After §22 (fo 22r) 'Explicit liber primus. Incipit secundus'. Other book-divisions added at various times: III §35 (27r), IV §54 (33v), V §73 (40r), VI §89 (46r), VII §110 (54r), VIII §143 (66v).

Verses (summarising the text) inserted at §§23 (22r), 35 (27r), 54 (33v), 73 (40r), 89 (46r), 109 (54r), 143 (66v), 163 (73v), 177 (80r). Printed by Hammer, 'Some Leonine summaries', pp. 117–19.

CONTENTS
?1–14: Dares Phrygius preceded by letter to Sallust as usual. Ed. Meister, *Daretis Phrygii De Excidio Troiae Historia*.

14v–88v: HRB.

88va/b: poem as in Douai, BM, MS. 882 and Valenciennes, BM, MS. 792. 'Hec Bernardus ego . . . gens aliena seruit amena.' Printed by Hammer, 'Some Leonine summaries', pp. 119–20. Walther, *Initia*, I.377, no. 7477.

?89–114v: Dudo of Saint-Quentin's History of the Norman Dukes. 'Inclito et pie uenerandi . . . Crastina uero die Ludouici pergentis . . .' Book III lacking. Ed. Lair,

'Dudonis Sancti Quintini De moribus'. On this manuscript see Huisman, 'Notes', pp. 125–26.

DESCRIPTION

SIZE 31 x 21 cm.

QUIRING No signatures.

RULING Two columns of 35 written lines, beginning above top ruled line.

SCRIPT Regular Protogothic minuscule (cf. Douai 882), heavy ticks on minims and descenders, short ascenders and descenders. Round **d** (nearly two-line) standard, round s occurs in final position, e-caudata is still found, and ampersand used for *et*. ?Written in N. France/Low Countries. For proportions and forms of **a, b, g,** etc. compare Lieftinck, *Manuscrits datés conservés dans les Pays-Bas*, I, pl. 95 (Bonne-Espérance, 1178–1193).

DECORATION Some large capitals divided geometrically and coloured; others with bold ink flourishes. Historiated initial on 66v reproduced by Loomis & Loomis, *Arthurian Legends*, pl. 340.

HISTORY

Olim Anchin (Benedictine Abbey, diocese of Arras) G.332, D.835.

BIBLIOGRAPHY

Hammer, 'Some Leonine summaries'.
Dehaisnes, *Catalogue général*, VI.635–36.

60   DOUAI, BIBLIOTHEQUE MUNICIPALE, MS. 882 (838)

Saec. xii *ex.*   Mediaeval provenance: Marchiennes (Benedictine)
198 fos   2nd fo: *Quicumque uelis mentem*

HRB 143r–197r   2nd fo: *habebat maximam*

§§1–3, 5–208. Dedicated to Robert of Gloucester.

Rubrics at §110 (171r) 'Incipit prologus in prophetia Merlini', §111 (171r) 'Incipit prophetia Merlini'.

Book-divisions: II §23 (147v), IIII (*sic*) §35 (151v), V §73 (160v), VI §89 (165r). No mark at §54 where a book-division is often made.

The last two of the additional verses found in Douai, BM, 880 appear in this manuscript at the same points in the text (§§163 and 177). The poems are found in a scribal portion different from, and apparently later than, the main part of the text.

CONTENTS

1r: blank except for scribbles of varying date.

1v: in Early Modern hand, 'Gesta Dei per Francos' – notes in Latin.

2ra: 'Uersus Sibylle de die iudicii'. 'Iudiciique die tellus sudore madescet . . . Recidet e celo ignisque et sulphuris amnis.' Cf. Augustine, *De Ciuitate Dei*, XVIII.23. Walther, *Initia*, I.501, no. 9907.

2ra: 'De breui subsistentia hominis', by Hildebert of Le Mans. 'Dic homo responde quid homo sit . . . mortua non oritur.' Ed. Migne, *Patrologia Latina*, CLXXI.1442. Walther, *Initia*, I.219, no. 4364.

2rb: 'Epytaphium cuiusdam'. 'Tu prope qui transis nec dicis . . . Ut mecum maneat in regione poli.' Walther, *Initia*, I.1023, no. 19501.

2rb: contents-list, in same hand as preceding: 'Hec continentur in isto uolumine'. 'De gestis Francorum Iherusalem (*sic*) regnantium . . . Item hystoria Hibdeberti (*sic*) Cinomannensis episcopi de Mahumeth.' Added in similar manner: 'Item hystoria Troie. Item hystoria Britonum'.

2v: 'Incipit inuentum quod fert prouerbia centum'. 'Domino seruure (*sic*) est regnare . . . Qui Deum diligit uitam eternam habebit. Amen.'

3ra: short poem in Leonine hexameters. '[ ]Quicumque uelis mentem conjungere celis . . . Post fletum cordis fugit omnis mencio sordis.' Not in Schaller-Könsgen or Walther, *Initia*.

3va–35ra: 'Incipiunt gesta Francorum Iherusalem (*sic*) expugnantium', anon. 'Anno Dominice incarnationis millesimo nonagesimo sexto . . . presentium siue preteritorum facinorum prodigia erant.' *Recueil des Historiens des Croisades, Historiens occidentaux*, III.487–543.

35rb: verses on leaders of the Crusades. 'Uenerandus Podiensis Aymarus episcopus . . . urbe capta Salomonis optinent regalia.' *Recueil des Historiens des Croisades, Historiens occidentaux*, III.543. Walther, *Initia*, I.1053, no. 20071.

35v–48rb: preface and text of Fretellus's *Descriptio de situ locorum*. With dedication to bishop of Olomouc, not that printed by Migne, *Patrologia Latina*, CLV.1038. 'Reuerentissimo patri et domino .H. Dei gratia Olomacensium antisti . . . et adhuc tenet Dei gubernante gratia.'

48rb: short note. 'Beda in exposicione super euangelium Luce. De monumento Domini ferunt qui nostra etate de Iherosolimis (*sic*) Britanniam uenerunt . . . rubicundo et albo dicitur esse permixtus.'

48v–49rb: 'Lamentatio de secunda uia Ihrosolimitana (*sic*)'. 'Hierusalem luge medio dolor orbis in orbe . . . Gloria cum luctu teritur quasi flos sine fructu.' Printed by Migne, *Patrologia Latina*, CLV.1095–98. Walther, *Initia*, I.412, no. 8166.

49v: 'Episcopi Ihrosolimitani (*sic*) .xl. .iii.'. 'Iacobus filius Ioseph . . . Symeon'. After closing rubric are added Daimbertus, Furemarus (added interlinearly), Gybelus, Arnulfus, Warmundus, Stephanus, Willelmus, and Folcherus.

49 bis r: 'Nomina Regum Iudee', from Saul to Amalricus; 'Comites Edessani'; 'Comites Tripolitani'; 'Principes Antiocheni'; 'Principes Galilee'. Lists mostly end with mid twelfth-century incumbent: Joscelin II de Courtenay, Raymond II, Bohemond III, and William de Bure respectively, Bohemond being the exception (1154–88).

49 bis v: 'Descriptio parrochie sancte Dei ciuitatis Iherosolime (*sic*)', from 'Cesariensis uero', to 'Comibeddamon (*sic*)'.

50r/v: 'Genealogia francorum regum. Hec est genealogia regis Karoli qui uocatus est magnus . . . Philipus genuit Ludouicum'. In thirteenth-century hand, names of Louis's son, and grandson, Philip, added.

51ra/b: 'Descriptio sanctuarii quod in palatio imperatoris Constantinopolim habetur'.

'Hoc est sanctuarium quod in capella imperiali . . . quorum duorum in eadem urbe quiescunt corpora.'

51va: 'Quomodo formata epistola fiat'. 'Greca elementa litterarum numeros . . . qui secundum Greca elementa significat "amen".' Also found in Paris, BN lat. 14193 (Hauréau, *Initia*, III.19r).

51vb: Latin/Greek/Hebrew numbers and alphabet.

52ra: 'Epistola beati Iheronimi (*sic*) presbiteri ad Damasum episcopum urbis Rome'. 'Beatissimo pape Damaso Iheronimus . . . missa de Roma Iherosolimam.'

52ra–53va: list of popes from Peter to Urban III (1185–86), with two continuations – Gregory VIII (1187) to Innocent III (1198–1216) and Honorius III to Alexander IV (1254–61).

53vb–69rb: 'Incipit prefatio beati Iheronimi (*sic*) presbiteri in libro de uiris illustribus'. Followed by *capitula* and text, 'Hortaris dexter ut tranquillum sequens ecclesiasticos . . . et nec dum expleta sunt'.

69v–70rb: 'Iheronimus (*sic*) ad Desiderium de .xii. scriptoribus'. 'Vis nunc acriter tui frater Desideri . . . ideo quasi umbra secus homines sunt.'

70v–109ra: 'Historia Iherosolimitana (*sic*) domn<i> Fulcherii Carnotensis' (according to closing rubric), preceded by prologue. 'Placet equidem uiuis prodest etiam mortuis . . . regio illa remansit ualde infirma.' Ed. *Recueil des Historiens des Croisades, Historiens occidentaux*, III.321–485.

109rb–110r: letter of Aymeric, patriarch of Antioch, to Louis, king of France. 'Anno ab incarnatione Domini .m.c.lxiiii. missa est hec epistola . . . in cuius manu corda sunt regum. Amen.'

110r–112ra: 'Quomodo Tyrus ab Alexandro rege capta sit excerptum ex decem libris historie eiusdem'. 'Tyrus et magnitudine et claritate ante omnes urbes Syrie Phenicisque memorabilis . . . sub tutela Romane mansuetudinis adquiescit.'

112ra/vb: 'Item ex eisdem libris hystorie Alexandri; quomodo Gaza ab eodem rege capta sit'. 'Igitur Alexander urbem Gazam obsidione cinxerat . . . quam geminato periculo Alexandri regis.'

113r–125va: 'Historia Gilonis cardinalis episcopi de uia Iherosolimitana (*sic*)', in verse. 'Hactenus (crossed out) intentus leuibus puerilia dixi . . . Hec ego composui Gilo nomine Parisiensis incola Tutiaci non inficiandus alumnus.' Ed. *Recueil des Historiens des Croisades, Historiens occidentaux*, V.727–51.

125vb–127va: 'Incipit Phisiologus'. 'Tres leo naturas et tres habet inde figuras . . . Cui sinon alii placeant hec metra Tibaldi.' Ed. Migne, *Patrologia Latina*, CLXXI.1217–24.

127va: 'Quomodo ignis habeatur de sole', note on fire. 'Cum de sole ignem uolumus habere . . . Sic natura quod diffusa facere non potuit collecta superauit.'

127va/b: various poems. 'De equipollentia uirginitatis sancte Marie', by Hildebert. 'Sol cristallus aqua dant qualemcumque figuram . . . mens humilis thus est inflata superbia pus est.' Ed. Scott, *Hildeberti Cenomannensis Episcopi Carmina*, pp. 54–55. Walther, *Initia*, I.963, no. 18366.

128ra–134v: 'Hystoria Hildeberti episcopi Cinomannensis de Mahumet', by Embricon of Augsburg. 'Heu quot sunt stulti . . . musa manum teneat et Mahumet pereat.' Ed. Cambier, *Embricon*.

135r/va: lament on the death of Charles the Good. 'Proh dolor ducem Flandrie defensorem ecclesie . . . hoc sunt digni supplicio quibus placet proditio.' Ed. Migne, *Patrologia Latina*, CLXVI.1045–48. Walther, *Initia*, I.768, no. 14804.

136: ruled but blank except for pen-trials etc. and verse at foot of rb.

137r–140r: 'Prefacio hystorie Troiane'. 'Cornelius nepos Salustio Crispo salutem . . . Troia uero a Troio rege dicta est.' Ed. Meister, *Daretis Phrygii De Excidio Troiae Historia*. Part of text only.

140va/b: 'De septem miraculis mundi'. 'Primum miraculum est Rome saluatio . . . et super .lxiiii(or).cxxvii(or). columne finem facium.'

140vb–141rb: notes on the French attack on Jerusalem. 'Anno Dominice incarnationis millesimo .c.xii. . . . aput castrum basilicas pagi Suessonici nobiliter oriundus.'

142ra: verse on fall of Troy. 'Pergama flere uolo . . . occisos rides occubuisse uides.' Added in rather later hand. Printed by Hammer, 'Some Leonine summaries', pp. 121–22. Walther, *Initia* I.723, no. 13985.

143r–197v: HRB.

197va–198ra: poem beginning 'Hec Bernardus' as in Douai, BM, 880. Printed by Hammer, 'Some Leonine summaries', pp. 119–20. Walther, *Initia*, I.377, no. 7477.

DESCRIPTION

SIZE 24 x 16 cm.

QUIRING Signatures suggest three separate volumes. A – I^8 (fos 2–9), II–V^8, VI ?^{10} (fos 42–49, 49 bis, 50), VII ?^{10} (?lacks 3: 51–59), VIII–IX^8, X^8 (fos 76–77, 77 bis, 78–82), XI ?^{6} (83–88), XII–XVII^8; B – I ?^{4} (fos 137–140), II ?^{2} (140 bis–141); C – I^8 (fos 142–146, 146 bis, 147–148), II–V^8, 181–198 uncollatable from microfilm.

RULING Two columns generally, but some lists in three. Writing below top line. A – 41 written lines per page. B – 52 lines. C – 39 lines but 38 after fo 181.

SCRIPT Whole volume to 180v (end of fifth quire of HRB) in similar script; Proto-gothic minuscule approaching two-line proportions, cf. Douai 880. In parts A and B, round d and *et*-nota are standard; the script here would concord with the compilation date for the lists of the 1180s. HRB in heavy, set script employing straight d and final s rather than round forms, and ampersand, not *et*-nota. No e-caudata. Script after fo 181r of later appearance. Compact, small and black, ?of early thirteenth century. Round d standard, 8-shaped d but no juncture.

HISTORY

Ex-libris of Saint Rictrudis, Marchiennes (Benedictine, diocese of Cambrai-Arras), in all three units (fos 2–136, 137–141, 142–198) and on B and C probably in same hand of late thirteenth century. *Ex-libris* found on verso of fly-leaf, 3r ('Sancte Rictrudis liber est hic Marchianensis'), 141v ('Sancte Rictrudis est liber marchianen-sis per quem seruatus maneat benedictus at per quem raptus anathema sit et maledictus siue Rogerus ego amendo'), 198v ('Sancte Rictrudis est liber Marchianesis', re-peated).

BIBLIOGRAPHY
Dehaisnes, *Catalogue général*, VI.637–43.
Hammer, 'Some Leonine summaries'.

61 DUBLIN, TRINITY COLLEGE, MS. 172 (B.2.7.)

Saec. xiv   Mediaeval provenance: ?
i + 414 pages   2nd fo: [*tan*]-*tas uariarum necessitatum* (p. 11)

HRB pp. 84–194
§§1–3, 5–208 [§177 acephalous]. Dedicated to Robert of Gloucester.
No opening or closing rubrics. At §111 (p. 142) in margin 'Prophetie Merlini'.
No book-divisions.
Opening of §177 absent; begins 'Ut igitur infamia'.

CONTENTS
p. 1: blank except for fifteenth-century note (illegible on microfilm).
p. 2: top half blank. Below, 'Incipit [liber secundus (erased)] De contracto ad eius tumulum sanato'. Text breaks off at foot of page. '[R]ebus humanis exemptus quam potens fuerit in diuinis beatus Edwardus . . . sustinere. Recolens.'
pp. 3–5: moral/religious matter written in small cursive hand.
Illegible on microfilm (p. 5 is an inserted slip).
p. 6: verso of slip. ?Blank.
p. 7: contents-list (?*ca* 1400) giving titles of *uitae*; titles of the genealogy (of English and Scottish kings) and HRB added in different hand.
p. 8: blank.
pp. 9–20: 'Incipit uita sancti Thome martyris Cantuariensis ecclesie archiepiscopi'. 'Sacrosanctam ecclesiam iugiter impugnat hostis antiquus . . . qui solus est super omnia benedictus in secula. Amen.' *BHL* 8180. Ed. Migne, *Patrologia Latina*, CXC.195–208.
pp. 21–64: 'Incipit prologus dompni Aelredi abbatis Rieuall. in uitam sancti Edwardi regis et confessoris'. 'Multis ueterum studio fuisse didicimus illustrium uirorum . . . ad laudem et gloriam Domini nostri Iesu Christi cui est honor in secula seculorum. Amen.' *BHL* 2423. Ed. Migne, *Patrologia Latina*, CXCV.737–90.
pp. 64–84: 'Et incipit genealogia regum Anglie et regis Dauid Scocie'. 'Quoniam de moribus optimis religiosi regis Dauid Scocie . . . quod ministerio litterarum posteris transmutamus. Amen.'
pp. 84–194: HRB.
pp. 195–226: 'Incipit prologus in uitam sancti Eadmundi gloriosissimi Anglorum regis et martiris'. 'Domino sancte metropolitane Dorobernensium ecclesie archiepiscopo Dunstano . . . ariditate ad testimonium presumptionis permanente.' Abbo of Fleury, *Passio sancti Eadmundi. BHL* 2393. Ed. Winterbottom, *Three Lives*, pp. 65–87. See Dumville & Lapidge, *The Annals*, pp. lix–lx.
pp. 226–230: 'Incipit inuentio cum translatione sancti Ragenerii militis et martiris

consanguinei sancti Eadmundi regis et martiris'. 'Temporibus Deo dilecti regis Anglorum Edwardi filii Ethelredi . . . cuius temporibus reuelatio facta est obiit anno Christi millesimo sexagesimo sexto.' *BHL* 7054b.

pp. 230–239: 'Incipit uita et passio sanctissimi Freemundi (*sic*) regis et martiris sancti Eadmundi regis et martiris ex sorore nepotis a quodam clerico Burghardo nomine . . .'. 'Ad laudem Domini nostri Iesu Christi ego Burghardus litteris anglicis et latinis instructus . . . per eum qui uiuit regnat et imperat in secula seculorum. Amen.' *BHL* 3144b.

pp. 239–243: 'Incipit uita sanctissimi Rumwoldi pueri confessoris filii regis North-amhimbrorum et filie Pende regis Merciorum'. '[L]egitur quia Christi magnalia enarrare . . . auxilante Domino nostro Iesu Christo qui cum Patre et Spiritu Sancto in Trinitatis unitate uiuit et regnat Deus per omnia secula seculorum. Amen.' *BHL* 7385. Edd. de Smedt, Van Hooff, de Backer *et al.*, *Acta Sanctorum Novembris*, I.685–90.

pp. 243–252: 'Incipit uita et passio beatissimi regis Oswaldi martyris a paganis interfecti'. 'Interfecto in pugna nobilissimo rege Eadwino . . . et regnat pro immortalia secula seculorum. Amen.'

pp. 253–259: 'Incipit uita sancte et Deo dilectissime Werburge uirginis'. '[F]ilia regum et sponsa Christi decentissima uirgo Werburga in Cestra ciuitate requiescit . . . Annuat inquam ipse saluator qui cum Patre et Spiritu Sancto in omnia secula regnat et dominatur. Amen.' *BHL* 8855. Ed. Migne, *Patrologia Latina*, CLV.97–110. See Rollason, *The Mildrith Legend*, pp. 26–27.

pp. 259–275: 'Incipit uita sancte Aetheldrethe uirginis .ix. kl. Iulii'. '[B]eata et gloriosa uirgo Etheldretha nobilissimis parentibus orta . . . Cui laus atque decus honor et pax gloria uirtus. Amen.' *Uita* and miracles (miracles beginning on p. 64, *BHL* 2638).

pp. 276–288: 'Incipit prologus in uitam sancte Mildrethe uirginis'. '[D]iuinus inter-pres Ieronimus Iob secundo transferens . . . diuina manus succurrisset . At prouida . . .' Ends imperfectly at top of page. *BHL* 5960. See Rollason, *The Mildrith Legend*, pp. 20–21.

pp. 289–316: 'Incipit epistola magistri Petri Blesensis ad dompnum Henricum abba-tum Croilandie de uita beati Guthlaci'. '[R]euerentissimo patri et domino dompno Henrico abbati Croilandie Petrus Blesensis Bathoniensis archidiaconus salutem . . . cui sit honor et gloria in secula seculorum. Amen.' *BHL* 3728.

pp. 317–334: 'Incipit prologus in uitam sancti Egwini episcopi et confessoris'. '[D]iuinorum series et altitudo mysteriorum quanto sepius recitatur . . . qui in sanctis suis est benedictus in secula. Amen.' *BHL* 2433.

pp. 334–343: 'Incipit uita sancti Uulganii heremite et confessoris'. '[ ]gitur gloriosus Christi confessor Uulganius de Christianissima Anglorum gente editus est . . . per omnia secula seculorum. Amen. Amen.' *BHL* 8746.

p. 344: blank.

pp. 345–381: 'Cum diabolus pronus et sollicitus humani generis inimicus intrasset in cor Iohannis . . . a Deo beneficia graciosa. Cui sit honor et gloria in secula seculorum. Amen'. *BHL* 3976.

pp. 381–394: 'Incipiunt miracula que in diuersis locis fiebant post mortem beati Honorati'. 'Translato igitur sanctissimo Honorato ad societatem ciuium supernorum

. . . Richus attamen eo anno conuersans plurimi in Domino religiose obdormiuit.' *BHL* 3976.

pp. 394–398: 'Postquam Karolus in sancta et uenerabili senectute migrauerat ab hac uita . . . et monasterii Lyrinensis interitum et ruinam'. *BHL* 3976.

pp. 399–400: blank.

p. 401: column written in informal hand (account of clash in France between clerics and townspeople).

p. 402 a/b: in documentary hand of ?later fourteenth century, brief description of progress of events from the beginning of the world to Charlemagne and his successors until the false prophet. 'Qant dieux establi le mond a durer .uii. anz . . . per lespeye.'

p. 402 b: twelve lines in different but similar hand. 'Cambria Carnaruan Angliis natus dabit Ag[ ] . . . in superis premium percepto fine tenebit.'

pp. 403–405: various prophecies in hand similar to that on p. 402.

p. 403a: 'Iste sunt prophetie diuerse a diuersis prophetante de sexto Hibernie qui uocatur dominus'. 'Rex Anglie et Francie et sextus dominus Hibernie . . . Sed prima causa sibi promissa remanebit.'

p. 403a: 'Item uersus illius sompniatoris uiri religiosi per quos uersus cognoscitur sextus Hibernie'. 'Illius imperium gens barbara senciet illum . . . Plus dabit hic orbi quam dabit orbis ei.'

p. 403a/b: 'Uersus uaticinales de Normannia de eodem sexto'. 'Anglia transmittet leopardi lilia galli . . . Imperium mundi sub quo dabit hic heremita.'

p. 403b: 'Uersus cuiusdam nomine Gildas per quantum tempus regnabit idem sextus'. 'Ter tria lustra tenent cum semi tempore sexti . . . Huic terram spernens sancto (*sic*) ethere scandit'.

p. 403b–404a: Vision of St Thomas of Canterbury. 'Quando ego Thomas Cantuariensis archiepiscopus exul ab Anglia . . . in quodam uase plumbeo, etc.'

p. 404a–405a: 'Hec prophecia Merlini Siluestris Anglorum regi Edwardo secundo huius nominis tercio reuelata est per spiritum sub testimonio duorum sanctorum'. 'Sicut rubeum draconem . . . multa prelia erunt in mundo fidei legum et in[ ]ciones erunt.'

p. 405a: added in informal hand. 'Solis in occasu leopardi . . . usque diem.'

p. 405b: 'Lilium in meliori parte manebit et ueniet in terram leonis . . . et transibit in terram promissionis'. Prophecy of the Lily, the Lion and the Son of Man: see Ward, *apud* Ward & Herbert, *Catalogue of Romances*, I.314.

p. 405b: 'Hec sequens prophecia Rome fuit [inuenta]'. 'Cesaris imperium per tempora longa patebit . . . Dignus erit pica ceteris erit hec [ ]ca.' Walther, *Initia*, I.116, no. 2307.

405b: 'Tolle capud milia cancri ter simule fiet . . . solis et lune bell[ ] sunt primitiue'.

p. 406: blank.

p. 407–414a: prophecy of John of Bridlington. 'Febribus infectus requies fuerat michi lectus . . . Ad mortem tendo morti mea carmina pendo.' Walther, *Initia*, I.316, no. 6296. Ed. Wright, *Political Poems*, I.128–211.

p. 414: 'Sex septem et ter decem si tranfieris (*sic*) ad Bethleem . . . dux gregis in Achonia'.

p. 414r: 'Regere clam cupiunt telluris regia apri . . .'

p. 414b: two other prophecies (illegible). 'Prophecia tradita beato Eadmundo de

Pontiniac[ ] per beatam uirginem Mariam' (two lines). 'H. patre defuncto reget . . . E. postea mira.' Edmond of Pontigny.
'Uersus sequentes composuit quidem spiritus ut dicitur.' 'Anno [ ]ephas mille canus catulus et cocadrille . . . ' Walther, *Initia*, I.58, no. 1128. Also in Cambridge, University Library, MS. Kk.6.16.

DESCRIPTION
QUIRING Some catchwords. Text and quiring frequently coincide, resulting in some irregularly sized quires. I ?^{8} (+ 2 after 1: pp. 1–20), II–III^8, IV^8 (pp. 53–68), V–XI^8, XII^8 (8 canc.: pp. 181–194), XIII–XV^8, XVI^6 (6 canc.: pp. 243–252), XVII–XVIII^8, XIX^2 (pp. 285–288), XX–XXII^8, XXIII ?^{6} (5–6 canc.: pp. 337–344), XXIV–XXV^8, XXVI^8 (pp. 377–392), quiring of pp. 393–414 not reconstructable from microfilm.
PRICKING Not visible on microfilm.
RULING Single column of 35 lines for main text. Written below top ruled line, double vertical boundary-lines, frame of double line running along top, foot and outer margins (to p. 344). Ruling irregular in added sections at ends.
SCRIPT Formal Gothic bookhand in at least one hand. Two-line proportions, tops of ascenders cleft. Juncture of **e** and **o** after **b**, **d**, and **p**, and occasionally **h**. **t** pierced, **a** has two-compartment form. Diagonal hairlines on **i** but otherwise few. **h** and round **r** trail slightly below line. Script of additions in several English hands, apparently somewhat later than the main text, using long **r**, curled **e**. Varying degree of formality. Some hands disciplined with light minims and heavy vertical strokes, as well as some angularity in the bowl of **d**.
DECORATION Minor capitals have elaborate filigree inside the letter with long trailing lines in the margin. Other capitals blocked out in colour with ivy-leaf decoration. Some historiated initials.

HISTORY
Ker rejected St Peter's, Westminster, as the provenance of this manuscript: *Medieval Libraries*, p. 197.

BIBLIOGRAPHY
Abbott, *Catalogue*, p. 22.

62 DUBLIN, TRINITY COLLEGE, MS. 493 (E.2.24)

Saec. xiii$^{2/ex.}$ Mediaeval provenance:
ii + 121 + i fos   2nd fo: *est ab Italia*

HRB 1ra–74ra
§§1–3, 5–208. Dedicated to Robert of Gloucester.
Rubrics at §1 (1ra) 'Incipit prephacio (*sic*) Galfridi Monumetensis ad Robertum comitem Claudiocestrie de hystoria Britonum a tempore Bruti primo rege Britonum usque ad tempus Cadawaladri (*sic*) filii Cadewallonis (*sic*)', §5 (1rb) 'De discripcione

(*sic*) Britannie', after §208 (74ra) 'Explicit liber Bruti quem Galfridus Monemutensis transtulit de britannico sermone in Latinum'. No book-divisions. Chapters numbered to §110 ('116').

Numerous marginalia.

At top of column following the end of HRB (74rb), in similar script (perhaps in red): 'Qui prolixitatem de regibus Britonum desiderat librum grandem Galfridi Arturi quem magister Henricus Huntedonensis archidiaconus apud Beccum inuenit querat ubi predicta diligenter et prolixe tractata'. This is a reworking of the end of Henry of Huntingdon's *Epistola ad Warinum*: ed. Howlett, *Chronicles*, IV.75 (*ex. inf.* Neil Wright).

Prophecies double-spaced but no commentary written.

CONTENTS
i–ii: cut from larger sheet written in formal large textura (inside of bifolium blank) with script now running vertically. Devotional text.
1ra–74ra: HRB.
74v: blank, not ruled.

75r–121vb: 'Incipit prologus de gestis Francorum'. 'Cum animaduerterem quam plurimos et fere omnes homines de gestis regum Francorum dubitare . . . occasionem dicens quod nisi treuga.' Mutilated at end but probably finished near top of 121vb. Nothing legible after the end of 121va. Part printed by de Wailly, 'Examen', pp. 403–5.
iii: as i–ii. Recto blank.

DESCRIPTION
QUIRING Two codicologically distinct units, in separate, but similar, hands. a², ?I–VIII⁸, ??IX¹² (?lacks 11–12: fos 65–74); X–XII¹², XIII ?¹² (?lacks 12, + 1 after 11: 111–121 + iii).
PRICKING Outer margin only.
RULING Two columns of 40 lines, written below top ruled line. Single vertical boundary-lines sometimes with double line ruled in side margins. B – similar with 41 lines, except for 75r/v which is single-column.
SCRIPT Gothic bookhand. Compressed, short ascenders, heavy strokes, minims not broken. t pierced, a generally two-compartment, final round s, crossed *et*-nota. Juncture of e and o after d. In one hand ascenders have flat tops, and straight-backed d is common.
B – similar to that of HRB but aspect more bristly, tall final s usual (round form occurs) and e and o are close to juncture after b, h, and p, as well as d. Ascender of round d sometimes trails to left. Some ascenders are tagged.
DECORATION HRB – unfiligreed capitals. More than one colour. B – filigreed initials.

HISTORY
Note in ?fourteenth-century hand on ii v 'Brutus cum gestis Francorum' suggests that the two parts of the volume were connected at an early date. 'John Crane' written in

sixteenth-century hand on several folios (ii r, 120v, 121v). On 121v it is found with the names ?Deryke ffrennyngham? and Edmund Tylney, written in the same hand.

BIBLIOGRAPHY
Abbott, *Catalogue*, p. 73.

63   DUBLIN, TRINITY COLLEGE, MS. 494 (E.5.7)

Saec. xii/xiii or xiii *in.*   Mediaeval provenance: ?
120 fos   2nd fo: *Lauinie eamque*

HRB 1r–76v
§§1–3, 5–110, 118–204 'Alanum Salomonis nepote et ab illo'. Dedicated to Robert of Gloucester ('Odbert<us> dux Glaurenie').
Rubrics at §1 (1r) 'Incipit editio G\a/ufredi Arturi Monumetensis de gestis Britonum', §5 (1r) 'Laus Britanie', §110 (43v) 'Prologus'.
Text dislocated at end. Fos 75–76 (§190 'conuentionem sua'–195 'toti Gallie non minimum') should follow 72v (ends §190 'possideret cum autem'). Text on 73r follows from 76v. No loss.

CONTENTS
1r–76v: HRB.
77ra–112ra: Vision of the monk of Eynsham (seen in 1196). 'Usu notissimum habetur quod diem terris sole post tenebras noctium reportante paulatim . . . honor potestas uirtus et magnificentia regnumque et imperium in secula seculorum. Amen.' Ed. Salter, *Eynsham Cartulary*, II.285–371. (This manuscript not listed by Salter.)
112v–113v: blank, ruled.

114r–120v: '[ ]ncipiunt ysagoge Porphirii ad predicamenta Aristotil[is]'. 'Huius tituli inscriptio nouit ad quid sit [ ] operis . . . nam neque ergo etc. Q. differre non recipiant magis et minus talis est ro..' ?Commentary on the Latin translation of the Greek.

DESCRIPTION
QUIRING Some catchwords. ?I–V⁸, quiring of fos 41–120 not reconstructable from microfilm.
PRICKING ?Trimmed away.
RULING HRB – single column of 27 lines, written above top ruled line, single vertical boundary-lines. *Visio* – two columns of 33 lines, written above top ruled line. *Ysagoge* – single column of 42 lines.
SCRIPT Beginning of HRB in strange disjointed script. No shading, descenders do not taper or end in tick or foot. Some ascenders have flat top. Final s tall. *Et*-nota crossed. Round s found in abbreviations. Some Insular abbreviations: .H. used for *enim* and dotted u for ut. Appearance of similar script (uncrossed *et*-nota) in Visio indicates that it must postdate 1196. Several other hands in HRB. All use final tall s but have more lateral compression. Crossed or uncrossed *et*-nota used. **de** compen-

dium found, as also fused **de** and **do** sometimes. *Ysagoge* – small, laterally compressed script. **a** has no head. *et*-nota, round **d** usual, but ampersand and straight-backed **d** found. Final **s** tall or round. Insular *enim* and *est* compendia used.

DECORATION Romanesque capitals in HRB and *Visio*. No capitals completed in *Ysagoge*.

BIBLIOGRAPHY
Abbott, *Catalogue*, p. 73.

64 DUBLIN, TRINITY COLLEGE, MS. 495 (E.4.30)

Saec. *xiv* (post$^{1/4}$)   Origin: ?Britain
125 fos   2nd fo: *propter tria castella* (2r)
                                      ?Originally 1r: [ ]*ibus Pictis et Scotis*

HRB 1r–111v
§5 '[ ]ibus Pictis et Scotis'–§208. Dedicatory section lost.
Rubric after §208 (111v) 'Et hec dicta sufficiunt per Dominum nostrum Iesum Christum. Explicit Brutus'.
No book-divisions.

CONTENTS
1r–111v: HRB (acephalous).
111v: notes recording extent of kingdoms of Deira, Bernicia, Northumbria and Mercia etc. with date 1343 (or 1346?). Printed by Dumville, 'Anecdota'.
112r–123v: sermon on purgatory.'[ ]n omnibus operibus tuis memorare nouissima tua et in eternum non peccabis.' '[ ] ses tres ?chers freres et soeurs en Dieu a tantz yoeux . . . de ceo nous defender Dieu. Amen.'
124–125: two flyleaves. Apparently taken from fourteenth-century account. Verso of first leaf and recto of second blank.

DESCRIPTION
QUIRING I^{12} (lacks 1: fos 1–11), II–IX^{12}, X^{12} (5–12 lacking: fos 108–111), XI ?^{12} (fos 112–123), b^2 (fos 124–125). Signatures on first recto of II–X.
PRICKING Trimmed away?
RULING HRB – none visible but single column of 27–31 folios written. 112–123 written in single column of 25–28 lines. Double outer boundary-lines on some folios. Written below top ruled line.
SCRIPT HRB in several Anglicana hands. Long **r** with little shoulder, simple unlooped form of **e**, crossed *et*-nota, 8-shaped **g**, looped two-compartment **a** throughout. Tops of ascenders angled down to the right; ascenders of majuscule letters sometimes split. Height of **a** and sigma-shaped **s** above other letters varies with hand. Sermon perhaps later. More florid version of documentary script. Tapering descenders, flourishes on tail of **y**, other hairlines. Thick uprights. Looped **d**, unlooped **e**. 2-shaped **r** descends below line. Long **r**. Ascenders turn down at right. *Et*-nota crossed.

DECORATION   None. In sermon, larger version of the same script used for rubrics.

BIBLIOGRAPHY
Abbott, *Catalogue*, p. 73.

65 DUBLIN, TRINITY COLLEGE, MS. 496 (E.6.2)

Saec. xiv[1]   Mediaeval dedication: Wymondham, Norfolk (Benedictine)
234 fos (229 foliated)   2nd fo: [*Leodi*]-*cen. .c. aieccenn. monasterien. Muricen.*

HRB 9r–123v
§§1–3, 5–208. Dedicated to Robert of Gloucester.
Rubrics at §6 (10r) 'De aduentu Enee in Italiam et natiuitat[e] Bruti', §110 (64v) 'Prologus de profeciis Merlini', §111 (65r) 'Incipiunt prophecie Merlini', §118 (71v) 'Expliciunt prophetie . . .', after §208 (123v) 'Explicit', and (124r) 'Explicit hic Bruti de gestis iste libellus cuius uirtuti congaudeat anglica tellus'. Rubrics at many chapter-divisions.
No book-divisions.
Prophecies glossed; glosses printed by Hammer, 'An unedited commentary'.

CONTENTS
1r–7r: acephalous. List of metropolitans and other ecclesiastical offices in western Europe (legible from 1v 'Sclavonia' and 'Hungaria' to 3r 'Scocia' 'Hybernia') then in Antioch and the East. Compare Miraeus, *Notitia episcopatuum*, pp. 65–91.
Ends with list of European kings.
7v–8v: in different hand, on Ages of the World. 'Prima etas ab Adam usque ad Noe; secunda a Noe usque ad Abraham . . . et in septima ueniet manifestus et indicaturus.'
9r–123v: HRB.
124r–125r: 'De Stephano rego set melius de ipso cau[ ]ur in exposiccione Merlini'. Notes on twelfth- and thirteenth-century kings from Stephen.
'Stephanus filius comitis Blesensis qui fuit affinis Willelmi Rufi regnauit .xviii. annis . . . .' Ends with note of death of Simon de Montfort at Battle of Evesham.
125v–126r: reckonings mentioning foundation of Wymondham. 'Anno ab origine mundi .vi.(m).D.ix. Ab incarnacione Domini .m.ccc.x. . . . A prima christianitate in Anglia .m.c.xl.vii..'
126v: notes on foundations of religious orders added underneath in different ink, similar hand. 'Dccccxii. incepit (*sic*) ordo Cluniacensis . . . .mccxxx. transiit sanctus Benedictus.'

127r: blank.
127v–128r: diagram 'Situs Anglie cum suis prouinciis et episcopatibus'. Circle enclosing six-petalled figure. Each section describes the early kings and the location of the bishoprics of one region.
128r–134r: account of English kings to Edward I accompanied by genealogical

diagram. 'Iste Britrichus regnauit in Westsex qui fuit unus ex quinque regibus . . . et uocatus est Eadwardus qui successit patri suo in regn[um].'

134v–137r: poem in praise of Edward I. 'Gesta regis cupio Edwardi referre quem scimus ab omnibus regibus differre . . . deprecor ut Dominus sibi prestet regna polorum.' Accompanied by line drawings of animals etc.

137v: another genealogical diagram (incomplete) describing children of Edward I.

138r/v: blank.

139r–161r: commentary on Geoffrey's *Prophetie Merlini*. '[Cir]ca prophetie presentes exposicionem uidelicet Ambrosii Merlini siue uatis Ambrosii . . . Truncabit namque maiora robora minoribus uero tutelam prestabit.' Ed. Hammer, 'An unedited commentary', pp. 82–88. See Eckhardt, *The Prophetia Merlini*, p. 12(–13), n. 44.

161, 161*, 162–164: blank except for a few brief notes (see below, HISTORY).

165r–177v: 'Breuis recapitulacio regum Cantuariorum' and similar accounts for East and West Saxons. 'Anno Dominice incarnacionis .cccc.xlix. secundum cronica Anglorum antiquissima Horsus frater . . . in uilla regia que Middeltune d[ ] edificauit.'

177v–179r: 'De quodam miraculo sancti Edwardi confessoris'. 'Anno gratie .m.lxvi. quamuis rex Edwardus secularibus curis multum esset occupatus . . . non siue lacrimis plangebatur amarissime.'

179r/v: 'De Woden et eius genealogia'. 'Anglorum siue Saxonum cum Britonibus hucusque altercacionibus prosecutis restat nunc . . . qui fuit Adam qui fuit Dei.'

179v–180v: 'Ut ex .v. filiis Uoden reges Anglorum originem habuerunt'. 'Iste igitur Woden .vii. filios legitur procreasse . . . sed uarias genologias (*sic*) admittunt.'

181r–188r: 'Anno Domini .m.cc.lxxi. dominus Henr. de Alemania interfectus est audiendo missam in ecclesia sancti Nicolai . . . anno Domini .m.ccc. septimo anno regni regis Edwardi .xxxv.'.

188v–190, 190*, 191, 191*: blank.

192r–215r: 'Anno Cesaris Octauiani Augusti .xl.ii. ebdomado iuxta Danielis prophetiam . . . et pre nimia angustia nouiter geniti'. Chronology of events in early Christian history.

215r–223v: 'Incipiunt descripciones quedam de sitibus ciuitatum et locorum circa Ierusalem'. 'Descripsi breuiter fines situsque locorum pagina sacra . . . studio temporare satagas.' Bede, *De Locis Sanctis*. Ed. Fraipont *apud* Geyer *et al., Itineraria*, pp. 251–80.

224r–225r: names of Norman nobles and noble families (in informal hand). 'Maundeuile . . . [G]atesdene e Munguinerey.'

225v and following folio (unnumbered) blank.

226r–227v: *Mirabilia Britannie*. 'Primum miraculum est stangnum iumonium (*sic*) . . . [ ] lapides'. Ed. Dumville, 'Anecdota'.

227v: 'Tres filii Noe diuiserunt orbem in tres partes . . . Uenedochia id est North Wales [ ]'. Ed. Dumville, *ibid*. This and the previous item found also in Cambridge, Sidney Sussex College, MS. 75, Oxford, Bodleian, MS. Oriel 16 and Madrid, Biblioteca Nacional, MS. 6319.

227v–229r: *Uaticinum* (*sic*) *Merlini Scoti* (according to final rubric). 'Catulus leonis in lup[ ] conuertetur . . . iacet in foresta de [ ]annerie.'

229v and following folio blank.

DESCRIPTION

QUIRING Some catchwords. Conjectural reconstruction from microfilm – I ?⁸ (1–8), ?II–IV ?¹², V–VII¹², VIII ?¹² (83–94), fos 95–122 uncollatable; IX ?¹² (127–138); 139–164 uncollatable, X–XI¹², 189–191 ?⁶ (lacks ?6); XII ?¹², XII–XIII⁸, XIV ?⁶ (220–225), XV ?⁶ (unnumbered blank, 226–229, unnumbered blank).

PRICKING Visible in outer margin.

RULING HRB single column of 29 lines. Single vertical boundary-lines. Written below top ruled line. Ruling of rest of volume very variable, even within text. Often 26 or 32 lines.

SCRIPT HRB in shaded Anglicana. Thick, tapering descenders; ascenders turn over to right at top. Looped **d** and two-compartment **a**, crossed *et*-nota. Cursive **r** does not descend below the line. Final long s usual but sigma-form found in all positions. Rest of volume except for 127–138 and 192–223 written in similar script, several hands. Split ascenders occasionally found; final tall s usual, short **r**. Four-line proportions. 127–138 written in smaller, more formal script. Thick pen considering smallness of script. Crossed *et*-nota, two-compartment **a** sometimes constructed of two straight strokes. No juncture. Final s tall. Minims not broken. 192–223 in bookhand similarly with tall final s but juncture of **e** and **o** after **b, d, h**, and **p**. Change of hand at *De Situ* but similar usages continue.

DECORATION Unfiligreed capitals.

HISTORY

Reckonings on 125v–126v indicate East Anglian origin, perhaps Wymondham, Norfolk. On fo 164 'Obutus (*sic*) Anablinae ni Kyrnan ionoti et? Kyniani filia ac Iohannis Edmundi Lynche uxor eius anima propicietur Deus amen anno Domini 1573 die uero mensis Iunii 13.o'. There were Kenians in Westmeath in the seventeenth century. This volume was not listed by Ker, *Medieval Libraries*.

BIBLIOGRAPHY

Abbott, *Catalogue*, p. 74.
Hammer, 'An unedited commentary', pp. 81–89.

66 DUBLIN, TRINITY COLLEGE, MS. 514 (E.5.3)

Saec. xiv   Mediaeval provenance: St Augustine's Abbey,
                                                                    Canterbury (Benedictine)

254 + ii fos (+ 92*)   2nd fo: *Telamon primus opidum*

HRB 15r–77r

§§1–3, 5–184, 186–208 [with *Merlinus iste* passage after §110, 51r]. Dedicated to Robert of Gloucester.

Rubrics at §1 (15r) 'Incipit prologus Galfridi Monemitensis in sequenti hystoria', at §5 (15r) 'Descriptio britannice insule. Primum capitulum', §109 (49r) 'Prefacio hystorie et epistola de interpretacione propheciarum Merlini', §111 (49v) 'Prophetie Merlini ex mistica pugna draconum', after §117 (51r) 'Explicit Merlinus', after §208 (77r) 'Hic explicit historia Britonum'.

Rubrics at many chapter-divisions.

Book-divisions: II §54 (30v), III §98 (45r), IV §143 (60v).

Commentary on Prophecies (unedited): Eckhardt, *The Prophetia Merlini*, p. 13 & n. 45.

Second Variant Version. Hammer's siglum D: Emanuel, 'Geoffrey of Monmouth's *Historia*', p. 104.

CONTENTS

1r: not shown on film – blank.

1v–2r: closely written in informal fourteenth-century hand (illegible). Title, 'Littera consolator[ ] de morte'.

2v: fourteenth-century contents-list recording present contents. *De professione monachorum* follows HRB according to original hand. Material now separating them listed separately (underneath) in different hand but of similar date.

Underneath, text continued from recto.

3r–14r: 'Incipit epistola Cornelii ad Salustium Crispum in Troianorum historia quem Greco a Darete historiographo facta est'. 'Cornelius Salustio Crispo suo salutem . . . Palamonem Epistrophum Scidium.' Ed. Meister, *Daretis Phrygii De Excidio Troiae Historia*.

Ends at top of 14r, Rest of folio blank.

15r–77r: HRB.

77r/v: in different, more informal, later-looking hand. '[ ]n ciuitate romana sunt quinque ecclesie que patriarchales dicuntur . . . Diaconus cardinalis sancte Agathe. Diaconus car-.' *Liber prouincialis*, truncated at end. Cf. Miraeus, *Notitia episcopatuum*, pp. 65–91.

78r/v: 'Prophetie aquile que reportaui de domo Glasconie'. 'Arbor fertilis a primo trunco decisa . . . qui pacificato regno occidet.' Ed. Schulz, *Gottfried*, pp. 463–65.

79r: 'Arbor fertilis a primo trunco etc . . . quo hec expleantur expectet'. Brief commentary on preceding text.

79v–89r: 'Expo[sicion]es prophecie Merlini' (late mediaeval title). 'Sedente itaque Uortigerno rege Britonum super ripam . . . confligent uenti diro sufflamine et sonitum inter sidera conficient.' Geoffrey of Monmouth, HRB, §§111–117, with commentary.

89r: on Welsh place-names. 'Uallis fluuius super angl. mons Snowdonne . . .'

89v: 'Niueus quoque senex etc. id est legatus cum potencia . . . salutem Maioris Britannie, etc.'.

89v–92v: 'Incipit prophetia sibille'. 'Sibille generaliter dicuntur omnes femine prophetantes . . . Et ipsi regnabunt cum illo in secula seculorum. Amen. Amen.' Ed. Sackur, *Sibyllinische Texte*, pp. 177–87.

92*: blank, ruled (unfoliated.)

93r–116v: ?later hand. 'Tractatus iste qui est de professione monachorum tres habet partes.' 'In prima forma professionis monachorum professionis declaratur . . . qui autem requirunt Dominum animauertunt omnia benedictus Deus.'

117r–137v: 'Incipit sinonima Ysidori Yspaniensis archiepiscopi'. 'Uenit nuper ad manus meas quedam scedula . . . supra uitam meam places.' Ed. Migne, *Patrologia Latina*, LXXXIII.827–868.

138r–146r: 'Incipit Leo papa de conflictu uiciorum atque uirtutum', by Ambrosius Autpertus. 'Apostolica uox clamat per orbem . . . Tu autem homo Dei studio actende que dico.' Bloomfield, *Incipits*, pp. 52–53, no. 0455. Ed. Migne, Patrologia Latina, XVII.1057–74; XL.1091–1103; LXXXIII.1131–44; CXLIII.559–75.

146v–161r: 'Incipit liber florum collectus et continuatus de diuersis libris summi et comp[]alis doctoris Augustini . . .'. 'Da mihi Domine scire et intelligere quis sit . . . Te prestante. Qui uiuis Deus per omnia s. s. Amen.'

162r–165v: 'Incipit dissuasio Ualeriani ad Ruffinum de uxore ducenda'. 'Loqui prohibeor et tacere non possum . . . sed ne Horesten (*sic*) scripsisse uidear. Uale.' Edd. & transl. James *et al.*, Walther Map: *De Nugis Curialium*, pp. 288–313.

165v–178v: 'Incipit speculum spiritualis amicitie'. 'Primum quid sit amicicia arbitror disserendum ne uideamur inaniter pingere . . . et misericordie iudicem intercedat' (also found in Oxford, St John's College, MS. 190).

178v–182r: written closely in informal fourteenth-century hand (cf. flyleaves at end). Latin, of devotional nature.

183r–204v: 'Incipit tractatus domini pape Innocencii de contemptu mundi'.'Domino et patri karissimo Petro Dei gratia Portuensi episcopo . . . Discedite a me maligni in ignem' (truncated). Ed. Maccarrone, *Lotharii cardinalis (Innocentii III) de miseria*.

205r–254v: 'Seneca de naturalibus questionibus'. 'Grandinem hoc modo fieri si tibi affirmauero . . . nec enim flumini dulcior gustus.' Beginning at Book IVb. Ed. Gercke, *L. Annaei Senecae naturalium quaestionum*, pp. 160–.
Two flyleaves closely written in Latin, pious/devotional material (cf. after 178).

DESCRIPTION

QUIRING Catchwords as far as quire XI. Also signature .i. at foot of 212v. a^2, I^{12} (fos 3–14), II^{12} (11–12 canc.: fos 15–24), III–V^{12}, VI–VII^8, VIII singleton (remainder of larger quire: fo 77); IX^{12} (78–89), X^4 (90–92, blank leaf); XI–XVII^{12}, XVIII^4 (177–180), fos 181–182 ?singletons, XIX^{12}, XX^{12} (11–12 canc.: fos 195–204), XXI–XXII^8, XXIII^8 (221–228), XXIV^8 (+ 1 before 1: 229–237), XXV^8, XXVI ?^{10} (1 lacking: fos 246–254)^b.

PRICKING Mostly trimmed away but visible in outer margin of fos 78–92 and in Seneca (fos 205–254).

RULING HRB and Dares in single column, 35/36 lines, written below top ruled line, single vertical boundary-lines. Majority of rest of volume with similar layout, 35–39 lines. Final item (thirteenth-century, Seneca) also in single column of 38/39 lines, but written above top ruled line, and double vertical boundary-lines.

SCRIPT HRB and Dares (also 93–115) in formal version of cursive with long, leftward-turning descenders on f, s etc. Written with thick nib. Crossed *et*-nota. Round d almost two-line or with long ascender. Final s round. Juncture of e and o after b, d, h, p. a has two-compartment or Caroline form. Liber *prouincialis* in monoline fourteenth-century cursive. Prophecies in Anglicana with looped ascenders, thick uprights, crossed *et*-nota, simple minuscule e. 116–182 – formal textura. Juncture of e and o after d, h, and p. Several hands. 183–204 – informal Gothic bookhand with looped two-compartment a, crossed *et*-nota; some juncture (not usually after o), flat top on double l. The Seneca (205–254) is the earliest part of the volume. Small, thirteenth-century four-line script. Small headed a; no real juncture.

DECORATION Capitals with simple filigree.

HISTORY

Recorded in catalogue of St Augustine's, Canterbury, as gift of John de London: Ker, *Medieval Libraries*, pp. 42, 244. This identification confirmed by *ex-libris* written in same fourteenth-century Anglicana hand as the contents-list on 2v which it precedes, 'Liber Iohannis de Lond[ ] de [ ] continentur'.

BIBLIOGRAPHY

Abbott, *Catalogue*, pp. 77–78.

67 DUBLIN, TRINITY COLLEGE, MS. 515 (E.5.12)

Saec. xiii/xiv   Mediaeval provenance: ?Wales
69 fos   2nd fo: *locutionem et comedendi*
                                 2nd fo (13r): [*Hecu*]-*ba et liberis*

HRB 21rb–65va

§§5–108, 111–208. Dedication absent.

Rubrics at §5 (21rb) 'Incipit hystoria Britonum a Galfrido Arturo Monemut\h/ensi de britannica lingua in Latinum translata', after §208 (65va) 'Explicit' and, added in secretary-hand, 'historia Britonum'.

No book-divisions marked but initials at §§5, 6, 23, 54, 90, 98, 111, 116 'Tres fontes', 118, 143, 163.

First Variant Version. Wright's siglum D. Marginalia show collation against another First Variant text: Wright, *The Historia Regum Britannie of Geoffrey of Monmouth*, *II*, pp. lxxx–lxxxii.

CONTENTS

1r: diagram of tree of knowledge.

1v–3r: 'Compendiosus extractus de epistola Aristotilis ad Alexandrum de conser[ ] sanitatis et dispo[sitio]ne regni' (rubric at top of page in informal hand). 'Domine .T. gratia uero regine Yspanie Iohannes Yspanie salutem . . . cogitaciones pessimas et tristissimas frequentes habere.'

3r/v: 'Prophetia aquile Sephtonie' (double-spaced). '[S]icut rubeum draconem albus expellet . . . qui pacificato regno occidit.' Ed. Schulz, *Gottfried*, pp. 464–65.

4: blank leaf.

5r–7v: acephalous. 'est pastor Admeti . . . Sed ne Horestem scripsisse uidear. Uale.'
Walter Map, *Dissuasio Ualeriani ad Ruffinum de uxore ducenda*. Edd. & transl. James
et al., Walter Map: *De Nugis Curialium*, pp. 288–313.
?8–9: blank.

10r/vb: 'Incipit genealogia ueterum uirorum ab Adam usque ad Brutum successiue
descendentium hoc modo. Adam pater generis humani genuit Seth . . . id est a Bruto
usque ad Cadwaladrum.' Also in Exeter Cathedral, MS. 3514.
10vb–11ra: genealogy of the Trojans. '[C]yprius quidam filius Yawan in Cypro insula
primo regnauit . . . a Britonibus Psedeyn nominatur.' Also found in Exeter 3514 and
Cardiff 2.611.
11rb: 'In hystoria Anglorum libro quinto de Calixto papa scribitur . . . qui semel
Romam irent'.
11va: 'Uir quidam magnus in Anglia . . . et in ultimo prorsus articulo ecclesie sue
proposse defecit'.

12ra–21rb: 'Daretis Frigii Entellii hystoria de uastacione Troie incipit. A Cornelio
Nepote Salustii de Greco in Latinum sermonem translata. Incipit prologus. Cornelius
Nepos Salustio Crispo suo salutem'. 'Cum multa uolumina legerem Athenis curiose
. . . Protenorem et alios quinque. Hactenus id Frigius Dares mandauit litteris.' Compare ed. Meister, *Daretis Phrygii De Excidio Troiae Historia*.
21rb–65va: HRB.
65va/b: 'Hec sunt nomina regum qui possederunt totum regnum Anglie et hic patet
quot annis regnauit unusquisque'. 'Aluredus qui primus totum regnum Anglie possedit
. . . Eadwarthis filius eius regnauit.' Ends with Edward I whose regnal years have been
added in a later hand (the continuation ends at Henry IV).

66ra: 'Culmen opes subolem pollentia regna triumphos . . . quem regnum Christi
promeruisse uides'. Epitaph of Ceadwalla, quoted by Bede, *Historia Ecclesiastica*,
V.9. Printed from Paris, BN, lat. 6040, by Hammer, 'An unrecorded *Epitaphium
Ceadwallae*'.
66ra/b: 'Primus rex Romanorum Romulus. Cui successit Numa Pompilius . . . Si
lapides plurimi dic ubi contigui'.
66va–69vb: 'In primis animetur confitens ut peccata sua humiliter et pure confiteatur
. . . decimarum extorsio frequens excommunicato'.

DESCRIPTION
QUIRING No signatures or catchwords.
fos 12–65 separately foliated (i–xliii) in the fifteenth century or later.
RULING Dares and HRB in two columns of 41 lines; single vertical boundary-lines;
written below top ruled line. 1v–3v – single column of up to 44 lines; Prophecies
double-spaced. 5r–7v – single column, 37 lines. 10–11 – double column, variable
(43–46 lines). 66–69 – two columns, 46–48 lines.
SCRIPT Dares and HRB in informal Gothic bookhand. Short ascenders and descend-
ers, minim-area not particularly compact but juncture of **e** and **o** after **b**, **d**, **p**, and

sometimes **h**. Two-compartment **a**, pierced **t**. Uncrossed *et*-nota. Some ascenders slightly tagged or have flat tops (as has **ll**). Final s usually cedilla-form or round but sometimes tall. 1–7 not unlike HRB. Similar usages and untidy aspect (but more forking of ascenders), but in 5r–7v **a** is round with little or no head. 10–11 and 66–69 in Anglicana with split-topped ascenders and fairly long descenders. Crossed *et*-nota. Sigma-s in final position and two-compartment a often rise above minim-letters. More than one hand. The script of none of these additions seems to postdate the early fourteenth century.

DECORATION HRB and Dares have filigreed capitals and rubrics in split-topped Anglicana.

HISTORY
Marginalia in Middle Welsh, 39r: printed by Wright, *The Historia Regum Britannie of Geoffrey of Monmouth, II*, p. lxxxii. Other marginal notes on Welsh name-forms. Notes in Latin in Anglicana hand of early fourteenth century.

BIBLIOGRAPHY
Abbott, *Catalogue*, p. 78.
Hammer, *Geoffrey*, pp. 6–7.

68 EDINBURGH, NATIONAL LIBRARY OF SCOTLAND, MS. ADV. 18.4.5

Saec. xiv[1]   Mediaeval provenance:
xvi (paper) + 90 + xvi (paper) fos   2nd fo: *De consuetudine seruanda*

HRB 40ra–90vb
§§5–108, 111–113.9, 117.73–208. Dedication absent. Rubrics at §5 (40ra) 'Incipit historia Britonum a Galfrido Arturo Monemutensi de britanica lingua in Latinum translata', after §208 (90vb) 'Qui scripsit carmen sit benedictus. Amen'.
No book-divisions indicated by rubrics but capitals at §§5, 6, 35, 43, 54, 90, 111, 118, 143, 161, 177.
Lacuna caused by loss of three folios after 67v (which ends §113.9 'iugum perpetue'; 67r begins §117.73 'sua supponat').
First Variant Version. Wright, siglum S: *The Historia Regum Britannie of Geoffrey of Monmouth, II*, pp. xc–xci.

CONTENTS
i–ii: Early Modern flyleaves. i r Eighteenth-century title and *ex-libris* inscription (see below, HISTORY).
ii r contents-list and second *ex-libris* (seventeenth-century).
1r–29va: 'Incipit epistola magistri Philyppi super librum qui dicitur Secreta secretorum'. 'Domino suo excellentissimo in cultu religionis christiane strenuissimo . . . ad

meliorem et probabiliorem partem.' Ed. Steele, *Opera hactenus inedita Rogeri Baconi*, V.25–172.

29va–40ra: 'Daretis Frigii Entellii hystoria de uastacione Troie incipit a Cornelio nepote Salustii de Greco in Latinum sermonen (*sic*) translata. Incipit prologus. Cornelius nepos Salustio Crispo suo salutem'. 'Cum uolumina multa legerem Athenis curiose ... Protenorem et alios quinque. Athenus (*sic*) id Dares Frigius mandauit literis, etc.' Compare ed. Meister, *Daretis Phrygii De Excidio Troiae Historia*. 40ra–90vb: HRB.

DESCRIPTION

SIZE 25 x 17 cm.

QUIRING I–V^{12}, VI^{12} (lacks 8–10: 61–67), VII^{12}, VIII^{10} (lacks 10, probably blank: 82–90).

PRICKING Outer margins only.

RULING Two columns of 35/36 lines. Narrow, double outer boundary-lines; divided central margin.

SCRIPT Informal bookhand with short ascenders and descenders. Juncture of **e** and **o** after **b**, **d**, **h**, and **p**. Looped two-compartment **a** usual but Caroline form also occurs. *Con*-symbol and 2-shaped **r** fall beneath the line. 8-shaped **g**. Final **s** usually round. Crossed *et*-nota. In **b**, **h**, **p**, etc., bowl of letter beginning to be separated from ascender.

DECORATION Filigreed capitals (red, blue).

HISTORY

Belonged to Sir Henry Savile: Watson, *The Manuscripts of Henry Savile of Banke*, pp. 28–29.

On ii r under contents-list, '1629. Ja: Balfournius Kynardiae miles leo armorum rex' (James Balfour). i r in ?eighteenth-century hand, 'Ex libris Bibliothecae Facultatis Iuridicae Edinburgi'.

BIBLIOGRAPHY

Beattie *et al.*, *National Library of Scotland. Summary Catalogue*, p. 59.

Cunningham, 'Latin classical manuscripts', pp. 74–75.

69 ETON, ETON COLLEGE, MS. 246
(*OLIM* PHILLIPPS 25145)

Saec. xiii^2 or later   Mediaeval provenance: ?England or Wales

iii + 60 fos   2nd fo: [*mi*]-*libus* (sic) *muniuit*

HRB 1r–60v.

§§6–108, 111–203 'quanta non poterant uini' (foot of 59v; last folio has been mutilated); end of §208 discernible at foot of 60v. Dedicatory section and §5 absent. No original rubric but above §6 in Secretary hand (1r), 'Historia Bruti'.

CONTENTS

i r/v: sixteenth-century Welsh verse.

ii–iii r: blank.

iii: blank except for note on verso (?sixteenth-century): 'Cronica nulla canit Britonica bella peracta / Nequit enim bella lingua referre tua / primus et illo parens Brutus te uincere cepit / postea te uincit gens maledicta minis / tempus adest ut fata parant depellere gentem / quam ?bonus ut fateor nullus amare queat'.

1r–60v: HRB.

60: mostly torn away.

DESCRIPTION

SIZE 18.5 x 13 cm.

QUIRING a^4 (4 lacking), I–IV^{12}, V^{12} (12 mutilated: 49–60).

PRICKING Visible in outer margin only.

RULING One column of 35–36 lines with ruling above top written line and single vertical boundary-lines.

SCRIPT Compact Gothic minuscule. Size and relative thickness of pen affect usage. Juncture of e and o after d, but not with h or p. Tall s found finally, t not always pierced, a sometimes has two-compartment form but is more often small-headed. *Et*-nota is crossed. Hairline over double l.

DECORATION Capitals with basic filigree.

HISTORY

Flyleaf suggests sixteenth-century Welsh provenance: Ker, *Medieval Manuscripts*, II.792–93. Recorded by Hammer as in the possession of John Tydesley Jones: 'Some additional manuscripts', p. 240.

BIBLIOGRAPHY

Dumville, 'The manuscripts of Geoffrey of Monmouth's *Historia*', p. 121.

Hammer, 'Some additional manuscripts', p. 240.

Ker, *Medieval Manuscripts*, II.792–93.

70   EXETER, CATHEDRAL LIBRARY, MS. 3514

Saec. xiii + **xiii/xiv**   Mediaeval provenance: Wales, ?Whitland (Cistercian)
534 pp.   2nd fo: *Ex tunc armaricata*

HRB pp. 94–218a

§§1–3, 5–208. Dedicated to Robert of Gloucester.

Rubrics at §5 (p. 95a) 'Incipit historia Britonum a Galfrido Arturo [canc.] Monemutensi de britannica lingua in Latinum translata', §6 (p. 95b, margin) 'Explicit descripcio Britannie insule. Incipit liber primus', after §208 (p. 218a) 'Explicit'.

Book-divisions: I §6 (p. 95b), II §23 (p. 106a), III §35 (p. 115b), IIII §54 (p. 125b), V §73 (p. 137a), VII §143 (p. 181).

First Variant Version (although includes §§1–3 and 109–110, usually omitted from the First Variant). Wright siglum E: *The Historia Regum Britannie of Geoffrey of Monmouth, II*, pp. lxxxii–lxxxvi.

Prophecies glossed: printed by Hammer, 'Bref commentaire', pp. 113–17.

CONTENTS

Contents-list written in fourteenth-century ?Anglicana hand on recto of ii r.

pp. 1–6b: 'Metodius martir Christi de fine seculi' (in top margin, informal hand). '[S]ciendum namque est nobis fratres karissimi quo[modo] in principio creauit Deus celum et terram ... Per omnia secula seculorum. Amen.' Compare ed. Sackur, *Sibyllinische Texte*, pp. 59–96.

pp. 7–8: blank except for fifteenth-century note on p. 8.

pp. 9–10a: genealogy. 'tam genuit Seth. Seth genuit Enos ... Edwardus rex Anglie genuit Iohannem Henricum et Alphonsum qui in minoribus premature descesserunt'.

pp. 10b–18: 'De aduentu Anglorum in Britanniam' (rubric in informal hand). '[ ]nno ab incarnacione Domini .cccc.xlviii. Martianus cum Ualentiano ... et sanctus Beda uenerabilis presbiter.' Ends in A.D. 734. Derived from Annals of St Neots: see Dumville & Lapidge, *The Annals*, p. lii.

pp. 19–21a: 'Incipit epilogium de obitu beati atque eximii doctoris Bede qui Giruuinensis monasterii presbiter extitit doctorque precipuus', by Cuthbert. '[ ]ilectissimo in Christo collectori Cuthuuino Cuthbertus ... ineruditio lingue facit.' Ed. Dobbie, *The Manuscripts of Caedmon's Hymn*, pp. 119–27. See Dumville & Lapidge, *The Annals*, pp. l–lii.

pp. 21b–30a: genealogy of French kings to Philip IV (1285–1314). '[P]rimus omnium regum Francorum qui apud illos more regio regnauit ... Philippus genuit Lodouicum qui duxit filiam et heredem regis Nauarre.'

?pp. 31–35 blank.

pp. 36–37: diagram of ten concentric circles spread across double page. The rings marked from the centre 'spera lune, spera mercurii ... spera nona'.

p. 38: ?blank.

p. 39: smaller, simplified version of previous diagram with 'Terra' at centre. Another small diagram of concentric circles beneath. One ring contains drawing of dragon, outside which is written 'En annus Ego sum sic sol se circuit in quo qui fluxit pridem status nunc temporis Idem'.

p. 40: circular diagram with eight-petalled design – large four central petals contain descriptions of qualities of humours and points of compass; names of the winds entered in smaller intermediate petals.
Beneath, diagram of 'Sol' heading ring of eight spheres.

p. 41–42: ?blank.

pp. 43–52: 'Beda de ymagine mundi' (Honorius of Autun). '[ ]peculum mundi ad instruccionem eorum quibus deesse copia librorum ... ad hanc dicunt Brendanum uenisse insulas circumiuimus etc.' Incomplete. Ed. Migne, *Patrologia Latina*, CLXXII.119–33.

p. 53: 'OT' map surrounded by text. 'Uentorum quatuor principales species sunt quorum primus ab oriente subsolanus ... unde illud poete a latis austri et cetera hiis similia.'

pp. 54–56a: 'Incipit genealogia uirorum ab Adam usque ad Brutum'. 'Adam pater generis humani genuit Seth ... Anno ab incarnacione Domini .d.c.lxxxix. Finit genealogia regum Britannie successiue regnancium a primo ad ultimum id est a Bruto usque ad Calawadrium.'

p. 56b: retrograde genealogy from Welsh kings to Adam. '[L]ewelinus filius Griffini filius Lewelini . . . Enos filius Seth filius Adam filius Dei.'

pp. 56b–57b: Trojan genealogy. '[C]yprius quidam filius Ieuan in Cipro insula primus regnauit . . . a Britonibus Preda\e/ nominatur'. Also in Dublin, Trinity College, MS. 515 and Cardiff 2.611.

pp. 57b–58a: 'Incipit genealogia Anglorum'. '[ ]thelwldus (*sic*) fuit Egbricti. Egbrictus fuit filius Elmundi . . . Hic post cataclisma a Noe genitus reperitur.'

pp. 58a/b: 'Incipit genealogia Normannorum et unde originem ducunt'. '[N]ormanni origine Dani .clccc.vi. (*sic*) ab incarnacione Domini anno duce quodam Rollone nomine . . . Iohannes frater eius iunior. Henricus .iiii. filius.'

pp. 58b–60a: '[H]ec est mensura Anglie uel Britannie in longitudine .D.CCC. miliaria id est a Penpenwyth . . . Staffortsyra .D. hyde unde .s. syra anglice latine dicitur prouincia et ponitur pro uicecomitatu'.

p. 60a/b: continues. 'Kynegilfus fuit primus rex Anglorum christianus . . . Huic successit Henr. secundus nepos Henr. primi ex filia et uixit .xxxiiii. annis.'

pp. 61–66b: 'Genealogia regum Francie'. '[ ]nno primo Graciani et Ualentiniani imperatorum . . . et iste similiter rotam fortune expertus est.'

pp. 67–93: 'Daretis Frigii Entelli hystoria de uastacione Troie incipit a Cornelio nepote Salustii de Greco in latinum sermonem translata. Incipit prologus. Cornelius Nepos Salustio Crispo suo salutem'. '[C]um multa uolumina legerem Athenis curiose . . . et alios quinque. Actenus id Dares Frigius mandauit litteris.' Compare ed. Meister, *Daretis Phrygii De Excidio Troiae Historia*.

pp. 94–218a: HRB.

pp. 219–222: blank.

---

pp. 223–226: Episcopal lists (in five columns except for p. 226) of Canterbury, Le Mans, Poitiers, Nantes, Amiens, Beauvais, Sens, Paris, Orléans, Senlis, Jumièges (abbots), Tours, Angers, Saint-Wandrille (abbots).

pp. 226–450a: 'In hoc uolumine continetur hystoria Anglorum nouiter edita ab Henrico Huntendunensi archidiacono libri .x.'. *Capitula*-list; then text begins 227a. 'Cum in omni fere litterarum studio . . . spiritus es caro sum te nunc intrante reuixi.' Edition of 1148: Greenway, 'Henry of Huntingdon and the manuscripts', pp. 106 & 114.

450b: in Anglicana hand. 'Apres cestui Roi Estephene regna Henri le filz emperice et fuit coronne a Westm. . . . et la conquist le .vii.'

pp. 451a–506a: 'Incipiunt capitula in hystoriam Normannorum et tendentem in reges Anglorum de Ricardo primo'. Text begins 453a. 'Postquam Willelmus Lungespee filius Rollonis . . . Uenit Pandulfus legatus Norwicensis electus.' Ends at 1215.

p. 506b: blank.

---

pp. 507–519b: *Chronica de Wallia*. 'Annus m.c. nonagesimus ab incarnacione Domini . . . a quibusdam exhereditatis et aliis malefactoribus qui incendia multa commiserunt'. Ed. Jones, ' "Cronica" ', pp. 29–41. See Hughes, *Celtic Britain*, pp. 77–79.

pp. 520–'523' (521): genealogy. 'Resus filius Griffini filius Resi magni habuit sex filios . . . Lewelin. Iorwerd. ualidissimi.' Ed. Jones, ' "Cronica" ', pp. 41–42.

p. '523'(521): 'In conquestu terre inter dominos de Cayreu . . . Septimus Dauid qui fuit episcopus Men.'. Ed. Jones, ' "Cronica" ', p. 42.

pp. '523'–'528': 'Cronica ante aduentum Domini anno .cccc.xl. fuit exidium [ ] . . . et maxima pars exercitus sui cecidit. Cui successit.' Truncated. Final section (pp. '527–528') printed by Jones, ' "Cronica" ', pp. 42–44. See Hughes, *Celtic Britain*, pp. 76–77.

pp. 529–553: blank except for a few notes.

p. 530: notes in French on Scottish kings written in fourteenth-century Anglicana. Also Early Modern notes on river (?Ouse) in Bucks., Beds., and Hunts.

p. 532: Early Modern genealogy, Brutus to Riwallo, and in the same hand on p. 53 there are Latin notes on Galfridian British history.

DESCRIPTION
SIZE 25.2 x 18.7 cm.
QUIRING I⁴ (pp. 1–8), II⁸, III⁴ (pp. 25–32), IV¹⁴ (lacks 13, + bifolium after 3: 33–62), V¹⁶, VI–X¹², XI⁴ (pp. 215–222), XII–XX¹², XXI⁶ (pp. 439–450), XXII–XXIII¹², XXIV¹² (+ one before 1: pp. 501–526), XXV⁴ (pp. 527–534).
PRICKING Visible in both margins in quire XII, otherwise in outer margin only.
RULING Two columns with single vertical boundary-lines; written below top ruled line except for fos 223–442. Dares and HRB 32 lines. Elsewhere 33–38 lines.
SCRIPT Dares and HRB in same formal Gothic bookhand (not fractura). Shaded, short ascenders and descenders. Straight-backed **d** frequent. Two-compartment **a**, **t** hardly pierced, uncrossed *et*-nota. Juncture of **e** and **o** following **d**, **p**, and sometimes **b** and **h**. Final **s** usually round but cedilla-form also found. Double **l** occasionally flat-topped. Tops of other descenders have slight hairline forks. Several other hands – some with more lozenging. Some have tall as well as round final **s**, crossed *et*-nota, or lack two-compartment **a**.
DECORATION No completed capitals.

HISTORY
Original volume (now fos 223–506) containing texts relating to English history extended at both ends in the late thirteenth- or early fourteenth-century.
Nature of *Chronica de Wallia* suggests that this took place at the Cistercian house of Whitland, Wales: Beverley Smith, 'The "Cronica de Wallia" '.

BIBLIOGRAPHY
Dumville, 'An early text', pp. 10–12.
Hammer, 'Bref commentaire'.
Hammer, *Geoffrey*, pp. 5–6.
Hammer, 'Some additional manuscripts', p. 240.
Ker, *Medieval Manuscripts*, II.822–25.
Ker & Watson, *Medieval Libraries*, p. 68.
Poole, *Report*, pp. 30–33.
Wright, *The Historia Regum Britannie of Geoffrey of Monmouth, II*, pp. lxxxii–lxxxvi.

71   FIRENZE, BIBLIOTECA LAURENZIANA, MS. XVII. DEXTR.6

Saec. xii*med.*/2   Mediaeval provenance: Florence, Friars Minor
ii + 137 +? fos   2nd fo: *nomen honorandum quia Latine*

HRB 56r–137v.

§§1–3, 5–208 [203 (*ex.*) –208 partly gone, as last folio has been mutilated]. Dedicated
to Robert of Gloucester.

Rubrics at §1 (56r) 'Incipit prologus Gaufridi Monimutensis ad Robertum comitem
Claudiocestrie in historiam de regibus Maioris Brittannie que nunc Anglia dicitur,
quam hystoriam idem Gaufridus nuper transtulit de Brittannico in Latinum', §5 (56v)
'Explicit prologus. Incipit liber primus', §110 (91r) 'Incipit prologus de prophetiis
Merlini', §111 (91v) 'Explicit prologus. Incipit prophecie', after §208 (137v) 'Explicit
liber .xi. historie de regibus Britanniam quam Gaufredus Monumutensis de Britannica
in Latinum transtulit'.

Rubrics after 71v in a more cursive and slightly later-looking hand than the original.
Book-divisions: I §5 (56v), II §23 (66r), III §35 (71v), IIII §54 (77r), VI §89 (91r),
VII §109 (100r), VIII §118 (105r), IX §143 (144r), X §163 (122v), XI §177 (129v).

CONTENTS

Flyleaves: contents-list and *ex-libris* inscriptions in late mediaeval hand.

1r–41v: 'Incipit prologus beati Augustini contra achademicos'. 'Cum ergo re-
liquissem . . . hominem sibi aptum.' 'Utinam romaniane hominem sibi aptum . . . et
citius quam speraueram fecimus.' Ed. Migne, *Patrologia Latina*, XXXII.905–58.

41v–42v: introductory note to following work. 'Per idem tempus inter illos . . . cum
sint plures idemque capitales.'

42v–55v: Augustine, *De ordine rerum.* 'Ordinem rerum Zenobi consequi ac tenere
cuique proprium . . . non solum cum Deo esse non mihi uidetur.' Truncated. Ed.
Migne, *Patrologia Latina*, XXXII.977–1020.

56r–137v: HRB.

DESCRIPTION

QUIRING Early signatures in section preceding HRB, beginning .i. (8v), .ii. (15v) and
then continuing regularly to .vii. on 55v. I⁸, II⁸ (6 lacking: 9–10, 12–13, 14–15),
III–VII⁸. No indication of quiring in HRB. The two sections were joined before the
writing of the contents-list on the flyleaf, as it quotes the late mediaeval foliation which
runs through the whole volume.

PRICKING Visible at outer edges only.

RULING Single column throughout; written above top ruled line. fos 1–55, 26–27
lines. HRB, 23–34 lines.

SCRIPT Protogothic minuscule with no Gothic symptoms. Written in several hands
of varying practice and aspect but generally rounded and of four-line proportions. One
uses *et*-nota, round d but no round s, another uses e-caudata, no round d but the *et*-nota.
Ampersand occurs, as does final round s. Augustine in a similar script but in different
hands.

DECORATION Rare in HRB. Plain Romanesque capitals at book-divisions. Opening initial is in two colours.

HISTORY
On flyleaf, in ?fourteenth-century hand: 'Iste liber est ad usum armarii conuentus Florentini Deo gratias fratrum minorum', followed by a list of contents. Opposite, another inscription: 'Iste liber est conuentus sancte crucis de Flor. ord. minorum continens infrascripta opera in facie proxime sequenti N° clxxxiii.' (in fifteenth-century hand). Listed in eighteenth-century among collection from Santa Croce, Florence: Bandinius, *Catalogus Codicum Latinorum Bibliothecae Mediceae Laurentianae*, IV.506–7.

BIBLIOGRAPHY
Bandinius, *Catalogus Codicum Latinorum Bibliothecae Mediceae Laurentianae*, IV.506–7.

72   FIRENZE, BIBLIOTECA NAZIONALE CENTRALE, MS. B. R. 55 (A.4.2591)

Saec. xiv   Mediaeval provenance: Florence Abbey
i + 55 fos   2nd fo (the original lacking): *hec conuenient sacerdotes*

HRB 3v–52rb
§§1–3, 5–208. Dedicated to Robert of Gloucester.
Rubric at §1 (3va) 'Incipit hystoria Britonnum' (*sic*). Running title. No book-divisions.
After §208 (52rb) 'Diuina gratia hunc librum concessit michi ad utendum in uita mea'.

CONTENTS
i: blank except for note of contents and shelfmark on verso (same on foot 1r).
1r–3v: acephalous, most of 1a erased. Account of the Tiburtine sibyl. 'Fuit igitur hec sybilla Priamidis regis filia . . . iudicii signum tellus sudore madescet.'
3va–52rb: HRB.
52v–53v: ?erased text. Line drawings of men on horseback on 53v (?? post-mediaeval).
54r: blank.
54v: line drawing of men at table, etc.
55r: line drawing, ? of two kings (?mediaeval).

DESCRIPTION
QUIRING Some catchwords. I^{12} (1 lacking, + one before 1: i, 1–11), $II–IV^{12}$, V $?^8$ (48–55).
PRICKING Not visible on microfilm.
RULING Two columns throughout, 47 lines. Single vertical boundary-lines. Written below top ruled line.

SCRIPT Small round two-line form of Gothic minuscule, ?of southern European form. Flat hairline tops or tags on ascenders. Uncrossed *et*-nota. Juncture of **e** and **o** after **b**, **d**, **p**, and other fusion of curved letters (**oe** etc.). Two-compartment **a**, pierced **t**. Final **s** round. **d** usually round and two-line, but straight-backed form occurs.
DECORATION Capitals, several colours, in squares of filigree.

HISTORY
On 1r and 52r (in same ?Humanist hand) 'Abbatie Florentine .[ ].89.7c' (several candidates).

BIBLIOGRAPHY
Dumville, 'The manuscripts', p. 149.

73 GLASGOW, UNIVERSITY LIBRARY, MS. U.7.25 (331)

Saec. xiii$^{1/med.}$ Mediaeval provenance: ?England
iv (mutilated) + 81 + 2 + iv fos   2nd fo: *Eneas cum Ascanio*

HRB 1r–83r
§§1–3, 5–103 (*ex.*), 128 (*med.*) –200 (*med.*). Dedicated to Robert of Gloucester. Rubrics at §1 (1r) 'Prologus', after §3 (1r) 'Incipit primus liber de situ et de regibus Britannie et qui prius [ ] inhabitauerunt', §8 'Pandraso regi' (2v) 'Littere Bruti Pandraso regi', and occasionally at other chapter-divisions.
Book-divisions: I §5 (1r), II §35 (16r), III §54 (22v), V §89 (38v). Lacuna between 46v (§103) 'tunc petebat ipse uero diem et locum nominasse' and 47r 'Cui Merlinus si perpetuo' (§128). Text breaks off on 81v in §200 'cur solus aberat'. Continued in Secretary hand 'cum ceteri Saxonum principes' –§202 'eam memoratus est' (82r–83r). 83v blank.
No other contents. Material completing HRB fills first three sides of final quire. Remainder blank. Interpolation after §5 as found in Cambridge, St John's College G.16, London, BL, Cotton Vespasian E.x, and Oxford, Bodleian, Rawlinson B.148.

DESCRIPTION
SIZE 19.5 x 12 cm.
QUIRING Some catchwords and signatures. Modern paper flyleaves before and after text. a^4 (parchment, lacks 4); I^{12}, II^{10}, III–IIII^{12}, V lacking, VI–VII^{12}, VIII ?^{12} (lacks 12: fos 71–81); XI ? (fos 82–83 + four blank leaves; stub before, mutilated leaf after).
PRICKING Not visible on microfilm.
RULING Single column of 28 lines; written below top ruled line except for the final quire which is frame-ruled and has 24–26 lines.
SCRIPT Bulk of text in a regular and even Gothic with usual proportions but without any breaking or great angularity. Juncture of **e** and **o** after **d**. **a** has the two-compartment form, the horizontal of **t** is pierced, and the *et*-nota is usually crossed. *Est*-compendium is found. Final quire in rapid cursive with simple round **a**, looped **e**, flat-topped **g** and slanting descenders.

DECORATION Plain, unfiligreed capitals.

HISTORY

Extensive annotation in Anglicana hands. On mutilated leaf after blank leaves which follow text, (upsidedown) in ?Early Modern hand, 'T. Ashe'.

BIBLIOGRAPHY

Dumville, 'The manuscripts', p. 119.
Young & Henderson Aitken, *A Catalogue*, p. 267.

74 GLASGOW, UNIVERSITY LIBRARY, MS. U.7.26 (332)

Saec. xiv ?[1]   Mediaeval provenance: Syon Abbey, Isleworth (Bridgettine)
iv + 127 fos   2nd fo: *que Hercules uellet*

HRB 25r–124r.

§§1–3, 5–82 'ex quo namque amplicuimus', 84 'Leuiter deinde subdendam'–208. Dedicated to Robert of Gloucester.

Rubrics at §1 (25r) 'Incipit edicio Gaufridi Arturi Monsmutenensis' (*sic*), after §208 (124r) 'Explicit hystoria britannica Galfridi Monemutensis' (added in similar but later-looking hand).

No book-divisions before the Prophecies, then V §111 (82r), VI §118 (90r), VI §143 (99r).

Hiatus in text after §82 caused by loss of fo 79. Now replaced by blank leaf.

CONTENTS

i–iv: blank parchment.

1r–16v: 'Hic incipit prologus Daretis Frigii de bello troiano'. 'Cornelius Nepos Salustio Crispo . . . Pasenionem (*sic*) Epistropum (*sic*) Scedium.' Ed. Meister, *Daretis Phrygii De Excidio Troiae Historia*.

16v–22r: 'Liber sibille' (from rubric on 22r). '[S]ibille generaliter omnes femine prophantes (*sic*) . . . et sulphurus annis.' Ed. Sackur, *Sibyllinische Texte*, pp. 177–87.

22r–23r: 'Augustinus in libro de ciuitate Dei'. '[I]n hiis latinis uersubus (*sic*) . . . Iesus Christus Dei saluator.' Note on verses which end preceding Sibylline prophecies, quoted by Augustine in *De Ciuitate Dei*, XVIII.23.

23v–24v: blank.

25r–124r: HRB.

124r–125r: extracts (added) from Chronicle of Matthew Paris. 'Anno Domini .d.cccxcii. Bonefacius sedit in cathedral. . . . Eadgaro filio Eadwardi cum filiabus predictis.' Faded to illegibility in places. Compare Luard, *Matthaei Parisiensis monachi Sancti Albani chronica*, I.423 & 526.

125v–127: blank except for note on 127v, 'Dares Frigius et Brutus [ ]'.

DESCRIPTION
SIZE
QUIRING a⁴, I–II¹², III⁸, IV–V¹², VI¹² (+ one blank leaf after 12: fos 57–69), VII¹², VIII⁸, IX–X¹², XI¹⁴ (114–127).
PRICKING Visible at outer edge.
RULING Single column of 26–42 lines.
SCRIPT Written in several hands using different types of English cursive. Varying from heavy, sprawling, flattened script without many cursive features to upright Anglicana with long descenders and ascenders (split or looped tops). Long cursive r and looped round d are common throughout the volume.

HISTORY
The volume matches an entry in the Syon Abbey catalogue of 1504 x 1526 (Cambridge, Corpus Christi College, MS. 141):
K11 que Hercules
t16 Liber Daretis Frigii de bello Troiano. Prophetia Sibille Tibertine.
Gaufridus Arturi de historia Britonum.
Ed. Bateson, *Catalogue*, p. 80.
On final flyleaves, in Early Modern hand: 'W. Machin'.

BIBLIOGRAPHY
Dumville, 'The manuscripts', p. 115.
Ker, *Medieval Libraries*, p. 185.
Young & Henderson Aitken, *A Catalogue*, pp. 268–69.

75 HEIDELBERG, UNIVERSITÄTSBIBLIOTHEK, MS. 9.31

Saec. xiii¹   Provenance: Salem (Cistercian), dioc. of Konstanz
272 pages   2nd fo (original lacking): *ceteros habitarem*

HRB pp. 3–123
Acephalous. §7 'libarentur. Quod leuiter fieri'–§208. Dedication lost.
After §208 (p. 123) 'Explicit historia Britonum' (original rubric).
No book-divisions.

CONTENTS
pp. 3–123: HRB.
p. 123: 'De etymologyis nominum subiectorum', brief notes (ink faded) following HRB. 'Armorica siue [ ]auia id est minor Britannia . . . qui fluuius leo (. . .).' Also found in Aberystwyth, NLW 13210, London, BL, Cotton Titus A.xxvii, Lambeth Palace, MS. 401 and Oxford, Bodleian, MS. Digby 196. Ed. Dumville, 'Anecdota'.
pp. 123–125: '[I]n diebus illis affixus est Iesus . . . de morte uita ita ut ira redire.' In different but near contemporary hand. Lower half of pages 125–126 cut down (below text on p. 125).
p. 126: blank.

pp. 127–143: 'Incipit prologus in purgatorio sancti Patricii episcopi'. Attributed to Henry of Sawtrey. 'Patri suo in Christo preoptato domino .H. . . . transferat in requiem beatorum.' With prefatory material as indicated by Ward, *Catalogue of Romances*, II.435–52. Epilogue abbreviated. *BHL* 6511.

pp. 143–195: 'Incipit uisio cuiusdam monachi de claustro Cinesheim in regno Angliae.' Account of vision of monk of Eynsham seen in 1196 and recorded by a monk of Coggeshall. 'Usu notissimum . . . regnumque et imperium in secula seculorum amen.' Ed. Salter, *Eynsham Cartulary*, II.285–371.

(195–227: collection of ecclesiastical anecdotes)

pp. 195–196: 'Mirum quod contigit in regno Anglie in episcopatu Norwicensi'. 'Temporibus Henrici regis secundi . . . de huiusmodi euentibus narrentur.'

pp. 196–198: 'Item aliud mirum quod in eodem episcopatu contigit'. 'Aliud quoque mirum . . . cupiditate ambo discedunt.'

pp. 198–199: 'Uisio de inpudicis sacerdotibus'. 'Quidam abbas genere anglicus qui prefuit cuidam abbatie . . . ad exitum uite sue feliciter. Amen.'

pp. 199–201: 'De angelo qui proiecit carbonem in ore monachi'. 'Ut autem presentes atque futuri . . . quanto minus si me ipsum pacauero (*sic*) prius.'

pp. 201–204: 'De monacho qui non credebat animam esse inmortalem'. 'Quidam monachus adolescens . . . seriem pluribus enarrauit.'

pp. 204–205: 'De feruore cuiusdam nouitii erga beatissimam Dei genitricem Mariam'. 'Quidam nouicius in quadam congregatione . . . et in triumphandis hostibus robustior.'

pp. 205–206: 'Quomodo conuersus uidit spiritum illusorium'. 'Contigit in quadam congregatione . . . et desides (*sic*) defraudamus.'

pp. 206: 'Quomodo ad signum crucis demon euanuit'. 'Quidam clericus litteris admodum . . . eum eisdem cruciandos.'

pp. 206–209: 'De quodam sacerdote'. 'Fuit igitur presbiter quidam opinionis . . . et amplius noli peccare.'

pp. 209–214: 'Uisio cuiusdam nouitii in Hyspania'. 'Ad gloriam eterni regis comprobatur . . . et gloriam Domini nostri Iesu Christi qui uiuit et regnat per omnia secula seculorum. Amen.'

pp. 214–219: 'Uisio cuiusdam monachi in Uacellis claustro'. With prologue. 'Quicquid exit? similis . . . qui cum patre et spiritu sancto uiuit et regnat per omnia secula seculorum. Amen.'

pp. 219–223: 'De quodam monacho aput Cluniacum'. 'Erant quidam Iohannes . . . in ?angelorum lucis.'

pp. 223–224: 'De nouitio qui crimen confiteri noluit'. 'Duo nouitii erant in quadam congregatione ordinis Cisterciensis . . . differe non metuit.'

pp. 224–225: 'Quod in Sauigniensi cenobio contigit de corpore Domini'. 'Quid in Sauigniensi monasterio contigerit de domno Hamone . . . atque diuinis aspectibus presentabat.'

p. 225: 'Quid contigit cuidam monacho celebranti'. 'Quoddam etiam preclarum miraculum . . . ut credimus contemplatur.'

p. 226: 'De monacho qui egredi disposuerat'. 'Extitit quidam Iohannis monachus Cluniacensis . . . que sibi acciderant.'

pp. 226–227: 'De monacho qui ignem in horreis iniecit'. 'Quidam monachus in Lewensi monasterio Cluniacensi . . . corporum expulerunt.'

pp. 227–272: 'Scriptoris uite beati Columbe confessoris incipit prima prefatio', with two prologues. 'Beati nostri patroni uitam descripturus . . . et opere excercere quod docuit per eiusdem.' By Adomnán. *BHL* 1886.

p. 273: notes in different hands. Top eight lines in nearly contemporary hand, 'Dominus ad Abraham in semine tuo et percutiet principes Moab.' Below, twelve lines, 'Quid est mundus. Mundus est incessabilis circuitus . . . presagium tempestatum'.

DESCRIPTION

QUIRING No signatures or catchwords.

PRICKING In both margins (visible in HRB).

RULING One column throughout of 38 lines in HRB, otherwise variable (34–46).

SCRIPT HRB in stiff and upright minuscule approaching Gothic. Juncture of **de** standard but not of **d** with **o**. Round **d** standard but tall **s** generally used except in final position. *Et*-nota standard. 8-form of **g**, small-headed **a**. Little lateral compression but lines closely spaced. Apparently Continental script of early thirteenth century or later. Rest of volume in different hands of similar type and date.

DECORATION Capitals with flourishes of same colour as main letter.

HISTORY

Two *ex-libris* inscriptions, 'Iste liber est domus beate Marie uirginis in Salem' (p. 273), in hands of (i) ?late thirteenth and (ii) fourteenth or fifteenth century, the second in a formal Gothic. Salem was founded in 1138 in the line of the abbey of Morimond.

BIBLIOGRAPHY

Dumville, 'The manuscripts', pp. 149–50.

Pertz, 'Handschriften der Universitätsbibliothek zu Heidelberg', p. 582.

76 LEIDEN, BIBLIOTHEEK DER RIJKSUNIVERSITEIT, MS. B.P.L. 20

Saec. xii *med.* (*ante ca* 1160)   Mediaeval provenance: Le Bec,
                                                                        Normandy (Benedictine)
iv + 107 + i fos   2nd fo: *ut per succedentia*

HRB 60r–101va

§§1–3, 5–208. Dedicated to Robert of Gloucester.

Rubrics at §1 (60r) 'Incipit prologus Gaufridi Monimutensis (*sic*) ad Rodbertum comitem Claudiocestrie in hystoriam de regibus Maioris Brittannie que nunc Anglia dicitur quam hystoriam idem Gaufridus nuper transtulit de Brittannico in Latinum', §5 (60r) 'Explicit prologus. Incipit liber .i.', §110 (81r) 'Incipit prologus de prophetiis Merlini', §111 (81r) 'Explicit prologus. Incipiunt prophetie', after §208 (101v)

'Explicit liber decimus historie de regibus Britonum quam nuper de Britannico in Latinum transtulit Gaufridus Monemutensis'.

Book-divisions: I §5 (60r), II §23 (64r), III §35 (66v), IIII §54 (69v), V §73 (73r), VI §89 (76v), VII §109 (81r), VIII §118 (83r), IX §143 (87v), X §163 (92r), XI (96r).

CONTENTS

1: recto blank. Twelfth-century contents-list on verso. Printed by Dumville, 'An early text', pp. 3–4.

2r–31v: *Gesta Normannorum Ducum*, F-redaction. Acephalous. 'dum per legatos a duce sepius obiurgaretur . . . quod ipse illis pro anima sua dabat.' Ed. Marx, *Guillaume de Jumièges.*

33ra–38va: 'Incipit prologus \Alcuini/ in uitam Caroli magni regis Francorum et imperatoris Romanorum'. 'Uitam et conuersationem et ex parte non modica res gestas . . . post obitum eius summa deuotione adimplere curauit.' Ed. Halphen, *Eginhard.*

38va–47ra: 'Incipit uita Alexandri regis magni Macedonis'. 'Egypti sapientes sati genere diuino primi feruntur . . . uino et ueneno superatus atque extinctus occubuit.' Ed. Kuebler, *Iuli Valeri Alexandri Polemi res gestae*, pp. 1–168.

Two folios lost after 36v.

47ra–51vb: 'Incipit epistola eiusdem ad Aristotelem magistrum suum de situ Indie'. 'Semper memor tui . . . et animi industria optimi Aristotelis indicium.' Ed. Walther Boer, *Epistola Alexandri.*

52r–59ra: 'Incipit adbreuiatio gestorum regum Francie'. 'Antenor et alii profugi . . . anno ab incarnatione Domini .m.c.xxx.vii..' Edd. Pertz, *et al.*, MGH, SS, IX.395–406.

59rb: blank.

59va: 'Genealogia comitum Flandrie'. 'Hidricus (*sic*) genuit Ingelramnum . . . nupsit amico comiti interrogat[ ].'

59vb: blank.

60r–101va: HRB.

101va–106rb: 'Incipiunt exceptiones de libro Gilde sapientis quem composuit de primis habitatoribus Britannie que nunc Anglia dicitur et de excidio eius'. 'A principio mundi usque ad diluuium anni .ii.cc.xl.ii. . . . in extremis finibus cosmi.' Ed. Faral, *La Légende*, III.5–61.

106rb/va: 'Miraculum quod contigit in quadam ecclesia beati Petri apostoli que sita est in urbe Constantia'. 'Anno ab incarnatione Domini .m.c.viii. indiccione prima Willelmus archiepiscopus . . . per totam diocesem [ ].' Excerpt from History of Orderic Vitalis: ed. & transl. Chibnall, *The Ecclesiastical History of Orderic Vitalis*, VI.264–66.

107: blank.

DESCRIPTION

SIZE 32.5 x 22.5 cm.

QUIRING Two volumes. (i) fos 1–59 – quires marked by letter, quires A-B lost; (ii) fos 60–107 – quires numbered (from .i., 67v). a ?1, [C]⁸ (+ one after 8: 2–10), D⁸, E⁸ (lacks 8: 19–25), F⁸ (lacks 1: 26–32), G¹⁰ (lacks 5–6 but replaced by unnumbered paper bifolium: 33–40), H⁸, I¹⁰ (+ one after 10: 49–59); I–V⁸, VI ?⁸ (100–107).

PRICKING In outer margins.

RULING Two columns of 47 lines. Double vertical boundary-lines and divided central margin.

SCRIPT (ii) in Protogothic minuscule with longish ascenders and descenders, various hands. Laterally compact. Final s tall or cedilla-shaped (occasionally round). a has small head. Round and straight-backed d equally common. e-caudata occurs. Ampersand usual but et-nota is found. Well-spaced ct-ligature. Tail of h often swings under the line. (i) similar to (ii) except for two older-looking hands. Several collaborating scribes. Hand at start of volume uses only ampersand; i is distinguished from other minims by a diagonal stroke beneath the line, g has straight back angled to left for tail. In other hands et-nota found with ampersand. Round and straight-backed d.

DECORATION Red, blue, and green unfiligreed capitals. Opening initial of second volume (start of HRB) constructed of foliate interlace on coloured ground with drawing of mounted knight leaping over the letter.

HISTORY

It has been argued that the copy of Gesta Normannorum Ducum which begins the first part of the volume was authorial, written by Robert de Torigni, creator of the F-redaction and monk of Le Bec, Normandy. This would place its writing about 1139. Certainly the volume was at Le Bec before the 1160s as it was by then joined to the second part of the present codex (which includes the HRB), being recorded in the library catalogue of that date. Arguments summarised by Dumville, 'An early text', pp. 2–4.

BIBLIOGRAPHY

Avril, 'Notes', p. 211.

Dumville, 'An early text'.

Hermans & Van Houts, 'The history of a membrum disiectum', especially pp. 37–39 (with plates).

Lieftinck, Manuscrits datés conservés dans les Pays-Bas, I.69.

Molhuysen, Bibliotheca Universitatis Leidensis: codices manuscripti, III.14–15.

Van Houts, Gesta Normannorum Ducum: een studie, pp. 229–31.

77   LEIDEN, BIBLIOTHEEK DER RIJKSUNIVERSITEIT, MS. VOSS. LAT. F.77

Saec. xiii/xiv (post 1282)   Mediaeval provenance: ? Normandy
190 + i fos (no fo 55)   2nd fo: Accidit ergo quoddam

HRB 75r–121v.

§§1–3, 5–208. Dedicated to Robert of Gloucester.

Rubrics at §1 (75r) 'Incipit prologus Gaufridi Monemitensis (sic) in librum de gestis regum Maioris Britannie que nunc Anglia dicitur ad Robertum comitem Glocestrie', §5 (75r) 'Explicit prologus. Incipit liber .i.', §110 (98v) 'Incipit prologus in librum .vii. qui continet prophetias Ambrosii Merlini', §109 (98v) 'Incipit prologus ad

Alexandrim Linlinensem episcopum', §111 (99r) 'Incipit liber septimus qui continet prophetias Ambrosii Merlini.

Book-divisions: I §5 (75r), II §23 (79v), III §35 (82v), IIII §54 (86r), V [ ], VI [ ], VII §111 (99v), VIII §118 (101v), IX §143 (107r), X §163 (111v), XI §177 (116r).

CONTENTS

1r: 'De humilitate Rollonis et quomodo reduxit corpus beati Andoeni archiepiscopi Rothomagensis'. 'Quante humilitatis Rollo fuit . . . quia quid magna humilitas nescit.' Ed. Duchesne, *Historiae Normannorum Scriptores*, p. 315.

1r–2r: 'Quoddam miraculum in tempore Rollonis'. 'Quidam uero aliud dicitur . . . pro anima sua dabat'. Ed. Duchesne, *ibid.*, pp. 315–17.

2r–50v: *Gesta Normannorum Ducum*, F-redaction (version of Robert de Torigni). Ed. Marx, *Guillaume de Jumièges*. 'Incipit epistola Willelmi Gemetricensis ad Willelmum ortodoxorum Anglorum regem in Normannorum ducum gestis.' 'Pio uictorioso atque ortodoxo summi regis nuptu . . . rex uictoriose atque orthodoxe.'

2v–50v: 'Incipiunt capitula primi libri historie Normannorum'. *Capitula*-list ends on 3r and is followed by main text. 'Ex quo Francorum gens resumptis uiribus . . . qui ante Lotharum imperauerat.'

50v: extract from Robert of Torigni's continuation to the work. 'Kalends Augusti quando . . . a domino Hugone archiepiscopo.' Ed. Howlett, *Chronicles*, IV.133.

50v–66r: further continuations. 'Stephanus rex Anglorum . . . et multi in ea perierunt.' Ed. Howlett, *ibid.*, IV.134–242.

66r–71v: 'Fundata est abbatia de ualle monte . . . a ciuitatibus et castellis Normannie receptus'. Ed. Duchesne, *Historiae Normannorum Scriptores*, pp. 1003–14.

71v–74v: final continuation. '.M.lxxx.vii. Obiit Guillelmus rex Anglorum . . . natus fuit Edoardus filius .H. regis Anglie.' Ed. Bouquet, *Recueil*, XVIII.343c–345.

75r–121r: HRB.

122r/v: 'Aquila prophetizans de Anglia'. 'Arbor fertilis a primo trunco . . . iniuriam qui pacificato regno occidet.' Ed. Schulz, *Gottfried*, pp. 463–65.

123v–130r: 'Hic incipit uita et conseruatio (*sic*) excellentissimi principis domini Karoli magni quondam imperatoris romani et regis Francie'. 'Uitam et conuersationem et ex parte non modica res gesta . . . summa deuotione adimplere curauit.' Ed. Halphen, *Eginhard*.

130r–138r: 'Antenor et alii profugi . . . et dux Acquitanorum anno ab incarnatione Domini .m.c.xxxvii.'. Ed. Waitz, *apud* Pertz *et al.*, MGH, SS, IX.395–406.

138v–139v: 'Cest la pes et lordenance fete entre excellenz princes loys roy de France et Henri roy dengleterre'. 'Henris par la grace de Dieu . . . .m.cc. cinquante nouisme el mois de Septembre.' Terms of the pact of 1259 between Louis IX and Henry III.

139v–143v: 'Citatio contra Guidonem de Monte facta a Gregorio papa .x.'. 'Gregorius episcopus seruus seruorum Dei . . . kalends Aprilis pontificatus nostri anno secundo' (A.D. 1273). Potthast, *Regesta*, II.1663, nos 20682 & 20712.

143v: French regnal list. 'Clodoueus primus rex Francorum .xxx. annis regnauit . . . Ludouicus filius eiusdem Ludouici .xlvii. annis.'

144r: notes on the officials, regions, peoples, etc., of the Holy Roman Empire, with note on foundation of Aachen. 'Tres Otones per successionem generis . . . corruent eternum satis uoluente suprema.'

144r/v: song of the war of the Welsh against the English. 'Trucidare Saxones soliti Cambrenses . . . est quam regnare longe plus conparare.' Walther, *Initia*, I.1021, no. 19462.

144v–160r: 'Incipit historia Mongalorum quos nos Tartaros appellamus', by Iohannes de Plano Carpini. 'Omnibus fidelibus ad quos presens scriptum peruenerit . . . siue perfectus illa que nondum erant conpelta (*sic*).' Ed. van de Wijngaert, *Sinica Franciscana*, I, pp. 27–130.

160r–190r: 'Excellentissimo domino et christianissimo .L. . . . interpretes et copiosas expensas'. William de Rubruc, *Itinerarium ad partes orientales*. Ed. van de Wijngaert, *ibid.*, I.164–332.

190v–191r: extract concerning Alexander story from Aethicus Ister, *Cosmographia*, §§31–41. 'Ut ait Ethicus ?philosophicus gens stultissima est . . . Alexander caspias portas muniuit.' Wuttke, *Die Kosmographie*, pp. 17–29 (see also p. cxxv).

191r: letter of Pope Martin IV, dated 10.1.1282. 'Martinus etc. dilectis filiis generali ministro. et prouinciabilis ministris . . . Datum .iiii. idus Ianuarii pontificatus nostri anno primo.' See Potthast, *Regesta*, II.1764, no. 21836. Underneath, a note in French, ?sixteenth-century.

191v: prophecy added in cursive hand of ? *ca* 1400. 'In terra laboris et promissionis fuit iamdiu . . . multi homines plagas.'

DESCRIPTION

SIZE 28.6 x 18.5 cm.

QUIRING No signatures or catchwords. I–V^8, VI^6 (41–46), VII–XXIV^8. Foliation skips from 54 to 56.

RULING Single column of 44 lines. Single boundary-lines. Ruling above top written line.

SCRIPT Small, compact Gothic bookhand. Juncture of e and o after b, d, h, p. Crossed *et*-nota and pierced t are standard; a generally has the two-compartment form. Some ascenders indented. h and x trail below the ruled line. The descender of p is not yet pierced.

DECORATION Elegant filigreed capitals. Some with more elaborate ornament and main part of the letter in two colours.

HISTORY

On foot of 1r: 'Po Petauius', Paul Petau. Some of the marginalia are in his hand (see de Meyier, *Codices Vossiani Latini*, I.163–67). Listed by Bernard in 1697 among the books of Isaac Voss: Bernard, *Catalogi*, II.1, p. 65, no. 2429.

The contents are nearly identical to a manuscript from St Mary's York, now Cambridge, Corpus Christi College, MS. 181: James, *A Descriptive Catalogue of the Manuscripts in the Library of Corpus Christi College*, I.425.

BIBLIOGRAPHY

de Meyier, *Codices Vossiani Latini*, I.163–67.
Van Houts, *Gesta Normannorum Ducum: een Studie*, pp. 327–39.

78 LENINGRAD, SALTYKOV – SHCHEDRIN STATE PUBLIC LIBRARY, LAT. F.IV.76

Saec. xv   Mediaeval provenance: Richard III, king of England (1483–85)
83 + i (?) fos   2nd fo: *partes Grecie et inuenit progeniem*

HRB 1r–79v
§§1–3, 5–208. Dedicated to Robert of Gloucester.
Rubrics at §1 (1r) 'Incipit distinctio Britannie liber primus', §5 (1r) 'Distinccio Britannie que nunc Anglia dicitur', §6 (1v) 'Incipit hystoria Britonum', §110 (39v) 'Incipit prologus de prophetia Merlini'.
Book-divisions: I §1 (1r), II §23 (8r), X §163 (62r). Others (modern) marked in margins (VI §89 31r, VII §109 39r).

CONTENTS
1r–79v: HRB.
79v–80v: 'Hic incipit prophecie aquile'. 'Arbor fertilis a primo trunco decisa . . . qui pacifico regno accidet.' Ed. Schultz, *Gottfried*, pp. 463–65.
80v–83v: 'Hic incipit arbor aquile Cheston. (*sic*)', commentary on the above, lemmata written in large textura, followed by exegesis. 'Arbor fertilis a primo decisa ad spacium trium iugerum. Arbor fertilis. sanguis Bruti interpretatur . . . pars uero tertia permanens uilis et uacua reperietur.' Found also in Cambridge, St John's College, MS. G.16.
Facing leaf: note on verso at foot in Russian.

DESCRIPTION
SIZE 29 x 21 cm.
QUIRING Paper manuscript. Arrangement indicated by catchwords. I–V^{16}, VI ? (81–83 + unnumbered blank(s)).
RULING Written mostly in single column of about 26–29 lines. No ruling visible on film. 81v–82v written in three columns.
SCRIPT Single hand. Rightward-leaning cursive with some angularity. Simple round form of a and pinched c-form of e. Top of t cuts the ascender as does flat top of g its uprights. Short r. Tops of ascenders (including round d) are looped but not completely angular. Textura found on 80v–81r is large and artifical-looking, with heavy diagonal feet on every minim.
DECORATION Lombardic capitals, (?red).

HISTORY
At the top right of 1r, signature of Richard III 'Ricardus R'. Immediately above it, that of Oliver Cromwell 'Cromwell.e 1656'. Under text on 83v at left, signature of James I 'James R' and at right, of Charles I 'Carolus R'. At the foot of 1r and 83v 'Ex Musaeo Petri Dubrowsky'.
This manuscript is evidently connected with a copy of the *Historia Troiana* of Guido delle Colonne, written in the same hand, which bears the same royal signatures and reached the same destination: it is now lat. F.IV.74 in the Saltykov –Shchedrin Library See Sutton & Visser-Fuchs, 'Richard III's books'.

BIBLIOGRAPHY
Sutton & Visser-Fuchs, 'Richard III's books'.
von Muralt, 'Handschriften der kaiserlichen Bibliothek', p. 793.

79   LILLE, BIBLIOTHEQUE MUNICIPALE, MS. 533

Saec. xii²   Provenance (1644): Loos (Cistercian)
57 fos   2nd fo: *agnita igitur ueterum*

HRB 1r–57
§§1–3, 5–197 'Eduuino relatum est' (breaks off at foot of 57v). Dedicated to Robert of Gloucester.
No opening rubric. On 33v before §110 'Incipit prologus de prophetia Merlini', before §111 'Explicit prologus. Incipit prophetia eiusdem'. At §177 (53v) 'Explicit .x. Incipit .xi.'. No other indications of book-divisions.
In hand of ?thirteenth century, in margin, running total of number of kings noted.
No other contents.

DESCRIPTION
SIZE 31 x 20.6 cm.
QUIRING No signatures or catchwords visible.
PRICKING In both margins.
RULING Two columns of 33 lines.
SCRIPT Clear, round Protogothic minuscule. Ascenders/descenders of about equal height to minims, little lateral compression, no juncture. Ampersand and *et*-nota occur, ? ampersand predominant. e-caudata occurs but not standard. Final round s rare. Straight and round d are found. Straight-backed g and small-headed a suggest Continental origin.

HISTORY
Catalogued as no. 85 among the books of Loos (Cistercian Abbey, diocese of Tournai) by Sanderus, *Bibliotheca*, II.118 (no. LXXV).

BIBLIOGRAPHY
Rigaux, *Catalogue général*, XXVI.405.

80   LINCOLN, CATHEDRAL LIBRARY, MS. 98 (A.4.6)

Saec. xii² + xiii + xv   Mediaeval provenance: ?midland England
185 fos   2nd fo: *eo uenerant grauiter*

HRB 20ra–106rb.
§§1–3, 5–208 [with *Merlinus iste* chapter after §117]. Dedicated to Robert of Gloucester.

Rubrics at §1 (19vb) 'Incipit prologus Gaufridi Monemutensis in sequentem hysto-
riam', §6 (21ra) 'Explicit descriptio Britannie insule. Incipit hystoria Britonum', after
§208 (106ra/b) 'Explicit ystoria Britonum'.
No book-divisions.
Second Variant Version. Hammer's siglum L: Emanuel, 'Geoffrey of Monmouth's
Historia', p, 104. Copy of Cambridge, UL, MS. Mm.5.29 with the addition of later
material after fo 169.
Prophetie §§111–113 with gloss, printed by Hammer, 'Another commentary'.

CONTENTS
1ra–15va: 'Incipit epistola Cornelii ad Salustium Crispum in Troianorum hystoria que
in Greco a Darete hystoriographo facta est'. 'Cornelius Salustio Crispo suo salutem
. . . Palamonem. Epistrophum. Scidium.' Ed. Meister, *Daretis Phrygii De Excidio
Troiae Historia.*
15va–19vb: 'Incipit prophetia Sibylle'. 'Sibylle generaliter omnes femine dicuntur
prophetantes . . . cum illo in secula seculorum. Amen.' Ed. Sackur, *Sibyllinische Texte*,
pp. 177–87.
20ra–106rb: HRB.
106rb–116vb: 'Incipi\un/t gesta Britonum a Gilda sapiente composita'. 'A principio
mundi usque ad diluuium anni .ii.cc.xlii. . . . in extremis finibus cosmi est.' Ed. Faral,
La Légende, III.5–61.
116vb–118ra: Bedan chronology. 'Quinquagesimo ergo quarto anno . . . qui sunt ab
exordio mundi usque in presens.' Also in Oxford, Bodleian Library, MS. Bodley 163.
118ra–120vb: 'Incipit libellus Bemetoli quem beatus Ieronimus de Greco in Latinum
transtulit uel composuit'. 'Anno .d.cccc. tricesimo mortuus est Adam . . . omnis honor
et perhennis in secula seculorum. Amen.' Compare ed. Sackur, *Sibyllinische Texte*,
pp. 59–96.
120vb–121rb: 'Hildricus Harlebecensis comes genuit Ingelramnum . . . Baldeuinum
et Willelmum'. Genealogical list of counts of Flanders.
121rb/va: 'Hec sunt nomina Francorum regum'. 'Clodoueus . . . Philippus. Lodouicus.'
121va–126va: description of Britain. 'Britannia igitur beatissima est insularum . . .
illam quam [ ]tus que semper in asperimis.' Henry of Huntingdon, *Historia Anglorum*,
I.1–13 (ed. Arnold, pp. 5–17).
126va–127rb: description of the geography of England with lists of the shires and
bishoprics. 'Anglia habet in longitudine .d.ccc. miliaria . . . Sstafordsire (*sic*) .d. hide.'
127rb–143va: *capitula*-list for following work. 'De Nectanabi prudentia . . . emisit
spiritum.' 'Incipiunt gesta Alexandri regis magni Macedonum'. 'Egypti sapientes fati
genere diuino primi feruntur . . . et ueneno superatus atque extinctus occubuit.' Ed.
Kuebler, *Iuli Valerii Alexandri Polemi res gestae*, pp. 1–168.
143va: 'Epitaphium'. 'Primus Alexandri pillea natus in urbe . . . ferroque regna lesit.'
Walther, *Initia*, p. 759, no. 14648.
143va/b: 'Quicquid in humanis constat uirtutibus altis . . . succubuit leto sumpto cum
melle ueneno'. See Hill, '*Epitaphia Alexandri*', p. 98. Walther, *Initia*, I.833, no.
15990.

143vb–152vb: 'Incipit epistola Alexandri regis magni Macedonum ad magistrum suum Aristotilem'. 'Semper memor tui etiam . . . nominis mei fama habeatur in gloria.' Ed. Walther Boer, *Epistola Alexandri.*

152vb–158va: 'Alexandri magni regis Macedonum et Dindimi regis Bragmannorum de philosophia per litteras facta collatio'. 'Sepius ad aures meas fando peruenit . . . quod a meliore prestantur.' Ed. Kuebler, *Iuli Valerii Alexandri Polemi res gestae*, pp. 169–89.

158vb–160rb: 'Parua recapitulacio de eodem Alexandro et de suis'. 'Tempore quo hic Alexander natus legitur . . . et egregie uicisse narratur.' Ed. Ross, 'Parva Recapitulacio', pp. 199–203. Followed by colophon, 'Exora Cristum (*sic*) qui librum legeris istum / ut scriptori det quicquid debetur honori'.

160rb–161ra: description of the holy sites at Jerusalem. 'Notum sit omnibus fidelibus statum ciuitatis Ierusalem sic esse dispositum . . . ciuitas Ierusalem capta fuit.'

161ra/va: 'Eodem die diuisio apostolorum'. 'Hec sunt reliquie apud Con[s]tantinopolim . . . caput sancti Pantaleonis martyr[is].'

161va–167vb: 'Incipit sermo quomodo primitus sancta arbor creuit in qua salus mundi pependit'. 'Sancta et diuina eloquia fratres iugiter . . . nunc et per omnia seculorum secula. Amen.' Ed. Mozley, 'A new text', pp. 117–27. (At this point, Mm.5.29 truncated.)

167vb–169ra: 'Sermo sancti Ieronimi de persecutionibus'. 'Frequenter diximus semper enim Christiani persecutionem patiuntur . . . qui in trinitate uiuit et regnat in secula seculorum. Amen.' Ed. Migne, *Patrologia Latina*, XL.1342–43.

(169ra/v: three notes)

169ra/b: 'Trium magorum nomina in libris inuenimus . . . filium hominis moriturum confessus est'. Ed. Migne, *Patrologia Latina*, LXXXIII.1293–1302 (incomplete). Dekkers, *Clavis*, p. 270, no. 1194. Lapidge & Sharpe, p. 209, no. 779.

169rb: 'Tribus modis diabolus securitatem mittit . . . seducuntur multi'.

169v: 'De preuaricatione Salomonis regis . . . uicesima Adriatina uicesima pri-'. Truncated.

170r–173r: 'Prophetia Merlini exposita' (thirteenth-century). 'Sedente itaque Wortogirno (*sic*) . . . Uenedotia id est Northuuallia rubebit materno.'

173v: 'Regula de .uii. etatibus'. 'Prima etas seculi ab Adam usque ad Noe . . . a captione Willelmi regis Scocie tunc fuit annus Domini .m.clxxv..' Added in late fourteenth century or later.

174r–181v: 'Hire bigynneth a bok wiche is callid Brut the cronycles of Engelonde'. 'This book tretith ond tellith of the kingis & principal lordis . . . wiche was dougtir [ ] heir . . .' Truncated.

182r–185rc: 'Iste (*sic*) sunt episcopi sub romano pontifice constituti qui non sunt in alterius prouincia in primis'. 'Hostiensis . . . Cantuaria, Dorobernia.'

185rc: 'Anglia habet in longitudine .dccc. milaria . . . In Anglia sunt .xxxii. enim scyre ut supra patet'. Copy of the start of the work found on 126v.

185rc: 'Nominum interpretacio'. Names of the archangels. 'Cum mane surrexeris ... omnes conuiue gaudebunt tibi.'

186v: 'Primus uirorum strenuorum illustrium'. 'Nouem nomina [ ]is erat Iosue ... ultimis in ordine uirorum illustrium.' From Josua to Godfridus (Godfrey de Bouillon).

DESCRIPTION

SIZE 29 x 19 cm.

QUIRING Catchwords. I–IV⁸, V⁸ (33–38, 38 bis, 39), VI–XX⁸, XXI¹⁰ (160–169); XXII⁴ (170–173); XXIII⁸ (174–181); XXIV ? (182–186).

PRICKING Outer margins only.

RULING Quires I–XX two columns of 29 lines, written above top ruled line. Prophecies of Merlin (Q. XXI) in single column of 32 lines. Brut (Q. XXII) single frame-ruled column, 34–40 lines written. Q. XXIV, 40 lines.

SCRIPT Original manuscript in several Protogothic hands. HRB in regular, fairly formal script written with wide nib. Short ascenders (with slightly flattened tops) and descenders. Straight-backed d and tall s standard in some hands but et-nota usual (ampersand found in some hands) and no e-caudata. Little lateral compression in places. Q. XXI in small but elongated thirteenth-century bookhand. Juncture of e and o after b, d, p. Final s tall or cedilla-shaped. Et-nota sometimes crossed, some occurrence of two-compartment a. Q. XXII in small, angular hand of fifteenth century or later. Leans to right. Ascenders with hairline, angularly-looped tops, pierced t, simple forms of e, and round a with angled sides. Q. XXIII in four-line script, minims disjointed, descenders tapered. Looped two-compartment a, final round s. No slant. Looped ascenders (not angular). Late fourteenth century or later.

DECORATION Minor capitals are plain Romanesque. Major capitals with stylised leafy scrolls and acanthus ornament.

HISTORY

186v foot, in sixteenth-century hand, 'Iste liber pertinet ad Thomam Tham[ ]'.

BIBLIOGRAPHY

Dumville, 'The manuscripts', p. 124.
Hammer, 'Another Commentary', pp. 589–601.
Hammer, 'Some additional manuscripts', p. 239.
Woolley, *Catalogue*, pp. 63–65.

81 *LONDON, BRITISH LIBRARY, MS. ADDITIONAL 11702

Saec. xiii/xiv   Origin: ?Southern France
88 fos   2nd fo: *ad Ascanium filium*

HRB 11r–88r

§§1–3, 5–21, 24 (*med.*) –32, 34–36, 39–179. Text ends without physical loss.
Nameless dedication.
No extant rubrics.

No book-divisions.

Fos 19–22 transposed: 18v ends §21 'quibusque prouinciis', continues on 20r 'repertos gigantes' with no loss of text. 20v ends §25 'in hunc diem appela-', completed on 19r '-tum est Brittannica lingua'. 19v ends §29 'id est Wintoniam', completed top 22r 'atque oppidum'. 22v ends §31 'Agganippo maritatur', continued on 21r 'Post multum uero temporis'.

Text jumps without physical break on 20v (line 5) from the end of §21 'in presentem diem dicitur' to §24 'Duxit itaque Locrinus' (line 6).

CONTENTS

1r–11r: 'Ab Adam usque ad diluuium anni .ii(m).xl.ii. . . . per infinita secula seculorum'. Ed. Dumville, *The Historia Brittonum*, III.61–105.
11r–88r: HRB. Text ends mid-recto.
88v: blank, ruled. Signs of erasure of two lines at top.

DESCRIPTION

SIZE 19 x 13 cm.
QUIRING Original catchwords. I–XI^8. Transposed folios 19–22 constitute central bifolia of Q. III.
PRICKING Apparent only in outer margin.
RULING Single column of 29–30 lines. Ruling above top written line. Single vertical boundary-lines.
SCRIPT Small, compact Gothic bookhand. Brown ink. Few descenders. a occasionally tall initially but often has small or no head, unlooped round d with tall diagonal ascender, 2-shaped r trails below line, final s more often straight than round, pierced t. Juncture of e and o following b, d, h, p. Bows of letters in juncture tend to come away from their uprights. Uncrossed *et*-nota. Straight-backed d occurs.
DECORATION Small plain filigreed capitals in red or red and blue, occasionally with purple.

HISTORY

Text of *Historia Brittonum* closely related to that of Paris, Bibliothèque nationale, MS. lat. 8048 (French, thirteenth-century): Dumville, *The Historia Brittonum*, III.33. On 88r in ?Early Modern ink capitals, 'Iste liber est meus Iouannes Pauolus de Feraris dictis de Bertois'. Note of purchase from Chevalier de Mortara in 1840 found on paper flyleaf at front of volume.

BIBLIOGRAPHY

Dumville, *The Historia Brittonum*, III.33.
Madden, *List of Additions*, 1840, p. 5.
Ward & Herbert, *Catalogue of Romances*, I.247.

Saecc. xii^2 + xv   Origin: ?Continental (?Low Countries)

72 + 16 fos   2nd fo: *Cumque a patre*

HRB 1r–85v

§§1–3, 5–166 (*ex.*) of original; §§166 (*ex.*) –208 supplied in fifteenth-century hand. Original ends at foot of 72v 'Iussit etiam Cadorem ducem'. Continued 73r 'Bedue-rumque', no loss of text. Dedicated to Robert of Gloucester.

No rubrics.

Book-divisions: II [ ], III §35 (17v), IV §54 (25v), V §73 (34v), VI §89 (41r), VII [ ], VIII §118 (54r), IX §143 (63v).

No book-divisions in fifteenth-century section.

No other contents but after §208 (85v) Latin notes in Early Modern hand taken from John Bale, *Scriptorum Britanniae Catalogus*. Same hand found on fo 1r. Rest of quire ruled but otherwise blank.

DESCRIPTION

SIZE 25 x 17 cm.

QUIRING A (twelfth-century) 1–72 – I–IX^8; B (fifteenth-century) 73–88 – X–XI^8. Single parchment flyleaves before and after.

PRICKING At outer edge only. In A sometimes very near to written space.

RULING A – single column of variable number of lines, 26–32 and even 41. Double vertical boundary-lines. Written above top ruled line. B – single column of 35 lines with single boundary-lines. Written below top ruled line.

SCRIPT A – several hands, in brown ink. Varies from quite rounded and large four-line script with some lateral compression in which e-caudata is frequent, straight-backed **d** occurs, ampersand is more common than *et*-nota, final **s** is tall, to smaller, less formal script with less continuity between letters and standard usage of *et*-nota only. Round **d** but tall final **s** are standard in this part of the manuscript. Straight-backed **g** not infrequent. B – regular *cursiua formata*. Prominent slanting descenders, tall crossed **t** and **g**, simple minuscule forms of **e** and **a**, looped ascenders, grey ink. **r** formed of v-like loop.

DECORATION A – bold capitals in blue or red with split shafts, foliate flourishes but no filigree ornament.

HISTORY

Erased *ex-libris* at top of 1r, not recovered under ultraviolet light. On front flyleaf: 'Purchased of Payne & Foss. 14 March 1846'.

BIBLIOGRAPHY
Madden, *Additions* 1846, p. 18.

Ward & Herbert, *Catalogue of Romances*, I.234.

83 *LONDON, BRITISH LIBRARY, MS. ADDITIONAL 33371

Saec. xii^2 Mediaeval provenance: ?
47 + i fos Present 2nd fo (original lost): *ibi monasterium*

HRB 28va–39v

Fragments only. §§1–3, 5 (*med.*), 19 (*ex.*) –21 (*ex.*), 25 (*in.*) –33 (*med.*), 40 (*med.*) –42 (*med.*), 55 (*med.*) –61, 99 (*med.*) –101 (*med.*), 105 (*med.*) –113 (*med.*), 116 (*med.*). Dedicatory section cut away.

Rubric at §1 (28va) 'Incipit prologus Gaufridi Monemutensis in hystoriis regum Britannie'; beside §106 (37ra), 'Historia Mellini', repeated above in hand of *ca* 1300. No book-divisions extant.

CONTENTS

1r–24v: *Liber historiarum gentis Anglorum Bede presbiteri Ceouulfum regem* (from final rubric, 24v), acephalous. 'facere solebat utpote nil proprie possessionis excepta ecclesia sua . . . et parere semper ante faciem tuam.' From III.7 to end, lacunose. Edd. Colgrave & Mynors, *Bede's Ecclesiastical History*.

25r–28r: *Epistola Alexandri regis ad Aristotilem magistrum suum* (from final rubric, 28r) also acephalous. 'capite solo oculo ad superuentum opinati Dei curiose intendebat . . . et animi industria optime Aristotiles indicium.' Ed. Walther Boer, *Epistola Alexandri*.

28v–39v: HRB.

(40r–47v: fragments of Peter Comestor, *Historia Scholastica*, ed. Migne, *Patrologia Latina*, CXCVIII.1053–1722).

40r/v: On Genesis, §§46–49. 'Ut pugnarent aduersus quatuor . . . hoc predictum est quia Saraceni uagi' (*ibid.*, CXCVIII.1094B–1096D).

41r–44v: On Genesis, §§68–82. 'in instanti putans . . . de quo dicit Ier. Sochot est usque hodie ciuitas' (*ibid.*, CXCVIII.1111B–1121D).

45r–46v: On Macchabees II, §§4–16. 'muneribus ut diceret quod cum armis descenderet . . . domum exstimaret. Edem' (*ibid.*, CXCVIII.1526B–1532A).

47r/v: On the Gospels, §§68–74. 'factum est secundum munere gratie . . . quasi .v. iii.' (*ibid.*, CXCVIII.1572C–1575D).

Blank parchment flyleaf.

DESCRIPTION

SIZE 24.5 x 34.5 cm.

QUIRING Signatures in Bede (IX 12v, X 15v, XI 21v, XII 24v). Some folios mounted. Fos 40–47 are of thicker, more suede-like parchment.

PRICKING Fos 1–39 – in both margins. 40–47 – outer margin only.

RULING Double columns with single vertical boundary-lines throughout. No ruling above top line. Bede 36 lines, *Epistola* & HRB 38, final section 37.

SCRIPT HRB and *Epistola* in same script: large, roundish, four-line. Little compression or angularity. No juncture. Round final s occurs, round d perhaps more common than straight form. e-caudata used incorrectly. Ampersand standard.

HISTORY
Bookplate of Edward Breeze of Morfa Lodge, Porthmadog. Note on flyleaves, 'Purchased at Sotheby's (Breeze sale, lot 328) 31. May 1888'.

BIBLIOGRAPHY
Scott, *Catalogue of Additions to the Manuscripts in the British Museum in the Years 1888–1893*, p. 5.

84 *LONDON, BRITISH LIBRARY, MS. ADDITIONAL 35295

Saec. xv (in, or soon after, 1422)   Origin: Collection made by John Streeche, canon of Kenilworth, Warwickshire.
280 fos   2nd fo: [ ]*ra personis urbs ciuibus*

HRB 137r–228v
§§1–3, 5–208. Dedicated to Robert of Gloucester.
Rubric on 136v: 'Incipit historia Britonum et quomodo Brutus primus rex Brutannie uenit in istam insulam cum gente sua post Troiam destructam fraude Attenor<is> et Enee qui Eneas postmodum Turno rege ab ipso deuicto regnauit in Italia Lauinia ducta ab eo filia regis Litinorum (*sic*) de qua filium Siluium genuit ut patet in sequenti historia'. §5 (137r) 'De Britannia insula', §111 (185v) 'Incipit prophetia Merlini. liber uii', after §208 (228v) 'Explicit historia libri Britonum que in octo libris continetur'. Other rubrics occasionally at textual divisions.
Book-divisions: II §23 (145r), III §35 (151r), IIII §54 (158v), V §73 (166v), VI §89 (175r), VII §111 (185v), 'Liber septimus post prophetiam' §118 (191r), VIII §143 (202r).

CONTENTS
i: blank, modern parchment.
1v: kalendar of saints (mounted on blank modern parchment).
2v (pasted to blank modern parchment): bookplate with I/S monogramme.
ii: blank, modern parchment.
3r–4r (mounted): poem on Troy. 'Pergama flere uolo fato Danaum data solo ... femina fatalis femina feta malis.' Ed. Hammer, 'Some Leonine summaries', pp. 121–22. Walther, *Initia*, I.723, no. 13985.
4v: poem. 'Digna perire mari pocius flammisue cremari ... Uicta Reso traci dempta dolis Ytaci.'
5r: kalendar of Saints (originally conjugate with 1v), also mounted on blank parchment.
6r–136v: 'Prologus operis sequentis'. Guido delle Colonne, *Historia destructionis Troie*. 'Licet cotidie uetera recentibus obruantur non nulla tamen uetera ... Anno Dominice incarnacionis millesimo ducentesimo octuagesimo septimo eiusdem prime indiccionis feliciter et anno [ ].' Ed. Griffin, *Historia destructionis Troiae*.
137r–228v: HRB.
229r–279v (232v blank, unruled): 'Et incipit historia regum omnium Anglorum ante

monarchiam et post expulsis Britonibus usque ad tempus regis Henrici post conquestum sexti que in quinque libris continetur' (rubric on 229v). History of England with
special reference to Kenilworth Priory. 'Apud Britones inconcussa stetit insule
monarchia . . . set fortunatus uictor ubique stetitur.' Ends with 18 lines of verse. Fos
265r–279v printed by Taylor, 'The Chronicle of John Streeche', pp. 146–87.

DESCRIPTION
SIZE 25 x 17.5/18 cm.
QUIRING Catchwords. I uncollatable (i, 1–2 [mounted], ii, 3–5, 6–12), II–XXVIII^8,
XXX ?^{4} (229–232), XXXI–XXXII^8, XXXIII^8 (1–4 replaced by 4 unnumbered modern
blanks: 249–252), XXXIV^{10} (1 lacking, replaced by unnumbered modern blank:
253–261), XXXV^8, XXXVI^8 (2 lacking, replaced by unnumbered modern blank):
270–276), XXXVII^4 (4 mounted, 3 modern unnumbered blanks: 277–280).
PRICKING For frame-ruling only.
RULING Frame in brown pencil. 28–34 lines written in HRB. 33–37 lines written
elsewhere.
SCRIPT Two distinct hands. HRB throughout in black, largish, Secretary-influenced
hand. Two-compartment a of minim height, small g, final sigma-shaped s. Ascenders
loop over, heavy uprights, some slant. 2-shaped et-nota, c and t difficult to distinguish,
e often like pinched c. Long r in rubrics but not text. Second hand is more compact
and cursive. Brown ink. Thinner pen. Looped d, sigma-shaped s, a has no head,
crossed et-nota, occasionally r is long.

HISTORY
The monogram of John Streeche is found on 2v and 136v. He was canon of the *cellula*
of Brooke or Broke, Rutland, from 1407 to 1425 when he resigned: Taylor, 'The
Chronicle of John Streeche', pp. 138–39. He composed the chronicle occupying
229r–279v of this manuscript and was also the scribe of BL, MS. Additional 38665:
Ker, *Medieval Libraries*, p. 271. Part of the present volume was written by Iohannes
Aston: *ibid.*. Also at top 6r in ?sixteenth-century hand, 'Thomas Maron'.
Bookplate of Ashburnham House (with date 1897) pasted inside front cover.

BIBLIOGRAPHY
Scott, *Catalogue of Additions to the Manuscripts in the British Museum in the Years
1894–1899*, pp. 240–42.
Taylor, 'The Chronicle of John Streeche'.

85   *LONDON, BRITISH LIBRARY, MS. ARUNDEL 10

Saec. xii *ex.*   Provenance (Early Modern): Cambrai
ii + 122 fos   2nd fo: *atque piscosis fluuiis*

HRB 2r–122rb
§§1–3, 5–184, 186–208. Dedicated to Robert of Gloucester.

No opening rubric. After §208 'Explicit historia Britonum' (N.B. last page in different hand from rest of HRB).

No book-divisions.

Second Variant Version, not known to Hammer: Crick, 'Manuscripts', p. 162. Interpolation (3r/v) before §6, 'Imperatorum constitutionem frustra obicitis catholici . . . qui publicis non sint dignitatibus implicati'.

No other contents. Flyleaves (i + 1) blank except for inscription i r (see HISTORY) and title, notes in French (?thirteenth-century) 1v.

No other contents. 122v and 123 not ruled, and blank except for a few pen-trials.

DESCRIPTION

SIZE 18 x 27 cm.

QUIRING Quire signatures. a^2 (i, 1), I–XV^8, XVI^2 (122–123).

PRICKING At outer edge only.

RULING Two columns of 24 lines, top line written, single vertical boundaries.

SCRIPT Large, formal, Protogothic minuscule, brown ink. Minims thickened at both ends but not broken, short ascenders, no juncture. *Et* not abbreviated (little abbreviation generally), no e-caudata, straight **d** used (perhaps a reflection of formality), final round s frequent. Last folio less calligraphic, more angular; crossed **t** and ampersand used.

DECORATION Red or pale blue Romanesque capitals with flourishes and curls in contrasting colour. Those at §§1 and 5 in gold outlined in black, with red and pale blue flourishes.

HISTORY

On verso of first flyleaf in small scratchy Early Modern hand: 'Liber ecclesie Cameracen.'. Stamp of Henry Howard of Norfolk at foot of 2r. Verso of final flyleaf, notes in French in informal hand of ?thirteenth-century, and notes in Latin recording death of Charles of Burgundy 153[6]. Note on i r: 'Walter G[ro]nsford translat[or] into Latin. 1828'. On i v in ?thirteenth-century hand 'Hystoria Britonum Gaufridi Monemitensis'.

BIBLIOGRAPHY

[Forschall,] *Catalogue of Manuscripts in the British Museum, N.S., 1: Part 1, The Arundel Manuscripts*, p. 3.

Ward & Herbert, *Catalogue of Romances*, I.224–25.

86   *LONDON, BRITISH LIBRARY, MS. ARUNDEL 237

Saec. xiii^1 Origin: ?Continental; provenance: ?English

ii (paper) + 64 fos   2nd fo: *ingere nituntur. Porro*

HRB 1r–64v

§§6–199 'et maximam partem sui exer-'. Dedicatory section absent without physical loss.

Note top 1r ?contemporary with rubrics 'Require prologum folio 3 ante finem istius libri qui incipit [ ]'.

Rubrics added (?*saec.* xiii/xiv).

No book-divisions.

Text related to version found in Bern, Burgerbibliothek, MS. 568 and Rouen, Bibliothèque municipale, MS. 1177 (U.74): Dumville, 'An early text', pp. 16–18, 22–23; Wright, *The Historia Regum Britannie of Geoffrey of Monmouth, I*, p. li.

No other contents.

DESCRIPTION

SIZE 25 x 16 cm.

QUIRING Occasional signatures indicate I–VIII⁸, with no loss at beginning. Early foliation in centre-top of each recto confirms this.

PRICKING In outer margin only.

RULING In brown pencil, one column of 31–34 lines, single vertical boundary-lines, top line generally written.

SCRIPT Compact, angular, and spiky, short ascenders and descenders, juncture of **de**, **do, po**. Round **d** two-line, *et*-nota uncrossed, **t** sometimes pierced, but **a** has small or upright head, not two-compartment form, final **s** is round, tall, or cedilla-shaped. Dark brown ink.

DECORATION Capitals in blue or orange-red with usual flourishes in the contrasting colour.

HISTORY

Marginal notes in various cursive hands, apparently English, of the fourteenth century.

BIBLIOGRAPHY

[Forschall,] *Catalogue of Manuscripts in the British Museum, N.S., 1: Part 1, The Arundel Manuscripts*, p. 70.

Ward & Herbert, *Catalogue of Romances*, I.241.

87   *LONDON, BRITISH LIBRARY, MSS. ARUNDEL 319 + 409

Saec. xiii²   Mediaeval provenance: ?Scotland
                                                                 (thirteenth century)

MS. 319

97 fos   2nd fo: *Saxonibus cesserunt*

HRB 16r–97v

§§1–3, 5–138 (*in.*), 143 (*in.*) –173 'rex Affricorum. Alphatima'. Dedicated to Robert of Gloucester.

Rubrics at §1 (6r) 'Incipit <editio Galfridi Monumetensis de gestis Britonum>' (no longer legible): see Ward & Herbert, *Catalogue of Romances*, I.232. §5 (16v) 'De situ Britannie et eius pulcritudine', §111 (72r) ?'Incipit prophecia Merlini'.

Book-divisions (*narraciones*): I §6 (17r), II §23 (26v), III §35 (33v), IV §89 (60r).

Loss of text between 86v (ends 'egressus est cum' §138) and 87r '.xv. annorum iuuenis' §143).

Interpolation of eight lines in §114 (73r) after opening sentence. 'Dolor conuertetur in gaudium cum matris in utero patrem filii trucidabunt. Orientis priuilegio gaudebit occidens et terrarum tam principes quam primates .vi. uestigia martiris adorabunt. Ex delicto geniti delinquunt in genitorem et precedens delictum fit causa sequencium delictorum. In ?matrum sanguinis sanguis instirget. (*sic*) et dispartibilis fiet afflictio donec Albania peregrinantis fleuit penitenciam. Quinti quadriga uoluetur in quartum et bis binario sublato. bina superstes regna calcabit'.

MS. 409
26 fos
HRB 1r–23r
§§173 'rex Hispanie. Hircatus rex' –208. No loss of text between MS. 319 and this. No rubrics but after §208 (23r) 'Et hec dicta sufficiant per Christum Dominum nostrum. Amen'.
No book-divisions.

CONTENTS
MS. 319
1r/v: blank except for name on verso, see below, HISTORY.
2r: verses. 'Si paribus uel disparibus constant elementis . . . Hec tibi signa dabunt quod defensor superetur.' Walther, *Proverbia*, IV.924, no. 28789. In Anglicana script ?*ca* 1300. Also found in BL, Royal 8.E.xvii.
Fifteenth-century contents-list.
2v–3r: medical recipes in various fourteenth- and fifteenth-century hands, Latin and English.
3v–4v: blank.
5r–6v: notes (Latin) for sermon. Names of sons of Israel, notes on Exodus.
7: blank, recto ruled.

8r–15r: abridged copy of Iulianus Pomerius, *De Uita Contemplatiua* (full unabbreviated text ed. Migne, *Patrologia Latina*, LIX.415–520). This copy imperfect in XXI.ii. 'In multumque reuisus sum uoluntati tue . . . et oues mee in deuorationem omnium.'

16r–97v: HRB.

MS. 409
1r–23r: HRB.
23r–24r: 'Prophecia Merlini Siluestris'. 'Sicut rubeum draconem albus expellet . . . qui pacifico regno occidet.' Ed. Schulz, *Gottfried*, pp. 464–65.
24v: blank except for name; see below.
24*r–25r: blank.
25v: document; see below.

DESCRIPTION
SIZE MS. 319 12 x 17 cm except for fos 8–15 (11 x 17 cm); MS. 409 12 x 17 cm.

QUIRING MS. 319 (tightly bound) I ?^{8} (8 lacking); II^8; III^{14} (16–29), IV–V^{12}, VI–VII^8, VIII^{16} (70–85), IX ?^{12}. MS. 409 I^{14}, II^8, parchment bifolium.

PRICKING Outer margin only in HRB and Q. II of MS. 319. Not visible in MS. 319, Q. I.

RULING HRB – single column, 27–29 lines written, single vertical boundary-lines. Written below top ruled line. MS. 319 – Q. I, single column, 40 lines or more; Q. II, single column, double vertical boundary-lines, 23–26 lines.

SCRIPT HRB rather crude at first. Letters widely spaced. Brown ink. Small-headed **a**, tall final **s**. Crossed *et*-nota. Some juncture of **do**, **po**, and **de**. 2-shaped **r** found after **a** as well as **o**. Hands of collaborating scribes are small and compressed, later in appearance with two-compartment **a**, pierced **t**, juncture of **e** and **o** after **b**, **d**, and **p**. Split ascenders. Minims lozenged at both ends. MS. 319, Q. I written closely in very small late thirteenth-century hand and hands of later date. MS. 319, Q. II in thirteenth-century hand. Upright and laterally compressed. Ampersand, little juncture, some splitting of tops of ascenders.

DECORATION Plain red capitals.

HISTORY

MS. 319 – name 'Henley' written in Humanist Cursive on 1v.

MS. 409 – document written on 25v issued in name of Alexander de Pundsoneby, rector of church of Kyrkam, Whithorn, in favour of a clerk, Robert de Gerroc, witnessed by Thomas, bishop of Whithorn, at Alnetun, and dated 1294: described by Ward, *apud* Ward & Herbert, *Catalogue of Romances*, I.233.

BIBLIOGRAPHY

Crick, 'The manuscripts', pp. 157–58.

[Forschall,] *Catalogue of Manuscripts in the British Museum. N.S., 1: Part 1, The Arundel Manuscripts*, pp. 93, 118.

Ward & Herbert, *Catalogue of Romances*, I.232, 233.

88 *LONDON, BRITISH LIBRARY, MS. ARUNDEL 326

Saec. xiii/xiv   Mediaeval provenance: ?Abingdon
134 fos   2nd fo (8r): *Recapitulacio Bede*

HRB 63r–122v.

§§1–3, 5–108, 111–189 'Adquiescentes igitur consilio eorum collegerunt graui'. Dedicated to Robert of Gloucester.

Rubrics at §1 (63r) 'Incipit prologus in hystoria Britonum', §5 (63r) 'Explicit prologus. Descripcio insule Maioris Britannie', after §108 (96r) 'Incipit indissolubilis prophetie Merlini liber de hystoriis Britonum', §118 (100r) 'Explicit prophecia Merlini'.

Book-divisions: II §23 (69v), III §35 (73v), IV §54 (78r), V §73 (84r), VI §89 (89r), VII §119 'Conuocato' (100v), VIII §135 (105r), IX §143 (107v), XI §177 'ut igitur infamia' (120r). Prophecies divided into *capitula*.

Interpolation after §5: 'Mirabilia Britannie insule' (§§63v–64r). 'Quoddam namque stagnum . . . et qualiter Troianos trans tot equora ista longe positis regnis in Britanniam adduxerit.' Ed. Dumville, 'Anecdota'.

CONTENTS

1r–6v: kalendar (twelfth-century). 'Prima dies mensis et septima truncat ut ensis Ianuarius habet dies .xxxi. et lunam .xxx. . . ..' From St Stephen to St Silvester (December). Includes Anglo-Saxon saints such as Aldhelm, Guthlac, Oswald, Dunstan. It bears some resemblance to St Albans texts but the number of female saints may suggest that it belonged to a nunnery, possibly Wherwell (*ex. inf.* Dr Nigel Morgan).

7r: fragment of text cut down from leaf in two columns.

7v: contents-list.

8r: 'Recapitulacio Bede presbiteri ob memoriam conseruandam eorum que distinctione temporum lacius digesta sunt'. 'Anno ante incarnacionem Dominicam .lx. . . . Gregorius papa misit Britanniam Augustinum.'

8v–9r: blank, unruled.

9v: more chronology. 'In principio erat uerbum . . . ab Adam usque ad natiuitatem Henric<i> regis filii Iohannis.'

10r–22r: 'Incipiunt cronica a principio mundi'. 'Primo creatus est Adam quasi annorum .xxx. . . . sanctus Thomas archiepiscopus translatus est <1221>. Hugo abbas Abendis obit et successit Rob. eiusdem loci camer..'

22v: blank, unruled.

23r–36v: 'In nomine sancte Trinitatis incipiunt gesta saluatoris Domini nostri Iesu [ ] que inuenit Theodosius magnus imperator in Ierusalem in pretorio Pontii Pilati in codicibus publicis'. 'Factum est in anno .xix. imperatoris Theodosii . . . omnia que gesta sunt de Iesu in pretorio meo.'

36v–40v: 'Quomodo crux Domini inuenta fuit'. '[P]ost peccatum Ade expulso de paradiso . . . cui est laus honor et imperium per omnia secula seculorum. Amen.' Ed. Hill, 'The fifteenth-century prose legend'.

40v–42r: 'Incipit de Antichristo'. 'De Antichristo scire uolentibus primo dicemus quare sic uocatur . . . ante secula iudicandum esse prefixit.' Anselm, *De Antichristo*, ed. Verhelst, *Adso Dervensis*, pp. 160–66, 157.

42r–50v: 'De expulcione Ade et Eue de paradiso'. 'Factum est cum expulsi essent Adam et uxor eius . . . cum factus fuisset Adam et non erat.' Truncated. Ed. Mozley, 'The "Vita Adae" ', pp. 128–48.

51r–54r: 'Arna et Emeria fuerunt sorores . . . ut induta pelleis tanquam seuo exempta domino triumpharet'.

54r–55v: 'Beatus Petrus apostolus ordinauit duos episcopos Linum et Cletum . . . ubi fuerunt omnes fere episcopi et abbates tocius Anglie'.

56r/v: 'Si quis ab occidentalibus partibus Ierusalem adire uoluerit . . . et ipse Abraham filium suum Ysaac immolare uoluit'.

57r–60v: 'Incipit liber Methodii episcopi et martiris de miliaribus mundi'. 'In nomine Domini nostri . . . opusculis suis collaudauit qui cum patre et spiritu sancto uiuit et regnat Deus per omnia.' Not the text of this name printed by Sackur, *Sibyllinische Texte*, pp. 60–96.

60v–63r: 'Incipit prophetia Sibille'. 'Sibille generaliter dicuntur omnes femine uates . . . in eternum cum Christo in secula seculorum. Amen.' Ed. Sackur, *ibid.*, pp. 177–87.

63r–122v: HRB.

123r–127v: annals and notes on popes and emperors from Boniface IV. 'Post passionem Domini anno sequenti beatus Petrus apostolus tenuit cathedram sacerdotalem . . . ut in hystoria sancti Pelagii plenius habetur.'

128r–134v: French history 640–1270. 'Nunc autem ad gesta Francorum stilus se uertat . . . esto Domini plebe sanctificator et custos et cum appropinquarum (*sic*) terminum.'

DESCRIPTION

SIZE 17 x 12 cm.

QUIRING I^6 (1–6); II^2 (7–8); III^{14}, IV^{16}, V^{10}, VI^2 (49–50), VII^{10}, VIII^{12}, IX^{16}, X^8, XI^{12}, XII^{14} (109–122), XIII^{12}.

PRICKING None visible.

RULING One column throughout of 37 or 38 lines in HRB (but occasionally 28–30). Most of volume ruled in 34–35 lines. Frame-ruling.

SCRIPT Volume written in compressed informal script after first quire. HRB in two-line Anglicana script with looped or split ascenders. **a** and **s** rise above minim height. **d** is looped, **g** almost two-line, *et*-nota is crossed. Long **s** occurs in all positions.

DECORATION Unfiligreed red capitals at beginning of books only.

HISTORY

Abingdon origin suggested by Ker on grounds of inclusion of material from that house, presumably meaning fos 10–22: *Medieval Libraries*, p. 2.

Name William Howarde on 1r in seventeenth- or eighteenth-century hand.

BIBLIOGRAPHY

[Forschall,] *Catalogue of Manuscripts in the British Museum, N.S., 1: Part 1, The Arundel Manuscripts*, p. 94.

Ward & Herbert, *Catalogue of Romances*, I.246.

89 *LONDON, BRITISH LIBRARY, MS. ARUNDEL 403

Saec. xii²   Mediaeval provenance: ?

18 fos   2nd fo: *mulieribus relictis atque infantibus*

HRB 1r–18v

Two fragments. §§82 (*ex.*) –103, 123 (*med.*) –143 (*in.*). No extant rubrics or book-divisions.

1r–10v §82 'Conano post hanc peticionem bellum ingerere' – §103 'Hengistum abire'. 11r–18v §123 '-nimiter resistunt et inuicem' – §143 'Defuncto igitur hiis Pendragon con-'.

No other contents.

DESCRIPTION
SIZE 21.5 x 14(.5).
QUIRING Two quires marked at the foot of the first recto .v. 1r, .vii. 11r. I^{10}, II ?^{8}.
PRICKING In outer margin only.
RULING Single column of 32 lines.
SCRIPT Single hand, brown ink. Four-line Protogothic (?cf. Continental). Some ascenders slightly indented at top, a has little head, straight-backed g. Round d, tall s standard. e-caudata very rare. No ampersand (*et*-nota used or *et* not abbreviated). No decoration.

HISTORY
Marginal annotation in Latin in Anglicana hand predating mid-fourteenth century. Stamp of Henry Howard foot first recto.

BIBLIOGRAPHY
[Forschall,] *Catalogue of Manuscripts in the British Museum, N.S., 1: Part 1, The Arundel Manuscripts*, p. 117.
Ward & Herbert, *Catalogue of Romances*, I.225.

LONDON, BRITISH LIBRARY, MS. ARUNDEL 409
See above, MS. Arundel 319

90 *LONDON, BRITISH LIBRARY, MS. COTTON CLEOPATRA D.viii

Saec. ?xiv/xv   Origin and mediaeval provenance: ?England
134 fos   2nd fo: *Quedam narracio de nobili rege*

HRB 8r–94r.
§§1–3, 5–208. Dedicated to Robert of Gloucester.
Rubrics at §1 (8r) 'Gaufridi Monemutensis de gestis Britonum. Prologus', §5 (8r) 'Britannie insule descripcio incipit', §109 (51r) 'Incipit prologus in prophecias Merlini', §111 (51v) 'Explicit prologus. Incipiunt prophecie Merlini' §118 (57r) 'Expliciunt prophetie', after §208 (94r) 'Explicit'.
Book-divisions: I §6 (8v), II §23 (16r), III §35 (21v), IV §54 (28r), V §73 (35r), VI §89 (42r), VII (*Prophetie Merlini* as indicated by rubric on 57r), VIII §118 (57r), IX §143 (67r), X §163 (76r), XI §177 (84r).
Prophetie §§111–115 glossed.
Poems at foot of many pages, as printed by Hammer from Paris, BN, lat. 4126: 'A note', pp. 230–33.

CONTENTS
1r: historical notes (folio damaged near binding). ' . . . Anno Domini millesimo .cc.lviii. apud Tewkesbury . . . ponda[rat?] .xl. libras.'

1v: notes of events 1258–1382. 'Summa annorum a creacione Adam usque ad incarnacionem [ ].' 'Quingentos decies cum bis centum numeratis . . . captus erat sic cum rex Francus accipe [ ].' Also verses as found in Oxford, Bodleian Bodley 622, 116r.

2r–3v: 'Quedam narracio de nobili rege Arthuro in sacr[ament]o altaris non credente plene qualiter confirmatus fuit in fide uere credens et quare inuitauit arma sua'. 'Dominus Deus uniuersorum conditor . . . per omnia secula seculorum. Amen.'

3v–5r: 'De origine gigantum in insula Albion olim habitancium et nomine insule que nunc Anglia dicitur'. 'Anglia modo dicta olim Albion dicebatur . . . et sic ueritas clarescit historie de primis habitatoribus huius terre.'

5r–6r: 'Compendium de Britannia siue Anglia'. 'Quoniam simplicioribus foret difficile prolixiores historias . . . uel pro ignauia amiserunt.'

6r/v: 'Sequitur de episcopatibus et primo de archiepiscopatu Eboracensi'. 'Archiepi-scopatus Eboracensis cui Euerwykeshire . . . quibus tota Northanhymbria subiacent (*sic*).'

6v: 'De archiepiscopatu Cantuarie'. 'Archiepiscopatus Cantuar. Episcopatus Rowcestrie . . . licet a Danis sepius infestarentur.'

6v–7r: 'Hit was an holy man and bylowet god . . . per a thowsand pound of gold etc.'. Followed by a Latin couplet.

7v: blank.

8r–94r: HRB.

94v: blank.

95r–107v: summary history of the Anglo-Saxon and Norman kings with the rubric 'Cadwaladrus autem abiectis secularibus propter Deum et regno terreno propter celeste Romam ueniens . . .'. 'Dic autem .xii. kalendis Maii migrauit ad Deum . . . qui omnes faceret ingredi.'

108r/v: added in Secretary hand, 'De regibus Anglie post conquestum', from William I to Henry IV. Continued to Henry VII.

109r–125r: series of anecdotes beginning 'Narracio quedam qualiter Christus ostendit se cuidam corporaliter inmissa'. 'Quidam presbiter religiosus ualde Plecgilis nomine . . . aperitur cor eius ad timendum Deum.'

125v: blank.

126r–132v: 'Lincolinensis in dictis bona exempla [ ]'. 'Si quis Romam Anglie in sui (*sic*) custodiam positam corrumperet . . . Set diuicie non possunt animam ingredi ergo nec implere.'

132v–133r: 'Cur homo torquetur. Ut ei meritum cumuletur . . . et dolor inferni sint memoranda tibi'.

133r: verse, seven lines. 'Ther ben fyue thynges yt lastynlych . . . the fythe is stedfast hope in the mercy of God.'

133r: verse. 'O quam iocundum quam dulce foret dominari . . . Non honor est sed onus assumere nomen honoris.' Walther, *Proverbia*, III.539, no. 19544.

133r/v: other verses in Latin and English in various hands.

134r/v: blank except for some notes on recto in English in fifteenth- and sixteenth-century hands.

DESCRIPTION

SIZE 24 x 17 cm.

QUIRING Indicated by catchwords. I ?⁸ (2 lacking: 1–7), II–XI⁸, XII⁸ (lacks 8: 88–94), XIII⁸, XIV⁸ (lacks 7–8: 103–108), XV–XVI⁸, XVII¹⁰ (125–134).

PRICKING Trimmed away.

RULING Frame-ruled. 37–39 lines written.

SCRIPT Cursive, Secretary-type but with width of bookhand. Grey ink. Some angularity in round **d**, and in looped tops of ascenders. Long cursive **r**, tall-backed **t**, occasional round **s**, simple backwards looped **e**-form, **a** above height of minims, two-compartment.

DECORATION Large capitals are blue in square of red ornament. Opening capital of HRB (8r) in gold on quartered solid ground of red and blue, with pale grey filigree.

HISTORY

Items on fos 2r–6v found in Oxford, Bodleian Library, MS. Bodley 622 (*S.C.* 2156), fos 1r–10r.

BIBLIOGRAPHY

Planta, *Catalogue of the Manuscripts in the Cottonian Library*, p. 583.
Smith, *Catalogus*, p. 142.
Ward & Herbert, *Catalogue of Romances*, I.249.

91 *LONDON, BRITISH LIBRARY, MS. COTTON GALBA E.xi

Saec. xiv   Mediaeval provenance: Canterbury, Franciscans
i + 155 fos   2nd fo: *De rege Lud magnifico*

HRB 5va–58vb.

§§1–3, 5–184, 186–205 'ut pristine potestate restitueretur'. Dedicated to Robert of Gloucester.

Rubrics at §1 (5va) '[Incipit prologus Gaufredi] Monumetensis in sequentem hystoriam', §5 (5vb) 'Descripcio britannice insule', §109 (34ra) 'Prefacio hystorici et epistola de interpretacione prophetiarum Merlini', §111 (34rb) 'Incipiunt prophetie Merlini ex mistica pugna draconum'.

Book-divisions: II §54 (19r), II §98 (30v), III §98 (29vb), IV §143 (44r).

Some chapters are numbered.

Second Variant Version. Hammer's siglum C: Emanuel, 'Geoffrey of Monmouth's *Historia*', p. 104.

CONTENTS

i r/v: document of 1495 from Thomas Palmer, provincial of Dominicans in England, to Agnes Cumbe, granting her prayers after her death.

1r/v: blank except for Early Modern contents-list on recto and notes on verso.

2ra–5rb: 'Incipiunt capitula hystori (*sic*) britannice'. 'Descripcio quantitatis et multimode opulencie . . . et anglice hystorie tractanda distribuit.' *Capitula*-list arranged in four books.

5va–58vb: HRB.

59r–110rb: 'Incipit hystoria Ierosolimitana abbreuiata. Cur Dominus terram sanctam uariis flagellis et sub alternis casibus se exposuit' (rubric on 59vb). Jacques de Vitry, *Historia orientalis*. Preceded by *capitula*-list. 'Terra sancta promissionis Deo amabilis . . . de die in diem expectantes.' Ed. Bongars, *Gesta Dei per Francos*, I.ii, pp. 1049–1124.

110v: blank except for ink drawing of dragon.

111ra–118va: 'Incipiunt gesta Alexandri regis Macedonum'. 'Egipti sapientes sati (*sic*) genere diuino primi feruntur . . . uino et ueneno superatus atque extinctus occubuit.' Ed. Kuebler, *Iuli Valeri Alexandri Polemi res gestae*, pp. 1–168.

118va: 'Epytaphium'. 'Primus Alexander pillea natus . . . se trementem ferroque regna lesit.' Walther, *Initia*, p. 759, no. 14648. Printed by Hill, '*Epitaphia Alexandri*', p. 97.

118va: 'Quicquid in humanis constat uirtutibus altis . . . occubuit leto sumpto cum melle ueneno'. Printed by Hill, *ibid.*, p. 98. Walther, *Initia*, I.833, no. 15990.

118va/b: 'Incipit prohemium epistole Alexandri'. 'Semper memor tui . . . que cura Alexandri tui complecti decuerant.' Continued on 121ra–125ra.

119ra–120vb: '[ ] Sybillis et de nominibus earum et de patria origine et actibus ipsarum a diebus Alexandri magni'. 'Sybille generaliter omnes femine dicuntur prophetantes . . . Et regnabit Dominus cum sanctis in secula seculorum. Amen.' Ed. Sackur, *Sibyllinische Texte*, pp. 177–87.

120vb–121ra: 'Principium hystorie magni Alexandri filii Philippi Macedonis usque ad Machabeos et reges Anthiocos inserendo Romanas hystorias sibi contemporaneas et hystoriam Appollinii (*sic*) Cyri'. 'Annis ab Adam quinque milibus .viii. lxxxviii. . . . quindecies centena milia Persarum cecidisse feruntur.' Extract from Godfrey of Viterbo, *Pantheon*. Ed. [Herold], *Pantheon*, cols 260–61.

121ra/b: 'Hic est finis imperii Persarum'. 'Hic est finis imperii Persarum . . . Hec de Alexandro Persayce breuiter tetigimus.' Extract from Godfrey of Viterbo, *Pantheon*. *Ibid.*, cols 262–63.

121ra–125ra: 'Epistola Alexandri magni Macedonis ad Aristotilem magistrum suum de omnibus mirabilibus que ipse uidit'. Continued from 120vb. 'Mense maio rege Persarum Dario . . . et industrie nostre ar[gumentu]m Aristotelis in perpetuum indicium.' Continued from 118vb. Ed. Walther Boer, *Epistola Alexandri*.

125ra: 'De Gog et Magog ex scriptis Ysidori', seven lines. 'Nota quod Alexander . . . et anichilatur.' Extract from Godfrey of Viterbo, *Pantheon*. Ed. [Herold], *Pantheon*, col. 267.

125ra–128vb: 'Hic incipit hystoria Romana mortuo Alexandro', a series of historical passages. 'Post mortem Alexandri in diuersis mundi partibus . . . cui multimodo celestis exercitus consona cantica simul cum eo cantant.' Extract from Godfrey of Viterbo, *Pantheon*. *Ibid.*, cols 270–316, 407–9, 415–17 (omitting verses).

128vb: Latin verses. 'De fonte olei qui fluxit in Tyberim'. 'Magna taberna fuit tunc emeritoria dicta . . . si super hiis debitas scripta sibilla legas.'

129r–154v: Chronicle of Martinus Polonus. 'Quoniam scire tempora summorum pontificum ac inperatorum (*sic*) . . . de expedicione et die expedicionis certificando.' Ed. Weiland, MGH, SS, XXII.397–474.

155r: divided into squares with faint notes ?on academic disciplines, texts etc.

155v: blank except for scribbles.

DESCRIPTION

SIZE 32 x 21.5 cm.

QUIRING All leaves now mounted separately.

PRICKING Excised but tears in outer margin suggest pricking along that edge.

RULING Two columns with single vertical boundary-lines. Written below top ruled line. 35 lines except on fos 129–154 which is ruled in a single column of 51–53 lines.

SCRIPT Most of volume in brown Gothic bookhand, not of most formal sort. Thick nib. Tops of ascenders tagged or split. Final s round, *et*-nota crossed, two-compartment looped **a**. Juncture of **e** and **o** after **b**, **d**. Fusion of other curved letters. Minims not broken. Martinus in small, monoline Anglicana hand. Split ascenders, short ascenders and descenders, sigma form of s, simple **e**, looped two-compartment **a** rising above other minim letters.

DECORATION In HRB red capitals without filigree in text but, at opening, red and blue capitals with scrolling along edge of text.

HISTORY

Top 1r, in cursive hand of the fourteenth century: 'Iste liber est de com[mun]itate fratrum minorum Cantuar. de procuracion[ ] . . . [ ]nfirmacionem fratris Hugo de Hertepol tunc minstri (*sic*) Anglie [ ]' (Franciscans). Ker, *Medieval Libraries*, p. 48.

BIBLIOGRAPHY

Planta, *Catalogue of the Manuscripts in the Cottonian Library*, p. 364.

Smith, *Catalogus*, p. 65.

Ward & Herbert, *Catalogue of Romances*, I.239–40.

92 *LONDON, BRITISH LIBRARY, MS. COTTON NERO D.viii

Saec. **xii/xiii** + xiv/xv + xvii   Mediaeval provenance: ?England
                                                            ?Colchester (late)

175 + 169 + 3 fos   2nd fo: *ergo Brutus et uirorum multitudinem*

HRB 3ra–63rb.

§§1–3, 5–208. Dedicated to Robert of Gloucester.

Rubrics at §1 (3r) 'Incipit prologus Gaufridi Monimutensis ad Robertum comitem Claudiocestrie in historiam de regibus Maioris Britannie que nunc Anglia dicitur quam historiam idem Gaufidus (*sic*) nuper transtulit de Britannico in Latinum', §5 (3r) 'Explicit prologus. Incipit liber primus', §110 (33v) 'Incipit prologus de prophetiis Merlini', §111 (33v) 'Explicit prologus. Incipiunt prophetie', after §208 (63rb)

'Explicit liber historie de regibus Britonum quem nuper de Britannico in Latinum transtulit Gaufridus Monemutensis'.

Book-divisions: I §5 (3r), II §23 (8v), III §35 (12v), IV §54 (17r), V §73 (22r), VI §89 (27r), VII §109 (33v), VIII §118 (37r), IX §143 (44r), X §163 (50v), XI §177 (56r).

CONTENTS

1: paper flyleaf with Early Modern contents-list on recto.

2: parchment flyleaf. Note about Geoffrey in sixteenth- or seventeenth-century hand on verso (mutilated at edge).

3r–63rb: HRB.

63rb–71rb: 'Incipiunt exceptiones (*sic*) de libro Gilde sapientis quem composuit de primis habitatoribus Britannie que nunc Anglia dicitur et de excidio eius'. 'A principio mundi usque ad diluuium anni .ii.cc.xlii. . . . quamuis habitasset in extremis finibus cosmi.' *Historia Brittonum*, in Gildasian recension, labelled as Book XII of HRB. Ed. Faral, *La Légende*, III.5–61.

71v: blank, unruled.

72ra–159vb: 'Incipit historia Normannorum'. 'Inclito et pie uenerando quem genus ornat sapientia decorat . . . Ricardus non solum ecclesie Fiscanni multa dedit sed etiam aliis ecclesiis.' Dudo of Saint-Quentin, History of the Normans. Ed. Lair, 'De Moribus'. On this manuscript see Huisman, 'Notes', p. 131.

160ra–169ra: 'Incipit uita Alexandri regis magni Macedonis'. 'Egipti sapientes sati genere diuino . . . uino et [uen]eno superatus atque extinctus occubuit.' Ed. Kuebler, *Iuli Valeri Alexandri Polemi res gestae*, pp. 1–168.

169ra–174va: 'Incipit epistola Alexandri regis magni magni (*sic*) Macedonum ad Aristotilem magistrum suum de situ Indie'. 'Semper memor tui . . . et animi industria optimi Aristotelis indicium.' Ed. Walther Boer, *Epistola Alexandri*.

174va–175ra: 'Numerus et nomina librorum uenerabilis Bede presbiteri'. 'In princi-pium Genesis usque ad natiuitatem Ysaace . . . quibus scriptura sancta contexta est.' Bede, *Historia ecclesiastica*, V.24, edd. Colgrave & Mynors, *Bede's Ecclesiastical History*, pp. 566–70.

175ra/b: 'Quidam prophetia Mellini Siluestris de regno Anglorum'. 'Mortuo leone iustitie surget albus rex . . . qui pacificato regno occidet.' Added in documentary hand perhaps not much later than main text. Ed. Schulz, *Gottfried*, p. 465.

175rb: notes, in fifteenth-century hand, on Empress Matilda and on Alexander.

175v: blank.

176ra–183ra: Giraldus Cambrensis, *Descriptio Kambrie*, first recension. 'Huberto Cantuar. archiepiscopi.' 'Ille ego qui quondam Hibernicam topographiam . . . pro hoc terrarum angulo respondebit.' Ed. Dimock, *apud* Brewer *et al.* (edd.), *Giraldi Cambrensis Opera*, VI.155–227. This version apparently composed after 1176 (see Dimock, *ibid.*, pp. xxiii–xxiv).

183ra–186rb: 'Disputacio inter clericum et militem super potestate commissa prefatis ecclesiasticis atque principibus terrarum . . .'. 'Miror optime miles paucis diebus . . . itaque Dominus est filius hominis et sabb[at]i.'

186rb–187ra: 'De origine gigancium in insula Albyon olim habitancium et de nomine eiusdem insule que nunc Anglia dicitur'. 'Anglia modo dicta olim Albyon dicebatur . . . historie de primis habitatoribus huius terre.'

187ra/va: 'De longitudine et latitudine Anglie et quod in ea .xxxii. comitatus et duo archiepiscopatus et .xiiii. episcopatus continentur'. 'Anglia habet in longitudine .dccc. miliaria . . . in Staffordshire .d. hide.'

188r–344va: Higden, *Polychronicon*, with continuation to 1376. 'In historico contextu cronographorum diligencia nobis delegato . . . in eorum sermonibus predicantes.'

345r–347r: 'Marianus libro tertio (*sic*) de monasterio Colecestrensi et eius fundatore'. 'Rex Willelmus iunior ciuitatem Colecestrie cum suis pertinentiis tradidit . . . quam tamen postea occupauerunt Richardenses.' Early Modern account of the foundation of the abbey of St John, Colchester. Printed by Astley, 'Mediaeval Colchester', pp. 122–28.

DESCRIPTION

SIZE 35 x 25.5 cm.

QUIRING Four units. A (3–71) – quire signatures beginning on 10v (I) indicate I–VIII⁸, then IX⁶ (2 lacking: 67–71). B (72–175) – signatures from I (79v) to IX (143v). I–XII⁸, XIII⁸ (3 and 6 singletons: 168–175). C (176–344) – with catchwords. I–V¹², VI¹⁰, VII–XIII¹², XIV ? (330–344). D (345–347) – paper. ? I⁴ (3–4 pasted together?).

PRICKING A–B – both margins. C – for frame-ruling.

RULING A–B – two columns of 39 lines. Double vertical boundary-lines, divided central margin, no ruling above top written line. C – two columns of 48 lines, single vertical boundary-lines. D – single column of up to 53 lines.

SCRIPT A–B – black, fairly large and formal four-line script. Minims not lozenged but joined by hairline ticks. Final s usually tall, occasionally high. Approaching juncture of e and o after p and d. *Et*-nota usually crossed. Ascender of round d often trails to left. Straight-backed form occurs only rarely. C – in paler ink. English script showing influence of Secretary hand. Looped ascenders, some angularity in bowls of g and looped d. r long or 2-shaped with descending hairline. e has cursive loop form. Descenders tend to be pointed. D – Humanist Caroline minuscule with 8-shaped g, final round s among the unCaroline forms.

DECORATION A–B – large capitals in red and green with scrolled/leafy decoration. Smaller capitals have split shafts, bosses, feathered ornament. C – blue or red enclosed in square of filigree. D – drawing at top in coloured inks of church at Colchester (printed by Astley) engraved by Hollar for Dugdale's *Monasticon*. Circles down the edge of the page (coloured in inks) contain the names of the abbots of Colchester.

HISTORY

This manuscript holds several works in common with Leiden B.P.L. 20 and its copy, BL, Cotton Vitellius A.viii + Cambridge, Gonville & Caius College, MS. 177/20, produced at Reading. It seems likely that the Leiden manuscript travelled to England early in its history. See Van Houts, *Gesta Normannorum Ducum: een studie*, pp. 49–50.

BIBLIOGRAPHY

Astley, 'Mediaeval Colchester', pp. 119–21.
Huisman, 'Notes', pp. 131–35, & three figures.
Planta, *Catalogue of the Manuscripts in the Cottonian Library*, pp. 238–39.
Smith, *Catalogus*, pp. 57–58.
Van Houts, *Gesta Normannorum Ducum: een studie*, pp. 196–98.
Ward & Herbert, *Catalogue of Romances*, I.230.

93 *LONDON BRITISH LIBRARY, MS. COTTON TITUS A.xviii + COTTON VESPASIAN B.x, fos 1–23 + COTTON FRAGMENTS xxix, fos 36–39

*COTTON TITUS A.xviii

Saec. xiv[1]   Mediaeval provenance: Durham
85 fos   2nd fo: *deponitur extra eodem*

HRB 14r–83r   2nd fo: *cum in uinculis abduxerat*

§§1–3, 5–208 [§5 compressed, 109–110 *pudibundus Brito* form]. Dedicated to Robert of Gloucester.

No original opening rubric but at top of 14r: 'Q. historia secundo fo, cum in uinculis' (fifteenth-century hand). Rubrics at §109 (50r) 'Uerba magistri', §111 (50r) 'Hic incipiunt prophetie Merlini', after §208 'Explicit historia Britonum que dicitur Brutus'.

No book-divisions but chapters numbered consecutively from 1–200.

CONTENTS

1r: blank.

1v: three contents-lists and an *ex-libris* inscription.

2r–6v: Innocent III, *De mysteriis missae*. 'Tria sunt in quibus precipue lex diuina . . . ut uult igitur Gregorius de [ ] in fine.' Ed. Migne, *Patrologia Latina*, CCXVII.773–.

7r–8r: 'Ordo officiorum dominicalium inter octo epiphanie et septuagesimam'. From fifteenth of the calends of February to third of calends of September (original end of text erased and written over).

8va–10vb: 'Golicus apochalissim ficmento (*sic*) posuit poetico ubi multor[um] uicia laus et iocundo depinxerat d[ ]'. 'A tauro torrida lampade cinchei . . . satis apperui cuique mortalium. Explicit.' Walther, *Initia*, p. 5, no. 91. Ed. Strecker, *Die Apokalypse*. Written over erasure in informal hand (fourteenth-century).

11r/v: originally tables as on 7r–8r but now erased.

12rb–13v: 'De ortu et uita sancti Wilfridi' (added rubric). 'Anno ab incarnatione uerbi Dei sexcentesimo quarto . . . duxit in pace.' Also in informal hand. Half column before this written but not legible. Ed. Migne, *Patrologia Latina*, CLIX.713–. *BHL* 8893.

14r–83r: HRB.

83va–85ra: 'Dialogus inter cor<p>us et spiritum cuiusdam potentis quasi examin[ ]'.
'Noctis sub silencio tempore brumali ... que dat unicumque prout operatoris.'
Walther, *Initia*, p. 610, no. 11894. Ed. Wright, *The Latin Poems*, pp. 95–106.

DESCRIPTION

SIZE 23.5 x 17 cm.

QUIRING (Original flyleaves now bound separately as Cotton Fragments XXIX, fos
36–39). A ?^{12} (+ 1 before 1: fos 1–13). B (HRB) Catchwords indicate regular
arrangement beginning at 14r. I–VI^{12}.

PRICKING In outer margin throughout.

RULING HRB in single column of 33 lines.

SCRIPT HRB in fairly large Gothic bookhand. Brown ink. Juncture of e and o after
b, d, and p. *et*-nota crossed. Two-compartment looped a, pierced t. Short ascenders
and descenders. Script of 2–6 and 83v–85r similar to this but smaller. Script of
additions over erasure is informal, apparently English. Grey ink. Looped e and d, long
r ?late fourteenth-century.

DECORATION Blue capitals filigreed in red.

HISTORY

On 1v in fifteenth- or sixteenth-century hand: 'Liber Iohannis Wherton de Kirkebythore ex legacione Iohannis Milthorpp. auditoris in testimonio suo etc. Post obitum
eiusdem Iohannis Wherton liberetur priori et conuentui abbathis Dunelmensis, preceptoris suo spiritualis etc.'. Also under HRB on 83r: 'Iste liber constat Iohanni
Wherton. de Kirkebythore' (Westmorland).

Originally joined to Cotton Vespasian B.x (fos 1–23) with the endleaves Cotton
Fragments, xxix (fos 36–39): Ker, *Medieval Libraries*, p. 73; Ker & Watson, *Medieval
Libraries*, p. 30, n. 2.

*COTTON VESPASIAN B.x, fos 1–23

CONTENTS

1ra–11rb: *Uita sancti Brandani* (from final rubric), by Benedeit. 'Donna Aaliz la
\veine . . . Par lui enuunt plusur que mil.' Edd. Short & Merrilees, *Benedeit*, pp. 30–79.

11v–21rb: 'Incipit uita beati Brendani abbatis'. 'Sanctissimus itaque Brendanus filius
Finlocha nepotis althi . . . gloriose migrauit ad Dominum. Cui \est/honor et gloria in
secula seculorum. Amen.' ?*BHL* 1437.

21rb–22rb: 'Incipit uita Longini m[artyris]'. 'In diebus Domini nostri Iesu Christi fuit
quidam miles centurio . . . uirtus et imperium cum Patre et Spiritus Sancto in secula
seculorum. Amen.' *BHL* 4965.

22v: brief summary of the fifteen signs before doomsday. 'Ieronimus in annalibus
libris Hebreorum inuenit quindecim signa .xv. dierum ante diem Iudicii. Sed utrum
continue futuri sunt . . . et resurgent omnes.'

22v: verses in various fourteenth-century hands. Seven lines 'Tucius (*sic*) ut petere laici sub imagine romam . . . Sit potes in terris uiuere iure poli'. Four lines headed 'Mulieres ?p[re]cant', 'Per uisum propter uisum emisit lacrimas . . . In unguentis unxit pedes Domini unguento'. 'Mens cor cur cupiunt lex Christi uera iocunda . . . Anglorum nomen tollet rubei renouabit.' Underneath in fifteenth-century hand 'Die ?ueneris ante festum sancti Laurerencii (*sic*) Anno Domini .m.cccc. sexagesimo septimo incepit bellum inter duos dracones uidelicet album et rubeum etc.'

23r/v: blank except for name on recto (?sixteenth-century hand) 'Iohannes Wherton' and 'Wherton', and on verso, in fourteenth-century hand 'Amor et timor fauor et premium humanum peruertunt iudicium . . . '.

DESCRIPTION
SIZE 23.5/24.5 x 17 cm.
QUIRING I–II^8, III^8 (lacks ?8: 17–23).
PRICKING Where extant, in outer margins only. Sometimes second line of prickings nearer to edge of text.
RULING Two columns of 44 lines beginning below top ruled line. Single vertical boundary-lines.
SCRIPT Round type of bookhand, not large. Brown ink. Juncture of **e** and **o** after **b**, **d**, **h** and **p**. Tops of ascenders sometimes notched. Large-headed **a**, pierced **t**. Final **s** is often tall.
DECORATION Fos 1r–10v, blue or red initials filigreed in those colours or in blue-green.

*COTTON FRAGMENTS xxix, fos 36–39

CONTENTS
36r: musical stave with accompanying text 'Eue mater gracie stella claritatis . . . tuos natos morto strat[ ]s redde filio.' Notes beneath in two different hands dated 14[?5]9 and 1460.
36v: three staves with text which runs on below. '[A]ngelus ad uirginem subintrans in conclaue uirginis . . . post hoc exilium.'
37r: very faded, scarcely legible. Text in formal fourteenth-century hand mentioning St Oswulf.
37v: various illegible notes followed by list of contents found in Cotton Titus A.xviii.
38r: mostly illegible. Written in several hands, including main hand of 36r/v. Note in sixteenth-century hand at foot.
38v: blank except for lines at top written in mediaeval hand (illegible).
39r: Magna Carta. '[ ] Dei gratia rex Anglie domni Hibernie et Aquitan. . . . Inspeximus magnam magnam cartam domini .H. Dei gratia rex Anglie . . . in perpetuum omnis libertates subscriptas.'
Several lines underneath in informal fourteenth-century hand followed by note in later hand dated 1342.

39v: writing at top, illegible except for date 1360.

BIBLIOGRAPHY
Ker & Watson, *Medieval Libraries*, p. 30, n. 2.
Planta, *Catalogue of the Manuscripts in the Cottonian Library*, p. 513.
Short & Merrilees, *Benedeit*, pp. 6–7.
Smith, *Catalogus*, p. 122.
Ward & Herbert, *Catalogue of Romances*, I.243.

94 *LONDON, BRITISH LIBRARY, MS. COTTON TITUS A.xxv

Saec. xiii/xiv   Mediaeval provenance: ?Britain
139 fos   2nd fo: *cito remige fuge*

HRB 106r–117v
§§177–206 'a Sergio papa con-'. Dedication lost.
No extant rubrics or book-divisions.

CONTENTS
1r–35v: Annals of Boyle. From Adam to 1201, 1224–38, 1251–. Written in hands of
varying date. 'Hoc anno natus est Enos . . . David mac Celling archiepiscopus' (final
lines illegible). Printed by Freeman, 'The Annals'. See also Flower, *apud* O'Grady &
Flower, *Catalogue*, I.4–14.

36r–71r: fifteenth-century. 'Here foloweth the manere and fourme of sekyng and
offeryng and also of the berung and translacione of three holy and worshipfull. kingis
of Coleyn. Iasper Melchyor and Balthaser.' 'Sithe of these three worshipfull kynges
. . . that in heuene above all. kingis and seyntys sittith and regneth Crist Iesus. Amen.'
English translation of John of Hildesheim, *Historia trium regum*. Ed. Horstmann, *The
Three Kings*.
71v: blank.

72r–93: different fifteenth-century hand. 'Uia noua diuersarum regionum proprieta-
tum declaratiua disposicio terre sancte.' Ludolphus de Sudheim. 'Reuerendissimo in
Christo patri ac domino domino suo gracioso Balduwino de Detenuordia Padeburnen.
ecclesie episcopo . . . et omnia loca maritima pro parte.' Truncated. Ed. Deycks,
Ludulphus. De Itinere.

94r–104v: prophecy of John of Bridlington. In fifteenth-century hand, on paper.
'Febribus [in]fectus requies fuerat mihi lect[ ] . . . Ad mortem tendo morti mei [ ].'
Walther, *Initia*, I.316, no. 6296.
105r: extract from Urban V, *Agni Dei*. 'Balsamus et munda cera cum crismatis unda
. . . Tantum pars minima quantum ualet integra [ ].' Thorndike & Kibre, *A Catalogue*,
col. 173.

105r/v: verses and recipes in various hands in Latin and English.

106r–117v: HRB.

118r–139v: documents in Latin and French, of the fifteenth and sixteenth centuries (mentioning Henry VI and VII, London, Huntingdon).

DESCRIPTION

SIZE 21 x 14 cm.

QUIRING Six volumes: A, C, E, F, parchment; B, D paper. A not collatable; B I–III^{12}; C I^{12}, II^{10}; D I^{12}; E I^{12}, F I^{12}, II ?^{10}. Catchword on 117v.

PRICKING In both margins for A, otherwise none extant.

RULING Two columns of 32 written lines. Single vertical boundary-lines, two lines; written below top ruled line.

SCRIPT HRB in large and fairly formal bookhand. Brown ink. Bristly angled tops to minims and ascenders. At least two hands. Crossed t, final s tall, round, or high. Short ascenders and descenders. Juncture of e and o after b, d, h, and p. Crossed et-nota. Double l has hairline top. Other volumes in variety of scripts.

DECORATION Blue capitals with red filigree.

HISTORY

'There is no reason to believe that the fragments in this volume have any original connection with the manuscript of our annals. It was Sir Robert Cotton's habit to bind manuscript fragments of the same size together': Freeman, 'The Annals', IV.336.

BIBLIOGRAPHY

Planta, *Catalogue of the Manuscripts in the Cottonian Library*, p. 515.
Smith, *Catalogus*, pp. 124–25.
Ward & Herbert, *Catalogue of Romances*, I.244.

95 *LONDON, BRITISH LIBRARY, MS. COTTON TITUS A.xxvii

Saec. xii/xiii   Mediaeval provenance: St Augustine's,
                                                                            Canterbury
219 fos   2nd fo: [*mar*]-*cia omnibus artibus*

HRB 9r–87r.

§§1–3, 5–184, 186–208. Dedicated to Robert of Gloucester.

No opening or closing rubrics extant. At §5 (86r) 'Incipit desc[ ] Britannie ins[ ]', §6 (9v) 'De origine Britonum qualiterque Brutus iuxta presagium patrem ac matrem peremit et in Grecia Troianorum reliquiarum dux effect[ ] sit', §109 (52r) 'Prefacio hystorici et epistola de interpretacione propheciarum Merlini', §111 (52v) 'Incipiunt prophecie Merlini ex mistica pugna draconum'. Other rubrics at chapter-divisions. No final rubric.

Book-divisions: II §54 (29r), III §98 (47r), IV §143 (66v). Each book is subdivided into chapters.
Second Variant Version. Hammer's siglum R: Emanuel, 'Geoffrey of Monmouth's *Historia*', p. 104.

CONTENTS
1r: (paper) blank except for Early Modern contents-list and ?pressmark.
2r: blank.
2v–8r: 'Incipiunt capitula hystorie britannice'. 'Descripcio quantitatis et multimode opulencie . . . et anglice historie tractanda distribuit.'
8v: blank.
9r–87r: HRB.
87r/v: note on British genealogies. 'Alii asserunt alium fuisse Brutum a quo Britannia dicta est . . . usque ad Decium Ualerianum anni sunt .lxix..' Extract from the *Historia Brittonum*. Ed. Dumville, *Histories and Pseudo-histories*.
87v–88r: note on placenames in HRB. 'Armorica siue Latauia id est Minor Britannia . . . et lapidem insignum triumphi erexit.' Ed. Dumville, 'Anecdota'.
88v: blank.
89r–105v: 'Incipit prologus sequentis operis'. 'Leges quas dicunt Edwardi regis ex Cnudi primum institutione diductas esse . . . Deus omnipotens omnibus nobis indulgeat sicut ei uelle sit. Amen.' Partially ed. Liebermann, *Quadripartitus*, pp. 83–99.
105v–174v: 'Incipiunt leges que Aeluredus rex scribere fecit'. Laws from Alfred to Cnut, preceded by *capitula*-list (ending on 106r). 'Locutus est Dominus ad Moysen dicens . . . oculus bouis .v. denariis et uacce .iiii. denariis.' Partially ed. Liebermann, *Quadripartitus*, pp. 112–18, 119–22, 122–24, 125, 126, 127, 129, 130–31, 132, 133, 134–35, 137–38, 139, 140–42, 143–49, 150–66.
175r/v: blank except for list of sins, sacraments, etc. on verso.
176ra–181vb: Marbodus, *De Lapidibus*. 'Euax rex Arabum legitur scripsisse Neroni . . . quamque dare solet uinum fugat ebrietatem.' Thorndike & Kibre, *A Catalogue*, col. 530.
182r–185v: letter of Prester John, §§1–96. 'Presbiter Iohannis potencia et uirtute Dei . . . acsi omni genere ciborum essemus impleti.' Ed. Zarncke, 'Der Priester Johannes', pp. 909–22.
185v–186v: '[B]ritannia insula autem quodam Bruto consule Romano dicta est . . . et intrauit in ostium Tamesis'. Ed. Dumville, *Histories and Pseudo-histories*.
186v (remainder) –187r: blank.
187v–206r: *Gesta Alexandri*. '[E]gypti sapientes fati genere diuino primi feruntur . . . uino et ueneno superat atque extinctus occubuit. ' Ed. Kuebler, *Iuli Valeri Alexandri Polemi res gestae*, pp. 1–168.
206v–216v: *Epistola Alexandri*. '[S]emper memor fui (*sic*) tui etiam . . . nominis mei fama habeatur in gloria.' Ed. Walther Boer, *Epistola Alexandri*.
216v: *Epitaphium Alexandri*. 'Primus Alexander pillea natus in urbe . . . se trementem ferroque regna lesit.' Walther, *Initia*, I.759, no. 14648.
216v–217r: '[Q]uicquid in humanis constat uirtutibus altis . . . succubuit leto sumpto

cum melle ueneno'. Twenty lines. See Hill, *'Epitaphia Alexandri'*, p. 98. Walther, *Initia*, I.833, no. 15990.

217v–219v: blank.

DESCRIPTION

SIZE 18.5 x 13.5/14 cm.

QUIRING Some folios remounted. Manuscript now too tightly bound for collation. ?New unit begins after 88v. Parchment is more suede-like, script different. However, script and decoration from 182r, and perhaps 175r, resemble that of HRB.

PRICKING At outer edge, now mostly trimmed away.

RULING fos 1–88 in single column of 27–28 lines; written above top ruled line; single vertical boundary-lines. 88–174 as before but 24 lines. 176–181 in two columns of 27 lines. 182–186 as for HRB. 187–219 23–26 lines.

SCRIPT Brown four-line script, heavy strokes considering small size. Several hands. No juncture. Forked tops to ascenders of **b, l, d** (straight-backed form frequent). Final **s** tall. Uncrossed *et*-nota but ampersand still common. Horizontal of **t** has hairline cross-stoke at left end. Short ascenders and descenders. 89–160r in blacker and more formal script. Round **d** nearly two-line, minims lozenged at top and thickened at foot. 160v–174v in thirteenth-century hand; tall, thin, with no juncture. Ascender of round **d** trails to left, *et*-nota sometimes crossed. Remainder of volume in various hands apparently contemporary with the script of HRB, betraying influence of documentary script. No juncture, brown ink.

DECORATION Red and green capitals with occasionally elaborate scrolled outline-ornament. Shafts of letters sometimes decorated. In laws – plain green, red, or blue capitals.

HISTORY

No. 895 in late fifteenth-century library catalogue of St Augustine's, Canterbury: Ker, *Medieval Libraries*, p. 43; James, *The Ancient Libraries*, pp. 293, 518.

BIBLIOGRAPHY

Planta, *Catalogue of the Manuscripts in the Cottonian Library*, p. 516.
Smith, *Catalogus*, p. 125.
Ward & Herbert, *Catalogue of Romances*, I.231–32.

96 *LONDON, BRITISH LIBRARY, MS. COTTON TITUS C.xvii

Saec. xii*med./2*   Mediaeval provenance: ?England
ii + 46 + iv fos   2nd fo: *claro genere Dardani ortam*

HRB 1r–46v.

§§1–3, 5–208. Dedicated to Robert of Gloucester.

Only original rubric at §1 (1r) 'Incipit prologus in historia Britonum'. Added rubric at §112. Also closing sentences of §68 (from 'Eodem tempore Petrus', 15r) and §77 (from 'Inter ceteros utriusque', 16v) written in red.

No book-divisions.

No other contents but flyleaves (i–ii) with title and note of donation in William Dugdale's hand (on iir). Flyleaves after HRB blank.

DESCRIPTION

SIZE 24 x 17 cm.

QUIRING a² (i–ii), I–IV¹⁰, V mounted bifolium, VI⁴, b⁴.

PRICKING In outer margin only.

RULING In one column of 38 lines. No ruling above top written line, single vertical boundary-lines.

SCRIPT Two distinct types of hand. Brown ink. 1–24 – formal, tall, and upright with use of ampersand and *et*-nota, and round and straight-backed **d**. **e**-caudata is found (often incorrectly used) and occasionally final round s. Laterally compressed. Strange aspect as a later corrector has crossed the **t**'s (by extending the uprights) and dotted the **i**'s. 25–46 – rounder and more looped with *et*-nota predominating over ampersand but with retention of straight-backed **d** and **e**-caudata. Descenders extended at foot of some pages. Final round s frequent. Thickenings on shoulder of tall s and tops of ascenders.

DECORATION Main capital has brown inked outline with red and green filling. Other initials are red or red and green with split stems or foliate decoration.

HISTORY

On 46v: 'Datus sum ego liber presens per Thomam Botelarem Estopiensis ecclesie rectorem magistro Thome Ludlowe de la Moorehowse, armigero generoso eiusdem predicte ecclesie uero et indubitato patrono. Uigesimo die mensis aprilis .v. feria tercia in ebdomeda sancti Paschatis anno Domini 1568 litera dominicali C#'. Same sixteenth-century hand seen in marginalia. Botelar also owned a volume of William of Malmesbury: Oxford, Bodleian Library, MS. Laud misc. 729 (*S.C.* 30593).

On iir: 'Ex dono Edoardi Walter equ[itis] aurati Garterii, regis armorum principalis', written in the hand of William Dugdale (according to Ward & Herbert, *Catalogue of Romances*, I.203).

BIBLIOGRAPHY

Planta, *Catalogue of the Manuscripts in the Cottonian Library*, p. 563.

Smith, *Catalogus*, p. 128.

Ward & Herbert, *Catalogue of Romances*, I.203.

97 *LONDON, BRITISH LIBRARY, MS. COTTON VESPASIAN A.xxiii

Saec. xiv²   Mediaeval provenance: ?England

5 + 112 + 1 fos   2nd fo: *Eneas post Troianum*

HRB 4r–106v.

§§1–3, 5–208. Dedicated to Robert of Gloucester.

Rubrics at §1 (4r) 'Incipit prologus in historiam de regibus Maioris Britannie que nunc

Anglia dicitur', after §3 (4r) 'Explicit prologus', at §110 (56r) 'Incipit prologus de prophetiis Merlini', §111 (56v) 'Explicit prologus. Incipiunt prophetie', after §208 (106v) 'Explicit liber undecimus historie de regibus Britonum'.

Book-divisions at §5 (4v) I, §23 (14r) II, §35 (20v) III, §54 (28r) IV, §73 (36v) V, §89 (45r) VI, §109 (56r) VII, §118 (62r) VIII, §143 (73v) IX, §16 (84v) X, §177 (94r) XI.

CONTENTS

i: blank parchment.

ii, iii: paper flyleaves. Blank except for Early Modern contents-list on iii r.

1r–2r: parchment flyleaves written in an Early Modern hand. 'Contenta historiae Galfredi Monumetensis.' 'Haec historia britannico . . . sermone coscripta (*sic*) fuit.' Referenced summary of the contents of HRB.

3r/v: flyleaf.

4r–106v: HRB.

107r–115v: 'Mandata Christi secundum magistrum Philippum quondam abbate de Leycistria' (from rubric on 115v) (begins under erasure at top of recto). 'Eor (*sic*) als mykyll as euerylke man whyls he lyffys in yis warld es a pyllgrum . . . wt. hys preciouse blode ?boght huse. Amen.'

DESCRIPTION

SIZE 24 x 17 cm.

QUIRING Flyleaves – one parchment, two paper, three parchment; three parchment stubs. From 4r – I–VIII^{12}, IX^4, X ?^{4} (4 lacking: 104–106); from 107r – I^8 and two singletons.

PRICKING In outer margin.

RULING In one column throughout with single vertical boundary-lines and ruling above top line. A – 30 lines with ruling for title across top margin. B – 34 lines.

SCRIPT Formal, two-line Gothic semi-quadrata. Ascenders short with indented or tagged tops. Feet on **r**, **n**, and **m**. Juncture of **e** and **o** following **b**, **d**, **p**, etc., and **a**, too, is sometimes joined to a preceding letter. **t** is pierced, **a** does not always have the two-compartment form but its headstroke is pointed, **x** is barred. Tall **s** and straight-backed **d** are found. Final **s** usually round. *Et*-nota is double-barred. B – greyer ink, the more cursive form of script used for vernacular texts. Textura display-script suggests a later date than that of A.

DECORATION Capitals in light or dark blue and red with fine filigree. Large blue and red initials with more elaborate decoration at book-divisions. Geometric designs etc. used to fill space after end of section of text. Red rubrication. B – cruder initials in blue within square of red filigree.

HISTORY

Under text on 1r ? name of Robert Cotton (partly erased).

BIBLIOGRAPHY

Planta, *Catalogue of the Manuscripts in the Cottonian Library*, p. 437.

Smith, *Catalogus*, p. 104.

Ward & Herbert, *Catalogue of Romances*, I.241–42.

Saecc. **xiii**^{2} + **xiv**^{2} + xv   Mediaeval provenance: ?England
394 fos   2nd fo (3r): *penarum. Et tunc angelus*

HRB 272r–355v; 356r–369v.

§§1–3, 5–175 'uno ictu interficiebat. Diffugie-'. Continued without loss to §208 in hand of later fourteenth-century. Dedicated to Robert of Gloucester.

Rubrics at §1 (271v) 'Incipit Brutus', above §1 (272r) 'Prologus', at §5 (272r) 'Incipit primus liber de situ et de regibus Britannie et qui post eam inhabitauerunt', at §108 (320v) 'Uerba Merlini', §109 (321r) 'Uerba auctoris', §111 (321r) 'Incipiunt uaticinia Merlini coram Uortegirno edita', after §208 (369v) 'Explicit liber historie gentis Britonum'. Occasional rubrics at chapter-divisions.

Book-divisions: I §5 (272r), III §35 (288r), VI §89 (311r), VII §118 (326v), VIII §143 (337v).

CONTENTS

1r/v: blank except for Early Modern contents-list on verso.

2r: 'Iuramentum prestandum per regem in coronatione sua . . . super altare protinus prestito coram cunctis'.

2v–5r: 'De assumpcione beate Marie uirgine'. 'Sciendum est fratres karissimi et omnibus fidelibus exponendum . . . per eum qui uiuit et regnat per omnia secula seculorum. Amen.'

5r: memoranda of two happenings in 1332 and 13(55). Completed in hand of 2r in which is then written 'Iuramentum quod faciet imperator domino pape in sua coronacione . . .'

5v: account of 'Pope Joan'.

6r–43v: 'Bestiarum. De omnibus bestiis'. 'Bestiarum uocabulum proprie conuenit leonibus . . . usque ad capud aliquo ictu collidatur debilis reddita.'

43v–59v: 'Incipiunt tropi in theologica facultate a magistro Willelmo Linc. ecclesie cancellano collecti'. 'Dei dona deprehensamus . . . uel uti pati uel omittere.' William de Montibus, *Tropi*.

59v–85r: 'Quidam tractatus de naturis animalium'. *Capitula*-list. 'Primus titulus sentenciarum generalium methaphisicarum (*sic*) . . . de naturali pietate et amicitia animalium et de contrario.' Text begins 61r. 'Ex operacione docti auctoris est iudicare . . . quia ualde amicus eius est.'

85v: blank.

86r–119r: 'Ymago mundi', Honorius of Autun. 'Incipit epistola Henrici ad Henricum.' 'Henrico septiformi spiritu in trina fide illustrato . . . Anno ab incarnacione Domini millesimo centesimo decimo.' Ed. Migne, *Patrologia Latina*, CLXX.119–?193.

119r: six-line verse. 'Sum uia uis dux pons requies pax gloria lux fons . . . Querere se queri (*sic*) quatuor hec mala sunt.'

119r–122v: prognostics for Mondays. 'Luna prima Adam creatus est . . . sang. min. ante horam .iii. oportet.'

123v–125v: 'De proprietatibus' (running title). 'In corpore humano nouem sunt mensure . . . curcilis (*sic*) est sella consulis uel in qua portabatur rex.'

125v–199r: 'Incipit hic nostri pulcrum numerale magistri et cancellarii Nichol. de Monte Willelmi' (rubric at foot of 125v). 'Deus unus est. Contra apostolus ait . . . in aliis opusculis nostris copiosius sunt exarata.' On the *Numerale* and the *Tropi* (above) of William de Monte, see MacKinnon, 'William de Montibus'.

199r–200ra: 'Unus Deus. Unus Dominus. Una fides. Unum baptisma . . . De preroga-tiuis beate uirginis'. Collection of biblical/religious ones, twos, threes, etc. (to twelve).

200ra–271v: 'Incipit uita sancti Thome martyr. et confessor. Cant[uarie] ecclesie archiepiscopi a magistro Eadwardo exposita'. By Edward Grim. 'Professores arcium seculo proprios singuli conatus habent . . . et statutas in regno Anglorum promulgaret.' Ed. Robertson, *Materials*, II.353–450. Apparently incomplete here. *BHL* 8182.

272r–355v: HRB.

356r–369v: HRB, continued.

369v–390r: brief chronicles of the English kings to 1346. 'Sequitur de quibusdam regibus qui postea in Anglia regnauerunt. Notandum igitur quod postquam Saxones sibi Angliam subiugauerant . . . Item bellum Dunielmensem fuit anno Domini millesi-mo CCC.xl.vi. etc.'

390r–391r: 'De Edwardo Carnaruan.'. 'Anno gratie millesimo cccvi . . . et decollare fecit commitem (*sic*) de Arundell..' Fifteenth-century continuation.

391v–392v: in Secretary-influenced hand. 'De origine gigantum in insula Albion id est Britannia Maior que modo Anglia dicitur habitancium et nomine insule.' 'Anglia modo dicta olim Albion dicebatur . . . et sic ueritas clarescit historie de primis habitatoribus huius terre.'

392v–393v: blank except for scribbles.

DESCRIPTION

SIZE 19 x 12.5 cm.

QUIRING Some catchwords. I^4, II^{16} (?+ one before 1: 5–21), III–IX^{16}, X^{16} (1 excised from second half of quire: 134–148), XI–XIV^{16}, XV ?^{16} (16 cancelled: 213–227), XVI–XXIII^{16}, XXIV–XXV^{12}, XXVI^{12} (380–391), XVII^2 (392–393), a singleton (blank).

PRICKING Outer edge only (in margin or along edge of text).

RULING HRB in single column of 33 lines. Single vertical boundary-lines. I–II the same. Fifteenth-century additions in single column of 32–35 lines.

SCRIPT 2–355 written in compact Gothic bookhand. Nearly two-line. Juncture of **e** and **o** after **d** and **p**. *et*-nota sometimes crossed, usually not. Round **s** finally and medially but tall **s** also found in all positions. Two-compartment **a** constructed of two vertical strokes or Caroline form. No trailing hairline on 2-shaped **r**, no flat-topped ascenders. After 356 in more informal fourteenth-century hand. Grey ink. No juncture, *et*-nota crossed, round **d** not looped, two-compartment **a** looped. Minims very upright. 390–393 – grey Secretary hand. Minims have feet. Tapering and slanted ascenders and descenders. Some angularity in bow of **d** and in 2-shaped **r**.

DECORATION 2–355 – red rubrics in hand close to that of text. Red or blue filigreed capitals.

HISTORY

In possession of Thomas Allen of Oxford (1540–1632): Watson, 'Thomas Allen of Oxford', p. 310.

BIBLIOGRAPHY

Planta, *Catalogue of the Manuscripts in the Cottonian Library*, p. 481.
Smith, *Catalogus*, p. 118.
Ward & Herbert, *Catalogue of Romances*, I.242–43.

99 *LONDON, BRITISH LIBRARY, MS. EGERTON 3142
(*OLIM* CLUMBER 47)

Saec. xiii/xiv	Mediaeval provenance: Holme St Benets
	(Benedictine), Norfolk +
	Hickling (Augustinian), Norfolk
iii + i (paper) + 204 fos	2nd fo: [*ue*]-*neri indulgens*

HRB 1r–80va

§§1–3, 5–208. Dedicated to Robert of Gloucester. Rubrics at §1 (1ra) 'Incipit liber de gestis Bruti editus a magistro Waltero Oxif. archidiacono', §5 (1rb) 'De mensura Britanie Maioris que nunc dicitur Anglia secundum longitudinem insule et latitud.', §109 (41v) 'De prophetia Merlini et eius actibus', §110 (41v) 'Hic rogauit Lincoliensis episcopus de translacione prophecie .M.', §111 (41v) 'De bello draconum et de significatione belli per Merlinum', after §208 (80v) 'Explicit liber Bruti et de gestis Britanorum usque ad tempus et aduentum Anglorum'.

No book-divisions.

Extra passage found after §117 (46rb/va) 'Super literis que ab aliquibus ex malicia et a nonnullis ex ignorancia tacita ueritate ... delegatus etiam sue cognitionis offi[cium]? nullatenus interponat' cancelled with line. Copy of a letter of Pope Innocent III to Master Aimon, canon of St Andrew's, Poitiers (October 18, 1208): see Wright, *The British Museum: Catalogue of Additions 1936–1943*, I.334; Potthast, *Regesta*, I.304, no. 3519.

CONTENTS

Three blank modern parchment flyleaves followed by correspondence concerning the chronicles found in the volume (nineteenth-century).

1r–80va: HRB.

81r–83v: short description of England including Heptarchy, bishoprics and shires, Benedictine monasteries in the province of Canterbury. 'Anglia que quondam dicebatur Britannia insularum regina merito a philosophis nuncupatur . . . De Blakeberge.'

83v–101v: Chronicle of Holme St Benet's to 1294. 'Dominus noster Iesus Christus Deus et Dei filius conceptus est . . . Rex cepit medietate cler. et decimam laycorum.'

101v–104v: original annal-numbers continue to 1532. Entries made in different hands by monks of Hickling, Augustinian priory in Norfolk. Last is for 1503. First contemporary Hickling entry perhaps 1343 (recording birth of Thomas de Offord).

105r–200v: Chronicle attributed to John of Oxenedes. 'A principio mundi usque ad diluuium anni duo milia ducenti et .xl. duo ... magister Robertus de Wynchelese archidyaconus Midelsexie et canonicus sancti Pauli London..' Ed. Ellis, *Chronica Johannis*.

201r–204v: blank. Ruling on 201r, 202v notes and list of regnal years from William I to Edward I, 204v notes (see below, HISTORY).

DESCRIPTION

SIZE 24.5 x 16.5 cm.

QUIRING I–VII^8, VIII–IX^{12}; ?X–XVII^{12}, XVIII ?^{10} (177–196), XIX^{12} (197–204).

PRICKING Outer edges only.

RULING Two columns of 36 lines throughout. Ruling above top written line. Single vertical boundary-lines but double line ruled in outer margin on many folios.

SCRIPT Brown Gothic bookhand, not quadrata. Looped two-compartment **a** or Caroline form, pierced **t**, two-line round **d**. Final **s** tall or round. Tops of ascenders tagged to left. Double **l** has flat top. Straight-backed **d** occurs. Crossed *et*-nota. Short ascenders. Juncture of **e** and **o** following **b**, **d**, **h**, **p**. Also *Verschrenkung* of **co**, etc.

DECORATION Blue or red capitals in square of filigree. Blue-green also used in filigree. Main capitals are inhabited. Letter-form in blue, outline of creature in red inside round of letter and background cross-hatched in red.

HISTORY

Record of succession of abbots of St Benet's (ending at 1294) in chronicle on 83v–101v suggests its origin. Continuators were canons of Hickling, Norfolk: Romilly *apud* Ellis, *Chronica Johannis*, pp. xxxvii–xxxviii. See also Ker, *Medieval Libraries*, pp. 102 and 101.

Book-plate of John Towneley on recto of paper flyleaf preceding text. One candidate (1697–1782) described by J. G. Alger: ed. Lee, *Dictionary of National Biography*, LIX.100–1.

In Early Modern hand on 202v 'Kentyng de Walcotte' and in ?fifteenth-century hand on 204v 'Thomas Gregory'. At top of 1r 'Wm. Herbert 1771', of Cheshunt.

BIBLIOGRAPHY

Hammer, 'Some additional manuscripts', p. 241.

Wright, *The British Museum: Catalogue of Additions to the Manuscripts 1936–1945*, I.334–35.

Flower, 'Manuscripts from the Clumber collection', pp. 81–82.

Dumville, 'The manuscripts', pp. 123–24.

100 *LONDON, BRITISH LIBRARY, MS. HARLEY 225

Saecc. **xii**$^{2/ex.}$ + xv   Origin and mediaeval provenance: ?England

ii + 76 + 6 fos   2nd fo: *uaticinium suum. Nam ut*

HRB 3r–78r

§§1–3, 5–208. Dedicated to Robert of Gloucester.

Rubrics at §111 (41r) 'Hic incipit Merlinus'.
No book-divisions.

CONTENTS
1: flyleaf, mainly blank, some scribbles of various dates.
2: flyleaf, closely written in current hands ?fourteenth century.
3r–78r: HRB.
78v–79v: 'Cestre lepistre de Sibille'. 'La lupart euassaillant la Roiaume de Ffraunce serra tiel et si fier . . . car deuant le sepulcre nostre seign[ ] il brandira le gleyfe.'
80r/v: late mediaeval note on recto; verso blank.
81–84: flyleaves as fo 1.

DESCRIPTION
SIZE 14 x 24 cm.
QUIRING a (1–2), I–IX^8, X ?^{6} (75–80), b ?^{4} (81–84).
PRICKING Both margins.
RULING Single column of 33 lines. Top line written. Double vertical boundary-lines.
SCRIPT Homogeneous. Tall, laterally compressed minuscule. Dark brown ink. Round **d**, tall **s** standard. *Et*-nota and ampersand found. Tops of ascenders slightly indented. Opening word of chapter in capitals (ink). No signs of juncture.
DECORATION Plain Romanesque capitals. Buff, green, red. Blank line-ends at end of chapters filled with two interlocking wavy lines (red).

HISTORY
(From inscription on 79v, legible only under ultra-violet light) owned, in fourteenth century by Guido de Waynflete, Augustinian *frater* and later by Sir Simonds D'Ewes (1602–50) (no. 904 in his list in BL, Add. 22918): Wright, *Fontes Harleiani*, pp. 349, 341; Watson, *The Library of Sir Simonds*, p. 207.

BIBLIOGRAPHY
Wanley *et al.*, *A Catalogue of the Harleian Manuscripts*, I.71.
Ward & Herbert, *Catalogue of Romances*, I.222.

101 *LONDON, BRITISH LIBRARY, MS. HARLEY 536

Saec. xii   Origin and mediaeval provenance: ?England
6 fos   2nd fo: *Excepit illum rex*

HRB 56r–61v
56r–57v. §126 '-nam istam et nisi' –§130 'Necessaria apposuisset leuius'
58r–61v. §166 'decem milibus comitatus' –§171 'contra turmam Achilli regis'.
No rubrics or book-divisions but capitula numbers added in late Gothic textura (red). Bound up with unrelated manuscripts (twelfth- to fifteenth-century); apparently post-mediaeval arrangement.

DESCRIPTION

SIZE 21 x 14 cm.

QUIRING Not visible. Text suggests a², b⁴.

PRICKING Only extant for boundary-lines.

RULING Two columns of 30 lines. Top line written. Single vertical boundary-lines.

SCRIPT Brown ink. Four-line Protogothic minuscule, small for type of script. Minims and descenders have hairline tick. Ampersand, round or straight-backed **d**, occasional final round **s** but tall form usual. Tail of **g** generously rounded and ends in hairline stroke.

DECORATION Romanesque capitals in dark green or red. Some have scroll decoration in other colour.

HISTORY

Top of 1r 'Johannes Dee', with date 1549. On John Dee (1527–1608), mathematician and astrologer, see Wright, *Fontes Harleiani*, pp. 126–27. No. T.55 in the list of Dee's books drawn up in 1583: James, *Lists of Manuscripts*, p. 55. Note in hand of Simonds D'Ewes (1602–50) on fo 35: Wright, *Fontes Harleiani*, p. 131.

BIBLIOGRAPHY

Watson, 'Bibliographical Notes'.

Wanley *et al.*, *A Catalogue of the Harleian Manuscripts*, I.343.

Ward, *Catalogue of Romances*, I.226.

102 *LONDON, BRITISH LIBRARY, MS. HARLEY 3773

Saecc. **xii/xiii** + ?xi   Origin: ?Continental

105 fos   2nd fo: *Pontificum gesta breuitate*

HRB 7r–57r

Seven fragments.

7r–14v §30 'in multa frustra contritus est' –§40 'a tempore attauorum suorum reseruatus'

15r–16v '§129 '-rentur. Lauabant namque' –§132 'uasis medicamentorum'

17r/v §101 'meum preterire consilium' –§102 'Sed bonitati eius ilico'

18r/v §113 'signabit. Pedes latrantium' –§115 'Ex Conano precedet aper'

19r–20v §79 'licet et Turbren' –§82 'Undique associabat. Postmodum'

21r–22v §88 'diligebant. Nec deerant' –§90 'manibus uestris pel-'

23r–57r §137 'mittebant. Arridebat ei' –184, 186–§208.

Dedication lost.

After §208 (57r) 'Explicit hystoria Brittonum'.

No extant book-divisions.

Second Variant Version. Hammer's siglum H: Emanuel, 'Geoffrey of Monmouth's *Historia*', p. 104.

CONTENTS

1r/v: 'Prologus sequentis operis' ('uidelicet in hystoriam Britonum' added). 'Cum olim poete grandisonis pompare modis sua ficmenta (*sic*) solerent . . . quod ex istis uersibus aduertere possunt.' (The first lines recast the opening of the *Carmen Paschale* of Caelius Sedulius: *ex inf.* Dr Neil Wright.)

1v: verses concerning contents. 'Super hystoriam Brittonum'. 'Actus famosos reges Britonum generosos . . . Error nox Treueris cessat uergit renouatur.'

2r–6r: 'Pontificum gesta breuitate profatur honesta / urbis Agrippine discreto singula fine / Stringens atque premens dumtaxat pagina presens'. Chronicle of see of Köln to 1237. 'Apud Agrippinam nobilem ciuitatem Gallie . . . Quadragesima non. Heinr. Bunnensis prepositus successit'.

6r/v: continued in several hands of thirteenth century.

7r–57r: HRB.

57r–74: 'Incipit descriptio uniuersi orbis que et mundi mappa dicitur'. 'Decriptio (*sic*) h. uniuersitati orbis comparata . . . que ad agnitionem ueritatis uenire. Amen.'

75r–102r: 'De origine Gallorum Trebirorum', Chronicle of see of Trier. 'Anno ante urbem Romam conditam millesimo .ccc. . . . et Meginero cedit episcopatus.'

102r–103r: 'Prima dedicatio quam constituit rex Salomon'. 'Prima dedicatio a Salomone . . . in seculum seculi laudabunt te.'

103v: 'De penitentia et liberatione Salomonis'. 'Ieronimus in .viii. x. libro super Ezechielem . . . ab eterno interitu liberantur.'

103v–104r: 'Dissonantia Ambrosii et Ieronimi. De penitentia Salomonis Ambrosius de libro regum'. 'Edificauit Salomon Astaroth ydolum . . . prius eliminare.'

104r: 'De locis sanctis. De liberatione Ade Ambrosius ad Marcellum'. 'In hac urbe immo in hoc loco . . . illuminabit te Christe.'

104r/v: 'Item de liberatione Ade'. 'Quia librum quam (*sic*) scribitur de penitentia Ade . . . uicium sui baptismatis lauacro pregauit (*sic*).'

104v–105v: 'Greg. ad Augustinum'. 'Cum enixa fuerit mulier . . . eripi non potest.' Extract from Bede, *Historia ecclesiastica*, I.27. Edd. Colgrave & Mynors, *Bede's Ecclesiastical History*, pp. 90–. 'Iohannes tercius papa episcopis Germanie et Gallie'. 'Petrus princeps . . . successori suo Clementi.'

105v: 'Ex concilio Tolerano cap. xii'. 'Dictum est quod in plerisque locis . . . et auariciam presumentes.'

DESCRIPTION

SIZE 26.5 x 17.5/18 cm.

QUIRING Some signatures on first recto of quire. I⁶, II⁸ (.iii.), III (fos 15–18: partly mounted; .ix. at foot of 17r), IV⁸ (lacks 3–6: .vii.), V⁸ (.xii.), VI⁸ (.xiii.), VII⁸ (.xiiii.), VIII⁸ (.xv.), IX⁸ (.xvi.), X⁸ (.xvii.), XI (fos 71–74). Second volume I⁸ (lacks 6: fos 75–81), II–IV⁸.

PRICKING Outer edge only.

RULING Single column except for 2r–6v (in 2). No ruling above top written line. 1r/v, 26 lines, double vertical boundary-lines. 2r–6v, 2 columns of 29 lines. HRB, single

vertical boundary-lines, 25–26 lines. 57r–74v, 22–23 lines. 75r–105v, 29–30 lines, drypoint.
SCRIPT fos 1–74 in dark brown ink, large Protogothic minuscule. Very rounded script with split or tagged ascenders. Generously spaced. Juncture of **do**. Round **d** frequent, final round **s** standard, found occasionally medially. Descenders extended when at foot of page. **g** straight-backed. When starting a line, horizontal of **t** and ascender of **d** trail into margin. 75–105 in earlier script with no round **d** and rare *et*-nota. Brown ink. **g** has dropped waist. **ct**-ligature well-spaced and joined at top.
DECORATION Large red and sometimes green capitals with foliate flourishes, split shafts etc.

HISTORY
Purchased for Harley by Nathaniel Noel in 1716 as reported in note at top of 1r: Wright, *Fontes Harleiani*, p. 253.
On the associations with Belgium and the Köln-Trier areas of other items acquired at the same time: Watson, 'An early thirteenth-century Low Countries booklist', pp. 43–44.

BIBLIOGRAPHY
Wanley *et al.*, *A Catalogue of the Harleian Manuscripts*, III.60.
Ward & Herbert, *Catalogue of Romances*, I.223–24.

103 *LONDON, BRITISH LIBRARY, MS. HARLEY 4003

Saec. xiii *ex.*   Origin and mediaeval provenance: ?Britain
iii (paper) + 151 + 10 (paper) + iv   2nd fo: *sitam uel inclinans*

HRB 81r–141v
§§1–3, 5–208. Dedicated to Robert of Gloucester. Rubrics at §1 (81r) 'Galfridi Arturi Monutensis (*sic*) de gestis Britonum prologus incipit', §5 (81r) 'Britannie insule descripcio', §6 (81v) 'Explicit descripcio. Incipit liber primus de gestis Britonum', §109 (111v) 'Incipit prologus de prophethiis (*sic*) Merlini', §111 (111v) 'Incipiunt hic prophethie Merlini', §118 (115r) 'Expliciunt prophethie Merlini. Incipit liber vii', after §208 (141v) 'Explicit liber'.
Book-divisions: II §23 (87r), III [ ], IV §54 (95v), V §73 (101r), VI §89 (105v), VII §118 (115r), VIII §143 (122r), IX §163 (128v), X §177 (134v).

CONTENTS
1+, 1–2: paper flyleaves. Blank except for note of sale on 1+; 1r, circular diagram whose segments contain descriptions of the kingdoms of the Heptarchy; contents-list (2v).
3r–37r: 'Incipit Hybernie hystorie distinctio prima de situ Hybernie uariaque eiusdem natura', Giraldus Cambrensis, *Topographia Hibernica*. 'Hybernia post Britanniam insularum maxima . . . quicquid a tanta maiestate fuerit iniunctum.' Ed. Dimock, *apud* Brewer *et al.* (edd.), *Giraldi Cambrensis Opera*, V.9–204.

37r–78r: 'Incipiunt capitula in duos libellos liber iste liberatur'. *Expugnatio hibernica*, Giraldus Cambrensis. *Capitula* ('Primus continet de exilio Dermicii ...') followed by text (38r) 'Requisitis et multociens ut indita nostri temporis gesta ... cum suus ex merito quemque tuebitur honor assequamur'. Edd. & transl. Scott & Martin, *Expugnatio hibernica*, MS. Hb, p. xxxviii).

78r–80v: 'Anno ab incarnacione Domini .m.clxvii. Dermicius rex Lagenie tranfretauit (*sic*) in Angliam ...'. Annals. Year-numbers extend to 1484 but last entry in original hand is at 1279 (79v) 'Hoc anno in crastino Prothi et Iacincti aplicuit (*sic*) R. Bigod comes Northfolchie mar. Anglie apud insulam'. Other entries in pencil at 1306, 1311, and 1313 (79v–80r), the last recording the succession of Walter Reginaldus following death of Robert, archbishop of Canterbury.

81r–141v: HRB.

142r–153v: continuations in same script. From Ine to William Rufus, end truncated. 'Successit igitur Calwalladro Ina ... et uiriliter insultabant ....'

154r–163v: paper, written in Early Modern hand. 'Iohannes Maior Scotus [ ] in tractato suo de gestis Scotorum li[ber] i c[apitulum 9] sic ait.' 'Scoti ab Hibernicis originem traxisse ... et eorum auxilienses uires regum haben[ ]es affunde (*sic*).' Extract from John Major, *Historia maioris Britannie*, fo XVII v – ?
Followed by five blank leaves.

DESCRIPTION
SIZE 21.5 x 15 cm.
QUIRING Three separate volumes – Giraldus; HRB and continuation; Early Modern paper manuscript. a^4 (lacks 4: 1+, 1–2), I–II^{12}, III^{14}, IV–VI^{12}, VII^4; VIII–IX^{12}, X^{10} (1 canc.), XI–XIII^{12}, 150 singleton, XIV^4 (1 lost, 3–4 mutilated: 151–153); 154–163, paper.
PRICKING None extant.
RULING Single column throughout. Giraldus 39 lines, double vertical boundary-lines, ruling above top written line. HRB 36–47 lines. Ruling above top written line, single vertical boundary-lines. Early Modern section unruled. 23 lines written.
SCRIPT HRB and continuation in small brown Anglicana. Several similar hands, most with split ascenders. Proportions vary from almost two-line upwards but never four-line. Crossed *et*-nota, long r. Final s has sigma-form. Giraldus in small brown bookhand with cursive features. Forked tops to ascenders. Crossed *et*-nota, two-compartment a but t hardly pierced. Juncture of e and o following b, d, p, but not h. ii flat-topped. Minim area not especially compact. Antiquarian addition in informal, rapid, ligatured hand. Looped d, e, two-compartment a.
DECORATION HRB – blue capitals with red. Unflourished red or blue capitals in Giraldus.

HISTORY
Owned by William Cecil (1520–98), and later Thomas Jett (until 1731): Wright, *Fontes Harleiani*, pp. 99, 205.

BIBLIOGRAPHY

Wanley *et al.*, *A Catalogue of the Harleian Manuscripts*, III.103.
Ward & Herbert, *Catalogue of Romances*, I.244–45.

104 *LONDON, BRITISH LIBRARY, MS. HARLEY 4123

Saec. xiv (1349)   Origin: ?Dyst (?=Diest, Brabant)
i + 172 fos (including unnumbered blank)   2nd fo: *ultramodum admiratus est ipsos*

HRB 2r–49rb.

§§1–3, 5–208. Dedicated to Robert of Gloucester.

No opening rubric. After §208 (49rb/va) 'Explicit hystoria de gestis regum Britannie quam Bruti appellamus quam scripsit Albertus filius Iohannis Alberti presbiter de Dyst. Orate pro eo omnes quicumque hanc hystoriam studiose inspexeritis perlegendo. Finito libro anno a natiuitate Domini .1300.49. mensis Decembris. In uigilia Lucie uirginis'.

CONTENTS

1: blank except for list of contents scribbled on verso in Early Modern hand.
2r–49v: HRB.
50r–126rb: *Liber de casu Troie* (from final rubric), Guido delle Colonne. Preceded by *capitula*-list. Text begins 54r 'Si et cotidie uetera recentibus obruant nonnulla . . . Anno Dominice incarnationis 1000.100 87 eiusdem prime indictionis feliciter'. Ed. Griffin, *Historia Destructionis Troiae* (MS H, *ibid.*, p. xii).
126v + following folio: blank.

127r–159r: 'Incipit cronica fratris Martini domni pape penitentiarii et capellani'. 'Quoniam scire tempora summorum pontificum Romanorum . . . et filius eius Phylippus in Franciam rediens coronatus est in epyphania sequenti.' von den Brincken, 'Studien', p. 526 (class IIIa).
159v + following fo: blank.
160r–165va: on the Six Ages of the world. 'Adam annorum .cxxx. genuit Seth cui superuixit annis .dccc. . . . aduersum quos Uespasianus in ingenti milicie transmissus plurimas urbes Iudee cepit.'
165va–167rb: 'Cursus et ordo temporum'. 'Prima ergo etas continet annos iuxta Hebreos nulle sexcentos quinquaginta sex . . . ut etas decrepita ipsa tocius seculi morte finienda.'
167rb: 'De Alexandro'. 'Uixit autem Alexander .xxxii. annos . . . uino et ueneno superatus atque extinctus occubuit.' Final part of Iulius Ualerius, *Gesta Alexandri*.
167v–170v: 'Liber prouincialis in districtu romano'. 'Tyburtinus Beatinus Anagninus . . . Apulei Ytalici singulis annis.'
171ra/va: 'Mappa mundi' (from final rubric). 'Iste sunt partes mundi: Asia, Europa, Affrica. Regiones Asye . . . Cesarea, Yleptis, Bizantium, Clipea.'
171vb: blank.

DESCRIPTION

SIZE 31 x 19.5 cm.

QUIRING I^8 (?+ 1 before 1: 1–9), II–VI^8, VII^4 (50–53), VIII–XV^8, XVI^{10} (118–126 + blank), XVII–XVIII^{10}, XIX ?^{10} (147–156), XX ?^{16} (13, 15 + one other cancelled: 157–169), XII ??^{2} (170–171). Coincidence of text and quiring in first volume.

PRICKING Visible at outer edges only.

RULING Two columns throughout. 46 lines in HRB. Ruling above top written line. 52 lines in second unit.

SCRIPT Small and round. Ascenders have indented tops. *Et*-nota is crossed, **a** has two-compartment form, and **t** is pierced. Juncture of **e** and **o** after **b**, **d**, and **p**, but not **h**. 2-shaped **r** has a hairline. Round **d** unlooped. Ascenders have indented tops. Brown ink. From 127r the script is a more formal Gothic hand approaching quadrata. Upright minims (even in round **d**), lozenged top and bottom giving jagged edge to minim space but not broken. Final **s** round. **t** pierced.

DECORATION Blue or chalky red initials, filigreed if blue.

HISTORY

Dyst, mentioned in colophon after HRB (49r/v), identified by Ward (*Catalogue of Romances*, I.236) as Diest in Brabant, Belgium. Spelling *Dist* well attested in the twelfth and thirteenth centuries, one usage of *Dyst* recorded in thirteenth century: Gysseling, *Toponymisch Woordenboek*, I.270.

BIBLIOGRAPHY

Wanley *et al.*, *A Catalogue of the Harleian Manuscripts*, III.118.
Ward & Herbert, *Catalogue of Romances*, I.236.
Wright, *Fontes Harleiani*, p. 48.

105 *LONDON, BRITISH LIBRARY, MS. HARLEY 5115

Saec. xiv *ex.* or xv   Mediaeval provenance: England
i + 150 + ii fos   2nd fo: *De ciuitate Samarcham*

HRB 88ra–150ra

§§1–3, 5–108, 111–208. Dedicated to Robert of Gloucester.
Rubric at §1 (88ra) 'Incipit historia regum Britannie Maioris secundum Galfridum Monemutensem', after §208 (150r) 'Explicit'.
No book-divisions.

CONTENTS

1r/v: flyleaf from thirteenth- or fourteenth-century book closely written in two columns.

2ra–47vb: 'Incipit liber domini Marci Pauli de Uenetiis de diuisionibus et con-sue[tu]dinibus orientalium regionum'. 'Librum prudentis honorabilis ac fidelissimi domini Marci Pauli ... ad diuersas prouincias et regiones deferuntur.' Compare Iwamura, *Manuscripts*.

47vb–86vb: 'Iste liber intitulatur flos historiarum terre orientis quem compilauit frater Hayconus . . .'. 'Diuiditur autem liber iste in quatuor partes . . . et conseruet qui potens est Deus in secula seculorum. Amen.' Ed. *Recueil des historiens des Croisades, Documents arméniens*, II.225–363.

87ra–88ra: 'Prohemium'. Story of Albina. 'Ab origine mundi circa annos tria milia et nungentos (*sic*) septuaginta fuit in Grecia quidam rex potentissimus . . . et insulam ex eorum nomine Britanniam uocauerunt sic inferius continetur.'

88ra–150ra: HRB.

150rb: note in English ?sixteenth-century hand.

150v: blank except for sketch of foliage and coat-of-arms.

150* blank.

151r: notes in fifteenth-century hand (Latin) concerning property of Robert Grey. Also medical recipes.

151v blank.

152 flyleaf as fo 1.

DESCRIPTION

SIZE 31.5 x 20.5 cm.

QUIRING Signatures. a singleton (fo 1), I–XII^{12}, XIII^8 (lacks ?6: 146–150, 150*, 151), b singleton (fo 152).

PRICKING For boundary-lines only.

RULING Two columns of 43 lines. Single vertical boundary-lines at gulley, double at outer edge. Ruling above top written line.

SCRIPT Grey-brown ink. Formal, nearly two-line bookhand resembling quadrata but minims not broken. Crossed *et*-nota. Round final s. Straight-backed d occurs. Two-compartment a constructed of vertical lines joined by hairlines. Round section of d and c angled. Pierced t.

DECORATION Minor initials blue, often in square of red filigree. Large capitals in blue and red with more elaborate filigree in red or violet.

HISTORY

Notes on final flyleaf concerning Robert Grey and 'Stynysford', one dated 1440.

BIBLIOGRAPHY

Wanley *et al.*, *A Catalogue of the Harleian Manuscripts*, III.247.
Ward & Herbert, *Catalogue of Romances*, I.245–46.

106 *LONDON, BRITISH LIBRARY, MS. HARLEY 6358

Saecc. **xii/xiii** + xiii^1 + xiv/xv   Mediaeval provenance: ?

86 + i fos   2nd fo: *ocupant. Deinde regem*

HRB 2r–58v.

§5–108, 111–208. Dedicatory section absent.

Rubrics at §5 (2r) 'Incipit prologus in hystoriam Britonum', at §6 (2r) 'Explicit prologus. Incipit hystorie Britonum liber primus. De Enea, Ascan[ ]', §111 (31v) 'Prophetia Merlini incipit', §118 (35r) 'Explicit prophetia Merlini'.

Book-divisions: I §6 (2r), II §22 (7r), III §35 (11v), IIII §54 (16r), V §73 (21v), VI §98 (27v), VII §111 (31v), VIII §118 (35r), IX §143 (40v), X §163 (46r), XI §177 (52r).

First Variant text. Wright, siglum H: *The Historia Regum Britannie of Geoffrey of Monmouth, II*, pp. lxxxvi–lxxxvii.

CONTENTS
1: flyleaf. On recto contents-list of ?sixteenth-century in pink ink. Verso blank.
2r–58v: HRB.
58*: blank.
59: blank with *ex-libris* and notes on verso (see below, HISTORY).

60r–83r: 'Turpinus Dei gratia archiepiscopus Remensis ac sedulus Karoli magni imperatoris consocius . . . Beatus Matheus apostolus et euangelista sua predicacione ad Dominum conuertit'. Ed. Meredith-Jones, *Historia Karoli*.

83v: 'Ex genere Priami fuit Moroueus . . . Ludouicus genuit Philippum qui nunc regnat'.

83v: 'Anno ab incarnacione Domini .dccc.lxxvi. Rollo cum suis Normanniam pene-trauit . . . et regnauit prope annis .xi. mortuo rege Ricardi successit Iohannes qui [ ]. Amen'. This and the preceding note also follow the *Historia Turpini* in Cambridge, Clare College, MS. 27, Corpus Christi College, MS. 292, and St John's College, MS. G.16.

84r: blank.
84v–86v: various extracts from chronicle of Chester in informal hand ? *ca* 1400 (rapid Secretary-hand with long cursive **r**, two-compartment **a** and no angularity in bow of **d**, etc.).

DESCRIPTION
SIZE 20 x 15 cm.
QUIRING No original signatures in HRB but added (?Early Modern). HRB apparently separate from Turpinus. I⁸ (+ 1 before 1: 1–9), II–VII⁸, VIII⁴ (lacks 4: 58, 58*, 59–60); IX–XI⁸; XII⁴ (lacks 4).
PRICKING Trimmed away in HRB. None visible at inner edges.
RULING One column throughout. HRB mostly in 37 lines, ruling indistinct. From 42r more distinct – 16 lines, top line written, double vertical boundary-lines. Turpinus has 30 lines, top line written, single vertical boundary-lines.
SCRIPT HRB in two types of hand, changing at 42r. A – four-line Protogothic with some lateral compression. Straight-backed **d** more frequent than the round form, final tall s retained, rare appearance of **e**-caudata, but standard use of the *et*-nota not ampersand. Insular *est*-compendium, and cursive **de** digraph found. B – rounder and more ordered with predominance of round **d** over other form but no final round s. Thickenings at base of minims, rounded tops to letters. *Enim*-compendium used.

et-nota again standard. Turpinus in later hand with juncture, crossed *et*-nota and filigreed capitals.

DECORATION Red Romanesque capitals (in A, chalky, orange-pink pigment is used) with one rubricator throughout HRB, now purple-grey.

HISTORY

Turpinus arguably written for Randulf de Blandeville, count of Chester, and is the earliest extant manuscript of the so-called C-Coeur de Lion version of that text: see de Mandach, *La Geste de Charlemagne*, pp. 130, 133. On verso of leaf following 58, late fifteenth- or sixteenth-century hand: 'Iste est liber Ricardi Blysset', perhaps to be identified with the Blysset who entered Magdalen College, Oxford, in 1488: Wright, *Fontes Harleiani*, p. 74. John Dee's mark on 60r and 83v and notes on 58v; also owned by D'Ewes: *ibid.*, pp. 127, 131; Watson, *The Library of Sir Simonds*, p. 245 (no. 60 in list of 1624).

BIBLIOGRAPHY

Dumville, 'The manuscripts', p. 119.

Hammer, *Geoffrey*, p. 7.

Wanley *et al.*, *A Catalogue of the Harleian Manuscripts*, III.247.

Ward & Herbert, *Catalogue of Romances*, I.235–36.

Wright, *The Historia Regum Britannie of Geoffrey of Monmouth, II*, pp. lxxxvi–lxxxvii.

107 *LONDON, BRITISH LIBRARY, MS. LANSDOWNE 732

Saec. xii/xiii	Origin and mediaeval provenance: ?England
71 fos	2nd fo: *Eneas excidium urbis cum*

HRB 1r–68v

§§1–208. Dedicated to Robert of Gloucester and Waleran of Meulan.

Rubrics at §1 (1r) 'Hic incipit liber Brut<i> de gestis Anglorum' (?late thirteenth-century). No other rubrics or book-divisions.

CONTENTS

1r–68v: HRB.

69r–71v: Anglicana hand (fourteenth-century) 'De unccione regis in regem'. 'De quo consecrandus est nouus rex . . . De officio pincernarum serui et comes Arundell..'

71v: beneath, in pencil. 'Nomina regum Anglie' (?fourteenth-century). Ends 'Marganus'; opening illegible.

DESCRIPTION

SIZE 19 x 13 cm.

QUIRING I–VIII^8, IX^8 (lacks ?8: fos 65–71).

PRICKING In both margins.

RULING Single column of 32 lines, double vertical boundary-lines. Top line written. *De Unccione* in 37 lines, written below top ruled line, single vertical boundary-lines. SCRIPT Small compact script similar to glossing script. Ampersand, round **d**, and tall **s** standard, but straight-backed **d** occurs. Initial **a** tall. No signs of juncture. Insular *enim*-compendium used. In *De Unccione*, tops of ascenders are turned over, not split. **a** and sigma-s rise above very short minims.

DECORATION Romanesque capitals in red, green and buff. Some with scrolled decoration in other colours.

BIBLIOGRAPHY

Ellis & Douce, *A Catalogue of the Lansdowne Manuscripts*, II.165.
Hammer, 'Remarks', p. 525.
Ward & Herbert, *Catalogue of Romances*, I.233–34.

108 *LONDON, BRITISH LIBRARY, MS. ROYAL 4.C.xi

Saecc. xi + xii*med./2* + xiii   Mediaeval provenance: Battle (Benedictine), Sussex
286 + fo fos   2nd fo: *editione uulgata. AB HIC*

HRB 222rb–248vb.

§§6–184, 186–208, 1–3, 5. Dedicated to Robert of Gloucester.

Rubric at §1 (222rb) 'Incipit historia Brittonum', at §111 (236r) is added in informal hand ?*ca* 1300 'Incipit prophetia Merlini'. No other rubrics but running title 'Historia Britonum' across facing pages.

Book-divisions added in ?late fourteenth or fifteenth century: II §23 (224v), III §35 (226v), IIII §54 (228v). *Capitula* numbered (late mediaeval).

Second Variant Version. Hammer's siglum B: Emanuel, 'Geoffrey of Monmouth's *Historia*', p. 104.

CONTENTS

1r–21vb: *Liber beati Ieronimi super Danielem* (from final rubric). 'Contra prophetam Danielem . . . in ipsorum libris poterit inuenire.' Ed. Glorie, *S. Hieronymi presbyteri opera, Pars 1, Opera exegetica, 5*, pp. 771–944.

21vb–22va: 'Expositis ut potui que in Danielis libro iuxta Hebraicum continentur . . . tunc querendum est quid ei respondere debeamus'. Ed. Glorie, *ibid.*, pp. 945–50.

22va–57va: 'Incipit explanationum in Osee prophetam beati Ieronimi presbiteri liber primus ad Pammachium'. 'Si in explanationibus omnium prophetarum . . . et in resurrectionem multorum in Israel.' Ed. Adriaen, *S. Hieronymi presbyteri opera, Pars 1, Opera exegetica, 6*, I.1–158.

57va–68va: 'Incipit prologus beati Ieronimi presbiteri ad Pamachium in explanationem Iohel prophete'. 'Non idem ordo est duodecim prophetarum apud septuaginta interpretes . . . super omnia tabernacula Iacob.' Ed. Adriaen, *ibid.*, I.159–209.

68va–96vb: 'Incipit explanationum in Amos prophetam ad Pammachium \liber primus/'. 'Amos propheta qui sequitur Iohelem . . . cuius promissio lex nature est.' Ed. Adriaen, *S. Hieronymi presbyteri opera, Pars 1, Opera exegetica, 6*, I.211–348.

97ra–102ra: 'Incipit liber eiusdem in explanationem Abdie prophete'. 'Dum essem paruulus ut paruulus loquebar . . . in illius sententiam transgredere.' Ed. Adriaen, *ibid.*, I.349–74.

102ra–110rb: 'Liber beati Ieronimi presbiteri super Ionam' (from final rubric). 'Triennium circiter fluxit postquam quinque prophetias interpretatus sum . . . qui comparantur iumentis insipientibus et assimilantur eis.' Ed. Adriaen, *S. Hieronymi presbyteri opera, Pars 1, Opera exegetica*, 6, I.377–419.

110vb–131va: 'Incipit explanationis in Micheam . . .'. 'Micheas in quem nunc commentarios dictare cupio . . . Egiptias extruat ciuitates.' Ed. Adriaen, *ibid.*, I.421–524.

131va–142va: 'Incipit liber explanationum beati Ieronimi presbiteri super Naum prophetam ad Paulam et Eustochium'. 'Iuxta septuaginta interpretes in ordine duodecim prophetarum . . . irruit quidem sed ingredi non potest.' Ed. Adriaen, *S. Hieronymi presbyteri opera, Pars 1, Opera exegetica*, 6, II.525–78.

142va–159rb: 'Incipit prologus beati Ieronimi presbiteri in explanationem Abbacuc prophete ad Chromatium'. 'Primum Chromati episcoporum doctissime scire nos conuenit . . . et cantores ceteros beati meo carmine superabo.' Ed. Adriaen, *ibid.*, II.579–654.

159rb–172ra: 'Incipit prologus eiusdem doctoris in explanationem Sophonie prophete ad Paulam et Eustochium'. 'Antequam Sophoniam aggrediar qui nonus est in ordine duodecim prophetarum . . . indigere expositione non arbitror.' Ed. Adriaen, *S. Hieronymi presbyteri opera, Pars 1, Opera exegetica*, 6, II.655–711.

172ra–179rb: 'Incipit prologus beati Ieronimi presbiteri in explanationem Aggei prophete ad Paulam et Eustochium'. 'Anno secundo Darii regis Persarum . . . Dominus dabit euangelizanti uerbum uirtutem multam.' Ed. Adriaen, *ibid.*, II.713–46.

179ra–212va: 'Incipit liber .i. explanationum beati Ieronimi in Zachariam ad Exuperium Holosarium episcopum'. 'Ultimo iam autumni tempore . . . quem de domo Dei asseruit auferendum.' Ed. Adriaen, *S. Hieronymi opera, Pars 1, Opera exegetica*, 6, II.747–900.

212va–222rb: 'Incipit prologus explanationis eiusdem beati Ieronimi in Malachiam prophetam ad Mineruium et Alexandrum'. 'Ultimum duodecim prophetarum Malachi interpretari uolumus . . . in Helia Iohannem intelligens.' Ed. Adriaen, *ibid.*, II.901–42.

222rb–248vb: HRB.

249rb–278r: Wace, *Roman de Rou*. 'Pur remembrer des ancesurs les feiz les diz e les murs . . . quin uelt auant faire sin face.' Ed. Holden, *Le Roman* (on this manuscript see *ibid.*, III.19–21.

278rb–279va: Miracle of Sardenai. '[ ] nom de la seinte trinite et si cum uint en autorite et cum en escrit trouai le miracle de Sardenai . . . qui uit et regne et regnera per seculorum secula. Amen.' Ed. Raynaud, 'Le miracle de Sardenai', pp. 531–37.

280ra–286vb: French metrical version of chronicle of Turpin. 'Ueirs est que li plusurs unt oi uolentiers e oent encore de Karlemaine . . . Philippe engendra Looys le enfant ki uiue et uaille.' Datable 1206 x 1223: Holden, *Le Roman*, III.20.

DESCRIPTION

SIZE 34.5 x 26 cm.

QUIRING Two overlapping sets of signatures (10v–217v, 209r–218r), transition occurring mid-text. I–XV^{10}, XVI^{10} (3 cancelled: 150–158), XVII–XXI^{10}, XXII^{10} (8 lacking: 209–217), XXIII^{10} (2, 8 lacking: 218–225), XXIV–XXV^{12}, XXVI–XXVIII^{8}, XXIX^{6} (274–279), XXX^{8} (280–286, 286*). Cumulative volume: HRB added to earlier volume, then Wace added after HRB. Final quire possibly separate.

PRICKING Fos 1–248 – in outer margin only. Turpin – both margins.

RULING Two columns throughout except for 249v–279v (verse) in three columns. Single boundary-lines. 50 lines before 223r with divided central margin, but 55 after 223v with change of hand. Single vertical boundary-lines; writing above top line. Wace in 46 lines. Turpin in 61 lines, double vertical boundary-lines, divided central margin.

SCRIPT Varying dates. 1r–223r in late Caroline minuscule, some angularity but basic proportions retained. e-caudata, ampersand. HRB – four-line Protogothic, some compression but still rounded. Ampersand standard, e-caudata found, initial a sometimes tall, round d occurs but straight form predominates. Final s standard. 8-shaped g. Brown ink. Wace etc. in small glossing hand. Round d, tall final s, de approaching juncture. Uncrossed *et*-nota. ?*ca* 1200. Turpin has later appearance. Juncture of de and do. Final s tall, however. *Et*-nota crossed. ?Early thirteenth-century.

DECORATION Romanesque capitals in purple, red, green, and brown. Opening rubric in pale blue. In commentaries (fos 1–222), red decorated capitals. Red or green in Wace, some filigreed. Red or blue in Turpin with contrasting filigree.

HISTORY

On 286*v in hand of perhaps *ca* 1300: 'Liber monasterii de Bello'.

Ex-libris in formal late Gothic bookhand on 1r, 'Liber monasterii sancti Martini de Bello Cicestr. dioc.'.

On the English associations of the text of the commentary on Habbakuk see Ker, *Books, Collectors and Libraries*, p. 76, n. 9.

BIBLIOGRAPHY

Dumville, 'The manuscripts', p. 119.

Ward & Herbert, *Catalogue of Romances*, I.277.

Warner & Gilson, *Catalogue of Western Manuscripts*, I.89.

109 *LONDON, BRITISH LIBRARY, MS. ROYAL 13.A.iii

Saec. xiv/xiv   Origin and mediaeval provenance: ?England
136 fos   2nd fo: *et Umbri uelud tria brachia*

HRB 1r–133r.

§§1–3, 5–162 'sub numero leuiter non caduntur cadebant', 164–208. Dedicated to Robert of Gloucester.

Only extant rubric after §208 (133r) 'Explicit liber Britonum'.

No book-divisions.

Hiatus before §164 not caused by physical loss. §162 ends near foot of 104v 'caduntur cadebant' and §164 begins beneath it 'Dispositis itaque'.

CONTENTS

1r–133r: HRB.

133v–134v: Hymn to the Virgin. 'Illustrata luce prima lux illustrans . . . beatum esse sine termino.' Staves drawn but no musical notation.

134v–135v: Second hymn. 'Uirgo parens gaudeat uirgo semper pura . . . intercurrat gessibus nostris fantasia.' With unfinished musical notation. Walther, *Initia*, I.1077, no. 20526.

135v–136r: about a prophecy. 'A quodam phitonico dudum in Cambria fuerat . . . ad sidera conuolebat.' Also found in London, BL, MSS. Cotton Claudius E.viii (1va/b) and Cotton Faustina A.viii (117ra/b).

136v: Hymn to St Peter (later hand). 'Cum [ ] Petrus in cruce uenit . . . cum hoc dixisset ait: Nolite.' With music.

DESCRIPTION

SIZE 18.5 x 11.5 cm.

QUIRING Catchwords at regular intervals ending on 130v. I–X^{12}, XI^{10}, XII ?^{6}.

Material following HRB seems to have been added on blank leaves at end of quire.

PRICKING Only visible for boundary-lines, at corners of written area.

RULING Single column of 28 written lines with writing below top ruled line and double vertical boundary-lines.

SCRIPT HRB in heavy shaded script of nearly two-line proportions. Juncture of e and o after b, d, h, and p. a is contructed of two vertical strokes joined by hairlines, t is pierced, 2-shaped r does not trail beneath the ruled line. *Et*-nota is crossed. Some ascenders are slightly tagged. Nearly black ink. Hymns in smaller and finer hand (except that on 136v).

DECORATION In HRB capitals are red or blue, filigreed with those colours or blue-green or brown.

HISTORY

Apparently in England at an early point as there are many marginal sketches (in brown pencil) of English towns (Leicester, York, etc.) which are labelled in an Anglicana hand of not later than the mid-fourteenth century. Also sketches of coats of arms. (For plate see Astley, 'Mediaeval Colchester', p. 118.)

At top of 1r, in pseudo-epigraphical capitals: 'Ponticus Virunius'. Lodovico da Ponte (1467–1520), a commentator on the Classics, produced an abridgment of the *Historia* (printed by Giles, *Galfredi Monumetensis Historia*, I.ii, pp. 3–53). He was born and died in Italy.

BIBLIOGRAPHY

Astley, 'Mediaeval Colchester', pp. 117–19.

Ward & Herbert, *Catalogue of Romances*, I.237.

Warner & Gilson, *Catalogue of Western Manuscripts*, II.74–75.

Saec. xiv ?[1]   Mediaeval provenance: ?Boston (Dominican), Lincolnshire
ii + 236 fos (includes 13 unnumbered fos + 161*)   2nd fo: *ut si forte a sibi*

HRB 99r–161v.

§§5–189 'despexerant perditum irent'. Early chapters abbreviated (to §8).
No rubrics or book-divisions.

CONTENTS
i: blank except for contents-list on verso (fourteenth-century?) which gives present
contents in the same order.

1r/v: blank.

2r–15r: 'Incipit libellus de ortu Alexandri et interfectione Nectancaby'. Iulius Ualerius, *Gesta Alexandri.* 'Prini (*sic*) sapientes Egipti . . . uino et ueneno superatus atque
extinctus occubuit.' Ed. Kuebler, *Iuli Valeri Alexandri Polemi res gestae*, pp. 1–168.

15v–23va: 'Incipit epistola Alexandri ad Aristotilem in qua continentur gesta ipsius
Alexandri'. 'Semper memor tui . . . et animi industria optime Aristotiles indicium.'
Ed. Walther Boer, *Epistola Alexandri.*

Following two (unnumbered) folios blank.

24ra–58va: 'Quoniam scire tempora summorum pontificum Romanorum ac imperatorum necnon et aliorum primi ipsorum contemporanorum (*sic*) . . . Nicholaus .3.
natus Ro. anno Dominice .m.cc.77. sed.'. Martinus Polonus. Ed. Weiland, MGH, SS,
XXII.397–474. See von den Brincken, 'Studien', p. 529 (class VIa).

58v (under text) and following 3 fos (unnumbered) blank.

59r–83va: Martinus, Chronicle of the Emperors. 'Post natiuitatem Domini nostri Iesu
Christi . . . terminum transfretaturum.'

83vb: blank.

84ra: written in a similar hand. Top trimmed away.

84rb/v + 6 following (unnumbered) fos: blank.

85v, 86v + 87r/v: written in pencil in informal hand (?early fourteenth century). Rectos
of 85 and 86 blank.

88r/v: blank except for prologue to following work on vb.

88vb–98vb: 'Dares de gestis Troianorum et Grecorum' (from final rubric). 'Cornelius
nepos Salustio Prisco salutem . . . bellum uero istud post diluuium fuit anno .d.cc.16.
actum est.'

99r–161v: HRB.

161* + following two (unnumbered) folios blank.

162r–189v: religious treatise. 'Sicud in apoteca dicuntur aliter omnis homo quod
desiderat inuenit . . . sicut debitor est ut ueritatem.' Breaks off.

190r–223r: 'Incipit liber primus mineralium qui est de lapidibus tractatus primus de
lapidibus in communi'. 'De mixtione et coagulacione sicut autem et congulacione
. . . de subalib. (*sic*) causis metallorum per hunc modum.' Thorndike & Kibre, *A
Catalogue*, p. 368. By Albertus Magnus (according to rubric at foot of 190r), on whom
see Thorndike, *A History of Magic*, II.524, n. 3. Fauser, *Die Werke*, p. 74 (shelfmark
there given incorrectly as Royal 13.A.15).

223r/v: '[ ] partet etiam accidencia cong[ ]scere ... ad habet superficere'. In small late quadrata, ?fifteenth-century.

DESCRIPTION

SIZE 18.5 x 13.5 cm.

QUIRING Generally indicated by catchwords. a 2 (fos i + 1), I^{12} (2–13), II^{10} (14–23); III $?^8$ (24–31), IV–VI^8, VII $?^6$ (fos 56–58 + 3 unnumbered); VIII–X^8, XI^6 (fos 83–84 + 4 unnumbered), XII^6 (2 unnumbered + 85–88), XIII^{10}, XIV $?^6$ (99–104), XV–XVII^8, XVIII^{10}, XIX^{12}, XX^8, XXI^6 (fos 159–161* + 2 unnumbered blanks); XXII^{16}, XXIII^{12}; XXIV–XXV^{12}, XXVI^{10}. Several units of text but joined at an early date as contents-list (1v) in fourteenth-century hand suggests. (Possible breaks after fos 23, 83, 161, 189.)

PRICKING Mostly trimmed away. Where extant are only for boundary-lines.

RULING Two columns of 25–34 lines in HRB. Fos 162–198 (religious tract) frame-ruled.

SCRIPT All of volume written in Anglicana except for last item (*De Mineralibus*) which is in Gothic bookhand (broad nib, simple strokes, juncture of **de** and **po**, crossed *et*-nota, brown ink). HRB mostly in idiosyncratic hand (found from 24r onwards) – deliberate, disjointed upright strokes. Ascenders have slightly split tops. Round looped **d** is written with a backwards ductus; both tall and round **s** occur in all positions. **a** is high and Caroline in form, short **r** is almost 3-shaped, *et*-nota is crossed. End of HRB in less compressed hand, also with split ascenders but with long cursive **r**.

DECORATION Crude and simple red initials. In *De mineralibus*, red or blue filigreed capitals.

HISTORY

Recorded by John Leland as belonging to the Dominican convent of Boston: Ker, *Medieval Libraries*, p. 11.

BIBLIOGRAPHY

Ward & Herbert, *Catalogue of Romances*, I.237–38.
Warner & Gilson, *Catalogue*, II.76.

111 *LONDON, BRITISH LIBRARY, MS. ROYAL 13.D.i

Saec. xiv/xv (*post* 1385)   Mediaeval provenance:
                                        Church of St Peter's, Cornhill, London
255 + i (incl. 2 unnumbered blanks)   2nd fo: *de Burgundia terra*

HRB 175r–21va.

§§1–3, 5–108, 111–208. Dedicated to Robert of Gloucester.

No original opening rubric but before §111 (193vb) 'Explicit historia usque adhuc et incipit prophetia Ambrosii Merlini quam dixit ex precepto Uortigerni regis Britonum', after §208 (212va) 'Ualete. Explicit historia de gestis Britonum'.

No book-divisions.

Related to Cambridge, UL, MS. Dd.1.17, especially in the compression of §179. Other omissions include the prologue to the Prophecies and the absence of the first sentence of §177 (which here begins 'Ut igitur').

CONTENTS

1r/v: blank except for note on verso, 'Liber ecclesie sancti Petri super Cornehill'.

2r: Early Modern contents-list.

2v: late Gothic contents-list, and *ex-libris* as on 1v.

3r–9ra: lists prefatory to the *Polichronicon*. 'Abraham bdon dux Israel . . . de Zoro-babel.'

9ra/b: account of the Ages of the world. 'Prima etas seculi ab Adam . . . secundum Orosium .v.cc. secundum Martinum .v.xcix. [ ] uerissimos .v.cxcvi..'

9va: 'Beatus Augustinus 2o de mirabilibus sacre scripture . . . dies et dimidia'.

9vb + following folio (9*) unnumbered and blank.

10ra–172rb: 'Prologus in historiam polichronicam'. 'Post preclaros artium scriptores . . . non plus uiguit in discrecione ?quam unus puer .viii. annorum.' In seven books, to 1377. Edd. Babington & Lumby, *Polychronicon*.

172rb–174vb: continuation. 'Richardus de Bordeus filius domni Edwardi . . . episco-pus Dunelmensis moritur, senex multorum dierum.'

175ra–212va: HRB.

212v–222rb: 'Gestus Karoli regis Francorum' (from final rubric). 'Gloriosissimus Christi apostolus Iacobus . . . magis enim deficeret manus et calamus quam historia.' Ed. Smyser, *The Pseudo-Turpin*.

222v–225rb: letter of Henry of Huntingdon to King Henry. 'Cum mecum propter ea que responsione tua accepi tractarem . . . nec plus ad presens dicam de tua generacione siue progenie sanctissima. Ualete.'

225rb–236vb: 'Testamentum prophetarum' (according to final rubric). 'Transcriptum testamenti Ruben . . . ad diem exitus eorum de terra Egypti.'

237ra–242rb: summary chronicle A.D. 1 to 1208. 'Anni ab incarnacione Domini anno primo .viii. kalendii Ianuar. Christus natus est . . . recurrentibus inter illos nunciis inferto.'

242v–243rb: chronicle from 1140 B.C. to 1385 A.D.. 'Anni ab orbe condito ad urbem Rome conditam . . . anno Domini .m.ccc.lxxv. rex Ricardus Anglie intrauit Scotiam.'

243rb/va: 'Descripcio corporis Christi'. 'Legitur in annalibus Romanorum . . . ante suam assumpcionem fuit etatis .lxiii. annorum.'

243va/b: 'Descripcio beate Marie'. 'Fuit beata Maria stature medie . . . summa per annum .ix. .ccc. anni.'

243vb–244ra: 'Mirabilia Hybernie'. 'Hybernia diuiditur in .iiii. . . . unde ex isto ruano (*sic*) dicitur oldruaunt (*sic*).'

244ra: 'Mirabilia Anglie'. 'Uentus egreditur de monte qui uocatur Peek . . . asportauerit in eundem locum eum inireient.'

244ra/b: 'Mirabilia orientis'. 'India tercia pars orbis estimatur . . . quare discurrendo tot mala facis.'

244rb/va: 'Fontes'. 'Sardinia est insula in mari . . . et uocem facit dulcem et canoram.'

244va/b: 'Montes'. 'Mons Olimpi est in Grecia . . . sicut uix teste Petro Iacobo et Iohanne.'

244vb–245ra: notes on pilgrimages. 'Notandusque ab Anglia ad Romam sunt mille miliaria . . . omiserunt graciosum munus Dei eis oblatum.'

245rb–246vb: 'Incipit libellus de tribus partibus mundi . . .'. 'Tres sunt partes mundi: Asia, Affrica, Europa . . . ibi omnia animalia uiuunt piscibus et sunt alba etc.'

246vb: 'Recapitulacio omnium terrarum ciuitatumque tocius mundi primo de Asia Anglice lingua'. '[Th]is world ys delyd al on thre . . . these bene alle in Asya.'

246vb–247ra: 'Iste sunt terre et ciuitates Affrice'. 'By [th]at other syde is Aufrike . . . By the see syde of Irlond.' Brown & Robbins, *The Index*, p. 584, no. 3653.

247ra: notes on taxation and measurements. 'Summa taxacionis spiritualis temporalis uirorum ecclesiasticorum prouincie Cantuar. cum dioc. . . .'

247v–248rb: 'Incipit expositio Danielis prophete quod uidit et disposuit in Babilonia . . .'. 'Aues qui uiderit contra se pungrare (*sic*) iracundiam signat . . . scilicet zizannia sanctiare machinas uel scandalum .s..' See Buhler, 'Two Middle English Texts'.

248rb/va: note on weights and measures. 'nota quod tria grana ordei me spice faciunt pollicem . . ..'

248va/b: 'De .xv. signis .xv. dierum precedencium diem iudicii Ieronimus in annalibus Hebreorum quindecim signa quindecim dierum .i. dies'. 'Maria omnia exaltabuntur in altitudine . . . et eadem crux humeris angelorum Christo descendente de celis portabitur etc.'

249ra–254vb: 'Liber septimus qui est ultimus historie Polichronice' (from final rubric). 'Hoc eodem anno non. Iunii natus est regi Edwardo .iii. . . . et quid grauius longam continuacionem diu post ea habuerunt.'

Next folio blank and unnumbered.

DESCRIPTION

SIZE 32 x 24 cm.

QUIRING Indicated by catchwords. I^{12} (+ 2 before 1 – fos 1–2: 1–9, 9*, 10–13), II–III^{12}, IV^8 (38–45), V^{10} (4 cancelled: 46–54), VI–VIII^{12}, IX^{10} (91–100), X–XV^{12}, XVI^{16} (15–16 excised: 173–186), XVII^{12}, XVIII^8, XIX^6, XX–XXII^{12}, XXIII^6 (+ 1 after 6: 249–254, 254*).

PRICKING Visible for boundary-lines only.

RULING Two columns of 54 lines – no ruled text-lines visible but writing evenly spaced. Written below top ruled line. Vertical line drawn in side margins about 2 cm from boundaries of text.

SCRIPT Grey/brown ink or black. Gothic bookhand of the formal sort. Short ascenders with tops tagged to the left, juncture of **d** with **e** and **o** but not of **h** or **p**. **t** is well pierced, **a** has looped two-compartment form, final round **s** is standard but tall **s** occurs in other positions. *Et*-nota is crossed. Some hairlines as from horizontal of final **t**. Aspect strongly reminiscent of that of Cambridge, UL, MS. Dd.1.17.

DECORATION Red running titles, blue or red paragraph-marks. Capitals in square of filigree. Major initials (in blue and red) have scrolling along edges of text.

HISTORY

Ex-libris in formal Gothic hand, yellow-brown ink on 1v and 2v: 'Liber ecclesie sancti Petri super Cornehill'. Ker, *Medieval Libraries*, p. 221.

BIBLIOGRAPHY
Ward & Herbert, *Catalogue of Romances*, I.248.
Warner & Gilson, *Catalogue of Western Manuscripts*, II.107–9.

112 *LONDON, BRITISH LIBRARY, MS. ROYAL 13.D.ii

Saec. xii *ex.* or later   Mediaeval provenance: Margam (Cistercian), Glamorgan
174 fos   2nd fo: *carn[u] pro[n]us omniumque fere*

HRB 124r–173v.
§§1–3, 5–208. Dedicated to Robert of Gloucester.
At §1 (124r) 'Gaufridi Arturi Monemutensis de gestis Britonum prologus incipit', at §5 (124r) 'Birtannie (*sic*) insule descriptio', §109 (148v) 'Incipit prologus in prophecias Merlini', after §110 (148v) 'Explicit prologus. Incipiunt prophecie', 118 (151v) 'Expliciunt prophetie Merlini'. No closing rubric.
Book-divisions: I §6 (124r), II §23 (128v), III [ ] but space for rubric at §35 (131v), IV §54 (135v), V §73 (140r), VI §89 (143v), (VI ends after §108, 148v), VIII §118 (151v), IX§143 (157r), X §163 (162v), XI §177 (167r).
Prophetie Merlini §§111–115 glossed in fourteenth-century Anglicana hand.

CONTENTS
1v–3v (1r stuck down to modern paper flyleaf): flyleaves with notes in late mediaeval hand on kings of England, etc.
4r–110ra: 'Incipit prologus Willelmi monachi Malmesberiensis in libro primo de gestis regum Anglorum'. 'Res Anglorum gestas Beda uir maxime doctus et minime superbus . . . seu oblatione muneris seu de linimento fauoris.' Ed. Stubbs, *Willelmi Malmesbiriensis monachi de gestis regum Anglorum*. MS. Ce: *ibid.*, I.lxxx–lxxxii.
110ra–123vb: 'Incipit prologus Willelmi Malmesberiensis in libros nouelle historie missos Roberto comiti Gloecestrie'. 'Domino amantissimo .R. filio regis Henrici . . . sed hec in uolumine sequenti Deo uolente latius expedientur.' Ed. Potter, *The Historia Novella*, MS. Ce 1 (*ibid.*, p. xl).
124r–173v: HRB.
174r: blank except for scribbles and pen-trials.
174v: stuck down to modern paper flyleaf.

DESCRIPTION
SIZE 37 x 26 cm.
QUIRING Indicated by signatures. a ?⁴ (lacks 1: 1–3), I–XX⁸, XXI¹⁰, b singleton (174).
PRICKING In both margins.
RULING In two columns of 41 lines. Double vertical boundary-lines and sub- divided central margin. Top line written.
SCRIPT Very formal – large, black, homogeneous throughout. Upright and rather angular. Minims unbroken but some lozenged at top. Standard use of ampersand is a

reflection of formality. Straight-backed **d** and final tall **s** are found as well as the round form. Curved suspension-mark. Little abbreviation.
DECORATION Coloured capitals primarily for book-divisions. Usually simple Romanesque shapes: pale brown, red, purple and green or blue.

HISTORY
Inscription in large Gothic textura under text on 173v: 'Liber monachorum sancte Marie de Margan', Cistercian abbey, Glamorgan. Second *ex-libris* of this house on 1v dated the ninth year of Henry V. Ker, *Medieval Libraries*, p. 129.

BIBLIOGRAPHY
Ward & Herbert, *Catalogue of Romances*, I.228.
Warner & Gilson, *Catalogue of Western Manuscripts*, II.109.

113 *LONDON, BRITISH LIBRARY, MS. ROYAL 13.D.v

Saec. xiii[1] (*post* 1206)   Origin and provenance: St Albans (Benedictine)
i + 201 + i fos (incl.   2nd fo: *inferebant. Nec eos hoc modo*
unnumbered leaf after fo 152)

HRB 1r–37vb
§§1–3, 5–208 [§§109–110 in *pudibundus Brito* form]. Dedicated to Robert of Gloucester.
Running title above §1 (1r): 'Gesta Britonum'. At §6 (1r) 'De aduentu Enee in Italiam et natiuitate Bruti' and similar summaries at most chapter-divisions; before §109 (20r) 'Prologus Galfridi in uaticinationes Merlini', at §111 (20r) 'Incipiunt uaticinia Merlini Ambrosii', after §208 (37vb) 'Explicit hystoria Britonum. Et de ambagibus Merlini'. No book-divisions.

CONTENTS
ir/v: blank but on verso, ?fifteenth-century shelfmark 'De almariolo in primo gradu B primus liber' and contents-list.
1r–37vb: HRB.
38r–43rb: 'Incipiunt gesta Britonum a Gilda sapiente composita', *Historia Brittonum*. 'A principio mundi usque ad diluuium anni .ii.cc.xlii. . . . in extremis finibus cosmi.' Ed. Faral, *La Légende*, III.5–61.
43rb–45ra: 'Nota Britannie admirabiles 79 c[ ] piscibiles fertilitates'. 'Britannia igitur beatissima est insularum . . . quos diximus aduenientes sibi locum patrie fecerunt.'
45ra–50vb: 'Incipit prefatio de subsequenti uisione que contigit in Estsexia'. 'Multifarie multisque modis olim Deus loquens patribus in prophetis . . . quam ex perplexis et profundis theologie disputationibus.' Thurkill's Vision (seen in 1206). Ed. Schmidt, *Visio Thurkilli*.
51ra–132va: 'Incipit prologus domni Willelmi monachi in libro primo de gestis regum Anglorum'. 'Res Anglorum gestas Beda uir maxime doctus et minime superbus . . . qui non erraui eligendi iudicio.' Ed. Stubbs, *Willelmi Malmesbiriensis monachi de gestis regum Anglorum*. MS. Cd: *ibid.*, I.lxxxiii–lxxxiv.

132va–142rb: Book VI, *Historia nouella*. 'Domini amantissimo Roberto filio regis Henrici . . . ab his qui interfuere ueritatem accepero.' Ed. Potter, *The Historia Novella*, MS. Cd (*ibid.*, p. xl).

142rb–151vb: 'Incipit quidam tractatus Alredi abbatis Rieuallis ad Henricum ducem Normannie postea regem Anglie de uita et moribus quorundam regum Anglie'. Aelred of Rievaulx, *Genealogia regum*. 'Illustrissimo duci Normannorum et Aquitanorum et comiti Andegauensium . . . et augeat suam excellentissime et illustrissime domine.'

151vb: 'Uisio cuiusdam sic alloquentis regem Malcolmum', 14 lines. 'Cur sic care taces? . . . quidque tuis mandas? Perpetuo ualeant.' Ed. Skene, *Johannis de Fortun. Chronica*, p. 452. Walther, *Initia*, I.197, no. 3945. Four-line poem added underneath in ?fifteenth-century hand. 'Tu quis eras pridem . . . .'

152ra/b: description of the shires and bishoprics of England. 'Anglia habet in longitudine .D.CCC. miliaria . . . Stafordscire .d. hide.'

152rb: list of Counts of Flanders. 'Hildricus Harlebeccensis comes genuit Ingelramnum . . . et ex ea duos filios suscepit Baldewinum et Willelmum.'

152rb: 'Hec sunt nomina Francorum regum'. 'Clodoueus . . . Philippus Lodowicus.' 152v + following folio blank, unruled.

153ra–200vb: 'Incipit prologus domni Willelmi monachi in libro primo de gestis pontificum Anglorum'. 'Prima sedes episcoporum post Christianitatem Anglorum Cantuarie habita est . . . heremeticam exercere ibi uitam.'

Final flyleaf: blank recto. Scribbles and drawing (? late mediaeval) on verso.

DESCRIPTION

SIZE 38 x 28 cm.

QUIRING Crude signatures or catchwords in faint brown pencil indicate coincidence of text and quiring. i + I–VI^8, VII^2 (fos 49–50); VIII–XIX^8, XX^8 (2 cancelled: 147–152 + blank); XXI–XXVI^8 + i.

PRICKING In both margins.

RULING Two columns of 56 lines, top line written. Subdivided central margin, double vertical boundary-lines with two lines drawn parallel to them in side margins (about 2.5 cm from text).

SCRIPT Formal early Gothic book-hand. Minims lozenged, ascenders have flat tops with slight hairline, juncture of e and o after b, d, and p (not h), and general fusion of curves. Straight-backed d still found frequently, ampersand is standard in some parts of book, final s not always round.

DECORATION Red or cobalt blue capitals with filigree. Opening initials large, elaborate and handsome with filigree in red and blue.

HISTORY

On 1r, above text: 'Hic est liber sancti Albani de libraria conuentus', in fifteenth-century formal hand (red). In similar hand on 37v after HRB: 'Hic est liber qui per quorundam neglegenciam fuerat deperditus. Sed per industriam uenerabilis nostri in Christo patris et Domini domni Iohannis abbatis sexti huic monasterio erat restitutus et assignatus librarie conuentus', thus implying that the book was reclaimed for St Albans through the efforts of John Whethamstede (abbot 1420–40 and 1451–64). The *ex-libris* on 1r is repeated in the same hand after the *Historia Brittonum* (45ra).

That the book was at St Albans at an early stage is confirmed by Vaughan's identification of the hand of Matthew Paris in certain rubrics and marginalia: 'The Handwriting of Matthew Paris'.
Annotated in sixteenth century by Polydore Vergil: Hay, *Polydore Vergil*, p. 86.

BIBLIOGRAPHY
Thomson, *Manuscripts from St Albans*, I.98–99, no. 35.
Vaughan, 'The Handwriting of Matthew Paris', pp. 381–82, 391, 393.
Ward & Herbert, *Catalogue of Romances*, I.229.
Warner & Gilson, *Catalogue of Western Manuscripts*, II.110.

114 *LONDON, BRITISH LIBRARY, MS. ROYAL 14.C.i (FOS 20–137) + COTTON NERO C.v (FOS 162–285)

ROYAL 14.C.i (FOS 20–137)

Saec. xiv *in.*   Mediaeval provenance: Norwich Cathedral (Benedictine)
i + 140 fos (incl. 3 unnumbered leaves)   2nd fo (21r): *Iudicauit*
                                                          Israel cuius destructio

HRB 80r–137r
§§1–3, 5–208 [+ *Merlinus iste* passage after §117, 112v–113r]. Dedicated to Robert of Gloucester.
No rubrics or book-divisions.
Second Variant Version. Hammer's siglum A: Emanuel, 'Geoffrey of Monmouth's *Historia*', p. 104.

CONTENTS
20r–74r: 'Cronica Romanorum composita a fratre Martino penitenciario domini pape et capellano' to 1277. 'Quoniam scire tempora summorum pontificum Romanorum ac imperatorum . . . et ibidem in ecclesia sancti Laurencii est sepultus.' See von den Brincken, 'Studien', p. 528 (class IIIb).
75r–79v: 'Romanum imperium siue post mortem siue post deposicionem Frederici imperatoris II . . . nec poterant conuenire de electione pape per plures annos uidelicet per .iii. annos'.
80r–137r: HRB (constituting first of three books of the History by Bartholemew Cotton as indicated by final rubric on 280vb of Nero C.v).
137v: blank, unruled.

LONDON BRITISH LIBRARY, MS. COTTON NERO C.v (FOS 162–285)

CONTENTS
162r–280vb: second and third books of History of Bartholemew Cotton. 'Incipit historia anglicana s[cilicet] liber secundus de regibus anglis. dacis. et normannis.'

'Attestantibus antiquorum cronographorum testimoniis . . . Elyensis cont[erminatur] Licoln. Norwyc. London..' Third book begins on 255r after blank leaf, 254r/v (final rubric 'Explicit tractatus de archiepiscopis et episcopis Anglie compilatus a fratre Bartholomeo de Cotton. monacho Norwyc. Anno gracie .m.cc.xcii. cum .ii. precedentibus libris s[cilicet] primo de regibus Britonum et secundo de regibus Anglis. Dacis et Normannis cuius anime propicietur Deus. Amen'.)
281: blank, recto ruled.

282r–283r: 'In ista bulla continetur causa secunde combustionis ecclesie Nor.'. '[ ]regorius episcopus seruus seruorum Dei uenerabilibus fratribus Londoniensis et Eliensis episcopis salutem et apostolicam benedictionem. Habet dil[ec]torum filiorum . . . non fecerint mencionem. Datum apud urbem Nete.m .iii. id. Marcii pont. nostri. Anno primo.'
283v: blank but note at top in ?sixteenth-century hand.
284–285: blank, ruling on 284 only.

DESCRIPTION
SIZE Royal 14.C.i (20–137) – 32 x 22 cm. Cotton Nero C.v (162–285) – 32.5 x 23 cm.
QUIRING Royal 14.C.i (20–137) I–IV^{12},V ?^{12} (stubs before 4 and 10: 68–79), VI–IX^{12}, X ?^{10} (128–137). Fos 20–56 – catchwords on many folios but not indicative of quiring. Some catchwords for quiring extant after that.
Cotton Nero C.v (162–285) I^4 (1 cancelled: 162–164), II^{10}, III–VIII^{12}, IX^{12} (9–12 cancelled: 247–254), X^{12} (9 cancelled: 255–265), XI^{16} (265–281); XII^4 (1, 4 singletons).
RULING Royal 14.C.i (20–137) + Cotton Nero C.v (162–285) – single column of 35 lines. Single vertical boundary-lines; written below top ruled line.
Episcopal lists in Nero C.v, 263r–281r, written in two columns.
SCRIPT HRB (+ Nero C.v, 162r–280vb) – dark brown ink. Anglicana formata. Large, four-line. Ascenders occasionally split. Long r, looped two-compartment a (upper compartment sometimes not joined). Feet on minims. Juncture of e and o after p and b but not d. Same script fos 20–79.
Nero C.v, 281–285 – more elongated and compressed script than above. ?Slightly later. Also in brown ink. Flourished and rightward-leaning. Two-compartment a, long r, uncrossed et-nota, crossed t.
DECORATION Blue or red filigreed capitals. Blue-green also used in filigree. Elaborate opening capital with areas of solid colours (blue with pink and grey) with white highlights and some gold. Animals and grotesque faces painted in full colour in margin of Martinus Polonus. See Sandler, *Gothic Manuscripts*, II.55. Nero C.v, 162–280 as HRB. No decoration in Nero C.v, 282–285.

HISTORY
Fos 1–19 of Royal 14.C.i belong to MS. Cotton Claudius D.vi (from St Albans). Remainder of Royal 14.C.i (20–137) belongs to Cotton Nero C.v, from Norwich.
Inscription on 285v of Nero C.v, 'Lix. Galfridi de Smalbergh. mo[nach]i est' in fourteenth-century hand. Acquired by Norwich cathedral soon after writing (before

ca 1325): see Ker, *Books, Collectors and Libraries*, p. 258; also Ker, *Medieval Libraries*, p. 138 and n. 6.

BIBLIOGRAPHY
Ward & Herbert, *Catalogue of Romances*, I.238.
Warner & Gilson, *Catalogue of Western Manuscripts*, II.132–33.

115 *LONDON, BRITISH LIBRARY, MS. ROYAL 15.C.xvi

Saec. xiv *ex.* or xv
iv + 184 + ii fos

Mediaeval provenance:
Hospital of St Thomas of Acon, London
2nd fo: *uiolare debebant*

HRB 146r–183v
§§1–3, 5–208. Dedicated to Robert of Gloucester.
Rubric after §208 (183va) 'Explicit liber qui uocatur Brutus'. Also by §111 (165r) in informal hand in margin 'Hic incipiunt uaticinia Merlini'.
No book-divisions.

CONTENTS
i–iv: flyleaves. Blank except for contents-list on i v and notes on i v and iii r (see below, HISTORY).
1r–59va: 'Tabula super Ouidium de transformatis . . .'. *Capitula*-list followed by text. 'Abbas a monarcho occiditur ueneno . . . Exurge Domine adiuua nos et redime nos seu libera nos.' Partly edited by van der Bijl, 'Petrus Berchorius'. See also Engels, 'L'édition critique de l'Ovidius moralizatus de Bersuire'.
59vb–71ra: 'Incipit philobiblon'. 'Uniuersis Christi fidelibus ad quos tenor presentis scripture peruenerit Ric. de Bury . . . ac eius de[inde] concedat perpetuum fruibilis faciei conspectum. Amen.' Ed. Altamura, *Riccardo da Bury*, pp. 71–134 (on this MS. (R2), see p. 28).
71r–85vb: 'Alanus de planctu nature'. 'In lacrimas risus insuccus gaudia uerto . . . prior mistice apparitionis reliquit aspectus.' Ed. Migne, *Patrologia Latina*, CCI.451–82.
86ra–145rb: 'Excidium Troianum', Guido delle Colonne. 'Licet cotidie uetera recentibus obruant nonnulla . . . Anno Dominice incarnacionis millesimo ducentesimo septimo eiusdem prime indiccionis feliciter.' Ed. Griffin, *Historia Destructionis Troiae*. Griffin's MS. R (p. xiv).
145v: blank.
146r–183va: HRB.
183vb–184ra: 'Prophetia aquile'. 'Arbor fertilis a primo trunco decisa . . . Tunc probitas generosa pacietur nulli irrogari iniuriam qui pacificato regno occidet.' Ed. Schulz, *Gottfried*, pp. 463–65.
184v and following two unnumbered folios blank.

DESCRIPTION

SIZE 35 x 24 cm.

QUIRING a^4 (?), I–XI^{12}, XII ?^{12} (+ 1 after 12, fos 133–145), XIII–XV^{12}, XVI ?^{6} (?6 excised: 182–184, 2 blanks). Catchwords.

PRICKING Only visible for vertical boundary-lines.

RULING Two columns of 52 lines. Single vertical boundary-lines, ruling above top written line.

SCRIPT Aspect more formal than letter-forms. Dark ink. Short ascenders and descenders. Tops of ascenders angled over. s is round when final, long in other positions. Pierced t. Looped two-compartment a. Juncture of e and o after d only. Crossed *et*-nota. Barred x. Cursive long r. Looped ascenders on b, h, l.

DECORATION Blue capitals in squares of red filigree. Blue or red paragraph marks in text.

HISTORY

In fifteenth-century hand on i v, 'Ex dono uenerabilis uiri domini Henrici Spycer canonici de Wyndesor.' (?Windsor), followed by contents-list.

Note on iii r 'Caucio magistri Iohannis Nele magistri domus sancti Thome de Achon. London. exposita penes uenerabilem uirum rectorem de Ashrugge. pro quodam uolumine omelias Origenis super Iesum Naue necnon super alios libros biblie continenti quod quidem uolumen habet in 2o fo. Amalech Et quod ibi'. The Hospital of St Thomas Acon was on Cheapside. Ashrugge is Ashridge, Bucks.: Ker, *Medieval Libraries*, pp. 126, 4.

On 183v, in Early Modern hand, 'Liber domus sancti Thome de Acon London. ex dono domini Iacobo comitis Ormundie'.

BIBLIOGRAPHY

Ward & Herbert, *Catalogue of Romances*, I.239.
Warner & Gilson, *Catalogue of Western Manuscripts*, II.170.

116 *LONDON, BRITISH LIBRARY, MSS. SLOANE 281 + 289

Saec. xv   Mediaeval provenance: ?
i + 14; 195 fos   2nd fo: *In principio erat uerbum* (MS. 289, fo 3)

HRB 120r–183r.

§§1–3, 5–108, 111–208. Dedicated to Robert of Gloucester.

Note in hand of text at top 120r: 'Notandum quod in pluribus locis istius libri error sit tam in denotacione annorum quam temporum et e contra[ria] differunt uero in eisdem margines a infratexto secundum tamen auctores et historiagrophos (*sic*). Crede plus margini quam infratexto'. Rubrics at §1 (in margin, 120r) 'Prologus', at §5 (120r) 'Explicit prologus', §118 (156r) 'Explicit prophetia Merlini', after §208 (183r) 'Explicit'.

Capitula marked at §5 (120r) I, at 'Quoddam namque' interpolation (120v) II, and also at §§6, 23, 35, 54, 73, 89, 118, 119 'Conuocato autem clero'. Prophecies divided into *capitula*.

Additional section after §5 on 120v–121r as in London, BL, MS. Arundel 326: 'Quoddam namque stagnum . . . Britanniam adduxerit'.

Some compressions in the text, for example in §§150 and 177.

CONTENTS

MS. 281

1r: contents-list (Early Modern, paper) indicating original position of MS. 281 before MS. 289.

2r: note in humanist minuscule '[ ] de triplici questione cuiusdam philosophi'. 'Quis non natus mortuus est . . . perdurat exemplo.'

2v: note remarking on discrepancy between the work copied (unspecified) and the *Polichronicon* (presumably of Higden).

3r: chronology as in Arundel 326. 'In principio erat uerbum et uerbum erat apud Deum . . . usque ad natiuitatem Henrici regis filii Iohannis.'

3v–14v: 'Incipiunt cronica a principio mundi'. 'Primo creatus est Adam . . . Anno Domini .m.cc.xx. sanctus Thomas archiepiscopus translatus est.'

As Arundel 326 but omitting final entry.

Following folio blank and unnumbered.

MS. 289

1r–51r: 'Primus tractatus'. 'Satagentibus igitur plenam historie noticiam . . . ut uarietas mecum multimoda uestium uariacione designetur.' Compilation containing geographical and historical information about the British Isles taken, according to contents-list on 281, 1r, from the works of Higden, William of Malmesbury, Henry of Huntingdon, and others.

51r: 'Sciendum quod iste liber in pluribus aggreditur . . . qui scrutatus renes et corda diuidens ing[ ]re prout uult. Amen'.

51v–59v: '[U]espasianus regnauit quasi annis .viii. qui pecunie auidus sed non iniuste auferens . . . lesus de ledente uindictam non repecii'.

60r–70v: 'In nomine sancte Trinitatis incipiunt gesta saluatoris Domini nostri Iesu Christi que inuenit Theodosius magnus imperator in Ierusalem in pretorio Poncii Pilati in codicibus puplicis'. 'Factus est in anno .xix. imperatoris Theodosii . . . omnia que gesta sunt de Iesu in pretorio meo.' Ed. Kim, *The Gospel of Nicodemus.*

70v–73v: 'Post peccatum Ade expulso de paradiso . . . cui est laus honor et imperium per omnia secula seculorum. Amen'. Ed. Hill, 'The fifteenth-century prose legend of the Cross before Christ', pp. 212–22. Bloomfield, *Incipits*, p. 336, no. 3966.

73v–79v: 'Factum est cum expulsi essent Adam et uxor eius Eua . . . et usque in seculum'. Ed. Mozley, 'The "Vita Adae" ', pp. 128–48.

79v–82v: 'Anna et Emeria fuerunt sorores . . . ut induta pelleis tamquam seuo exempta domino triumpharet'.

82v–83v: 'Beatus Petrus apostolus ordinauit duos episcopos . . . ubi finerunt omnes fere episcopi et abbates tocius Anglie'.

84r/v: on Jerusalem and its environs. 'Si quis ab occidentalibus partibus Ierusalem adire uoluit . . . ubi et ipse Abraham filium suum Isaac immolare uoluit.'

85r–88r: 'In nomine Domini nostri Iesu Christi incipit liber Metodii episcopi ecclesie Pateruensi<s> . . . de primo mundi milliare'. 'Sciendum namque cum nobis . . . qui cum patre et spiritu sancto uiuit et regnat Deus per omnia secula.'

88r–91r: 'Incipit prophetia sibille'. 'Sibille generaliter dicuntur omnes femine uates . . . cum Christo in secula seculorum. Amen.' Ed. Sackur, *Sibyllinische Texte*, pp. 177–87.

91r–92v: 'De Antechristo (*sic*)'. 'Scire uolentibus primo dicemus quare sic uocatur . . . qui ea hora seculum iudicabit qua ante secula iudicandum esse prefixit.' Anselm, *De Antichristo*, ed. Verhelst, *Adso Dervensis*, pp. 160–66 & 157.

92v–95v: 'De errore et legibus Machometi'. 'Tempore pape Bonefacii quinti . . . et acies mente minimo grauaretur.'

96r–108r: 'Ex Martino Polono'. 'Anno sequenti pro Christo post passionem Domini beatus Petrus . . . ut saccinos qui intitulantur de pma. sn. de ualle uiridi et cons.'

108v: 'Respice prophetiam Merlini c[apitulum] .xvii. et c[apitulum] .xviii. licet non in toto subsequenti plane patet tamen in aliquo bene patet simulari'. 'Notandum quod anno Domini 1068 . . .'

109r–115v: '[P]hillipus rex Macedonie secundum Trogum . . . heri premebat hodie premitur a terra'. Alexander Story from Higden, *Polichronicon*, iii.26–30. See Arnold, 'The Source of the Alexander history in B. M. MS Sloane 289'.

115v–119v: 'Reuelacio et prophetia Sancti Edwardi regis et confessoris'. '[R]ex .E. sanctus Dei confessor . . . eo successit filius Ricardus per .x. annos regnaturus ut patet alibi post[ ].'

120r–183r: HRB.

183r/v: tract on the Anglo-Saxon heptarchy. 'Ab Adam usque ad Brutum . . . felix qui poterit mundum contempnere.'

184r: 'Hec sunt nomina regum Maioris Britannie sic digesta'. 'Brutus . . . Yni.'

184v: 'Angli Saxones Marciani principis tempore Beda testa . . . sed erat insula adhuc in .vii. regna diuisa'.

185r: 'Hec sunt nomina regum postquam Saxones et Angli regnare ceperunt'. 'Adelstanus . . . Henricus eius filius sextus.' Continued in different hands from Edward IV to Henry VII.

185v–186r: diagram describing contents of each of kingdoms of Heptarchy.

186v–195v: 'Fuit autem primus Aelli rex Australium Saxonum . . . regis frater australium Uuallosium'. Truncated. Extends to Harthacnut.

DESCRIPTION

SIZE 18.5 x 14 cm.

QUIRING Some catchwords. Paper singleton (fo 1), I^{14} (2–14, 14*); II^{10}, $III–IV^{12}$, IV^{10}, V^{16} (6 cancelled, 1, 16 detached: fos 45–59), VI^{12} (1–2, 11–12 detached: 60–71), VII^{12} (1–2, 11–12 detached: 72–83), VIII^{12} (1, 12 detached: 84–95), IX^{12} (96–107), 108–109 mounted singletons, X^{10} (6 cancelled: 110–118), 119–121 mounted singletons, XI^{8} (122–129), 130–135 mounted singletons, XII^{8} (136–143), 144–149 mounted singletons, XIII^{8} (150–157), 158–161 mounted singletons), XIV^{12} (162–173), 174–179 mounted singletons, XV^{12} (180–191), 192–195 mounted singletons, 195* paper singleton.

PRICKING None extant.
RULING Faint pencil frame. Single column, 36–37 lines written.
SCRIPT Small neat Secretary-hand. Grey-brown ink. Horizontal top of g pierces the upright strokes of the letter to form the top compartment. Simple round form of a, e has pointed top or cursive loop form, looped d, tall-backed t. Long descenders but script not splayed. Leans to right. Little angularity in looped letters.
DECORATION Simple red capitals in HRB. Preceding line-ends filled with geometric patterns.

HISTORY
Catalogued in 1697 among books of Francis Bernard F.R.C.P.: Bernard, *Catalogi*, II.i, p. 90.

BIBLIOGRAPHY
Scott, *Index to the Sloane Manuscripts*, p. 207.
Catalogus librorum manuscriptorum Bibliothecae Sloanianae, pp. 45–46.
Ward & Herbert, *Catalogue of Romances*, I.250.

117 *LONDON, BRITISH LIBRARY, MS. STOWE 56

Saec. xii *ex.*   Origin: ? Continental
ii + 184 + i (paper) fos   2nd fo: [*Christia*]-*ni orationis gratia*

HRB 111vb–185va.
§§1–3, 5–208. Dedicated to Robert of Gloucester.
Rubrics at §1 (111vb) 'Prologus sequentis operis', §5 (112rb) 'Incipit Britannice hystorie liber primys (*sic*)', after §208 (185va) 'Hunc primum scripsi socios donet Deus ipsi'.
Book-divisions: I §5 (112rb), II §23 (118vb), III §35 (123va), IV §54 (129rb), V §73 (135va), VI §89 (141vb), VII §111 (150ra), VIII [ ], IX §143 (162va), X [ ], XI §177 (177r).

CONTENTS
i + 1: ?Early Modern flyleaves, blank except for contents-list on 1v in imitation textura.
2r–59rb: 'Incipit prologus in historia de Iehrusalem'. 'Baldricus Burguliensium fratrum abbas . . . post hunc Arnulfus oriundus uterque cikes (*sic*).' History of Baudri de Bourgueil, ed. *Recueil des historiens des Croisades, Historiens occidentaux*, IV.9–111.
59rb–63vb: summary of Norman history to the accession of Henry I, abridged from William of Jumièges's chronicle and its continuation. 'Tempore Ludouici cognomento nichil fecit . . . sicque cum angelia etiam Normanniam optinuit.' (See Van Houts, *Gesta Normannorum Ducum: een studie*, p. 51.)
64ra–75ra: 'Incipit epistola Cornelii ad Crispum Salustium in Troianorum historia que in Greco a Darete hystoriographo facta est'. 'Cum multa Athenis studiosissime agerem inueni . . . Palamonem. Epistrophum. Scidium.' Ed. Meister, *Daretis Phrygii De Excidio Troiae Historia*.

75ra–87vb: 'Incipit historia Appollonii regis Tyrii'. 'Fuit quidem rex Antiochus nomine . . . et aliud bibliothece sue.' Ed. Kortekaas, *Historia Apollonii regis Tyri*.

87vb–99va: 'Hystoria de Alexandro rege magno Macedonum'. 'Egipti sapientes fati de genere diuino primi feruntur . . . uino et ueneno superatus atque extinctus occubuit.' Ed. Kuebler, *Iuli Valeri Alexandri Polemi res gestae*, pp. 1–168.

99va–106vb: 'Incipit epistola Alexandri regis magni Macedonum ad Aristoulem (*sic*) magistrum suum de itinere et situ Indie'. 'Semper memor tui . . . animo et industria optime Aristotile sponde.' Ed. Walther Boer, *Epistola Alexandri*.

106va–111vb: 'Incipit epistola Alexandri ad Dindimum regem Bragmannorum'. 'Sepius ad aures . . . quod dante meliora prestantur.' Ed. Kuebler, *Iuli Valeri Alexandri Polemi res gestae*, pp. 169–89.

111vb–185va: HRB.

DESCRIPTION

SIZE 27.5 x 21.5 cm.

QUIRING Regularly in eights from fo 2. i and 1 are additions. a² (i, 1), I–XXII⁸, followed by 4 paper flyleaves + parchment binding scrap then paper leaf written in English, ?sixteenth-century hand.

PRICKING In both margins.

RULING In two columns of 34 written lines, single vertical boundary-lines. Written above top ruled line.

SCRIPT Continental? Broad and uncompressed but some breaking in the Gothic manner. No juncture but **de** written closely. Straight-backed **d** is rare. Ascender of the round form often trails just above preceding letters. Uncrossed *et*-nota standard, final round s rarely used. g has straight-backed form with round bow.

DECORATION Capitals mostly plain red, green, or brown ink. Some with outlining and scrolled decoration.

BIBLIOGRAPHY

Scott, *Catalogue*, I.33–36.

118 *LONDON, COLLEGE OF ARMS, MS. ARUNDEL 1

Saec. xiv   Origin: ?England
i + viii (paper) + 236 + i fos   2nd fo: *-dos suos in salosus maris*

HRB 55ra–90vb

§§1–3, 5–208 [§§109–110 *pudibundus Brito* form]. Dedicated to Robert of Gloucester.

Rubrics at §1 (55ra) 'Incipit prologus Gaufredi Monemutensis in sequente hystoria', §5 (55ra) 'Descripcio Britannie insule', after §208 (90vb) 'Explicit'.

No book-divisions.

CONTENTS

i: parchment flyleaf with a few notes (see below, HISTORY).

Small paper quire of eight inserted before fo 1. Foliated 1–5 (+ 3 unnumbered folios): 1r–6r contain index to HRB in angular fifteenth-century hand, with additions in another hand of similar date. 'Assaracus cum Bruto et eorum adherentibus minutis . . . Ysias prophetabat 68.' Remainder of quire blank.

1ra/b: 'Paradysus locus est in oriente longo [ ]ris tractatu a nostro habitabili segregatus cuius uocabulum a Greco in Latinum uersum dicitur ortus . . . Nilus non procul ab Athlante monte. Tygris et Eufrates in Armenia'.

1rb: 'Diuisio totius mundi'. 'Uniuersus orbis diuiditur in tres partes uidelicet in Asiam Affrica[m] et Europam. Ista sunt regna et prouintie Asie . . . Ybernia Orcadia.' 15 lines.

1rb–2ra: 'Incipiunt mirabilia Anglie' (30 items). 'Primum mirabile est Thenderhale. Secundum Pollendrith. Tertium de albo equo cum pullano suo . . . et sunt aues ex sua natura boni saporis et apte ad comedendum.'

2ra/b: 'De comitatibus Anglie' on shires and bishoprics of England. 'In Anglia sunt .xxxii. schire que uocantur comitatus quidam maiores et quidam minores . . . Ducentas uero in latum continens.'

2v: blank, unruled.

3r: map of the world – three land-masses (Asia, top; Europe, left; Africa, right) with Mediterranean in centre.

3va/b: 'Hic Iulius Cesar diuinis humanisque rebus singulariter instructus . . . et per consequens audaciores'.

4ra–7vb: 'Hic tractatus de mappa mundi'. 'Mundus describitur rotundus cuius alia pars est habitabilis alia inhabitabilis . . . et attende in principio formam mundi.'

8ra–13rb: 'Hic tractat de primo elemento quo est terra' (rubric at foot of 7vb for first of fourteen chapters). 'Deus mundum id est terram rotundum formauit . . . in omnium gaudio et deliciis perseuerabit ad quod nos perducat etc.'.

13rb–23va: 'De ymagine mundi', Honorius of Autun. 'Ad instructionem multorum quibus deest copia librorum . . . Quinta etate apud Babilonem signum Nabugodonosor ann. .xliiii. Sibilla .vii. Cumana claruit et Ezechiel.' Ed. Migne, *Patrologia Latina*, CLXXII.119–75.

23vb–54va: 'Incipit hystoria ierosolimitana abreuiata. Capitulum primum. Cur Dominus terram sanctam uariis flagellis sub alternis casibus exposuit'. No *capitula*-list. 'Terra sancta promissionis Deo amabilis et sanctis angelis uenerabilis . . . de die in diem expectantes.' Jacques de Vitry, *Historia orientalis*. Ed. Bongars, *Gesta Dei per Francos*, I.ii, pp. 1049–1124.

54vb: blank.

55ra–90vb: HRB.

91ra–151vb: 'De omni Hybernensium', annals from A.D. 75 (Rodericus of the Picts) ending with correspondence of Edward III with Emperor Louis, Pope Clement VI, etc. 'Gurguint filius Belini magni regis Britonum . . . ex quibus nisi d[ ]s auertat g[ ]nia ti-.' Also found in London, BL, Harley 5418. See Hardy, *Descriptive Catalogue*, II.527.

152r–175vb: 'Incipit prologus de gestis Francorum'. 'Cum animaduerterem quam plurimos . . . ad preces legati treugas per spacium .v. annorum dedit.' See de Wailly, 'Examen', especially, pp. 403–5.

176ra–180vb: 'Willelmus Gemmeticensis monachus de gestis Normannorum ducum'. 'Iaphet .ii. Noe filius genuit filium quem Magog nominauit . . . ?[muni]ciporum presidii robustius uallari uerens ac adutatus fastigio.' Truncated at end. Not included by Van Houts, *Gesta Normannorum Ducum: een Studie.*

'180'ra–'185'va (181–186): 'Liber Ioachym et Anne uxoris eius de ortu beate Marie matris Christi'. 'Erat uir in Israel Ioachim ex tribu Iuda . . . et Tyberius [ ] eius suscepit imperium.'

185va–188vb: 'De factis Iudeorum in Iesum que inuenit Theodosius magnus in Ierusalem in pretorio Pontii Pilati in codicibus publicis'. 'Anno .xiii. imperii Tyberii Cesaris imperatoris Romanorum et ?Lodis regis Galylee . . . omnia que gesta sunt de Iesu in pretorium meum.' Ed. Kim, *The Gospel of Nicodemus.*

189ra–194ra: 'Incipit Dares Phrygius de troiana distructione translatus de Greco in Latinum'. 'Cornelius Salustio Crispo suo salutem . . . Andromachem et Helenum in milia .cc. hucusque historia Daretis scripta est.' Ed. Meister, *Daretis Phrygii De Excidio Troiae Historia.*

194rb/va: 'Incipit liber Thephrasti (*sic*) de nupciis'. 'Fertur aureolus Thephrasti liber de nupciis in quo querit an uir sapiens ducat uxorem . . . quam quos uelis nolis habere cogaris.' Migne, *Patrologia Latina*, XXIII.276–78B.

194v–198r: 'Incipit epistola Alexandri magni regis Macedon?u[m] ad magistrum suum Aristotilem summum philosophum de situ Indie et eiusdem uastitate'. 'Semper memor sum tui . . . et animo et industria optime Aristotile ponderares.' Ed. Walther Boer, *Epistola Alexandri.*

198rb–200vb: 'Incipit epistola Alexandri ad Dindimum magistrum Bragmanorum'. 'Sepius ad aures meas fando peruenit Romam . . . quod a meliore prestantur.' Ed. Kuebler, *Iuli Valeri Alexandri Polemi res gestae*, pp. 169–89.

200vb–206vb: 'Ortus et uita et obitus Macedonis Alexandri regis magni'. 'Egipti sapientes fati genere diuino primi feruntur . . . uino et ueneno superatus atque extinctus occubuit.' Ed. Kuebler, *Iuli Valeri Alexandri Polemi res gestae*, pp. 1–168.

206vb–207rb: 'Epithoma de ortu uita et obitu Alexandri Macedonum regis magni memorie digna'. 'Quoniam non est humane nec ineuitabiles ?casus transire . . . nisi fortuna infelicior eos emulacione uirtutis in perniciem mutuam armasset.' Same found in Paris, Bibliothèque nationale, MS. lat. 4126.

207ra–214rb: 'In ciuitate Anthiocha rex fuit nomine Antiochus . . . in templo Diane Ephesiorum aliud bibliothece sue exposuit'. Ed. Kortekaas, *Historia Apollonii regis Tyri.*

214rb–226va: 'Incipit liber [el]ucidarii'. 'Sepius rogatus a discipulis quasdam questiunculas . . . et uideas regem glorie in suo decore et uideas bona Ierusalem omnibus diebus uite tue. Amen.'

226vb–227va: 'Incipit liber de Antichristo reg[ ]e. Ieronimus', by Adso. 'Excellentissime ac regali dignitate pollenti Deo dilec[tissim]e omnibusque sanctis amabili monochorum magistri . . . qua ante secula iudicandum esse prefixit.' Ed. Verhelst, *Adso Dervensis*, pp. 20–30.

227va–234va: 'Incipit liber prouincialis ubi sunt omnes ciuitates mundi. [ ]'. 'In ciuitate romana sunt quinque ecclesie que patriarchales dicuntur . . . Et de edificatione urbis usque ad natiuitatem Christi .d.cc.lii. annos.' Compare ed. Miraeus, *Notitia episcopatuum*, pp. 65–91. List of metropolitans and other prelates, towns and castles opposing the Church in the Holy Land, notes on Eastern and Western emperors.

234vb: Vision of Thomas, in fifteenth-century hand. 'Quando ego Thomas Cant. archiepiscopus exul ab Anglia fugiebam . . . Et hec omnia sibi tradidi inclusa in uase plumbeo.'

235: slip. Blank except for note in Latin on recto dated 1488, twenty-third year of reign of Edward IV.

DESCRIPTION

SIZE 37 x 23 cm. Paper quire 29.5 x 22.5 cm.

QUIRING Catchwords. I^4 (1 cancelled, + 8 after 1: fos a, i–viii + 1–2), II^8 (fos 3–10), III–VII^8, VIII^4 (51–54); IX–XII^8, XIII^4 (87–90), XIV–XX^8, XXI^8 (6–8 lacking: 147–151), XXII–XXIV^8; XXV^8 (176–180, 180*–182), XXVI^6 (183–188), XXVII–XXXI^8, XXXII^8 (7 cancelled, 8 cut down: fos 229–235). A mediaeval foliation begins on 56r (start of HRB) but no change in layout from preceding section.

PRICKING Where extant, visible in outer margin only.

RULING Two columns of 50 lines. Single vertical boundary-lines, ruling above top written line.

SCRIPT Small, compact Gothic bookhand with cursive features. Short ascenders and descenders (tapering). Long s, f, and r hang below line. Round d with tall ascender. Round s in final position. Crossed t. a (two-compartment) rises above minim-letters. *Et*-nota crossed or uncrossed. Juncture of e and o after b, d, h, and p. Weak grey ink. Most of volume in same script. Annals following HRB in more cursive script with split ascenders. Hands smaller and more compact towards end. Index to HRB in informal fifteenth-century hand using long r, looped e, and looped two-compartment a when in initial position. Angular looped d and ticked-down tops of ascenders. Addition on 234vb in grey ink, four-line cursive with some angularity.

DECORATION Full-colour pictures on 3r and 3v: figures in foreground, backgrounds squared (blue or purple) with geometric designs. Main capitals are red and blue, inhabited, and sometimes accompanied by scrolling of same colours along edges of written area. Small capitals are blue in square of red filigree.

HISTORY

At the foot of the recto of the flyleaf before text, in fifteenth-century hand, 'Cronica quondam Th[o]m[ae] Walmesford'.

Notes in the hand of John Dee. His signature in small letters, top 91r.

BIBLIOGRAPHY

Black, *Catalogue of the Arundel Manuscripts*, pp. 1–4.

Saec. **xiv** (*post* 1307) + xiii   Mediaeval provenance: ?England
216 + ii (numbered) fos   2nd fo: *anno uite religione*
         2nd fo ('181'r): *cum hostibus congressa est*

HRB '180'r–'210'v (182–212)
Acephalous. §§84 'Galliam euolans uniuersos populos'–208. Dedication lost. Final
rubric in contemporary hand (?not that of scribe) 'Explicit'. Other rubrics occasionally.
No book-divisions.

CONTENTS
1r–'165'r (168): 'Incipit prologus in librum qui flores hystoriarum intitulatur', continuation of Chronicle of Matthew Paris by Matthew of Westminster. 'Temporum
summam lineamque descendentem ab exordio mundi ... de genero inferius plus
dicetur.' Ed. Luard, *Flores historiarum*. See Hardy, *Descriptive Catalogue*, III.314.
'165'r (168): 'Incipit compilatio cronicarum recollecta ab anno Domini .m.ccc.viii.
per magistrum Adam Meriemouth canonicum Lond. de contingentibus in annis
sequentibus'. (Continues without a break from *Flores historiarum*). '[Q]uoniam ut
scribitur per antiquos res audita perit ... pro eo quod dominus rex episcopum
Couentr[ie].' On Merimouth see Stubbs *apud* Thompson (ed.), *Adæ Murimuth.
Continuatio Chronicarum* .
'165'v (168): blank except for note at foot.
'166'r (169): diagrammatic genealogy (Latin) of French kings from Saint Louis to
Edward, king of England (son of Isabella and grandson of Philip of France).
'166'v (169): blank.
'167'r (170): blank except for note on recto, ?fourteenth-century.

'168'r–'173'v (176): 'Quoto anno ab incarnatione Domini Britanni qui primum
Britanniam incolebant fidem Christi in primis susceperunt'. 'Anno dominice incarnationis .c.lxii. Eleutherius papa undecimus ... Willelmum Ric[ardum] Henricum et
postquam .xx. annis mensibus .x..' In hand of *ca* 1200.
'174'ra/b (177): continued in fourteenth-century hand. 'Et diebus .xxviii. genti Anglorum prefuit regnum ... cui successit Edwardus filius eius anno Domini millesimo
ccc.xxvii..'

'174'v–'175'r (177–178): blank but notes in Early Modern hand on '175'r.
'176'ra–'177'va (179–180): in hand of ? late fourteenth century, succession of the
bishops of Norwich. 'Norwic. episcopatus .viii..' '[ ] rege orientalium Anglorum
Sigeberto regnante primus episcopus fuit Felix ... de primis fructibus a domino papa
Clemente' (entry for 1299). Continued in Secretary-type hand to 180r. '[ ] etiam
instrumenta predecessorum suorum episcoporum Norwici ... ad ecclesiam suam per
arcidiaconum Norwici intronizatus est.' Last entry is dated 1356.
'178'va–'179'ra (181–182): in similar hand. 'Sequenti uero die Alexander prior

conuocato capitulo . . . Cui successit per eleccionem cap. Norwic. uia spiritus sancti.' ('179' originally stub only; verso blank.)

'180'r–'210'v (183–213): HRB.
'211'r–'213'v (214–216): blank, rectos ruled only.
'214'–'215' (217–218): paper flyleaves.

DESCRIPTION
SIZE 27.5 x 28 cm.
QUIRING I–XIV^{12}, XV ?^{4} (1–2 excised: 169–170); XVI^2 (171–172), XVII ?^{4} (+ 1 after 4: 173–177); XVIII^4 (?+ 1 after 4: 178–182); XIX–XX^{12}, XXI^6, XXII^4 (213–216), b paper (217–218). Signatures marked in *Flores historiarum* (A). Incorrectly paginated.
PRICKING Not visible in C but in outer margin in A, B, and D.
RULING HRB (D) in single column, single bounds; written below top ruled line. 40 then later 46 lines. A – in single column of 40 lines; B and C double column of 35 and 44 lines respectively.
SCRIPT HRB and A in Anglicana hands, brown ink. HRB in two portions corresponding with different numbers of lines (second begins '204'r). First hand has looped, not split, ascenders, thick uprights with little distinction between minim-letters. Two-compartment **a** is slightly above minim-height, **e** does not have the cursive curl form. Second hand has fewer loops but similar thick upright strokes and treatment of ascenders. Both hands have the long cursive **r**. A – in several hands resembling the first of HRB. B – dark brown or black ink in smallish compact hand resembling glossing script. Uncrossed *et*-nota, round **d** but tall **s**. Laterally compressed and quite angular but no juncture. C – in grey-black ink. Four-line formalised cursive with pinched lobes to letters, especially **g** (although round **d** is not entirely angular). Tops of ascenders are angled downwards but do not turn back towards ascender.
DECORATION Only in B – red rubrics with red or green Romanesque initials.

HISTORY
Pressmark of Norwich Priory on '165'v, O.xlviii. (C), see Ker, *Books, Collectors and Libraries*, p. 264. First section of book (Matthew of Westminster's chronicle) has been associated with St Paul's, London (James & Jenkins, *A Descriptive Catalogue*, II.293), but this has been rejected by Ker (*Medieval Libraries*, p. 121). Fos 171–177 were originally part of Lambeth Palace 104 (fos 1–208), an Exeter volume containing the *Polichronicon* (Ker, *ibid.*, p. 83, n. 4).
Fos '176'–'179' belong to Lambeth Palace MS. 192 and came originally from BL MS. Additional 15759, a Norwich copy of Higden's *Polichronicon*: Ker *apud* Bill, *A Catalogue of Manuscripts in Lambeth Palace Library*, pp. 12–13. Ker identified hand of John Bale on '177'r (?180) and noted rusty mark left by chain on 178.

BIBLIOGRAPHY
James & Jenkins, *A Descriptive Catalogue*, II.292–95.
Todd, *A Catalogue*, p. 13.

120 *LONDON, LAMBETH PALACE, MSS. 379+357

MS. 379

Saec. **xii²** (+ xv)

Mediaeval provenance:
? Lanthony (Augustinian), Gloucestershire

68 + 64 + ii fos

2nd fo: *in ipsos dirigem*

HRB 1r–68v

§§1–3, 5–208. Dedicated to Robert of Gloucester.
Rubrics at §1 (1r) 'Incipit edicio Galfridi Arturi Monemutensis de gestis Britonum',
§5 (1r) 'Descriptio insule', §6 (1v) 'Narratio hystorie', §73 (25r) 'Hystoria de Lucio
rege', §89 (31r) 'Hic incipit historia Gratiani regis', §110 (39r) 'Prologus', §111 (39r)
'Hic incipit prophetia Ambrosii Merlini', after §208 (68v) 'Explicit Brut[ ]'.
No book-divisions.

CONTENTS
1r–68v: HRB.
68v: under HRB, verses (four lines) in fourteenth-century hands, repeated. 'Rex uirgo
stultus uir femina pissis (*sic*) auarus. . . .' Walther, *Initia*, I.878, no. 16790. Edd. James
& Jenkins, *A Descriptive Catalogue*, II.523.

69r–130r: fifteenth-century. 'Stimulus amoris diuini etc..' 'Liber iste qui stimulus
amoris in dilectissimum et piium (*sic*) Iesus . . . sic ergo finiatur noster tractatus ut
laudet Deum omnis spiritus. Amen.'
Followed by two blank unruled unnumbered leaves.

DESCRIPTION
SIZE 24 x 16.5 cm.
QUIRING Signatures in HRB (.iii. 24v to .vi. 48v). Catchwords in *Stimulus*. I–VIII⁸,
IX⁴; X–XVII⁸.
PRICKING Outer margin only.
RULING HRB in single column of 31 lines. Written below top ruled line. Double
vertical boundary-lines. B Single column of 37 written lines. Written below top ruled
line, single vertical boundary-lines.
SCRIPT HRB in Protogothic minuscule (?Anglo-Norman). Dark brown ink. No round
s. Round d frequent. *Et*-nota usual but ampersand found at opening. Little abbrevia-
tion. Minims and descenders end in small tick if finished at all, thickening at top.
Variable size but constant number of lines.
B Grey ink. Four-line informal Gothic with angularity in round a, and g but not round
d (which has looped ascender). 2-shaped r trails below the line. Cursive looped e
occurs.
DECORATION HRB Red or green Romanesque capitals. Opening initial green with
simple red outline ornament. B Blue capitals in squares of red filigree.

MS. 357

Saec. xv   Mediaeval provenance: ?Lanthony or Duleek, Ireland
ii (paper) + 111   2nd fo: *qm. illam non ignorans*

CONTENTS

1r–29v: 'Incipit tractatus Ricardi heremite super .lx. lecciones mortuorum'. 'Parce michi Domine nichil enim sunt ?dies mei . . . a quo nos Christus liberet qui cum patre et spiritu sancto regnat in eternum. Amen.'

30r: blank, ruled.

30v: two notes on confession mentioning Armagh added ?in later fifteenth-century hand.

31r–35v: 'Cronica cuiusdam amici ueritatis in argumentum fundacionis canonicorum regularum sancti Augustini doctoris et episcopi'. 'Frater quidam ordinis . . . ordinis beati Augustini doctoris et episcopi ac patris gloriosi.'

35v–38r: 'Incipit ars predicandi abbreuiata a magistro Hugone de Sneyth de ordine predicatorum'. 'Sic dilatandi modus est sermonibus aptus . . . ' (four lines of verse). 'Diuide thema quandoque alia facta autem diuisione . . . alia uero naturalia spectant ad alios speculantes.' See Little & Pelster, *Oxford Theologians 1280–1302*, p. 100.

38r–40v: 'Incipit prefacio Hug[onis] de Sancto Uictore in librum de laude caritatis'. 'Seruo Christi Petro Hugo gustare et uidere quam suauis est Dominus . . . et mansionem in nobis facere qui cum Deo patre et spiritu sancto uiuit et regnat Deus per omnia secula seculorum. Amen.'

41r: 'Incipit tractatus Hug[onis] de Sancto Uictore de .vii. uiciis'. 'Septem sunt uicia. Superbia [inuid]ia ira . . . et iniquitatis opera oriuntur.' Bloomfield, *Incipits*, p. 470, no. 5473. Ed. Migne, *Patrologia Latina*, CLXXVI.525c–526b.

41r–42r: 'Liber magistri Hugonis quot modis impugnatur humilitas' (Hugh of Saint-Victor). 'Duobus modis dia[boli?] . . . maiori attestacione firmare concupiscit.' Ed. Migne, *Patrologia Latina*, CLXXVII.565–67.

42v–45r: 'Meditaciones beati Bernardi de lamentacione beate uirginis Marie et passione filii sui'. 'Quis dabit capiti meo aquam et oculis imeis (*sic*) ymbrem lacrimarum . . . Christus qui cum Deo patre etc.' Cf. Skerret, 'Two Irish translations of the Liber de passione Christi'.

45r/v: 'Oracio Bernardi'. 'Aue et gaude sancte Dei angele . . . loqui semper et facere Amen.'

45v–61v: 'In nomine patris et filii et spiritus sancti et uirginis matris Dei. Amen. Proposicio magistri Ricardi archiepiscopi Ardmahcam (*sic*) . . . '. Richard FitzRalph, archbishop of Armagh, *Propositio* presented at Avignon, 1357. 'Nolite iudicare secundum faciem . . . iuxta peticionem quam feci.'

61v–63v: 'De ualidis mendicantibus'. 'Queritur an dandum sit ualido mendicanti . . . ab omni specie mali abstinendum sit id est tess. .v..'

63v–66v: 'De ualidis mendicantibus'. 'Utr[u]m uiri ad corporales labores ualidi . . . quem amplius non uidebit etc.'

67r–70v: blank.

71r–72r: ?'M[emoran]dum de beato Augustino et quid de eo scribunt doctores inter cetera'. 'Beatus pater Augustinus apposuit non solum animum . . . doce me et sana me.'

72v–77r: larger hand. 'In festo sancti Kyernani episcopi et confessoris ad ui'. 'Salue Kenane honor Midencium iubarum ecclesie doctor . . . inclinaui modice aurem meam et excepi illam.' Ed. Hughes, 'The Offices', pp. 363–71.

77r/v: late textura. 'Ista est prophecia beate Hildegardis monialis . . . .' 'Insurgent gentes que comedent peccata populi . . . scienciam uiarum uestrarum nolumus etc.'

78r–111r: earlier hand. 'Burnelli speculum merito liber iste uocatur / Ex cuius sub specie stultorum uita notatur.' 'Suscipe pauca tui ueteris Will[elm]e Nigelli . . . Quam cum uirtutum munera scripta iacent.' Ed. Wright, *The Anglo-Latin Satirical Poets*, I.11–145.

DESCRIPTION

SIZE 24.5 x 17 cm.

QUIRING a 2 (paper), I^4 (1–4), $II–III^8$, IV^6, V^4 (27–30); $VI–X^8$ (ending 63–70); XI^{14}, XII^{12}, XIII^8, XIV^8 (lacks 8: 105–111), b^2 (paper).

PRICKING QQ. I–V pricked at outer edge. Elsewhere pricking visible only for boundary-lines.

RULING Single column throughout. QQ. I–V 40–41, single vertical boundary-lines. QQ. VI–X 36–37 lines. QQ. XI–XIV frame-ruled, 40–41 written, except for 72–77 (single column of 26 lines, double vertical boundary-lines).

SCRIPT QQ. I–V four-line script. Watery black ink. Angular g, d, q, and looped ascenders. Two-compartment a. QQ. VI–X similar but with cursive loop form of e. Fos 72–77 – aspect of formal textura but cursive forms: long r, looped ascenders. 111r–178 in faded brown cursive script. Angular minuscule e or looped form. Two-compartment a, final sigma-shaped s, long r.

DECORATION Lombardic red capitals. Rubrics throughout in enlarged version of script of text. Blue used as well on fos 72–77.

HISTORY

MS. 379

Early Modern *ex-libris* inscription on second part of volume (at foot of 69r) 'Sub de Ro: le: Fe: K. J. H.'?. Same mark found in Cambridge, University Library, MS. Dd.10.32 and elsewhere, including in the catalogue of Leicester cathedral library: see James & Jenkins, *A Descriptive Catalogue*, p. 480. MS. 379 ascribed provenance of Lanthony secunda (Glos.) by Watson on account of its connection with MS. 357: *Medieval Libraries*, p. 43.

MS. 357

Note on 111r in sixteenth-century hand 'Ioh[ ] Gatte'. Presence of Office of St Kenen (Cianan) suggested to James that the manuscript originated at Duleek, an Irish cell of Lanthony (the source of many books now at Lambeth), the Augustinian priory. Other Irish associations are indicated by the note on 35v mentioning Armagh. Ker (*Medieval Libraries*, p. 110) tentatively attributed the volume to Lanthony itself. See also Hughes, 'The Offices', pp. 349–50.

The two volumes are unrelated by script – the HRB must have circulated independently from the rest of the material here for three hundred years, at least (on the basis of their respective dates).

They have been associated on the grounds of having belonged to one of the thirty volumes broken up and rebound (to create ninety volumes) during the rearrangement of the library by Archbishop Sancroft (1617–93). This book contained ten items marked '33' and an eleventh 'Galfridus Monemuthensis de gestis Britonum' marked '55' which was removed. Sancroft later reidentified this tentatively as MS. 379 fos 1–68. His conjecture now stands on the grounds that '[This] is the only Geoffrey of Monmouth now at Lambeth which can be identified with the Geoffrey formerly at the end of L.ζ.18': Ker, *apud* Bill, *A Catalogue of Manuscripts in Lambeth Palace Library*, pp. 13–14 & 7–8.

BIBLIOGRAPHY
Dumville, 'The manuscripts', p. 119.
James & Jenkins, *A Descriptive Catalogue*, II.522–23, 478–81.
Todd, *A Catalogue*, pp. 50, 47.

121 *LONDON, LAMBETH PALACE, MS. 401

Saec. xiv   Mediaeval provenance: ?
iii + 129 fos   2nd fo: *collaudauit opemque suam ei*

HRB 19ra–100v
§§1–3, 5–208. Dedicated to Robert of Gloucester.
Rubrics at §1 (19ra) 'Galfridi Arturi Monemutensis Britonum liber. Incipit prologus', §5 (19rb) 'Explicit prologus. Incipit Britannie insule descriptio'.
No rubrics at Prophecies or after §208.
Book-divisions: I §6 (19va), II §23 (26vb), III §35 (31vb), IV §54 (38ra), X §163 (81vb), XI §177 (90vb).
Prophecies of Merlin glossed, §§112–113.

CONTENTS
Three parchment flyleaves: mostly blank except for scribbles (see below, HISTORY), and Early Modern contents-list on verso of the third.
1ra–14ra: 'Incipit hystoria Daretis Troianorum Frigii de Greco translata in Latinum a Cornelio Nepote' (rubric at 1rb following usual preface). 'Cornelius Salustio Crispo suo salutem . . . Palamonem Epistrophum Scidium.' Ed. Meister, *Daretis Phrygii De Excidio Troiae Historia*.
14ra/b: additional paragraph. 'Nescit mens nostra fixum seruare tenorem . . . tot nostras facies mutat sentencia formis.'
14rb–18ra: prophecy of the Erythraean Sibyls. 'Sibille generaliter omnes / femine dicuntur prophetantes . . . et ipsi regnabunt cum illo in secula seculorum. Amen.' Ed. Sackur, *Sibyllinische Texte*, pp. 177–87.
18ra/b: 'Assercio cuiusdam philosophi'. 'Quenam summa boni . . . non posse et uelle nocere.'

18va/b: note on place-names in HRB. 'Armorica siue Latauia id est minor Britannia . . . et lapidem in signum triumphi erexit.' (Found in Aberystwyth, NLW, 13210, and elsewhere.) Ed. Dumville, 'Anecdota'.

19ra–100v: HRB.

101: blank.

102ra–117rb: 'Incipiunt gesta Alexandri regis Macedonum'. 'Egipti sapientes sati genere diuino primi feruntur . . . uino et ueneno superatus atque extinctus occubuit.' Ed. Kuebler, *Iuli Valeri Alexandri Polemi res gestae*, pp. 1–168.

117rb/va: 'Epitaphium'. 'Primus Alexander pillea natus in urbe . . . se trementem ferroque regna lesit.' Walther, *Initia*, I.759, no. 14648.

117va/b: 'Quicquid in humanis constat uirtutibus altis . . . occubuit leto sumpto cum melle ueneno'. Walther, *Initia*, I.833, no. 15990.

117vb–126vb: 'Incipit epistola Alexandri magni regis Macedonum ad magistrum suum Aristotilem'. 'Semper memor tui . . . nominis mei fama habeatur in gloria.' Ed. Walther Boer, *Epistola Alexandri*.

(127–129: flyleaves with notes in various hands)

127ra: in informal hand predating the mid-fourteenth century, complaint of Christian subjects of Mohammedans. 'Non te decipiat falsus error et simulata suasio tirannorum . . . et calamitatis fugiatis miseriam in futuro.'

127ra/b: letter of Peter of Aragon to Charles, king of Jerusalem. '[ ]agnifico principi domino Karolo regi Ierusalem illustri Petrus Aragonum . . . que experte nostra dixerint oraculo uiue uocis.'

127rb: letter of Charles to Peter. 'Karolus regis Francie filius ducatus Apulee . . . quo latitas uisitabunt.'

127rb: in later fourteenth-century hand. 'Hybernia continet .ix. uiginti cantredas . . . habunt .v. suffrag..'

127v: verses on the Virgin Mary in fourteenth-century hand. 'Aue nostre spes salutis auferens obprobrium . . . contra fructum noxium.'

128v–129r: verses (see James & Jenkins, *A Descriptive Catalogue*, II.558). 'Nato nobis saluator celebremus cum honore diem natalitium . . . transit adesse.'

129v: blank.

DESCRIPTION

SIZE 22.5 x 16 cm.

QUIRING a⁴ (1 lacking: i–iii), I¹², II⁶ (fos 13–18), III–VIII¹², IX¹² (lacks 11: 91–101), X¹², XI¹² (adds one after 12), b⁴ (1 lacking: 127–129). Some catchwords.

PRICKING Only extant for boundary-lines.

RULING Two columns of 35 lines. Ruling above top written line, central margin divided. Single boundary-lines with outer frame of double line in margins at foot and outer edge.

SCRIPT Black ink, formal semi-quadrata. Short ascenders and descenders. Juncture varies with the hand: in one hand fusion of e and o after d, b, and p, but often no real juncture in other hands. *Et*-nota is crossed or uncrossed. Tall s usual, straight-backed and round d are common. a does not have two-compartment form. Double l has a flat top.

DECORATION   Very fine. Rubrics in red in main hand. Main capitals are blue and red with fine red in-filling and feathered scrolling. Minor capitals flourished.

HISTORY
On ii r, in fifteenth- or sixteenth-century hand 'Quod N. Locke'. On ii v in different hand 'Nicholaus Locke est possessor huius liber ex [ ]'.
128r in fifteenth- or sixteenth-century hand 'Bryngewode in Wigmorelande. Thomas Ercove'.

BIBLIOGRAPHY
James & Jenkins, *A Descriptive Catalogue*, II.556–58.
Todd, *A Catalogue*, p. 52.

122/123 *LONDON, LAMBETH PALACE, MS. 454

Saecc. xiii/xiv + xii + xii/xiii
i + 204 fos

122 *LONDON, LAMBETH PALACE, MS. 454, 28r–123r

Saecc. xiii/xiv   Mediaeval provenance:?
                                    2nd fo: [ ]*neas post Troianum bellum*

HRB 28r–123r
§§1–3, 5–208. Dedicated to Robert of Gloucester.
No rubrics or book-divisions.

123 *LONDON, LAMBETH PALACE, MS. 454, 124r–204r

Saec. xii$^{med./2}$ + xii/xiii   Mediaeval provenance:
                                    ? 2nd fo: *Brittannis Saxonibus*

HRB
§§1–3, 5–109, 110–134 (*ex.*), 166 (*ex.*) –170 (*ex.*). Dedicated to Robert of Gloucester.
Extensive rubrics in body of text beginning §33 (141v) 'Ysaias et Osee prophetabant et Roma conditur', as in Oxford, Bodleian, Fairfax 28.
Book-divisions: III §35 (143r).
Hiatuses in text mostly caused by physical loss. 196v ends 'et ut tantum' (§134), 197r begins 'Regin, Mapelaut' (§166). 204v ends 'Hec .iiii. agmina' (§170).
Written in round English early-looking hand to 188r (end of §109), 188v blank. 189r–204v are written in later hand of small glossing type (§110–208).

CONTENTS (122/123)

i: ruled. Blank except for notes on recto, contents-list (?Archbishop Sancroft's) on verso.

1: blank except for various pious notes on recto.

2v–8r: in ?fifteenth-century formal vernacular hand 'Thus stondith this kalender to undirstond it in his foorme . . . ond thei be of the north partie'.

8v–22r: tables of figures.

22v–25v: diagrams of eclipses.

26r: device constructed of concentric circles of parchment pivoted about central point and marked with compass rose etc. ?For calculating dates.

26v–27v: blank (except for notes on verso, see HISTORY).

28r–123r: HRB.

123v: notes in various late mediaeval hands.

124r–204v: HRB.

DESCRIPTION

SIZE (fos 28–123) 19.5 x 13.5/14 cm. (fos 124–204) 19.5 x 13 cm.

QUIRING Series of signatures in first HRB manuscript, from .ii. 51v to .uii. 111v. Three discrete units. I (i, 1–5), II⁶, III–IV⁸ (ending 27v); I–VIII¹² (ending 123v); I–VII⁸, VIII ?⁸ (+ 1: 180–188), IX–X⁸.

PRICKING Trimmed away.

RULING Fos 28–123 – single column, 28 lines, single vertical boundary-lines, written above top ruled line. Fos 124–204 – single column, no ruling above top written line, single vertical boundary-lines. 27 lines (to fo 188), 44 or 33 (to fo 194), 31 (to 204).

SCRIPT 28–123 – rather irregular hand with short ascenders and descenders. Crossed *et*-nota, final s tall or round. Straight-backed **d** as well as round. Juncture of **e** and **o** after **d** and **p**. **a** does not have two-compartment form; occasionally straight-backed with decoratively waved top. Ascenders slightly indented at top, that of **b** is tagged. Fos 124–204 – first hand (to fo 194) very round Protogothic minuscule. Dark brown ink. Straight-backed **d**, tall s, e-caudata, ampersand and uncrossed *et*-nota. Round **d** and s rare. Well spaced. After 194v written in more than one later-looking hand. Initially small glossing-type script. *Et*-nota, round **d** but tall s and no juncture. One hand uses crossed *et*-nota.

DECORATION None completed fos 28–123; fos 124–194 have red Romanesque capitals. After change of hand on fo 194, red or blue capitals with simple filigree.

BIBLIOGRAPHY
Dumville, 'The manuscripts', p. 119.
James & Jenkins, *A Descriptive Catalogue*, II.628–29.
Todd, *A Catalogue*, p. 58.

124 *LONDON, LAMBETH PALACE, MS. 503

Saec. xiv ?*med.*/2   Mediaeval provenance: Richard ap Robert,
                              chantry-priest of St Anne's, Shaftesbury
iv + 111 + iii fos   2nd fo: *restat parare ut insequentibus*

HRB 1r–111r
§§1–3, 5–208. Dedicated to Robert of Gloucester.
No original rubrics or book-divisions.
64v blank (after §117).

CONTENTS
i: stuck down. On verso running vertically '[ ]onesby is'?.
ii r/v: blank except for note on verso (see below, HISTORY).
iiir: name 'Thomas Lambarde', repeated on iv r with date July 3, 1637 and note 'Lent my cosen Godfrey'.
iv v: notes by William Lambarde on Arthur taken from Ponticus Virunnius, John Bale, John Leland.
1r–111r: HRB.
111v: notes in Early Modern and mediaeval hands.
v–vii: parchment. Some notes.

DESCRIPTION
SIZE 22 x 13 cm.
QUIRING a^4 (i–iv), I–II^{12}, III^{10}, IV^6, V–IX^{12}, X^{12} (lacks 12: 100–111), b^4 (?lacks 4: v–vii). Catchwords.
PRICKING In outer margin.
RULING Single column of 30–31 lines. Ruling above top written line. Single boundary-lines with ruling in outer margin. Double-line at outer edge on some folios.
SCRIPT Ordered and upright Anglicana. Brown ink. Fluent and regular. Looped two-compartment **a** and sigma-shaped **s** rise slightly above minim letters. Tapering descenders. Laterally compressed. Long **r** cleft. Heavy loop on round **d**.
DECORATION Blue or red capitals. Opening initial seems originally to have been two-colour filigreed letter with scrolling along margin in the fourteenth-century manner.

HISTORY
111r, note beneath text in ?fifteenth-century hand: 'Liber domini Ricardi ap Robert cantarist. sancte Anne infra monesterium (*sic*) Sheftonie' (i.e. chantry-priest of St Anne's at the monastery of Shaftesbury).
On same folio, 'W. Lambarde 1565', William Lambarde, the Kentish antiquary. 'Franciscus Bernard M. D. codicem hunc bibliothecae Lambethanae D. D. Decembris .xxx. A. D. MDCLXXXIV' ii v.
On final flyleaf 'Ioh[anne]s Cokke', fifteenth-century hand.

BIBLIOGRAPHY
Dumville, 'The manuscripts', p. 119.

James & Jenkins, *A Descriptive Catalogue*, pp. 707–8.
Todd, *A Catalogue*, p. 65.

125 MADRID, BIBLIOTECA NACIONAL, MS. 6319 (F.147)

Saec. xii ?[2]   Mediaeval provenance: ?England
74 fos   2nd fo: [*par[ ]*]-*ulis et mulieribus*

HRB 1r–74r
§§1–3, 5–208. Nameless dedication.
No original rubrics but above §1 (1r) in ?fourteenth-century hand 'Incipit liber Bruti
cum prophetia Merlini', and above that in Early Modern hand 'Galfridus Monumeten-
sis'.
No book-divisions.
Numerous corrections in margin and over erasures.
Glosses on Prophecies in cursive hand apparently of the thirteenth century.

CONTENTS
1r–74r: HRB.
74r: account of division of world. 'Post diluuium tribus filiis Noe orbem terrarum
parcientibus . . . et repleuerunt Europiam.'
74r/v: *Mirabilia Britannie*. 'Primum siquidem miraculum Britannie stangnum Lum-
monoim in Scotia . . . [ ].' Ed. Dumville, 'Anecdota'. Both this and the preceding text
(from the *Historia Brittonum*) follow HRB in Cambridge, Sidney Sussex College, MS.
75 and Oxford, Bodleian, Oriel College, MS. 16.

DESCRIPTION
QUIRING No original signatures but one catchword (8v). Otherwise fourteenth-
century catchwords. I⁸, II ?⁶, III–IV⁸, V⁴, VI⁶, VII–IX⁸, X ?¹⁰ (65–74).
PRICKING Visible in outer margin only.
RULING Single column of 33 or 34 lines (Prophecies, 31 lines).
SCRIPT Several collaborating hands. Four-line Protogothic minuscule. Minims have
thickenings or ticks top and bottom but no angularity. *Et*-nota and round **d** standard
in some hands, but ampersand and straight-backed **d** used elsewhere. e-caudata found
rarely. Obvious change of hand on 15r.
DECORATION Romanesque capitals. Some split shafts.

HISTORY
Annotations in Anglicana script suggest later mediaeval English provenance. In Early
Modern hand on 74v 'Thomas Nortonus', possibly Thomas Norton of Bristol whose
Ordinall was printed by Ashmole, *Theatrum chemicum Britannicum*, pp. 1–106.

BIBLIOGRAPHY
Hammer, 'Some additional manuscripts', p. 236.
Dumville, 'The manuscripts', p. 126.

MANCHESTER, JOHN RYLANDS UNIVERSITY LIBRARY, MS. LAT. 216
See 165 Paris, Bibliothèque Nationale, lat. 4999A.

126 MONTPELLIER, BIBLIOTHEQUE DE L'UNIVERSITE (ECOLE DE MEDECINE), MS. 92

Saec. xii ²/ᵉˣ.   Mediaeval provenance: ?Pontigny (Cistercian)
204 fos   2nd fo: *sexum puella concepisset*

HRB 1r–81v
§§1–3, 5–208 but §§83–84, 174, 179, and 184 in abbreviated form. Nameless dedication.
Rubrics at §1 (1r) 'Incipit prologus Gaufridi Monemutensis in historiis regum Britannie', §5 (1r) 'Incipit liber historiarum regum Britannie', after §208 (81v) 'Explicit hystoria regum Britannie translata a Gaufrido Monemutensi'.
No book-divisions.
Abbreviated sections: §83 ends 'acquieuit ei Octauius', §84 begins 'Igitur post acceptum regnum Britannie affectauit Maximianus sibi Gallias subiugare'; §174 opens 'Ad aciem Arturi repellunt. Arturus uero uisa strage suorum abst..'; §179 '.N. Gloecestrensis' to 'Ecclesia sepultus est' omitted; §184 truncated after 'gentem patrie subiugauit'. Same compressions in Bruxelles, BR, MS. 9871–9874, and Paris, BN MS. lat. 5233 (see also HRB MSS. 151, 173, 175)

CONTENTS
1r–81v: HRB.
81va/b: notes on the bishops of Ireland. 'Metropolitanus Armachie . . . Episcopum de Celmunduach.' Ed. Lawlor, 'A fresh authority for the synod of Kells', p. 18.
82r–204va: 'Incipit praefacio uenerabilis Bede presbiteri in historia Anglorum'. 'Gloriosissimo regi Ceoluulfo . . . et parere semper ante faciem tuam.' Edd. Colgrave & Mynors, *Bede's Ecclesiastical History* (possibly English c-type: *ibid.*, pp. lx–lxi).
204va/b: blank after Bede except for scribbles (thirteenth- and fourteenth-century).

DESCRIPTION
SIZE 32.9 x 23.1 cm.
QUIRING No signatures visible on microfilm.
PRICKING In both margins.
RULING In two columns of 33 lines. Written above top line. Single vertical boundary-lines, central margin divided vertically (in Bede, divided into 3).
SCRIPT Very regular and upright, relatively unabbreviated; script and space between lines about equal. Script of Bede almost two-line. Ampersand standard, round s finally, round d (two-line) occurs occasionally. Script of Bede similar but e-caudata used. Not unlike Anglo-Norman type but ?Northern French.
DECORATION Elaborate opening capitals with complex stylised foliate filling.

HISTORY
Answers entry in twelfth-century catalogue of library of the Cistercian abbey at
Pontigny (diocese of Auxerre) printed by Libri, *Catalogue général*, I.715. M.
Peyrafort-Bonnet expressed some caution about the identification.

BIBLIOGRAPHY
Libri, *Catalogue général*, I.320.
Peyrafort-Bonnet, 'La dispersion d'une bibliothèque médiévale', p. 111.

127 MONTPELLIER, BIBLIOTHEQUE DE L'UNIVERSITE (ECOLE DE MEDECINE), MS. 378

Saec. xii   Mediaeval provenance: ?
68 fos   2nd fo: *fecisse exulatus*

HRB 1r–68v
§§1–3, 5–208. Dedicated to Robert of Gloucester.
Rubrics at §1 (1r) 'Prologus Galfridi in istoria Britannorum, §5 (1r) 'Finit prologus
incipit istoria Britannorum'. No closing rubric.
No book-divisions.
Dislocation of fos 35–38. 34v (§107 'apparebat mihi in') should be followed by 36r
(§107 'specie pulcherimi iuuenis'); 38r (§112.2 'colla sub pedibus) should follow 36v
(§112.2 'succursum prestabit et'); 38v (§115.20 'flumine sanguine ma-') should be
followed by 35 (§115.20 '-nabunt. Tunc erumpent' – §116.39 'genus uolucrum a[ ]-');
37 (§116.39 '-nuntiabit sibi' – §116.61 'populum germinabit') should precede 39r
(§116.61 'Delicie principes').
No other contents.

DESCRIPTION
QUIRING Single catchword, on 64v, and dislocated folios suggest possible conjectu-
ral reconstruction: I–VIII⁸, IX ?⁴ (65–68).
PRICKING Visible at some outer edges.
RULING In single column of 41–42 lines.
SCRIPT In several hands of similar type. *Et*-nota standard but ampersand occurs in
final position in some words. Round d standard medially, round s finally (but tall form
is found). e- and q-caudata occur. ?Continental; cf. script of Lille, BM, 533 etc.

BIBLIOGRAPHY
Libri, *Catalogue général*, I.436.

128 NEW HAVEN (CONN.), YALE UNIVERSITY, MS. 590
(*OLIM* PHILLIPPS 2324)

Saecc. **xii**^{2} + xiii *in.*   Mediaeval provenance: Roche (Cistercian), Yorkshire
ii + 131 fos   2nd fo: *proueniunt. Habet et nemora*

HRB 1r–114v

§§1–207 'sub duce Adelstano qui primus inter eos diadema portauit'. Dedicated to Robert of Gloucester and Waleran of Meulan.
No rubrics or book-divisions.
Same dedication and truncated ending found in Cambridge, UL, MS. Ii.1.14.

CONTENTS
i: slip of ?document written in fourteenth-century Anglicana hand.
ii: shelfmark and ?various *nomina sacra*. Name and stamp of Phillipps. Verso blank.
1r–114v: HRB.

115r–122v: in later hand on separate quire. French moralising poem. 'Tel quide a leger sa greuance/ Qui creut e duble sa pesance . . . U il sun od les benurez.'
123ra–129rb: 'Ici comence li romanz des romanz'. 'Molt dei\t/ bons estre kar li notis en est granz . . . Quil li ust son peche pardone.' Followed by couplet. Ed. Lecompte, *Le Roman des Romans.*
129v–130r: formulas for exorcism. 'In nomine patris et filii . . . defendat me ab omnibus malis. Amen. Amen. Amen.', etc.
130v: blank except for brief note in Early Modern hand giving page references for certain items in HRB.
131r/v: cut from larger leaf containing readings from Old Testament.

DESCRIPTION
SIZE 23.2 x 16.6 cm.
QUIRING Some catchwords (24v, 32v, 62v). I–IV^8, V–VII^{10}, VIII–XIII^8, XIV^8 (5–8 lacking: 111–114), XV^8, XVI^8 (+ 1 after 8: 123–130 + 131).
PRICKING Both margins.
RULING Two columns, written above top ruled line, mainly 35 written lines, 25 in places. French in two columns of 40 lines. Single vertical boundary-lines.
SCRIPT Rather round and irregular Protogothic. Round **d** and tall or high final **s** usual but straight-backed **d** occurs. Ampersand standard in part of manuscript, uncrossed *et*-nota in others. Tail of **h** swings below the line. **a** has small head. Some lateral compression with *de* approaching juncture in places. Flattened thickenings on ends of minims, ascenders and descenders. French written in small, compact hand with juncture of **e** and **o** after **d** and **p**. Ascenders have slightly forked tops. Final **s** tall. Upper part of **a** remains open. Wace in hand of more primitive aspect and no real juncture. Final round **s**.
DECORATION Romanesque capitals with simple ornament inside letter. Red or green.

HISTORY

On ir and 1r, Roche Abbey pressmark 'VIII.E'. Occasional notes in English cursive hand in text. After it left the Phillipps collection it was recorded by Griscom as in the possession of T. Fitzroy Fenwick: *The Historia*, p. 52. Bequeathed to Yale University by Norman Holmes Pearson.

BIBLIOGRAPHY

Dumville, 'The manuscripts', p. 120.
Ewert, 'An early manuscript of the "Roman des Romans" '.
Griscom & Jones, *The Historia*, pp. 20 and 51, n. 2.
Ker & Watson, *Medieval Libraries*, p. 58.

129 NEW HAVEN (CONN.), YALE UNIVERSITY, MS. 598

Saec. xiii ?*med*.   Mediaeval provenance: ?
105 fos   2nd fo: [*Her*]-*culem collaudauit*

HRB 14rb–101vb.
§§1–3, 5–208. Dedicated to Robert of Gloucester.
Rubrics at §1 (14ra) 'Incipit prefatio Gaufridi Monemutensis in hystoriam Britonum', §109 (58v) 'Prologus Gaufridi in prophetiam Merlini', §110 (58v) 'Epistola [. . .]' (worn), §111 (58v) 'Prophetia Merlini de regibus Britonum', closing rubric illegible.
Book-divisions: III §35 (28v), V §73 (42v), VI §89 (49v), XI §177 (91ra).
Also signs of rubrication at §23 (23r).

CONTENTS

1r–14ra: Dares Phrygius, History of the Trojans. 'Cornelius nepos Salustio Crispo . . . Palamonem Epistropum Scidium.' Ed. Meister, *Daretis Phrygii De Excidio Troiae Historia*.
14rb–101vb: HRB.
102ra/b: 'De origine Normannorum'. 'Normanni origine Dani .dccc.lxxx.vi. ab incarnatione Domini anno . . . Uuillelmus filius eius. Heinricus frater eius.' Cf. Hugh of Saint-Victor, *Excerptiones allegoricae*, X.10, ed. Migne, *Patrologia Latina*, CLXXVII.284. Also in Paris, BN, MSS. lat. [13935 +] 5508.
102v–105v: 'Incipiunt quedam miracula uenerabilis patris nostri Benedicti a quodam huius monasterii monacho in Rich[ ] [?con]dita . . .' (rubric 102rb). 'Totus orbis gratuletur sed precipue letetur . . . adiuuet nos trinitas summe benedicta. Amen.'

DESCRIPTION

SIZE 27 x 18.6 cm.
QUIRING Indicated by catchwords beginning on 8v (none on 104v). I–XIII⁸, XIV singleton (105).
PRICKING In both margins.
RULING Two columns of 29 written lines. Written below top ruled line. Single vertical boundary-lines.

SCRIPT Gothic bookhand. Tall and laterally compressed throughout. Juncture of **d** with **e** and **o**. Ascenders often tagged to the left or split. Ascender of **d** often trails to the left. The horizontal of **t** is just pierced but **a** has the old Caroline form. *Et*-nota is usually crossed.

DECORATION Plain red or blue capitals (rarely filigreed).

HISTORY
On the front flyleaf in an eighteenth-century hand: 'John Barwick 62'. Book-plate of Sir Edward Cholmeley Dering. From bequest of Norman Holmes Pearson.

130 NOTRE DAME (INDIANA), UNIVERSITY OF NOTRE DAME LIBRARY, MS. 40

Saec. xv (after 1414)   Mediaeval provenance: ?England
iii + 57 fos   2nd fo: ?

HRB 13vb–35vb
??§§1–3, 5–208. Dedicated to Robert of Gloucester.
Rubrics at §1 (13vb) 'Translacio Gaufridi Arciri (*sic*) Monemutensis de gestis Britonum', §5 (13vb) 'Prologus', after §208 (35vb) 'Explicit historia Britonum'.
Book-divisions: I §6 (14ra), II §54 (19va).

CONTENTS
i–iii: blank paper.
1r: note concerning contents of manuscript, dated 1560.
1v–2v: blank.
3ra–10vb: *Cronice Martini* (from final rubric). 3ra and 3va bear genealogy of Jewish kings from Achas 4480 to 1571. '[S]ecundum Orosium ad Augustinus (*sic*) a creacione mundi ad urbem Rome conditam . . . Johannes .23. anno Domini 1414 celebrauit consilium in Constancia ciuitate Alemannie ubi et ipse depositus est.' Derived from the Chronicle of Martinus Polonus. Ed. Weiland, MGH, SS, XXII.397–474.
11r/v: blank paper.

12r/v: blank.
13ra/b: 'De prima inhabitacione regni Anglie etc.'. 'Ab origine mundi circa annos tria milia et uigentos septuaginta . . . nomine Britanniam uocauerunt sicut patet in sequenti.'
13rb: 'Genologia Priami regis Troie et Enee usque ad Brutum'. 'Ciprus quidam filius Cetini in Cypro insula primus regnauit . . . Iaphet filius Noe.'
13va/b: 'De forma quorundam ducum Grecorum et Troianorum', taken from the *Historia Troiana* of Dares Phrygius (Book XII). Ed. Meister, *Daretis Phrygii De Excidio Troiae*, pp. 14–16.
13va: 'Dares Frigius qui historia Troianorum scripsit . . . affabilem uerecundam animo simplici pia[m].'

13va/b: 'Priamum regem Troianorum uultu pulcro magnum uoce . . . animo simplici largam daps[ilem]'.

13vb–35vb: HRB.

36: blank paper.

37r/v: blank.

38ra–39ra: 'Incipit liber Methodii de millenariis seculi'. 'In nomine Ihesu Christi incipit liber Methodii episcopi ecclesie Paterenys . . . in opusculis suis collaudauit.' 'Sciendum namque est nobis fratres karissimi . . . uiuit et regnat Deus per infinita secula seculorum. Amen.'

39ra/va: *Hec de historia ecclesiastica secundum Bedam de Britania et maxime gencium Anglorum* (from final rubric). 'Uerum ea que temporum distruccione latius digesta sunt ob memoriam conseruandam breuiter recapitulari placuit. Anno igitur ante incarnacionem dominicam 68 . . . ad lucem propriam est reuersa.' Begins with *Historia ecclesiastica* I.ii. ?Brief summary only.

40r/v: blank.

41r/v: blank.

42ra/va: anonymous English chronicle to 1412 from Noah, Sem, Iaphet, to Woden, to Alfred, Edward, William I etc. 'Ab hiis tribus filiis Noe textuntur generaciones lxxii post diuisionem in edificatione Babel . . . magistri suspecti dicebantur de lollardria.' Note on 46vb 'Ab Henrico tertio usque ad finem est totum de cronicis Cestrensis'. Not correct: see Corbett, *Catalogue*, p. 180.

48r–57v: blank.

DESCRIPTION

SIZE 34 x 28 cm.

QUIRING Parchment and paper: fos i–iii, 11–12, 36–37, 40–41, 48–57 paper, remainder parchment. Paper leaves bear mid sixteenth-century watermark (Briquet, *Les filigranés*, II.638, type 12801–12802); some form blank wrappers to separate the four parchment manuscripts. I¹² (iii, 1–11); II¹², III¹² (lacks 11: 24–36), II and III enclosed between paper leaves fos 12:36; IV⁴ (37–40: 37 and 40 paper); V⁸ (lacks 8: 41–47, 41 paper); VI⁸ (blank paper), VII² (56–57, blank paper).

PRICKING

RULING A – two columns; B – two columns, frame-ruled, 70 lines written; C as B with 64–75 lines; D – two columns.

SCRIPT HRB in mixed Anglicana/Secretary hand. Two-compartment **a** and **g**. Looped ascenders on **b, h, l**, but that on **d** is forked. Short broken **r**. Upright but tapered descenders on **f** and long **s**. A – mixed Anglicana/Secretary with single-compartment **a**, two-compartment **g**, short broken **r**, thin and upright ascenders on **f** and long **s**. Brown ink. C – Anglicana. Horned, two-compartment **a**, two-compartment **g**, long **r**, looped final **e**, looped round **d**. D – upright Anglicana, some Secretary features. Short **r** more frequent than long form, single compartment **a** standard.

DECORATION A – names of popes etc. encircled, arranged in two columns linked by coloured bar. B–D – red and blue capitals or blue with red filigree, all in same hand.

HISTORY

Common rubrication for texts in B-D suggests that they were copied in the same place. Frontispiece on 1r gives account of contents and ends 'all whiche being likelye to have bene confounded for wast parchement in a chaundeless hande, was preserved, bought and newe bounde at the chardge of Valentyne Leigh in the yere of oure Lorde godd 1560. Per Ualentinam Leigh'. (This date agrees with that of the watermark of the paper wrappers.)

BIBLIOGRAPHY

Corbett, *Catalogue*, pp. 177–81.
Crick, 'The manuscripts', p. 159.

131 OLOMOUC, NATIONAL OLOMOUC REGIONAL ARCHIVE, MS. 411

Saec. xv   Mediaeval provenance: ?
63 fos   2nd fo: *uel argenti siue ornamentorum*

HRB 1r–63rb
§§1–3, 5–208. Dedicated to Robert of Gloucester.
Rubrics at §111 (margin, 53va) 'Hic incipiunt prophetie Merlini', and after §208 (63rb) 'Explicit cronica regum Britannie'. In margin by §180 (57r) 'Lapides Merlini' and other occasional marginal rubrics.
No book-divisions.
No other contents but a preliminary note concerning the text is dated 1808.

DESCRIPTION

SIZE ?
QUIRING Some catchwords extant. I–III^8, ?IV–V^8, VI ?^{8}, VII ?^{8}, VIII (57–63).
PRICKING None visible.
RULING Two columns, 35 lines. Single vertical boundary-lines.
SCRIPT Round and calligraphic Gothic bookhand (cf. Italian). Thick-nibbed. Short ascenders and descenders. Uncrossed *et*-nota. Round d is a two-line letter. Single-compartment a. Juncture of e and o after b, d, h, p and also *Verschrenkung* of other rounded letters. Final m written as figure 3. Initial a resembles Greek lambda, with no cross-stroke. Final s round. Single minim written where space occurs at the end of a line of text.
DECORATION 1r has full-colour heavily-painted border (around whole page) of scrolls etc. (not like Gothic filigree) with angels and two crests (arms not discernible) at foot. Opening c also painted in full colour, filled with fighting figures (knights). Other capitals alternate colours with contrasting filigree (elaborate, almost geometric). Some descenders at foot or ascenders at head extended and decorated in the same way.

HISTORY

Apparently in mediaeval binding. Note on inserted leaf (9.2.1808) begins 'Johannes

Jos. L. Baro a Buol bibliothecarius Olomucensis ecclesiae legentibus salutem dicit
. . . '. At foot 1r in ?eighteenth-century hand, 'Ex Bibl. Cath. ecclae. Olom.'.

BIBLIOGRAPHY
Crick, 'Manuscripts', p. 159.
Wattenbach, 'Reise nach Österreich', p. 683.

132 *OXFORD, ALL SOULS' COLLEGE, MS. 35

Saec. xiii[1]   Mediaeval provenance: (thirteenth-century)
                                              in possession of Scottish scholar
i + 182 + i fos (incl. 73*, 108*)   2nd fo: [*sedi*]-*bus uagos geminum futurum*
                                              2nd fo (154r): *inter armatos quo impetus*

HRB 152v–180vb
§§6–108, 109–110 *pudibundus Brito* form, 118 in *Merlinus uero incipiens* form,
119–204'ad Cornubiam inhabitauit'.
?Contemporary additions: §§1–3, 5 + 109–118 (fos 152v, 166r–168v).
Original lacks dedicatory section. Nameless dedication in additions.
No rubrics in original but in additions at §1 (152v) 'Incipit liber de gestis Anglorum
ante aduentum Christi a Gauterio editus', §5 (152v) 'De insulis Britannie' and in less
formal hand in red after §5 'Post sequitur Q. Eneas etc.'.
No book-divisions.
Additions have same format and decoration as original part of volume and the script
is similar. The Prophecies are written on two extra leaves (whiter parchment than the
rest) inserted into Q. XVIII after 166. Text ends 166v §105 ('tantam cladem') and
continues without loss on 169r 'inspexisset Uortegirnus'. 167r–168v contain additions
from §109 'non alter in clero' to §118 'cum autem haec et alia prophetasset Merlinus',
linked into original text on 169 with *signes de renvoi*. Note in ?later thirteenth-century
hand at the foot of 166v 'Uerte duo noua folia et inuenies quid sequ[ ]tur "tantam
cladem" uidelicet "inspexisset" etc.'.

CONTENTS
i: paper. ?Seventeenth-century contents-list and inscription of ownership (see below,
HISTORY).
1r–136ra: William of Malmesbury, *Gesta regum Anglorum*. 'Res Anglorum gestas
Beda uir maxime doctus et minime superbus . . . qui non erraui eligendi iudicio.' Ed.
Stubbs, *Willelmi Malmesbiriensi monachi de gestis regum*. His MS. Ao (*ibid.*,
I.lxix–lxxii).
136ra–151vb: 'Incipit prologus .W. monachi in nouella historia Anglorum ad Robertum comitem Gloecestrie'. 'Domino amantissimo Roberto filio regis Henrici . . . qui
interfuere ueritatem accepero.' Ed. Potter, *The Historia Novella* (MS. Ao, *ibid.*,
p. xxxix).
152r: blank, unruled.
152va–180vb: HRB.

DESCRIPTION

SIZE 24.5 x 19 cm.

QUIRING I–III^8, IV–VII^{10}, VIII^8 (65–72, 72*, 73), IX–XI^{10}, XII^{10} (104–108, 108*, 109–112), XIII–XVI^{10} (ending fo 152); XVII^8, XVIII^8 (+ two before 7: 161–170), XIX^8, XX^2.

PRICKING Visible in both margins in both parts of book but often at outer margin only.

RULING Two columns throughout. HRB – 48–49 written lines, written above top ruled line; single outer boundary-lines with divided margin between columns. Fos 1–151 – 41 lines, written below top ruled line; double outer boundary-lines.

SCRIPT HRB mostly in minute glossing hand. Larger and heavier on first few folios. Tall final s, small-headed a, round d with long ascender. No juncture. Uncrossed et-nota. Additions in similar script but final s more frequently round. William of Malmesbury in blacker, less compressed script with spiky aspect. ?Slightly later than HRB. e and o approaching juncture with preceding d and p.

DECORATION Red or light green capitals in HRB, including additions. Red only in first part of volume.

HISTORY

Letters of mid-thirteenth century written by Scottish scholar in the margins of the first part of the volume: see Ker & Pantin, 'Letters of a Scottish Student at Paris and Oxford c. 1250'. At foot of 121r, note in hand dating at least from the fifteenth century, 'Est liber hic sancti Martini Louaniensis'. On flyleaf in ?seventeenth-century hand, 'Iste liber fuit quondam sancti Martini Louaniensis [ ] emptus fuit in bibliotheca Gudiana'. Cottineau notes an Augustinian priory Val Saint-Martin, at Leuven: *Répertoire*, I.1663. N. R. Ker noted that the manuscript did not bear the name of Vlimmerius, an Early Modern book-collector associated with Leuven who was known to have possessed English manuscripts: Ker, 'English manuscripts owned by Johannes Vlimmerius and Cornelius Duyn', p. 206, n. 3.

BIBLIOGRAPHY

Coxe, *Catalogue of Manuscripts in the Library of All Souls' College*, pp. 9–10.

133 *OXFORD, ALL SOULS' COLLEGE, MS. 39

Saec. xiv^1 (?$^{in.}$)   Origin: ?Northern England
ii (paper) + 120 fos + iv (2 parchment, 2 paper)   2nd fo: *ut a regibus et principibus*

HRB 1r–74v + 74v–78r

§§1–3, 5–197 'cum decem milibus militum quos ex'. Completed in antiquarian hand. §197 'ei rex Salomon'–§208. Dedicated to Robert of Gloucester.

Rubrics at §1 (1r) 'Incipiunt historie regum Britannie que nunc dicuntur Angli[ ]', §111 (37v) 'Incipit de Merlino', sixteenth-century final rubric (78r) 'Explicit'. Rubrics at many chapter-divisions, like at §21 'At Corineus' (7r) 'Hic agit de Corineo et Cornubea'.

No book-divisions.

CONTENTS

1r–78r: HRB.

78v: blank.

79r–86r: English history from the Anglo-Saxons to Edward I, in French. 'Iadis al tens des Engleys soleyt Engletere estre en cinke partyes et a cinke reys . . . Apres ly fu roy Edward son fiz ke conquist Gales et Escose.'

86v: blank.

87r–103v: Peter Langtoft's chronicle on the wars of Edward I in England and France (French verse). 'Ky uoet oyr de rays coment chescon uesquist / E lylle ke brutus bretayne apeler fist . . . For he has ouer hipped / His tipet[ ] es tipped / his tabard es come.' Only last few lines in English. Legge, 'A list of Langtoft manuscripts', p. 20.

104r–105v: 'Hec sunt staciones quas statuit beatus Gregorius. In primis omnibus ad sanctum Petrum uenientibus .vii. anni relaxantur uota fracta si ad ea redierint peccata oblita offensa patrum et matrum sine [ ] inieccione'. Account of boundaries and church-dedications in Rome under Pope Gregory I. '[?Dona] in septuag. ad sanctum Laurenc. extra muros. . . [?Dona] post pascha ad sanctum Pancracium .iii. ann. .iii. quadr. .xl. d.'

106r–107v: *Indulgencia* of Pope Gregory I. 'Omnibus Christi fidelibus cognoscere desiderantibus que uel quante sint indulgencie . . . quarta pars omnium scelerum relaxatur et durat indulgencia per .viii. dies.'

107v–109r: genealogy from Rollo of Normandy to Richard I of England. 'Primus Normannus dux Rollo qui et Robertus dictus est regnauit in Angl. .xxx. ann. . . . et genuit ex ea fil. Edward. et Edmund. et filias.'

109v–110v: 'Anno Domini .m.cc. octog. nono passio ministrorum domini .E. regis Angl. secundum opera sua'. 'Edwardus rex quidam nobilis abiit in regione longin-quam accipere sibi tributum . . . et dominus qui reddet unicuique secundum opera sua.'

110v–111r: 'Sumpserunt turbyt. weg. brun. .lii. rey perit lyt . . . est ubi solamen quod sunt superacta grauati / Est cito dampnati totus populus ferat. Amen'.

111r: 'Peractis a natiuitate Domini .cccc. et nonaginta quinque ann. Kerdike regnauit .xv. ann. . . . Stephanus rex r[egnit] .xviii. ann.'. Regnal list of English kings from kings of Wessex to Stephen.

111v–112r: account of shires and bishoprics of England. 'Anglia habet in long[itudine] occies .c. miliare s[cilicet] a Renwaterstrece (*sic*) qui locus est ultra montem sancti Michaelis . . . Staffordsire (*sic*) in qua sunt .D. hyde.'

112r: 'Quatuor sunt uie regie constructe in Anglia . . . quod in ueteribus scriptis eorum inuenitur'.

112v: blank.

113r–117v: 'Sanctissimo in Christo patri domino .B. diuina prouidencia sacrosancte Romane ac uniuersalis ecclesie summa pontifici . . .'. 'Infra scripta non in forma nec in figura iudicii . . . per tempora diuturna.' Dated 1301. Ed. Stones, *Anglo-Scottish Relations*, pp. 192–218.

117v–120v: 'Memorandum quod anno Domini .m.ccc. tercio circa festum natiuitatis beate Marie contigit casus qui subscribitur de Bonifacio papa . . .', letter sent by William de Hundleby of Lincoln, *procurator* in Roman curia, concerning disturbance at Anagni in 1303. 'Ecce reuerende patri in uigilia natiuitatis beate Marie anno Domini supradicto . . . in tam modico tempore sicut nos hic uidimus. Datum Rome die ue[ ]s prox. ante festum sancti Michaelis. Anno Domini supradicto.'
No fo 121.
122 and following leaf blank except for notes (see below, HISTORY).

DESCRIPTION
SIZE 23.5 x 15.5 cm.
QUIRING a^2 paper, I^8, II^{10}, III–V^8, VI^{10} (43–52), VII–VIII^8, IX^8 (8 cancelled: fos 69–75); X ?^{8} (+ three before 1: 76–86), XI–XII^8, XIII^{10}, XIV^8 (113–120), b^2 fos (122, unnumbered blank).
PRICKING None extant.
RULING Single column throughout, 32–24 written lines in HRB. Single vertical boundary-lines; written below top line. Rest of volume 25–32 lines, variable. Verses 29–31 lines.
SCRIPT Similar throughout volume. Largish, disciplined Anglicana. Brown ink. Ascenders tagged at left, split, or turned down to the right. Looped **d** and two-compartment **a**. Long **r** descends only just below the line. **e** usual simple form, **t** pierced, small 8-shaped **g**. **a** usually rises above minim letters. Final **s** is high or round. Uncrossed *et*-nota.
DECORATION Red or blue capitals, rarely filigreed. Opening initial blue filigreed with red.

HISTORY
Note of death of T. Bromley in 1587 on 122r printed by Coxe: *Catalogue of Manuscripts in the Library of All Souls' College*, p. 10. Next leaf blank except for note on recto in sixteenth-century hand 'Liber Georgii Bromley ex dono patris sui charissimi Georgii Bromley militis anno Domini 1586 regnante Elizabetha pacifica', repeated underneath in different, perhaps rather later hand. Anglicana script indicates English origin. Known distribution of Langtoft's Chronicle is Northern English: Legge, *Anglo-Norman*, pp. 72–73.

BIBLIOGRAPHY
Coxe, *Catalogue of Manuscripts in the Library of All Souls' College*, pp. 10–11.

134 *OXFORD, BODLEIAN LIBRARY, MS. ADD. A.61 (*S.C.* 28843)

Saec. xiii   Mediaeval provenance: English
54 fos   2nd fo: [*pa*]-*trem inuenando*

HRB 1ra–53vb
§§1–208. Dedicated to Robert of Gloucester and Waleran of Meulan. Above §1 (1r) 'Hic incipit brutus Anglie', 'Prologus'. No closing rubrics.

Book I only marked (§5, 1rb).

QQ. II and IV transposed without loss of text. Fos 29–36 (§58 'Dominum Iulii abicientes'– §90 'Plebs usus belli ignaria (*sic*)') should precede fos 17–28 (beginning §90 'que ceteris negotiis).

No other contents.

Shield drawn under HRB (53v) and different one on facing recto. 54v blank except for fifteenth-century note on Dionysiac cycle.

DESCRIPTION

SIZE 17 x 13 cm.

QUIRING I–II^8, III^{12}, IV^8, V^{14}, VI^4 (51–54). IV should follow II. No catchwords.

PRICKING Occasionally visible at outer edge.

RULING Two columns throughout with *ca* 38 x 46 written lines. Sometimes written below top ruled line. Double or single boundary-lines.

SCRIPT Several small and often cursive hands of glossing type. Varying degrees of informality and irregularity. Least formal hand has deeply split ascenders and simple, crude letter-forms; tall decorated ascenders on the first line of a page as in documentary hands. *Et*-nota crossed in places, a has both Caroline and two-compartment form, juncture of de occurs but none otherwise. Round d standard, tall final s usual. g crank-tailed. Insular *enim*-compendium found. Dark brown ink.

DECORATION Small plain red capitals without filigree except (in ink) at §§1 and 5.

HISTORY

On 54v, in fifteenth-century hand, now barely visible: 'Iste liber est fratris Guillelmi de Buria de [. . .] Roberti ordinis fratrum pred[icatorum]: Hunt *et al.*, *A Summary Catalogue of Western Manuscripts in the Bodleian*, V.515.

BIBLIOGRAPHY

Hunt *et al.*, *A Summary Catalogue of Western Manuscripts in the Bodleian*, V.515.

135 *OXFORD, BODLEIAN LIBRARY, MS. BODLEY 233 (*S.C.* 2188)

Saec. xiv^1 Mediaeval provenance: ?Britain
vi + 107 + ii fos   2nd fo: [*super*]-*ueniente. Ascanius regia*

HRB 1r–105ra.

§§1–3, 5–208. Letter of Arthur interpolated after §178.

Dedicated to Robert of Gloucester.

Rubrics at §1 (1ra) 'Incipit liber qui uocatur Brutus per Galfridum Monemutensem a Britannico in Latinum translatus. Prologus', §110 (52va) 'Incipit prologus de prophetia Merlini et liber vii', §111 (52vb) 'Explicit prologus. Incipit prophetia eiusdem'. Book-divisions: II §23 (10ra), III §35 (16vb), IIII §54 (24va), V §73 (33ra), VI §89 (41rb), VII §110 (52va), VIII §143 (71rb), IX §163 (82va), X §177 (92rb). 94ra/b, after §178 'anno ab incarnacione Domini .dxlii.', rubric '[L]ittere quas misit Arturus inuictus rex Britannie. Hug. capillano de Branno super sequanam cum palefrido. Anno

Domini .m.c.lvii.'. 'Arturus Dei gratia . . . pro dignitate tue promocionis famulabitur' – Arthur's letter, also found in Aberystwyth, NLW, Llanstephan 196, Bodleian, Rawlinson B.189, and Würzburg, UB, M.ch.f.140.

CONTENTS

i–iii: parchment flyleaves. On i r ?court records in late fourteenth-century hand, mentioning people of Solihull, Estote, ?Gerton (or Derton).

iiii: taken from book written in Anglicana hand of before mid-fourteenth century (two columns). Additions on verso, 'Incipiunt gesta Bruti in X libellis diuisi quorum primus habet xxiiii (altered to .xxv.) capitula . . .'.

Anecdotes va/b. 'Erat quedam mulier in habitu uiri quondam . . .', 'Erat aliquando quidam clericus magne pompe . . .', etc.

v ra/b: verses in couplets. 'Crux cara Christicolis celso consecrata creatoris . . . mortis noctem perimens fac nos frui luce [ ]. Amen.' Walther, *Initia*, I.173, no. 3468.

In same hand. 'Responsio cuiusdam spiritus incantatori super fatis pape Bonefacii et regis Edwardi parum ante mortem eorum.' 'Caput inficitur uirtutis in ocio . . . tunc adequabitur fortuna gremio.'

Verso. Top written in small hand (? *ca* 1300) 'In natura anime duplex est potencia siue uis . . . et tres uires anime i[de]o tum sunt septem'.

vi r/v: prophecy of Eagle of Shaftesbury. 'Mortuo leone iusticie surgit rex albus in Britannia . . . et rumor operis alpes transcendet.' Ed. Schulz, *Gottfried*, p. 465. Interrupted by note on king Cadwallo (vi recto) and prophecy (vi verso) in different hand: 'Reperitur in quodam tractatu sancti Molingi qui in libris Hibn. uocatur beatus spiritu prophetico plen. de illo quem Merlinus Ambrosius uocat sextum Hibn. sic.'. 'Animus eius adeo generosa probitas replebitur . . . per graciam a seipso.'

vi v: other prophecies. 'In ultimis diebus draconis albi semen eius triphanam spargetur . . . et uacua remanebit.' Followed by note connecting Eagle of Shaftesbury version of Merlin prophecies ('Sicut rubeum draconem') with St Edward. Another prophecy, attributed to Merlinus, 'Uersus reperti in quodam libro Merlini Celidonii de illo quem Merlinus Ambrosius uocat sextum Hibern..' 4 lines. 'Fit per te mundus tibi regnum sexte rotundus . . ..' 'Idem uersus liberati per angelum Alano sancto uiro cognomine sompniator petenti certum signum a domino ad cognoscendum quis foret ille quem Merlinus Ambrosius uocat sextum Hibern..' 'Illius imperium gens barbara senciet illum . . . Plus dabit hic o<rb>i quam dabit orbis ei.' Walther, *Initia*, I.441, no. 8731. 'Item uersus de Normannis superuenientibus ad subiugandum regnum Anglorum.' 'Pax erit illorum breuis . . . et gens priorum' (2 lines).

1r–105ra: HRB.

105ra: under HRB in fourteenth-century hand. 'Cum fuerint anni completi mille ducenti . . . corruet Anglorum gens perfida fraude suorum' (5 lines). Followed by four lines of verse, 'Corruet amborum genus et gens ense priorum . . ..' *De aduentu Antichristi.* Walther, *Initia*, I.181, no. 3617. Beneath, note on Merlin's prophecy concerning conquest of Ireland.

105rb: in hand of HRB. 'Ces sunt les noms des reys Bretons qui primes conquistrent que ore est appelle Engletere.' 'Deuant la natiuite nostre seygnur Iesu Crist en

Engletere . . . Doresete Suthamp-.' Truncated at end. Compare extract from Brut found in Bodleian Library, MS. Tanner 195, 129r–138r.

106ra/b: (in same hand). 'Henrici primi fuerat rex iste secundus . . . Tempore longeuo sensus uigor sit in illo.'

106ra–107ra: 'Cognomina conquisitorum Anglie cum bastardo et cito post uenientium'. 'Bastard. Baignard. Brassard . . . Costentin. Cheu. Parleben.' Compare Hardy, *Descriptive Catalogue*, II.5.

107ra: verses concerning prophecies etc. 'Uersus directi cuidam sancto in uisione.' 'Rex rectus nichil est rectus rex se regit . . . Hiis explanatis perceptis rex erit aptus.' 'Uersus per quant. temporis sextus durabit.' 'Ter tria lustra tenent cum semi tempora sexti . . . Hinc terrena spuens sanctus super ethera scandit.'

107rb: 'Uersus magistri Mich[ael]is le poter de Corn[ ]'. 'Cur homo ?delinquis linquisque Deum tibi d[ira] . . . Hiis te collaudo sic et metra claud[o].' Walther, *Initia*, I.196, no. 3921.

107v: 'De la entendante de Escoce a Engleterre'. Account of dominion of English kings over Scotland from Edward the Elder to ?Edward I (damaged at end). 'Fet a remenbrer que le rey Edward le primer . . . et subiettion et fealtee des reys de Scoce.' Final two flyleaves from late Gothic musical manuscript.

DESCRIPTION

SIZE 28 x 20 cm.

QUIRING a^2 (+ 1 paper after 1), b $?^4$ (?1 cancelled), I^8 (fos 1–8), II–IX^{12}, X^4 (lacks 4: 105–107), c^2. Some catchwords.

PRICKING In both margins.

RULING Two columns throughout. 30 lines written; written below top ruled line.

SCRIPT ?Semi-quadrata. Large. Dark brown ink. Short ascenders and descenders. Ampersand used. Juncture of e and o after b, d, and p; some *Verschrenkung* of other letters. Final round s.

DECORATION Blue or red capitals with trailing filigree in the contrasting colour (also in blue-green). Major capitals are in blue and red with solid grounds.

HISTORY

Initials and mark of Ralph Barlow on fo 1 (Barlow presented the manuscript to the Bodleian in 1606).

BIBLIOGRAPHY

Hunt *et al.*, *A Summary Catalogue of Western Manuscripts in the Bodleian*, 2.1, p. 251.

136 *OXFORD, BODLEIAN LIBRARY, MS. BODLEY 514 (*S.C.* 2184)

Saecc. xii *ex.* + xiii *in.*   Mediaeval provenance: Jervaulx, Yorkshire (Cistercian)

i + 91 fos   2nd fo: *et saltus nemorum*

HRB 1ra–34vb

§§1–208. Dedicated to Robert of Gloucester and Waleran of Meulan.

No original opening and closing rubrics but at §118 (*sic*) (20vb) 'Incipit prophetia Merlini'.

No book-divisions. After §208 is added in a thirteenth-century cursive hand, 'Explicit historia Britonum monasterii Ioreuallis'.

CONTENTS

i: contents-list on recto in thirteenth-century documentary hand. Verso blank except for *ex-libris* inscription (see HISTORY).

1ra–34vb: HRB.

35r–36r: blank (vertical foldline). Only 35r ruled.

36v: two columns written in informal hand of the twelfth century. 'Homo quidam tres habuit amicos dispariter amicos ... post penitendi inducias admissa.' A tale of repentance. Bloomfield, *Incipits*, p. 213, no. 2411.

37r–46vb: 'Liber de signis pronosticorum infirmitatum siue ad salutem siue ad mortem attinentium incipit'. 'Intellectus enim significationis rerum non minus est iuuamentum ... et hec est sicut [ ]animus et sicut precepimus.'

46vb–54rb: 'Quoniam humana corpora assidue interius exteriusque dissoluuntur ... unde corpora desiccantur'. Petrus Mussandina, glosses on *Prognostica* of Hippocrates. Thorndike & Kibre, *A Catalogue*, col. 1277.

54rb–55vb: medical treatise. 'Intentio Philareti est in hoc opere pulsuum elementiam cum utilitate ostendere ... et uix occurrit digitis defectumque nature significat.' Commentary on Philaretus, *De pulsibus*. Thorndike & Kibre, *A Catalogue*, col. 763.

56r/v blank, erased text on recto running sideways.

57r: blank except for medical notes on humors (etc.) in thirteenth-century hands.

57v–62vb: ?commentary on Galen's *Techne*. '[C]um inter omnia corpora humanum corpus tum proprie forme inpressione ... que sit utilis que inutilis ad medicinam discernant'.

63r: medical notes in hands as on 57r. Verso blank.

64r–71vb: anonymous commentary on Hippocrates' *Liber Aphorismorum*, imperfect at both ends. 'et manentes constitutiones borea id est frigide ... eam spasmi cito consummitur primum.' Kibre, 'Hippocrates latinus', p. 255.

72r–87v: 'Tractaturi de iudiciis'. 'Primo de preparatoriis iudiciorum dicemus ... ab omni sacerdote intrepide Christi ministeria.' Treatise on aspect of Roman law.

88r–89r: 'Quomodo post quadringentos decem et octo annos corpus beati Cuthberti incorruptum sit inuentum et in nouam ecclesiam translatum'. 'Inter hec tam frequentium miraculorum opera ... tot sanctorum reliquias ibidem conspiciunt.' See Colgrave, 'The post-Bedan miracles', p. 317.

89v–91v: blank except for notes (see HISTORY).

DESCRIPTION

SIZE 23 x 16.5 cm.

QUIRING a singleton, I–III^8, IV^{12} (25–36: stitching clear after 6); V–VI^8, VII^4 (53–56); VII^8 (8 lacking: 57–63); IX^8; X–XI^8; XII^4 (88–91).

PRICKING Outer margins only except Q. XII where in both margins. In HRB extant only for boundary-lines.

RULING Double columns except for Q. XII. HRB 45–47 lines written, single vertical boundary-lines, written above top line; QQ. V–VII – 39–40 lines, sometimes written below top ruled line; Q. VIII – 57 lines; QQ. IX–XI – 55–59 lines; Q. XII – 35 lines, single column, double outer boundary-lines, top line written.

SCRIPT HRB in extremely small, dark brown glossing-script. Straight-backed **d** and tall **s**. *Et*-nota standard. Several hands. No e-caudata. Round **d** occasionally used. **a** usually has small head. **ct**-ligature. Not very heavily abbreviated. Other items seem rather later, in various hands. Mostly small minuscule of the early thirteenth century with Caroline **a**, round **d**, uncrossed *et*-nota, no juncture ?because of size. Straight-backed **d** in places. Varying degrees of abbreviation. 88r–89r, however, written in more formal hand, larger script. Final s round or tall. Crossed *et*-nota. **de** approaching juncture. Round **d** standard.

DECORATION HRB – mostly unfiligreed red or blue capitals. Very elaborate initials at §§1, 6 and 110 constructed of complex interlace incorporating acanthus scrolls and, at §5, spotted animals; ink outline, coloured in blue, brown and green (outline only at §110). Elsewhere plain red capitals but blue initial filigreed with red at 72r.

HISTORY

Final rubric (thirteenth-century) consititutes earliest mark of ownership, see above. On i verso, in capitals ?*ca* 1300 'Liber sancte Marie de Ioreualle'. Jervaulx *ex-libris* repeated on 91r. Early Modern notes: 90v 'Bassetur ?Thones (or Jhones) Camb:Brittan. 1634', 91r 'Arthur Gilroy' (same on i verso), 91r (sixteenth-century) 'Nicholas Lynneby Ioannensis'. Nicholas Lymbie, admitted to St John's College, Oxford, in 1582, gave two other manuscripts to the Bodleian, S.C. 1979 and 2183: Stevenson & Salter, *The Early History of St. John's College*, p. 362.

BIBLIOGRAPHY

Hunt *et al.*, *A Summary Catalogue of Western Manuscripts in the Bodleian*, 2.1, p. 249.

*OXFORD, BODLEIAN LIBRARY, MS. BODLEY 585 (*S.C.* 2357)

See Cambridge, University Library, MS. Dd.6.7 (324).

137 *OXFORD, BODLEIAN LIBRARY, MS. BODLEY 622 (*S.C.* 2156)

Saec. xiv² + xiv¹　　　　　Mediaeval provenance: England, ?Glastonbury
i + 116 fos　　　　　　　　　2nd fo (2r): *coniurauerat postulauit*
　　　　　　　　　　　　　　2nd fo (13r): [*Tur*]*-nus rex Rutulorum*

HRB 12r–112r

§§1–3, 5–208. Dedicated to Robert of Gloucester.
Rubrics above §1 (12r) 'Gaufridi Monemutensis de gestis Britonum prologus incipit', at §5 (12r) 'Britannie insule descripcio', §6 (12v) 'Incipit liber Britonum', §109 (62r) 'Explicit liber .vi. Incipit prologus in prophetias Merlini', §111 (62r) 'Explicit prologus. Incipiunt prophetie', §118 (68r) 'Expliciunt prophetie. Sequitur liber octauus unde supra', after §208 (112r) 'Explicit. Explicit'.
Book-divisions: II §23 (21v), III §35 (27v), IV §54 (35r), V §73 (43v), VI §89 (51v), [VII] §109 (62r), VIII §118 (68r), IX §143 (79r), §163 (89v), XI §177 (99v).
Prophecies glossed: gloss unpublished – see Eckhardt, *The Prophetia Merlini*, p. 12.

CONTENTS
i: on recto, opening line of prophecy of John of Bridlington (? *ca* 1400); a few notes on verso in ?fifteenth-century hands in Latin and English.
1r–4r: 'De origine gygant[um] in insula Albion olim habitancium et nomine insule que nunc Anglia dicitur'. 'Anglia modo dicta olim Albion dicebatur et habebat . . . et sic ueritas clarescit historie de primis habitatoribus huius terre.' In Anglicana hand with split ascenders.
4r–6r: 'Conpendium de Britannia siue Anglia'. 'Quoniam simplicioribus foret difficile prolixiores hystorias . . . uel pro ignauia amiserint.' Also found in London, BL, MS. Cotton Cleopatra D.viii.
6r/v: 'Sequitur de episcopatibus et primo de archiepiscopatu Eboracensi'. 'Archiepiscopatus Eboracensis cui Euerwycscire. Lancastrescire et Notinghamscire subiacent . . . a Danis sepius infestarentur.'
6v: 'De Normanniis' (*sic*). 'Anno ab incarnacione Domini .m.lxvi. a conuersione uero Anglorum .cccc.lxx. . . . ad suum arbitrium commutans.'
6v–10r: 'Quedam narracio de nobili rege Arthuro in sacramento altaris nunc plene credente qualiter confirmatus fuit in fide factus uere credens et quare mutauit arma sua'. 'Dominus Deus uniuersorum conditor . . . et sepultus est in insula Auallone in cimiterio monachorum inter duas magnas pirannides.' Taken from the Chronicle of John of Glastonbury. Also found in London, BL, MS. Cotton Cleopatra D.viii.
10v–11r: blank, unruled.
11v: sixteenth-century inscriptions of ownership (see below, HISTORY) and contents-list recording all present contents.

12r–112v: HRB.
112v–115v: blank except for verses in hand of ? *ca* 1400 on 113v ('Omnipotens Deus hic faciet te uince[re] paruo . . .') and a few place- and personal names from HRB on 115v.
116r: verses in English (6 lines). 'Wan y was pore than was y fre . . . To day y was

riche and now have y nouth.' Brown & Robbins *The Index*, p. 636, no.3970. 'A scheld of red a crosse of grene . . . Among his en[ ]s thar he no3t quake' (6 lines) *ibid.*, p. 16, no. 91. 'That in thi mischef forsakit ye . . . that in thy nede wernet ye' (4 lines) *ibid.*, p. 522, no. 3280. Entered in fifteenth century or later. The last found also on verso of flyleaf preceding text. Note in Latin at foot 'Ad cognoscendum utrum mulier sit impregnata uel non . . ..'
116v: blank.

DESCRIPTION
SIZE 17 x 12 cm.
QUIRING a uncollatable (fos i–ii paper + blank unnumbered leaf, fo iii parchment, fos 1–10, 2 stubs, fo 11); I^8 (fos 12–19), II–XI^8, XII^8 (100–107). Catchwords and signatures.
PRICKING In outer margin.
RULING Two columns of 30 written lines. Written below top line; single vertical boundary-lines.
SCRIPT Informal Gothic bookhand. **r** and **s** do not trail below the line. Small, heavy, rather ugly script with flat tops to some ascenders; descenders have angled stroke at foot. Two-compartment **a**, unpierced **t**. Occasional juncture of **e** with **d** and **p**, not **h**. Ampersand is used for *et*. Round **s** frequent even medially, although tall form is also found in all positions. Round **d** has long ascender.
DECORATION Red or blue capitals with simple trailing filigree at start of HRB but plain capitals otherwise.

HISTORY
Material on fos 4r–10r has Glastonbury associations. Some is found in the Glastonbury manuscript Cambridge, Trinity College, MS. R.5.33 (100r/v). On 11v in ?late fifteenth-century hand: 'Liber domini Iohannis More emptus a magistro Thomas ?Quirk'; then, added, 'Et iam m[agistri] Iohannis Cole de dono domini Iohannis Clerk' (one John Clerk was bishop of Bath and Wells 1523–41). Beneath contents-list (in hand of first note, 11v) 'Constat J:[Cliffe]' (Hunt *et al.*, *A Summary Catalogue of Western Manuscripts in the Bodleian*, II.i, p. 234). At foot in sixteenth-century hand, 'Liber Willelmi Derlyngton'.

BIBLIOGRAPHY
Hunt *et al.*, *A Summary Catalogue of Western Manuscripts in the Bodleian*, II.i, p. 234.

138 *OXFORD, BODLEIAN LIBRARY, MS. BODLEY 977 (*S.C.* 27602)

Saec. xiv^1 $^{(?in.)}$ Mediaeval provenance:
153 fos   2nd fo (5r): [*Tro*]-*ianorum nunciatum est mirandam*

HRB 28r–151r
§§1–3, 5–108, 110–184, 186–208. Dedicated to Robert of Gloucester.

Rubrics at §1 (28r) 'Incipit prologus Galfridi Monemutensis in sequenti historia', §5 (28v) 'Descripcio britannice insule. Primum capitulum', §6 (29r) 'De origine Britonum qualiter Brutus iuxta presagium patrem peremit et matrem et in Grecia Troianarum reliquiarum dux efectus sit' (similar commentary at every textual division), §110 (95v) 'Incipit edicio Galfridi Monemutensis de dictis Merlini', §111 (95v) 'Prophecie Merlini ex mistica pugna draconum', §118 (102v) 'Explicit Merlinus . . .', after §208 (151r) 'Explicit hystoria Britonum'.

Book-divisions: II §54 (60v), III §98 (88r), IIII §143 (116r).

Second Variant Version. Hammer's *siglum* G: Emanuel, 'Geoffrey of Monmouth's *Historia*', p. 104.

CONTENTS
(1–3: flyleaves)

1r: notes in cursive late mediaeval hand. 'O sancta Appolonia ora pro nobis [ ] ex toto corde me pre[ ]' and similar notes.

1v, 2r: two shields with fleur-de-lys motif, name Walton, and other notes. Fifteenth- or sixteenth-century.

2v: in small neat hand (fifteenth-century), 'Iesus mey lady help. . . .' and moral sayings.

3r: sketch of crucifix.

3v: notes in rough Secretary-type hand recording a theft from the house of a chaplain in Lincolnshire.

4r–26r: 'Incipit epistola Cornelii ad Salustium Crispum in Troianorum historia que in Greco a Dareto hystoriographo facta est'. 'Cornelius Salustio Crispo suo salutem . . . Palamonem. Epistrophum. Scidium.' Ed. Meister, *Daretis Phrygii De Excidio Troiae Historia*.

26r (foot)–27v: blank.

28r–151r: HRB.

151v: list of place-names with facing gloss (same hand as above). 'Ytalia: ubi nunc Roma . . . Cardorcanensen. Orcanye. Augustudunum [ ].'

152r: erased text.

152v–153r: prognostications (in Secretary-hand). 'Ianuarius quando tonitr<u>um est in mense Ianuarii . . . Nouembris.'

153v: blank.

DESCRIPTION
SIZE 14.5 x 9.5 cm.

QUIRING a⁴ (1 mutilated: fos 1–3), I–II¹², III–VI¹⁰, VII¹², VIII¹⁴, IX–XIII¹⁰, XIV ?¹⁰ (144–153). Some catchwords.

PRICKING Trimmed away.

RULING Single column throughout of 25–29 lines (27 lines average). Narrow double vertical boundings and double line across top and foot margins. Ruling above top written line. Flyleaves not ruled.

SCRIPT HRB in small, rather crude and heavy minuscule. Letters spaced because of small size. Two-compartment a, round or high final s, t not very pierced, crossed

et-nota. Juncture of **o** with **d** and **p** and of **e** with **d**. Flat top to double **l**, ascenders slightly indented or tagged at top. 2-shaped **r** frequent. Brown ink.
DECORATION Red unfiligreed capitals. Medial capitals in text highlighted in red.

HISTORY
On outer wrapping (parchment, taken from 1523 court-roll), 'Ex dono Hen. Northcote M. D. coll. Exon. Soc. A.D. .M.DCC. iii/iv'. This part of the manuscript owned by Thomas Allen: Watson, 'Thomas Allen of Oxford', p. 292.

BIBLIOGRAPHY
Hunt *et al.*, *A Summary Catalogue of Western Manuscripts in the Bodleian*,V.296–97.

139 *OXFORD, BODLEIAN LIBRARY, MS. DIGBY 67 (*S.C.* 1668), fos 57–68

Saec. xii *ex.* (or xii/xiii)   Provenance: ?
104 fos (12 of HRB)

HRB 57r–68v
Fragments.
57r–59v: 'Domino in Ierusalem' (§28) – 'Sed quia discordia sese' (§35).
60r–62v: '-am petentes. Obtulerunt' (§43) – 'Gaio Iulio Cesari' (§55).
63r–68v: 'Resistunt ergo et ipsi' (§166) – 'in occidentalibus regni' (§186).
No rubrics or book-divisions extant.

CONTENTS
Found in volume of fragmentary manuscripts of various dates and sizes, largely dating from the thirteenth century or later.
No neighbouring fragment is compatible in size or appearance with HRB fragments.

DESCRIPTION
(57r–68v only)
SIZE 21 x 16 cm.
QUIRING I ?^{8} (lacks 4–5), II ?^{8} (lacks 1, 8).
PRICKING At outer edges only.
RULING Two columns of 36 lines. Double boundary-lines, divided central margin, no ruling above top written line.
SCRIPT Minuscule of angular aspect, with some lateral compression. Nearly black ink. Round **d** frequent but straight-backed form is more common, final s is tall or high. Apparently no e-caudata. **a** when initial is often high. Pinched curve of **h**, **g** almost crank-tailed. *Et*-nota used. Thickening on tops of some ascenders.
DECORATION Red or pale blue capitals with simple contrasting line-decoration inside the letter or scrolling outside it.

HISTORY
Fos 85–116 (a philosophical collection) were numbered 28 in the catalogue of 1410 of Merton College, Oxford: Powicke, *The Medieval Books*, pp. 133–34 and p. 68; Ker, *Medieval Libraries*, p. 147.

BIBLIOGRAPHY

Macray, *Catalogi codicum manuscriptorum Bibliothecæ Bodleianæ, Pars IX*, cols 73–76.

OXFORD, BODLEIAN LIBRARY, MS. DIBGY 196 See appendix

140 *OXFORD, BODLEIAN LIBRARY, MS. DOUCE 115 (*S.C.* 21689)

Saec. xiv¹ (?1313–27)   Mediaeval provenance: ?
73 fos (+ 9b, 10b, 59b; no fo 19)   2nd fo: *petiuitque nemor abdita*

HRB 1r–68v
§§6–208 [§§109–110 in *pudibundus Brito* form]. Dedicatory chapters absent.
Rubrics after §208 (68v) 'Explicit'.
Book-division II §23 (6v).

CONTENTS
1r–68v: HRB.
68v–69r: in same hand with note at end, 'Isti uersus reperiebantur in sarcophago cuiusdam sollempnis clerici in urbe Rome et per quosdam ibidem existentes Anglicos Anglie transmissi'. 'Gallorum leuitas Germanos iustificabit . . . sub quo tunc uana cessabit gloria cleri.' Walther, *Initia*, I.353, no. 7015. Ed. Holder-Egger, 'Italienische Prophetieen', pp. 125–26.
69r–72v: '[Q]ui uoet oir et uoet sauer de rey en rey de heir en heir . . . Bellum de Euesham fuit scco. Non. Augusti anno Domini .m.cc.xl.quinto'. French prose Brut chronicle to 1274. Stengel, 'Elf neue Handschriften', pp. 278–79; Vising, *Anglo-Norman Language and Literature*, pp. 66–67, and p. 92. In hand contemporary with that of HRB.
72v: same hand. '[D]e archiepiscopis ecclesie Christi Cantuar. quantum uixerint et quantum ecclesia uacauit'. 'August. xvi annis . . . Walterus.' Ends with Walter Reynolds, 1313–27, whose length of tenure of the see is not entered.
73r: blank.
73v: shield and note in fourteenth-century hand, 'Edwardus Dei gratia rex Anglie dominus Hibn.'. Inscriptions of ownership (see below, HISTORY) and other notes.

DESCRIPTION
SIZE 22 x 13.5 cm.
QUIRING I–VIII⁸, IX⁶ (65–70), X², ?singleton (73).
PRICKING Mostly trimmed away.
RULING Single column of 36–37 written lines. Written below top ruled line.
SCRIPT Brown ink, Anglicana hand of more formal type. Small minim-letters with very long tapering descenders and thick uprights. Hairline wisps on minims and suspension marks, etc. Split ascenders. Two-compartment **a** and circular form of **s** are within height of minims. Uncrossed *et*-nota. Lines fairly widely spaced. Ordered aspect.

DECORATION Red or blue filigreed capitals.

HISTORY

On 73v in fifteenth-century hand, beside coat of arms, 'Iste liber constat Iohanni Stwarde militi filio Io. Scotangli militis ex dono prepotens[ ] et nobilissimi don. dompni ducis Bedfor[ ]'; perhaps donor is therefore George Neville (1470–77): Hunt *et al.*, *A Summary Catalogue of Western Manuscripts in the Bodleian*, IV.527.

Underneath, in somewhat later hand, 'Iste liber constat Ricardo Stywarde filio Tho. Stywardis anno Domini 149[0]'.

Other fifteenth-century notes on same folio, 'Iohannes Seneschallus', 'Connyngesburgh'.

Top 1r, Early Modern hand, 'Sir Duncan Stuart Bart.'.

BIBLIOGRAPHY

Hunt *et al.*, *A Summary Catalogue of Western Manuscripts in the Bodleian*, IV.526–27.

141 *OXFORD, BODLEIAN LIBRARY, MS. FAIRFAX 28 (*S.C.* 3908)

Saec. xii*med./2*   Origin: ?English
viii + 91 fos   2nd fo: *Rutulorum et cum illo*

HRB 1r–90v

§§1–3, 5–208. Dedicated to Robert of Gloucester.

Opening and closing rubrics added in hands of ? *ca* 1300, above §1 (1r) 'Liber Bruti et continet quater .xx. et .x. folia et .cc. et .v. capitula', after §208 (90v) 'Explicit liber Bruti'. Extensive original rubrics in text beginning at §27 'Genuit', 'Ciuitas Eboraci conditur a rege Ebrauco et rex David regnat in Iudea . . . '. Cf. London, Lambeth Palace, MS. 454 (b).

Book-division: III §35 (17r). Marginal *capitula*-numbers added, perhaps at same time as rubrics.

CONTENTS

'ii'–'ix': added parchment flyleaves, mostly blank.

'ii' r/v: notes in Fairfax's hand, mostly in English. On the recto they concern Geoffrey's work, naming Ponticus Virunnius and quoting Selden's note on 'Poly-olbion' (*sic*). On verso: 'Transcriptum ex perantiquo MSo penes [ ] in octauo nuper prioratui de Bolton in Crauen comitatu Eboracensi spectante, cui titulus correctorius secundum ordinem bibliae una cum aliis tractatibus de Algarismo [ ]' (note at foot of page), copied from MS. Fairfax 27. 'Facta est uisio quod mirabilis in claustro Cister. ordinis Tripoli . . . in tanta tranquilitate noua audiente de Antichristo.'

1r–90v: HRB.

91r: flyleaf. Recto written in very cursive late mediaeval hand. Verso blank except for seventeenth-century note.

DESCRIPTION

SIZE 20 x 14.5 cm.

QUIRING a^8, I–XI^8, XII^4 (3 lacking: 89–91).

PRICKING In outer margin only.

RULING Single column, 30 lines. Ruling not visible.

SCRIPT Dark brown ink. Four-line Protogothic minuscule. Not especially regular or laterally compressed. Stubby appearance, thick vertical strokes. Ampersand very frequent but uncrossed *et*-nota also found. e-caudata rare. Tall final s standard but round form also found. Straight-backed **d** perhaps more common than round form. Tail of **g** descends from back of letter in a straight line. Thickening on shoulder of tall s. Prepositions often joined to following noun.

DECORATION Original rubrics in bright red. Initials are simple Romanesque capitals, some with leafy scrolls or bosses, in red or green (which penetrates membrane).

HISTORY

Signature 'Fairfax' on 1r, at top right.

BIBLIOGRAPHY

Hunt *et al.*, *A Summary Catalogue of Western Manuscripts in the Bodleian*, II.2, p. 787.

142 *OXFORD, BODLEIAN LIBRARY, MS. JESUS COLLEGE 2

Saec. xv   Mediaeval provenance: ?

iv + 232 + ii fos   2nd fo: *regna[ui]t .xxix. annis*

HRB 1r–232v

§§6–208. (Part of §§64 and 75 omitted). Dedicatory section absent.

Rubrics at §6 (1r) 'Incipit historia Britonum', §110 (95r) 'Incipit prohemium siue littera tranmissa domino Alexandro Lincoln. episcopo in prophetias Ambrosii Merlini', before §111 (95v) 'Explicit prologus. Incipiunt uaticinia Ambrosii Merlini qui floruit circa annum Domini .cccc.xxx. in tempore Uortigerni regis Britannie', after §208 (232v) 'Explicit historia Britonum'.

Heavily interpolated, often with comparative historical material (Roman, for example), and adapted. Some material taken from Chronicle of Martinus Polonus (ed. Weiland, MGH, SS, XXII.397–474, from pp. 398–403, 408, 448). The beginning of the Eagle of Shaftesbury prophecy of Merlin (which usually circulates independently of Geoffrey's work) found after §117 (145r/v) 'Arbor fertilis a proprio trunco decisa ... in hac tribulacione remedium'. Ed. Schulz, *Gottfried*, pp. 463–65.

Prophecies of Merlin (§111) glossed (fos 96r–97v).

No other contents (two blank parchment flyleaves after 232).

DESCRIPTION

SIZE 21.5 x 15 cm.

QUIRING Paper with parchment flyleaves. a^4 (unnumbered blank followed by i–iii), I–XXIX^8, b^2. Catchwords.

RULING Single column of 14–21 lines. Prophecies in 8–9 lines. Generous margins. often containing commentary or added text.
SCRIPT Dark grey ink. Large and rapid informal bookhand. Pierced **t**, looped two-compartment **a**, long cursive **r**, 8-shaped **g**, final sigma **s**. Angularity in bowl of looped round **d**, **st**-ligature, looped tops of ascenders.
DECORATION Some ink capitals (Lombardic).

BIBLIOGRAPHY
Coxe, *Catalogus codicum manuscriptorum qui in collegiis aulisque Oxoniensibus hodie adservantur*, II.7, p. 1.

143 *OXFORD, BODLEIAN LIBRARY, MS. JONES 48 (*S.C.* 8956)

Saec. xiv   Mediaeval provenance:
                              Furness (fifteenth-century), Cistercian (Lancs.)
vi + 9–140 fos   2nd fo: [*po*]-*testate sublimatus condidit*

HRB 9r–140v
Fragmentary. §§5–51 (*ex.*), 68 (*ex.*) –108, 109–110 *pudibundus Brito* form, *Merlinus uero incipiens* chapter, 111–117 (*ex.*), 119 (*in.*) –173 (*med.*).
Dedicatory chapters absent.
Rubrics at §111 (79v) 'Incipiunt prophecie Merlini'.
Book-divisions: I §6 (9v), II §23 (23v), III §35 (34r), V §72 (46v), VI §89 (60v), 'ultimus' §143 (108v).
Lacuna between 44v (ends §51 'ab hac luce migrans', end of quire) and 45r ('sit euangelium quod scripserat' §68). Interpolation, after §110, begins 'Merlinus uero incipiens coram rege Uortigerno prophetare'. Last two sentences of §117 omitted (ends 'prorumpent Pliades') (89r); §119 'Rumore itaque' begins 89v. Cf. Aberystwyth, NLW, MS. Peniarth 43 and Oxford, All Souls' College, MS. 35. Text truncated at foot of 140v, 'et Walwanus quibus meliores pre-' (§173).
No other contents. 1–2 blank paper. 3–8 parchment, blank except for fifteenth-century note on origin of world (6r, upsidedown) and *ex-libris* (7v).

DESCRIPTION
SIZE 15 x 8.5 cm.
QUIRING a¹⁴ (2, 4–7, 10, 12, 14 lacking: fos 3–8), I–XI¹². Catchwords, including last folio.
PRICKING Trimmed away.
RULING Single column of 28 lines. Single vertical boundary-lines; written below top ruled line.
SCRIPT Same throughout. Small, regular, informal English. Round, slightly tapering, descenders; ascenders turned down at top, not split. 2-shaped **r** used rather than long form. Two-compartment **a**, pierced **t**, looped **d**. **f** and **s** descend below the line. Final round **s**. No real juncture but **o** and **e** written close to preceding **d**. Brown ink.
DECORATION Rather crude blue capitals with red filigree. Initial letters of sentences

sometimes highlighted in light brown. Initials at §§5 and 6 in blue and red filled with filigree and at §5 with scrolling along edge of text.

HISTORY
On 7v, upsidedown, now very indistinct, 'Istum librum emit frat. [ ] de Dalton abbas huius mon[ ]': William, abbot of Furness 1412–23 (see Hunt *et al.*, *A Summary Catalogue of Western Manuscripts in the Bodleian*, III.42). Ker, *Medieval Libraries*, p. 89.

BIBLIOGRAPHY
Hunt *et al.*, *A Summary Catalogue of Western Manuscripts in the Bodleian*, III.41–42.

144 *OXFORD, BODLEIAN LIBRARY, MS. LAT. HIST. b.1, FRAGMENT 2

Saec. ?xiv/xv[1]
2 fos   Origin: English

HRB 2r–3v
Two fragments. 2r/v: 'fau[ces ill]ius cum gladio' (§116.54) – 'Quod prius uitabis. hinc' (§118).
3r: 'Quicumque etenim pro confratribus' (§147 *in.*) – 'peticioni adquiscens 'ueniam donauit' (§149).
No extant rubrics or book-divisions.

DESCRIPTION
SIZE fo 2, 26.5 x 14.5 cm; fo 3, 26.5 x 17 cm.
QUIRING Conjugate leaves. Originally separated by approximately eight leaves.
PRICKING None extant as trimmed into edge of text.
RULING Not visible but single column, 33 lines written.
SCRIPT Ink now worn. Minuscule using long **r**, looped two-compartment **a**, final **s** sigma-shaped, crossed **t**, crossed *et*-nota, looped ascenders. Some angularity. Dark brown-grey ink.
DECORATION No capitals completed.

HISTORY
Belongs to volume of fragments.

BIBLIOGRAPHY
East, 'Manuscripts', pp. 483–84.

145 *OXFORD, BODLEIAN LIBRARY, MS. LAT. MISC. b.17, fo 10

Saec. xii*med./2*   Mediaeval provenance: ?English

HRB
10r §193 'Uersus Armoricam dirigerent' –§194 'preter Romanos qui'.

10v §194 '-runt numquam eam deinceps habuerunt' –§195 'agris exterminarent. Dignum tamen'.

No extant rubrics. *Capitula*-numbers, apparently early, in red: .xiii. §194, .xiiii. §195. Low values of the numbers suggest arrangement in subdivided books, rather than serial *capitula*-numbers.

DESCRIPTION
SIZE 20.2 x 15.5 cm. Cut down at top with loss of a little text (?3–4 lines).
PRICKING None extant.
RULING Single column, single vertical boundary-lines.
SCRIPT Brown ink. Rather irregular four-line Protogothic. Occasional e-caudata. Final round s and round d occur but tall and straight-backed forms much more frequent. Ampersand. Insular *est*-compendium. ct-ligature. h has pinched top.
DECORATION Simple Romanesque capitals in red or green.

HISTORY
This volume of fragments was formerly shelved as B.2.16 in the library of Lord Clifden at Lanhydrock, Cornwall: Hammer, 'Some additional manuscripts', pp. 241–42; Dumville, 'The manuscripts', p. 166.

BIBLIOGRAPHY
Hammer, 'Some additional manuscripts', pp. 241–42.

146   *OXFORD, BODLEIAN LIBRARY, MS. LAT. MISC. e.42 (*S.C.* 36220)

Saec. xii²   Origin: ?S. England
iv + 5–52 + ii

HRB 5r–52v
Fragmentary. §§54–124 (*med.*), 127 (*ex.*) –137 (*med.*), 138 (*ex.*) –165 (*med.*), 171 (*ex.*) –184 (*med.*). Dedicatory section lost.
Rubrics at §109 (27ra) 'Incipit prologus uaticiniorum Merlini', §110 (27ra) 'Epistola ad Alexandrum', §111 (27rb) 'Incipiunt uaticinia Merlini ad Alexandrum Lincolniensem episcopum missa', §143 (39rb) 'Incipit de Arturo uiro famosissimo'.
No book-divisions extant.
Text begins on 5r 'prosapia nos Romani et Britones' (§54).
Lacunae between fos 33v (ends 'per nasale Cassidis atque totis', §124) and 34r (begins 'nobiles pro patria defunctos', §127), between 37v (ends 'petiuitque prouintiam', §137) and 38r (begins 'suum et exuta specie', §138), and between 48v (ends 'Cuius dum cacumen', §165) and 49r (begins 'querele quia undique', §171). 52v ends 'fugauit eum a ciuitate in ciuitatem do-' (§184).

CONTENTS
1r–4v: fragment of music manuscript (? *ca* 1200 or later).
5r–52v: HRB.
53r–54v: fragment, truncated at both ends, of commentary on Boethius' *De hebdo-*

madibus by Gilbert of Poitiers (of about same date as liturgical fragment). 'nam Plato et Cicero unione species sunt idem homo . . . ut corporalitas et corpus hu-.' See Häring, 'Texts concerning Gilbert of Poitiers', p. 191

Modern note on binding recording removal to a separate folder of a fragment of treatise on Roman law (twelfth-century) too large to be bound with this manuscript, MS. Lat. misc. e.42*. This work has been identified as part of a commentary on Placentinus, *Summa codicis*: Legendre, *Miscellanea britannica*, p. 492, n.2.

DESCRIPTION
SIZE 20.5 x 15 cm.
QUIRING I⁴; II⁴ (mounted leaves, + one before 1: fos 5–9), III–V⁸, VI⁸ (1, 6 lacking: 34–39), VII⁸, VIII 5 mounted leaves (lacuna between 1 and 2), lacuna, IX² (mounted: 53–54). Some catchwords.
PRICKING At outer edge in HRB.
RULING HRB in two columns of 31 lines. No ruling above top line, divided central margin. A – 15 staves but trimmed down at head. C – single column, bottom lines trimmed away leaving about 37 lines.
SCRIPT HRB in handsome, clear, black, four-line Protogothic. Round s is rare, both forms of d used equally, e-caudata is found, *et*-nota is standard. Rounded thickenings on ends of minims and on tall s. High initial a occurs. Letters are narrow but not packed together.
DECORATION Extant large initials have elaborate scrolling; minor capitals in pale blue, red, green, and pale brown. Initial at §111 (27rb) is constructed of two biting dragons whose tails form scrolls: red, blue, green with ink outline. Also at §143 (39rb) large interlaced initial with animal head, coloured with ink outline. Minor capitals are Romanesque with bosses and split shafts of letter.

HISTORY
Elizabeth Parker McLachlan has noted a similarity between the initials in this manuscript and those in Winchester manuscripts: 'In the wake of the Bury Bible', pp. 222–23, n. 47.
On 54r, 'Liber Guil[lelmi] Mart[ini] emptus 14 Aug. 1568 precium 3s. 4d': Hunt *et al.*, *A Summary Catalogue of Western Manuscripts in the Bodleian*, VI.434. Emden read this as William Marshall, fellow of Merton College: *A Biographical Register of the University of Oxford A.D. 1501 to 1540*, p. 382, a judgement shared by Ker, 'Oxford College libraries', p. 506, n. 2.
Bought for the Bodleian from L. Morshead of Treniffle, Launceston, 1913.

BIBLIOGRAPHY
Hunt *et al.*, *A Summary Catalogue of Western Manuscripts in the Bodleian*, VI.434.

147 *OXFORD, BODLEIAN LIBRARY, MS. LAUD MISC. 579 (*S.C.* 1496)

Saec. xv   Origin: English
iv + 273 pages (incorrectly foliated)   2nd fo (p. 3): *conciuium prosapia moratus*

HRB pp. 1–134

§§1–3, 5–208. Dedicated to Robert of Gloucester.

Rubrics at §1 (p. 1) 'Incipiunt gesta regum Britonum qualiter composita sunt', §109 (p. '69') 'Incipit prologus de propheciis Merlini inclitissimi iwenis (*sic*)', §110 (p. '69') 'Epistola', §111 (p. '70') 'Incipiunt prophecie Merlini', after §208 'Finis huius oposculi (*sic*) etc.'.

Book-divisions: I §5 (p. 1), II §23 (p. 13), III §35 (p. 21), IV §54 (p. 31), V §63 'Cumque postmodum' (p. 38), VI §89 (p. 54), VII §118 (p. 77), VIII §143 (p. '82'), IX §163 (p. '105'), X §177 (p. '118').

CONTENTS

pp. i–iv: blank flyleaves.

pp. 1–'134': HRB.

p. '135': blank.

pp. '136'–'269': 'Incipit cronica fratris Martini penitenciarii domini pape et capellani rubrica etc.'. 'Quoniam scire tempora summorum pontificum Romanorum ac imperatorum . . . et animauit ad suscepta negotia sollicite prosequenda.' Ed. Weiland, MGH, SS, XXII.397–474.

270–273: blank; 270–271 ruled.

DESCRIPTION

SIZE 29.5 x 21 cm.

QUIRING Catchwords. a^2 (pp. i–iv), I^{10}, II^{10} (pp. 21–29, 2 unnumbered pages, pp. 30–38), III–IV^{10}, V^{10} (pp. 79–95, 95*, 96–97), VI^{10}, VII^{10} (10 excised: pp. 118–135), VIII–XII^{10}, XIII^{10} (pp. 236–240, 242–248, 250–256), XIV^{10} (9 excised, 10 stuck down on to binding: pp. 257–264, 266–273).

PRICKING Visible for boundary-lines only.

RULING Single column of 38 lines. Ruling above top written line.

SCRIPT Humanist minuscule of the Caroline type. Pierced **t**, round **s** even medially but tall form also, round **d** as well as straight-backed form. Ascenders have plain tops or small approach strokes. **e** often suspended by '. **g** constructed of sigma-shape with rightward hooked tail.

DECORATION In same hand as Oxford, New College, MS. 228 (dated 1452) and Oxford, St John's College, MS. 98: Pacht & Alexander, *Illuminated Manuscripts*, III.94. Major capitals have letter in raised gold (or silver) on solid ground of purple-brown and blue (quartered) and speckled with groups of three white dots. Opening capital (p. 1) similar but inside letter, detailed painting of winged ox lying on a book; elaborate leafy flourishes in margins. Rubrics in strange red capitals, apparently imitating Rustic Capitals, but letters are frequently barred. Minor capitals in plain blue or red.

HISTORY

English binding *ca* 1465 by 'Scales' binder I: Hunt *et al.*, *A Summary Catalogue of the Western Manuscripts in the Bodleian*, I.572.

Fo 1, erased inscription 'Garde Iolye quod Brugge'. Also 'quod Brugge' in Secretary hand after final rubric of HRB (p. 134) and final flyleaf (p. 274) with sketch of coat of arms and in sixteenth-century Secretary hand 'arma Brugge' and ?'R. du Brugge', later Bridges family: Pacht & Alexander, *Illuminated Manuscripts*, III.94. Laud's *ex-libris* foot of fo 1.

BIBLIOGRAPHY

Coxe, *Catalogi codicum manuscriptorum Bibliothecæ Bodleianæ, Partis II, fasciculus I*, col. 414.

Hunt *et al.*, *A Summary Catalogue of Western Manuscripts in the Bodleian*, I.64.

Pacht & Alexander, *Illuminated Manuscripts*, III.94, no. 1090.

148 *OXFORD, BODLEIAN LIBRARY, MS. LAUD MISC. 592 (*S.C.* 1388)

Saec. xii*med.*/2   Mediaeval provenance:
7 fos   2nd fo: *Festinantes itaque nuntii*

HRB

§103 'pugnare incepisset' – 'patuerat. Securi igitur' §120 (*med.*). Dedicatory section absent.
No extant rubrics or book-divisions.
No other contents.

DESCRIPTION

SIZE 25.3 x 17.5 cm. Trimmed quite close to text.
QUIRING Stitching between fos 5 and 6 suggesting I^{10} (lacking ?8–10). Fos 38–44 of a larger volume.
PRICKING Trimmed away.
RULING Two columns of 40 lines. Central margin generally divided.
SCRIPT Large, regular, four-line Protogothic minuscule. Brown ink. Little lateral compression. Practice varies between hands. In first, *et*-nota is more usual than ampersand, final round **d** and round **s** occur, though rare. In second, ampersand and straight-backed **d** are standard, final round **s** is found, **t** has short diagonal stroke at right end of cross-stroke. e-caudata occurs in both hands.
DECORATION Large Romanesque capitals in faded red and green, occasionally with split shafts or filigree decoration in contrasting colour.

HISTORY

1v, Laud's *ex-libris* with the date 1635.

BIBLIOGRAPHY

Coxe, *Catalogi codicum manuscriptorum Bibliothecæ Bodleianæ, Partis II, fasciculus I*, col. 421.

East, 'Manuscripts', p. 483.

Hunt *et al.*, *A Summary Catalogue of Western Manuscripts in the Bodleian*, I.60.

149 *OXFORD, BODLEIAN LIBRARY, MS. LAUD MISC. 664 (*S.C.* 1048)

Saec. xiv   Origin: ?S. England
115 fos   2nd fo (3r): *dirutis meniis in desertis locis*

HRB 2r–115v
§§1–3, 5–151 (*in.*), 161 (*in.*)–199. 'Merlinus iste' interpolation after §117.
Dedicated to Robert of Gloucester.
Rubrics above §1 (2r) 'Incipit edicio Galfridi Mo\ne/mutensis de gestis Britonum.
Prologus', at §5 (2v) 'Descripcio Britannie', §111 (64r) 'Liber .vii. de prophetia
Merlini'.
Book-divisions: I §6 (3r), II §23 (13r), III §35 (21r), V §73 (40v), VI §89 (50r), VII
'Prologus' §109 (63v), VII §111 (64r), VII (*sic*) §118 (72r), VIII §143 (87r), IX §163
(92v), X §177 (104v).
Prophecies §§112–114 glossed. Text double-spaced for this purpose on 64v–66r.
Lacuna between foot 91v (§151 'Scotorum populo petiuit rex') and top 92r (§161
'Dicendi fuerat').
Text is broken off foot 115v 'in haec uerba clamarent'.

CONTENTS
1r: blank.
1v: in hand similar to that of HRB. 'Rex Eluredus et beatus Neotus fratres fuerunt
... et ipsa sancta Edburga sponsa Iesu Christi.' Similar note found in Bodley 451 (*S.C.*
2401), fo 120. Printed by Braswell, 'Saint Edburga of Winchester', p. 304, n. 53.
1v: in two columns 'Nomina regum Anglorum'. 'Aldredus pater Aluredi ... Haraldus
qui perdidit Angliam regnum .ix. mensibus.'
2r–115v: HRB.

DESCRIPTION
SIZE 19 x 13.5 cm.
QUIRING Tightly bound, some stitching visible. Conjectural reconstruction only. No
catchwords. a singleton (fo 1), I–III^8, IV ?^{8}, V ?^{10}, VI–VIII ?^{10}, IX ?^{6}, X ?^{8}, XI^8, XII^{10},
XIII ?^{2}, XIV^8.
PRICKING All trimmed away.
RULING Single column of 28 lines with double vertical boundary-lines. Written
below top ruled line. Double line at edge of lower and outer margins.
SCRIPT Gothic bookhand with lozenged minims but roundness in other letters like
b, **g**, round **d**, and round **s**. Nearly two-line but round **d** is a three-line letter. Ampersand
and *et*-nota; two-compartment **a** constructed of vertical strokes joined by cross-
strokes; pierced **p** and **t**; x has hairline bar. Tall s is found. 2-shaped **r** broken.
DECORATION Elaborate at book-divisions: letter (blue and red) is filled with leaf
pattern left in reserve and is filigreed. Otherwise capitals are large and plain.

HISTORY
Nunnaminster or Pershore origin suggested on basis of reference to Edburga (1v) but
rejected by Ker: *Medieval Libraries*, p. 384.
Laud's usual *ex-libris* inscription is on 2r and is dated 1633.

Note on 40r in hand of Archbishop Ussher: Hunt, *apud* Coxe, *Catalogi codicum manuscriptorum Bibliothecæ Bodleianæ, partis II, fasciculus I*, col. 577.

BIBLIOGRAPHY

Coxe, *Catalogi codicum manuscriptorum Bibliothecæ Bodleianæ, partis II, fasciculus I*, col. 421.

Hunt *et al.*, *A Summary Catalogue of Western Manuscripts in the Bodleian*, I.44.

150 *OXFORD, BODLEIAN LIBRARY, MS. LAUD MISC. 720 (*S.C.* 1062)

Saecc. xiii² + xiii/xiv   Provenance (seventeenth-century): Durham
251 fos   2nd fo: *Item post eum regnauit*

HRB 3r–133a r
§§1–3, 5–208 [§§109–110 'Pudibundus Brito', §§42–43, 95 compressed]. Dedicated to Robert of Gloucester.
Rubrics at §1 (3r) 'Incipit prologus in historia Brittonum. 19', §5 (3v) 'Explicit prologus. Incipit hystoria Brittonum', §8 'Pandraso regi' (5r) 'Littera', §109 (69r) 'Incipit prologus de prophetia Merlini', §111 (69v) 'Incipit prophetia Merlini', no final rubrics. Many rubrics at chapter-divisions.

CONTENTS
1r–2r: 'Nomina regum a Bruto primo rege Britonum in Britannia regnancium. . .'. From Brutus to Cadwaladr. Same script as HRB.
2v: blank except for scribbles.
3r–133a r: HRB.
133a v–133b v: blank.
134r/v: in same hand as HRB, notes to readers of Giraldus Cambrensis marked 'Lectori'. 'Leccio certa prodest uaria delectat. Si ergo legendo proficere queris . . . et stilus elegancios inuenitur.'
134v–137v: 'Introitus in recitacionem', prologue to following work. 'Consideranti mihi quam breuis et fluxa sit uita . . . nobile laudetur ocium inter negocia multa.'
137v–244r: 'Incipiunt capitula libri Giraldi Kambrensis de mirabilibus Hybernie' followed by prefatory letter (142v) and text (143v). 'In tres particulas libellus iste distinguitur . . . ignem accendens.' Text 'Hibernia post Brittanniam insularum maxima . . . quicquid a tanta maiestate fuerit iniunctum'. Ed. Dimock, *apud* Brewer *et al.* (edd.), *Giraldi Cambrensis Opera*, V.9–204 (this manuscript discussed *ibid.*, V.xxv–xxvi, late edition).
244v: blank.

245r–249r: in Anglicana hand (early fourteenth-century), excerpts concerning Scotland taken from various chronicles with note (at foot of 249r) 'Ista autem peticio proposita fuit in Gallico in presentia regis et multorum de utroque regno'. 'Anno Domini nongentesimo primo. Edwardus monarcha cognomento senior filius Alusedi (*sic*) . . . de consilio uestro ad iusticiam faciendam et seruandam.'

249v: 'Carta Ric[ardi] regis de regno Scocie', to archbishops, bishops, counts, barons, *ministri*, etc. 'Ric[ardus] Dei gratia rex Anglie . . .' 'Sciatis nos karissimo sanguineo nostro Willelmo . . . et heredibus nostris. Testibus hiis Baldeuino archiepiscopo et ceteris archiepiscopis et episcopis et multis aliis.' Ed. Stones, *Anglo-Scottish Relations*, pp. 12–17.

250v: poem (fifteenth-century hand) 'Miles amat lepores'. Walther, *Proverbia*, II.886, no. 14839. Note 'Qui cupit alterius oculo depon[ere] labem Primitus ex proprio depulat ipse trabem'.

251–252: blank except for scribbles.

DESCRIPTION

SIZE 20 x 13.5 cm.

QUIRING I^2 (1–2), II–VIII^8, IX^{12} (+ 1 after 1: 59–71), X–XVI^8, XVII^8 (8 excised: 128–134), XVIII^8 (one cancelled from first half of quire: 135–141), XIX–XXIII^8, XXIV^{10} (?10 lacking: 182–190), XXV^8 (191–198), XXVI–XXX^8, XXXI^6 (239–244); XXXII–XXXIII^4.

PRICKING At outer edges only.

RULING Single column of 25 lines in HRB, 26 in Giraldus. Written below top ruled line, single vertical boundary-lines. Additions (245r onwards) in similar format but 22–27 lines.

SCRIPT HRB in shaded semi-quadrata with short ascenders and descenders. Two-compartment **a** usually, with pinched top; pierced **t**; crossed *et*-nota. Round **d** is standard but straight-backed form occurs, round **s** is used finally. 2-shaped **r** is used. Juncture of **e** and **o** after **b**, **d**, **h**, **p**, even initial **u**. Fusion of other rounded letters: **ba**, **da**, **ha**, **ce**, **co**, **oe**. Brown ink. Giraldus similar. Scottish material in dark brown ink, four-line Anglicana. Split and looped ascenders and heavy vertical strokes. **a** is above minim-height. Minims difficult to distinguish. Long **r**. Apparently written before the mid-fourteenth century.

DECORATION HRB and Giraldus have unfiligreed blue or red capitals with red rubrics. Filigree on opening capital, however, and alternate red and green flourishes along margin. Giraldus has illustrations of *mirabilia* in colour with ink details. Some excised. See Pacht & Alexander, *Illustrated Manuscripts*, III.43, no. 462.

HISTORY

On 2v in seventeenth-century hand 'Augustini Lindsill ex dono amicissimi Antonii Maxton'. Augustine Lindsell (*ob*. 1634), later bishop of Hereford, was, like Laud, a chaplain of Richard Neile, bishop of Durham, who made him a prebendary of that see in 1619. Lindsell's name is found in six Laudian manuscripts, five from Durham given by Antony Maxton, prebendary of Durham: Hunt, *apud* Coxe, *Catalogi codicum manuscriptorum Bibliothecœ Bodleianœ, Pars II*, pp. x–xi. Durham mediaeval provenance rejected by Ker, *Medieval Libraries*, p. 76, and Ker & Watson, *Medieval Libraries*, p. 34. Laud's *ex-libris* with date, 1633, on 3r.

BIBLIOGRAPHY

Coxe, *Catalogi codicum manuscriptorum Bibliothecœ Bodleianœ, Pars II*, cols 511–12.

Hunt *et al.*, *A Summary Catalogue of Western Manuscripts in the Bodleian*, I.45.

151 *OXFORD, BODLEIAN LIBRARY, MS. NEW COLLEGE 276

Saec. xiii[1]   Mediaeval provenance: Belle-Perche (Cistercian),
                                               diocese of Montauban, France
136 fos (+ 63*)   2nd fo: [*uberta*]-*te glebe temporibus suis*

HRB 1r–136r
§§1–3, 5–208 [§§83–84, 173–174, 179, 184 compressed]. Nameless dedication.
No opening rubric, but in late mediaeval textura at foot of 1r, 'Ystoria Bruti primi
regis Britannie Maioris id est Anglie modo'.
Only original rubric after §208 (136r), 'Explicit'.
No book-divisions.
No other contents.

DESCRIPTION
SIZE 19 x 13 cm.
QUIRING I–VII^8, VIII^8 (57–63, 63*), IX–XIII^8, XIV^6 (104–109), XV–XVII^8, XVIII^4
(4 lacking: 134–136). Catchwords.
PRICKING In outer margin only.
RULING 1–81r in single column of between 22–30 written lines. 81v–136r in double
column of 24–27 written lines. Written below top ruled line, single vertical bound-
ary-lines.
SCRIPT Weak brown ink. Script similar throughout but change of hand 81v, coincid-
ing with change of format. Wide nib for size of script, producing simple strokes.
Four-line bookhand. In first hand straight-backed **d** still frequent, final **s** usually round
but also tall. Round **d** standard in second hand, juncture of **do**, final high **s**. No
substantial lateral compression or angularity in either hand.
DECORATION Blue or red capitals with fairly elaborate filigree in red or violet.
Capitals within text sometimes given ink flourishes. Some filigree in shape of fantastic
creatures (as on 67r).

HISTORY
Written in pale brown ink along outer edge of 1r in ?thirteenth-century textura
(possibly contemporary with manuscript's production), 'Liber monasterii belle per-
tice'. *Bella Pertica* is the Cistercian abbey Belle-Perche, founded in 1143, daughter
of Clairvaux, in diocese of Montauban, Tarn-et-Garonne: Cottineau, *Répertoire*, I,
cols 332–33.
Top 1r, in ?sixteenth-century hand, 'Thome Martini liber'. Thomas Martyn, master in
chancery, bequeathed the book to New College in 1584: Emden, *A Biographical
Register of the University of Oxford A.D. 1501 to 1540*, p. 735.

BIBLIOGRAPHY
Coxe, *Catalogus codicum manuscriptorum qui in collegiis aulisque Oxoniensibus
hodie adservantur*, I.7, p. 97.

152 *OXFORD, BODLEIAN LIBRARY, MS. ORIEL COLLEGE 16

Saec. xv[1]   Mediaeval provenance:
ii + 232 fos   2nd fo: *De Brendano Hibn.*

HRB 9v–48vb
§§1–3, 5, 12 (*med.*) –208. Dedicated to Robert of Gloucester.
No opening rubric but after §208 (48rb) 'Explicit historia Brittonum'.
Book-divisions: II §23 (12v), V §111 (29v), VI §118 (31v).
Text missing after end of §5 which finishes 9vb. 10r begins 'inuenirem quos ad liberandum' (§12).
Followed by *mirabilia* as in Cambridge, Sidney Sussex College, MS. 75 and Madrid, Biblioteca Nacional MS. 6319. Final rubric to HRB follows them.

CONTENTS
Flyleaves formed of nineteenth-century notes on this manuscript by 'Mr Petrie of Stockwell' bound in.
1r–8ra: reference tables to accompany Higden's *Polichronicon* (as in BL Royal 13.D.i). 'Abraham, Adon dux Israel . . . Zerobabel.'
8rb: note on ages of the world as in BL Royal 13.D.i. 'Prima etas seculi ab Adam usque ad diliuium (*sic*) . . . secundum uerissimos .v.cxcvi..' 'Nota de etatibus secundum cursum libr..' Brief list of ages of world with chapter references to *Polichronicon*, in different fifteenth-century hand.
8v–9r: blank but frame-ruled.
9v–48rb: HRB.
48va/b: following HRB is list of *mirabilia*. 'Post diluuium tribus filiis Noe orbem terrarum parcientibus in tres partes . . . ut magnum uel paruum inuenitur.'
50r–222r: 'Prologus primus in historiam policronica'. 'Post preclaros arcium scriptores . . . sub anno gracie millesimo ccc.xliiii. per ?iusiones per papam factas cessauit.'
222r–230vb: continuation to A.D. 1377. 'Et ne quis deinceps tales promissione afferret . . . unus puer .viii. annorum.' Cf. BL Royal 13.D.i (but compared by Coxe with that in Cambridge, Corpus Christi College, MS. 147: *Catalogus codicum manuscriptorum qui in collegiis aulisque Oxoniensibus hodie adservantur*, I.5, p. 6).
231: blank stub.
232r/v: blank except for unimportant note on recto (?fifteenth-century).

DESCRIPTION
SIZE 35 x 24.5 cm.
QUIRING Paper flyleaves. a⁸ (1–8), I¹² (9–18: two lacking from first half of quire), II–XIV¹², XV¹² (lacks 1: 175–185), XVI–XVIII¹², XIX ?¹² (no. 11 is unnumbered stub, 10 cut down: fos 222–232). Catchwords.
PRICKING For frame-ruling.
RULING Frame only, for two columns. 53–55 lines written.
SCRIPT Grey-brown ink. Fairly angular formalised cursive. Quite rapid. Some angularity in round **d**, **o**, but not **g**. Long or short **r**, uncrossed *et*-nota, pierced **t**. **e** resembles a pinched **c** or has cursive loop form. Simple round **a**. No heavy slanting descenders.

Ascenders turn down at top. First quire in more shaded and formal script with crossed *et* and less cursive form of **e**. Similar to remainder, however.

DECORATION Blue capitals in square of red filigree. Empty half-lines are often filled with pattern in red. Capitals larger and more deliberate in first quire.

BIBLIOGRAPHY

Coxe, *Catalogus codicum manuscriptorum qui in collegiis aulisque Oxoniensibus hodie adservantur*, I.5, p. 6.

153 *OXFORD, BODLEIAN LIBRARY, MS. RAWLINSON B.148 (*S.C.* 11519)

Saec. xiii *med.*   Mediaeval provenance:
88 fos   2nd fo: *Ibi cum a Latino rege*

HRB 1ra–88rb
§§1–3, 5–108, 111–208. Dedicated to Robert of Gloucester.
Rubrics after §3 (1rb) 'Incipit primus liber de situ et regibus Britannie qui prius eam inhabitauerunt', §108 (46r) 'Uerba Merlini', §111 (46v) 'Incipiunt uaticinia Merlini coram Uortegirno rege edita'.
Book-divisions: II §35 (16ra).
Other contemporary notes. Top 1r 'Presens huic operi sit gratia [. . .]ncupinatis aliut'. After §208 (88vb) 'Librum scribendo compleui fine iocundo / Promisso precio sum dignus iure peracto', first and last lines of verses found in Cambridge, St John's College, MS. G.16 and (Paris, BN lat. 4999A +) Manchester, John Rylands University Library, MS. lat. 216: *Colophons*, VI.398, no. 22509. Interpolation after §5 (1vb) 'Anno ante incarnationem Domini .m.c.lvii. et ante condicionem Rome . . . annis peractis'. Also found in Cambridge, St John's College, MS. G.16, Glasgow, UL 331, and London, BL Cotton Vespasian E.x.
No other contents.

DESCRIPTION
SIZE 16.5 x 11 cm.
QUIRING Tightly bound. I–II[10], III[12], IV[10], V[16] (43–58), VI[8] (59–66), VII[14] (67–80), VIII ?[8] (unnumbered stub after 8: 81–88).
No catchwords, one signature .iii. foot 32v.
PRICKING None extant.
RULING Two columns of 28 written lines. Written below top ruled line; single vertical boundary-lines.
SCRIPT Very balanced and regular, ? single hand. Brown ink. Round s initially and in abbreviations; final s is tall or high. Double-barred *et*-nota. Juncture of **e** and **o** after **b, d, p**, but not **h**. Some flat-topped ascenders. **a** generally two-compartment. **t** barely pierced.
DECORATION Red rubrics in hand of text. Blue capitals with simple red trailing filigree.

HISTORY

Notes on 88v in an antiquarian hand, listing British and English historians (Giraldus, Geoffrey, etc.), then recording events in early Anglo-Saxon period.

BIBLIOGRAPHY

Macray, *Catalogi codicum manuscriptorum Bibliothecæ Bodleianæ, Partis V, fasciculus 1*, col. 500.

154 *OXFORD. BODLEIAN LIBRARY, MS. RAWLINSON B.168
(*S.C.* **15441**)

Saec. xiii ?[1/med.]   Mediaeval provenance: ?
55 + 5 fos   2nd fo: *Erectus igitur in ducem conuocat*

HRB 1r–54v + 55r–59v

§§1–3, 5–189 'iniuit cum Brocmail'. §189 ('qui pauciori numero') –§208 supplied in eighteenth century. Dedicated to Robert of Gloucester.
No original rubrics or book-divisions.
No loss of text in §189 between 54v (end of mediaeval section) and modern supply.
Note on 55r in continuator's hand 'Continuat. e codice ueteri MS. (ad initium regni, ut uidetur, Eduardi [pri]mi in membranis exarato) misu (*sic*) mutuo dato a Guilielmo Beckett chirurgo Abingtoniensi Sept. 19. 1730'. Beckett's manuscript unidentified. No other contents extant. HRB preceded by number of paper flyleaves, blank except for first recto (see HISTORY).

DESCRIPTION

SIZE 23.5 x 16 cm.
QUIRING I[10], II[14], III[8], IV[8] (8 lacking: 33–39), V[8] (8 lacking: 40–46), VI[8]; VII[8] (7 blank, 8 stuck down: 55–59). Q. VII (eighteenth-century) in paper.
PRICKING At outer edges.
RULING Single column of 32/33–36 written lines. Single vertical boundary-lines; written below top ruled line. Supply has ruling for margins only. 35–42 lines written.
SCRIPT Several hands, black/dark brown ink.
First hand is angular and compact. Tops of minims lozenged. Occasional two-compartment **a**. Some juncture of **e** and **o** after **d** and **p**. Pierced **t**, crossed *et* or ampersand, tall, high or round s finally (round usual). Other hand smaller with less juncture, final tall s, ampersand and crossed *et* but some tagged ascenders. Another hand with similar usage to first, compressed and spiky; no juncture of **p**, however. Supply in small script with long **r**, simple minuscule **a** and **e**, and looped ascenders. Many ligatures.
DECORATION Mostly plain blue or red capitals. Some with ink filigree.

HISTORY

On recto of first paper flyleaf 'Suum cuique Tho. Hearne Maii 21 M.DCC.XXII. Ex dono amici pereruditi Richardi Graves, de Mickleton prope Campden in agro Gloucestriensi armigeri Galfridus Monumethensis sed mancus ad finem'. Beneath, in hand

243

of continuator 'I have since perfected it from another MS. in the hands of Mr. Wm. Beckett of Abbington, Berks.'.

BIBLIOGRAPHY

Macray, *Catalogi codicum manuscriptorum Bibliothecæ Bodleianæ, partis V, fasciculus*, col. 513.

155 *OXFORD, BODLEIAN LIBRARY, MS. RAWLINSON B.189 (*S.C.* 11550)

Saec. xiv *ex.* or later   Mediaeval provenance: Hatfield Peverell,
                                                                        Essex (Benedictine)
i + 181 fos (no fo 138, adds 26*, 141*)   2nd fo: *Euolutis a mundi*

HRB 4r–117v
§§1–3, 5–56, 57–208. Dedicated to Robert of Gloucester.
No opening or closing rubrics. At §110 (59r) 'Incipit prologus de prophecia Merlini', §111 (59v) 'Explicit prologus. Incipit prophecia eiusdem'.
Book-divisions: II §23 (13r), V §73 (36v), VI §89 (46v), VIII §143 (80v).

CONTENTS
i: blank except for note (on verso) glossing Latin place-names, '[ ] North Wales, Demecia South Wales, Neustria Normannia . . .', etc.
1r/v: (cf. 119 ff.) 'De antiquis urbibus Britannie'. 'Regio Britannie quondam fuit .xxviii. nobilissimis ciuitatibus insignita . . . in confinio Loegrie et Kambrie. Salopia.'
2r–3r: On the settlement of Britain. 'Euolutis a mundi constitucione tribus millibus nongentis saxaginta (*sic*) et decem annorum circulis . . . producat terra animam uiuentem.' Cf. Cambridge, University Library, MS. Dd.6.7.
3v: blank except for *ex-libris*; see below.

4r: 'Littere quas misit Arturus inuictus rex Britannie Hugoni capellano de Branno super sequanam cum palefrido'. 'Arturus Dei gratia . . . pro dignitate tue promocionis famulabitur.' Same occurs as interpolation in HRB in Bodley 233 and as preface (as here) in Aberystwyth, NLW Llanstephan 196, and Würzburg, Universitätsbibliothek, MS. M.ch.f.140.
4r–117v: HRB.
117v–119r: Eagle of Shaftesbury version of Prophecy of Merlin. 'Sicut rubeum draconem albus expelleret . . . iniuriam qui pacificato regno occidet.' In same hand as HRB. Ed. Schulz, *Gottfried*, p. 464–65.
119r–180v: 'Incipit liber quem composuit uenerabilis Beda presbiter de gestis Anglorum quem scribi fecit Will.s de Writele' (this name cancelled and in same hand in margin is added 'Iohannis Bebset quondam prior de Hatffeld Peuere[ll] ad utilitatem legentium cuius anime propicietur Deus') – extracts from Bede's Ecclesiastical History, prefaced by *capitula*-list. Text (119v) 'Anno ab incarnacione Domini centesimo quinquagesimo sexto Antonius cognomento uerus . . . sed breuitatem sermonis

in eruditio lingue facit'. Ends with Cuthbert, *De obitu Bede*, ed. Dobbie, *The Manuscripts of Caedmon's Hymn*, pp. 119–27 (see also *ibid.*, p. 92). See Colgrave & Mynors, *Bede's Ecclesiastical History*, p. lx; Laistner & King, *A Handlist*, p. 99. The whole in smaller and later-looking hand.

DESCRIPTION

SIZE 27.5 x 19 cm.

QUIRING a⁴ (?4 cancelled: fos 1–3), I⁸ (4–11), II⁸, III⁸ (20–26, 26*), IV–XVI⁸, XVII⁸ (131–137, 139), XVIII⁸ (140–141, 141*, 142–146), XIX–XXII⁸, XXIII² (179–180). Catchwords. HRB volume (QQ. I–XVI) extended at both ends in fifteenth century, resulting in present arrangement.

PRICKING At outer edge.

RULING One column throughout. HRB and Prophecies of Merlin written in 35 lines, starting below top ruled line. Bede and fos 1–4 frameruled with variable number of lines (34–48).

SCRIPT HRB in very large, heavy script (brown ink). Version of informal Gothic script but written with wide-nibbed pen and so given formal, shaded appearance. Lines closely packed. f and tall s sometimes descend below the line. Round s (sigma-shaped) found initially. Round d, two-compartment a, short r. No juncture. Minims upright with small approach-strokes, not lozenged. Tops of ascenders looped over. 2-shaped r has descending hairline. Round d and looped two-compartment a. Uncrossed loop-form of *et*-nota. Additions in four-line script, watery grey ink. Tops of ascenders turned down, angular g and d (round). Simple round form of a. Fos 1–3 in hand different from that of 119–179 (Bede) but similar script.

DECORATION Blue capitals with trailing red filigree in both phases of book.

HISTORY

Note at top of 1r 'Hic liber reppertur (*sic*) in monasterio S. Albani 1537'. Inscription on 3v, 'Liber prioratis de Hatfeld. Peuerell. Ex dono domini Iohannis Bebseth. De licencia Willelmi abbatis'. The abbot in question would be William Heyworth, abbot of St Albans 1401–20: Ker, *Medieval Libraries*, p. 267. Benedictine priory of Hatfield Peverell, Essex, was a cell of St Albans.

Note on 3r in hand of Sir John Prise: Colgrave & Mynors, *Bede's Ecclesiastical History*, p. lx. ?Same hand found in margins of 1r and 178r.

BIBLIOGRAPHY

Macray, *Catalogi codicum manuscriptorum Bibliothecæ Bodleianæ, partis V, fasciculus 1*, col. 524.

156 *OXFORD, BODLEIAN LIBRARY, MS. RAWLINSON C.152
(*S.C.* 12016)

Saecc. (xiii + xiii *ex.* +) xii *med.*   Mediaeval provenance: ?
i + 98 + 82 + i fos   2nd fo (original lost): *Et enim uenientes*
    2nd fo: *quem sexum puella concepisset*

HRB 99r–182v.

§§1–3, 5–190 (*in.*), 193 (*in.*) –203 (*ex.*) [109–110 in *pudibundus Brito* form]. Dedicated to Robert of Gloucester.

Rubrics at §1 (99r) 'Gaufridi Mon\u/tensis de gestis Britonum secundum Caratonum editio (*sic*)', §5 (99r) 'Explicit prefac[ ]. Liber incipit primus', §111 (145v) 'Prophetie Merlini Britonis', §158 'Lucius rex' (166r) 'Epistola Lucii Tiberii'.

Book-divisions: I §5 (99r), II §54 (120r), III §109 (145r).

Two leaves lacking from final quire, resulting in loss of text between 178v (ends 'pacto pacem inter' §190) and 179r (begins 'per Albaniam itinere' §193). Breaks off at foot of 182v §203 'Britannia ira Dei deserta quam uos'.

CONTENTS

Parchment flyleaf: on verso, fourteenth-century note concerning first item.

1r–14v: part of *Testamenta duodecim patriarcharum*, imperfect at both ends. 'Benedixit omnes sanctos ab Abel usque nunc . . . et habitauerunt in Egypto usque ad diem exitus eorum ex terra Egypti.'

15r–98v: 'Incipit hystoria Ierosolimitana abbreuiata. cap. .i. Cur Dominus terram sanctam flagellis et sub alternis casibus exposuit' (rubric on 16v). 15r–16v *capitula*-list. Text 16v–98v 'Terra sancta promissionis Deo amabilis . . . de die in diem expectantes'. Jacques de Vitry, *Historia orientalis*. Ed. Bongars, *Gesta Dei per Francos*, I.ii.1049–1124.

99r–182v: HRB.

Final flyleaf (183) with notes and verses on recto in hands of *ca* 1300 (religious) and 1400 (historical).

DESCRIPTION

SIZE 30 x 16.5 cm.

QUIRING 3 units, of which the last (HRB) is the oldest. HRB has some signatures (beginning .III. on 115r), catchwords, and separate late mediaeval foliation. a ?⁴ (2–4 excised), I ?⁸ (1–4 lacking: 1–4), II¹² (11–12 lacking: 5–14); III–IX¹² (marked by catchwords); I–X⁸, XI ?⁶ (+ 1 before 1, 5–6 lacking: 179–183).

PRICKING Visible in outer margin in all parts of volume.

RULING Single column throughout. HRB has double vertical boundary-lines, 38–39 lines, starting below top ruled line; drypoint ruling in places. A and B have 37 lines, single boundary-lines and ruling above top line.

SCRIPT HRB in tall, four-line Protogothic minuscule with almost Caroline aspect. Lines well spaced and letters separated. Small flat tops to ascenders. Brown ink. Round s found occasionally, in medial or final position. Only straight-backed d used in one hand, but round form as well occurs elsewhere. Ampersand is usual and e-caudata is used but not always correctly. Formality breaks down from 181v with the appearance of a more irregular and angular hand. Round d is found as well as the straight form; *et*-nota is used; script maintains four- line proportions and spacing of letters.

A and B in formal Gothic bookhand. A is more monoline, more disjointed and less two-line than B and lacks juncture. t is pierced and a occasionally has two-compartment form. B later in aspect with heavy upright strokes and tagged tops to ascenders, same forms of **a** and **t** as in A, but flat top on double **l**. Juncture of **e** and **o** after **b**, **d**, and **p**. Final **s** occasionally tall. Crossed *et*-nota. Round **d** with long ascender. DECORATION HRB has large Romanesque capitals (3–6 lines deep) in red. Some split shafts or bosses. A and B have filigreed capitals (blue, red) but in A they are less skilfully decorated.

BIBLIOGRAPHY

Macray, *Catalogi codicum manuscriptorum Bibliothecæ Bodleianæ, partis V, fasciculus 2*, col. 63.

157   *OXFORD, BODLEIAN LIBRARY, MS. RAWLINSON D.893 fos 27–28 (*S.C.* 13659)

Saec. xiii[1]   Mediaeval provenance:
2 fos

HRB 27r–28r

§§178 (*ex.*) –181 (*ex.*), 183 (*in.*) –184, 186 (*med.*)–(*ex.*), 206 (*med.*) –208.
'Explicit' after §208 (28r).
?Outer bifolium of quire. 27r §178 'Aschillus [ ] Dacie rex . . . regnum [ ] que regni' §181. 27v §183 'robustus armis . . . exaltacione transtulero' §186. 28r §206 'ut uideret si reuelatio' –208. Leap in text mid-page on 27v from end of §184 'patebat' to 186 (*med.*) 'Successerunt quo Britonum'.

CONTENTS

28v: part of *Prophetie Merlini*, HRB §§111–112.4 scarcely legible now. '[Ita?]que Uortigirno . . . tempora super eneum . . ..' Last line illegible. Part of volume of very miscellaneous fragments of many different sizes.

DESCRIPTION

SIZE 14.5 x 10 cm. Trimmed down with some loss of text.
PRICKING Trimmed away.
QUIRING Conjugate leaf, perhaps outer bifolium of quire.
RULING Single column of 34 lines extant; about 4–5 lines lost.
SCRIPT Rather crude minuscule with little lateral compression. Brown ink. Uncrossed *et*-nota, round **d** and final tall or high **s** standard. No juncture, piercing of **t**, or two-compartment **a**, but aspect suggests thirteenth-century date. Small size accounts for lack of juncture.
DECORATION Single crude ink capital without filigree.

HISTORY

Note in fifteenth-century hand on final flyleaf of volume 'It[em] recepi a Ioh[ann]e'. Collection prefaced by letter of 28.4.1731 from Robert New of the Middle Temple to Thomas Hearne sent to accompany the bundle of fragments which presumably now form this volume, and were originally owned by John Le Neve.

BIBLIOGRAPHY

Macray, *Catalogi codicum manuscriptorum Bibliothecæ Bodleianæ, partis V, fasciculus 4*, cols 75–87.

158 *OXFORD, BODLEIAN LIBRARY, MS. TANNER 195 (*S.C.* 10021)

Saec. xiv   Mediaeval provenance: English
iii + 4–139 fos   2nd fo: gone. Present 2nd folio mutilated

HRB 4–98r
Beginning mutilated (fos 4 and 5 tiny fragments of parchment); text from 6r. §36 'copiam Norguenwensium' –§208. Dedicatory section lost.
No extant rubrics or book-divisions.

CONTENTS
i–iii: blank except for contents-list on verso of iii in ?fourteenth-century hand. 'Contenta huius libri sunt h[ec] subscripta. In ?primo cronica uersificata de gestis Edwardi. Penitentiale. magistri Roberti de Flamesborogh. Quidam tractatus de a. uiciis. Secreta secretorum Aristotilis ad Alexandrum. Quidam tractatus imperfectus de ?confessione. Hugo de Vienna de ?penitentia. Cronica de gestis Bruti et aliorum regum Britannie. Constituciones domini Roberti Lincoln. episcopi'. Volume now very imperfect.
4r–98r: HRB.
98r–100r: 'Quo tempore Saxones siue Angli uenerunt in Britanniam', from Ralph of Diceto. 'Tempore Uortigerni regis Britones crebro afflicti . . . et eorum regna dominio suo subiecerunt.' Described by Hardy, *Descriptive Catalogue*, II.234.
100va–102va: lists of kings of the Anglo-Saxon Heptarchy (Wessex, Kent, Essex, Northumbria, Anglia, Mercia, Sussex). 'Reges Westsexie Cerdicnis .xvii. . . . . Edelwoldus.'
102va–128v: 'Uide lector et perpende quanta nomina quam cito ad nichilum deuenerunt . . . igitur accepit rex.' Ends mid-page. Rest of verso blank.
129r–138r: 'Ici commencerent le Bretons a regner. Ces sunt les noms des roys bretons ke primes furent en Bretanie le grande ke ore est apele Engletere'. 'Deuant la natiuite nostre seygnour . . . sun fiz ke nasqui en Gales.' From French Brut Chronicle: Vising, *Anglo-Norman Language and Literature*, pp. 66–67 and p. 93.

DESCRIPTION
SIZE 23 x 16.5 cm.
QUIRING a⁴ (4 lacking: i–iii), I (4 singletons: 4–7), II–XI¹² , XII (3 mounted singletons: 128–130), XIII ?⁸ (8 mutil.: 131–138), b² (2 lacking). Catchwords.
PRICKING For boundary-lines only.
RULING Single column of 27 lines. Single vertical boundary-lines. Written below top ruled line. Text in two columns for king-lists on 100v–101v.
SCRIPT Large and fairly formal bookhand but no lozenging. Brown ink. Small tick on tops of minims. Two-compartment a constructed of verticals joined by hairlines.

Final **s** is high (cedilla-shaped), tall, or round. Crossed *et*-nota. Juncture of **e** and **o** after **d** and **p** and fusion of other curved letters (**co, va, ho**, etc.). In **b, h, p**, upright of letter tends to be detached from rest.

DECORATION Unfiligreed blue or red capitals.

BIBLIOGRAPHY

Hackman, *Catalogi codicum manuscriptorum Bibliothecæ Bodleianæ, Pars IV*, col. 633.

159 *OXFORD, BODLEIAN LIBRARY, MS. TOP. GEN. c. 2
(*S.C.* 3118), pp. 22–41

Saec. xvi

HRB pp. 21–41.
John Leland's precis of HRB, including some extracts. Seems to have been vulgate text.
Notes headed 'Ex libro Galfredi quem de uita Merlini Syluestris scripsit uel potius e Britannico sermone in carmen Latinum transtuli<t>'. Book-divisions marked but added by Leland, as he explains in note on p. 26 'Ex .i. cap. 2 libri Lelandus quamquam exemplar manuscriptum non habebat librorum diuisiones'. The whole printed by Hearne, *Joannis Lelandi antiquarii De rebus Britannicis collectanea*, III.17–43.

BIBLIOGRAPHY
Dumville, 'The manuscripts', p. 123.
East, 'Manuscripts', p. 484.
Hunt *et al.*, *A Summary Catalogue of Western Manuscripts in the Bodleian*, II.1, 591.

160 *OXFORD, CHRIST CHURCH, MS. 99

Saec. xiii²   Mediaeval provenance: ?
i + 260 + i fos   2nd fo: *troas reuersus est*

HRB 1r–42r
§§1–3, 5–208. Dedicated to Robert of Gloucester.
Rubrics at §1 (1r) 'Incipit prologus in gestis Bruti et ceterorum regum Britannie'. No other rubrics, no book-divisions.

CONTENTS
1r–42r: HRB.
42v: blank.

43r–46r: *Liber qui dicitur prouincialis in quo iniantur* (sic) *omnes patriarche metropolitani archiepiscopi cum eorum suffraganeis qui subsunt sacrosancte Romane ecclesie* (from final rubric). 'In ciuitate Romana sunt quinque [ ] que patriarchales dicuntur . . . archiepiscopatus Colocensis qui dicitur Bodo nullum habet suffraganeum.' Compare Miraeus, *Notitia episcopatuum*, pp. 65–91.

46v–50v: 'Quoniam scire tempora summorum pontificum Romanorum ac imperatorum . . . ipsa autem ciuitas continuis .xxvii.'. Part of chronicle of Martinus Polonus. Ends in consulship of Lucius Censorinus and Martus Maulius, 602 years from the foundation of the city.

51r–113va: 'Incipit prephatio uenerabilis Bede presbiteri in libro ecclesiastice historie gentis Anglorum'. 'Gloriosissimo regi Ceolwlfo Beda famulus Christi et presbiter in Domino salutes . . . apud omnes fructum pie intercessionis inueniam. Amen.' Edd. Colgrave & Mynors, *Bede's Ecclesiastical History*. On this manuscript, *ibid.*, p. lvii. Rest of 113v blank.

114r/va: 'Incipit epilogium de obitu eximii doctoris Bede qui Girwinensis? monasterii presbiter extitit doctorque precipuus' (rubric written at foot of page in informal hand). '[ ]ilectissimo in Christo lectori Cuthwino Cuthbertus condiscipulus . . . inerudicio lingue facit.' Ed. Dobbie, *The Manuscripts of Caedmon's Hymn*, pp. 119–27 (this manuscript not mentioned).

114va–115ra: account of period of the conversion of the Anglo-Saxons. '[ ]n nomine Domini nostri Iesu Christi. Beatus Augustinus a beato Gregorio Romane urbis episcopo ad predicandum genti Anglorum in Britanniam missus . . . Eadbaldus rex ad laudem Dei et sui genitricis construxit.'

115rb/vb: 'He sunt notaciones de sanctis in Anglia pace? requiescunt'. '[ ]anctus Albanus prothomartir Anglorum iuxta locum qui uocatur <W>etlingacester requiescit . . . [S]ancta Mere<w>enna abbatissa in loco qui dicitur Rumesige prope amnem Taerstan requiescit.' Cf. Liebermann, *Die Heiligen Englands*, pp. 10–16.

116r–137r: 'Incipiunt secreta secretorum Aristotilis ad magnificum regem Alexandrum'. 'Domino suo excellentissimo in cultu religionis Christiane strenuissimo . . . qui dominatus fuit toto orbi dictus monarchia in septemtrione.' Ed. Steele, *Opera hactenus inedita Rogeri Baconi*, V.25–172.

137r–139r: 'Disputacio magistralis inter ducem et philosophiam de hominis cotidiana concepcione. Intencio philosophi'. 'Cum sit homo animal rationale . . . uel propter nimiam raritatem.' Herrmann, 'Un remaniement', p. 256.

139r–140v: 'Incipit tractatus Aristotilis de quatuor humoribus'. 'Elementum est simpla et mi[n]ima pars corporis . . . et humida sicut et sanguis.'

140v: 'Enplastre qest apele grace dieu'. 'Lenplastre qest apele grace dieu . . . seient reseruy a bon us e en saune garde etc.'

141r–196v: 'Incipit cronica fratris Martini penitenciarii domini pape et capellani R[omane]'. 'Quoniam scire tempora summorum pontificum Romanorum ac imperatorum . . . et animauit ad suscepta negocia sollicite prosequenda.' Ed. Weiland, MGH, SS, XXII.397–474.

196v–201vb: in two columns. '[A]lienum est omne quicquid optando euenit / [A]b alio expectes alteri quod feceris . . . Heredis fletus sub persona uisus est / Furor sit illesa sepius pac[ient]ia.' Walther, *Proverbia*, I.91, no. 789.

202r–211v: 'Factum est autem in anno quinto decimo imperii Tiberii Cesaris imperatoris Romanorum et Herodis . . . quia ipsum credimus Dei filium qui cum patre . . .', etc. Compare ed. Kim, *The Gospel of Nicodemus.*

212r–225v: series of anecdotes and exempla. '[I]n urbe Bizantea fuit quidam qui nominis sui famam uolens extendere . . . iuxta nomen Marie que sunt in terra.'

226r–260ra: 'Incipit prologus in librum de missarum officiis editum a domino Innocencio papa tercio'. 'Tria sunt in quibus precipue lex diuina consistit . . . totum continue censui subscribendum.' Ed. Migne, *Patrologia Latina*, CCXVII.773–916.

260rb: added in small glossing hand. '[ ]aborem in ludum uertit fructus consideracio . . . labor tibi non solum erit non difficilis uerum eciam fiet delectabilis.'

Flyleaf: note in fourteenth-century hand.

DESCRIPTION

SIZE 17 x 25.5 cm.

QUIRING a singleton (fo i), I^{12}, II^{14}, III^{16} (16 cut down: fos 27–42); IV^8, V $?^{14}$ (1 canc.: 51–63), VI–VIII^{12}, IX^{10}, X $?^4$ (+ two after 4: 110–115), XI–XIX^8, XX^{10} (188–197), XXI^4, XXII–XXVII^8, XXVIII^{10} (+ 1: 250–260), b singleton. Catchwords.

PRICKING In HRB in outer margins only. Same throughout except QQ. XXVII and XXVIII.

RULING HRB – two columns of 40 lines. Single vertical boundary-lines. Written below top ruled line. Layout variable elsewhere. Martinus – single column, 49 lines. Bede – two columns of 40–42 lines. Fos 116–196 – single column of 38 lines; 196v–201v – same, two columns; 202–225 – single column, 36 lines; fos 226–260 – two columns of 54 lines.

SCRIPT HRB in brown bookhand, fairly regular and small. Minims compact but not broken. Two-compartment **a**, pierced **t** except for opening few folios. Juncture of **e** and **o** after **b, d, h**. Uncrossed *et*. Final **s** round, tall, or cedilla-shaped. *Liber prouincialis* in late thirteenth-century script. Round **d** with tall ascender. Juncture following **d** and **p**. Bede in small hand of glossing type with crossed *et*-nota, some juncture. Similar to that in HRB. Brown ink. Fos 116–225 – formal version of Anglicana. Looped **d** and two-compartment **a**, small minims, long descenders, split-topped ascenders, *et*-nota sometimes crossed. Fos 226–260 – small brown thirteenth-century bookhand. Unpierced **t**, Caroline **a**. Juncture of **e** and **o** after **d, h, p**.

DECORATION Blue or red unfiligreed capitals at start of HRB, most not completed. Red capitals elsewhere except for last item (226–260) in which there are red or blue capitals, some with filigree.

BIBLIOGRAPHY

Kitchin, *Catalogus codicum manuscriptorum*, p. 44.

161 *OXFORD, MAGDALEN COLLEGE, MS. LAT. 170

Saec. xii/xiii   Mediaeval provenance: Eye, Suffolk (Benedictine)
ii + 112 + ii fos   2nd fo: *Dimicantibus ergo illis*

HRB 1r–110v

§§1–3, 5–166 (*med.*), 167 (*med.*) –170 (*med.*), 166 (*med.*) –167 (*med.*), 170 (*med.*) –208. Dedicated to Robert of Gloucester.

No original opening or closing rubrics. At §111 (56r) 'Prophetia Merlini', also at §78 (37r) 'De natiuitate Helene regine' and §88 (42r) 'Undecim milia uirginum'. No book-divisions.

Dislocation (without loss) in text after 90v (ends 'et eiusdem capite' §166). This should be followed by fos 93–94 ('amputato ad equos' §166– 'turpiter amisissent' §167). Text on 91r continues from that on 94v (begins 'nisi fortuna optatum' §167). Text on 92v continued on 95r (§170 'ex inprouiso obuiaremus' and 'atque ipsos segregatim'). Fos 91–94 constitute the central bifolia of Quire XII. The dislocation must have been caused by a copying error as it cannot be rectified by rearrangement of the leaves.

CONTENTS

i–ii: blank parchment bifolium before text with first recto pasted on to binding. College bookplate on verso of ii.

1r–110v: HRB.

111: ruled but blank except for note at foot of verso in hand close in date to that of text 'Am. confitemini Domino quoniam bonus. Am. michi autem nimis honora'.

112: not ruled. Recto blank. Verso, diagram of concentric circles (unlabelled) drawn in pencil with verses beneath in fourteenth-century Anglicana hand 'Nocte tota pluit redeunt spectacula mane . . . sic uos non uobis fertis aratra boues'. Vergilius to the Emperor Octavian. Walther, *Initia*, I.610, no. 11887.

iii–iv: parchment bifolium with last verso pasted to binding, *ex-libris* inscription on recto (see below).

DESCRIPTION

SIZE 16.5/17 x 12.5/13 cm.

QUIRING Mostly indicated by catchwords. a², I–XIV⁸, b². Some leaves scrappy – text on fos 43 and 52 written across patch stitched over hole in membrane.

PRICKING Outer margins only.

RULING Single column, 25 lines. Double vertical boundary-lines; written above top line.

SCRIPT Small minuscule (?of glossing type), nearly black ink. Juncture of **e** and **o** after **d** frequent. Ampersand and crossed *et*-nota. Final s round, tall, occasionally cedilla-shaped. Several forms of round **d**, straight-backed **d** also. Hairline flat tops on ascenders of **b, h, l. t** unpierced, no two-compartment **a**. Script has marked lateral compression towards end of volume.

DECORATION Green or red Romanesque capitals. Sometimes simple scrolled decoration in the other colour.

HISTORY

On iv r, in hand of ?late fourteenth century, 'Iste liber est monasterii beati Petri de Eye in comitat. Sowtffolch. oms. eumm. iu.[ ]' (end lost). Benedictine alien priory of St Peter, cell of Bernay: Ker, *Medieval Libraries*, p. 86. Also College shelfmark at foot of 1r. ?Seventeenth-century title at top of 1r, 'Gaufridus Monemutensis'.

BIBLIOGRAPHY

Coxe, *Catalogus codicum manuscriptorum qui in collegiis aulisque Oxoniensibus hodie adservantur*, II.2, p. 78.

162 *OXFORD, MAGDALEN COLLEGE, MS. LAT. 171

Saec. xii^2 Mediaeval provenance: Tynemouth (Benedictine), Northumberland
ii + 96 + i fos   2nd fo: *ad mare insederunt*

HRB 1r–96v

§§1–3, 5–108, 117.73–208. Dedicated to Robert of Gloucester. Rubrics at §1 (1r) '[G]alfridi Monemutensis de gestis Britonum incipit prologus', §5 (1v) 'Explicit prologus. Incipit Britannie descriptio', §6 (2r) 'Incipit liber'; no final rubric.

Book-divisions: I §6 (2r), II §23 (11r), III §35 (18r), IIII §54 (26r), V §73 (34v), VI §89 (42r), VIII §118 (35r), IX §143 (64v), X §163 (74v), IX (*sic*) §177 (84v).

Capitula-numbers marked for each chapter (in red).

Hiatus caused by excision of prophecies after 52v (§108 ends at foot). 53r begins 'Pensa libre oblique pendebat' §117.73. The excision of the prophecies may postdate the note of contents (fifteenth- or sixteenth-century) now only faintly visible on i v, which mentions the prophecies as book 7 of Geoffrey's History.

No other contents. Blank bifolium before text, with first leaf pasted to binding and college book-plate on its verso. Note on verso of ii ?*ca* 1400, 'Armorica parua Britannia. Albania id est Scocia. Uenodocia id est Northwallia. Demecia id est Suthwallia'. Blank leaf after text, pasted to binding.

DESCRIPTION

SIZE 15 x 10.2 cm.

QUIRING No quire signatures extant. a^2 (fos i–ii), I–V^{10}, VI ?^{10} (3–8 cancelled: 51–54), VII^{10}, VIII^{10} (4, 8 cancelled, no loss: 65–72), IX–X^{10}, XI ?singleton (fo 93, mounted), XII ??^{6} (?3, 5 cancelled, 6 stuck down: 94–96, iii).

PRICKING Outer edges only.

RULING Drypoint, apparently. Single column, 28 lines. Single vertical boundary-lines, written above top line.

SCRIPT Small, rather idiosyncratic, Protogothic minuscule, more than one hand. Aspect seems earlier than certain individual forms suggest. Long descenders with leftward curve, including long s and r. Uncrossed *et*-nota standard. a has small head. **de** and **do** approaching juncture. Straight-backed **d** also and tall final s. ct-ligature. e-caudata occasionally. g with large open loop.

DECORATION Romanesque capitals in red, brown or green. Some main capitals have foliage scrolls and decoration in more than one colour.

HISTORY
Provenance given by Ker & Watson, *Medieval Libraries*, p. 66.

BIBLIOGRAPHY
Coxe, *Catalogus codicum manuscriptorum qui in collegiis aulisque Oxoniensibus hodie adservantur*, II.2, p. 78.

163 PARIS, BIBLIOTHEQUE DE L'ARSENAL, MS. 982 (7.H.L)

Saec. xiv² Mediaeval provenance: Jean le Bègue (fifteenth-century)
188 fos 2nd fo: [*inhabi*]-*tat humanum genus*

HRB 168vb–188rb
§§5–108, 111–208. Dedicatory chapters absent.
Rubrics at §5 (168vb) 'Incipit hystoria Britonum ab antiquis Britonibus tracta', §6 (168vb) 'Incipit narracio', §111 (178va) ' . . . Incipit .vii. de prophetiis Merlini', after §208 (188rb) 'Explicit hystoria Britonum a Galfrido Arthuro de britannico in Latinum translata est [canc.]. Deo gracias'. Beneath, in same hand, 'Bos portat spinam de qua facit auca rapinam. quod rapit auca boui fit uitulo uel oui'.
Book-divisions: II §23 (170va), III §35 (171vb), IV §54 (173rb), V §73 (175ra), VI §90 (176va), VII §111 (178va), VIII §118 (179vb), IX §143 (182ra), X [ ], XI §?177 (185vb).
Note in margin beside §111 (178va) 'Hic deest prologus'.
First Variant Version. Wright, *siglum* R: *The Historia Regum Britannie of Geoffrey of Monmouth: II*, pp. lxxxix–xc.
The *Uera Historia de Morte Arthuri* is interpolated in its entirety between §§178 and 179: Wright, *ibid.*, p. xc; ed. Lapidge, 'An edition', pp. 79–83.

CONTENTS
1r: contents-list. Formal Gothic hand.
1ra: in two columns, informal hand. 'Gennadius auctor ait.' 'Orosius presbiter hispanus genere uir eloquens et historiarum cognitor . . . Honorio imperium tenente.'
1ra/b: 'Incipit prefaciuncula in Orosio'. 'Orosius presbiter Zaraconensis Hispanus genere . . . miraque breuitate contexuit.'
1rb–42va: 'Incipit prologus libri Orosii de ormesta mundi feliciter'. 'Paulus Horosius Aurelio episcopo salutem. Preceptis tuis parui beatissime pater Augustine . . . per te iudicanda si deleas. Amen.' Migne, *Patrologia Latina*, XXXI.663–1174.
42va: (in different hand) 'Nota quod Gelasius papa urbis Rome de Orosio sic dicit . . . miraque breuitate contexuit'.
42vb: 'Uersus de excellencia huius operis Orosii' (in same hand as preceding note). 'Hic est magnarum dictus liber historiarum . . . simus gaudentes et Christi pace fruentes. Amen.'

42vb–47vb: 'Breuem temporum per generationes et regna primus ex nostris Iulius Affricanus ... Deo fauente reperatur esse porrectum'. In same hand as 1–42va. (47vb–48vb: Isidore, *Historia Gothorum, Wandalorum et Sueuorum*. Ed. Mommsen, *Chronica minora*, II.268–303)

47vb–48ra: 'Incipit Gothorum historia fato (*sic*) edita prologus'. 'Gothorum antiquissima origo de Magog filio Iaphet fuit ... et ipsam Hispaniam uidit.'

48ra/va: 'Incipit Wandalorum historia'. 'De .cccc.xliiii. ante biennium inruptionis Romane urbis ... usque ad Gilimeri interitum.'

48va/b: 'Incipit Sueuorum cuius supra era .cccc.xlvi. Sueui principe Hemerico cum Alanis ... Quid manasse .c2xxxii. annis scribitur'.

48vb–53rb: 'Era dcx2xiiii Romanorum 2xii'. 'Eraclius imperio coronatus ... qui annorum mundi seriem conscripserunt.'

53v: blank.

54ra–111va: Chronicle of Rodrigue Ximines. 'Serenissimo et inuicto et semper augusto domino suo Fernando Dei gratia regi Castelle ... '. *Capitula*-list, 54ra–55va. Text, 56ra. 'Serenissimo et inuicto semper Augusto ... hic noluimus (*sic*) iterare.' Ed. Cabanes Pecourt, *Rodericus Ximenius*.

112v–114rb: glossary in three columns, from 'Acies. Qui honeste spiritum in acie proffundere non uult turpiter debet ... ' to 'Genitalia' (*sic*) '. ... et ingnata (*sic*) uoce iudicum tribum alia polluuntur li[ber] .vii. c. de testa.'

144v: blank.

115ra–160vb: 'Beda de gestis Anglorum' (running title). 'Gloriosissimo regi Ceoluul-fo Beda famulus Christi et presbiter ... et parere semper ante faciem tuam.' Edd. Colgrave & Mynors, *Bede's Ecclesiastical History*. (Descendant of ninth-century manuscript at Nonantola in the later Middle Ages: *ibid.*, p. lxx.)

160vb–161va: 'Incipit epistola Ieronimi ad Eugelium presbiterum. De Melchisidech'. 'Misisti michi uolumen adesnoton (*sic*) et nescio utrum tu de titulo nomen subtraxeris ... tanto nocuerit corporis ualitudini.' Epistola 73. Ed. Hilbert, *Sancti Eusebii Hieronymi Epistulae*, II.13–23.

161va–164ra: 'Incipit exp[ositi]o Bede super Tobiam'. 'Sancti patris Tobie liber et in superficie litere salubris patus patet ... Credo iudere bona dum in terra uiuencium.'

165r–168vb: 'Incipit epistola Cornelii ad Crispum Salustium in Troianorum hystoria que in Greco a Darete hystoriagrapho facta est. Cornelius Gayo Crispo Salustio'. 'Cum multa Athenis studiosissime agerem ... Neoptolemus. Pentesileam.' Compare ed. Meister, *Daretis Phrygii De Excidio Troiae Historia*.

168vb–188rb: HRB.

DESCRIPTION

SIZE 36 x 24.5 cm.

QUIRING Apparent coincidence of text and quiring. Possible reconstruction from catchwords: I–III^{10}, IV–V^8, VI^8 (?8 canc.–end of text: fos 47–53); VII ?^{2} (54–55), VIII–XII^{10}, XIII^{10} (lacks 10: 106–114); XIV–XIX^8, XX ?^{2} (163–164); XXI–XXIII^8.

PRICKING Not visible on film.

RULING Two columns, 46 lines.

SCRIPT Several different hands, two main types of script in volume. HRB and Dares in small, round, four-line minuscule. Prominent descender on g and ascender on round d. a round with no head. Flat top on double l. Juncture of e and o after b, d, p. Bede in more compact, shaded, and recognisably Gothic script but also round. Juncture of e and o after d, h, and p. Two-compartment a, pierced t. Short ascenders and descenders. Most of Orosius in similar script with notes at either end in hand similar to that of Dares/HRB. Ximenes in script intermediate between the two styles.

DECORATION Red rubrics. Red or blue capitals. Minor initials lack filigree but have simple vertical line ornament. Major capitals in two colours with dense filigree around letter.

HISTORY

188r: Signature (now illegible) 'A bele Viegne', anagram used by Jean le Bègue, who in 1411 and 1413 (under Charles VI) compiled inventories of the Bibliothèque royale, then housed at the Louvre, Paris: Delisle, *Le Cabinet*, I.46. *Ex-libris* of Collège de Navarre, Paris, entered in a ?sixteenth-century hand on 188rb and 1r: 'Pro libraria regalis collegii Campaniae als. Nauarrae' (188rb).

BIBLIOGRAPHY

Crick, 'The manuscripts', p. 157.
Hallaire, 'Quelques manuscrits de Jean le Bègue'.
Martin, *Catalogue des manuscrits de la Bibliothèque de l'Arsenal*, II.205–7.
Wright, *The Historia Regum Britannie of Geoffrey of Monmouth, II*, pp. lxxxix–xc.

164 *PARIS, BIBLIOTHEQUE NATIONALE, MS. LAT. 4126

Saec. xiv + xiv/xv   Origin: Yorkshire (?Hulne or Carmelites, York)
297 fos (incl. 157*)   2nd fo: *quatenus non extendi*

HRB 134va–211vb
§§1–3, 5–208. Dedicated to Robert of Gloucester.
Rubrics at §1 (134va) 'Cronica Galfridi Monemutensis' (added in the later hand). 'Incipit ystoria Britonum' (original), after §208 (211vb) 'Explicit cronica Galfridi Monumetensis in hystoriam Britonum'.
Running title 'Brutus', then 'Uortigernus', 'Merlinus' etc.
No book-divisions.
Opening of §43 omitted. After penultimate sentence of §42 (ending 'deditioni coegerunt') §43 begins 'et petentes Romam cum tota multitudine', omitting usual first phrase (cf. Oxford, Bodleian Library, MSS. Jones 48 and Laud misc. 720). Prophecies of Merlin have continuous marginal gloss (Inc. 'Sedente itaque eo id est deliberante ... impetu fortune feretur'). Ed. Hammer, 'A commentary on the *Prophetia Merlini*', pp. 6–18.
Poems of Iohannes Beuerus in margins of many pages in a somewhat later hand: Hammer, 'The poetry of Johannes Beverus'. Cf. BL Cotton Cleopatra D.viii. See Hammer 'Note', pp. 230–34.
Across lower margin on many folios in different hand (? cf. gloss to Prophecies), grey

ink, historical notes on early British history comparing HRB with extracts from *Annales* of Alfred of Beverley: discussed by Hammer, 'Note', pp. 226–27.

CONTENTS

1r: blank.

1v: world map, Jerusalem at centre.

2r: blank.

2v: late fourteenth-century contents-list. Last three lines erased (after 'Uisio Cyrilli cum comento (*sic*) abbatis Ioachym').

3ra–4ra: 'Decretalis contra fratres procurata per magistrum Ricardum fitz Rauf archiepiscopum de Armagh'. 'Innocentius episcopus seruus seruorum Dei dilectis filiis abbati Westmonasterii, priori sancti Bartholomei in Smethfeld . . .' (Inc.) 'Frequentes actenus . . . contrarium edita non obstante. Datum anno .viii. kalends Septimb. pontificatus nostri anno quinto.' *Decretales* of Innocent VI against the mendicant friars (25.8.1357).

4rb: blank.

4va–6va: decretals on privileges of mendicants by Benedict XI. 'Benedictus episcopus seruus seruorum Dei ad perpetuam rei memoriam . . . et Pauli apostolorum eius se nouerit incursurum. Datum Laterani tercio decimo kalend. Martii pontificatus nostri anno primo.'

7ra–9ra: Boniface VIII on the same. 'Bonifacius episcopus seruus seruorum Dei ad perpetuam rei memoriam super cathedram preminencie pastoralis . . . et professores eorum habentes affectu beniuolo.'

9rb: blank.

9va/b: prophetical poem. 'Regnum Scotorum fuit inter cetera regna . . . Per mundi metas lilia subtus erunt.' Walther, *Initia*, I.864, no. 16547. Printed from this manuscript by Skene, *Chronicles*, pp. 117–18.

10ra/vb: 'Uas electionis', decretals of John XXII against John de Poliaco. 'Iohannes episcopus seruus seruorum Dei uenerabilibus fratribus patriarchis archiepiscopis et episcopis ac dilectis filiis electis . . .' (Inc.) 'Uas eleccionis doctor eximius et egregius predicator . . . Iohannes efficaciter repromisit Datum Auinion. octauo kl. Augusti. Pontificatus nostri anno .v.'.

10vb: 'Te adoro creatorem . . . absque participacione corporis tui qui uiuis'.

11ra–12ra: 'Incipit tractatus magistri Stephani medici Hugonis episcopi Dunelmi de quodam prodigio . . .'. 'Quidam senex habitabat in solitudine deserti . . . sequentis uite at cor. disciplina plenius emundaret.'

12rb–13vb: 'Incipit de diuersis signis et prodigiis mundi que fecit Deus ut tereret (*sic*) homines que descripsit sanctus Patricius Ybernie episcopus'. Patrick, bishop of Dublin (1074–84), *De mirabilibus Hibernie*. 'Plurima mira malum signancia signa futurum . . . Gloria spiritui sancto per secula cuncta. Amen . . .' See Bieler, *Codices Patriciani latini*, pp. 10–11.

14ra–18ra: 'Incipit cosmigrafia Prisciani'. 'Lectionum peruigili cura comperimus senatum . . . uel numerum gencium commonencium.' Ethicus Ister. Ed. Riese, *Geographi latini minores*, pp. 71–91.4 (where text diverges from printed edition).

18ra–19ra: continues but not according to printed text. 'In mari occeano . . . id est quatragesima pars sextarii.'

19ra/vb: 'Incipit itinerarium mar.'. 'Incipit itnarium (sic) maritimum que loca nauigaturi tangere debeant . . . per fluuium arelatum i[ ] p[ ] .xxx..'

20ra–21rb: 'De tribus mundi partibus et de distribucione tocius orbis montium et fluuiium (sic)'. 'Disposuit cursus sumpnius moderator aquarum . . . Cynnamus est arbor cynnama que generat.'

21va–22va: 'Mensura tocius terre secundum Romanos doctissimos guomonica (sic) racione certissime comprobata'. 'Terre tocius ambitus omnisque plenus circuitus iuxta Romanorum dimensionem est tredencies (sic) et quindecies centena milia passuum . . . in Cartaginem apud Hyberos que mox colonia facta est Peni condiderunt.'

22va–26va: 'Incipit descripcio Orosii de tribus partibus mundi quomodo orbis terrarum quem inhabitabat genus humanum antiquis au<c>toribus distributus et diuisus sit triphar[iam]'. 'Dicturus sum et scripturus ab orbe firmato . . . Nec de Affrica plura que memorentur occurrunt.'

26va–27rb: 'De situ Albanie que in se figuram hominis hominis (cancelled) habet quomodo fuit primitus in septem regionibus diuisa quibusque nominibus antiquitus sit uocata et a quibus inhabitata'. 'Opere precium puto mandare . . . annis .xvi. in Pictiuia feliciter regnauit.' Ed. Anderson, *Kings and Kingship*, pp. 240–43.

27rb–29va: 'Cronica de origine antiquorum Pictorum'. 'Picti propria lingua nomen habet . . . qui tribuit magnam ciuitatem Brechne domino.' Ed. Anderson, *Kings and Kingship*, pp. 243–53.

29va–31ra: 'Cronica regum Scottorum .ccc.x.iiii. annorum'. 'Fergus filius Erie ipse fuit primus . . . filius Dei uiui.' Ed. Anderson, *Kings and Kingship*, pp. 253–58.

31ra–32ra: 'Qualiter acciderit que memoria sancti Andree apostoli amplius in regione Pictorum que nunc Scocia dicitur quam in ceteris regionibus sit et quomodo contigerit quod tante albi[ ]e ibi facte a[ ]tus fuerunt quas multi adhuc seculares uiri iure hereditario possident'. 'Andreas qui interpretatur . . . castra receperunt.' Ed. Anderson, *Kings and Kingship*, pp. 258–60.

32rb/vb: blank.

33ra–45ra: 'Liber Petri Amfulsi' (from final rubric). 'Dixit Petrus Amfulsus seruus Iesu Christi compositor huius libri . . . Illis de pretio contendentibus sompnus euanuit. Amen.' Edd. Hilka & Söderhjelm, *Die Disciplina clericalis*.

45ra–48rb: 'Hic incipit prologus in libro Methodii martiris'. 'In nomine Christi incipit liber Methodii . . .'. Text 'Sciendum namque nobis fratres karissimi . . . Qui uiuit cum patre et spiritu sancto per infinita secula seculorum. Amen.' Cf. ed. Sackur, *Sibyllinische Texte*, pp. 59–96.

48v: blank.

49r–96vb: *Liber Giraldi Kambrensis de mirabilibus Hybernie* (from rubric on 50va), First Recension. Prologue 'Consideranti mihi quam breuis et fluxa sit uita . . .', *capitula*, then text (53ra) 'Placuit excellencie uestre inuictissime Anglorum rex . . . quicquid a tanta maiestate fuerit iniunctum'. Ed. Brewer, *Opera*, V.3–202. On this manuscript see O'Meara, 'Giraldus Cambrensis', p. 178.

97v–105ra: Letter of Alexander to Aristotle. 'Semper tui memor . . . et animi mei operam et industriam optime Aristotiles ponderares.' Ed. Walther Boer, *Epistola*

Alexandri. Final section continues beyond printed text 'Per hec mea magna que tibi scripsi . . . humanis rebus excesserim posteritatis hystorie relinquo'.

105ra–106va: 'Pulchre et conuenienter Pompeius Trogus huic loco subditur cuius ita ?refert hystoria. Quoniam non est humane nature ineuitabiles casus transire . . . nisi fortuna eos emulacione uirtutis in perniciem mutuam armauisset'. Found as 'Epithoma de ortu uita et obitu Alexandri' in London, College of Arms, MS. Arundel 1.

106va–107vb: 'Incipit metrum in destruccione Troianorum'. 'Diuiciis ortu specie uirtute triumphis . . . Arte sed non parta ligneus egit equus.' Simon Chèvre d'Or. Cf. Boutemy *et al.*, 'La Version parisienne du poème de Simon Chèvre d'Or', pp. 269–86 & p. 267, n. 1. Walther, *Initia*, I.234, no. 4645.

107vb–119va: 'Incipit epistola Corneli<i> ad Crispu<m> Salustium in Troianorum historia que in Greto (*sic*) a Darete historiagrapho facta est'. 'Cornelius nepos Salustio Crispo suo salutem . . . hucusque Daretis Frigii historia conscripta est.' Ed. Meister, *Daretis Phrygii de Excidio Troiae Historia.*

119va/b: continuation. 'Quis Troianorum quem Grecorum occidit . . . et Polixenam filiam eius interfecit.'

119vb–120va: 'Pergama flere uolo fata (*sic*) Danais data solo . . . Tot clades numero scribere si potero'. Ed. Hammer, 'Some Leonine summaries', pp. 121–22. Walther, *Initia*, I.723, no. 13985.

120va–132v: 'Incipit prefacio in historia Britannorum extracta a libro qui dicitur policronicon'. 'Adest Britannia iuxta promissum seriosius describenda . . . uestium uariacione designetur.' Higden, *Policronicon*, Book I. Edd. Babington & Lumby, *Polychronicon*, II.2–174 (preamble to the opening *capitula*-list different from that printed).

133ra/va: Hildebert, *Uersus de excidio Troiano* (according to final rubric). 'Uiribus atque minis Danaum Troia (*sic*) data ruinis . . . sic gens Romulea surgit ab Hectorea.' Ed. Migne, *Patrologia Latina*, CLXXI.1451–53. Walther, *Initia*, I.1081, no. 20582.

133va–134va: 'De primis auctoribus siue scriptoribus historiarum'. 'Primis autem apud nos Moyses diuine historie cosmographiam de inicio mundi conscripsit . . . ad earum cognicionem utile promittamus.'

134va–211vb: HRB.

212r/vb: 'Sequitur continuacio regum Saxonum secundum cronicas \Alfridi Beuerlacensis/ (?over erasure but in same hand) et Henrici Huntingdon . . . ' (rubric on 211vb). 'Breuis recapitulacio tocius precedentis opusculi.' 'Britones origine Troiani . . . nec eam postea recuperauerunt.' Ed. Hammer, 'Note', pp. 227–28.

212vb–213ra: 'Incipit prefacio de historia Anglorum'. 'Finito regno Britonum . . . reges habere ceperunt.' Cf. ed. Hearne, *Aluredi Beuerlacensis Annales*, p. 77 (beginning of Book VI).

213ra–242ra: 'Incipiunt excerptiones de historiis Anglorum et unde Angli uenerunt et originem duxerunt'. 'Aduenerant autem sicut Beda refert . . . translatum est regnum Anglie ad Normannos.' Cf. ed. Hearne, *Aluredi Beuerlacensis Annales*, pp. 78–152 (continues beyond printed text which ends at 251vb; continuation begins 'Datus est etiam episcopatus Conuentrensis (*sic*)').

242ra–252ra: 'Incipiunt excerpta de gestis regum Normannorum in Anglia secundum

Alfridum Beuerlacensem'. 'Primum ostendendam est . . . cum regnasset .xxxv. annis et .iiii. fere mensibus.'

252rb–281vb: 'Sequitur continuacio hystorie secundum cronicam Ranulphi monachi Cestrensis in suo Policronicon usque ad Edwardi tercii regis tempora . . . '. 'Mortuo Henrico primo successit Stephanus . . . Scocia concordiam ecclesia libertatem.'

282ra/b: 'Erat Gilbertus Anglicus magnus iste theologus . . . nec eo unus processerit in misteriis'.

282rb–283rb: 'Epistola Cirilli ad abbatem Ioachim'. 'Domni tocius diuine sapientie . . . tabellas deposuit et in ictu disparuit.'

282vb: 'Pato (*sic*) hoc tempore scriptum in presentis scripture articulo coarcatum . . . ut sic quasi Dominus temporum uideatur'.

282vb–294va: 'Prophecia Cirilli heremite de monte Carmeli'. 'Tempore annorum Christi millesimo .cc.l.iiii. Februar. kalendis viii . . . magna capucia post tergum in modum cornu.'

294va–295rb: 'Epistola abbatis Joachim ad Cirillum heremitam de monte Carmeli'. 'Stelle manenti in ordine sanctitatis . . . ad ipsum incenderit quod ipsi descripserint.'

295rb/va: paragraphs concerning preceding text. 'Ego frater Petrus Maymeti . . . existens scolaris Parys. istum libellum . . . scripsi . . . .' Identified as Pierre Maymet, bachelier sentiaire 1339, *ob.* 1348: Samaran & Marichal, *Catalogue des manuscrits*, II.488.

295v–296r: 'Epistola sancte Hildegardis ad Colonicensem de futura tribulacione clericorum et de nouis religiosis . . . deinceps in fortissima ui rectitudine persistent. Amen'. In smaller, less formal hand.

DESCRIPTION

SIZE 31 x 18.5 cm.

QUIRING a^2 (1–2), I–II^8, III^{10}, IV^4 (29–32); V^6, VI^2, VII^8; VIII–XI^{12}, XII^{12} (1–3, 10–12 singletons: 97–108), XIII^8, XIV^6 (117–122), XV^8, XVI^6 (131–136), XVII^{10}, XVIII^{12} (147–151, 151*, 152–157), XIX–XXII^{12}, XXIII^4 (206–209), XXIV^2, XXV– XXXII^8, XXXIII^8 (7–8 lacking: 276–281), XXXIV^{10}, XXXV fos 292–296.

PRICKING Pricking in outer margin only except for QQ. XXXI–XXXII where pricking in both margins.

RULING Mostly two columns, 36 lines, single vertical boundary-lines, written below top ruled line. Decretals likewise but 34–43 lines. Fos 282r–295r – 51–52 lines, double vertical boundary-lines.

SCRIPT Several hands, some quite late-looking. 33–105, 134v–211v – rounded Gothic bookhand with short ascenders and descenders. Earliest-looking hand of volume. Dark brown ink. Final s round. Juncture of e and o after b, d, and p, not h. Fusion of other curved letters. Crossed *et*-nota. Two-compartment a. Tops of ascenders have hairline tag at left. Decretals in hands not found in rest of volume. Late. Angular, resembling quadrata. Pale grey-brown ink. Pointed tops to minim-letters and two-compartment a. Hairlines, crossed *et*-nota. 2-shaped r trails below the line. fos 11–32 – grey ink, four-line minuscule with long r, barred x, final round s, looped two-compartment a, juncture of e and o after d and p. 2-shaped r trails below the line. Upright and laterally compressed. 106–134va – in more angular hand than that immediately preceding it (more like that of 11–32). Written over erasure above the beginning of HRB, mid-folio 134va.

212r–246rb – slightly later in appearance. Several other hands.

DECORATION HRB – main initials are blue and red with red filigree, minor capitals filigreed (blue or red). After 106, capitals are blue in a square of red filigree.

1–32 and after 212 – unfiligreed red capitals.

HISTORY

Name of Robert Populton recurs in manuscript (on 11ra, 13va, 134va, 212va, 213ra, 252ra) with formulae such as 'Ora pro Popilton qui me compilauit', 'Ora pro Populton qui me fecit scribi'. On Robert Populton of York, see Hammer, 'Note', p. 230; Anderson, 'The Scottish materials', p. 235; and especially Levison, review, pp. 113–14. Examination of the manuscript suggests that Populton extended a preexisting historical collection written in a Gothic script of ?earlier fourteenth century, more formal than that of the hands associated with his own compilation. 33r–105r in the early hand but after 105v continued mid-quire on singletons (fos 106–108) in 'Populton' hand. 134va–211vb similarly in this earlier-looking hand. 134r and certainly 134va (top) seem to have been written (in a 'Populton' hand) over erasure.

Name of Populton absent from these suggested earlier sections, except for entry on 134va, in an identifiably 'Populton' hand, over erasure. According to this analysis of the compilation, the pre-Populton manuscript contained Petrus Alphonsus, *Liber Methodii*, Giraldus Cambrensis, *Epistola Alexandri*, and Geoffrey's *Historia*.

At head of fo 1r 'Cod. Colb. Regius 3896', and at foot 'Gulielmus Cecilius mil. D. de Burghley', indicating ownership by Lord Burghley and Jean-Baptiste Colbert (ob. 1683).

BIBLIOGRAPHY

Anderson, *Kings and Kingship*, pp. 235–40.

Anderson, 'The Scottish materials'.

Avril & Stirnemann, *Manuscrits enluminés*, pp. 163–64, no. 204.

Hammer, 'A commentary on the *Prophetia Merlini*'.

Hammer, 'Note'.

Hardy, *Descriptive Catalogue*, II.170–71.

Levison, review, pp. 113–14.

[Mellot,] *Catalogus*, III.549–50.

Samaran & Marichal, *Catalogue des manuscrits*, II.488.

Skene, *Chronicles of the Picts*, plates of fos 28–29 before p. 3.

165 PARIS, BIBLIOTHEQUE NATIONALE, MS. LAT. 4999A + MANCHESTER, JOHN RYLANDS LIBRARY, MS. LAT. 216
(*OLIM* BN LAT. 4999A, ITEM 8)

*PARIS, BIBLIOTHEQUE NATIONALE, MS. LAT. 4999A

Saec. xii/xiii
25 + 93 fos

Mediaeval provenance: ?
2nd fo: *Regnum Argiuorum incoat*

CONTENTS
A (MS. Barrois 251)

1r–25r: Chronicle arranged according to the Ages of the World.
'Prima etas in exordio sui continet creacionem mundi . . . obiit Richardus rex Anglorum et dux Normannorum comes Andegauis et Aquitanorum.'

25v: in ?fifteenth-century hand, 'Nota sequentes historiographos'. 'Pompeius Trogus. . . de [ ]ipio.'

B (MS. Barrois 244)

1r–47r: *Liber epistolaris Iheronimi* (*sic*) *presbiteri* (from final rubric), brief chronicle of popes from Damasus to Adrian I (772), beginning with a letter of Jerome (ed. Migne, *Patrologia Latina*, XXX.293). 'Beatissimo pape Damaso Hieronymus. Gloriam sanctitati (*sic*) tue . . . sepultus est in basilica beati Petri apostoli .vi. kal. Iani. inditione quarta.'

47v: 'Nomina episcoporum Cenomannice urbis' (in different hand to preceding but of similar date). 'Donnus (*sic*) Iulianus episcopus sedit anni .xl.vii. menses .iii. dies .x. . . . Donnus Hugo episcopus sedit anni .vii. menses .iii. dies .xvii. cessauit episcopatus menses .xi.'

48r–51v: 'Prophecia sibille tiburtine' (rubric in later hand). 'Sibille generaliter omnes femine dicuntur . . . et ipsi regnabunt cum illo in secula seculorum. Amen.' Ed. Sackur, *Sibyllinische Texte*, pp. 177–87.

52r–75rb: 'Incipit liber de tribus circunstantiis (*sic*) gestorum id est personis locis temporibus'. 'Fili sapientia thesaurus est . . . sub se constituit.' First part ed. Green, 'Hugo of St Victor De tribus maximis circumstantiis gestorum'.

75v: 'De nominibus imper[ ] Constantinopo[ ]'. 'Michael curo palates . . . Iohannes porfirogenitus filius eius.'

C (MS. Barrois 250)

76r–86r: 'In nomine Dei summi incipiunt gesta saluatoris Domini nostri Iesu Christi que inuenit Teodosius magnus imperator in Ierusalem in pretorio Poncii Pilati in codicibus publicis.' 'Factum est in anno nono decimo imperii Tyberii Cesaris imperatoris Romanorum . . . in codicibus publicis pretorii sui.' Ed. Kim, *The Gospel of Nicodemus*.

86r–92r: 'In hoc codice continetur libellus Bede presbiteri de locis sanctis Ierusalem quem a discipulis maiorum adbreuiando cumposuit (*sic*)'. List of contents 'De situ Ierusalem . . . De Constantinopoli . . .'. 'Situs Ierusalem urbis pene in orbem circumdatus . . . si lectionis orationisque studio tibi temperaret (*sic*) satagas.' Bede, *De Locis sanctis*. Ed. Fraipont *apud* Geyer *et al.*, *Itineraria*, pp. 251–80. Dekkers, *Clavis*, p. 521, no. 2333. Spaces left in text (?for illustrations).

92r: large shield at foot.

92v: blank except for inscription and signature in Early Modern hand (see below, HISTORY).

93r: list of archbishops of Rouen in several Early Modern hands.

From no. 74, Hugo de Orge to no. 81, Charolus a Borlom[ ]o.

93v: blank.

DESCRIPTION

SIZE Much cut down. A 16.2 x 11.8 cm. B 17 x 12.5 cm. C 17 x 12.1 cm.

QUIRING Too tightly bound for collation.

PRICKING Trimmed away.

RULING Mostly single column, 32–41 lines, very variable. Occasionally four columns for lists in B.

SCRIPT Similar throughout, several hands. Small brown glossing-type, four-line Protogothic. Round **d** and final tall s standard but straight-backed **d** and round s also found. Small-headed **a**. *Et*-nota standard.

DECORATION Blue capitals with some red ornament in B but mostly plain red capitals. Some of lists in Hugh of Saint-Victor have arcaded tops like canon tables.

HISTORY

Signature on 92v ?'Picard.' One Jean Picard (ob. 1615) was among the librarians of the Bibliothèque royale: Delisle, *Le Cabinet*, II.232.

HRB listed as eighth item (now John Rylands Library, MS. lat. 216), following *De locis sanctis*, in Mellot's 1744 catalogue (as cited below).

BIBLIOGRAPHY

Mellot, *Catalogus*, IV.28.

Delisle, *Catalogue*, pp. 203–5.

MANCHESTER, JOHN RYLANDS LIBRARY, MS. LAT. 216

Saec. xiii/xiv   Provenance: ?

?75 fos   2nd fo: *At Brutus ob predictam*

HRB 1r–75v

§17 'Uictoriam tum adepti spoliis eorum' –109, §110 'Coegit me . . . nobilitatis tue dilectio', §§111–208. Dedicatory section lost.

Rubrics at most chapter-divisions. §108 (35v), 'Uerba Merlini', §109 (35v), 'Uerba auctoris'. Verses after §208 (75v) 'Librum scribendo compleui fine iocundo / Scribere non posco rquiescere (*sic*) fessus hanelo / Hec Rogere tibi pro posse polita peregi / Mente, manu, lingua, tandemque labore peracta / Ne precor indignum reputes ne semper amicum / Promissis precio sum dignus iure peracto' (hand of text). Cf. Cambridge, St John's College, MS. G. 16: *Colophons*, V.259, no. 16787.

Book-divisions: II §35 (8v), III §89 (27r), IIII §111 (36r), V §118 (40r), VI §143 (60r). No other contents but 2 paper flyleaves after 75v.

DESCRIPTION
QUIRING Catchwords indicate I–IX^8, X ? (fos 73–75).
PRICKING In outer margin.
RULING Single column throughout of 30 lines, narrow double vertical boundary-lines.
SCRIPT Anglicana with tall, thick, split ascenders. Looped s, long r, two-compartment a rising above minim letters, round s standard in final position, crossed et-nota, two-line g. Heavily shaded loop on d (always round).
DECORATION Unfiligreed capitals. Rubrics in double-sized version of script of text.

HISTORY
On recto of second flyleaf after text: 'Cornely Duyn Aemstelredamensis, Haga comitis Hollandia anno MDCxii'. Not noted by Ker, 'English manuscripts owned by Johannes Vlimmerius and Cornelius Duyn'. Catalogued with the Barrois manuscripts at Ashburnham Place in 1861: *Catalogue of the manuscripts at Ashburnham Place*, II, no. 223 (catalogue unpaginated). Printed notice 'From the library of George Dunn of Woolley Hall, near Maidenhead'.

BIBLIOGRAPHY
Fawtier, 'Hand-list of Additions to the Collection of Latin Manuscripts in the John Rylands Library, 1908–1920', pp. 187 & 195.
Hammer, 'Some additional manuscripts', p. 239.

166 *PARIS, BIBLIOTHEQUE NATIONALE, MS. LAT. 5233

Saec. xii *ex.*   Mediaeval provenance: ?
159 fos   2nd fo: [*brittan*]-*niis aliquantulum usque ad*
HRB 97va–155va
§§1–3, 5–208. §§83, 84, 173–174, 179, and 184 compressed. Nameless dedication.
Rubrics at §1 (97rb) 'Incipit prologus Gaufridi Monemutensis in historia regum Britannie', §111 (127v) 'Prophetia Mellini'.
No book-divisions.

CONTENTS
1r–97rb: 'Incipit prefatio uenerabilis Bede presbiteri in historia Anglorum'. 'Gloriosissimo regi Ceoluulfo . . . semper ante faciem tuam. Amen.' Edd. Colgrave & Mynors, *Bede's Ecclesiastical History*. Text of Continental m-type: *ibid.*, p. lxiv.
97va–155va: HRB.
155va–159va: 'Incipit passio sanctorum martyrum Uincentii Orontii et Uictoris'. 'Anno septimo Diocleciani et Maximiani . . . et regnat per infinita secula seculorum. Amen.' *BHL* nos 8670–71.

DESCRIPTION
SIZE 41 x 29.5 cm.

QUIRING I–XIX⁸, XX⁴ (153–156), XXI⁴ (4 lacking: 157–159). Indicated by signa-tures usually, but on XVI and XVII by catchwords.

PRICKING Visible often in both margins.

RULING Two columns throughout, with double boundings and division of the central margin into two (but three on 1r–8v). 38 lines, written above top ruled line.

SCRIPT Rounded, massive Protogothic in most of volume. Laterally compressed, fairly canonical. Round **d**, uncrossed *et*-nota standard. Round **s** usual in final position but tall form occurs there. **e**-caudata is used occasionally. Straight-backed **g**. Subsi-diary hand (beginning at 124vb) is more compact, shaded, and angular with the ascender of initial **d** sometimes trailing into the margin, giving a later appearance. Straight-backed **d**; ampersand and **e**-caudata occur occasionally. Tops of minims are lozenged.

DECORATION Red, green, pale brown capitals with single-line scrolling in contrast-ing colour. Red rubrics.

HISTORY
Top of 1r: 'Cod. Colb.'. Jean-Baptiste Colbert (ob. 1683), for a time librarian of the Bibliothèque royale, whose collection of 8000 volumes entered that library in 1732: Delisle, *Le Cabinet*, I.439.

BIBLIOGRAPHY
Mellot, *Catalogus*, IV.57.

167 *PARIS, BIBLIOTHEQUE NATIONALE, MS. LAT. 5234

Saecc. xii²/ᵉˣ· + ?xvi   Mediaeval provenance:
      Saint-Jean, Amiens (Premonstratensian)
ii + 150 fos   2nd fo: *nulla ualet*
            2nd fo: *natus fuerat*

HRB 95r–150v
§§1–3, 5–119, 124–203 'reliquie patriam factis' (foot 150v). Dedicated to Robert of Gloucester.

Rubrics at §1 (95r) 'Incipit prologus in libro de gestis Britonum', §5 (95r) 'Descriptio brittannice insule', §110 (123r) 'Incipit prologus prophetie Merlini', §111 (123r) 'Explicit. Incipit prophetia Merlini'.

Book-divisions: II §23 (100r), III §35 (103v), IV §54 (108r), V §73 (112v), VI §89 (117r). Also spaces left, apparently for rubrics, at §§143 (132v) and 177 (144v).

Some dislocation of text of §§124–128 and 143–147 due to the transposition of the first and second bifolia of a quire of eight (B, Q.V). No loss of text. 127 should follow 128 and 134 should precede 133.

CONTENTS
1r–94va: 'Incipit prologus uenerabilis Bede in ecclesiasticam historiam gentis Anglo-rum'. '[ ]loriosissimo regi Cioluulfo . . . semper ante faciem tuam. Amen.' Prologue

265

and opening (1r–2v) supplied in ?sixteenth-century hand. Original copy begins
'Autem bellum quarto imperii sui anno ... '. Edd. Colgrave & Mynors, *Bede's
Ecclesiastical History*. Text of Continental m-type: *ibid.*, p. lxiv.

90v–91r left blank mid-text, with loss of some text within V.21 (90r ends 'Pecunia
tua tecum sit in perditionem . . . Sed et tuam nunc prudentiam rex admoneo', Colgrave
& Mynors, *Bede's Ecclesiastical History*, pp. 548 and 550).

94vb: blank.

95r–150v: HRB.

DESCRIPTION

SIZE 30.5 x 22 cm.

QUIRING Signatures indicate that Bede and HRB constitute two separate volumes,
each arranged in eights. a^4 (4 excised), I^8 (1–3 lacking, bifolium substituted: 1–7),
II–XIII^8; (HRB) I–IIII^8, V ?^{8} (1:8 and 2:7 transposed), VI–VII ?^{8}.

PRICKING Visible at outer edge only in HRB but in both margins in Bede.

RULING Two columns throughout. A – 34 lines; B – 33 lines.

SCRIPT Upright minuscule tending to angularity but with little lateral compression.
Hands vary in roundness or spikiness but share use of straight-backed g, uncrossed
et-nota, tall s in final position, and both straight and round **d** (straight predominates).
e-caudata occurs sometimes in one hand. Small-headed **a**. Continental script (? North
France/Low Countries).

DECORATION Mostly plain capitals, some with split shafts (both straight and wavy)
in red, green, and blue. §§1 and 5 in HRB are multicoloured with foliate scrolls. In
Bede's *Historia*, capitals are red, some with split ornament.

HISTORY

On 91r (otherwise blank), in formal documentary hand of perhaps saec. xv, note
concerning the foundation of the Premonstratensian order and the establishment of
religiosi at Saint-Firmin, Amiens ('Ambn.') in 1126 and their later move outside
Amiens to a *cenobium* popularly called St John the Baptist's. (See also Colgrave &
Mynors, *Bede's Ecclesiastical History*, p. lxiv.) (The Premonstratensian house of
Saint-Jean, Amiens, was originally founded in the priory of Saint-Firmin before being
transferred to a new site in 1136: Cottineau, *Répertoire*, I, cols 85–86.)

BIBLIOGRAPHY
Mellot, *Catalogus*, IV.56.

168 *PARIS, BIBLIOTHEQUE NATIONALE, MS. LAT. 5697

Saec. xv ?[1]   Mediaeval provenance: ?
296 fos (foliated for 297 but omits 215)   2nd fo: *Illa aprucium dicta est*

HRB 135r–225v (224)
§§1–3, 5–208. Nameless dedication.

Rubrics at §1 (134v) 'Incipit hystoria Britonum'. 'Incipit', (135r) 'Incipit hystoria Britonum. Rubrica', §5 (135r) 'Explicit prefacio. Incipit hystoria. Rubrica'. Also in ink in hand of text beside §111 (180r) 'Incipit pro[ ] Merlini'.
No book-divisions.

CONTENTS
1r–134v: 'Incipit hic hystoria Troiana. Rubrica', Guido delle Colonne. 'Sicet (*sic*) cotidie uetera recentibus obruam . . . m. ducentessimo octuag. septimo eiusdem prime [?indicione] feliciter. Amen.' Ed. Griffin, *Historia Destructionis Troiae*.
135r–225v(224): HRB.
226r–248r: 'Incipit liber historie famosisimi (*sic*) Karoli magni quomodo tellurem hispannicam et Galiciam potestate Sarracenorum liberauit de h. quod apostolus Iacobus Karolo nunciauit'. 'Gloriosissimus ?igitur Christi apostolus . . . ipse Fredericus regnauit etc.' Ed. Meredith-Jones, *Historia Karoli*.
248v–249v: blank.
250r–295r: 'Flauii Uegetii Ren[ ] illustris uni epithoma rei militaris libri ?uniuerso quinque incipiunt feliciter R'. 'Primus liber eleccionem edocet [ ]onum . . . in rubro et in nigro. Bartholus.' Ed. Lang, *Flavi Vegeti Renati Epitoma*.
295v–297v: blank. ?Early Modern signature on 297v (not legible).

DESCRIPTION
SIZE 26.5 x 18.5 cm.
QUIRING Very tightly bound (impossible to microfilm). Catchwords indicate I–XVII^{12}, XVIII^{12} (205–214, 216–217) XIX ?^{8} (218–225); XX–XXI ?^{12}; XXII^{12} (250–261), XXIII–XXIV^{12}; XXV ?^{12} (286–297).
PRICKING Outer margins only.
RULING Single column of 30 or 31 lines. Single vertical boundary-lines, ruling above top written line.
SCRIPT Similar throughout but perhaps several hands. Weak brown ink. Four-line late mediaeval script. Horned-c form of e, simple round a, final s round but long elsewhere. Tapering descenders but little slope. Tops of ascenders looped under but not angular. Pierced t, round d, 2-shaped r. Juncture of po. Some angularity but nowhere very marked.
DECORATION Red rubrics in script of text but with exaggeratedly tall ascenders. Opening capitals on 1r, 135r, 226r, etc., have grey and gold leaf-type flourishes in margin, sometimes with red, blue, white, and other colours. Minor capitals are blue or red in a square of red or blue filigree.

BIBLIOGRAPHY
Mellot, *Catalogus*, IV.149.

169 *PARIS, BIBLIOTHEQUE NATIONALE, MS. LAT. 6039

Saec. xiv   Origin: ?Italian
58 fos   2nd fo: *In tantum autem milicia*

HRB 1r–58v

§§1–3, 5–208. Dedicated to Robert of Gloucester.

No opening rubric. After §208 (58v) 'Explicit britannicus magistri Ualterii partinens (*sic*). Finito libro sit laus et gloria Cristo'. Other rubrics at §110 (31v) 'Incipit prologus de prophetia Merlini', §111 (31v) 'Explicit prologus Merlini. Incipit prophetia eiusdem', §137 'Aderat inter' (40v) 'Hic incipit ystoria Arturi' and similarly at some other chapters.

Book-divisions rubricated at §109 (31v) VII, and §163 (47v) X only but indications for rubrics in margin at §54 (15v) IIII, §89 (25r) VI , §143 (41v) IX, §177 (52v) XI. Other large capitals at §§ 5 (1r), 6 (1v), 23 (7r), 35 (11r), 73 (20v).

No other contents.

DESCRIPTION

SIZE 33 x 21.5 cm.

QUIRING Catchwords. I–VI⁸, VII⁶, VIII ?⁴ (55–58).

PRICKING None extant.

RULING One column of 39–40 written lines. Double vertical boundary-lines. Written below top ruled line.

SCRIPT Round, Italian minuscule; *littera bastarda*/humanist. Most letters sit on the line, short ascenders and descenders. Simple straight strokes but minims often finished top and foot. Juncture of **b** and **d** with **e**; **b, d,** and **p** with **o**. Vertical mark at end of line if no word there, no words broken across lines.

DECORATION Initials at chapter-divisions usually of simple form with vertical hatching. Elaborate major capitals enclosed in a square filled with block colours (blue, red, grey, green) with white highlighting. Initials for §§1 and 5 (1r) are historiated (?author portraits) in same colours as major initials, with letter in gold frame.

HISTORY

On fo 1 'Ant. Lancelot' and in a different hand 'Codex Lancellot 16. Regius 10210'. Antoine Lancelot (ob. 1740) bequeathed his collection of 206 manuscripts to the king of France in 1733: Delisle, *Le Cabinet*, I.409.

BIBLIOGRAPHY

Mellot, *Catalogus*, IV.195.

170 *PARIS, BIBLIOTHEQUE NATIONALE, MS. LAT. 6040

Saec. xii*med./2*   Mediaeval provenance: English
ii + 59 + ii fos   2nd fo: *Eneas post Troianum*

HRB 1r–59v

§§1–208 but §§31–60 are found after 60–87 because of the transposition of quire II.
Dedicated to Robert of Gloucester and Waleran of Meulan.

No contemporary rubrics or book-divisions.

§6 begins at top of new leaf; preceding column is mostly blank.

Q. V, containing part of *Prophetie Merlini* and following chapters, is in a different
hand: 'tonantis et inter' (§114) 33r to 'Gorlois reputaretur adesse' (§137) 39v; last
folio of quire (after 39) excised. 40r continues from 39v with no loss of text.

QQ. II and III transposed: 8v ends 'Interrogante igitur' (§31), 17v completes this
phrase, 'illo Gornorilla prius'; 9r opens 'eius prefatis palis' (§60) which follows from
foot 24v 'peteret naues'; 25r opens 'nullam commixtionem' (§87) which follows from
16v 'possiderent. Et ut'.

CONTENTS

i–ii: later flyleaves with scribbles and sketches in late mediaeval hand.
1r–59va: HRB.
59vb: 'Epitafium Ceaduualli regis Anglorum in ecclesia Sancti Petri in Roma'.
'[C]ulmen opes sobolem pollentia regna triumphos . . . omnium inimicorum suorum
dominabitur.' Bede, *Historia ecclesiastica*, V.7. Schaller & Könsgen, *Initia*, p. 140,
no. 2961. Ed. Hammer, 'An unrecorded *Epitaphium Ceadwallae*'. Perhaps in slightly
later hand than that of HRB.
60–61: blank except for pen-trials and other scribbles (including sketches of mythical
creatures) in various twelfth- and thirteenth-century hands.

DESCRIPTION

SIZE 27 x 18 cm.
QUIRING a², I⁸, III⁸, II⁸, IV⁸, V⁸ (lacks 8: 33–39, different hand), VI–VII⁸, VIII⁴, b ?⁴
(2–3 excised: 60–61). Transposition of quires II and III had happened before late
mediaeval numbering of bifolia according to quire (each folio in 1st half of quire given
quire number).
PRICKING Visible in outer margin only. No extant pricking on many folios.
RULING In two columns of 36 lines.
SCRIPT Unruly Protogothic, basic roundness but descenders and minims ticked. e-
and q-caudata found, round d occurs but is not standard, *et*-nota usual. High but not
round final s occurs. Dark brown ink. ?Anglo-Norman. For script cf. Cambridge,
University Library, MS. Mm.5.29 or Bern, Burgerbibliothek, MS. 568. Fos 33–39 –
later looking hand, more upright and laterally compressed. *et*-nota standard. Round d
very frequent but e-caudata still used. Paler ink.
DECORATION Red Romanesque initials, with foliate flourishes at §§1 and 6.

HISTORY

Book-plate of Foucault inside binding (Nicholas-Joseph Foucault, member of the

269

Académie des Inscriptions, ob. 1721: Delisle, *Le Cabinet*, I.374). On 1r: 'Ant. Lancelot' (Antoine Lancelot, ob. 1740). 'Galfredus Monemethencis' (?sixteenth-century hand). English early history suggested by the script and by notes on 60v (thirteenth-century) 'Sim. uicecomes de Norhant. sira fu[ ]am de hisoriis salt. mando tibi quatinus quam cicius poteris ad me uenias nam ibimus apud Lundonias' (upside-down), and by marginal notes in Anglicana hands.
Also on 61r in ?sixteenth-century hand 'Roberte Recors bok'.

BIBLIOGRAPHY
Avril & Stirnemann, *Manuscrits enluminés*, pp. 39–40, no. 65.
Hammer, 'An unrecorded *Epitaphium Ceadwallae*'.
Mellot, *Catalogus*, IV.195.

171 *PARIS, BIBLIOTHEQUE NATIONALE, MS. LAT. 6041

Saec. xiii *ex.* / xiv[1]   Mediaeval provenance: ?
iii + 78 + ii fos   2nd fo: *eius mortua est*

HRB 1r–77v.
§§1–3, 5–199, [200–205 compressed], 206–208. Nameless dedication (§3).
Rubrics at §1 (1r) 'Incipit in historia Britonum prefacio Gaufridi Monemitensis', §111 (41r) 'Incipit prophecia Merlini'. After §208 (77v) 'Benedictus Marie filius. Amen'.
Leap in the text mid-page (76v) from §200 'et Ioduuaaldum fratris sui filium bellis' to §205 'purificati ab Alano auxilium petiuit'. No physical break.
No other contents. 78 blank except for note on recto 'La bataille dentre le roy Artur et Mordreuc son nepuen fut lan v.xlii.'. Final two flyleaves from large-format glossed book written in formal thirteenth-century hand.

DESCRIPTION
SIZE 24.5 x 16 cm.
QUIRING Catchwords indicate quiring in eights. a⁴ (4 lacking: i–iii), I–IX⁸, X⁶, b².
PRICKING Visible at outer edges.
RULING One column throughout with single vertical boundary-lines, 31 lines. Written below top ruled line.
SCRIPT Minuscule of prickly aspect. Minims broken, **a** usually has two compartments separated by a hairline stroke, the horizontal of **t** is pierced, final **s** is round, *et*-nota is crossed. Fusion of curves: **b**, **c**, and **p** with **o**; **a** and **e** with **d**. Tops of ascenders are slightly indented and sometimes tagged. Brown ink.
DECORATION Red capitals with blue filigree. Initial letters in text highlighted in red.

BIBLIOGRAPHY
Mellot, *Catalogus*, IV.195.

172 *PARIS, BIBLIOTHEQUE NATIONALE, MS. LAT. 6041A

Saec. xiv   Origin: ?Italian
ii + 213 fos + ii   2nd fo: *Troianos et oppida*

HRB 1r–56ra.

§§1–3, 5–208. Dedicated to Robert of Gloucester.
No opening rubric. In small script in margin at §109 (77v) 'Incipit prologus de
Merlino', §110 '.vi. .vii. incipit', §111 'Explicit prologus. Incipit prophecia eiusdem'.
After §208 (56ra): 'Explicit iste liber scriptus feliciter. Amen'.
No book-divisions.

CONTENTS
Flyleaf Bv: fourteenth-century contents-list. Prophecy of Thomas of Canterbury in
?fifteenth-century (*cursiua formata*) hand. 'Quando ego Thomas Cantuarien. . . . in
quodam uase plumbeo.'
1r–56ra: HRB.
56rb: blank.
56v–104va: *Chronicon* of Robert Abilaut (according to Hauréau, *Initia*, III.157v). 'In
primordio temporis ante omnem diem . . . quam tocius studuit reformare.'
104vb: note (in same hand) on military manoeuvres in S. France. 'Anno Domini
.mclxxviii. . . . a Lodouice rege Francie.'
105ra–124va: compilation of cronicles of First Crusade. 'Episcopo Uiuariensi domino
meo . . . nunc et semper in seculorum secula. Amen.' Extracts from Raymond
d'Aguilers, *Historia Belli Sacri* and *Gesta Francorum*: France, 'Note sur le manuscrit
6041A'.
124va–127ra: 'Incipit prefacio in libro Sibille'. 'Sibille generaliter omnes . . . et ipsi
regnabunt in secula seculorum. Amen.' Ed. Sackur, *Sibyllinische Texte*, pp. 177–87.
127ra–128rb: '[ ]um requisicio facta fuisset ab Herode . . . Ego Thomas israelita omnia
que uidi recordatus sum scripsi sermonibus meis de i[ ]u et ipse qui debet iudicare
seculum per ignem et reddere unicuique secundum opera sua et regnas in secula
seculorum amen'. Version of Gospel of Thomas, cf. Tischendorf, *Evangelia Apocrypha*, pp. 164–68.
128v: blank.
129ra–131va: 'Incipit liber Athanasii patriarche ciuitatis magne Alexandrie de passione ymaginis Domini saluatoris que crucifixa est a Iudeis . . .' (rubric following
prologue). 'Apud Cesaream . . . atque indiuisum semper manet inperium. Amen.' Ed.
Migne, *Patrologia Graeco-latina*, XXVIII.811–20.
131va/b: 'Incipit tractatus ex libro translatus in Latinum a domino Simra archiatrali
de quodam linteo diuinitus transformatum qui in hac sollempnitate ualde congruit'.
'Redemptor igitur et saluator . . . saluator orbis terre nostrique memor digneris esse.'
131vb–132va: 'Item exemplar epistole Domini saluatoris que directa est per acianiam
cursorem ad Abagarum regem Edissene ciuitatis'. 'Beatus es qui me credisti . . . ad
laudem et gloriam Domini saluatoris per omnia secula seculorum. Amen.' On the
correspondence between Abgar and Christ see James, *The Apocryphal New Testament*, pp. 476–77.

132va–143vb: 'Sanctus Brendanus filius Finiloche alcide genere cogenis . . . Prestante domino nostro Iesu Christo cuius honor et inperium sine fine permanet in secula seculorum. Amen'. *Nauigatio Sancti Brendani* (not listed by Kenney, *The Sources*), ed. Selmer, *Navigatio. BHL* 1436.

144ra–160rb: 'Turpinus Dei gratia Remensis archiepiscopus . . . ad Dominum conuertit'. Pseudo-Turpinus, ed. Meredith-Jones, *Historia Karoli.*

160va–178rb: 'Testamenta .xii. patriarcharum et primo de Ruben'. 'Transcriptum testamenti Ruben . . . usque ad diem exitus eorum ex terra Egypti.' Followed by list of the twelve patriarchs.

178va–179vb: 'Incipit passio secundum Nichodemum de passione et resurreccione atque assentione Domini nostri Iesu Christi de uisitatione Adam aliorumque et de expoliatione inferni [ ]'. 'Audistis fratres karissimi que acta sunt . . . regnum meum ministri mei utique re-', truncated (loss of one or more quires after Q. XV).

180ra–213rb: Hayton, *Flos historiatus.* 'Diuiditur autem liber iste in quatuor partes . . . Alexandri finita istoria fracolino per multos annos sit uita. Amen.' Ed. *Recueil des Historiens des Croisades, Documents arméniens*, II.255–363.

213v: blank.

Final flyleaf taken from two-column glossed book. ?In Continental script (*post* 1250).

DESCRIPTION

SIZE 30.5 x 19.5 cm.

QUIRING Flyleaves A-B, I–III^{12}, IV^{14} (13–14 excised: 37–48), V–XIV^{12}, XV^{12} (4 excised: 169–179); XVI–XVII^{12}, XVIII^{10}, flyleaf. Catchwords. Loss after Q. XV evident from truncated text and unmatched catchword on 179v.

PRICKING None extant.

RULING Two columns of 44–45 lines, but 47 lines in quires XVI–XVIII.

SCRIPT Gothic bookhand. Heavily shaded with thick verticals, largely two-line script. t pierced, high or round s standard in final position, a small-headed (not two-compartment). *Et*-nota uncrossed. Juncture of d and b with e, fusion of groups of curved letters, for example p, o, c. Hairline top to double l and general roundness suggest date in fourteenth rather than thirteenth century.

DECORATION Red or blue capitals have simple flourished ornament with vertical hatching in violet or red. Two-colour letters with more elaborate filigreed decoration at major divisions.

HISTORY

Written in Italian script: France, 'Note sur le manuscrit 6041A', p. 414. Once in possession of Roger de Gaignières: *ibid.*

BIBLIOGRAPHY

France, 'Note sur le manuscrit 6041A'.
Mellot, *Catalogus*, IV.195.

173 *PARIS, BIBLIOTHEQUE NATIONALE, MS. LAT. 6041B

Saec. xii *ex.*   Mediaeval provenance: ?
67 fos   2nd fo: [*dif*]-*fugeret occupauit*

HRB 1r–46ra
§§1–3, 5–208. Some compressions: §§83–84, 173–174, 179, 184. Nameless dedication.
Rubrics at §1 (1r) 'Incipit prologus Gaufridi Monemutensis in hystoriis regum Britannie', and at top in informal hand (? *ca* 1200) 'Gesta Britonu[m] et gesta Francorum .ii. libro', after §3 (1ra): 'Explicit prologus' and, in red, 'Incipit hystoria'. No closing rubric, no book-divisions.

CONTENTS
1r–46ra: HRB.
46va–67va: (after *capitula*-list) 'Incipit gesta Francorum'. 'Principium regni Francorum eorumque originem uel gentium illarum ac gesta proferamus . . . et alias quam plurimas eccllesias (*sic*). Amen.' *Liber historie Francorum.* Ed. Krusch, MGH, SS, rer. Mer., II.238–327, 1. 20. Departs from printed text after '. . . expetunt in auxilium'; continues 'et munera multa ei tribuunt . . .'.
Rest of 67 blank except for note in later mediaeval hand.

DESCRIPTION
SIZE 32.5 x 23.5 cm.
QUIRING Signatures indicate arrangement in eights. I–VII⁸, VIII ?⁸, IX ?⁴ (lacks 4: 65–67).
PRICKING In both margins.
RULING Two columns of 47 written lines. Single boundary-lines, written above top ruled line.
SCRIPT HRB written in closely packed lines of a large and heavy Protogothic minuscule. Little angularity or lateral compression. e-caudata occurs occasionally, round d more frequent than straight-backed form, round and tall s found in final position, uncrossed *et*-nota standard. Ligatures using majuscule forms found at line-ends (for example, N + s). *Gesta* (codicologically inseparable from HRB) in more upright and compact script. Dark brown ink.
DECORATION Romanesque capitals with some foliate flourishes or split uprights in pale blue, red, dark green. Very large capitals at §§1 and 5 filled with interlace.

BIBLIOGRAPHY
Mellot, *Catalogus*, IV.195.

174 *PARIS, BIBLIOTHEQUE NATIONALE, MS. 6041C

Saec. xv ?[1]   Mediaeval provenance: ?
72 fos   2nd fo: *moratus est Brutus*

HRB 1r–71va

§§1–3, 5–208. Dedicated to Robert of Gloucester. Rubrics at §111 (38v) 'Explicit prologus. Incipit prophecia eiusdem Merlini' and after §208 (71va) 'Explicit hystoria Britonum a tempore Bruti usque ad tempus Cadualadri scripta'.
No book-divisions.
No other contents. Notes and pentrials on 71va and b, and at top of 72r.

DESCRIPTION
SIZE 30.5 x 21.5 cm.
Paper manuscript with parchment outer bifolia in first and fifth quires.
QUIRING Catchwords indicate I–IV^{12}, V^{14}, VI^{10}.
RULING Frame-ruled in two columns but individual lines ruled in places. 38, 40–45 lines.
SCRIPT *Cursiua* type. Fairly rounded; thick strokes; prominent and slightly slanting descenders, looped ascenders. **d** is looped, **a** and **e** have simple forms. Top of **g** is horizontal and pierced by the vertical strokes of the letter. Little angularity in tops of ascenders or round **d**. Brown-grey ink.
DECORATION Simple red capitals. Red rubrics.

HISTORY
On 1r, 'Cod. Colb. 1579'.
On 71v: 'Ex libris Jo. le Fevre Caulopolitani [ ]'? indicating ownership of Henri du Cambout, Duc de Coislin, bishop of Metz (1697–1732).

BIBLIOGRAPHY
Mellot, *Catalogus*, IV.195.

175 *PARIS, BIBLIOTHEQUE NATIONALE, MS. LAT. 6230

Saec. xii   Mediaeval provenance: ? (?Continental origin)
194 fos   2nd fo: *Britannia insula optima*

HRB 3r–194v

§§1–3, 5–208. §§83–84, 173–174, 179 and 184 compressed. Dedicatory phrase omitted but supplied in correcting hand (?antiquarian).
No original opening rubric but title in modern hand 'Galfridi Monemutensis historia'. Only original rubric found after §208 (194v) 'Explicit'; and in cursive hand of ? *ca* 1300 'Liber istorie Britonum' is added.
No book-divisions.
No other contents – fos 1–2 flyleaves (ruled as for rest of book but blank except for Early Modern title on 1r, 'Historia Britannie').

DESCRIPTION

SIZE 17 x 12 cm.

QUIRING Catchwords indicate arrangement in tens beginning at fo 3. a^2 (1–2), I–XVII^{10}, XVIII^{10} (+ 1 after 5: 173–183), XIX^{10} (184–193), singleton (194), flyleaf.

PRICKING Outer margin only.

RULING ?Drypoint. one column of 19–20 lines. Written above top ruled line.

SCRIPT Large, four-line, upright and clear Protogothic. Angular. Black ink. Round d more frequent than the straight form. Et-nota and tall final s used. a has small head which is sometimes split and joined to the preceding letter. Straight-backed g. Apparently Continental.

DECORATION Romanesque initials with some bosses, split shafts and simple scrolling. Red and cobalt blue.

HISTORY

On 3r, 'Cod. Colb.'. Jean-Baptiste Colbert. Under text on 194v, signature of indeterminate date, 'galleren: :n:'. Possibly Galleranus Nicolaus, founder of the College of Quimper in Paris, where Ivo Cavellatus, the first editor of the HRB, worked. On Nicolaus, see Griscom, *apud* Griscom & Jones, *The Historia*, p. 11, n. 3.

BIBLIOGRAPHY

Mellot, *Catalogus*, IV.218.

176 *PARIS, BIBLIOTHEQUE NATIONALE, MS. LAT. 6231

Saec. xii$^{med./2}$ Mediaeval provenance: ?Anglo-Norman

29 fos (i + 27 + i)   2nd fo: *nobilia flumina thamensis*

HRB 1r–28r

§§1–3, 5–43 (end) 'et in turmis resociare. Crebras etiam'. Nameless dedication (§3). Rubrics at §1 (1r) 'Incipit prologus in historia britonum', §5 (1v) 'Explicit prologus. Incipit hystoria Brit[onum?] [ ]'.

No book-divisions.

No other contents but flyleaves (fos 1 and 29) from twelfth-century ?confraternity book (list of names against dates): Drogo, Vitalis, Hugo, Fulco, Rainerius, etc.

DESCRIPTION

SIZE 18.5/19 x 13 cm.

QUIRING Some quire-markings. a (singleton), I–III^8, IV ?3 singletons (25–28), b (singleton).

PRICKING In outer margin only.

RULING One column of 28 lines.

SCRIPT Heavy and stiff Protogothic minuscule (?Continental) with short ascenders and descenders. Brown ink. Heavy uprights with hairline ticks. Small-headed a, straight-backed g. Et-nota, round d, and tall final s are usual, but ampersand, straight d, and round or high s occur. e-caudata rare. Little lateral compression.

DECORATION Mostly large unfiligreed initials sometimes with simple decoration inside letter. Chalky bright red.

HISTORY
On 1r 'Codex Bigotianus 357'. Collection of the Bigot family, begun in Rouen in the early seventeenth century by Jean Bigot, entered royal collection in 1706: Delisle, *Le Cabinet*, I.322–29. Notes in Early Modern hand at top of 1r, 28v, and elsewhere.

BIBLIOGRAPHY
Mellot, *Catalogus*, IV.218.

177 *PARIS, BIBLIOTHEQUE NATIONALE, MS. LAT. 6232

Saecc. xv (or later) + xii^2 Mediaeval provenance: ?
117 fos   2nd fo: *germina conueniunt*

HRB 2r–117v
§§1–3, 5–208. Opening and end supplied in round mannered cursive script (?*cursiua bastarda*).
2r–10r (§15 'auro et argento donatur') in later hand. 10r was blank first recto of twelfth-century quire. 110r–117v added in the later hand (text from §194 'genti Anglorum' to end). Dedicated to Robert of Gloucester (dedication occurs in added section).
Rubrics at §1 (2r) 'Incipit brutus siue hystoria regum Britannie Maioris a Bruto ipsius primo rege usque ad Cadualladrum ultimum ipsius regem' (fifteenth-century), §34 (20v) 'De Dumuallone Mollutio', §72 (37r) 'Ut Lucius rex Christianitatem \in/ insulam constituit', §97 (50v) 'Ut Uortegirnus consul Geuiseorum factus est rex' and other rubrics passim; §109 (58r) 'Incipiunt uaticinia Merlini secundum eundem Gaufridum Bonemutensem. Liber vi', §111 (58v) 'Incipiunt uatticinia Merlini', after §208 (117v) 'Explicit historia regum Britannie Ma[ ] a Bruto ipsius primo rege usque ad Cadualadrum regem ultimum ipsius inclusiue. Deo gratia'.
Book-divisions: III §35 (21r), IIII §73 (37v), VI §89 (45v), VI (*sic*) §109 (58r).
Prophecies §§112–115 have marginal and interlinear gloss.
Note on Merlin (not usual *Merlinus iste* passage) added in margin 58v.
No other contents.

DESCRIPTION
SIZE 20 x 14 cm.
QUIRING Some catchwords. a singleton (fo 1), I–X^8, XI^4 (82–85), XII–XIV^8; XV^8.
PRICKING Small round holes at outer edge.
RULING Single column, 25 lines.
SCRIPT Original section in heavy, upright, Continental Protogothic minuscule. Four-line proportions, lateral compression. Ampersand and straight-backed **d** apparently more frequent than *et*-nota and round **d**. Second hand has round final s and juncture of **de** but straight-backed **d** still found. Straight-backed g with flat top piercing vertical

strokes. Fifteenth-century additions in very round canonical script with trailing hairline on 2-shaped r and other letters. t has tall back.

DECORATION Original section has capitals in red, green, and blue. Some bosses and split shafts, some simple filigree in contrasting colour.

HISTORY
Top fo 2r 'Codex Colb. 5154' (Jean-Baptiste Colbert).

BIBLIOGRAPHY
Mellot, *Catalogus*, IV.218.

178 *PARIS, BIBLIOTHEQUE NATIONALE, MS. LAT. 6233

Saec. ?xiii/xiv   Mediaeval provenance: ?
81 fos   2nd fo: *Akalon qui prope fluebat*

HRB 4r–81r
§§6–208 [§§109–110 in *pudibundus Brito* form]. Dedicatory chapters absent.
Rubrics at §111 (42r) 'Incipit exposicio libri Merlini' continued as commentary in margin, after §117 (49r) 'Explicit', after §208 (81r) 'Explicit'.
Prophecies glossed, text double-spaced from §112 'Aper etenim Cornubie' –§117. Similar, less complete, gloss in BN lat. 4126. Ed. Hammer, 'A commentary on the *Prophetia Merlini*', pp. 6–18. Second gloss (siglum Y) found also in London, British Library, MS. Cotton Claudius B.viii (copy of Prophecies only); printed by Hammer, 'A commentary on the *Prophetia Merlini*', pp. 413–31.
No other contents. 1r–3v blank paper flyleaves.

DESCRIPTION
SIZE 23 x 15.3 cm.
QUIRING Catchwords. Flyleaves (1–3), I^{12} (4–15), II–III^{10}, IV^{12}, V^{10}, VI^{12}, VII ?^{12} (70–81).
PRICKING Outer margin only.
RULING Single column of 35 lines. Written below top ruled line.
SCRIPT Brown ink. Book-hand with short ascenders and descenders. Juncture of o and e with d and p. a is Caroline, not two-compartment. t and p pierced. Final s usually round, occasionally tall. Crossed *et*-nota. Flat top on double l.
DECORATION Blue or red capitals with simple trailing filigree in red and green-blue.

HISTORY
At foot 4r '[P] Pithou'. Much of Pierre Pithou's manuscript-collection acquired by Jacques-Auguste de Thou in 1596, whence it entered the collection of Jean-Baptiste Colbert, which became part of the Bibliothèque royale in 1732: Delisle, *Le Cabinet*, I.470–72. On date of glosses to prophecies, see Eckhardt, *The Prophetia Merlini*, pp. 11–12.

178   BN, LAT. 6233

BIBLIOGRAPHY
Brugger, 'Zu Galfrid von Monmouth's Historia', pp. 276–77.
Eckhardt, 'The date'.
Mellot, *Catalogus*, IV.218.

179 *PARIS, BIBLIOTHEQUE NATIONALE, MS. LAT. 6275

Saec. xii ?*med.*   Mediaeval provenance: ?
104 fos   2nd fo: *siluestribus apris* (original lost).

HRB 1r–104v
Acephalous. §§15 'quieuit ei tota multitudo . . . '–95 'summisisset. Cepit igitur', §§96 'illam per Uortegirnum'–208 'in Latinum sermonem'. Dedicatory section lost.
Only rubrics extant are at §194 'Dolendum' (98v) 'Responsio Salomonis regis ad Caduallonem'. Lines left before §109 (49r).
No book-divisions.
Text lost in §§95–96 because of loss of folio between 41v and 42r. Closing words of §208 excised.
No other contents.

DESCRIPTION
SIZE 16.8 x 10.8 cm.
QUIRING Signatures. a², I⁶ (1–3 lost: ? = 8, 1–5 lost), II⁸ (fos 4–11), III–V⁸, VI⁸ (lacks 7: 36–42), VII–XI⁸, XII⁸ (4–5 singletons: 83–90), XIII¹⁰ (fos 91–100), XIV ?⁸ (5–8 lacking). Membrane scrappy in places.
PRICKING At outer edge only.
RULING In one column of 22 lines.
SCRIPT Protogothic with four-line proportions. Little lateral compression, g-form particularly spacious. Brown ink. Indented tops to minims. Sporadic use of e-caudata and even **ae** spelling, ampersand occurs but *et*-nota usual; round **d** similarly more frequent than straight form. **a** is small-headed and **g** straight-backed. Apparently Continental.
DECORATION Simple red capitals.

BIBLIOGRAPHY
Mellot, *Catalogus*, IV.223.

180 *PARIS, BIBLIOTHEQUE NATIONALE, MS. LAT. 6432

Saec. xiv ?¹ + xii²   Mediaeval provenance: ?Britain
32 + 35 fos   2nd fo: *albedineitas nigredineitas*

HRB 33r–67v
Three fragments.

33r/v: §15 'respondit. Quoniam aduersi dii'–§18 'ad tartara detrudere'.
34r–51v: §27 'Stadiatl. (*sic*) Egron. Has omnes' –§116.44 'ipsumque totum deu-orabit'.
52r–67v: §119 'applicuit Aurelius Ambrosius' –§197 'et filius eius Offridus cum'. Dedication lost.
No rubrics or book-divisions.

CONTENTS
1r–32v: 'Incipit prologus loyce (*sic*) Ocham'. 'Dudum me frater et amice carissime . . . dum hec est uera animal est.' William of Ockham's *Summa Logice*, truncated after part III.3, cap. 18. Ed. Boehmer *et al.*, *Uenerabilis inceptoris Guilliemi de Ockham Summa Logicae*. This MS. no. 62: *ibid.*, p. 30*.

33r–67v: HRB.

DESCRIPTION
SIZE A (Ockham) – 28.5 x 20 cm. B (HRB) – 28.5 x 18 cm.
QUIRING Catchwords in Ockham only. I–IV⁸; (HRB) I² (+ 1 before 1: 33–35), II–V⁸.
PRICKING A – none visible; B – in outer margin.
RULING In two columns throughout. A – 57–62 lines (?frame-ruling); B – 43 lines.
SCRIPT A – broad pen for size of script; short, thick strokes. Round d, pierced t, final s round, single-compartment a. Compressed and highly abbreviated like a scholastic manuscript. Brown-grey ink.
B – four-line Protogothic with some compression of the minim area. Thickenings on the top of minims. *Et*-nota and round d standard (straight form also found), but tall s finally (round s rare), and occasional appearance of e-caudata. Brown ink.
DECORATION A – red, unfiligreed initials. Also paragraph marks. B – lobster-red Romanesque initials.

HISTORY
Notes in British hands as at foot of 43r in hand of ?*ca* 1300. On 60r 'Edwardus Dei gratia rex Angl[iae]'. ? Welsh at foot of 36v, 41v–42v.

BIBLIOGRAPHY
Mellot, *Catalogus*, IV.242.

181 *PARIS, BIBLIOTHEQUE NATIONALE, MS. LAT. 6815

Saec. xiv/xv   Mediaeval provenance: Milan, Visconti-Sforza family (A.D. 1426)
213 + i fos   2nd fo: [*opinio*]-*nes uniuersos elig*[ ]
                                               2nd fo: *Ante in exitu nemoris*

HRB 178vb–213va
§§1–3, 5–203 'sed summi regis potentia'. Dedicated to Robert of Gloucester.
Rubrics at §1 (178vb) 'Incipit prologus Gaufridi Monimutensis ad Robertum comitem Claudiocestrie in historiam de regibus Maioris Britannie que nunc Anglia dicitur quam

279

historiam idem Gaufridus nuper transtulit de Britannico in Latinum', §5 (178vb) 'Explicit prologus. Incipit liber primus'.

Other book-divisions at §23 (182ra) II, and ends of books marked at §117 (198vb) VII, §143 (203ra) VIII, §163 (206va) IX, §177 (210ra) X. Large initials at other chapters where book-divisions are usual.

CONTENTS

1r–26rb: 'C. Iulii Solini siue grammatici polihistor ab ipso editus et recognitus de posito orbis terrarum et de singulis mirabilibus que in mundo habentur'. 'Quoniam quidam impatientius quam studiosius opusculum . . . ad nuncupationem suam congruere insularum qualitatem.' Ed. Mommsen, *C. Iulii Solini Collectanea*.

26v: blank.

27ra–45ra: 'Incipit historie Romane liber primus', Eutropius. 'Primus in Ytalia ut quibusdam placet . . . quam ad maiorem scribendi diligentiam reseruamus.' Ed. Droysen, MGH, AA, II.6–182.

45ra–53va: continues. 'Hucusque ystorie Eutropius composuit. Cum tamen aliqua Paulus Diaconus addidit . . .' Text 'Anno ab urbe condita millesimo centesimo decimo octauo Ualentinianus . . . insequenti Deo presule libello promenda sunt.' Ed. Droysen, MGH, AA, II.185–224.

54: blank.

55ra–80va: 'Prologus que sit Germania uel que gentes eam inhabitent'. *Capitula*-list followed by text. 'Septentrionalis plaga . . . cura Francorum Abbarumque (*sic*) pacem custodiens.' Paulus Diaconus, *Historia Longobardorum*, edd. Bethmann and Waitz, MGH, SS, Lang, pp. 47–187.

80va–82vb: *Historia Gothorum*. 'Gothorum antiquissimum esse regnum certum est . . . ad istum Sisebutum anni ducenti .liiii..'

82vb–83rb: *Historia Uandalorum*. 'Quandali cum Alanis et Sueuis pariter Hispanias ingrediuntur . . . et Uuandalorum interitum anni .cxxiii. et menses .vii..'

83rb/va: *Historia Sueuorum*. 'Sueui duce Hemerico rege . . . quod mansit annis .cxxvi..'

83va–84rb: 'Post mortem Catheline . . . et multe alie innumerabiles'. Text concerning Fiesole and Florence. Ed. Crivellucci, 'Per l'edizione', pp. 63–64.

85r–110vb: 'Quoniam scire tempora summorum pontificum ac imperatorum . . . mortuus est Rome et in Lateransi ecclesia sepelitur'. Martinus Polonus. Ed. Weiland, MGH, SS, XXII.397–474.

111ra–178va: 'De Gaio Gallicula eiusque genere et conuersatione ante imperium'. 'Gaius Gallicula post Augustum . . . Tyberium natum ex Druso filio naturali nepotes.' 170rb/vb blank. Thomas Tuscus (of Pavia). Partial edn by Ehrenfechter, MGH, SS, XXII.490–528.

178vb–213va: HRB.

213vb blank.

Blank folio following 213.

DESCRIPTION

SIZE 34 x 24 cm.

QUIRING Catchwords suggest arrangement mainly in twelves, with smaller units at

the end of texts since text and quiring coincide. I–II^{12}, III^{14}, IV^{12}, V ?^{4}, VI–VII^{12}, VIII^6; IX–X^{12}, XI^{14} (109–122), XII–XVIII^{12}, XXIX ?^{8} (207–213, unnumbered blank).
PRICKING Not visible.
RULING Two columns of 55 lines throughout; double vertical boundary-lines; written below top ruled line.
SCRIPT Round and compact with simple forms. Short ascenders and descenders, occasionally ascenders tagged at the left. Juncture of **b**, **d**, and **p** with **e** and **o**. Presumably Italian. Black ink.
DECORATION Major initials blocked out with solid colours (gold, purple, green, blue, brown) into a square, white highlighting. Minor initials are red or blue with filigree. Running titles in alternate red and blue capitals.

HISTORY
Catalogued in 1426 among books of the Visconti-Sforza family. See Pellegrin, *La Bibliothèque des Visconti et des Sforza*, pp. 144–45.

BIBLIOGRAPHY
Crivellucci, 'Per l'edizione', pp. 62–65.
Mellot, *Catalogus*, IV.281.

182 *PARIS, BIBLIOTHEQUE NATIONALE, MS. LAT. 7531

Saec. xiv^1 Provenance: Milan, Visconti-Sforza family (A.D. 1426)
311 fos (incl. 31*, 62*, 132*, 202*)   2nd fo: *scierunt nunc altera*

HRB 235va–260vb
§§1–3, 5–208. Nameless dedication.
Rubrics at §1 (235va) 'Incipit liber de gestis Anglorum ante aduentum Christi a Gauterio editus', §5 (235vb) 'De insula Britannie', after §208 (260vb) 'Finit hystoria regum', and in different hand 'Explicit hystoria regum Anglorum' (lower margin).
No book-divisions.

CONTENTS
1ra–2ra: 'Epitoma d[ ]hilo[ ]', Hugh of Saint-Victor, *Epitome in Philosophiam*. 'Sepe nobis Indaleti . . . ad reliqua liber euadet.' Printed by Baron, 'Hugonis de Sancto Victore, *Epitome Dindimi in philosophiam*', pp. 105–18.
2ra: 'Philosophia'. Table of curriculum subjects and disciplines arranged in four columns, 'Latina ethica theorica o[ ]ica.'
2rb–8vb: Hugh of Saint-Victor, *De Grammatica*. 'Quid est grammatica . . . uexit ad urbes.' Ed. Leclercq, 'Le "de grammatica" de Hugues de Saint-Victor'.
9ra–24vb: Hugh of Saint-Victor, *Chronicon*. '[F]ili sapientia thesaurus est . . . Honorius 2. sedit an[no] 5 m[ensis] 2.' Ed. Waitz, MGH, SS, XXIV.88–97.
25ra–va: Hugh of Saint-Victor, *De Ponderibus et mensuris*. 'Proportiones rerum in ponderibus et mensuris considerantur . . . miliare et dimidium.' Ed. Baron, 'Hugues de Saint-Victor lexicographe'.

25va–26ra: 'Multa in scriptura sacra occurrunt . . . qui Iacobum interfecit'.

26ra–27ra: '[S]piritalis diiudicat omnia . . . ad uerum bonum cooperante natura'. Hugh of Saint-Victor, *Miscellanea*, Book I, tit. i. Ed. Migne, *Patrologia Latina*, CLXXVII. 469–77.

27ra/b: Hugh of Saint-Victor, *De Uerbo incarnato*: *Collatio* II. 'Uerbum caro factum est. Quod uerbum? Dei . . . id est humana natura non persona.'

27rb/va: Hugh of Saint-Victor, *De Uerbo incarnato*: *Collatio* I. '[D]um medium silentium . . . preparatum est ab inicio seculi. Amen.'

27vb–28ra: Hugh of Saint-Victor, *De unione corporis et spiritus*. '[Q]uod natum est ex carne caro est . . . rationem scientiam facit'. Ed. Migne, *Patrologia Latina*, CLXXVII.285–89.

28ra/b: 'Theophania est apparitio diuina . . . et amor uirtutis'. Hugh of Saint-Victor, *Miscellanea*, Book I, tit. lxxxiii. Ed. Migne, *Patrologia Latina*, CLXXVII.518.

28rb: '[I]mplete ydrias aqua . . . illuminato dulcescit'. Hugh, *Miscellanea*, Book I, tit. lxxxii. Ed. Migne, *Patrologia Latina*, CLXXVII.517–18.

28rb: 'Egredimini filie Syon . . . exhibebit sublimis'. Hugh, *Miscellanea*, Book I, tit. cxvii. Ed. Migne, *Patrologia Latina*, CLXXVII.543.

28rb/va: 'Ferculum Salomonis cor exercitatum . . . pertineas'. Hugh, *Miscellanea*, Book I, tit. lx. Ed. Migne, *Patrologia Latina*, CLXXVII.503.

28va: unidentified works, ? from Hugh's *Miscellanea*. 'Uoca[ ] . . . ad quod tu uis.'

28va–29ra: '[F]ratres debitores sumus non carni . . . que tamen sepe sunt (altered to *fiunt*) occasio penitencie'. Hugh, *Miscellanea*, Book I, tit. cxix–cxxix. Ed. Migne, *Patrologia Latina*, CLXXVII.544–49.

29ra/b: 'Indica mihi quem diligit anima mea . . . adepta consolemini'. Hugh, *ibid.*, tit. cxxxi–cxxxii. Ed. Migne, *Patrologia Latina*, CLXXVII.549.

29rb/va: Hugh, *De Uerbo incarnato*: *Collatio* III. 'Omnia per sapientiam Dei . . . Magnificat a. m. d. etc.' Ed. Migne, *Patrologia Latina*, CLXXVII.315–24.

29va/b: 'De duabus portis mortis' (opening section in extract from Hugh's *Miscellanea*, 'Qui cupiditate peccant . . . siue ad aquilonem'. Hugh, *Miscellanea*, Book I, tit. cxxxiii–cxxxv. Ed. Migne, *Patrologia Latina*, CLXXVII.549–50.

29vb–30ra: 'Deus noster et cibus . . . ut in illo haberet beatum esse'. Hugh, *ibid.*, Book I, tit. cxliii–cli. Ed. Migne, *Patrologia Latina*, CLXXVII.552–55.

30ra/b: 'Pelias (*sic*) fugiens Iezabel . . . Post exercitum uniuersum puluerem'. Hugh, *ibid.*, Book I, tit. cix–cxi. Ed. Migne, *Patrologia Latina*, CLXXVII.538–40.

30rb/vb: *Tractatus de gestis Francorum regum* (from final rubric). Continuation of tract from 215v. Written in same hand, marked by note and *signes de renvoi*. 'Uenationem exerceret iudicio diuino . . . Deus per omnia secula seculorum. Amen.'

31ra–129ra: 'Incipit prologus libri de sacramentis ab inicio usque ad finem in unam seriem disponitis', Hugh of Saint-Victor. '[L]ibrum de sacramentis Christi . . . Et qui erit infinita sine fine.' Ed. Migne, *Patrologia Latina*, CLXXVI.173–618.

129rb–167vb: Hugh of Saint-Victor, Commentary on the Heavenly Hierarchy of Dionysius the Areopagite. '[I]udei signa querunt et Greci sapientiam . . . in quo sapientia transcendit sanctitas condescendit.' Ed. Migne, *Patrologia Latina*, CLXXV.923–1154.

167vb–210rb: Thomas Aquinas, Commentary on *De diuinis nominibus* of Dionysius the Areopagite. '[T]unc autem O beate . . . et unus Deus uiuens et regnans per omnia secula seculorum. Amen.'

210rb–215va: 'Incipit tractatus de gestis Francorum regum'. 'Eo itaque tempore apud Grecorum regna . . . in quadam silua.' Continued on 30rb.

216ra–235: *De Officiis ecclesiasticis* (mutilated at beginning). 'Esuriui et non dedistis mihi manducare . . . totum tempus quod Deo non cogitas exst[ ]a perdidisse .d.'

235va–260vb: HRB.

260vb–261vb: 'Incipit quedam primo in theologica nisi lucerna etc.' (rubric at foot of page). *Sermo* of Jacques de Lausanne. 'Lucerna pedibus meis uerbum tuum . . . et sic epistole Pauli.'

262ra/b: Prologue to *Adnotationes* on Pentateuch, Hugh of Saint-Victor. '[ ]esiderius proprium nomen est. Hinc Desiderii mei . . . Greca quam Latina et Ebrea quam Greca.' Ed. Migne, *Patrologia Latina*, CLXXV.29–32.

262rb–264va: Hugh of Saint-Victor, *De Scripturis et Scriptoribus sacris*. '[L]ectorem diuinarum scripturarum . . . a Iuda Iudei.' Ed. Migne, *Patrologia Latina*, CLXXV.9–24. Last chapter absent.

264va–268va: Hugh of Saint-Victor, 'De nuncupatione genesis'. 'Liber iste qui primus est diuinorum . . . id est eos natos tenuit Ioseph super genua.' Ed. Migne, *Patrologia Latina*, CLXXV.32–.

268va–270rb: Hugh, 'Incipiunt note de Exod.'. 'Locus in qua . . . cui uolueri etc.' Ed. Migne, *Patrologia Latina*, CLXXV.62 (line 13)–74.

270rb–271vb: 'Incipit liber Leuitici'. 'Liber Leuiticus hebraice dicitur uaiechra . . . non oportebat redimi.'

271vb–273ra: Hugh, explanatory notes on Book of Judges with note on Ruth. 'Liber iudicum qui Hebraice sophthim dicitur . . . tolle calciamentum.' Ed. Migne, *Patrologia Latina*, CLXXV.87–96.

273ra–275va: Hugh, explanatory notes on Book of Kings. 'Liber regum apud nos . . . de manu regis Syrie.' Ed. Migne, *Patrologia Latina*, CLXXV.95–113.

275va–276rb: 'Cumque uenisset dies altera tulit stragulum . . . potest in hoc seculo'.

276va–277rb: '?Resens seculum distinguitur in duos status . . . tempore Achaz regis Iuda'.

277ra–281rb: 'Incipit liber de gestis Karoli magni a Turpino archipresule editus' (rubric in lower margin). 'Gloriosissimus namque Christi apostolus Iacobus . . . uiuit et regnat Deus per infinita secula seculorum.' Ed. Meredith-Jones, *Historia Karoli*.

281rb/v: ?Concordance. 'De 4 [ ] Gregorius super Ez[echielem] omel. 2. 3. 4 . . . De timore [ ]'.

282ra–284ra: Hugh of Saint-Cher, *Speculum Ecclesie*. 'Dicit apostolus ad Ephesios sexto . . . hominem bonis operibus.' Identified by Hauréau (*Initia*, II.41). Ed. Jaumar, *Speculum ecclesie*.

284ra–288ra: History of Apollonius of Tyre. 'Fuit quidam rex in Antiocha ciuitate . . . aliud bibliothece sue.' Ed. Kortekaas, *Historia Apollonii regis Tyri*. (Stuttgart recension.)

288ra–304va: *Rationale diuinorum officiorum*, Jean Beleth, incomplete. 'Tutor uniuersitatis rerum altissimus et creator . . . et alie due Marie matres Iacoborum.' Ed.

Douteil, *Iohannis Beleth*, pp. 3–229, l. 28 (this manuscript not listed by Douteil). Blanks left between some sections.
304vb–307v: blank.

DESCRIPTION

SIZE 35.5 x 24 cm.

QUIRING I¹² (lacks 6), II¹⁴ (lacks 1: 12–24), III⁶, IV¹² (31, 31*, 32–41), V¹², VI¹² (54–62, 62*, 63–64), VII–XI¹², XII¹² (125–132, 132*, 133–135), XIII–XVII¹², XVIII¹² (196–202, 202*, 203–206), XIX¹⁰ (1 excised: 207–215), XX–XXII¹², XXIII¹⁰, XXIV¹² (262–273), XXV ?¹² (274–285), XXVI¹², XXVII¹² (11–12 lacking: 298–307), singleton (blank flyleaf). Foliation incorrect (duplication of fos 31, 62, 132, 202).

PRICKING In both margins.

RULING Text in two columns (tables sometimes more). Very variable number of lines, 50–76. Usually double outer vertical boundary-lines. Written below top ruled line.

SCRIPT Several different hands writing fairly small, abbreviated minuscule. Mostly black ink. Hands have different aspects and practices. Two hands use small-headed **a**, round **d** and lack juncture, but of these one uses final high s and uncrossed *et*-nota, while final tall s and crossed *et*-nota are found in the other. A further hand is later-looking with bowls of letters coming away from the uprights, some juncture. Several scribes used wide nib producing thick, simple strokes.

DECORATION Some red rubrics in hand of text. A few plain red initials at the opening of the volume.

HISTORY

Catalogued in 1426 among books of the Visconti-Sforza family, Milan: Pellegrin, *La Bibliothèque des Visconti et des Sforza*, pp. 155–56. Pellegrin notes entry on 308v in hand very similar to that of librarian of Pavia 'Plurima libri ualde peregrini ut patet in prima fatie huius' (*ibid.*, p. 156).

BIBLIOGRAPHY

Goy, *Die Überlieferung der Werke Hugos von St. Viktor*, pp. 9, 11, 40, 45, 50, 53, 57, 85, 88, 90, 96, 144, 191, 456, 479.
Mellot, *Catalogus*, IV.370.

183 *PARIS, BIBLIOTHEQUE NATIONALE, MS. LAT. 8501A

Saec. xii²   Origin: ?Saint-Vincent (Benedictine), Metz
131 fos   2nd fo: *adesse prenuntiabantur*

HRB 63v–129v
§§1–3, 5–208. Nameless dedication.
Rubrics at §1 (63v) 'Incipit liber in regum historiis qui Britanniam ante incarnationem Christi inhabitauerunt et postea successerunt', §5 (63v) 'Explicit prologus. Incipit

liber metas Britannie et quicquid in ea fertile siue delectabile inuenitur describens. Capitulum I', after §208 (129v) 'Explicit'. Other rubrics at chapter divisions occasionally.

No books but original *capitulum*-numbers at the end of every section marked by an initial.

CONTENTS

Paper flyleaves, one with contents-table.

1r/v: 'Incipit de ordinatione et uita Sancti Patricii episcopi et apostoli Scotorum'. 'In illo tempore Sanctus Patricius erat apud Scotos . . . et electis Dei gaudet in secula seculorum. Amen.' *BHL* 6501.

1v: continuation of previous work. 'Quatuor modis coequantur Moyses et Patricius . . . breuiter nunc liceat terminare.' This and the *Uita* printed by Dumville, *The Historia*, III.105–7. See also Bieler, *Codices Patriciani latini*, p. 45.

1v: three lines of notes, 'Unde accepit initium genealogia Franchorum' from Anchises to Charlemagne. See Faral, *La Légende*, I.288, n. 2. Also in [Paris, BN, MS. lat. 9768 +] Rome, BAV, MS. Reg. lat. 1964: Schroeder, 'Zwei Genealogien'.

1v–11r: 'Incipit historia magni Alexandri regis Macedonum'. 'Egiptii sapientes . . . atque extinctus occubuit.' Ed. Kuebler, *Iuli Valeri Alexandri Polemi res gestae*, pp. 1–168.

12r–15v: 'Prima interrogatio Alexandri ad Dindimum'. 'Sepius ad aures . . . criminosis apud nos.' *Collatio* I, ending incomplete. Ed. Kuebler, *ibid.*, pp. 169–85 (full text ends on p. 189). Followed by poem: 'Nunc euuangelii textum scribendo sequutus'.

16r–22v: 'Semper memor tui . . . Aristoteles inditium'. Letter of Alexander to Aristotle, ed. Walther Boer, *Epistola Alexandri*.

Followed by twenty-two line verse: 'Armipotentis Alexandri hic conscripta tenentur . . . Pi[ ]nia prescitis dat et ut promissa fuerunt.'

23r–32rb: 'Incipit relatio de\Matho/mete'. 'Quisquis nosse cupis patriam Machometis . . . Iherusalem (*sic*) nostris cesserunt menia Francis.' Walther, *Initia*, I.76, no. 1494.

32va: verses by Ausonius. 'Est et non cunctis monosillaba nota frequenter . . . Qualiter uita hominum quam monosillaba uersant.' Ausonius, *Opuscula* 7.4. Also in Auxerre, BM, MS. 91. 'Ter binos deciesque nouem superexit in annos . . . Cetera secreta nouit Deus arbiter eui.' Schaller & Könsgen, *Initia*, p. 720, no. 16238.

32vb–33r: 'Nulle sunt occultiores insidie . . . quam luxuria est'. Also in Auxerre, BM, 91.

33v–36v: 'Uisio Gugtini prius canonici postea monachi . . . huius instabilis uite clausit horam'. Ed. Migne, *Patrologia Latina*, CV.771–80.

36v–37v: 'Miraculum Sancti Iheronimi de leone'. 'Quadam namque die . . . neque finentur in secula seculorum. Amen.'

37v–39v: 'Ab Adam usque ad diluuium anni .ii.cc.xlii. . . . qui est era .dclxvi.v. dccclvii.'. Annals or reckonings from Old Testament times to the Roman Emperors. Also in Auxerre, BM, 91.

40r–63r: 'Liber Ethici Philosophi'. 'Phylosophorum scedulas sagaci indagatione . . . catalogo compescuit.' Ed. Wuttke, *Die Kosmographie*.

63v–129v: HRB.

130r–131v: 'Incipiunt lude (corr. to ludi) Senece de obitu Claudii Neronis'. 'Quid actum sit in celo . . . noli mihi inuidere.' Text truncated. Ed. Russo, *L. Annaei Senecae Divi Claudii Apocolocyntosis*, pp. 45–96 (on this MS., p. 23). See also Reynolds, *Texts and Transmission*, p. 362.

DESCRIPTION
SIZE 25 x 19.5 cm.
QUIRING Indicated by signatures at foot of first recto of the quire. A-B^8, C^{10} (8 lacking), D-H^8, I^8, K-L^8, M^6 (90–95), N^6 (96–111), P-Q^8, R^4 (128–131).
PRICKING In both margins.
RULING Single column of 36 lines, occasionally 29; top line written. Occasionally in two columns.
SCRIPT Brown ink. Protogothic minuscule in several hands. Round **d** and ampersand are standard, final **s** is tall. Minims and ascenders have indented tops. Some lateral compression but basic roundness retained. Thick upright strokes with hairline ticks. In one hand, the horizontal of **t** has diagonal stroke at right end.
DECORATION Capitals occasionally of Romanesque split and bossed type, red. ?Initials at §§1 and 5 in HRB added (ink interlace). Larger initials are more elaborate with stylised foliage ornament.

HISTORY
Association with Saint-Vincent, Metz, suggested by opening of *Uisio Guetini* (33v) in this manuscript, which contains the phrase, 'Et nos fratres eius ipso narrante scripsimus, serui sancti Uincentii Mettis': Dolbeau, 'Anciens possesseurs', p. 215. Manuscript later in possession of Claude Dupuy: Omont, *Anciens inventaires*, IV.206.

BIBLIOGRAPHY
[Mellot,] *Catalogus*, IV.532.

184 *PARIS, BIBLIOTHEQUE NATIONALE, MS. LAT. 12943

Saecc. xi (or xii^1) + **xii** (*ante* 1181)

Mediaeval provenance:
Saint-Germain-des-Prés (Benedictine)

iii + 149 + ii fos

2nd fo: [*roman*]-*norum auxilia que*
2nd fo: *ultramodum admiratus est*

HRB 97r–148v
§§1–3, 5–208. No dedication.
Rubrics at §1 (97r) 'Incipit prefacio magistri Gaufridi Monemutensis in historia Britonum', §5 'Explicit prefatio. Incipit historia', §111 (124ra) 'Incipit prophetia Merlini', §118 'Explicit prophetia Merlini', after §208 (148vb) 'Explicit historia de primordio Britannie Maioris que nunc Anglia uocatur'.
No book-divisions.

CONTENTS

A–B: flyleaves apparently from liturgical manuscript (text and music) in formal black thirteenth-century bookhand.

C: paper flyleaf with Early Modern list of contents.

1r–89va: 'Incipit prefatio Bede presbiteri in historiam Anglorum'. 'Gloriosissimo regi Ceoluulpo (*sic*) . . . et parere semper ante faciem tuam.' In five books, edd. Colgrave & Mynors, *Bede's Ecclesiastical History*. m-text: *ibid.*, p. lxiv.

89a/b: notes on consanguinity. 'Beatus Ysidorus de consanguinitate sic loquitur . . . anathema sit.' This text follows Bede's *Historia* in early Caroline copies and their descendants (see Colgrave & Mynors, *ibid.*, pp. lxii, lxiv).

89vb: 'Item ex decreto Gregoris pape iunioris'. 'Inuenimus etiam in aliorum decretis . . . uestrum fiat exitium.'

90r–96rb: Adomnán, *De locis sanctis*. 'Arculfus episcopus gente Gallus . . . legamus elementum.' Ed. Bieler, *apud* Geyer *et al.*, *Itineraria*, pp. 183–234. Dekkers, *Clavis*, p. 521, no. 2332.

97r–148v: HRB

149r/va: charter of Saint-Germain concerning Hugh, abbot 1162–81. 'Inter domnum Hugonem abbatem sancti Germani de Pratis et Iohannem de Marci euit contentio . . . .'

150–151: flyleaves (as A-B, above).

DESCRIPTION

SIZE 29 x 21 cm.

QUIRING Later numbering of bifolia within quire (A1–4 etc.). a² (+ 1 paper after 2), I–XI⁸, XII⁸ (8 mutilated and backed: 89–96); (HRB) XIII–XVIII⁸, XIX⁶ (5–6 pasted together: 145–149), b² (150–151). HRB physically distinct from Bede but not charter.

PRICKING In outer margins only.

RULING In two columns throughout. Bede 42 lines written, *De Locis* 41–42 lines, HRB 42 lines.

SCRIPT Bede and *De locis* in eleventh-century hand, brown ink. HRB in Protogothic minuscule becoming disjointed and shaky in places. Short ascenders and descenders. Upright strokes have jagged tops. No juncture, roundness retained but some lateral compression. *Et*-nota and round **d** standard. **a** with very small head, **t** with pierced horizontal, **g** straight-backed (and crank-tailed form found in one hand). Final **s** tall, not round.

DECORATION In Bede, rubrics in red capitals. Rather rough initials in red, green, or blue, sometimes with crude foliate scrolls. HRB has initials in red or blue with some simple scrolled ornament.

HISTORY

At the foot of 149va in thirteenth-century hand: 'Iste liber est Sancti Germani de Pratis. Quicumque eum furauerit anatema sit. Amen'. Also on 1r modern (?eighteenth-century) *ex-libris*.

BIBLIOGRAPHY
Delisle, 'Inventaire des manuscrits latins de Saint-Germain-des-Prés', p. 544.
Samaran & Marichal, *Catalogue des manuscrits*, III.311 + plate.

185 *PARIS, BIBLIOTHEQUE NATIONALE, MS. LAT. 13710

Saec. ?xv²   Mediaeval provenance: ?
iii + 244 fos   2nd fo: *Nectanbanus autem incognitus*

HRB 83r–218r
§§1–3, 5–208. Dedicated to Robert of Gloucester.
Rubrics at §1 (83r) 'Galfridi Arturi Monemutensis de gestis Britonum liber incipit.
Prologus', after §208 (218r) 'Explicit hic liber qui nuncupatur brutus'.
Rubric in Early Modern hand before §109 (151v) 'Incipiunt uaticinia Merlini'.
No book-divisions but major capitals at §23 (96r), §35 (105r), §54 (116r), §73 (127v),
§89 (138r), §109 (152r), §111 (152v), §118 (159v), §143 (175r), §163 (189r), §177
(202r).
Text displaced without loss. Bifolium 181:188 should follow 182:187: resulting
disruption of text in §155 and §§159–160.

CONTENTS
i–iii: flyleaves, blank except for Early Modern contents-list on ii r.
1r–75v: 'Incipit liber magni Alexandri imperatoris quem librum inter apocriphos
computamus'. 'Sapientissimi namque Egiptii scientes mensuram terre . . . usque ad
Christi Domini natiuitatem computantur anni .d.c.xiii..'
76r–82v: blank.
83r–218r: HRB.
218v–222v: blank.

223r–244r: printed book. *Tractatus racionis et consciencie de sumpcione pabuli
salutiferi corporis Domini nostri Iesu Christi* (from final rubric), Matthew of Cracow.
'Multorum tam clericorum quam laicorum querela est non modica . . . regnat in
seculorum. Amen.' See Hain, *Repertorium*, I.2, nos 5803, 5805.
244v: blank.

DESCRIPTION
SIZE 21 x 14.3 cm.
QUIRING Paper. a² (+ 1 before 1), I–VI¹², VII¹⁰; VIII–XVIII¹², XIX⁸ (fos 215–222);
XX¹⁰, XXI¹². QQ. XX–XXI (fos 223–244) a printed book.
PRICKING Visible in outer margin occasionally in HRB.
RULING Single column, frame-ruled. 1–75v 32–33 lines written, HRB 30 lines, 223–
244 30 lines.
SCRIPT (A and B) four-line script written with wide nib. Heavy upright ascenders
but that of round d diagonal. Simple round a, e like pinched c (horned). Long s often
tall in ligature, final s is round. t and c very similar. 2-shaped r. Grey ink.

223r onwards printed with painted capitals. Basically Caroline forms with round **d** (juncture with **e** and **o**) and final round **s**.
DECORATION Small, plain capitals in red and blue. Major capitals are formed of two colours with blue on the inside of the letter. Opening capital (1r) filigreed.

HISTORY
On 2r 'Ex libris Iohannis le Feron[ ] caulopolitani [ ] maiestatis hystoriographi[ ]', and similarly on 218r: see Delisle, *Le Cabinet*, II.377. Modern notice in manuscript states that it came from the 'Coisliniana, olim Segueriana' library, which Henri du Cambout, duc de Coislin, bishop of Metz, bequeathed to Saint Germain-des-Prés (1732).
Shield ?of Jean Budé, book-collector and father of Guillaume Budé, librarian of Fontainebleau under François I: Delisle, *Le Cabinet* II.377; I.181.

BIBLIOGRAPHY
Delisle, 'Inventaire des manuscrits latins de Saint-Germain-des-Prés', p. 239.

186 *PARIS, BIBLIOTHEQUE NATIONALE, MSS. LAT. 13935 + 5508

*PARIS, BIBLIOTHEQUE NATIONALE, MS. LAT. 13935

Saec. xiii/xiv   Mediaeval provenance: ?
80 fos   2nd fo: *Ebraucum genuerat*

HRB 1r–80v.
Imperfect at both ends. §24 'obuiam rege Hunorum'–§29 (*med.*), §10 (*ex.*) –§20 (*med.*), §29 (*med.*)–§195 'cum fabricatoribus suis susceptio'. Dedicatory section lost. No extant rubrics or book-divisions.
The dislocation of §§10–20 (which are found after §29) is not physical: the first block of text ends on 2v (§29) 'Condidit etiam Kaerguem'. The sentence is completed from §10 'castra tentoria ab hostium . . .'. The text continues from §10 to §20 'et audatior nullus excepto Corineo inerat' (7r). Here it moves after a linking section 'Hic solus solo gladio suo .d.c. . . . et a terge hostes scelerate inuadit audatiores' to the place in §29 where the text had been broken off earlier, 'idem Guntoniam atque oppidum montis Paladur . . .'.
The two halves of §29 are marked by *signes de renvoi* and on 7r there is a marginal note: 'Quere superius tale signum'.
The Prophecies are glossed.
No other contents.

DESCRIPTION
SIZE 22.5 x 17.5 cm.
QUIRING Catchwords indicate I–X^8 extant (presumably with the loss of a quire at either end).
PRICKING, RULING, SCRIPT, DECORATION See below.

289

HISTORY
From the library of Henri du Cambout, Duc de Coislin, bishop of Metz (1697–1732), which he bequeathed to Saint-Germain in 1732.

BIBLIOGRAPHY
Delisle, 'Inventaire des manuscripts latins de Saint-Germain-des-Prés', p. 250.

*PARIS, BIBLIOTHEQUE NATIONALE, MS. LAT. 5508

Saec. xiv[1]   Mediaeval provenance: ?
70 fos (2–71)   2nd fo: *sua inquietationem incipere*

HRB 2ra–5va
Fragment. '-territus iugiles circa' §196–§208.
No rubrics. Next text follows immediately under §208.

CONTENTS
No folio 1.
2ra–5va: HRB.
5va/b: note on the origins of the Normans and the Norman dukes.'Normanni origine Dani .dccc.lxxxvi. ab incarnatione Domini . . . Henricus frater eius.' Cf. Hugh of Saint-Victor, *Excerptiones Allegoricae*, X.10. Ed. Migne, *Patrologia Latina*, CLXXVII.284. Also found in New Haven, Yale UL, MS. 598.
6ra–7vb: apocryphal letter of Emperor Manuel of Constantinople to Robert of Flanders, by Robert of Reims. 'Domino et glorioso comiti Flandrensium Rothberto . . . mercedem habeatis in celum. Amen'. Ed. Hagenmeyer, *Die Kreuzzugsbriefe*, pp. 146–49.
7vb–69vb: Robert of Reims,*Historia hierosolymitana*. 'Uniuersos qui hanc hystoriam legerint . . . et gloriatur Deus per omnia secula seculorum. Amen.' Ed. Migne, *Patrologia Latina*, CLV.667–758.
Folio lost after 7v (which ends 'dictionum inculta'; 8r begins 'Persarum gens extranea').
69va/b: letter of the patriarch of Jerusalem and the bishops of the East. 'Hierosolimitanus patriarcha et episcopi tam greci quam etiam latini . . . Christi uere nos committimus'. Ed. Hagenmeyer, *Die Kreuzzugsbriefe*, pp. 146–49.
69vb–71vb: 'Aegyptii sapientes genere . . . Dei deorum pulcherrimi'. *Gesta Alexandri* (Epitome by Iulius Ualerius), final quire(s) lost. Ed. Kuebler, *Iuli Valeri Alexandri Polemi res gestae*, pp. 1–168.

DESCRIPTION
SIZE 23 x 18 cm.
QUIRING Catchwords indicate quiring in eights. ?I[8] (lacks 1, 8: 2–7) – loss of 8 indicated by modern note in the manuscript on 7v – then II–IX[8].
PRICKING At outer edge only.
RULING 30 lines, two columns. Ruling above top written line.

SCRIPT Gothic book-hand of a simplified, disjointed aspect. Occasional juncture of o and e after d and p. Also fusion of ba found, but juncture is infrequent. *Et*-nota is sometimes crossed. t is usually pierced, a sometimes has the two-compartment form but is often rounded with a small head. Minuscule r has a foot. s always has the tall form. The *est*-compendium is found. Ascenders occasionally have flat tops or tags. Dark brown ink.

DECORATION Capitals have simple filigree or feathered ornament in contrasting colour (light blue, red). Some initial letters in body of text picked out in red.

HISTORY
Colbert's *ex-libris* on 2r. Also at foot 2r 'Jac. Aug. ?Thuuni'. The collection of Jacques-Auguste de Thou, formed in the late sixteenth and early seventeenth centuries, came into the collection of Jean-Baptiste Colbert in 1680: Delisle, *Le Cabinet*, I.470–72.

BIBLIOGRAPHY
Crick, 'Manuscripts', pp. 158–59.
Crick, 'The manuscripts', pp. 158–59.
[Mellot,] *Catalogus*, IV.125.

187 *PARIS, BIBLIOTHEQUE NATIONALE, MS. LAT. 15073

Saec. xvi?   Provenance: ?
iii + 181 + i fos   2nd fo: *diuersorum colorum*

HRB 1r–181v
§§1–3, 5–208. Dedicated to Robert of Gloucester.
Rubric after §208 (181v) 'Deo gratias et sic est finis huius libri'.
No book-divisions.

CONTENTS
i: document written in Latin and French in informal hand of approximately similar date to rest of manuscript. Verso blank.
ii: blank.
iii: blank recto but notes on *Historia* on verso 'R[ ] sequuntur hic habentur.
Historia regum Britannie Maioris ab eius exordio scilicet a Bruto primo rege . . .'.
At least two hands.
1r–181v: HRB.

DESCRIPTION
SIZE 21 x 15 cm.
Paper but i and final flyleaf are parchment.
QUIRING First half of each bifolium in quire numbered. a⁴ (4 excised), I–XXII⁸, XXIII ?⁶ (6 lacking: 177–181), singleton.
RULING Frame-ruled. 23 lines written.
SCRIPT Rapid and informal. Splayed aspect due to slanting strokes. Ascenders and

descenders lean and curl under at ends. t-like c, t has tall upright, e often has cursive loop-form, a is simple and round, sometimes horned. s round when final, long in other positions. Weak grey ink.

DECORATION Double-sized formal angular script used for opening words after an initial. Capitals are unfiligreed but have ornate shape. Opening initial blue with red, elsewhere capitals blue or red.

HISTORY
On iii v 'Picardus'. ?Jean Picard (ob. 1615), librarian of Bibliothèque royale: Delisle, *Le Cabinet*, II.232.

BIBLIOGRAPHY
Delisle, 'Inventaire des manuscrits latins de Saint-Victor', p. 70.

188 *PARIS, BIBLIOTHEQUE NATIONALE, MS. LAT. 17569

Saec. xii/xiii　　　　　　　Provenance: Chaalis (Cistercian), diocese of Senlis
i + 148 + i fos　　　　　　　　　　　　　　　2nd fo: *ciuitas. Cui puer*

HRB 35vb–102rb
§§1–3, 5–208. Dedicated to Robert of Gloucester.
Above §1 (35vb) 'Prologus sequentis operis', at §5 (36ra) 'Incipit Britannice hystorie liber i'. No closing rubric but scribal verse (102r) 'Hunc primum scripsi. Socios donet deus ipsi'. Also in London, BL, MS. Stowe 56.
Book-divisions: I §5 (36ra), II §23 (42va), III §35 (47rb), IV ?trimmed away, V §73 (58vb), VI §89 (64ra), VII §111 (71va), VIII ?trimmed away, IX §143 (82vb), X §177 (95ra).

CONTENTS
1r–13vb: 'Incipit historia Apollonii regis Tyrii'. 'Fuit quidam rex Antiochus nomine . . . et aliud bibliothece sue.' Tegernsee recension. Ed. Kortekaas, *Historia Apollonii Regis Tyri*, pp. 279–411.
12vb–23vb: 'Hystoria de Alexandro rege magno Macedonum'. 'Egypti sapientes fati de genere . . . atque extinctus occubuit.' Ed. Kuebler, *Iuli Valeri Alexandri Polemi res gestae*, pp. 1–168.
23vb–30vb: 'Incipit epistola Alexandri regis magni Macedonum ad Aristotilem magistrum suum de itinere et de situ Indie'. 'Semper memor tui . . . et industria optime Aristotile sponde.' Ed. Walther Boer, *Epistola Alexandri*.
30v–35v: 'Incipit epistola Alexandri ad Dindimum regem Bragmanorum'. 'Sepius ad aures meas . . . aut inuidie quod dante meliora prestantur.' *Collatio Bragmannorum* (i), ed. Kuebler, *Iuli Valeri Alexandri Polemi res gestae*, pp. 169–89.
35v–102r: HRB
102v: blank.
103ra–104rb: *capitula*-list for following work. 'De origine urbis Rome et temporibus eius . . . Item insule gorgados.'

104va–146vb: 'Incipit liber Solini Iulii. De situ orbis terrarum et de diuersis que in mundo continentur'. 'Cum et aurium clementia ... insularum qualitatem.' Ed. Mommsen, *C. Iulii Solini Collectanea.*

146v–147r: notes on geography of countries in northern Europe. 'Porweghe (*sic*) in hac terra lucet sol ... Erregweite Kentyre Nessunt Man.'

147r–148v: mutilated, blank.

Blank parchment flyleaf.

DESCRIPTION

SIZE 31 x 23.8 cm.

QUIRING Contemporary signatures. a (singleton), I–XVIII[8] (VII unmarked; signatures VI on 48v and VIII on 64v, apparently no losses), XIX ?[8] (3–4 mutilated, 5–8 lacking: 145–148).

PRICKING Generally in both margins.

RULING Heavy and well defined, in two columns of 36 lines. Single vertical boundary-lines, top ruled line written.

SCRIPT Formal and disciplined minuscule throughout book, nearing Gothic proportions but little angularity and no juncture. Large and clear. Very short ascenders and descenders. Flat-topped minim space. In HRB round **d** is almost standard, round s frequent, ampersand predominates, e-caudata occurs rarely. Top of **d** trails into margin at times. Dark brown ink.

?N. France. Cf. Samaran & Marichal, *Catalogue des manuscrits*, III, pl. xxxv (Paris, BN, MS. lat. 8898, Soissons, *ca* 1180–1190) for script and capitals.

DECORATION Small capitals with single-line foliate scrolls. Red, green, dark and light blue, pale brown. Larger capitals have similar but more elaborate decoration, sometimes in two colours.

HISTORY

In cursive hand of perhaps late twelfth century in middle of 148r (mutilated): 'Liber Sancte Marie Karoliloci quisquis eum abstu[l]it furco uel rap. ... et anatema erit'. Same repeated underneath in slightly later hand in which is added '.R. Dei patientia Ego Guibert promitu'. Carolilocus is the latinised form of Chaalis, the name of a Cistercian abbey, daughter of Pontigny, founded 1137.

Also on 1r in modern hand 'L'Egl. de Paris', at foot 1r in Early Modern hand 'Ant. Loisel'. Antoine Loisel, grandfather of Claude Joly, who, in 1680, endowed Notre Dame with a collection of manuscripts including some derived from Loisel: Delisle, *Le Cabinet*, I.431.

BIBLIOGRAPHY

Delisle, 'Inventaire des manuscrits de Notre-Dame', p. 514.

189 *PARIS, BIBLIOTHEQUE NATIONALE, MS. LAT. 18271

Saec. xii^2 Mediaeval provenance: (?Continental origin)
105 fos   2nd fo: *ne Laomedon impure ferret*

HRB 18r–105v

§§1–3, 5–208. Nameless dedication.

Rubrics at §1 (18r) 'Incipit in historiam Britannorum prefatio Gaufridi Monomutensis', §5 (18r) 'Explicit prefatio. Incipit hystoria', after §208 (105v) 'Explicit'. Erasure
under §208. Not legible. Other rubrics added in rough capitals ?Early Modern, as on
1r.

No book-divisions.

CONTENTS

1r/v: parchment flyleaf with contents-list on recto in capitals (Early Modern) and
inscription of ownership on verso (see below, HISTORY).

2r–17v: 'Hystoria Daretis Frigii de uastatione Troie. Incipit prologus Cornelii'.
'Cornelius nepos Salustio Crispo suo salutem . . . Palamonem Epistropum S\c/ydium.'
Ed. Meister, *Daretis Phrygii de Excidio Troiae Historia*.

18r–105v: HRB.

DESCRIPTION

SIZE 20.5 x 14 cm.

QUIRING a singleton (fo 1), I–XIII^8. Some catchwords.

PRICKING At outer edge only.

RULING Single column of 28 lines throughout. No ruling above top written line.
Double vertical boundary-lines.

SCRIPT HRB in several different hands. Rather small, nearly black, four-line Protogothic of Continental sort. e-caudata occurs, *et*-nota is more frequent than ampersand.
Round **d** is standard in one hand but straight-backed form is found elsewhere.
Occasional final round s. No juncture or fusion. Heavy ticks on minims and descenders. Uprights often thick. Straight-backed g.

DECORATION Capitals mostly not completed but where present they have simple
single-line decoration inside letter mostly. In red or light blue.

HISTORY

Erasure under text on 105v.

On 1v in ?seventeenth-century hand, 'Ex libris et bibliotheca Johannis Petri'.

BIBLIOGRAPHY

Delisle, 'Inventaire des manuscrits de Notre-Dame', p. 549.

Saec. xiv ?[1]   Provenance (1641): Tournai, Saint-Martin (Benedictine)
iii + 242 + ii fos   2nd fo: *quo ad Gallias*

HRB 1r–129r
§§1–3, 5–208. Dedicated to Robert of Gloucester.
Rubrics at §110 (68r) 'Incipit prologus de prophetia Merlini', §111 (68v) 'Explicit prologus. Incipit prophetia eiusdem', after §208 (129r) 'Explicit'.
Book-divisions: II §23 (14r), III §35 (22r), IV §54 (31v), V §73 (43r), VI §89 (53v). No other book-divisions rubricated but large capitals at §118 (75v), §143 (90r), §163 (103r), §177 (115r).

CONTENTS
i: two-column ?German, ?fourteenth-century, upsidedown. 'Noch begin en ?wt uer-henen . . . .'
ii: blank except for unimportant notes in late mediaeval and Early Modern hands (upsidedown) on recto.
iii: on recto 'Hic liber est ?G[ ] Ma[ ]t[ ]' ?sixteenth-century' and Early Modern contents-list on verso (recording present contents).
1r–129r: HRB.
129v: blank.

130r–229v: 'Liber poenitentialis' (title in ?sixteenth-century hand), Thomas of Chobham (incomplete). 'Cum miseraciones Domini sint super omnia opera . . . cuius actio censetur esse mortale peccatum.' Ed. Bloomfield, *Thomae de Chobham Summa confessorum*. Ends at p. 226 '. . . sicut alii faciebant noluit'; last paragraph on 229v apparently not printed 'Est enim consensus mortis . . . mortale peccatum'.
230r–242r: 'Ut confessionem et decorem uiduas . . . qui adhuc habet usum contrarium regule'.
242v: blank.
iv: blank except for notes on verso; ?associated with date given there, 1562.
v: recto blank. Notes on verso (running vertically) in late mediaeval hands.

DESCRIPTION
SIZE 25 x 17 cm.
QUIRING Catchwords throughout. Quire signatures beginning I (137v) indicate separate volume beginning at fo 130. a^2 (+ 1 before 1), I–XV^8, XVI^{10} (1 excised, no loss of text: 121–129); I–XII^8, 330–242 uncollatable, b ?2 singletons (iv–v).
PRICKING Outer margin only.
RULING Single column throughout. A – 24 lines. B (after 130r) – 26 lines. Single vertical boundary-lines, ruling above top written line.
SCRIPT HRB – throughout in Gothic bookhand (formal but not quadrata). Largish. Dark brown ink. Juncture of e and o after b, d, p (not h) and fusion of uo etc. Pierced t and p. Two-compartment a (looped, not straight-sided), crossed *et*-nota. Double l is flat-topped. Some ascenders have slightly tagged tops. Second volume in blacker, more lozenged and broken script.

DECORATION Large capitals in blue and red with elaborate red filigree and alternate red and blue scrolls along margin. Otherwise red or blue filigreed capitals. B – has no major capitals but minor capitals as in HRB.

HISTORY
Matches entry of Sanderus in his list of the books of the Benedictine abbey of Saint-Martin, Tournai, *Bibliotheca*, I.116.
Olim A–F. Didot (nineteenth-century collector). Entry in Humanist cursive on 242v names '[ ]uillet' and '[ ]ouillet' with other notes.

BIBLIOGRAPHY
Omont, 'Nouvelles acquisitions du Département des Manuscrits', p. 14.

191 PARIS, BIBLIOTHEQUE SAINTE-GENEVIEVE, MS. 2113

Saec. xii²   Mediaeval provenance: ?
ii + 66 fos   2nd fo: *potestate Pandrasi regis*

HRB 1r–66v
§§1–3, 5–208. Dedicated to Robert of Gloucester.
At §1 (1r) 'Incipit prologus Gaufridi Monemutensis in librum de gestis regum Maioris Britannie que nunc Anglia dicitur ad Rotbertum comitem Gloecestrie', §109 (32v) 'Explicit liber sextus. Incipit prologus in librum septimum qui continet prophetias Ambrosii Merlini', §110 (33r) [ ]ncipit prologus ad Alexandrum Lincolniensem episcopum', §111 (33r) 'Incipit liber .vii. qui continet prophetias Merlini Ambrosii', no closing rubric.
In 11 books: I §5 (1r), II §23 (7v), III §35 (11v), IV §54 (16v), V §73 (22r), VI §89 (26v), VII §109 (32v), VIII §118 (37r), IX §143 (45v), XI §177 (59r).
No other contents.

DESCRIPTION
SIZE 25.5 x 17.8 cm.
QUIRING Signatures and stitching indicate I–VII⁸ and VIII¹⁰.
PRICKING In both margins.
RULING Single column, double vertical boundary-lines, 31–37 lines.
SCRIPT Four-line Protogothic, angular aspect. e-caudata, straight **d** and ampersand are found (but *et*-nota is more frequent). g often has an open bow especially in hand beginning on 35v, which is rounder in aspect, uses round **d**, has short ascenders and descenders.

HISTORY
On paper fly-leaves, 1753 *ex-libris* of Sainte-Geneviève.
DECORATION Most capitals are plain but at book-divisions etc. they have bosses or flourishes and outline decoration in a contrasting colour.

BIBLIOGRAPHY
Kohler, *Catalogue des manuscrits de la Bibliothèque Sainte-Geneviève*, II.264–65.

192 PHILADELPHIA (Pa), THE FREE LIBRARY, MS. E.247

Saec. xii²/ᵉˣ·   Mediaeval provenance: ?
1–7, 9–16, 29–77 fos   2nd fo: *& rege suo precedente*

HRB 1r–38v.

§§1–3, 5–36 (*ex.*), 43 (*in.*) –88 (*ex.*), 155 (*med.*) –204 'subdendam si in illam'.
Dedicated to Robert of Gloucester.
No original rubrics but on 1r in hand of fourteenth century or later: 'Historia Galfridi'.
No book-divisions.

CONTENTS
1r–38v (8, 17–28 lost): HRB.
39: lacking.
40r–77v (51–55, 65–68 lacking): 'Epistola Willelmi ad Robertum comitem', preface
followed by William of Malmesbury's *Gesta Regum*, lacunose and truncated.
'Domino uenerabili et famoso comiti . . . crebrarum eius orationum iudex . . . .' (Book
III). Ed. Stubbs, *Willelmi Malmesbiriensis monachi de gestis regum.*

DESCRIPTION
SIZE 27 x 19 cm.
QUIRING In eights as indicated by the original signature .ii. on 16v. Collation
provided by Griscom, *apud* Griscom & Jones, *The Historia*, pp. 39–40. I⁸ (lacks 8:
1–7), II⁸, III lost (?8: 17–24), IV⁸ (1–4 lacking: 29–32), V⁶ (33–38), VI ?; I⁸ (40–47),
II⁶ (4–6 lacking: 48–50), III–V lost (?eights, no allowance made in foliation), VI⁸ (1–3
excised: 56–60), VII⁸ (1, 8, lacking; 6–7 excised: 61–64), VIII ?⁴ lost (65–68), IX¹⁰
(1 lacking: 69–77), X (?4) lost.
PRICKING Visible at inner edges.
RULING Two columns of 50–56 lines in HRB and 55–56 in *Gesta Regum*. Top line
written.
SCRIPT Small, rather untidy Protogothic of four-line proportions. Round **d**, *et*-nota
predominate over the straight-backed form and ampersand. Tall **s** is standard. No
e-caudata. No juncture. The *est*-compendium is found. Similar script in *Gesta Regum.*
DECORATION Perhaps not contemporary with the book's production. Resembles
typical thirteenth-century filigreed capitals. Red, blue, and sometimes green: Griscom
& Jones, *The Historia*, p. 38.

HISTORY
Formerly Griscom E.17: Dumville, 'The manuscripts', p. 122.

BIBLIOGRAPHY
De Ricci & Wilson, *Census*, II.1161.
Griscom & Jones, *The Historia*, pp. 37–40 + plate.

PHILLIPPS 3117
See Appendix I.

297

193 REIMS, BIBLIOTHEQUE MUNICIPALE, MS. 1430

Saec. xii/xiii   Mediaeval provenance: ?
37 fos   2nd fo: *tantum facinus fecisse*

HRB 1r–37va

§§1–3, 5–140 'In hostes conducerent' (37va). Dedicated to Robert of Gloucester. No original opening rubrics. After §110 (29v) 'Explicit prologus. Incipit prophetia eiusdem'.
No book-divisions.
No other contents. 37vb blank except for later scribbles.

DESCRIPTION
A + 37 fos + B + 2 (outer fly-leaf apparently joins to A).
QUIRING I–III⁸, IV⁶ (lacks 6: 25–29), IV⁸. Fo A before 1, B after 37.
PRICKING No inner prickings visible.
RULING In two columns of 41–42 lines. Top line written. Single vertical boundaries. On 29v which contains §§109–110, inner column written only.
SCRIPT Four-line Protogothic minuscule. Juncture of **po** but not **de**. Round **d** standard but other form appears, uncrossed *et*-nota usual but ampersand also used, final round s occurs occasionally. Retention of early features suggests date not later than the early thirteenth century.

BIBLIOGRAPHY
Loriquet, *Catalogue général*, XXXIX.2, pp. 667–68.

194 ROMA, BIBLIOTECA APOSTOLICA VATICANA, MS. OTTOBONI LAT. 1472

Saec. ?xiii   Mediaeval provenance: ?
iii + 130 fos   2nd fo: *non stilus ignoret*

HRB 92r–127r

§§1–3, 5–208. Dedicated to Robert of Gloucester.
Rubrics at §1 (92r) 'Incipit liber magistri Gaufridi Monemutensis quem transtulit de Britannico in Latinum de regibus Britannicis', after §208 (127v) 'Explicit liber de regibus Britannicis quem Gaufridus Monemutensis transtulit de Britannico in Latinum'.
No book-divisions.

CONTENTS
i: ? fourteenth-century contents list on verso.
ii: notes in French in hand similar to that of main text.
1r–28r: *Liber magistri Gaufridi Anglici Uinosaluo de artificio loquendi* (from final rubric on 28v), Geoffrey de Vinsauf. 'Papa stupor mundi si dixero papa nocenti ...

298

crescere non poteris quantum de iure mereris.' Ed. Gallo, *The Poetria nova*, pp. 14–128.

28r: notes. 'Si uetus exemplum non sufficit ecce nouellum . . . et in thalamo serat posteriore.'

28v–30r: notes. 'Hic est numerus annorum a creatione primi hominis usque ad presens tempus . . . ubi primum regem Faronnidum sibi constituunt.'

30r–48v: 'Incipiunt gesta Francorum', (and in Early Modern hand 'Guillelmi Armoricii de gestis Philippi Magnan. regis Franc.'), William Brito. 'Gesta Francorum regis Philipi magnanimi que ipse preclare gessit a primo anno . . . pannos .d.cc.tarum marcharum precio estimatos.' Ed. Delaborde, *Oeuvres de Rigord et de Guillaume*, I.168–320. See also p. 315, no. 5.

49r–50vb: 'Hic incipit tractatus de honestate clericorum'. 'Intepuit subito tenui mens nostra calore . . . que tam lectoris quam sua lucra cupit.' Ed. Reiffenberg, ['Histoire littéraire, poème sur le costume clérical'], pp. 81–94.

50vb–51ra: 'Pontificis uestis auro byssoque iacinto . . . et scind?[ere] flamen neget illis atque leuamen'.

51rb–52r: originally blank but notes added in ?sixteenth-century hand on 51rb running on to top 51v. The rest is blank.

52v–56r: 'Hic est summa uiciorum'. Diagram of vices and virtues. 'Ex uirulenta radice superbie nascitur pestifera proles . . . Pro suis deliciis nimis esse sumptuosum.' Bloomfield, *Incipits*, p. 185, no. 2053.

56v–61v: *Optimum notabile de confessione* (from final rubric). 'Templum Dei (*sic*) sanctum est quod estis uos . . . .' 'Sermo iste quamuis omnis tangat . . . id est confessionem cum decore uiduisti.' Robert Grosseteste, *Templum Domini*. Bloomfield, *Incipits*, pp. 516–17, no. 5982.

61v–68r: 'Incipiunt cronica episcoporum Metensium a tempore beati Clementi usque ad diem hunc'. 'Metis est ciuitas antiqua in Galliarum prouincia . . . manus munda pudica caro.'

68v–69r: On fasting. 'Letanie in anno bis fiunt. In festo sancti Marci quedam letania . . . Quarto ex eo quod demones a Deo illud timent.'

69v–70v: 'Incipit prologus de uita Antichristi', by Albuin. 'Heriberto Coloniensi episcopo Albininus suorum omnium seruorum ultimus . . . qua ante secula iudicandi esse prefixit.' Ed. Verhelst, *Adso Dervensis*, pp. 68–74, and p. 59.

71r–81v: 'Incipit liber primus Lotharii cardinalis qui postea dictus est Innocencius tercius de miserabili humane condicionis ingressu'. *Capitula*-list on 71r, text begins 71v. 'Domino patris karissimo P. Portuensi episcopo Lotharius indignus diaconus . . . Qui est benedictus in secula seculorum. Amen.' Ed. Maccarrone, *Lotharii Cardinalis (Innocentii III) De miseria*.

82r–88r: 'Incipit speculum anime'. Bernard of Clairvaux, *Meditationes*. 'Multi multa sciunt et senique (*sic*) ipsos nesciunt alios inspiciunt . . . qui uiuit et regnat in secula seculorum. Amen.'

88r–91r: 'Incipit prologus de reuelatio Methodii martiris quomodo fuit ei reuelatum de principio ac fine mundi'. 'Rogasti karissime pater ut librum karissimi Methodii martiris atque pontificis . . . et percuciet (*sic*) eos in momento temporis.'

91r–92r: HRB §§106–110 'tue mulcerent', §§205 'reperarent. Quod cum'–208, crossed through. Hiatus comes between end 91v and top 92r (stub visible).
92r–127v: HRB.
127v–128v: 'Hec de historia ecclesiastica Britanniarum (*sic*) et maxime gentis Anglorum ... multisque et uerbo et conuersatione saluti fuit et hec dicta sufficiant'. ?Epitome of Bede.
128v–129v: 'De scriptura canonica recipienda'. List of biblical books and their contents.
129v–130r: 'De presbiteris qui se aperte reprobi libidinis conuersatione Deo reprobabiles exibent ... bono proposito ligantur'.
130r: underneath, in same hand in French, notes on the Ages of the World mentioning Godfrey, king of Jerusalem (?Godfrey de Bouillon, ob. 1100).

DESCRIPTION
QUIRING Catchwords. a², I–VII⁸, VIII ?⁴ (57–60); IX–XI⁸, XII ?¹⁰ (lacks 9–10: 85–92), XIII ?⁶, XIV⁸, XV⁴, XVI⁸, XVII⁸ (2, 7 singletons), XVIII ?⁴ (127–130).
PRICKING Outer margin.
RULING ?Not ruled. 42–54 lines written, very variable. Single column, variable width.
SCRIPT Similar throughout. Very rapid and informal scholastic-looking hand. No juncture. Ascenders looped when ligatured to preceding letter. Long s descending below the line. a has little or no head. e formed of two strokes. r short but heavily-cleft (almost like v).
DECORATION Unfiligreed capitals, more than one colour.

HISTORY
Initials foot 1r and last verso ?'E. T. S.'.
Shelfmark 'Q.VI.27' and date, 1578, on flyleaf.

BIBLIOGRAPHY
Les Manuscrits de la Reine, p. 90.

ROMA, BIBLIOTECA APOSTOLICA VATICANA, MS. OTTOBONI LAT. 3025
See appendix II.

195 ROMA, BIBLIOTECA APOSTOLICA VATICANA, MS. PAL. LAT. 956

Saec. xii (with xiv)   Mediaeval provenance: ?
62 + 129 fos   2nd fo: *quod respondit erat manifestare*

HRB 1r–62va.
Acephalous. §27 'Britannie suscepit et .lx. annis tenuit' – §208.
§100 'Puelle daretur regi et ut peterent'– §119 'Nec mora cum crastina dies' written in fourteenth-century hand on inserted folios (26r–32v). Dedicatory section lost.

No rubrics or book-divisions.

CONTENTS
1r–62va: HRB.

63–64: blank except for title on both rectos.
65r–191v: 'Continuatio historiarum Helmodi scripta ab Arnoldo abbate Lubecense ad episcopum Racesburgensem'. 'Domino et patri Philippo Racesburgensis ecclesiae antistiti . . . laus et gloria Christo. Amen.' Ed. Lappenburg, *apud* Pertz, *Arnoldi Chronica.*

DESCRIPTION
QUIRING Extant signatures indicate arrangement in eights and the loss of the first quire. II–IV^8, V^{10} (lacks 3), VI ?^{6} (lacks 6: 34–38), VII–IX^8. Q. V has undergone later alteration: the original outer bifolium was retained (fos 25:33) but a new quire of eight, minus the second leaf, was inserted inside it. The new section is in a formal Gothic book-hand of perhaps the fourteenth century. 63r–191 are a separate paper manuscript.
PRICKING In either outer margin only or both margins, depending on scribal portion.
RULING Two columns throughout. Most of HRB in 35 lines; outer bifolium of V 36 lines; body of V 36 lines.
SCRIPT HRB in a roundish Continental Protogothic of the heavy, upright sort. a has little head, g is often straight-backed. e-caudata and ampersand are found but usage of round d and final round s varies according to individual practice. No signs of Gothic compression or juncture. 63–191 written in a humanist cursive.
DECORATION Capitals have Romanesque shapes, usually with simple, single-line foliate or scrolled ornament. Some are more elaborate.

196 ROMA, BIBLIOTECA APOSTOLICA VATICANA, MS. PAL. LAT. 962

Saecc. xv + xvi + xiii^2 Mediaeval provenance: ?
158 fos   2nd fo: *dirigitur uobisque*
       2nd fo: *affatus est. Egregie*

HRB 118r–157v.
§§1–3, 5–208. Nameless dedication (§3).
No extant opening rubric. After §208 (157v): 'Explicit historia regnum [corr. regum] Britannie'. No other rubrics or book-divisions.

CONTENTS
1r–62r: Robert of Reims, *Historia hierosolimitana.* 'Uniuersos qui hanc hystoriam legerint . . . et glorificatur Deus.' Ed. Migne, *Patrologia Latina*, CLV.667–758.
62r: letter of patriarch of Jerusalem and bishops of the East. 'Iherosolimitanus patriarcha et episcopi tam Greci quam Latini . . . uere nos commitimus.' Ed. Hagenmeyer, *Die Kreuzzugsbriefe*, pp. 146–49.
62r–64r: letter of Emperor Manuel to Robert of Flanders. 'Domino et glorioso comiti

Flandrensis Roberto ... sed mercedem habeatis in celis in perpetuum. Amen.' Ed.
Hagenmeyer, *ibid.*, pp. 129–38.
64v: blank.

64Ar/v: blank.
65r–67r: 'De methodo historiae ecclesiasticae'. 'Totum opus distribuetur ... decla-
mationibus et digressionibus.'
67v: blank.

68r/v: blank.
69r–117v: 'Primum caput de argumento in libri'. 'Multae grauesque res in consider-
ationem iis uenire solent ... atque tenacius in fixae manens.'
117A–C: blank.

118r–157v: HRB.
158: French document (?fifteenth-century) on verso. Recto blank.

DESCRIPTION
QUIRING Several manuscript books apparently, of which the HRB is the oldest unit.
It bears a late mediaeval foliation, 46–97, not found in the rest of the manuscript. 1–64
?fifteenth-century paper; 64A–67 paper leaves written in humanist cursive; 68–117
paper written in antiquarian hand; 118–157 parchment, thirteenth-century.
PRICKING ?For boundary-lines only.
RULING HRB in single column of 42–60 lines.
SCRIPT HRB in highly compressed rapid Gothic minuscule. Thick, simple strokes.
Indented or forked tops to some ascenders. a has no head except occasionally when
initial. *Et*-nota is crossed. Juncture of e and o with b, d, p, etc.

HISTORY
On 64r in formal Gothic bookhand: 'Explicit passaigum (*sic*) magnum pet'. Io.
Wissenburg'.

197 ROMA, BIBLIOTECA APOSTOLICA VATICANA, MS. REG. LAT. 692

Saec. xii^2 Mediaeval provenance: ?
ii + 88 + ii fos   2nd fo: [*fidu*]-*ciam maximam in illis*

HRB 1r–48va.
§§1–3, 5–208. Dedicated to Robert of Gloucester.
No contemporary rubrics or book-divisions.

CONTENTS
i r: Latin document in fifteenth- or sixteenth-century cursive hand.
i v: blank but in sixteenth-century hand of Secretary type 'Charles par la grace de[ ]'.

ii: largely blank. Sixteenth-century *ex-libris* at top right of recto torn away. Contents-list in Early Modern hand on verso.

1–48va: HRB.

48vb–51rb: 'Britannia occeani insula cui quondam Albion nomen fuit . . . hic campano gramine corda tumet'. Bede, *Historia ecclesiastica*, I.i–x. Edd. Colgrave & Mynors, *Bede's Ecclesiastical History*.

51rb–59vb: 'Uita et conuersatio gloriosissimi imperatoris Karoli . . .'. 'Uitam et conuersationem et ex parte non modica res gestas . . . post obitum eius summa deuotione adimplere curauit.' Ed. Halphen, *Eginhard*.

59vb–82vb: 'Cum gesta priscorum bona mala ue maxime . . . condita erat nobiliter sepeliuit'.

82vb–88vb: 'Uita Theodorici Gothorum regis' (according to final rubric). 'Primo regum Francorum . . . cuius rex esset affinitatis expers.'

89–90: flyleaves as i–ii. 90v bears document as i r. Elsewhere notes in Latin, sixteenth-century apparently.

DESCRIPTION

QUIRING Signatures (on foot first recto of quire, beginning II on 9r) indicate I–XI^8. 89–90 are singleton flyleaves.

PRICKING In outer margin only.

RULING Two columns of 40 lines. Top line written, single boundary-lines.

SCRIPT Upright, solid Continental Protogothic. Diagonal ticks or feet on minims and descenders. *Et*-nota standard, e-caudata infrequent, round d occurs fairly often. Final round s is found in some hands. a is triangular with small head and g is straight-backed. Ascenders have indented tops.

DECORATION Spaces left for capitals including half column before HRB (1ra) but none completed.

BIBLIOGRAPHY
Les Manuscrits de la Reine, p. 22.

198 ROMA, BIBLIOTECA APOSTOLICA VATICANA, MS. REG. LAT. 825

Saecc. xv or xiv *ex.*   Mediaeval provenance: ?
146 fos   2nd fo: *aduolantibus apibus*

HRB 1r–142r.

§§1–3, 5–208. Dedicated to Robert of Gloucester.

Rubrics at §1 (1r) 'Incipit hystoria regum Britonum a tempore Bruti eorum primi regis usque ad Cadualladrum ultimum inclusiue etc.', after §108 (72v) 'Incipit prologus prophecie uel uaticini Merlini' (end of fo blank), at §109 (73r) 'Incipit prologus de propheciis Merlini', at §111 (73v) 'Explicit prologus. Incipit prophecia', after §208 (142r) 'Explicit hystoria Bruti primi Britonum regis necnon aliorum regum sequencium usque ad Cadualladrum inclusiue ultimum regem Britannie Maioris etc.'.

No book-divisions.

CONTENTS

1r–142r: HRB.

142r–146r: 'Epystola Luciferi' (according to final rubric). 'Lucifer princeps tenebrorum tristicia profundi Acherontis regens ymperia . . . in robore promissorum.' Letter sent in 1350 to Clement VI, attributed to Henry of Hessen.

DESCRIPTION

QUIRING Indicated by catchwords. I–VI^{12}, V ?^{8} (*Prophetie Merlini*: 73–80), VI–X^{12}, XI ?^{6}.

RULING Frame-ruling. 27 or 28 lines written.

SCRIPT Fluent Secretary. Prominent tapering descenders without great slope. Minims hard to distinguish. Tops of ascenders broken and curled under. **d** is not yet angular. Top of **t** rises well above the cross-stroke. **a** has simple round form.

DECORATION Capitals are enclosed in square of filigree. Double-size textura script is used for significant opening words.

BIBLIOGRAPHY

Manuscrits de la Reine, p. 55.

199   ROMA, BIBLIOTECA APOSTOLICA VATICANA, MS. VAT. LAT. 2005

Saec. xii$^{med./2}$ Mediaeval provenance: ?

ii + 120 + 2 fos   2nd fo: *suaui soporis in ripis*

HRB 1r–69r.

§§1–208. Dedicated to Robert of Gloucester and Waleran of Meulan.

Rubrics at §1 (1r) 'Incipit historia regum Britannie'.

No book-divisions but divided into *capitula* which are numbered serially throughout.

CONTENTS

Flyleaves: fourteenth-century book. Rubric at foot verso 'Explicit liber Peryerminias (*sic*)'.

1r–69r: HRB.

69v–120v: 'Incipit prefatio apologetica Roberto monacho in historia Iherosolimorum' (Robert of Reims). 'Uniuersos qui hanc hystoriam legerint . . . [ ]uomodo uult miseretur et sanat. Amen.' Ed. Migne, *Patrologia Latina*, CLV.667–758.

DESCRIPTION

SIZE 22 x 15 cm.

QUIRING Sequence of original signatures to 65r indicates regular arrangement in eights. (Signatures located at centre foot of first folio of quire.) Despite ceasing of signatures, section following HRB is not separable and seems to be contemporary with it.

PRICKING Visible in outer margins only.
RULING In single column of 26 to 34 lines, very variable. Possibly unruled.
SCRIPT Several hands. Untidy, rather stiff Continental Protogothic. e-caudata occurs and ampersand is found although *et*-nota is more frequent. Round **d** is very common. Letters are extended at foot of page and the proportions of the whole are sometimes attenuated. Minims have cupped strokes at top.

BIBLIOGRAPHY
Griscom & Jones, *The Historia*, p. 32 & pl. II.

200 ROUEN, BIBLIOTHEQUE MUNICIPALE, MS. U.74 (1177)

Saec. xii²/ᵉˣ· Mediaeval provenance: Jumièges
  (late thirteenth-century), Normandy
302 + ii fos 2nd fo: *fluminum cursus auertent*

HRB 1r–59ra
§§6–208. Dedicatory sections absent.
Rubrics at 1r 'Incipit historia Anglorum edita a Gaufrido Monemutensi iussu Alexandri Linconiensis episcopi'.
No original book-divisions but these added in later hand at §§ 35 II (9v), 89 III (23v), 110 IV (30r), 118 V (33r), 143 VI (40r).
Text close to Bern 568: Dumville, 'An early text', pp. 16–17 and references.

CONTENTS
1ra–59ra: HRB.
59r–62ra: 'Anno ab incarnatione Domini quadragentesimo nono Mauritianus . . . eodem rege regnante', immediately beneath, in same hand, no rubric. Extracts from Bede, *Historia ecclesiastica*, I.15, I.23–25, I.34; II.1–3. Edd. Colgrave & Mynors, *Bede's Ecclesiastical History*. English c-text: *ibid.*, p. lxi.
62r–166r: 'In uolumine hoc continetur hystoria Anglorum nouiter edita ab Henrico Huntendunensi . . .', in ten books. Preceded by *capitula*-list, 'Primus liber est de regno romanorum . . . lectori prelibando notificaremus'. Text 'Cum in omni fere litterarum studio . . . Et animi pericula non reformidantis fuerit.' Edition of 1147. Greenway, 'Henry of Huntingdon and the manuscripts', pp. 108–12, esp. 109 (MS. Lc1).
166v–170v: continuation of above from 1147–57 as found in Chronicle of Robert of Torigni. 'Henricus filius ducis Gaufridi . . . et uocatus est.'
171r–172v: extract from continuation by monk of Le Bec covering years 1157–1160. 'Mense decembri apud Romam . . . Obiit Robertus.'
173r–275ra: 'Incipit prefatio ecclesiastice hystorie gentis Anglorum'.
'Gloriosissimo regi Cewlfo (*sic*) Beda famulus Christi . . . apud omnes fructum pie intercessionis inueniam. Amen.' Edd. Colgrave and Mynors, *Bede's Ecclesiastical History*. Rest of fo 275 blank.
276r–278rb: acephalous text. 'delatoris hamis intercipiebat. Crudelitate etiam qua consulem de Moretuil . . . et animi pericula non reformidantis fuerit.'

278v–282v: 'Incipit libellus Bede presbiteri de temporibus minor'. 'Tempora momentis . . . secundum .lxx. .v.dcccc.'

282v–288rb: 'Incipit libellus Bede de natura mundi'. 'Naturas rerum uarias labentis et eui . . . ad occidentem extenditur.' Ed. Jones, *Bedae uenerabilis Opera. Pars I. Opera didascalica*, I.189–234. Rest of folio blank.

289r–297va: 'Incipit liber Gilde sapientis de primis habitatoribus Britannie que nunc dicitur Anglia et de excidio eius'. *Historia Brittonum*. 'A principio mundi usque ad diluuium anni .ii.cc.xlii. . . . in extremis finibus cosmi.' Ed. Faral, *La Légende*, III.5–61.

297va–298: blank. 298 unruled.

299r–302r: Bede, *De Temporibus Minor*, repeated partially. 'Tempora momentis . . . Artaxerxes ann. .xl. Esdra legem.' Verso blank but ruled. See Dumville, 'An early text'.

DESCRIPTION

SIZE 32.4 x 23 cm.

QUIRING No signatures but layout, script, rubrication homogeneous throughout. Apparently the product of a disciplined scriptorium.

PRICKING At both edges.

RULING Two columns of 35 lines. Writing on top line. Single vertical boundary-lines.

SCRIPT Formal, monumental Protogothic minuscule of Anglo-Norman type, moving towards two-line script. Round **d** and final tall **s** more frequent than straight **d** and round **s**. *Et*-nota not ampersand. No juncture evident but minims close-packed.

DECORATION Fine capitals. Plain letter form with single-line flourishes.

HISTORY

On 302v, in late thirteenth or early fourteenth-century hand: 'Ego sum abbatie Gemmeticum', Jumièges, Normandy. Ownership restated at top 1r in Early Modern hand.

BIBLIOGRAPHY

Dumville, 'An early text', especially pp. 6–16.

Omont, *Catalogue général*, I.295–97.

201 ROUEN, BIBLIOTHEQUE MUNICIPALE, MS. 3069

Saec. xviii

vii + 119 fos (foliated 8–126)   2nd fo: *qui patrem et matrem*

HRB 8r–86r

§§1–3, 5–208. Dedicated to Robert of Gloucester.

200 chapters.

Collation of the 1508 edition against London, British Library, MS. Cotton Titus A.xviii supervised by Nicolas Brett for Dom Morice (Pierre-Hyacinthe, the Breton historian).

CONTENTS

1r: nineteenth-century note about this manuscript. Verso blank.

2r: letter of Nicolas Brett dated Angers, 18.7.1739, concerning the production of the transcript. Recipient unnamed. Verso blank.

3r/v: blank.

4r: title page signed 'Nal. Salmon Cler' dated 25.4.1739. 'Historiam Galfridi Monumetensis de origine et gestis regum Britannorum a Iohanne Badio Ascensio editam An. 1508 cum M.S. in bibliotheca Cottoniana, cui titulus Titus A. xviii.5 fideliter comparaui. Uariationes a libro typis exarato in marginem inserui.' Verso blank.

5r: note (in new hand) on Cotton manuscripts containing HRB: Nero D.viii, Galba E.xi, Titus A.xviii, and also on Royal 4.C.ix (*recte* 4.C.xi). Verso blank.

6r–7r: 'Memoire pour Londres envoye par D. Morice, historien de Bretagne'. Undated. Apparently written in same hand as the beginning of the transcript. Request to librarian of Cottonian library to compare the four copies of the *Historia* which it contains with each other and with Ascensius's text to determine whether what he printed was really the work of Geoffrey, bishop of St Asaph.

8r–86r: HRB.

86v–90v: blank.

91r–126r: in different hand, 'Ex chronico Nicolai Trivetti Dominicani ab anno MCXXXVI ad annum MCCCVII'. 'Ut autem iuxta nostram intentionem . . . Rediit itaque cardinalis Londonias super his certitudinem expectaret.' Ed. Hog, *F. Nicholai Triveti de ordine frat. predicatorum Annales*.

BIBLIOGRAPHY

Omont, *Catalogue général*, II.81.

202 SAINT-OMER, BIBLIOTHEQUE MUNICIPALE, MS. 710

Saec. xiv ?[1]   Provenance: ?Saint-Bertin

A + 176 + B fos   2nd fo: [*ciui*]-*tatis incola atque inquisita*

HRB 53v–95ra.

§§1–3, 5–109, 111–184, 186–208. Dedicated to Robert of Gloucester.

Rubrics at §1 (53v) 'Incipit prologus Gaufridi Monemutensis in libro de nominibus regum Britonum qui uocatur hystoria Bruti', no final rubric.

Book-divisions at §23 (58r) II, §35 (67r) III.

§110 omitted (mid-column).

Second Variant Version. Hammer's siglum O: Emanuel, 'Geoffrey of Monmouth's *Historia*', p. 104.

CONTENTS

1ra–41rb: 'Incipit prologus in uita Sancti Thome martyris Cantuarensis archiepiscopi', by Edward Grim. 'Professores artium seculi proprios singuli conatus . . . Thomam martyrium fecere subire beatum.' Edd. Robertson & Sheppard, *Materials*, II.353–450. *BHL* 8182.

41rb–51rb: 'Quedam breuis compilatio collecta ex pluribus libris hystoricis'. 'In principio temporis creauit Deus celum . . . Philippus frater ipsius tunc comes Pictauensis in regno successit.'

51rb: note on the foundations of various religious orders. 'Anno Domini nongentesimo .xii. incepit ordo Clugniacensis . . . ordo fratrum minorum.'

51rb–53rb: 'Dictum de Philomena'. 'Philomena preuia temporis ameni . . . ut me cantus uolucris doceat cantare.' Also found in Paris, Bibliothèque Nationale, MS. lat. 10710: Hauréau, *Initia*, IV.287v.

53rb: 'Hii omnes fuerunt episcopi Morinen.'. 'Autmondus . . . Ingerannus' then additional names. Morinen. probably for Morinensi, signifying Saint-Jean-au-Mont-les-Thérouanne.

53rb/vb: 'Initium ordinis Cartusiensis'. 'Sicut patres nostri narrauerunt nobis . . . que domus Cartusia nuncupatur.'

53vb–95ra: HRB.

95ra/va: 'Mirabilia Britannie insule'. 'Primum miraculum est stagnum lumonoy . . . et semper moueri uidebatur non longe a terra.' Ed. Dumville, 'Anecdota'.

95vb–97rb: 'De duobus militibus miracula'. 'Miraculum quoddam in regno imperatoris Alemannorum . . . et ad agnitionem ueritatis uenire. Amen.'

97rb–101vb: 'Incipit epistola Alexandri magni regis Macedonum ad magistrum suum Aristotilem'. 'Semper memor tui . . . animi industrie optime Aristotilis inditium.' Ed. Walther Boer, *Epistola Alexandri*.

101vb: continues 'De morte Alexandri', and ends with account of the twelve Alexandrias. 'Alexander solis et lune arboribus consultis ab altera illarum responsum accepit . . . et extremum uoluntatem suam secreto expressit.'

101v–102ra: 'Occasio mortis illius'. 'Occasio illius mortis . . . et ueneno superatus atque extinctus occubuit.' End of Iulius Ualerius, *Gesta Alexandri*.

102ra/b: 'Epytaphium Alexandri'. '[P]rimus Alexander pillea natus . . . occubuit leto sumpto cum melle ueneno.' Walther, *Initia*, I.759, no. 14648.

102rb/va: on items of Greek and Roman history 'De Lucio pario', 'De morte Cesaris', 'De Uirgilio et filia Neronis imperatoris'. 'Lucius Papirius consul . . . supra dorsum portantur.'

102va–103rb: 'Ab Adam usque ad Noe anni bis mille ducenti quadraginta duo . . . a Roma condita impletur'. Chronology from Adam to death of Robert, count of Flanders.

103rb–104ra: 'Hii omnes fuerunt Romani pontifices'. 'Petrus apostolus . . . Clemens V' in original hand (ending foot 103vb) with additions in several hands. Pontificate of Clement V, 1305–14.

104ra/b: 'Hii omnes fuerunt reges Francorum'. 'Moroueus . . . Philippus filius eius' (son of Louis who was grandson of St. Louis).

104va–105va: 'De Antichristo', by Adso. 'Omnes de antichristo scire uolentes . . . qua iudicandum esse predixit.' Ed. Verhelst, *Adso Dervensis*, pp. 22–30.

105va–107rb: 'Epistola presbiteri Iohannis imperatorum Romanorum'. 'Presbiter Iohannes potentia et uirtute Dei . . . et potestatem nostram.' Ed. Zarncke, 'Der Priester Johannes'.

107va–109rb: 'De ?Palumbo presbitero'. 'Fuit Rome uir quidam diues . . . et ego proculdubio pro pretio eius centum uaccas tibi dabo.'

109rb/vb: 'De historia beati Nicholai et de quodam priore miraculum'. 'Inter innumera uirtutem insignia . . . atque paratissimus ero.' *BHL* 6209.

109vb–110vb: 'De duobus ducibus altercantibus et per ostensionem animarum pacificatis'. 'Rem uobis fratres refero . . . enim est uirtutis angelo dignitatis.'

110vb: 'De primis parentibus Domini nostri Iesu Christi secundum carnem'. 'Maria mater Domini et Maria mater Iacobi . . . et serua t<u>um Tungressum episcopum.'

110vb–112vb: 'Tractatus magistri Hugonis de S. Uictore'. 'Ibo mihi montem Myrre . . . in unum congregamur.' *De amore sponsi ad sponsam.* Ed. Migne, *Patrologia Latina*, CLXXVI.987–94.

112vb–117va: 'Uisio Elysabeth ancille Domini quam uidit in S[ ]maugiensi cenobio de resurrectione beate uirginis matris Domini Iesu Christi'. 'In anno quo mihi per angelum Domini annuntiabatur . . . sit honor et gloria et gratiarum actio in secula seclorum. Amen.'

117va–118va: 'Alpha et w magne Deus hely . . . cum Moyse et Helya pium cantem alleluya. Amen'. Hildebert of Le Mans. Walther, *Initia*, I.43, no. 835.

118va–119va: 'Ecce labat mundus grauat . . . uoca (*sic*) mox est releuare paratus'. Walther, *Proverbia*, I.865, no. 6910.

119va–119 bis va: 'Quid decus aut forma . . . Hac facit a multis laudum sibi iura rependi'. Walther, *Proverbia*, IV.316, no. 25001.

119 bis va–122va: 'Dominus uobiscum uitando pericula iura . . . uiuendi munus sine fine dies parit unus'.

122va–124rb: 'Plurima cum soleant mores exercere sacros . . . Christo bissena custodia ponitur hora'.

124rb–126vb: 'Quedam prouerbia ex dictis antiquiorum'. 'Alba ligustra cadunt uaccinia . . . O mala tempora cur quia stercora tot peperunt.' Walther, *Proverbia*, I.87, no. 754.

126vb–133ra: 'Uita sancte Marie Egyptiace' (verse). 'Incipit hec phariae conuersio Sancte Marie . . . quid stulti proprium non posse et uelle nocere.'

133ra–165vb: *Iohannes Beleth, De Diuinis Officiis.* 'In primitiua ecclesia prohibitum erat . . . et iudeis fuisse auariorem.' Ed. Douteil, *Iohannis Beleth*, pp. 1–301, l. 73 (siglum Sa).

165vb: 'De inuentione sancte crucis'. 'Nunc de inuencione sancte crucis dicendum est cruce Domini inuenta est ab Helena . . . et postea uocatus est quiriacus.'

165vb–167rb: 'De sancto Iohanne euangel.'. 'Sanctus Iohannes qui supra pectus Domini in cena recubuit . . . qui habuerit uirtutes quas isti lapides signant.'

167rb–168vb: 'Omelia Addonis', Paulus Diaconus. 'Quis est homo diues nisi Christus . . . qui uiuit et regnat per omnia secula seculorum. Amen.' Ed. Migne, *Patrologia Latina*, XCV.1370–75.

168vb–169ra: 'De triplici domo Dei'. 'Beati qui habitant in domo tua Domine . . . ut in nobis habitaret Iesus Christus Dominus noster.'

169ra/vb: 'De .iiii. modis contemplacionis'. 'Quatuor modis eximus per contemplacionem . . . et amplius ad archam redite noluit.'

309

169vb–170rb: 'Quod sit sanctificare ieiuniam'. 'Quia ieiuniantis Domini uictorias recensentes triumphum nostre salutis agnouimus . . . ut sustinenda doceret.'

170rb–174vb: 'Septem sunt peticiones in oracione dominica'. 'Pater m. septem sunt peticiones sicut .vii. dona spiritus et .vii. uirtutes . . . in ara cordis adoletur.'

175ra/vb: 'Sermo Sancti Augustini episcopi de unitate trinitatis et incarnatione Domini'. '[ ]egimus sanctum Moysen populo Dei precepta . . . que in celis sunt et que in terris.' Ed. Migne, *Patrologia Latina*, XXXIX.2196–98. See Dekkers, *Clavis*, p. 91, no. 368, Sermon 245 (possibly by Syagrius).

175vb–176vb: unidentified. 'Conuenio uos o iudei qui usque in hodiernum diem negastis filium Dei . . . testimonium non est uerum.'

176v: blank except for contents-list in spidery secretary-hand.

DESCRIPTION

QUIRING Catchwords indicate arrangement primarily in eights.

RULING Two columns of 48 lines with ruling above top written line.

SCRIPT Compressed formal Gothic book-hand, approaching quadrata. Juncture of e and o with b, p and d (sometimes h). a has two-compartment form, t is pierced, *et*-nota crossed, final s standard.

DECORATION Capitals are filigreed quite elaborately.

HISTORY

If list on 53r refers to the bishops of Thérouanne, then it would seem that this manuscript, throughout its history, can be associated with the region of St-Omer.

BIBLIOGRAPHY

Douteil, *Iohannis Beleth*, I.229*–232*.

Michelant, *Catalogue général* III.313–14.

203 SALISBURY, CATHEDRAL LIBRARY, MS. 121

Saec. xii^{2/ex.}
i + 64 + i fos

Mediaeval provenance: ?
2nd fo: *Brutus telum in ipsos*

HRB 1r–64v.

§§1–3, 5–208. Dedicated to Robert of Gloucester.

Rubrics at §1 (1r) 'Incipit edicio Galfridi Arturi Mon[ ] de gestis Britonum', along fore edge of 1r 'Incipit edicio Galfridi Arturi Monemutensis de gestis Britonu[m]'. §5 (1r) 'Descriptio insule', §6 (1v) 'Narratio istorie', §89 (27v) 'Hic incipit istoria Gratiani regis', §110 (35r, in margin) 'Prologus', §111 (35r) 'Hic incipit prophetia Ambrosii Merlini'.

Major capitals are found at places where book-divisions often fall (§§1, 5, 6, 23, 35, 54, 73, 89, 109, 111, 118, 143, 163, 177).

Post-mediaeval book-divisions at main initials (§§1, 23, 35, 54, 73, 89, 111, 118, 143). No other contents (flyleaves are modern paper).

DESCRIPTION
QUIRING Signatures indicate eight regular quires of eight.
PRICKING Visible at outer edge only.
RULING Single column of 34 lines.
SCRIPT Prickly four-line minuscule. Straight-backed **d** is still frequent but *et*-nota not ampersand is used and e-caudata is very rare. Tops of ascenders are angled and minims and descenders are ticked. g is crank-tailed. Final s tall.
DECORATION Heavy and elaborate Romanesque initials (geometric and foliate patterns).

HISTORY
Above rubric on 1r is the mediaeval shelfmark 'B II' and also in ?thirteenth-century hand 'Liber de gestis Bruti'. Many nota signs in margin. The manuscript was apparently at Salisbury in 1622 when Young catalogued the library but it was not included: see Ker, *Books, Collectors, and Libraries*, p. 204, n. 1 (and also p. 271).

BIBLIOGRAPHY
Lakin, *A Catalogue of the Library of the Cathedral Church of Salisbury*, p. 24.

204 SAN MARINO (CAL.), HENRY E. HUNTINGTON LIBRARY, MS. EL 34.C.9 (1121)

Saec. xv   Origin: ?English
54 fos   2nd fo: *doctrina Britonum*

HRB 1r–25va
§§66 (*in.*)–67 (*in.*), 71 (*ex.*)–208 [§§171–173 compressed, §§179, 181, 186, 200, 202 truncated]. Dedication lost.
Above §111 (9v) 'Prophetia Merlini' (repeated as running title on next folios), under §117, added in hand contemporary with text 'Et sic finit prophecia Merlini'. No final rubric.
No book-divisions but *capitula*-numbers in margin at each division.
Text begins (1ra) 'Deinde hortabatur Britones' §66. 1ra mutilated at foot, 1rb lost. 1vb begins 'quod possidebat optinuit' §71. First fifteen folios mutilated at foot and some in outer column.

CONTENTS
1–25va: HRB.
25va/b: 'Hec sunt nomina regum Anglie et tempora regni illorum' to Henry III (regnal length of Henry III originally unfinished but list continued in different but contemporary hand to Henry VI). 'Primus rex Anglie Hyne uocabatur ... Henricus filius eius.'
26r/v: 'R[ ]gibus Anglie post conquestum'. 'Sanctus Edwardus confessor rex Anglie ... et Edmundum comitem Cancie ...' End mutilated. Edward III is king last mentioned (in margin).

311

27r–28v: 'Prophetia de rege Edwardo .iii. et de sequela (*sic*) sua'. 'Tunc suscitabat dominus in Britannia . . . cessabunt reges esse quia ubique et erit nouum seculum.'

29ra–33rb: 'Incipit prologus fratris Nicholi Trevet de ordine predicatorum in annales regum Anglie qui a comitibus Andegauensibus suam traxerunt originem secundum lineam masculinam'. Book I only. 'Atheniensium Romanorumque res gestas certissimus auctor Salustinus (*sic*) . . . ante aliquot anno constructa.' Ed. Hog, *F. Nicholai Triveti de ordine frat. predicatorum Annales*, pp. 1–30.

33va–37ra: 'Incipiunt gesta Henrici secundi regis Anglorum qui primus erat eorum qui de comitibus Andegauensibus originem duxit secundum lineam masculinam' (rubric on 33r). 'Henricus filius Galfridi cognomento Plantageneth . . . earum fierent presules mortuo Ricardo episcopo London..'

37v: blank except for note in large Gothic script 'Dominus Nichola[us]'.

38ra–45v: poem on chess (with diagrams). 'Seignurs une poy entendez . . . et issi le supera desqes ac iuat.'

46v–54v: 'Dixit Petrus Amfusus (*sic*) seruus Christi Iesu compostor huius libri . . . sic que dura fuit mors . . .'. Mutilated at end. Edd. Hilka & Söderhjelm, *Die Disciplina clericalis*.

DESCRIPTION

SIZE 29 x 22 cm.

QUIRING ?Paper. Catchword at 14v but many folios damaged at foot.

RULING Fos 1–26 – two columns of 46–47 lines; fos 27–28 – single column of 44–45 lines; fos 29–37 – two columns of 45–48 lines; fos 38–45 – single column of 41–42 lines; fos 46–54 – single column of 48–50 lines.

SCRIPT More than one hand. Regular, compact, and angular four-line minuscule. Shaded. No slant. Descenders and minims end in point. Ascenders angled down, not curled under. Angular round **d** (large loop) and **g** (8-shaped). Simple two- stroke form of **e**, long or 2-shaped **r**, two-compartment **a**, sigma-type of final **s**.

DECORATION None extant.

BIBLIOGRAPHY

De Ricci & Wilson, *Census*, I.137–38.

205 SANKT GALLEN, STIFTSBIBLIOTHEK, MS. 633

Saec. xiii*in./1*   Mediaeval provenance (1461): Sankt Gallen (Benedictine)
130 pages   2nd recto: (p. 5) *eorum inquetudini*

HRB pp. 3–121

§§1–3, 5–208. Nameless dedication (§3): printed from this manuscript by Hammer, 'Some additional manuscripts', p. 237.

Rubrics above §1 (p. 3) 'Incipit prologus in Britannicam hystoriam', §5 (p. 3) 'Textus hystorie'.

No other rubrics or book-divisions.

CONTENTS

pp. 1–2: flyleaf. Blank except for nineteenth-century contents-list on verso.

pp. 3–121: HRB.

pp. 122–128b: 'Democritus dicit mulierem solum . . . sufficientia sibi hospicia facuerit'. Solinus, *Polyhistor*, I.54–.

pp. 128b–130: 'Presbiter Iohannes potentia et uirtute Dei rex regum terrenorum . . . acsi omni genere ciborum repleti simus'. Ed. Zarncke, 'Der Priester Johannes', pp. 909–22. §§1–96.

DESCRIPTION

QUIRING No signatures.

PRICKING Visible in outer margin.

RULING HRB in two columns, 34–35 lines. No ruling above top written line? Medical works similarly but in single column, returning to double column from p. 128.

SCRIPT HRB apparently in single hand. Script has proportions of Protogothic minuscule but juncture of e and o after d. Minims not broken. Wide nib. Straight-backed d frequent. t pierced. a has small head. Final s round or tall, occasionally high. Medical works in similar script but smaller and spikier with g resembling two o's arranged vertically and joined by line.

DECORATION Plain, single colour, rather crude. Sometimes stylised leaf-scrolls on major capitals. Simple line ornament on opening capital of HRB.

HISTORY

Recorded in the library catalogue of Sankt Gallen in 1461 (no. 1399): Lehmann, *Mittelalterliche Bibliothekskataloge*, I.116.

BIBLIOGRAPHY

Hammer 'Some additional manuscripts', pp. 236–38.

Scherrer, *Verzeichniss der Handschriften der Stiftsbibliothek von St Gallen*, p. 206.

206 SEVILLA, BIBLIOTECA COLOMBINA, MS. 7.3.19

Saec. xv or later   Mediaeval provenance: ?

84 fos   2nd fo: *puero qui patrem*

HRB 1r–83v.

§§1–3, 5–208. Dedicated to Robert of Gloucester.

No rubrics but after §208 (83v) 'Deo gracias. Amen'.

No other contents, fo 84 blank.

DESCRIPTION

QUIRING Catchwords indicate I–VII^{10}, VIII^8, IX ?^{4}(fos 79–83).

RULING Frame-ruled. About 36–39 lines written.

SCRIPT Late mediaeval cursive of the 'splayed' type. Heavy diagonal strokes form ascenders of round d (leaning to left) and most descenders (leaning to right). Minim-

letters hard to distinguish. Simple form of a and e. Long s is ligatured with following e (resembles mediaeval st-ligature).
DECORATION Only completed capitals on 1r. Large opening initial with filigree filling and plain small capital. Elsewhere, spaces left with larger gaps at §§ where book-divisions often occur.

BIBLIOGRAPHY
Ewald, 'Reise nach Spanien im Winter von 1878 auf 1879', p. 378.

207 STOCKHOLM, KUNGLIGA BIBLIOTEKET, MS. HOLM.D.1311

Saec. xii/xiii[1]   Mediaeval provenance: ?
ii + 47 fos   2nd fo: *Quomodo iterum cum Modredo*

HRB 2ra–47vb.
§§1–3, 5–208. Dedicated to Robert of Gloucester.
Rubrics at §1 (2ra) 'Incipit prefacio Gaufridi Monemutensis in hystoriam Brittonum', §5 (2rb) 'Explicit prefacio. Incipit liber primus historie Brittonum', §110 (25ra) 'Incipit prefatio Gaufridi Monemutensis in prophetiam Ambrosii Merlinii', §111 (25rb) 'Explicit prologus. Incipit prophetia Ambrosii Merlinii', no final rubric.
Book-divisions: I §5 (2rb); II §23 (6ra), III §35 (8va). Then in hand of ?*ca* 1400: IV §54 (12ra), V §73 (16ra), VI §87 (19va), VII ? (space for rubric at §118: 28ra), VIII §143 (33va), IX §163 (40rb). *Capitula*-numbers added throughout in same hand.
Second Variant Version. Hammer's siglum S: Emanuel, *'Geoffrey of Monmouth's Historia'*, p. 104.

CONTENTS
1ra–2ra: 'Incipiunt capitula in brittanicam hystoriam. Capitula libri primi'. *Capitula*-list for nine books. 'De qualitate et quantitate Brittannie . . . quod in ipso regnum Britonum defecit.'
2ra–47vb: HRB.

DESCRIPTION
QUIRING Some early signatures (.iii. on 24v, .iiii. on 32v, .v. on 40v). Also .iii. on 18v ?additional. Suggests I–V^8, VI ?^{8} (lacks 8: 41–47).
PRICKING In both margins.
RULING Two columns of 45 lines with no ruling above top written line.
SCRIPT Minuscule without Gothic angularity or compression. No juncture or piercing of t. Straight-backed d and tall s still occur but are not standard. Perhaps size affects usage of normal dating features. Uncrossed *et*-nota used. Cedilla-shaped s (found finally elsewhere) occurs in this manuscript in all positions. When starting a line, ascender of d, first stroke of U, horizontal of t trail into margin. Ascender of d elsewere is sometimes ticked down at the top. a is small-headed.
DECORATION Many initials have decoration of filigree, stylised foliage, circles etc. Major capitals are large and highly decorated.

HISTORY
Came into the Royal Library in the eighteenth century.

BIBLIOGRAPHY
Griscom & Jones, *The Historia*, p. 572.

208 TROYES, BIBLIOTHEQUE MUNICIPALE, MS. 273 bis

Saec. xii/xiii   Mediaeval provenance: Clairvaux (Cistercian)
40 fos   2nd fo: *que sibi moriens*

HRB 2r–39v
§§1–3, 5–208. Nameless dedication.
Rubrics at 1r 'Incipit prologus Galeridi in historia Britannorum', §5 'Explicit prologus. Incipit historia Britannorum'. No closing rubric.
No book-divisions.

CONTENTS
Flyleaves (1 and 40) contain document in French, ?fifteenth-century hand, mentioning Vitry, but no other extant contents.
Originally bound with Troyes, BM, MS. 433 (124 fos) which contains Baldwin of Ford, Sermones; Hugo, *De perfectione uite*, prefaced by letter to sister Heliundis; Bernard of Clairvaux, letters.

DESCRIPTION
QUIRING Some signatures, .iii. (25v), .iiii. (33v).
PRICKING Visible at outer edges only.
RULING Distinct. In two columns of 45 lines. Ruling above top line of script. Central margin divided in two.
SCRIPT In several hands. Regular heavy book-hand of late twelfth or early thirteenth century. Juncture of **de** occasionally, straight **d** as well as round (two-line) form. Lateral compression. Minims lozenged but not broken. Crossed *et*-nota standard but ampersand used mid-word. q- and e-caudata still found. ?N. French script.

HISTORY
Listed in 1472 library catalogue of Clairvaux (no. 1410) as larger volume of which the remainder is now shelved as MS. 433 in the same library.
See Vernet *et al., La Bibliothèque de l'Abbaye de Clairvaux*, p. 242.

BIBLIOGRAPHY
Libri, *Catalogue général*, II.134.

209 TROYES, BIBLIOTHEQUE MUNICIPALE, MS. 1531

Saec. **xiv** + xiii + xvi
466 fos

Provenance:? Trier
2nd fo: *De ciuitatibus Nazareth*

HRB 84v–169r

§§1–3, 5–185, 186–208. Dedicated to Robert of Gloucester.

Rubrics at §1 (84v) 'Incipit prologus Gauffridi Monemutensis in sequentem hysto-riam', §5 (85r) 'Descripcio ca. .i.', §109 (131v) 'Prefacio hystorici et epistola de interpretacione propheciarum Merlini R.', §111 (131r) 'Incipiunt prophecie Merlini ex mistica pugna draconum', after §208 'Explicit hystoria Britannica'.

Book-divisions: II §54 (107r), III §98 (116v), IIII §143 (147r). Also *capitula* numbers noted in margin.

Second Variant Version. Hammer's siglum T: Emanuel, *'Geoffrey of Monmouth's Historia'*, p. 104. Preceded by *capitula*-list as in Cambridge, University Library, MS. Ff.1.25; London, BL, MSS. Cotton Galba E.xi, Cotton Titus A.xxvii (all Second Variant manuscripts).

CONTENTS

1r–78r: 'Incipit hystoria Ierosolomitana abbreuiata. Capitulum primum. Cur Dominus terram sanctam uariis flagellis et sub alternis casibus se exposuit. R.' (rubric on 2v). *Capitula*-list followed by text (begins 2v). 'Terra sancta promissionis Deo amabilis . . . et sancta Romana ecclesia de die in diem expectantes.' Jacques de Vitry, *Historia orientalis*. Ed. Bongars, *Gesta Dei per Francos*, I.ii, pp. 1049–1124.

78v: blank.

'78'r–84v: 'Incipiunt capitula primi libri hystorie britannice'. 'Descripcio quantitatis et multimode opulencie . . . anglice ystorie tractanda distribuit.'

84v–169r: HRB.

169v: blank.

170r–176v: Arnulf of Lisieux. 'Ysagoge dictaminum ad epistolas componendas secundum magistrum Tramundum.' Truncated at end. Preceded by *capitula*-list (170r–171r). 'Artificiosa dictandi peritia ingenio uso et eruditione . . . prestolatur Brutus dedignatur . . . .'

177r–252r: 'Incipit cronica fratris Martini' (rubric on 177r). Martinus Polonus. 'Quoniam scire tempora summorum pontificum Romanorum ac imperatorum . . . ueniens in Syciliam est defunctus.' Ed. Weiland, MGH, SS, XXII.379–474.

252v: entered on blank verso in humanistic hand 'Sequuntur epistolæ Poggii Euarini Vergerii Quirini Uitalis Gasparini Arelii Guarinii Hermolai'.

253r–465v: Humanist correspondence as listed above.

DESCRIPTION

QUIRING Three mediaeval units with humanist correspondence bound in at the back. Catchwords. I–VI¹², VII ?⁶ (fos 73–78); VIII¹² (78–89), IX–X¹², XI¹⁰ (114–123),

XII ?[14] (124–137), XIII–XIV[12], XV ?[8] (162–169); XVI ?[8] (blank + 170–176); XVII–XXII[12], XXIII ?[4] (lacks 4: 249–251); letters (paper).

PRICKING Not visible.

RULING Single column throughout except for *capitula*-lists (in two columns). fos 1–169 – 33–34 lines, single vertical boundary-lines, ruling above top written line. 170–176 – single column, 28 lines, very narrow double vertical boundary-lines, no ruling above top written line. 177–252 – single column, 33–35 lines, ruling not visible.

SCRIPT 1–169 in informal Gothic bookhand, written with broad nib. Short ascenders and descenders. Ascenders tagged to left. Juncture of e and o after b, d and p, not usually after h. Final s round or cedilla-shaped, occasionally tall. 2-shaped r trails below the line. Crossed *et*-nota. t pierced, a has very small or no head. 170–176 – disciplined four- line script, Protogothic proportions (?early thirteenth-century). Final s tall, round d almost two-line. Straight-backed d occurs. Uncrossed *et*-nota. Fos 177–252 – later thirteenth-century, more informal. Short, broad script with forked ascenders, juncture of e after b, d, p, and sometimes h but o often not joined to preceding h or d. Crossed *et*-nota. Final s tall. Fos 253–465 – Humanist cursive, various hands.

DECORATION 1–169 – larger initials in two colours with filigree, minor initials filigreed as usual. 170–176 – unfiligreed capitals except for first which has simple line decoration. 177–252 – filigreed capitals.

BIBLIOGRAPHY
Libri, *Catalogue général*, II.642–44.

210 USHAW, USHAW COLLEGE, MS. 6

Saec. xii[2] + xii *ex.*   Mediaeval provenance: ?Kirkstall (Cistercians)
242 fos   2nd fo: *tria nobilia flumina*

HRB 61r–121v + 227r–242r; 3–60v + 122r–225v

Originally contained §§110–208 only [*Merlinus iste* passage after §117]. This unit, now 61r–121v + 227r–242r, was split after §178 'omnes fere duos' (with no loss of text) when §§1–109 was added (3r–60v), using the two blank folios at the beginning of the first quire (now 59–60); the text was continued from the break in §178 'qui in ambis' to the end of §187 (122r–124v). Dedicatory section absent in original.

Rubrics apparently date from time of additions.

Additional section dedicated to Robert of Gloucester.

Rubrics above §1 (3r) 'Galfridi Monemutensis in historia Britonum' and also in margin ?contemporary hand 'Prologus. Incipit', at §5 (3v) 'Hic incipit historia Britonum', summaries at some chapters in hand of 'Prologus' rubric at §1, §111 (61v) 'Hic incipiunt prophetie Merlini' (very faint), after §117 (70v) 'Explicit prophetia Merlini', after *Merlinus iste* chapter (70v) 'Quomodo Merlinus indicauit Uortig[ ] ?exitum uite sue . . . filiorum regis Constantinii [. . .]'. Very faint.

No book-divisions.

CONTENTS
1–2: flyleaves, apparently from book in twelfth-century English hand, extracts from sermon of Odo of Cluny: Levison, 'A combined manuscript', p. 42.
3r–60v: HRB §§1–109 (added).
61r–121v: HRB §§110–178 (*med.*) (original).
122r–124v: HRB §§178 (*med.*) –187 (added).
124v–225v: under HRB. 'De Sancto Augustino'. 'Anno gratie quingentesimo octogesimo secundo . . . Teobaldus Beccensis abbas Cantuariensis archiepiscopus effectus est.' Henry of Huntingdon, *Historia Anglorum*. Greenway, 'Henry of Huntingdon and the manuscripts', p. 108 (MS. U).
226: stub.
227r–242r: HRB §§178 (*med.*) –208 (original).
242v: blank except for unimportant notes (Latin) in fourteenth-century informal hand, Early Modern note of contents, and sixteenth-century signature, Thomas Killingbecke.

DESCRIPTION
SIZE 18.5 x 12.5 cm.
QUIRING Original in nine quires marked with signatures (I–VIII) and catchwords. Additions marked by catchwords only (some lacking); represented here by lower case Roman numerals. a^2 (fos 1–2), i–vii^8; I^{14} (3 cancelled: 59–71) II–V^8, VI^{10} (104–113), VII^8; viii–xvii^8, xviii^8 (202–207, 209–210), xix^8 (2 cancelled: 211–217), xx ?^{10} (?3, 7 singletons, 10 lacking, 9 cut down: 218–226); VIII^8, [IX]^8.
PRICKING Visible at outer edges in additions only.
RULING Single column throughout with top line written. Original – 21 lines (sometimes 20), double outer boundary-line. Additions – 23/24 lines (20–21 on 59v–60v), double inner and outer boundary-lines.
SCRIPT The whole volume written in English Protogothic minuscule. Script of original is taller and less compact than that of additions; round **d** frequent, final round **s** occurs, *et*-nota standard, e-caudata still found. Additions in less rounded script, no round **d** or s but no e-caudata; crossed *et*-nota standard. Ascenders sometimes indented and some descenders have feet.
DECORATION Similar in both. Romanesque capitals, mostly plain but some with foliate flourishes or contrasting scrolled decoration.

HISTORY
Northern English interest evident in annotations in body of manuscript, dating from before about 1200: Levison, 'A combined manuscript', pp. 44–49. Levison noted the Northern associations of the name Killingbecke (found on 242v), an abbot of the Cistercian Abbey of Kirkstall being Robert Killingbeck: *ibid.*, p. 49.

BIBLIOGRAPHY
Dumville, 'The origin of the C-text', esp. pp. 316–18.
Hammer, 'Some additional manuscripts', p. 241.
Levison, 'A combined manuscript'.

211 VALENCIENNES, BIBLIOTHEQUE MUNICIPALE, MS. 792 (589)

Saec. **xiv** *med./2* + xiii/xiv

Origin: ?English
Provenance (Early Modern): Vicoigne
(Premonstratensian), dioc. of Arras

265 fos

2nd fo: *potencie offendit. non est ei*

HRB 1r–54r
§§1–3, 5–208. Dedicated to Robert of Gloucester.
Rubrics at §1 (1r) 'Incipit prefacio in hystoria Brittannorum', §5 (1r) 'Sequitur hystoria', §110 (28r) 'Incipit prologus in prophecia Merlini Ambrosii', §111 (28r), 'Eplicit (*sic*) prologus. Incipit prophecia eiusdem', after §208 (54r) 'Explicit historia Brittannorum prima'.
Book-divisions: II §23 (6r), IIII §35 (9v), IV §54 (13v), V §73 (18r), VI §89 (22r), IX §143 (37v), X §163 (43r), XI §177 (48r).
This is a complete vulgate manuscript: Griscom seems to have derived his statement that this manuscript contained a lacunose or abbreviated text from the description to that effect made by Lièvre in the *Catalogue général*, XXV; cf. Griscom & Jones, *The Historia*, p. 569; Dumville, 'The manuscripts', p. 117.

CONTENTS
1r–54r: HRB.
54r: eight-line verse. 'Scripsimus Arturum quem Britto putat rediturum . . . Ceperit huic anime sit eden uel celica tempe.' *Colophons*, VI.492, no. 23365.
54va/b: 'Historia Brittannorum in uersibus'. 'Dardanus exulat alta perambulat et rutulorum . . . Hec lege que sequeris sicque peritus e<ris>.' The second also found in Douai, BM, MSS. 880 and 882. Ed. Hammer, 'Some Leonine summaries', pp. 119–20. Laid out differently here from Hammer's edition; corresponds with his ll. 29–70, 1–28.
55ra–82vb: 'Sequitur de eadem materia historia Britonum uersificata. O magistro Alexandro Nequam con[ ] ut credo et scripta dominum Cadiocum episcopum Uenetensem. Incipit historia Brittannorum uersificata' (rubric begins at foot of 54v). 'Primus ab Ytalia post patris fata relegat . . . Antistes uestro uiuat Chadiochus <in ore>.' Walther, *Initia*, I.759, no. 14643. Ed. Wright, *The Historia Regum Britannie of Geoffrey of Monmouth, IV*.
83r–84v: 'Incipit recapitulacio omnium predictorum in antiqua hystoria Britanorum sumpta ex cronicis Uincentii libro .xvii. capitulo .v. .vi. et .vii.'. 'Narrat antiqua Britaniorum (*sic*) hystoria quod Ascanius Enee Troiani filus (*sic*) . . . Hec facile ut a[ ] tota in ue[ ] p.'
Followed by note 'Hec omnia supraposita debent precedere capitulum .3. sequentis historie Willelmi Malmesberiensis in additione Uincentii . . .'.
84v–123v: '[R]es Anglorum gestas Beda uir maxime doctus . . . clamantes oppidanis ut portas'. William of Malmesbury, *Gesta regum*, to Book IV §308 (*med.*), Stubbs, *Willelmi Malmesbiriensis monachi de gestis regum*, II.362.
124r–125v: blank except for fragment of text.
126r–158v: text resumes 'Qui de Manona iniquitatis sibi amicos . . . cum fauore

omnium sibi dyadema imposuit.' Unidentified. Not apparently from William's *Gesta regum* or *Historia Nouella*.

158v: blank.

159r–224r: 'Incipit prologus in exposicione Mellini Ambrosii'. 'Cum multos rerum nouitate permotos (*sic*) quas in regno Anglie nostris temporibus . . . dicacionem Helie et Enoch.' Commentary of Alain de Lille on Galfridian Prophecies. Ed. *Prophetia Anglicana.*

224r–228v: 'Sequitur eius prophetia', HRB §§111–118. 'Sedente Uortegirno Britonum rege super ripam . . . quos aper Cornubie deuorabit.'

229r: 'Beda de situ Britannie.' 'Insula Britannie cui quondam Albion nomen fuit . . . et uocatur fossa tendit quia per Lincolniam.' Free adaptation of Bede, *Historia ecclesiastica*, I.i. Edd. Colgrave & Mynors, *Bede's Ecclesiastical History.*

229r: 'Commendacio Britannie'. 'Britannia sicut legitur [ ] insulas omnes est uel prima uel maxima . . . Continet etiam Scotiam totam.'

229r–230v: 'Incipit tractatus de mirabilibus Britannie'. 'Uentus Britannie egreditur de cauernis terre . . . Ab autem uocatur locus ille Rollendit[ ].' This and the preceding two items are also found in Cambridge, Corpus Christi College, MS. 59, fos 140r–142v.

231r–237r: 'Incipiunt annales de gestis Britonum de gestis Saxonum de gestis Danorum de gestis Normannorum. Prologus incipit', ending with the reign of King John. 'Ad expendiendas regni necessitates miliciam semper non credimus . . . Et sepultus est apud Wigorniam in ecclesia beate Marie.' Cf. Cambridge, Corpus Christi College, MS. 59, 142v–151r (?). Hardy, *Descriptive Catalogue*, III.46.

237v–238r: blank.

238v–259r: 'Incipiunt alia cronica breuissima a tempore aduentus Normannorum in Angliam de fortuitis in hiis diebus contingentibus'. 'Anno incarnacionis Domini .m.lxv. ciclus annorum magnus .D.xxxii. bis a natiuitate Christi . . . et ecclesias Anglicanas depilandas.' Also in Cambridge, Corpus Christi College 59, 151v–173r. See Hardy, *Descriptive Catalogue*, I.ii, p. 101.

259v: blank.

260r–265r: 'Magna carta', with documents associated with Henry III – charter of the forest, and two confirmations of other charters (1253) in his name.

'Henricus Dei gracia rex Anglie, dominus Hybernie, dux Normannorum Aquitanum et comes Andagau. . . . In primis concessimus Deo et hac presenti carta . . . anno regni nostri primo.'

DESCRIPTION
SIZE 33.5 x 22 cm.
QUIRING No catchwords or quire signatures visible on microfilm.
PRICKING Visible in inner margin in several places.
RULING 1–53r – single column, 40 written lines, written below top ruled line; 54r–82v – double column, 40 lines; 83r–84v – single column, 43–44 lines; 85–158 – single column, 40–41 lines; 159–228 – single column, 40–41 lines; 229–265 – single column, 40 lines.
SCRIPT HRB written in late-looking compact Gothic bookhand; **d**, **o**, etc., con-

structed of vertical strokes; flourishes on tails of g and 2-shaped r. Two-compartment a, final s tall or round. Fusion of a, d, e, and o with preceding d, and of a with b; fusion following p and h not usual.

Other hands often coincide with blocks of text. 85–158r, 260–265 – similar to script of HRB, different hands. 54–83 – earliest-looking part of volume. Minuscule with simple, unbroken strokes and very short ascenders and descenders. a has small head; final s is tall or round; *et*-nota is crossed; juncture of e and o with preceding b, d, and p. 83–84 + 159–222r – more flourished, informal script; cursive with small minim-area and heavy, tapering down-strokes (e.g. f, long s). Looped round d, uncrossed et-nota, two-compartment a, final s is sigma-shaped or round. Change of hand near foot of 175v. Similar usages (except for crossed *et*-nota) but plainer and heavier aspect. 229 – more formal and flourished hand with angled looped tops to ascenders.

DECORATION Initials in HRB are filigreed at main textual divisions but no ornament visible elsewhere. Capitals within the text are usually decorated with double hairline strokes, angular outlines, etc. 54–83 – plain capitals. Filigreed initials 85–158.

HISTORY
In Early Modern hand at foot 1r, 'Bibliothecae Viconiensis'. The Premonstratensian abbey of Vicoigne (*Uiconia*), founded in 1125, was in the diocese of Arras, in the *arrondissement* of Valenciennes whose town library acquired several of the abbey's manuscripts: Cottineau, *Répertoire*, II.3361–62. The contents of MS. 792 fos 229r–259r are also found in Cambridge, Corpus Christi College, MS. 59, 140–173r, a manuscript apparently compiled by a canon of Merton; this raises the possibility that our manuscript originated in England. Some of this material is also found in London, BL, MS. Cotton Faustina A.VIII.

BIBLIOGRAPHY
A.-F. Lièvre, *Catalogue général*, XXV.474–75.

212 WINCHESTER, CATHEDRAL LIBRARY, MS. 9

Saec. xiv (*post* 1334)   Mediaeval provenance: Southwell
220 fos   2nd fo: *Post peccatum Ade*

HRB 118r–217v.
§§1–3, 5–108, [109–110 added (at foot of 171v) in *pudibundus brito* form], 111–208. Dedicated to Robert of Gloucester.
Rubric at §1 (118r), mostly lost, 'Incipit hystoria [ ]'.
No book-divisions.

CONTENTS
1r: list of popes from Peter to John XXII (1311–34).
1v: list of emperors from Octavian to Frederick II.
2r/v: blank except for *ex-libris* inscription and contents-list on verso.

3r/v: 'Reuelatio Wilfredi archiepiscopi Eboracensis' (later title). '[S]anctus Wilfridus negociis suis Rome expletis . . . ampliauit honorifice et dotauit.'

4r–7r: 'Apocryphum de ligno crucis a superstiosis (*sic*) fictum ut crassis mendaciis sacrae scripturae contradicentibus plenum' (later title). 'Post peccatum Ade expulso eo de paradiso . . . uiuit et regnat trinus et unus. Amen.' Bloomfield, *Incipits*, p. 336, no. 3966. Ed. Hill, 'The fifteenth-century prose legend', pp. 203–22.

7r–101r: 'Quoniam scire tempora summorum pontificum Romanorum . . . Iohannes .xxii. qui nunc est'. Chronicle of Martinus Polonus, ed. Weiland, MGH, SS, XXII.379–474 with continuation to Pope John XXII (1311–34) ed. Holder-Egger, MGH, SS, XXX.1, pp. 715 & 709–11.

101v: blank.

102r–117r: 'Incipit epistola Cornelii ad Crispum Salustium in Troianorum hystoria que in Greco a Darete hystoriographo compilata siue facta est'.

'Cornelius Salustio Crispo . . . Neoptholemus Penthesileam.' Ed. Meister, *Daretis Phrygii De Excidio Troiae Historia*.

117v: blank, unruled.

118r–217v: HRB.

217v–220r: annals. 'Anno gratie .ciiii(x).v. Lucius Britannorum . . . usque coro[nacio]num regis Aluredi fluxerunt anni .m.xxxix..'

DESCRIPTION

QUIRING Volume seems, from script and layout, to be a unit.

PRICKING Not visible on film.

RULING Single column of 30 lines with double vertical boundary-lines. Ruling above top written line.

SCRIPT Gothic bookhand with crossed t, two-compartment a and crossed *et*-nota. Juncture of e and o with d and p and fusion of other letters (co etc.). Short ascenders, sometimes flat-topped. *-bus* abbreviation and 2-shaped r sometimes trail below the ruled line.

DECORATION Elaborate opening initial for HRB with filigree and ornament along edges of text. Plain capitals within text.

HISTORY

On 2v, in cursive hand of ?fourteenth century: 'Liber Helie de Counton. can. ecclesie Suthwellensis et prebende de Ouerhalle apud Northwell'. Underneath, in later mediaeval hand: 'Liber Marie Suthwellie in quo continetur reuelatio Sancti Wilfridi [ ] et quodam appocriphum . . . et cronica Martini . . . et historia Frigii Daretis . . . et historia Britonum. Cum breui enumeratione regum Anglie a tempore Lucii usque ad Eadwardum 2m . . .' (strip cut out of fo [ ]). Collegiate church of BVM: Ker, *Medieval Libraries*, pp. 181, 306.

BIBLIOGRAPHY

Dumville, 'The manuscripts', p. 128.

Holtzmann, 'Papsturkunden in England', II.1, p. 41.

213 WÜRZBURG, UNIVERSITÄTSBIBLIOTHEK, MS. M.ch.f.140

Saec. xvi

278 fos

Provenance: Würzburg, Schottenkloster Sankt Jakob
2nd fo: *comporta dixerunt magi*

HRB 2r–96v.

§§1–3, 5–208. Dedicated to Robert of Gloucester.

Rubrics at §1 (2r) 'Incipit prologus in historia de regibus et gente Brittonum', §5 (2v) 'De situ et quantitate Britt.', §110 (47v) 'Prophecia Merlini. Prologus', §111 (47v) 'Incipit prophecia Merlini', rubrics passim at textual divisions but no final rubric.

Book-divisions: II §23 (9v), III §35 (15v), IV §54 (22v), V §73 (30v), VI §89 (37v), VII §110 (47v), VIII §143 (64v), IX §165 (74r), X §179 (85r),

CONTENTS

1: flyleaf. ?Blank.

2r–96r: HRB.

96v–97r: addition to HRB as in Aberystwyth, NLW, MS. 196. Oxford, Bodleian, MS. Rawlinson B.189. 'Littere quas misit . . . pro dignitate tue promocionis famulabitur.'

97r–152v: 'Incipit prologus in historia Normannorum'. '[P]io uictorioso atque orthodoxo summi regis nutu Anglorum regi . . . inuenerunt rebelles resistere.' *Gesta Normannorum Ducum*, D-redaction. Ed. Marx, *Guillaume de Jumièges*.

153v–184v: 'Successiones episcoporum Wurgeburgensium'. 'Sanctus Kylianus cum sociis suis martyrium accepit . . . .' Latin episcopal list extending to Lorenz of Bibra (1495–1519), and extended in different hand to Konrad of Thungen (1519–40).

184v: blank.

185r–206r: documents relating to the history of Würzburg.

206v–223r: notes on the town of Würzburg by Heinric Kelner and names of popes, emperors, and bishops of Würzburg. 'In nomine Domini. Amen. Cum gesta antiquorum nos modernos sepius inducunt precogitare futura . . . Maximilianus filius eiusdem Friderici.'

223v–224v: blank.

225–230r: records of the bishops of Würzburg.

230r–231r: on fortifications and palaces of see of Würzburg.

231r–233r: documents relating to history of Würzburg.

233v–237r: legal formulae (including oaths).

237r–239r: documents concerning the history of Würzburg.

240r–248v: Swabian chronicle. 'In gotes namen. amen. Dye cronica ist gemacht meinem herren um Gemund Auspurger bistums . . . von Cristi geburt drewtzehen hundert und in dem siben und sybentzig jare.'

248v–249v: *Ein questio, dar in man probirt, das Keyser Ludwig ein rechter Keyser gewest ist.* 'Queritur utrum illi qui iurauerunt et promiserunt . . . non possunt tale iuramentum aliqualiter obseruare.'

249v–252r: excerpt from Chronicle of Martinus Polonus. 'Alexander imperator militarem disciplinam seuerissime rexit . . . thezaurus ibi remansit in hodiernum diem.' Ed. Weiland, MGH, SS, XXII.448–65.

323

252r–253r: concerning Regensburg.
253r–264v: Chronicle of the Roman Emperors. 'Homerus poeta describens inter omnia regna mundi . . . Marcii et regnauit.'
265r–266v: note in German.
267r–274v: *Ordo episcoporum.* 'Episcopus Hostiensis . . . et patriarche sunt quatuor.'
275r–277v: concerning persecution of Jews in Würzburg.
278: ?blank.

DESCRIPTION
SIZE 32.5 x 21.5 cm.
QUIRING Paper. I–XXXIX^8, XXXV^6 (273–278).
RULING Frame-ruled. 31–38 lines written.
SCRIPT Late cursive without slope. Minim letters hard to differentiate as are **c** and **t**. **r** is contructed of a sloping minim with a horizontal stroke. **d** has a looped ascender. Final round **s** is **c**-shaped. Flamboyant approach-strokes and suspension-marks .
DECORATION Initials not completed. Angular display script (not textura).

HISTORY
Thurn describes an inscription in humanist cursive at the end of the volume: 'Codex Ioannis Tritemii abbatis. De origine et gestis ducum regum et gentis Britonum libri X. De origine gentis Nortmannorum libri X. Successiones episcopum Wirciburgensium. Cathalogus omnium episcopatuum Christianorum': *Die Handschriften der Universitätsbibliothek Würzburg*, II.i, p.136.
In hand of the early seventeenth century, at top of 2r: 'Sancti Iacobi Scotorum Herbipoli'.

BIBLIOGRAPHY
Thurn, *Die Handschriften der Universitätsbibliothek Würzburg*, II.i, 136–40.
Van Houts, *Gesta Normannorum Ducum: een Studie*, pp. 212–13.

APPENDICES

I MANUSCRIPT IN PRIVATE HANDS

214 *PHILLIPPS, MS. 3117

Saec. xv
44 fos

Mediaeval provenance: ?English
2nd fo: *campos late spaciosos*

HRB 1v–44r
§§1–3, 5–108, 111–208. Dedicated to Robert of Gloucester.
Rubrics at §1 (1v) 'Incipit historia regum Britannie Maioris secundum Galfridum Monemutensem', §118 (26r) 'Incipit 2. liber Bruti', §124 (27r) 'De bello inter Eldol et Hengistum', §208 (44r) 'Explicit'.
No book-divisions.

CONTENTS
1r/v: Story of Albina. 'Ab origine mundi circa annos tria milia et nongentos septuaginta fuit in Grecia ... et insulam ex eorum nomine Britanniam uocauerunt sicut inferius continetur.'
1v–44r: HRB.
44r/v: in different hand (contemporary). *Capitula*-list to *Status imperii Iudaici*. Truncated. 'Status imperii Iudaici breuiter in hoc opusculo annotatus est ... et de epistola qua scripsit.' See Hammer & Friedmann, 'Status'.
Four parchment stubs visible.

DESCRIPTION
SIZE 32.5 x 23 cm.
QUIRING Indicated by catchwords. I–V⁸, VI⁸ (5–8 cancelled: fos 41–44).
PRICKING Trimmed away.
RULING Brown pencil. 44/45 written lines, writing below top ruled line; 46 in Q. VI. Single vertical boundary-lines.
SCRIPT Four-line cursive bookhand, fairly formal. Main hand roundish, leans slightly to the right. Cleft long r. Angularity in u and b, but not d and g. Pierced t, looped round d, looped two-compartment a, simple minuscule e (not loop-form). f and s have long descenders (final s round). Dark grey-brown ink. Final quire mostly in another hand with crossed *et*-nota, greater angularity.
DECORATION Red or blue Lombardic capitals. Opening capital (1r) parti-coloured.

HISTORY
Top 1r in ?eighteenth-century hand, 'Liber Iohannis Maynard de Medie (*sic*) Templo London.'
Marginal annotation (Latin) in several antiquarian hands, one in Humanist minuscule.

BIBLIOGRAPHY
Dumville, 'The manuscripts', pp. 164–65.
Griscom & Jones, *The Historia*, p. 563.

II   EXTRACTS FROM THE *HISTORIA*

It seems unnecessary as well as impracticable to attempt a comprehensive list of the numerous manuscripts including extracts of Geoffrey's *Historia*. Only one manuscript is described here, on the grounds of its resemblance to Bern, Burgerbibliothek, MS. 568, which belongs to a distinctive group of texts (on which see Dumville, 'An early text').

215   ROMA, BIBLIOTECA APOSTOLICA VATICANA, MS. OTTOBONI LAT. 3025

Saecc. xv/xvi; xii/xiii   Mediaeval provenance: ?
80 fos   2nd fo: *uires eorum*

HRB 13r–21r
Extracts from HRB §§31, 55, 111–117, 8 and 158. Speeches, letters and the *Prophetie*. Usual rubrics and book-divisions not appropriate here.
13r: extract from §31 'Indignans autem Leir olim ex Britonum . . . et pauperem esse patiuntur'.
13v: 'Epistola Cassibellauni regis Anglorum ad Gaium Cesarem'. §55 complete.
14r–20r: 'Uaticinia Merlini'. §§111–117 complete.
20v: extract from §8. 'Pandraso regi Grecorum Brutus dux reliquiarum Troie salutem . . . cum diligencia ascedant.'
20v–21r: extract from §158. 'Lucius rei publice procurator . . . restituere conabor.'

CONTENTS
1r–5v: Pope Paul II, letters excommunicating heretics and others. '[P]aulus episcopus seruus seruorum Dei ad perpetuam rei memoriam excommunicamus . . . non. aprilis pontificat [ ] anno secundo.' 1463.
6r/v: 'Casus nouiter reseruati summo pontifici'. 'Sanctissimus in Christo pater et dominus . . . nulli penitus suffragari.'

7r–9r: letter of Frederick Barbarossa to Hillin, archbishop of Trier. 'F. Romanus imperator et semper augustus dilecto suo .H. . . . prout domine dederit resistant.' Ed. Pertz, 'Mittheilungen', pp. 418–26.

9r/v: letter of Hillin to Pope Hadrian IV. 'Domino et patri .A. summo et uniuersali pontifici .H. . . . temporibus sunt.' Ed. Pertz, 'Mittheilungen', pp. 426–28.

10r–12v: Hadrian IV to archbishops of Trier, Mainz and Köln. '.A. seruus seruorum Dei dilectis in Christo fratribus .H. . . . quia non expedit fraternitati uestre et eidem. Amen'. See Jaffé [& Loewenfeld], *Regesta*, II.132–33, no. 10393.

13r–21r: HRB.

21r/v: blank after HRB.

22r–35v: 'Aueni fabula' (added title). '[R]ustica deflenti paruo iurauerat olim . . . expedit insignem promeruisse necem.' Ed. Guaglianone, *Aviani Fabulae*, pp. 5–74.

36r/v: blank.

37r: acephalous fragment of text. 'reprehensionis morsus sustineat . . . studis desuda-rem.'

37r/v: fragment of letter from Hadrian IV to Emperor Frederick. 'Adrianus episcopus seruus seruorum Dei dilecto filio suo [ ] . . .'. 'Lex diuina sicut parentes . . . usque ad sedem Petri reptase iam uideamus.' See Jaffé [& Loewenfeld], *Regesta*, II.144, no. 10575.

38r–44r: Greek.

46r–50r: 'Incipit ars organi'. 'Organum est cantus subsequens precedentem . . .' Musical manuscript.

51r–60v: 'Incipit reuelatio ecclesie Sancti Michahelis (*sic*) in monte qui dicitur tumba . . .'. 'Postquam gens Francorum Christi gratia insignita . . . et regnat dies clarus dies aeternus in longitudie (*sic*) dierum. Amen.'

60v–61r: 'Miraculum per sanctam Mariam de quodam rustico'. 'Erat quidem uir secularis rurali opera deditus . . . que cum eo in eternum sit benedicta. Amen.'

61v: blank.

62r–64v: 'Sermo Raddbodi episcopi in adnuntiatione sancte Marie'. 'Audiuimus fratres dilectissimi pastorem omnium . . . ante palmarum diem .v. frater festiuitatis terminum.'

65r–66r: 'Italia Gallia Africa Iispania Illiricus Trachia . . . Nomina prouinciarum uel ciuitatum quarundam regionis Italie'. 'In Italia sunt prouinciae numero .xvii. . . . Maxima Ualentiana.' Ed. Riese, *Geographi Latini minores*, pp. 130–32.

66r–67r: 'Nomina ciuitatum .cxxv. que sunt in prouincia solius regionis Gallie ..'. 'Ciuitas metropol. Uienesium. ciuitas Gennauensium . . . ciuitas Ualentium. Cf. Mommsen, MGH, AA, IX, 600–1.

67v–68v: 'Nomina pontificum sancte Romane ecclesie et quot annis uel mensibus seu diebus quisque eorum sedit'. To Calixtus II (1119–24).

69r–80r: Vergil, *Eclogues* I–X. Mutilated at beginning. 'Tytyre tu pat[ ] . . . Ite domum sature uenit hesperus i[te] capelle.' Ed. Coleman, *Vergil Eclogues*.

DESCRIPTION

SIZE 21.2 x 14/15 cm.

QUIRING Paper and parchment, composite collection. I^8 (flyleaves + 1–6); $II–V^{10}$ (7–36); VI ^{1} (parchment, fo 37); VII^8 (paper) VIII $?^6$ (?lacks 6: 46–50) (paper); IX^8, X^6 (parchment); XII^4 (65–68); XIII^8, XIV^4 (69–80).

RULING HRB frame-ruled. About 29 lines written. Variable layout elsewhere.

SCRIPT HRB section (7–36) in fifteenth-century hands. Begins in rapid and angular script with top of **g** piercing uprights, angled tops to ascenders, small-headed **a**. Other hand also has tapered descenders and looped **d** with simple form of **e** and round **a**, looped tops of ascenders sometimes pinched but bowl of **g** and **d** not yet angular.

fos 1–6 ?later fifteenth-century script. Other items twelfth- to fifteenth-century.

HISTORY

Owned by Paul Petau.

BIBLIOGRAPHY

Les Manuscrits de la Reine, pp. 68–69.

Pellegrin *et al.*, *Les manuscrits classiques*, I.827–28.

III MANUSCRIPTS NOT AVAILABLE FOR INCLUSION

It has proved impossible to obtain microfilms of the following.

[216] HALLE, UNIVERSITÄTS- UND LANDESBIBLIOTHEK, MS. STOLBERG-WERNIGERODE, Za 38

(Crick, 'Manuscripts', p. 160)

[217] MADRID, BIBLIOTECA NACIONAL, MS. R.202

(Dumville, 'The manuscripts', pp. 165–66)

IV MANUSCRIPTS WHOSE PRESENT LOCATION IS UNKNOWN

All those listed as extant by Griscom (*The Historia*, pp. 551–72) have been accounted for by David Dumville ('The manuscripts', pp. 114–22, 'Manuscripts', pp. 164–65, 166) who has also traced those in Griscom's list of unlocated manuscripts (section D:

The Historia, p. 580). Griscom gives a supplementary list of ten manuscripts (section E), those found in Hardy's catalogue of 1862 (*Descriptive Catalogue*, I.341–48) and which he had failed to locate. A little progress can now be made on these (N.B. the last on the list was destroyed by fire in 1694).

i. A group of four (Griscom's numbers 26–29) is clearly derived from Sanderus's catalogue of Belgian monastic libraries of 1741: the houses are listed in the same order and under similar name-forms Sanderus, *Bibliotheca*, I.224, 271, 310, 356). London, BL, Arundel 10 bears an Early Modern *ex-libris* 'ecclesie Cameracen.' (Cambrai). No known copy of the *Historia* can be identified as having belonged to any of the other houses: St. Peter's, Oudenbourg (near Bruges), Bonne Espérance (Premonstratensian), and Villers (Cistercian).

ii. The manuscript listed as Thorpe 1393 is to be found in one of the catalogues issued in 1836 by the antiquarian bookseller Thomas Thorpe of London ([Thorpe], *Catalogue*, p. 407):
'Bedae (Venerabilis) Historia Ecclesiastica Gentis Anglorum. – Gaufridi Monemutensis Hystoria Regum Britanniae. Two remarkably fine manuscripts of the thirteenth century, upon vellum, written in double columns, in a fine bold character, but both are unfortunately deficient of some leaves, in 1 vol. folio'.
This description would fit London, BL, MS. Add. 33371 which was bought for that library at Sotheby's in 1888 from the estate of Edward Breeze of Porthmadog.

iii. Fürstliches Bibl. Bückeburg, Schaumburg-Lippe. Hardy derived his knowledge of this manuscript from Lappenberg's reference in *A History of England* (I.xxx, n. 6) to 'an excellent MS.' of Geoffrey's text in the possession of the Prince of Schaumberg-Lippe. This private court library has been described as 'lacking in significance' (Buzás, *German Library History*, p. 330).

iv. Phillipps 18 or 58 (*olim* Bibliothèque Royez). A. N. L. Munby recorded the sale of Phillipps 18 to the National Library of Scotland where it is shelved as MS. Adv. 34.5.22: *Catalogus*, I. This manuscript, however, contains a History of the Dukes of Argyll: Beattie, *National Library of Scotland. Summary Catalogue*, p. 47. Munby did not record the fate of Phillipps 58.

v. Vatican 218 (does not correspond with that number in the present series of Vat. lat., Reg. lat., or Ottoboni manuscripts or with the old Reginensis catalogue: *Les Manuscrits de la Reine*.)

vi. *Olim* Henrici Langley *armiger* 38 (6986). The *Dictionary of National Biography* (XXXII.111) records a Henry Langley (1611–79), master of Pembroke College, Oxford, and canon of Christ Church. This does not seem to fit Bernard's description of Langley as *equ[es] de comitatu Salopiensi*: *Catalogi*, II.i, p. 216.

vii. To these may be added 'a MS. copy of Gildas or Nennius, together with Geoffrey of Monmouth's Historia Britonum' at Drummond Castle, reported by Thomas Innes in a letter of unspecified year. Innes was the author of a critical essay on the early inhabitants of Scotland, published in 1729. (See *First Report*, p. 18.)

V LOST MANUSCRIPTS OF THE *HISTORIA*

Bern, Burgerbibliothek, MS. 392 (see Crick, 'The manuscripts', pp. 159–60)
Tournai, Bibliothèque de la Ville, MS. 135 (see Crick, 'Manuscripts', pp. 160–61)

VI REVISED LIST OF ABRIDGMENTS OF THE *HISTORIA*

For previous lists of abridgments see Dumville, 'The manuscripts', p. 171.

Canterbury, Cathedral Library, MS. Add. 128/27a
East Berlin, Deutsche Staatsbibliothek, MS. Phillipps 1880
London, British Library, MS. Arundel 220
Paris, Bibliothèque nationale, MS. lat. 11107

VII MANUSCRIPTS OF THE *PROPHETIE MERLINI*

The following is based on a conflation of the list published by Caroline Eckhardt in 1982 ('The *Prophetia*', pp. 172–76) and the supplement provided by David Dumville (*apud* Crick, 'The manuscripts', pp. 161–62) with some additions and revisions.

Independent Copies
Alençon, Bibliothèque municipale, MS. 20, fos 53 and 56
Arras, Bibliothèque municipale, MS. 184 (163), fos 57r–61v
Boulogne-sur-Mer, Bibliothèque municipale, MS. 180 (+ 139 + 145),
    fos 72va–74v (= HRB MS. 16)
Bourges, Bibliothèque municipale, MS. 367, fos 28v–30r
Bruges, Bibliothèque de la Ville, MS. 428, fos 48vb–51rb (= HRB MS. 17)
Bruxelles, Bibliothèque royale, MS. II. 936 (1490), fo 92r/v
Cambridge, Corpus Christi College, MS. 313, fos 68–73
Cambridge, Corpus Christi College, MS. 476, fos 3–41
Cambridge, Fitzwilliam Museum MS. 379, fos 4v–8v
Cambridge, Peterhouse, MS. 177, fos 222r–227v
Cambridge, Trinity College, MS. R.7.23 (759), pp. 3–13
Cambridge, Trinity College, MS. O.1.17 (1041), fos 177r–181r (= HRB MS. 38)
Cambridge, University Library, MS. Dd.14.2 (848), fos 291r–297r
Cambridge, University Library, MS. Ff.1.27 (1160), pp. 610–618
Cambridge, University Library, MS. Gg.6.42 (1611), fos 214r–222r

Cambridge, University Library, MS. Oo.6.111 (3183), fos 21r–26r
Dublin, Trinity College, MS. 301 (C.3.19), fos 21r–25v
Dublin, Trinity College, MS. 514 (E.5.3), fos 79v–89r
Dublin, Trinity College, MS. 516 (E.5.10), fos 17r–22v
Dublin, Trinity College, MS. 517 (E.4.12), fos 135r–138v
Firenze, Biblioteca nazionale centrale, MS. II.I.75, fos 80v–82v
Den Haag, Koninklijke Bibliotheek, MS. 78.D.18, fos 1r–83v
Den Haag, Koninklijke Bibliotheek, MS. 78.D.18, fos 84r–87v
Laon, Bibliothèque municipale, MS. 109 (end flyleaf)
Liège, Bibliothèque de l'Université, MS. 369C, fos 143r–145v
Lincoln, Cathedral Library, MS. 98 (A.4.6), fos 170r–173r (= HRB MS. 80)
Lincoln, Cathedral Library, MS. 214 (C.4.1), fos 162v–166r
London, British Library, MS. Additional 25014, fo 119v
London, British Library, MS. Additional 40007, fos 40r–41v
London, British Library, MS. Arundel 66, fos 267r–268v
London, British Library, MS. Arundel 292, fos 61v–67v
London, British Library, MS. Cotton Claudius B.vii, fos 213r–215r
London, British Library, MS. Cotton Claudius B.vii, fos 224r–230v
London, British Library, MS. Cotton Cleopatra C.iv, fos 87r–93r
London, British Library, MS. Cotton Cleopatra C.x, fos 56v & 67r–69v
London, British Library, MS. Cotton Faustina A.viii. fos 110v–115v
London, British Library, MS. Cotton Nero A.iv, fos 65r–76r
London, British Library, MS. Cotton Tiberius A.ix, fos 2r–5r
London, British Library, MS. Cotton Titus D.vii, fos 32r–38r
London, British Library, MS. Harley 838, fos 92r–93v
London, British Library, MS. Royal 8.D.iii, fos 160v–163r
London, Lambeth Palace, MS. 527, fos 46–59
Montpellier, Bibliothèque de l'Université (Ecole de Médecine), MS. 142,
   fos 69v–106v
New York City, Columbia University Library, MS. Plimpton 266, fos 30r–32r
Oxford, Bodleian Library, MS. Bodley 91 (*S.C.* 1891), fos 95r–102v
Oxford, Bodleian Library, MS. Bodley 355 (*S.C.* 2444), fos 39r–41v
Oxford, Bodleain Library, MS. Bodley 623 (*S.C.* 2157), fos 22r/v and 83r–85r
Oxford, Bodleian Library, MS. Digby 28 (*S.C.* 1629), fos 162r–167v
Oxford, Bodleian Library, MS. Digby 98 (*S.C.* 1699), fos 72r–75r
Oxford, Bodleian Library, MS. Hatton 56 (*S.C.* 4062), fos 23r–26v
Oxford, Bodleian Library, MS. Lyell 35, fos 9v–16v
Oxford, Bodleian Library, MS. Rawlinson D. 893 (*S.C.* 13659), fo 28v (= HRB 157)
Oxford, Bodleian Library, MS. Top.Oxon.d.72 (*S.C.* 33675)
Oxford, Lincoln College, MS. 27, fos 183v–186v
Oxford, University College, MS. 97, fos 179v–185r
Paris, Bibliothèque nationale, MS. français 2001, fos 105v–110v
Paris, Bibliothèque nationale, MS. lat. 2321, fo 48
Paris, Bibliothèque nationale, MS. lat. 2599, fos 263v–266r
Paris, Bibliothèque nationale, MS. lat. 2935, fos 83r–86v

Paris, Bibliothèque nationale, MS. lat. 3319, fos 5r–9v
Paris, Bibliothèque nationale, MS. lat. 3522A, fos 42r–48v
Paris, Bibliothèque nationale, MS. lat. 6237, fos 18v–21r
Paris, Bibliothèque nationale, MS. lat. 6274, fos 63r–76v
Paris, Bibliothèque nationale, MS. lat. 7481
Paris, Bibliothèque nationale, MS. lat. 9422, fos 119v–122v
Paris, Bibliothèque nationale, MS. lat. 15172, fos 106v–112v
Princeton (N.J.), Princeton University Library, MS. 57
Roma, Biblioteca Apostolica Vaticana, MS. Ottoboni lat. 3025, fos 14r–20r
Roma, Biblioteca Apostolica Vaticana, MS. Reg. lat. 189, fos 19r–22v
Roma, Biblioteca Apostolica Vaticana, MS. Reg. lat. 807, fos 1v–6r
Roma, Biblioteca Apostolica Vaticana, MS. Reg. lat. 1534, fos 62r–66v
Roma, Biblioteca Apostolica Vaticana, MS. Vat. lat. 3820, fos 41r–43v
Rouen, Bibliothèque municipale, MS. U.134 (1403), fos 65v–69v
San Marino (Cal.), Huntington Library, MS. HM 1345, fos 107r–111r
Valenciennes, Bibliothèque municipale, MS. 543 (497), fo 36
Valenciennes, Bibliothèque municipale, MS. 792 (589), fos 224r–228v (= HRB 211)

Inserted into Other Texts
Cambridge, Corpus Christi College, MS. 26, pp. 66–69 (in Matthew Paris's *Chronica Maiora*)
Den Haag, Koninklijke Bibliotheek, MS. 71.E.44, fo 116r/v (in commentary of Iohannes de Rupescissa)
London, British Library, MS. Cotton Iulius A.v, fos 54r–57v (in Langtoft's Chronicle)
London, British Library, MS. Harley 53, fos 37v–40v (in St Albans chronicle)
London, British Library, MS. Harley 1620, fos 37v–39v (in Matthew Paris's *Chronica Maiora*)
London, College of Arms, MS. Arundel 22, fos 44r–47r (in English Chronicle of 'Maister Gnaor')
London, Lambeth Palace, MS. 6, fos 43r–48r (in St Albans chronicle)
Oxford, Bodleian Library, MS. Douce 207 (*S.C.* 21781), fos 40v–42r (in Roger Wendover's *Flores historiarum*)
Oxford, Bodleian Library, MS. Rawlinson B.150 (*S.C.* 11520), fos 16r–19v (in *Tractatus de Bruto abbreviato*)
Paris, Bibliothèque nationale, MS. lat. 2599, fo 270r/v (in commentary of Iohannes de Rupescissa)
Paris, Bibliothèque nationale, MS. lat. 14726, fos 95v–98r (in commentary of Iohannes de Rupescissa)

Deletions from the List
Alençon, Bibliothèque municipale, MS. 12 (contains HRB §§118–208 only)
Cambridge, University Library, MS. Gg.4.25 (1524), fo 65v (miscellaneous prophecies)
Dublin, Trinity College, MS. 496 (E.6.2), fos 139r–161r (commentary only, ed. Hammer, 'An unedited commentary', pp. 82–88)

VIII MANUSCRIPTS OF THE *UITA MERLINI*

Independent copies
London, British Library, MS. Cotton Vespasian E.iv, 112v–138v
York, Minster Library, MS. XVI.Q.14
London, British Library, MS. Cotton Cleopatra C.iv (extract)
London, British Library, MS. Harley 6148 (extract)

Inserted into Higden's *Polichronicon*
London British Library, MS. Cotton Julius E.viii
London, British Library, MS. Cotton Titus A.xix
London, British Library, MS. Harley 655
London, British Library, MS. Royal 13.E.i

ABBREVIATIONS

BAV	BblioteCa Apostolica Vaticana
BHL	*Bibliotheca hagiographica latina antiquae et mediae aetatis* (2 vols + supplement, Bruxelles 1898–1911)
BL	British Library
BM	Bibliothèque municipale
BN	Bibliothèque nationale
BR	Bibliothèque royale
DNB	L. Stephen (& S. Lee) (edd.), *Dictionary of National Biography* (63 vols, London 1885–1900)
HRB	*Historia regum Britannie*
Patrologia graeco-latina	J. P. Migne, *Patrologiæ cursus completus sive bibliotheca universalis, integra, uniformis, commodo, oeconomica omnium SS. patrum, doctorum scriptorumque ecclesiasticorum qui ab ævo apostolico ad usque Innocentii III tempora floruerunt. . .*, Ser. graeca (161 vols, Paris 1857–65)
Patrologia latina	J. P. Migne, *Patrologiæ cursus completus sive bibliotheca universalis, integra, uniformis, commodo, oeconomica omnium SS. patrum, doctorum scriptorumque ecclesiasticorum qui ab ævo apostolico ad usque Innocentii III tempora floruerunt. . .*, Ser. latina (217 vols + 4 index vols, Paris 1844–55)
MGH, AA	*Monumenta Germaniae Historica, Auctores antiquissimi* (15 vols in 13, Berlin/Leipzig 1877–1919)
MGH, SS	*Monumenta Germaniae Historica, Scriptores* (32 vols in 34, Hannover 1826–)
MGH, SS, Lang.	*Monumenta Germaniae Historica, Scriptores rerum Langobardorum et italicarum saec. vi–ix* (Hannover 1878)
MGH, SS, rer. Mer.	*Monumenta Germaniae Historica, Scriptores rerum Merovingicarum* (7 vols, 1884–1920)
NLS	National Library of Scotland
NLW	National Library of Wales
NS	new series
UB	Universitätsbibliothek
UL	University Library

BIBLIOGRAPHY

T. K. Abbott, *Catalogue of the Manuscripts in the Library of Trinity College, Dublin*
... (Dublin 1900)

M. Adriaen (ed.), *S. Hieronymi opera. Pars 1, Opera exegetica, 6. Commentarii in prophetas minores* (2 vols, Turnhout 1969–70)

A. Altamura (ed.), *Riccardo da Bury. Philobiblon* (Napoli 1954)

A. O. Anderson, M. O. Anderson, W. C. Dickinson (facs. ed.), *The Chronicle of Melrose from the Cottonian Manuscript, Faustina B.ix, in the British Museum* (London 1936)

M. O. Anderson, 'The Scottish materials in the Paris manuscript, Bib. Nat. Latin 4126', *Scottish Historical Review* 28 (1949), 31–42

M. O. Anderson, *Kings and Kingship in Early Scotland* (2nd edn, Edinburgh 1980)

F. E. A. Arnold, 'The Source of the Alexander history in B. M. MS Sloane 289', *Medium Ævum* 33 (1964), 195–99

T. Arnold (ed.), *Henrici archidiaconi Huntendunensis Historia Anglorum* (London 1879)

E. Ashmole, *Theatrum chemicum britannicum* (London 1752)

H. J. D. Astley, 'Mediaeval Colchester – town, castle and abbey – from manuscripts in the British Museum', *Transactions of the Essex Archaeological Society*, NS, 8 (1903), 117–35

F. Avril, 'Notes sur quelques manuscrits bénédictins normands du xie et du xiie siècle', *Mélanges d'archéologie et d'histoire (Ecole française de Rome)* 76 (1964), 491–525; 77 (1965), 209–48

F. Avril & P. D. Stirnemann, *Manuscrits enluminés d'origine insulaire vii e–xx e siècle* (Paris 1987)

C. Babington & J. R. Lumby (edd.), *Polychronicon Ranulphi Higden monachi Cestrensis* (9 vols, London 1865–86)

E. Baehrens (ed.), *Poetae Latini Minores* (5 vols in 4, Leipzig 1879–83)

J. Bale, *Scriptorum illustrium maioris Brytannie catalogus* (2 vols, Basel 1557–59)

A. M. Bandinius, *Catalogus codicum latinorum Bibliothecae Mediceae Laurentianae* (5 vols, Firenze 1774–78)

F. Barlow (ed.), *The Letters of Arnulf of Lisieux* (London 1939)

R. Baron, 'Hugo de Sancto Victore, Epitome Dindimi in philosophiam', *Traditio* 11 (1955), 91–148

R. Baron, 'Hugues de Saint-Victor lexicographe. Trois textes inédits', *Cultura neo-latina* 16 (1956), 132–37

W. Beattie *et al.*, *National Library of Scotland. Summary Catalogue of the Advocates' Manuscripts* (Edinburgh 1971)

J. Becquet & L. Hambis (edd.), *Jean de Plancarpin. Histoire des Mongols* (Paris 1965)

E. Bernard, *Catalogi librorum manuscriptorum Angliæ et Hiberniæ in unum collecti* (Oxford 1697)

J. Beverley Smith, 'The "Cronica de Wallia" and the dynasty of Dinefwr: a textual and historical study', *Bulletin of the Board of Celtic Studies* 20 (1962–64), 261–82

Bibliotheca Phillippica: Catalogue of manuscripts on papyrus, vellum and paper of the thirteenth century B.C. to the eighteenth century A.D. from the celebrated collection formed by Sir Thomas Phillipps (1792–1872): Tuesday 25 November 1969

L. Bieler, *Codices Patriciani Latini; a descriptive catalogue of Latin manuscripts relating to St. Patrick* (Dublin 1942)

J. Bignami-Odier, *Etudes sur Jean de Roquetaillade (Johannes de Rupescissa)* (Paris 1952)

E. G. W. Bill, *A Catalogue of Manuscripts in Lambeth Palace Library: MSS. 1222–1860* (Oxford 1972)

W. H. Black, *Catalogue of the Arundel Manuscripts in the Library of the College of Arms* (unpubl., London 1829)

F. Bloomfield (ed.), *Thomae de Chobham Summa confessorum* (Leuven 1968)

M. W. Bloomfield *et al.*, *Incipits of Latin Works on the Virtues and Vices, 1100–1500 A.D.* (Cambridge, Mass. 1979)

P. Boehner *et al.* (edd.), *Uenerabilis inceptoris Guillelmi de Ockham Summa Logicae* (St Bonaventure, NY 1974)

J. Bongars, *Gesta Dei per Francos sive orientalium expeditionum et regni Francorum hierosolimitani historia* (3 vols in 2, Hannover 1611)

M. Bouquet, *Recueil des historiens des Gaules et de la France* (24 vols in 25; vols 1–19 reed. Delisle, Paris 1869–80; vols 20–24, Paris 1840–1904)

A. Boutemy *et al.*, 'La Version parisienne du poème de Simon Chèvre d'Or sur la guerre de Troie (MS. lat. 8430)', *Scriptorium* 1 (1946/7), 267–88

A. Brandl, 'The Cock in the North. Poetische Weissagung auf Percy Hotspur (gest. 1403)', *Sitzungsberichte der königlich preussischen Akademie der Wissenschaften 1909* (Berlin 1909), pp. 1160–89

L. Braswell, 'Saint Edburga of Winchester: a study of her cult, a.d. 950–1500, with an edition of the fourteenth-century Middle English and Latin lives', *Mediaeval Studies* 33 (1971), 292–333

J. S. Brewer *et al.* (edd.), *Giraldi Cambrensis Opera* (8 vols, London 1861–91)

C. M. Briquet, *Les Filigranés: Dictionnaire historique des marques du papier dès leur apparition vers 1282 jusqu'en 1600* (4 vols, Paris 1907: rev. imp. ed. A. Stevenson, Amsterdam 1968)

J. Bromwich, 'The first book printed in Anglo-Saxon types', *Transactions of the Cambridge Bibliographical Society* 3 (1959–63), 265–91

C. Brown & R. H. Robbins, *The Index of Middle English Verse* (New York 1943)

E. Brugger, 'Zu Galfrid von Monmouth's *Historia Regum Britanniae*', *Zeitschrift für französische Sprache und Literatur* 57 (1933), 257–312

K. Buchner (ed.), *Anicius Manilius Severinus Boethius Philosophiae Consolationis libri quinque* (Heidelberg 1977)

C. F. Buhler, 'Two Middle English texts of the *Somnia Danielis*', *Anglia* 80.3 (1962), 264–73

L. Buzás, *German Library History, 800–1945* (Jefferson, NC 1986)

[M. D. Cabanes Pecourt (ed.)], *Rodericus Ximenius de Rada opera* (1793, facs. Valencia 1968)

G. Cambier (ed.), *Embricon de Mayence: La Vie de Mahumet* (Bruxelles 1962)

Catalogue of the manuscripts at Ashburnham Place (2 vols + appendix, London [1861])

Catalogus librorum manuscriptorum Bibliothecæ Sloanianæ (unpubl., 1837–40)

I. Cavellatus (ed.), *Britannie utriusque regum et principum origo et gesta insignia ab Galfrido Monemutensi ex antiquissimis britannici sermonis monumentis in latinum sermonem traducta: et ab Ascanio cura et impendio magistri Ivonis Cavellati in lucem edita* (Paris 1508; 2nd edn, 1517)

R. W. Chambers, *The Place of St. Thomas More in English Literature and History: being a revision of a lecture delivered to the Thomas More Society* (London 1937)

M. Chibnall (ed.), *The Ecclesiastical History of Orderic Vitalis* (6 vols, Oxford 1969–80)

B. Colgrave, 'The post-Bedan miracles and translations of St Cuthbert', in C. Fox and B. Dickens (edd.), *The Early Cultures of North-West Europe: H. M. Chadwick Memorial Studies* (Cambridge 1950), pp. 307–32

B. Colgrave & R. A. B. Mynors (edd.), *Bede's Ecclesiastical History of the English People* (Oxford 1969)

R. Coleman (ed.), *Vergil Eclogues* (Cambridge 1977)

Colophons de manuscrits occidentaux des origines au xvie siècle (6 volumes, Fribourg-en-Suisse 1965–82)

J. A. Corbett, *Catalogue of the Medieval and Renaissance Manuscripts of the University of Notre Dame* (Notre Dame, Indiana 1978)

L. H. Cottineau, *Répertoire topo-bibliographique des abbayes et prieurés* (3 vols, Macon 1935–70)

H. O. Coxe, *Catalogue of Manuscripts in the Library of All Souls College Oxford* (Oxford 1852)

H. O. Coxe, *Catalogi codicum manuscriptorum Bibliothecæ Bodleianæ, Pars II* (2 vols, Oxford 1858–85; rev. imp. by R. W. Hunt [single volume], Oxford 1973)

H. O. Coxe, *Catalogus codicum manuscriptorum qui in collegiis aulisque Oxoniensibus hodie adservantur* (2 vols, Oxford 1852)

J. Crick, 'Manuscripts of Geoffrey of Monmouth's *Historia Regum Britannie*', *Arthurian Literature* 7 (1987), 158–62

J. Crick, 'The manuscripts of the works of Geoffrey of Monmouth: a new supplement', *Arthurian Literature* 6 (1986), 157–62

A. Crivellucci, 'Per l'edizione della *Historia Romana* di Paolo Diacono', *Bollettino dell'istituto storica italiano* 40 (1921), 7–103

I. C. Cunningham, 'Latin classical manuscripts in the National Library of Scotland', *Scriptorium* 27 (1973), 64–90

W. L. Davies *et al.*, *Handlist of Manuscripts in the National Library of Wales* (Aberystwyth 1943-) (in progress)

C. de Clercq (ed.), *The Latin Sermons of Odo of Canterbury* (Bruxelles 1983)

A. de Mandach, *Naissance et développement de la chanson de geste en Europe: I, La Geste de Charlemagne et de Roland* (Paris 1961)

S. De Ricci & W. J. Wilson, *Census of Medieval and Renaissance Manuscripts in the United States and Canada* (2 vols + index, New York 1935–40)

C. de Smedt, W. van Hoofl, J. de Backer *et al.*, *Acta sanctorum Novembris* (4 vols in 5 + Propylaeum, Paris/Bruxelles 1887–1925)

N. de Wailly, 'Examen de quelques questions relatives à l'origine des Chroniques de Saint-Denis', *Mémoires de l'Institut Royal de France. Académie des Inscriptions et Belles-Lettres* 17.i (1847), 379–407

R. J. Dean & E. Kennedy, 'Un fragment anglo-normand de la *Folie Tristan* de Berne', *Le Moyen Age* 79 (1973), 57–72

C. Dehaisnes, *Catalogue général des manuscrits des bibliothèques publiques des départements* 6 (Paris 1878)

E. Dekkers, *Clavis patrum latinorum a Tertulliano ad Bedam* (2nd edn, Steenbrugge 1961)

H. F. Delaborde (ed.), *Oeuvres de Rigord et de Guillaume le Breton, historiens de Philippe-Auguste* (3 vols in 2, Paris 1882)

L. Delisle, *Le Cabinet des manuscrits de la Bibliothèque imperiale: étude sur la formation de ce depôt comprenant les éléments d'une histoire de la calligraphie, de la miniature, de la reliure, et du commerce des livres à Paris avant l'invention de l'imprimerie* (3 vols, Paris 1868–81)

L. Delisle, *Catalogue des manuscrits des fonds Libri et Barrois* (Paris 1888)

L. Delisle, 'Inventaire des manuscrits conservés à la Bibliothèque imperiale sous les nos 8823–11503 du fonds latin', *Bibliothèque de l'Ecole des Chartes*, 5th ser., 4 (1863), 185–236

L. Delisle, 'Inventaire des manuscrits latins de Saint-Germain-des-Prés', *Bibliothèque de l'Ecole des Chartes*, 6th ser., 3 (1867), 528–56; 6th ser., 4 (1868), 220–60

L. Delisle, 'Inventaire des manuscrits latins de Saint-Victor conservés à la Bibliothèque imperiale sous les numéros 14232–15175', *Bibliothèque de l'Ecole des Chartes*, 6th ser., 5 (1869), 1–79

L. Delisle, 'Inventaire des manuscrits latins de Notre-Dame et d'autres fonds conservés à la Bibliothèque nationale sous les numéros 16719–18613', *Bibliothèque de l'Ecole des Chartes* 31 (1870), 463–565

F. Deycks (ed.), *Ludulphus. De itinere terrae sanctae liber* (Stuttgart 1851)

V. DiMarco & L. Perelman, 'The Middle English Letter of Alexander to Aristotle', *Costenus* NS 13 (1978), pp. 49–109

E. van K. Dobbie, *The Manuscripts of Caedmon's Hymn and Bede's Death Song* (New York 1937)

F. Dolbeau, 'Anciens Possesseurs des manuscrits hagiographiques latins conservés à la Bibliothèque nationale de Paris', *Revue d'histoire des textes* 9 (1979), 183–238

H. Douteil (ed.), *Iohannis Beleth: Summa de ecclesiasticis officiis* (2 vols, Turnhout 1976)

A. Duchesne (ed.), *Historiae Normannorum scriptores antiqui* (Paris 1619)

D. N. Dumville (ed.), 'Anecdota from manuscripts of Geoffrey of Monmouth', *Arthurian Literature* (forthcoming)

D. N. Dumville, 'An early text of Geoffrey of Monmouth's *Historia Regum Britanniae* and the circulation of some Latin histories in twelfth-century Normandy', *Arthurian Literature* 4 (1985), 1–36

D. N. Dumville (ed.), *The Historia Brittonum* (10 vols, Cambridge 1985-)

D. N. Dumville, *Histories and pseudo-histories of the Insular Middle Ages* (North-ampton 1989)

D. N. Dumville, 'The manuscripts of Geoffrey of Monmouth's *Historia Regum Britanniae*', *Arthurian Literature* 3 (1983), 113–28; 4 (1985), 164–71; 5 (1985), 149–51

D. N. Dumville, 'The origin of the C-text of the Variant Version of the Historia Regum Britannie', *Bulletin of the Board of Celtic Studies* 26 (1974–76), 315–22

D. Dumville & M. Lapidge (ed.), *The Annals of St Neots with Vita Prima Sancti Neoti* (Cambridge 1985)

W. G. East, 'Manuscripts of Geoffrey of Monmouth', *Notes and Queries* 220 [N.S. 22] (1975), 483–84

C. D. Eckhardt, 'The date of the 'Prophetia Merlini' commentary in MSS. Cotton Claudius B.vii and Bibliothèque nationale fonds latin 6233', *Notes and Queries*, NS, 23 (1976), 146–47

C. D. Eckhardt, *The Prophetia Merlini of Geoffrey of Monmouth: a fifteenth-century English commentary* (Cambridge, Mass. 1982)

C. D. Eckhardt, 'The *Prophetia Merlini* of Geoffrey of Monmouth: Latin manuscript copies', *Manuscripta* 26 (1982), 167–76

H. Ellis (ed.), *Chronica Johannis de Oxenedes* (London 1859)

H. Ellis & F. Douce, *A Catalogue of the Lansdowne Manuscripts in the British Museum* (2 vols in 1, London 1812–19)

H. D. Emanuel, 'Geoffrey of Monmouth's *Historia regum Britannie*: a second variant version', *Medium Ævum* 35 (1966), 103–10

A. B. Emden, *A Biographical Register of the University of Cambridge to 1500* (Cambridge 1963)

A. B. Emden, *A Biographical Register of the University of Oxford to A. D. 1500* (3 vols, Oxford 1957–59)

A. B. Emden, *A Biographical Register of the University of Oxford A.D. 1501 to 1540* (Oxford 1974)

J. Engels, 'L'Édition critique de l'Ovidius moralizatus de Bersuire', *Vivarium* 9 (1971) 25–48

J. G. Evans, *Report on Manuscripts in the Welsh Language* I.i (London 1898)

J. G. Evans, *Report on Manuscripts in the Welsh Language* I.ii Peniarth (London 1899)

J. G. Evans, *Report on Manuscripts in the Welsh Language* II.i Jesus College Oxford; Free Library, Cardiff; Havod; Wrexham; Llanwrin; Merthyr; Aberdâr (London 1902)

J. G. Evans, *Report on Manuscripts in the Welsh Language* II.ii Plas Llanstephan; Free Library, Cardiff (London 1903)

J. G. Evans, *Report on Manuscripts in the Welsh Language* II.iii Panton; Cwrtmawr (London 1905)

P. Ewald, 'Reise nach Spanien im Winter von 1878 auf 1879', *Neues Archiv der Gesellschaft für ältere deutsche Geschichtskunde* 6 (1881), 219–398

A. Ewert, 'An early manuscript of the "Roman des Romans" ', *Modern Language Review* 23 (1928), 299–306

E. Faral, 'Geoffroy de Monmouth: les faits et les dates de sa biographie', *Romania* 53 (1927), 1–42

E. Faral (ed.), *La Légende arthurienne: études et documents* (3 vols, Paris 1929)

W. Fauser, *Die Werke des Albertus Magnus in ihrer handschriftlichen Überlieferung* (Aschendorff 1982)

R. Fawtier, 'Hand-list of additions to the collection of Latin manuscripts in the John Rylands Library, 1908–1920', *Bulletin of the John Rylands Library* 6 (1921/2), 186–206

First Report of the Royal Commission of Historical Manuscripts (London 1874)

R. Flower, 'Manuscripts from the Clumber collection', *British Museum Quarterly* 12 (1937/8), 79–82

[J. Forschall,] *Catalogue of Manuscripts in the British Museum. N. S. 1: Part 1 The Arundel Manuscripts* (3 parts in 1, London 1834)

I. Fraipont (ed.), *Bedae Venerabilis Opera. Pars III, Opera homiletica. Pars IV, Opera rhythmica* (Turnhout 1955)

J. France, 'Note sur le manuscrit 6041A du fonds latin de la Bibliothèque nationale: un nouveau fragment d'un manuscrit de l'*Historia Belli Sacri*', *Bibliothèque de l'Ecole des Chartes* 126 (1968), 413–16

A. M. Freeman (ed.), 'The Annals in Cotton MS. Titus A. xxv', *Revue Celtique* 41 (1924), 301–30; 42 (1925), 283–305; 43 (1926), 358–84; 44 (1927), 336–61

G. Friedrich (ed.), *M. Tulli Ciceronis opera rhetorica* (2 vols, Leipzig 1884–91)

E. Gallo, *The Poetria nova and its Sources in Early Medieval Rhetorical Doctrine* (The Hague 1971)

J. Gauthier, *Catalogue général des manuscrits des bibliothèques publiques de France* 13 (Paris 1891)

A. Gercke (ed.), *L. Annaei Senecae naturalium quaestionum libri VIII* (1907, facs. edn Stuttgart 1970)

P. Geyer *et al.* (ed.), *Itineraria et alia geographica* (Turnhout 1965)

J. A. Giles (ed.), *Arnulfi Lexoviensis episcopi epistolae ad Henricum II regem Angliae sanctum Thomam arch. Cant. et alios* (Oxford 1844)

J. A. Giles (ed.), *Galfredi Monumetensis Historia Britonum* (2 vols, London 1844/5)

R. Glorie (ed.), *S. Hieronymi presbyteri Opera. Pars I, Opera exegetica, 5* (Turnhout 1964)

R. Goy, *Die Überlieferung der Werke Hugos von St. Viktor: ein Beitrag zur Kommunikationsgeschichte des Mittelalters* (Stuttgart 1976)

A. Gransden, *Historical Writing in England i: c. 550 to c. 1307* (London 1974)

A. Gransden, *Historical Writing in England ii: c. 1307 to the Early Sixteenth Century* (London 1982)

W. H. Green, 'Hugo of St Victor De tribus maximis circumstantiis gestorum', *Speculum* 18 (1943) 484–93

D. E. Greenway, 'Henry of Huntingdon and the manuscripts of his *Historia Anglorum*', *Anglo-Norman Studies* 9 (1986), 103–21

N. E. Griffin (ed.), *Historia Destructionis Troiae* (Cambridge, Mass. 1936)

A. Griscom, 'The date of composition of Geoffrey of Monmouth's *Historia*: New Manuscript Evidence', *Speculum* 1 (1926), 129–56

A. Griscom & R. E. Jones (edd.), *The Historia Regum Britanniæ of Geoffrey of Monmouth with contributions to the study of its place in early British history* (New York 1929)

P. Grosjean, 'Catalogus codicum hagiographicorum Latinorum bibliothecarum Dubliniensium', *Analecta Bollandiana* 46 (1928), 80–148

A. Guaglianone (ed.), *Aviani Fabulae* (Turino 1958)

A. Gwynn, *The Writings of Bishop Patrick, 1074–1084* (Dublin 1955)

M. Gysseling, *Toponymisch woordenboek van Belgie, Nederland, Luxemburg, Noord-Frankrijk en West-Duistland (voor 1226)* (2 vols, [Brussels] 1960)

A. Hackman, *Catalogi codicum manuscriptorum Bibliothecæ Bodleianæ, Pars IV* (Oxford 1860)

H. Hagen, *Catalogus codicum Bernensium* (Bern 1875)

H. Hagenmeyer (ed.), *Die Kreuzzugsbriefe aus den Jahren 1088–1110* (Innsbruck 1901)

H. Hagenmeyer (ed.), *Fulcherii Carnotensis Historia Hierosolimitana* (Heidelberg 1913)

T. Hahn, 'Notes on Ross's checklist of Alexander texts', *Scriptorium* 34 (1980), 275–78

L. Hain, *Repertorium Bibliographicum* (4 vols, Stuttgart 1826–37)

E. Hallaire, 'Quelques manuscrits de Jean le Bègue', *Scriptorium* 8 (1954), 291–92

C. Halm (ed.), *Sulpicii Severi libri qui supersunt* (Wien 1866)

L. Halphen (ed.), *Eginhard: Vie de Charlemagne* (Paris 1923)

N. E. S. A. Hamilton (ed.), *Willelmi Malmesbiriensis monachi. De gestis pontificum Anglorum* (London 1870)

J. Hammer, 'Bref commentaire de la Prophetia Merlini du ms 3514 de la bibliothèque de la cathédrale d'Exeter', in ed. Hammer, *Hommages à Joseph Bidez et à Franz Cumont* (Brussels 1949), pp. 111–19

J. Hammer, 'A commentary on the *Prophetia Merlini* (Geoffrey of Monmouth's *Historia Regum Britanniae*, Book VII)', *Speculum* 10 (1935), 3–30; continuation *Speculum* 15 (1940), 409–31

J. Hammer, 'Another commentary on the *Prophetia Merlini* (Geoffrey of Monmouth's *Historia Regum Britanniae*, Book VII)', *Bulletin of the Polish Institute of Arts and Sciences in America* 1 (1942/3), 589–601

J. Hammer (ed.), *Geoffrey of Monmouth. Historia Regum Britanniae: a Variant Version edited from manuscripts* (Cambridge, Mass. 1951)

J. Hammer, 'Note on a manuscript of Geoffrey of Monmouth's *Historia Regum Britanniae*', *Philological Quarterly* 12 (1933), 225–34

J. Hammer, 'The poetry of Johannes Beverus with extracts from his *Tractatus de Bruto abbreviato*', *Modern Philology* 34 (1936/7), 119–32

J. Hammer, 'Remarks on the sources and textual history of Geoffrey of Monmouth's *Historia regum Britanniae*, with an excursus on the *Chronica Polonorum* of Wincenty Kadłubek (Magister Vincentius)', *Bulletin of the Polish Institute of Arts and Sciences in America* 2 (1943/4), 501–44

J. Hammer, 'Some additional manuscripts of Geoffrey of Monmouth's *Historia Regum Britanniae*', *Modern Languages Quarterly* 3 (1942), 235–42

J. Hammer, 'Some Leonine summaries of Geoffrey of Monmouth's *Historia Regum Britanniae* and other poems', *Speculum* 6 (1931), 114–23

J. Hammer, 'An unedited commentary on the *Prophetia Merlini* in Dublin, Trinity College, MS 496 E.6.2 (Geoffrey of Monmouth's *Historia Regum Britanniae*, Book VII)', *Charisteria Thaddaeo Sinko: quinquaginta abhinc annos amplissimis in philosophia honoribus ornato ab amicis collegis discipulis oblata* (Warsaw 1951) pp. 81–89

J. Hammer, 'An unrecorded *Epitaphium Ceadwallae*', *Speculum* 6 (1931), 607–8

J. Hammer & H. Friedmann, 'Status imperii iudaici', *Scriptorium* 1 (1946/7), 50–65

C. Hardwick *et al.*, *A Catalogue of the Manuscripts preserved in the Library of the University of Cambridge* (5 vols, Cambridge 1856–67)

T. D. Hardy, *Descriptive Catalogue of Materials Relating to the History of Great Britain and Ireland to the end of the reign of Henry VII* (3 vols in 4, London 1862–71)

N. M. Häring, 'Texts concerning Gilbert of Poitiers', *Archives d'histoire doctrinale et littéraire du Moyen Age* 37 (1970), 169–203

S. Harrison Thompson, *The Writings of Robert Grosseteste, bishop of Lincoln 1235–1253* (Cambridge 1940)

B. Hauréau, *Initia operum scriptorum latinorum medii potissimum aevi ex codicibus manuscriptis et libris impressis alphabetice digessit* (facs. edn, 8 vols, Turnhout 1973/4)

D. Hay, *Polydore Vergil: Renaissance historian and man of letters* (Oxford 1952)

T. Hearne (ed.), *Aluredi Beverlacensis Annales sive historia de gestis regum Britanniæ, libris IX* (Oxford 1716)

T. Hearne (ed.), *Joannis Lelandi antiquarii De rebus Britannicis collectanea* (6 vols, London 1774)

T. Hearne (ed.), *Thomae Sprotti Chronica* (Oxford 1719)

J. M. M. Hermans & E. M. C. van Houts, 'The history of a membrum disiectum of the Gesta Normannorum Ducum, now Vatican Reg. lat. 733 fol. 51*', *Mededelingen van het Nederlands Instituut te Rome*, NS, 9–10 (1982/3), 79–94

[B. J. Herold (ed.),] *Pantheon sive Vniuersitatis libri, qui chronici appellantur, XX, omnes omnium seculorum et gentium, tam sacras quam prophanas historias complectentes . . .* (Basel 1559)

L. Herrmann, 'Un remaniement de la *Philosophia* de Guillaume de Conches', *Scriptorium* 1 (1946/7), 243–59

I. Hilbert (ed.), *Sancti Eusebii Hieronymi Epistulae* (3 vols, Leipzig 1910–17)

A. Hilka & W. Söderhjelm (edd.), *Die Disciplina clericalis des Petrus Alfonsi (das älteste Novellenbuch des Mittelalters)* (Heidelberg 1911)

B. Hill, 'The fifteenth-century prose *Legend of the Cross before Christ*', *Medium Ævum* 34 (1965), 203–22

B. Hill, '*Epitaphia Alexandri* in English medieval manuscripts', *Leeds Studies in English* 8 (1975), 96–104 (with plate)

B. Hill, 'The Middle English and Latin versions of the *Parva Recapitulatio* of Alexander the Great', *Notes and Queries* 225 (1980), 4–20

J. H. Hill & L. L. Hill (edd.), *Petrus Tudebodus. Historia de hierosolymitano itinere* (Paris 1977)

T. Hog (ed.), *F. Nicholai Triveti de ordine frat. predicatorum. Annales* (London 1845)

A. J. Holden (ed.), *Le Roman de Rou de Wace* (3 vols, Paris 1970–73)

O. Holder-Egger, 'Italienische Prophetieen des 13. Jahrhunderts', *Neues Archiv der Gesellschaft für ältere deutsche Geschichtskunde* 33 (1907/8), 97–187

W. Holtzmann, 'Papsturkunden in England: 2 Band. Die kirchlichen Archive u. Bibliotheken; 1. Berichte u. Handschriftenbeschreibungen', *Abhandlungen der Gesellschaft der Wissenschaften zu Göttingen, philologisch-historische Klasse* (Berlin 1935)

K. Horstmann (ed.), *The Three Kings of Cologne: an early English translation of the 'Historia trium regum' by John of Hildesheim* (London 1886)

K. Horstmann (ed.), *Richard Rolle of Hampole of Hampole, an English Father of the Church and his followers* (2 vols, London 1895/6)

D. R. Howlett, 'A St Albans historical miscellany of the fifteenth century', *Transactions of the Cambridge Bibliographical Society* 6 (1972–76), 195–201

R. Howlett (ed.), *Chronicles of the Reigns of Stephen, Henry II and Richard I* (4 vols, London 1884–89)

K. Hughes, 'The offices of S. Finnian of Clonard and S. Cianan of Duleek', *Analecta Bollandiana* 73 (1955), 342–72

K. Hughes, *Celtic Britain in the Early Middle Ages*, ed. D. N. Dumville (Woodbridge 1980)

G. C. Huisman, 'Notes on the manuscript tradition of Dudo of Saint-Quentin's *Gesta Normannorum*', *Anglo-Norman Studies* 6 (1983), 122–35

R. W. Hunt *et al.*, *A Summary Catalogue of Western Manuscripts in the Bodleian Library at Oxford* (6 vols in 7 + index, Oxford 1922–53, repr. Munchen 1980)

D. Hurst (ed.), *Bedae Venerabilis Opera. Pars III, Opera homiletica. Pars IV, Opera rhythmica* (Turnhout 1955)

D. Huws and B. F. Roberts, 'Another manuscript of the Variant Version of the "Historia Regum Britanniae" ', *Bibliographical Bulletin of the International Arthurian Society* 25 (1973), 147–52

M-T. Isaac, *Les Livres manuscrits de l'abbaye des Dunes d'après le catalogue du xviie siècle* (Aubel 1984)

S. Iwamura, *Manuscripts and Printed Editions of Marco Polo's travels* (Tokyo 1949)

P. Jaffé [& S. Loewenfeld], *Regesta Pontificum Romanorum ab Condita Ecclesia . . .* (2nd edn, rev. W. Wattenbach *et al.*, 2 vols, Leipzig 1881–88)

M. R. James, *The Ancient Libraries of Canterbury and Dover* (Cambridge 1903)

M. R. James, *The Apocryphal New Testament being the Apocryphal Gospels, Acts, Epistles and Apocalypses* (Oxford 1925, rev. edn 1953)

M. R. James, *A Descriptive Catalogue of the Manuscripts in the Library of Corpus Christi College Cambridge* (2 vols, Cambridge 1912)

M. R. James, *A Descriptive Catalogue of the Manuscripts in the Library of Gonville and Caius College* (2 vols + suppl., Cambridge 1907–14)

M. R. James, *A Descriptive Catalogue of the Manuscripts in the Library of St John's College, Cambridge* (Cambridge 1913)

M. R. James, *A Descriptive Catalogue of the Manuscripts in the Library of Sidney Sussex College, Cambridge* (Cambridge 1895)

M. R. James, *A Descriptive Catalogue of the Western Manuscripts in the Library of Clare College, Cambridge* (Cambridge 1905)

M. R. James, *Lists of Manuscripts formerly owned by Dr. John Dee* (Oxford 1921)

M. R. James, 'Lists of manuscripts formerly in Peterborough Abbey', *Bibliographical Society Transactions, Supplement* 5 (1926)

M. R. James (ed.), rev. edn C. N. L. Brooke & R. A. B. Mynors, *Walter Map: De Nugis Curialium. Courtiers' Trifles* (Oxford 1983)

M. R. James, *The Western Manuscripts in the Library of Trinity College Cambridge. A Descriptive Catalogue* (4 vols, Cambridge 1900–4)

M. R. James & C. Jenkins, *A Descriptive Catalogue of the Manuscripts in the Library of Lambeth Palace* (2 vols, Cambridge 1930–2)

[A. Chappiel for] C. Jaumar (ed.), *Speculum ecclesie una cum speculo sacerdotum* in *Sermones optimi ac fecundissimi super pater noster: et Ave Maria: Augustini de leonissa: ordinis heremitarum divi presulis Augustini* [Paris *ca* 1500]

C. W. Jones *et al.* (ed.), *Bedae Venerabilis Opera. Opera Didascalica* (3 vols, Turnhout 1975–80)

T. Jones, ' "Cronica de Wallia" and other documents from Exeter 3514', *Bulletin of the Board of Celtic Studies* 12 (1946–48), 27–44

G. Kane & E. T. Donaldson (edd.), *Will's Vision of Piers Plowman, Do-well, Do-better and Do-best* (London 1975)

L. Keeler, *Geoffrey of Monmouth and the Late Latin Chronicles, 1300–1500* (Berkeley 1946)

J. F. Kenney, *The Sources for the Early History of Ireland: ecclesiastical. An introduction and guide* (New York 1929)

N. R. Ker, *Books, Collectors and Libraries: studies in the medieval heritage*, ed. A. G. Watson (London 1985)

N. R. Ker, *English Manuscripts in the Century after the Norman Conquest* (Oxford 1960)

N. R. Ker, 'English manuscripts owned by Johannes Vlimmerius and Cornelius Duyn', *The Library*, 4th ser., 22 (1941/2), 205–7

N. R. Ker, 'From "above top line" to "below top line": a change in scribal practice', *Celtica* 5 (1950), 13–15

N. R. Ker, *Medieval Libraries of Great Britain: a list of surviving books* (2nd edn, London 1964)

N. R. Ker, *Medieval Manuscripts in British Libraries* (3 vols, Oxford 1969–83)

N. R. Ker, 'Oxford College libraries in the sixteenth century', *Bodleian Library Record* 6 (1957–61), 459–536

N. R. Ker & W. A. Pantin, 'Letters of a Scottish Student at Paris and Oxford c. 1250', *Formularies which bear on the History of Oxford c. 1204–1420* (2 vols, Oxford 1942), II.472–91

N. R. Ker & A. G. Watson, *Medieval Libraries of Great Britain: A list of surviving books: supplement to the second edition* (London 1987)

P. Kibre, 'Hippocrates latinus: repertorium of hippocratic writings in the Latin Middle Ages III', *Traditio* 33 (1977), 253–95

H. C. Kim (ed.), *The Gospel of Nicodemus Gesta Saluatoris edited from the Codex Einsidlensis, Einsiedeln, Stiftsbibliothek, MS. 326* (Toronto 1973)

G. W. Kitchin, *Catalogus codicum MSS. qui in bibliotheca Ædis Christi apud Oxonienses adservantur* (Oxford 1867)

D. Knowles & R. N. Hadcock, *Medieval Religious Houses. England and Wales* (2nd edn, London 1971)

C. Kohler, *Catalogue des manuscrits de la Bibliothèque Sainte-Geneviève* (3 vols, Paris 1893–98)

G. A. A. Kortekaas (ed.), *Historia Apollonii regis Tyri: prolegomena, text edition of the two principal Latin recensions, bibliography, indices and appendices* (Groningen 1984)

B. Kuebler (ed.), *Iuli Valeri Alexandri Polemi res gestae Alexandri Macedonis* (Leipzig 1888)

K. F. Kumaniecki (ed.), *M. Tulli Ciceronis scripta quae manserunt omnia. Fasc. 3. De Oratore* (Leipzig 1969)

J. Lair (ed.), 'De Moribus et actis primorum Normanniae ducum auctore Dudonis Sancti Quintini', *Mémoires de la Société des antiquaires de Normandie*, 3rd ser., 3 (1858), 115–301

M. L. W. Laistner and H. H. King, *A Handlist of Bede manuscripts* (Ithaca 1943)

S. M. Lakin, *A Catalogue of the Library of the Cathedral Church of Salisbury* (London 1880)

C. Lang (ed.), *Flavi Vegeti Renati Epitoma rei militaris* (Leipzig 1885)

M. Lapidge, 'An edition of the *Uera historia de morte Arthuri*', *Arthurian Literature* 1 (1981), 79–83

M. Lapidge & R. Sharpe, *A Bibliography of Celtic-Latin Literature 400–1200* (Dublin 1985)

J. Laporte, 'Epistulae Fiscannenses. Lettres d'amitié, de gouvernement et d'affaires (XIᵉ-XIIᵉ siècles)', *Revue Mabillon* 43 (1953), 5–31

J. M. Lappenberg, *A History of England under the Anglo-Saxon Kings* (2 vols, London 1845)

J. Le Neve, *Fasti Ecclesiae Anglicanae, 1300–1541, II, Hereford Diocese*, ed. J. M. Horn (London 1962)

J. Le Neve, *Fasti Ecclesiae Anglicanae, 1300–1541, IX, Exeter Diocese*, ed. J. M. Horn (London 1964)

J. Leclercq, 'Le "de grammatica" de Hugues de Saint-Victor', *Archives d'histoire doctrinale et littéraire du moyen âge* 14 (1943–45), 263–322

I. C. Lecompte, *Le Roman des Romans: an Old French poem* (Paris 1923)

P. Legendre, 'Miscellanea britannica', *Traditio* 15 (1959), 491–97

M. D. Legge, *Anglo-Norman in the Cloisters: the influence of the orders upon Anglo-Norman literature* (Edinburgh 1950)

M. D. Legge, 'A list of Langtoft manuscripts, with notes on MS. Laud misc. 637', *Medium Ævum* 4 (1935), 20–24

P. Lehmann *et al.*, *Mittelalterliche Bibliothekskataloge Deutschlands und der Schweiz* (4 vols in 6, Munich 1918–79)

W. Levison, 'A combined manuscript of Geoffrey of Monmouth and Henry of Huntingdon', *English Historical Review* 58 (1943), 41–51

W. Levison, review of N. R. Ker, *Medieval Libraries of Great Britain: a list of surviving books* (1941), *Medium Ævum* 11 (1942), 111–15

G. Libri, *Catalogue général des manuscrits des bibliothèques publiques des départements* 1 (Paris 1849)

G. Libri, *Catalogue général des manuscripts des bibliothèques publiques des départements* 2 (Paris 1855)

F. Liebermann, *Die Heiligen Englands: angelsächsisch und lateinisch* (Hannover 1889)

F. Liebermann (ed.), *Quadripartitus, ein englisches Rechtsbuch von 1114* (Halle 1892)

G. I. Lieftinck, *Manuscrits datés conservés dans les Pays-Bas: catalogue paléographique des manuscrits en écriture latine portant des indications de date* (2 vols in 4, Amsterdam 1964–88)

G. I. Lieftinck, 'Pour une nomenclature de l'écriture livresque de la période dite gothique: essai s'appliquant spécialement aux manuscrits originaires des Pays-Bas médiévaux', in *Nomenclature des écritures livresques du ixe au xvie siècle* (Paris 1954) pp. 15–34

A. -F. Lièvre, *Catalogue général des manuscrits des bibliothèques publiques de France* 25 (Paris 1894)

A. G. Little & F. Pelster, *Oxford Theologians 1280–1302* (Oxford 1934)

R. S. Loomis & L. H. Loomis, *Arthurian Legends in Medieval Art* (London 1938)

H. Loriquet, *Catalogue général des manuscrits des bibliothèques publiques de France* 39.2 (Paris 1906)

H. R. Luard (ed.), *Matthæi Parisiensis monachi Sancti Albani Chronica majora* (7 vols, London 1872–83)

H. R. Luard (ed.), *Flores historiarum* (3 vols, London 1890)

G. Mac Niocaill, *The Medieval Irish Annals* (Dublin 1975)

M. Maccarrone (ed.), *Lotharii cardinalis (Innocentii III) De miseria humane conditionis* (1955)

H. MacKinnon, 'William de Montibus, a medieval teacher', *Essays in Medieval History presented to Bertie Wilkinson*, edd. T. A. Sandquist & M. R. Powicke (Toronto 1969), pp. 32–45

E. P. McLachlan, 'In the wake of the Bury Bible: followers of Master Hugh at Bury St Edmunds', *Journal of the Warburg and Courtauld Institutes* 42 (1979), 216–24

W. Macray, *Catalogi codicum manuscriptorum Bibliothecæ Bodleianæ. Pars V* (5 vols, Oxford 1862–1900)

W. D. Macray, *Catalogi codicum manuscriptorum Bibliothecæ Bodleianæ. Pars IX* (Oxford 1883)

W. D. Macray et al., *Report on Manuscripts in Various Collections* (8 vols in 7, London 1901–13)

F. Madden, *List of Additions to the Manuscripts in the British Museum in the Years 1836–1840* (London 1843)

F. Madden, *Catalogue of Additions to the Manuscripts in the British Museum in the Years 1846–1847* (London 1864)

J. Major, *Historia maioris Britannie tam Anglie quam Scotie* ([Paris] 1521)

G. D. Mansi, *Sacrorum conciliorum noua et amplissima collectio* 27 (Venezia 1784)

Les Manuscrits de la Reine de Suède au Vatican: réédition du catalogue de Montfaucon et cotes actuelles (Vatican 1964)

H. Martin, *Catalogue des manuscrits de la bibliothèque de l'Arsenal* (9 vols in 10, Paris 1885–94)

F. Marx (ed.), *M. Tulli Ciceronis quae manserunt omnia. Fasc. 1. Incerti auctoris de Ratione dicendi ad C. Herennium lib. IV* (Leipzig 1964)

J. Marx (ed.), *Guillaume de Jumièges. Gesta Normannorum Ducum* (Rouen 1914)

M. McKisack, *Medieval History in the Tudor Age* (Oxford 1971)

D. McKitterick, *Cambridge University Library. A History: the eighteenth and nineteenth centuries* (Cambridge 1986)

F. Meister (ed.), *Daretis Phrygii. De excidio Troiae historia* (Leipzig 1873)

[A. Mellot,] *Catalogus codicum manuscriptorum Bibliothecæ Regiæ* (4 vols, Paris 1739–44)

C. Meredith-Jones (ed.), *Historia Karoli magni et Rotholandi ou Chronique du pseudo-Turpin* (Paris 1936, repr. Genève 1972)

P. Meyer, 'Les manuscrits français de Cambridge: ii Bibliothèque de l'Université', *Romania* 15 (1886), 236–57

P. Meyer, 'Les manuscrits français de Cambridge: iii Trinity College', *Romania* 32 (1903), 18–120

K. A. de Meyier, *Codices Vossiani Latini* (*Bibliotheca Universitatis Leidensis Codices Manuscripti* XIII–XVI) (4 vols, Leiden 1973–84)

M. Michelant, *Catalogue général des manuscrits des bibliothèques publiques des départements* 3 (Paris 1861)

A. Miraeus, *Notitia episcopatuum orbis Christiani in qua Christianae religionis amplitudo elucet libri V* (Antwerp 1613)

P. Molhuysen, *Bibliotheca Universitatis Leidensis: Codices manuscripti III. Codices Bibliothecae Publicae latini* (Leiden 1912)

A. Molinier, *Catalogue général des manuscrits des bibliothèques publiques de France* 6 (Paris 1887)

T. Mommsen (ed.), *Chronica minora Saec. IV. V. VI. VII* (3 vols, Berlin 1891–98)

T. Mommsen (ed.), *C. Iulii Solini Collectanea rerum memorabilium* (2nd edn, Berlin 1895)

347

N. Morgan, 'Matthew Paris, St Albans, London, and the leaves of the "Life of St Thomas Becket" ', *Burlington Magazine* 130 (February 1988), 85–96

J. R. Mozley, 'The "Vita Adae" ', *Journal of Theological Studies* 30 (1928/9), 121–48

J. R. Mozley, 'A new text of the Story of the Cross', *Journal of Theological Studies* 31 (1930), 113–37

A. N. L. Munby (facs. ed.), *Catalogus librorum manuscriptorum in bibliotheca D. Thomæ Phillipps Bart. A.D.1837* (3 vols, Cambridge 1975)

T. R. Nash, *Collections for the History of Worcestershire* (2 vols, London 1781/2)

W. A. Nitze, 'The exhumation of King Arthur at Glastonbury', *Speculum* 9 (1934) 355–61

G. Nortier, *Les Bibliothèques médiévales des abbayes bénédictines de Normandie* (Paris 1971)

S. H. O'Grady & R. Flower, *Catalogue of Irish Manuscripts in the British Museum* (3 vols, London 1926–53)

J. J. O'Meara, 'Giraldus Cambrensis in Topographia Hibernie: text of the first recension', *Proceedings of the Royal Irish Academy* 52c (1948–50), 113–78

H. Omont, *Anciens inventaires et catalogues de la Bibliothèque nationale* (5 vols, Paris 1908–21)

H. Omont, *Catalogue général des manuscrits des bibliothèques publiques de France* 1 (Paris 1886)

H. Omont, *Catalogue général des manuscrits des bibliothèques publiques de France* 2 (Paris 1888)

H. Omont, 'Catalogue des manuscrits Ashburnham-Barrois récemment acquis par la Bibliothèque nationale', *Bibliothèque de l'Ecole des Chartes* 63 (1902), 10–68

H. Omont, 'Nouvelles acquisitions du Département des Manuscrits de la Bibliothèque nationale pendant les années 1909–1910', *Bibliothèque de l'Ecole des Chartes* 72 (1911), 5–56

G. Orlandi, 'Baucis et Traso', *Commedie latine del XII e XIII secolo*, ed. F. Bertini (5 vols, Genova 1976-), III.243–303

O. Pacht & J. J. G. Alexander, *Illuminated Manuscripts in the Bodleian Library Oxford* (3 vols, Oxford 1966–73)

M. B. Parkes, *English Cursive Book Hands 1250–1500* (Oxford 1969, rev. imp. Ilkley 1979)

J. J. Parry, 'A Variant Version of Geoffrey of Monmouth's *Historia*', in *A Miscellany of Studies in Romance Language and Literature presented to Leon E. Kastner*, edd. M. Williams & J. A. de Rothschild (Cambridge 1932), pp. 364–69

E. Pellegrin, *La Bibliothèque des Visconti et des Sforza, ducs de Milan, au XVe siècle* (1 vol + suppl., Paris 1955–69)

E. Pellegrin, 'Essai d'identification de fragments dispersés dans les manuscrits de bibliothèques de Berne et de Paris', *Bulletin d'information de l'Institut de recherche et d'histoire des textes* 9 (1960), 7–37

E. Pellegrin et al., *Les Manuscrits classiques latins de la Bibliothèque Vaticane* (2 vols in 3, Paris 1975–82)

E. Pellegrin, *Manuscrits latins de la Bodmeriana* (Cologny-Genève 1982)

G. H. Pertz (ed.), *Arnoldi Chronica Slavorum ex recensione I.M. Lappenbergii* (Hannover 1868)

G. H. Pertz, 'Handschriften der Universitätsbibliothek zu Heidelberg', *Archiv der Gesellschaft für ältere deutsche Geschichtskunde* 9 (1847), 579–87

H. Pertz, 'Mittheilungen aus dem Archiv der ehemaligen Abtei Malmedy, von Herrn Regierungsrath Ritz aus Aachen', *Archiv der Gesellschaft für ältere deutsche Geschichtskunde* 4 (1822), 412–34

M. Peyrafort-Bonnet, 'La Dispersion d'une bibliothèque médiévale: les manuscrits de l'abbaye de Pontigny', *Cîteaux: Commentarii Cisterciensis* 35 (1984), 92–128

F. Pfister, 'Die Historia de Preliis und das Alexanderepos des Quilichinus', *Münchener Museum für Philologie des Mittelalters und der Renaissance* 1 (1912), 249–301

F. Pfister (ed.), *Kleine Texte zum Alexanderroman: Commonitorium Palladii, Briefwechsel zwischen Alexander und Dindymus, Brief Alexanders über die Wunder Indiens nach der Bamberger Handschrift herausgegeben* (Heidelberg 1910)

J. Planta, *Catalogue of the Manuscripts in the Cottonian Library deposited in the British Museum* (London 1802)

C. Plummer (ed.), *Venerabilis Baedae opera historica* (2 vols, Oxford 1896)

R. L. Poole, *Report on Manuscripts in Various Collections* (Dublin 1907)

A. de Poorter, *Catalogue des manuscrits de la bibliothèque publique de la ville de Bruges* (Gembloux 1934)

K. R. Potter (ed.), *The Historia Novella by William of Malmesbury* (Edinburgh 1955)

A. Potthast, *Regesta pontificum Romanorum inde ab a. post Christum natum mcxcviii ad a. mccciv* (2 vols, Berlin 1874/5)

F. M. Powicke, *The Medieval Books of Merton College* (Oxford 1931)

Prophetia Anglicana, Merlini Ambrosii Britanni, ex incubo olim (ut hominum fama est) ante annos mille ducentos circiter in Anglia nati, vaticinia et praedictiones: a Galfredo Monumetensi latine conversae: una cum septem libris explanationum in eandem prophetiam excellentissimi sui temporis oratoris, polyhistoris & theologi Alani de Insulis . . . (Typis Ioachimi Bratheringii, Frankfurt 1603)

H. Prutz, *Kulturgeschichte der Kreuzzüge* (Berlin 1883)

J. Quicherat, *Catalogue général des manuscrits des bibliothèques publiques des départements* 4 (Paris 1872)

G. Raynaud, 'Le miracle de Sardenai', *Romania* 11 (1882), 519–37

Recueil des historiens des Croisades, Documents arméniens (2 vols, Paris 1869–1906)

Recueil des historiens des Croisades, Historiens occidentaux (5 vols, Paris 1844–95)

Recueil des historiens des Croisades, Historiens orientaux (5 vols, Paris 1872–1906)

B. Rehm (ed.), *Die Pseudoklementinen: II Rekognitionen in Rufins Übersetzung* (Berlin 1965)

[Baron de] Reiffenberg, ['Histoire littéraire, poème sur le costume clérical'], *Bulletins de l'Académie royale des Sciences et Belles-Lettres de Bruxelles* 9.2 (1842), 80–94

L. D. Reynolds (ed.), *L. Annaei Senecae Dialogorum libri duodecim* (Oxford 1977)

L. D. Reynolds (ed.), *Texts and Transmission: a Survey of the Latin Classics* (Oxford 1983)

A. Riese, *Anthologia latina siue poesis latinae supplementum* I (2 vols in 1, Leipzig 1869/70)

A. Riese (ed.), *Geographi latini minores* (Heilbronn 1878)

H. Rigaux, *Catalogue général des manuscrits des bibliothèques publiques de France* 26 (Paris 1897)

H. T. Riley (ed.), *Willelmi Rishanger quondam monachi S. Albani et quorundam anonymorum Chronica et Annales* (London 1865)

J. C. Robertson & J. B. Sheppard (edd.), *Materials for the History of Thomas Becket, archbishop of Canterbury* (7 vols, London 1875–85)

P. R. Robinson, *Catalogue of Dated and Datable Manuscripts c. 737–1600 in Cambridge Libraries* (2 vols, Cambridge 1988)

D. W. Rollason, *The Mildrith Legend: a study in early medieval hagiography* (Leicester 1982)

D. J. A. Ross, *Alexander Historiatus: a guide to medieval illustrated Alexander literature* (London 1963)

D. J. A. Ross, 'Parva Recapitulacio: an English collection of texts relating to Alexander the Great', *Classica et Mediaevalia* 33 (1981/2), 191–203

F. W. E. Roth, 'Lateinische Gedichte der XII.-XIV. Jahrhunderts', *Romanische Forschungen* 6 (1891), 9–16

C. F. Russo (ed.), *L. Annaei Senecae, Divi Claudii Apocolocyntosis* (2nd edn, Firenze 1955)

E. Sackur (ed.), *Sibyllinische Texte und Forschungen. Pseudomethodius, Adso und die Tiburtinische Sibylle* (Halle 1898)

H. E. Salter (ed.), *Eynsham Cartulary* (2 vols, Oxford 1907/8)

C. Samaran & R. Marichal, *Catalogue des manuscrits en écriture latine portant des indications de date, de lieu ou de copiste* (7 vols in 14, Paris 1969–84)

A. Sanderus (ed.), *Bibliotheca belgica manuscripta* (2 vols, Lille 1641–44)

L. F. Sandler, *Gothic manuscripts 1285–1385* (2 vols, Oxford 1986)

D. Schaller & E. Könsgen, *Initia carminum Latinorum saeculo undecimo antiquiorum* (Göttingen 1977)

G. Scherrer, *Verzeichniss der Handschriften der Stiftsbibliothek von St Gallen* (Halle 1875)

P. G. Schmidt (ed.), *Visio Thurkilli relatore, ut videtur, Radulpho de Coggeshall* (Leipzig 1978)

P. Schmitt, *Catalogue général des manuscrits des bibliothèques publiques de France* 56 (Paris 1969)

J. B. Schneyer, *Repertorium der lateinischen Sermones des Mittelalters für die Zeit von 1150–1350* (9 vols, Aschendorff 1969–80)

E. Schroeder, 'Zwei Genealogien', *Anzeiger für deutsche Alterthum und deutsches Literatur* 18 (1892), 298–99

A. Schulz (San Marte)(ed.), *Gottfried's von Monmouth, Historia Regum Britanniae, mit literar-historischer Einleitung und ausführlichen Anmerkungen, und Brut Tysylio, altwälsche Chronik in deutscher Uebersetzung* (Halle 1854)

A. B. Scott (ed.), *Hildeberti Cenomannensis episcopi carmina minora* (Leipzig 1969)

A. B. Scott & F. X. Martin (edd.), *Expugnatio hibernica by Giraldus Cambrensis* (Dublin 1978)

E. J. L. Scott, *Catalogue of Additions to the Manuscripts in the British Museum in the Years 1888–1893* (London 1894)

E. J. L. Scott, *Catalogue of Additions to the Manuscripts in the British Museum in the Years 1894–1899* (London 1901)

E. J. L. Scott, *Catalogue of the Stowe Manuscripts in the British Museum* (1 vol. + index, London 1895/6)

E. J. L. Scott, *Index to the Sloane Manuscripts in the British Museum* (London 1904, repr. Oxford 1971)

C. Selmer (ed.), *Navigatio Sancti Brendani Abbatis from Early Latin Manuscripts* (Notre Dame 1959)

M. C. Seymour, 'The English Manuscripts of Mandeville's Travels', *Transactions of the Edinburgh Bibliographical Society* 4 (1966), 169–210

I. Short & B. Merrilees (edd.), *Benedeit: the Anglo-Norman Voyage of St Brendan* (Manchester 1979)

T. Silverstein, *Visio Sancti Pauli: the history of the apocalypse in Latin together with nine texts* (London 1935)

D. W. Singer, *Catalogue of Latin and Vernacular Alchemical Manuscripts in Great Britain and Ireland dating from before the XVI century* (3 vols, Bruxelles 1928–31)

W. Skene (ed.), *Chronicles of the Picts, Chronicles of the Scots, and Other Early Memorials of Scottish History* (Edinburgh 1867)

W. Skene (ed.), *Johannis de Fortun. Chronica gentis Saxonum* (Edinburgh 1871)

R. A. Q. Skerret, 'Two Irish translations of the Liber de passione Christi', *Celtica* 6 (1963), 82–117

J. J. Smith (ed.), *Abbreviata cronica ab anno 1377 usque ad annum 1469* (Cambridge 1840)

T. Smith, *Catalogus librorum manuscriptorum Bibliothecæ Cottonianæ* (Oxford 1696)

H. M. Smyser (ed.), *The Pseudo-Turpin edited from Bibliothèque Nationale, Fonds Latin, MS. 17656 with an annotated synopsis* (Cambridge, Mass. 1937)

R. Steele (ed.), *Opera hactenus inedita Rogeri Baconi . . .* (16 fasc., Oxford 1909–40)

F. Stegmüller, *Repertorium Biblicum Medii Aevi* (11 vols, Madrid 1940–80)

E. Stengel, 'Elf neue Handschriften der prösischen Brut-Chroniken', *Zeitschrift für romanische Philologie* 10 (1886), 278–85

W. H. Stevenson & H. E. Salter, *The Early History of St. John's College Oxford* (Oxford 1939)

E. L. G. Stones (ed.), *Anglo-Scottish Relations 1174–1328: some selected documents* (Oxford 1965, rev. impr. 1970)

E. L. G. Stones & G. G. Simpson (edd.), *Edward I and the Throne of Scotland 1290–1296: an edition of the record sources for the Great Cause* (2 vols, Oxford 1978)

K. Strecker (ed.), *Die Apokalypse des Golias* (Rome 1928)

S. Strongman, 'John Parker's manuscripts: an edition of the lists in Lambeth Palace

MS 737', *Transactions of the Cambridge Bibliographical Society* 7 (1977–80), 1–27

W. Stubbs (ed.), *Willelmi Malmesbiriensis monachi de gestis regum Anglorum* (2 vols, London 1887–89)

A. F. Sutton & L. Visser-Fuchs, 'Richard III's books: VII Guido delle Colonne's *Historia destructionis Troiae*. VIII Geoffrey of Monmouth's *Historia Regum Britanniae*, with *The Prophecy of the Eagle* and commentary', *The Ricardian* 8 (1988), 136–48

C. H. Talbot, 'Notes on the library of Pontigny', *Analecta Sacri Ordinis Cisterciensis* 10 (1954), 106–68

F. Taylor, 'The Chronicle of John Streeche for the reign of Henry V (1414–1422)', *Bulletin of the John Rylands Library* 16 (1932), 137–87

E. M. Thompson, *Adæ Murimuth. Continuatio Chronicarum. Robertus de Avesbury De gestis mirabilibus regis Edwardi tertii* (London 1889)

R. M. Thomson, *Manuscripts from St. Albans Abbey 1066–1235* (2 vols, Woodbridge 1982)

L. Thorndike, *A History of Magic and Experimental Science during the First Thirteen Hundred Years of our Era* (6 vols, New York 1923–41)

L. Thorndike & P. Kibre, *A Catalogue of Incipits of Mediaeval Scientific Writings in Latin* (London 1963)

[T. Thorpe,] *Catalogue of upwards of Fourteen Hundred Manuscripts, upon Vellum and Paper* (London 1836)

H. Thurn, *Die Handschriften der Universitätsbibliothek Würzburg* (2 vols, Wiesbaden 1970–73)

C. Tischendorf (ed.), *Evangelia apocrypha adhibitis plurimis codicibus graecis et latinis maximam partem nunc primum consultis atque ineditorum copia insignibus* (Leipzig 1876)

H. J. Todd, *A Catalogue of the Archiepiscopal Manuscripts in the Library at Lambeth Palace* (London 1812)

G. J. Turner (ed.), *Brevia placitata* (London 1951)

M. S. van der Bijl, 'Petrus Berchorius reductorium morale liber XV: Ovidius moralizatus, cap. ii', *Vivarium* 9 (1971), 25–48

A-D. von den Brincken, 'Studien zur Überlieferung der Chronik des Martin von Troppau (Erfahrungen mit einem massenhaft überlieferten historischen Text)', *Deutsches Archiv für Erforschung des Mittelalters* 41 (1985), 460–531

J. van den Gheyn et al., *Catalogue des manuscrits de la Bibliothèque royale de Belgique* (13 vols, Bruxelles 1901–48)

E. M. C. Van Houts, *Gesta Normannorum Ducum: een studie over de handschriften, de tekst, het geschiedwerk en het genre* (Groningen 1982)

A. van de Wijngaert (ed.), *Sinica Franciscana I: itinera et relationes fratrum minorum saeculi XIII et XIV* (Brozzi 1929)

R. Vaughan, 'The handwriting of Matthew Paris', *Transactions of the Cambridge Bibliographical Society* 1 (1949–53), 376–94

D. Verhelst (ed.), *Adso Dervensis. De Ortu et tempore Antichristi necnon et tractatus qui ab eo dependunt* (Turnhout 1976)

A. Vernet *et al.*, *La Bibliothèque de l'abbaye de Clairvaux du xiie au xviiie siècle* (Paris 1979)

J. Vising, *Anglo-Norman Language and Literature* (London 1923)

J. Vogels, *Handschriftliche Untersuchungen über die englische Version Mandeville's* (Crefeld 1891)

von Muralt, 'Handschriften der kaiserlichen Bibliothek zu St. Petersburg', *Archiv der Gesellschaft für ältere deutsche Geschichtskunde* 11 (1858), 791–804

H. Walther, *Initia carminum ac versuum medii aevi posterioris latinorum: alphabetisches Verzeichnis der Versanfänge mittellateinischer Dichtungen* (1 vol. + suppl., Göttingen 1959–69)

H. Walther, *Proverbia sententiaeque latinitatis medii aevi: lateinische Sprichwörter und Sentenzen des Mittelalters in alphabetischer Anordnung* (6 vols, Göttingen 1963–69)

W. Walther Boer (ed.), *Epistola Alexandri ad Aristotelem ad codicum fidem edita et commentario critico instructa* (The Hague 1953)

H. L. D. Ward & J. A. Herbert, *Catalogue of Romances in the Department of Manuscripts in the British Museum* (3 vols, London 1883–1910)

H. Wanley *et al.*, *A Catalogue of the Harleian Manuscripts in the British Museum* (4 vols, London 1808–14)

G. F. Warner & J. P. Gilson, *Catalogue of Western Manuscripts in the Old Royal and King's Collections* (4 vols, London 1921)

E. G. R. Waters (ed.), *The Anglo-Norman Voyage of St. Brendan by Benedeit: a poem of the early twelfth century* (Oxford 1928)

A. G. Watson, 'Bibliographical Notes: an identification of some manuscripts owned by Dr. John Dee and Sir Simonds D'Ewes', *The Library*, 5th ser., 13 (1958), 194–98

A. G. Watson, *The Manuscripts of Henry Savile of Banke* (London 1969)

A. G. Watson, 'Thomas Allen of Oxford and his Manuscripts', *Medieval Scribes, Manuscripts and Libraries: essays presented to N. R. Ker* (London 1978), edd. M. B. Parkes and A. G. Watson, pp. 279–313

A. G. Watson, 'An early thirteenth-century Low Countries booklist', *British Library Journal* 7 (1981), 39–46

A. G. Watson, *Catalogue of Dated and Datable Manuscripts c. 435–1600 in Oxford Libraries* (2 vols, Oxford 1984)

A. G. Watson, *Catalogue of Dated and Datable Manuscripts c. 700–1600 in the Department of Manuscripts, The British Library* (2 vols, London 1979)

W. Wattenbach, 'Reise nach Österreich in den Jahren 1847, 1848, 1849', *Archiv der Gesellschaft für ältere deutsche Geschichtskunde* 10 (1851), 426–693

W. Wattenbach (ed.), 'Verse aus England', *Neues Archiv der Gesellschaft für ältere deutsche Geschichtskunde* 1 (1876), 600–4

K. F. Werner, 'Andreas von Marchiennes und die Geschichtsschreibung von Anchin und Marchiennes in der zweiter Hälfte des 12. Jahrhunderts', *Deutsches Archiv für Erforschung des Mittelalters* 9 (1952), 402–63

M. Winterbottom (ed.), *Three Lives of English Saints* (Toronto 1972)

G. E. Woodbine (ed.), *Glanvill: De legibus et consuetudinibus regni Angliae* (London 1932)

R. M. Woolley, *Catalogue of the Manuscripts of Lincoln Cathedral Chapter Library* (London 1927)

F. Wormald (ed.), *English Benedictine Kalendars after A. D. 1100* (2 vols, London 1939–46)

F. Wormald & P. M. Giles, *A Descriptive Catalogue of the Additional Illuminated Manuscripts in the Fitzwilliam Museum acquired between 1895 and 1979 (excluding the McClean Collection)* (2 vols, Cambridge 1982)

C. E. Wright, *The British Museum: Catalogue of Additions to the Manuscripts 1936–1945* (2 vols, London 1970)

C. E. Wright, *Fontes Harleiani: a study of the sources of the Harleian collection of manuscripts preserved in the Department of Manuscripts in the British Museum* (London 1972)

N. Wright (ed.), *The Historia Regum Britannie of Geoffrey of Monmouth, I: Bern, Burgerbibliothek, MS. 568* (Cambridge 1985)

N. Wright (ed.), *The Historia Regum Britannie of Geoffrey of Monmouth, II, the First Variant Version: a critical edition* (Cambridge 1988)

N. Wright (ed.), *The Historia Regum Britannie of Geoffrey of Monmouth, IV: the Gesta Regum Britannie* (Cambridge, forthcoming)

T. Wright (ed.), *The Anglo-Latin Satirical Poets and Epigrammatists of the Twelfth Century* (2 vols, London 1872)

T. Wright (ed.), *The Latin Poems commonly attributed to Walter Mapes* (London 1841)

T. Wright (ed.), *Political Poems and Songs relating to English History composed during the period from the Accession of Edw. III to that of Ric. III* (2 vols, London 1859–61)

T. Wright (ed.), *The Political Songs of England from the reign of John to that of Edward II* (London 1839)

T. Wright (ed.), *The Seven Sages in English Verse* (London 1845) [Percy Society XVI]

H. Wuttke (ed.), *Die Kosmographie des Istrier Aithikos im lateinischen Auszuge des Hieronymus aus einer Leipziger Handschrift* (Leipzig 1853)

J. Young & P. H. Aitken, *A Catalogue of the Manuscripts in the Library of the Hunterian Museum in the University of Glasgow* (Glasgow 1908)

F. Zarncke, 'Der Priester Johannes', *Abhandlungen der philologisch-historischen Classe der k. sächsischen Gesellschaft der Wissenschaften* 7 (1879), 829–1028

INDEX I: Contents

Listed by author then title: medieval authors placed under Christian name if other name is not a true surname (for example if a placename or descriptive title only) – otherwise listed under surname. Anonymous works are grouped together, where appropriate, under a general heading which is separated by a colon from individual details which follow. Documents are listed under name of issuing authority. Spelling has been normalised where necessary.

Gildas (cont.)
   see also Historia Brittonum, Prophecy
Gilo, *De uia Ierosolimitana* 60
Giraldus Cambrensis,
   Descriptio Kambrie 92
   Expugnatio Hibernica 1, 103
   Topographia Hibernica 1, 103, 150, 164
Glanvill, *De legibus et consuetudinibus regni Anglie* 6
Godfrey of Viterbo, *Pantheon*, extracts 32, 91
Grammatica:
   Differentie similium partium orationis 34
   Liber ermeneumatum 34
   'Littera est nota elementi . . .' 34
   'Nomen est pars orationis . . .' 34
   De numero iuxta latinos 34
   'Omnium uerborum perfectam . . .' 34
   Partes secundum ordinem litterarum alphabeti, from Isidore 34
   Partes per dispositionem litterarum alfabeti, from Priscian 34
   De patronimico 34
   Questiones on grammatical issues 34
   Quomodo epistola formata fiat 60
Greek 215
Gregory X (pope), *Citatio contra Simonem et Guidonem de Monteforte* 77
Grim, Edward, *Uita S. Thome Cantuariensis* (*BHL* 8182) 98, 202
Grosseteste, *see* Robert
Guido della Colonne, *Historia Troiana* 40, 84, 104, 115, 168. *See also* 78

Hadrian IV (pope), letters 15, 215
Hagiography:
   Uita Ade 88, 116
   Uita S. Aetheldrethe (*BHL* 2638) 61
   Uita SS. Albani et Amphibali (*BHL* 214) 42
   Passio SS. Alexandri et al. (*BHL* 266) 12
   Uita S. Ansberti 12
   Uita S. Amandi (*BHL* 332) 12
   Passio S. Anastasie 12
   Uita S. Austreberte (*BHL* 831) 12
   Passio S. Barbare (*BHL* 913) 19
   Miracula de S. Benedicto 12
   Nauigatio S. Brendani (*BHL* 1436) 172
   Uita S. Brendani (*BHL* 1437) 93
   Uita S. Brendani, verse (*BHL* 1445) 38
   Quodam scriptum de S. Brictio 12
   Passio SS. Crisanti et Darie 12
   Uita S. Cucufatis (*BHL* 1998) 12
   translation of S. Cuthbert 136
   Miracula S. Edwardi 65
   Uita S. Ecgwini (*BHL* 2433) 61
   Passio S. Euphemie 12
   Miracula post mortem S. Honorati (*BHL* 3976) 61
   Uita S. Hylarii 12
   Actus S. Iohannis theologi et Prochori eius discipuli (*BHL* 4323) 20
   Passio SS. Machabeorum (*BHL* 5111) 12

Robert of Reims, *Historia hierosolymitana* 186, 196, 199
Robert de Torigni, Chronicle (continuations) 77, 200
Rolle, Richard, of Hampole (ps.), *De uisitacione infirmorum* 40
Roman des Romans 128

Saracen – *see* Mahomet and Islam
Scotichronicon (extract) 24
Secreta Secretorum – *see* Alexander legend
Secreta Ypocratis 39
Seneca,
   Apocolocyntosis 183
   De naturalibus quaestionibus 66
   Dialogi 17
Seneca (ps.), *De remediis fortuitorum* 14
'Sermo quomodo primitus sancta arbor creuit' – *see* Legend of the Cross
Seuene Sages 40
Sibyl:
   account of Tiburtine Sibyl 72
   Cestre lepistre de Sibille 100
   Uersus Sibylle de die iudicii 60
   notes on Sibylline verse in Augustine's *De ciuitate Dei* 74
   see also Prophecy
Simon Chèvre d'Or, poem on destruction of Troy 164
Solinus, Iulius, *Polyhistor* 181, 188, 205 (extract)
Somnium beate Thome martiris 40 (lost)
Somnium ducis Gloucestrie 7
Speculum spiritualis amicitie 66
Status imperii Iudaici 13, 16, 21, 214
Stephanus, *medicus* of Hugh, bishop of Durham, *Tractatus de quodam prodigio* 164
Stimulus amoris 120
Streeche, John, Chronicle 99
Syluius, *see* Andreas

Testamenta xii patriarcharum 32, 40, 111, 156, 172
Theophrastus, *Liber de nupciis* 118
Three kings of Cologne 40
Thomas of Chobham, *Summa confessorum* 190
Thomas Tuscus, *De Gaio Gallicula* 181
Tibaldus, *Phisiologus* 60
Trivett, Nicholas, *Annales regum Anglie* 201, 204
Tudebode, Peter, *Historia de hierosolimitana itinere* 23
Tuscus, *see* Thomas

Ualerianus – *see* Walter Map
Ualerius, Iulius, *Gesta Alexandri* 2, 25, 38, 54, 76, 80, 91, 92, 95, 104 (extract), 110, 117,
   118, 121, 183, 186, 188, 202 (extract). Cf. 185. *Uita Theodorici* 197
Urbain le Courtois, poem on conduct and manners 38
Urban V, *Agni Dei* (extract) 94

Vegetius, *Epithoma rei militaris* 168
Vergil, *Eclogae* 215
Uersus Platonis de Deo 12

INDEX II: First lines of Latin verse

374

INDEX III: Origin and provenance

Including names of scribes and owners